RATOATH
PAST AND PRESENT

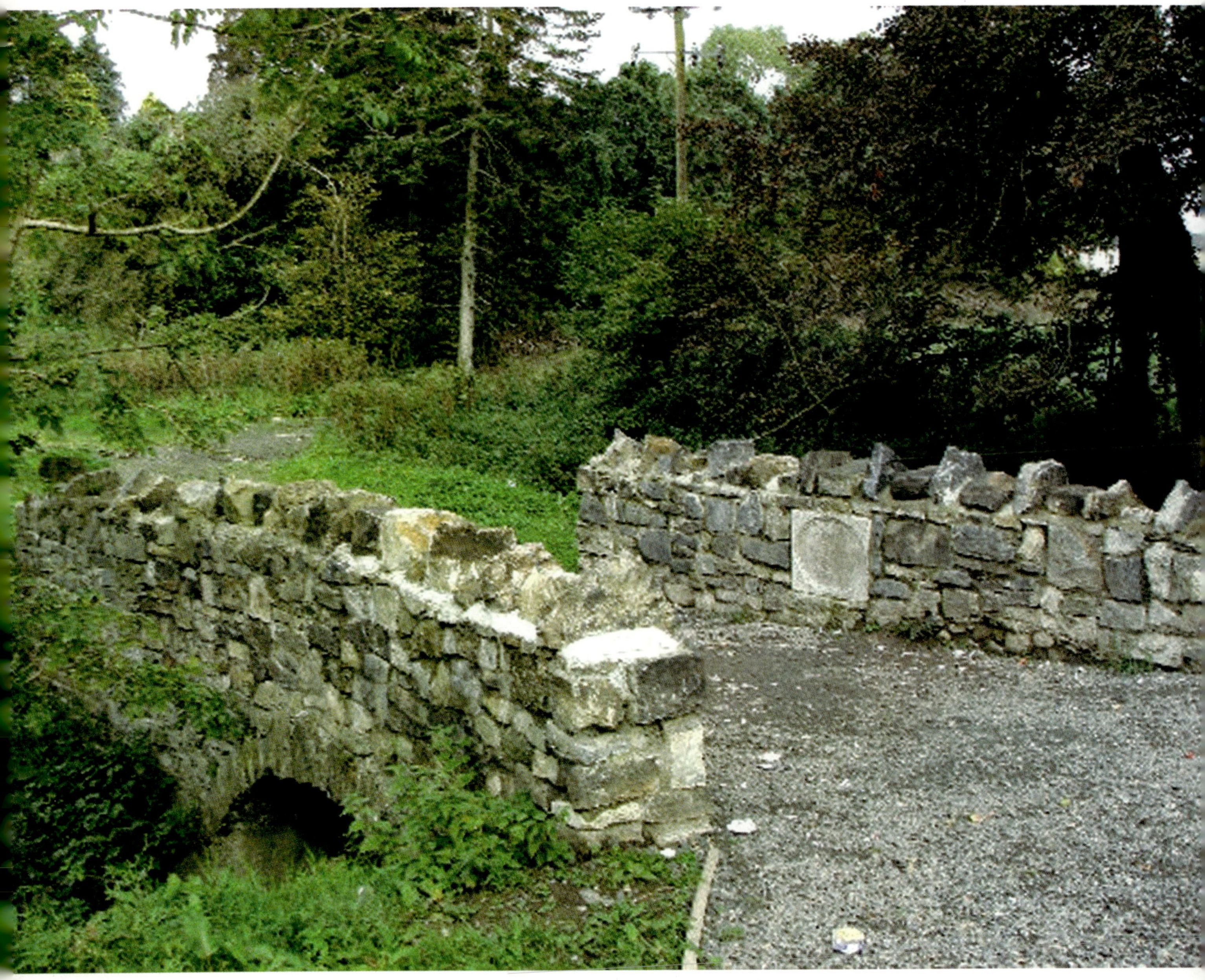

RATOATH
Past and Present

RATOATH HERITAGE GROUP

Published in 2008 by
The Ratoath Heritage Group

© The Ratoath Heritage Group

All rights strictly reserved. No part of this publication may be copied, reproduced, stored in a retrieval system, or transmitted in any form, or by any means, now known or hereafter invented, including written, electronic, mechanical, photocopying, recording or otherwise, except brief extracts for the purpose of review, without the written permission of the publisher and copyright owner.

The book is sold subject to the conditions that it shall not, by way of trade or otherwise, be lent, resold, hired out or otherwise circulated, without the publisher's prior consent, in any form of binding or cover other than that in which it is published and without similar condition including this condition being imposed on the subsequent publisher.

This publication has received support from the Heritage Council under the 2008 Publications Grant Scheme.

ISBN: 978-0-9560979-0-3 Hardbark
978-0-9560979-1-0 Paperback

Cover design: Susan Waine

Back Cover: Photograph of The Lough Lane, courtesy Mary Anne Halton
Frontispiece: James Corballis Esq. Bridge 1814 (The bridge and access path were restored during 2007)

Published by: Linden Publishing Services
Print origination: Susan Waine, Ashfield Press and typeset in 11.5 on 13 Quadraat, Frutiger and Academy Engraved
Printed by: Betaprint Limited, Dublin

For the People of Ratoath

Past and Present

LIST OF SPONSORS

McGarrell Reilly Homes, Ltd. (Sean Reilly)
Tattersalls Ireland
Bicycle Importer (Paul J. Maher)
Meadowbank Developments Ltd. (Francis McGee)
Franic Construction, Ltd. (Francis McGee)
Brazil & Co. (Steel Ltd.)
Fairyhouse Racecourse
Kathleen and Brian O'Neill
Paul and Paula Eiffe
John and Julia Long
Mary Wallace, T.D.
Roy and Patricia O'Sullivan
Danny and Ann Gaughan
Noel and Jenny Conway
Donnelly Providers, Ltd.
Donnelly Properties
Patrick Donnelly & Sons Construction, Ltd.
Paraic Sherry, Sherry Fitzgerald Sherry
Nicholas Killian
DNG Ronald Duff
Regina Doherty
Gerard Byrne
Noel and Agnes Eiffe
The Deering Family
Johnny and Anne Ryan
Brian and Bríd Conway, Glascairn Construction, Ltd.
The Flood Family
Daragh, Sheila and Dominic O Neill
Chris and Monica Maher and Family, Submersible Pump Services, Ltd., Fairyhouse Road
Paddy and Gretta Dolan & Family
Dessie and Maureen Brady
Johnny and Susan Brady
Terry and Cheryl Brady
Tony Darby and Family
Deliverance Transport Company, Ltd.
Paul & Mary Anne Halton
McConnan Estates, Ltd.
Financial Architests, Ltd.
Bank of Ireland, Ratoath
Dunboyne & District Credit Union, Ltd.
Property Partners Brady Fitzgerald Estate Agents (Ratoath)
The Heritage Council

An Chomhairle Oidhreachta
The Heritage Council

Contents

List of Sponsors	vi
Acknowledgements	xi
Foreword ~ Dermot Gallagher	xiii
Preface: Background to the Book ~ Joe Mannering, Chairman	xv
Introduction ~ Paul Halton	xvii
MAPS Various	xx

Local History

Ratoath: A Historical Perspective ~ Frances Maher	1
Lagore Crannóg ~ Tony Darby	9
Rathbeggan ~ Tony Darby	22
Townlands in Ratoath Parish ~ Ratoath Heritage Group	26
Lagore House ~ Beryl Donnelly	28
Thunder Family of Lagore and Ballaly ~ Beryl Donnelly & Frances Maher	37
1798 Rebellion in Meath ~ Ann Gaughan	39
Extracts from a Ratoath Diary: 1804-1898 ~ Frances Maher	42
'Coderliss' Grounds ~ Nick Killian	49
Ratoath Cemetery ~ Frances Maher	51
Archaeological Excavations and Discoveries in Ratoath in 2004 ~ Angela Wallace	58
Archaeological Discoveries on the N2 in Meath & Dublin ~ Maria FitzGerald	64
Through the Eyes of Archaeologists – The Ratoath Pot ~ Ratoath Heritage Group	77
Commemorative Monument in Steeplechase, Ratoath, 2008 ~ Bríd Ní Rinn	79
The Crickeens Ancient Burial Ground ~ Ratoath Heritage Group	80
Famine, Craftsmen and Mills ~ Chris Ward	81
Cattle Industry in Ratoath ~ Ciaran Buckley	83

Appreciation of Heritage

Ratoath Heritage Group & Activities ~ Ratoath Heritage Group	89
Heritage Day Walk ~ Ratoath Heritage Group	95

Church Matters

MAP of Meath Diocese	96
Priests who have served in Ratoath Parish (1405-2008) ~ Frances Maher	97
Vicars appointed to the Deanery of Ratoath ~ Frances Maher	101
Priests Native to the Parish of Ratoath ~ Ratoath Heritage Group	104
Recording Local Church History: Dean Cogan (1826-1872) ~ Frances Maher	106
Church of the Most Holy Trinity ~ Ratoath Heritage Group	107
Holy Trinity Church Remembers ~ Ratoath Heritage Group	112
Ratoath Parochial House ~ Ratoath Heritage Group	114
Family Surnames in Ratoath Parish in 1950's and 1960's ~ Parish Records	116
Father John Cogan (1898-1984) ~ Frances Maher	117
Father Frank McNamara ~ Ratoath Heritage Group	119
Father Gerry Stuart ~ Ratoath Heritage Group	120
Silver Jubilee Mass for Fr. Gerry Stuart – Address ~ Dermot Gallagher	121
Ordination of Fr. Derek Darby ~ Paul Halton	124
Remembrance Trees in Church Grounds ~ Ratoath Heritage Group	126

Education
>   Folklore Collection: Folklore from Ratoath and District ～ Paul Halton — 128
>   Patrick Keenan: A Successful Scholar of the 19th Century ～ Frances Maher — 136
>   Ratoath National School ～ Frances Maher — 138
>   Recollections on School in the 1940's ～ Gerard Ralph — 144
>   An Introduction to Ratoath School 2001 ～ Taidh McNamara — 145
>   Salmon of Knowledge Sculpture ～ Ratoath Heritage Group — 147
>   Rathbeggan National School ～ Frances Maher — 149
>   St. Paul's National School, Ratoath ～ Morag McGowan — 151
>   Ratoath College ～ Máire Ní Bhróithe — 153

Family and Friends
>   Barker Family ～ Patricia Barker — 155
>   Brady Family ～ Christopher J. Brady — 156
>   Christy and Kathleen Martin – The Bungalow, Ratoath ～ Noel & Sonny Martin — 158
>   Conway Family, Fairyhouse Road ～ Noel Conway — 162
>   Costello's Family Grocery Shop ～ May Ryan (née Costello) — 164
>   Dolan Family ～ Paddy Dolan — 165
>   Donnelly Family, Fairyhouse Road ～ Anne Donnelly — 167
>   Donohoe Family ～ Aggie Donohoe — 168
>   Doran Family, Tankardstown ～ Doran Family — 169
>   History of the Eiffe Family ～ Noel Eiffe Junior — 170
>   Family of Sarah and Dan Eiffe, Barrack House ～ Eiffe Family — 172
>   Everard Family, Bradystown ～ Paul Everard — 173
>   Everards, Rackenstown ～ Everard Family — 175
>   Foley Family, Lagore Road ～ Irene Foley — 176
>   Gerry Keogh & Family ～ Gerry Keogh — 177
>   Gorman Family, Ballybin ～ Geraldine Clarke — 180
>   John Caul, Fairyhouse ～ Anne Byrne — 181
>   Kennedys of Peacockstown ～ Frances Maher & Joe Mannering — 183
>   Keogh Family, Rackenstown ～ Maria Keogh — 185
>   Mahon Family ～ Mahon Family — 188
>   Mannering Family ～ Joe Mannering — 191
>   Mary Wallace TD, Minister of State & The Wallace Family ～ Ann Gaughan — 192
>   McCarthy Family ～ Mary Dinneny — 194
>   Moore Family ～ Moore Family — 195
>   O'Brien Family, Tankardstown ～ Ruaidri & Blathin O'Neill — 196
>   O'Neill Family, Pullwee Street ～ Mary O'Neill — 198
>   Rafferty Family ～ Joan King — 200
>   Richard and Christina Donnelly, The Commons ～ Mary O'Sullivan — 202
>   Roche Family Memories ～ John & Mary Roche — 204
>   Rooney Family, Glascarn ～ Bernie Dolan — 205
>   Rory & Petra Conway ～ Rory Conway — 206
>   Walls Family in Ratoath ～ Rose O'Neill — 207
>   White Family, Fairyhouse Road ～ Patrick (Shane) White — 209
>   White Family, Kilrue ～ David White — 210
>   Woods Family ～ Pat Woods — 212
>   Irish Nun is War Heroine ～ Ratoath Heritage Group — 213
>   In Memory of James Everard – Queen's Own Cameron Highlanders
>   Ratoath Heritage Group — 214
>   From Wilkinstown to the Padma Shri and other Stories ～ Gregory Peppard — 215

My Roots in Ratoath ～ Canon Pat Browne ... 223
Goodbye Ireland – a brief memoir ～ Dan Eiffe ... 225

Stories and Tales across the Decades
    Victorian Doctor ～ Chris Ward ... 232
    Royal Meath Dairy ～ Maeve Gallagher ... 234
    Farm Work & other Recollections of Ratoath ～ Michael McCarthy ... 235
    Ratoath Boys' Annual Bicycle Race, 1927 ～ Beryl Donnelly ... 238
    Working with Iona Airways and Aer Lingus ～ Michael Elliot ... 239
    Entertainment in Ratoath in the 1930's and 1940's ～ Nick Sherry ... 240
    Threshing in the Parish of Ratoath – 1940's ～ Gerard Ralph ... 242
    Fair Days in Ratoath ～ Noel Eiffe ... 243
    Drama Class in Ratoath 1936 – "The Merchant of Venice" ～ Ratoath Heritage Group ... 245
    Coming to Meath and Working in Park House ～ Mary Kate Gaughan ... 246
    Spitfire Crash at Ratoath ～ Tony Darby ... 252
    Emergency Harvest in 1946 & the Memories ～ Ann Gaughan ... 255
    Memories of a Lifetime ～ Frank Maher ... 258
    Life in Ratoath ～ Jimmy Ralph ... 260
    Early Memories of Ratoath ～ Nick Killian ... 262
    Poteen Maker of Glascarn ～ Noel Conway ... 263
    Memories of the Augustinian Convent and Nursing Home ～ Sister Clement ... 264
    Sisters of St. Augustine ～ Madeline O'Neill ... 266
    Remembering Confirmation Days in Ratoath ～ P. Flood, G. Ralph, L. Flood ... 268
    Ratoath Inn ～ Leo & Rose McGirl ... 270
    The Humours of Peacockstown, Ratoath ～ John Sheahan ... 271
    Newcomers to Ratoath … "21st Century Blow-Ins" ～ Maria & Paddy Dalton ... 273

Streetscapes and Landscapes
    A Journey through Ratoath – No longer a Village ～ Patrick Sherry ... 275
    Ratoath Song from 1940's ～ Patrick Sherry ... 279
    Growing up on the Dunshaughlin Road in the late 1950's ～ Tony Darby ... 280
    Well Road and Main Street ～ Noel Martin & Beryl Donnelly ... 301
    Skryne Cabinhill Road ～ Noel Eiffe ... 304
    Park House ～ Sheila Moorehead ... 305
    Royal Irish Constabulary Barracks, Ratoath ～ Paul Halton ... 306
    Cabinhill Townland ～ Peggy Byrne ... 307
    Kilbride Road ～ Joe Mannering ... 314
    Irish Street to Fairyhouse Racecourse ～ Frances Maher ... 316
    Curkeen House ～ Miriam Toole ... 320
    Darthogue (Doghtog) ～ Joan & Frank Deering ... 321
    Glebe House & Gardens ～ Mary Anne Halton ... 322
    Ratoath Manor ～ Ratoath Heritage Group ... 323
    Strand House ～ Anne Keogh ... 326

Associations and Clubs
    Active Age ～ Maureen Butler & Anne Brady ... 327
    Ratoath ICA ～ Anne Ryan ... 330
    Pioneer Association ～ Ratoath Heritage Group ... 332
    Badminton Club ～ Fiona Simpson ... 334
    Ratoath Bridge Club ～ Maureen Butler ... 335
    Ratoath Garden Club ～ Irene Hayes & Patricia Smith ... 336
    Ratoath Foróige Club – The Early Years ～ Gretta Judge ... 338

9th Meath Scout Group ~ John & Julia Long	342
Ratoath Athletic Club ~ Ronnie Quigley & Phil Bateson	344
First Soccer Games in Ratoath ~ Tony Darby	347
Ratoath Harps ~ B. Conway, D. O'Neill, J. Colfer, M. Tallant	351
History of Ratoath GAA ~ Ray Murphy	370
Ratoath Rugby Club ~ David Marrinan	399
Lagore & District Gun Club ~ Tony Darby	402
Pitch and Putt ~ Bróna Darby	405
Terry Fox Run ~ Willie Donohoe	410
Royal Lopez Chess Club ~ Dave Eccles	411

Horses for Courses

Creakenstown Point-to-Point Races ~ Gretta Kelly	413
Ward Union Staghounds ~ James Byrne & Ann Gaughan	418
Fairyhouse – Home of the Irish Grand National ~ Ratoath Heritage Group	425
Jockeys – Native to Ratoath ~ Joe Mannering	434
My Time with D.L. Moore at Old Fairyhouse ~ Paddy Woods	437
Through the Years with Tommy Carberry ~ Pamela Carberry	442
Legend of Pat Rogers of Ratoath ~ Ruth Rogers	447
Tom Dreaper and the Irish Grand National ~ Liam & Peter McLoughlin	454
Tattersalls (Ireland) ~ Sophie Hayley	456

Community

Ratoath Community Centre (1930's – 2008) ~ Nick Killian	459
Official Opening Address, President of Ireland, Mary McAleese ~ Nick Killian	466
Ratoath Population Trends ~ Paul Halton	467
Ratoath 1993 to 2008 – A study of a rapidly changing community Ratoath Heritage Group	468
New Urban Living; a study of social and civic life, 2003 ~ M.P. Corcoran, J. Gray & M. Peillon	471
Ratoath Independent Living Initiative 2008 ~ RILI Committee	482
Pride of Place in Ratoath ~ Ratoath Heritage Group	483
Community in Action in the New Millennium ~ Ratoath Heritage Group	486
Know your Neighbour Event, 2007 ~ Ratoath Heritage Group	488

Photographic Gallery

A Ramble Down Memory Lane	489
Getting Out and About	490
Holidays in Ireland	492
Close to Home	493
Childhood Memories Revisited – The Dunshaughlin Road	494
Ratoath Lads on Holiday Summer 2000	495
Street Life	496
Ratoath Club/Cub Celebrations	497
Lough Lane Flora – A Walk on the Wild Side	498
Mary Moore's Sweet Shop	499
Ecclesiastical and Social Functions	500
Lough Lane Stepping Stones	502
Conclusion ~ Ratoath Heritage Group	503
Bibliography	504

ACKNOWLEDGEMENTS

THIS PUBLICATION has been a labour of love and researching it was an enriching experience from start to finish. Ratoath Heritage Group is indebted to so many generous people without whom it would have been impossible to publish this book. Without the passionate commitment of all the contributors who wrote articles on a variety of topics, provided personal stories of their life and times, and entrusted us with their most precious photographs, *Ratoath, Past & Present* would not have seen the light of day.

For their written contributions and photographs from their personal and family archives we thank:-

Dermot Gallagher, Joe Mannering, Paul Halton, Frances Maher, Tony Darby, Beryl Donnelly, Ann Gaughan, Chris Ward, Ciaran Buckley, Angela Wallace, Maria FitzGerald, Bríd Ní Rinn, Fr. Derek Darby, Gerard Ralph, Taidh McNamara, Morag McGowan, Máire Ní Bhróithe, Patricia Barker, Finian Darby, Christopher J. Brady, Noel Martin, Sonny Martin, Noel Conway, Paddy Dolan, Anne Donnelly, Aggie Donohoe, Noel Eiffe Junior, Eiffe Family, Paul Everard, Eiffe Family, Everard Family, Irene Foley, Gerry Keogh, Geraldine Clarke, Anne Byrne, Maria Keogh, Mahon Family, Mary Dinneny, Moore Family, Ruaidri & Bláithín O'Neill, Mary O'Neill, Joan King, Patrick Kennedy, Mary O'Sullivan, John & Mary Roche, Bernie Dolan, Rory & Petra Conway, Rose O'Neill, Patrick (Shane) White, Pat Woods, Gregory Peppard, Canon Pat Browne, Dan Eiffe, Maeve Gallagher, Michael McCarthy, Michael Elliot, Nick Sherry, Noel Eiffe, Mary Kate Gaughan, Frank Maher, Jimmy Ralph, Nick Killian, Noel Conway, Sister Clement, Madeline O'Neill, Peggy Flood, Gerard Ralph, Lorna Flood, Maria & Paddy Dalton, Leo & Rose McGirl, Patrick Sherry, Peggy Byrne, Miriam Toole, Joan & Frank Deering, Fiona Simpson, Mary Anne Halton, Anne Keogh, Maureen Butler & Anne Brady, Anne Ryan, Irene Hayes, Patricia Smith, Gretta Judge, John & Julia Long, Ronnie Quigley, Phil Bateson, Brian Conway, Daragh O'Neill, Jimmy Colfer, Ray Murphy, David Marrinan, Bróna Darby, Willie Donohoe, Dave Eccles, Derek Brady, Gretta Kelly, James Byrne, Paddy Woods, Pamela Carberry, Ruth Rogers, Liam & Peter McLoughlin, Sophie Hayley, Lynch Family, Ita and Oliver Doran and Family, Flood Family, Kevin White, Bernie Lynch, Derek Maguire, Lil & Gerry O'Sullivan, Johnny Carey, Family of Mrs. Mary Mooney, Lagore, Peter Barrow (Photographer, European Photo Services), White Family, Kilrue. Seamus Farrelly (Photographer), Owen Hackett, Padraig Halton, James Cusack.

The generous support of our many sponsors, listed at the start of this book, is deeply appreciated and without them we would not have had the financial resources to bring the book to completion.

For their advice, information and shared recollections we wish to thank Mrs. Foley, Michael O'Reilly, Michael Kenny (Dunshaughlin), Michael Kenny (Dunboyne), Michael Thunder (now residing in Oslo), Fr. Derek Darby, Dermot Oates, Peadar Flanagan, Luke Ralph, Chris Dogget, Sheila Dennehy, Pat & Sheila Naughton, Elizabeth Madden, Desmond Toole, Florrie Martin, Fr. Peter Mulvany and Margaret Hobbs. Patricia and Anthony Andrews and Bill Compton who generously provided information on the Thunder Family. Anna Weglowska from Poland and Eamon Power from Aer Lingus.

We thank individuals in the Ratoath community and neighbouring parishes, and the families of committee members, who constantly assisted and supported the development of the project. We are indebted to them for their time and encouragement throughout the long process from inception to publication. Gathering information and stories meant long meetings at kitchen tables, in the Community Centre and the Parish Resource Centre. Our work involved visiting people in their homes, listening to and recording stories, researching in libraries and archives and even taking a trip or two outside the country. Long nights, weekends and holidays were spent researching, reading, scanning images, e-mailing updates, rewriting, editing and proofreading. A big "Thank You" to all concerned!

We especially wish to thank the Principals and staff of the local schools, staff of Ratoath Community Centre, Dunboyne and District Credit Union Limited, May Foley and Barbara Scally of Dunshaughlin Library, staff of Meath County Council and Navan Library, including Andy Gaffney, staff of the Royal Irish Academy, the National Archives, National Library of Ireland, Irish Folklore Department of UCD, Department of Education and Science, Public Records Office of Northern Ireland (PRONI) in Belfast, Central Statistics Office, Ordnance Survey of Ireland, Archaeology Section National Roads Authority, The Heritage Council, Palgrave Macmillan Ltd, Hampshire, UK, local newspapers and newsletters, *The Meath Chronicle*, *The Drogheda Independent*, *The Fingal Independent*, *Village Voice*, *Ratoath News* and *The Meath Echo* for permission to use reports, articles and other historically significant material. We also wish to thank Fr. Gerry Stuart, PP, and the staff of the Parish Office for their kind assistance.

A very special thanks to Dr. Mary Corcoran, Dr. Jane Gray and Dr. Michel Peillon, National University of Ireland, Maynooth, for the use of their research results on the population trends in Ratoath over recent years. We are indebted to Dermot Gallagher for writing the Foreword to the book.

We wish to express our thanks and deep appreciation to Ray Lynn, Adrienne Foran and all the staff at Betaprint for their professional advice and for undertaking the printing of this book. Finally, but not least, we wish to acknowledge the high quality work of Susan Waine, Linden Publishing Services, for the design and layout of this publication.

SPECIAL NOTE: We owe a great debt of gratitude to those who proofread articles, and those who corrected and confirmed dates and facts about local events in the past. Whilst every effort has been made to get all names, dates and events accurate, if any errors or omissions have occurred we apologise.

Foreword

THE PUBLICATION OF "Ratoath Past and Present" is extraordinarily timely. No less than the wider country, we have witnessed in our community over the last generation an era of unprecedented change. The pace, as much as the scale of that change, has been breath-taking. Overall, it has been a hugely positive experience. But it also raises major questions about the nature of our community and how we face the future.

That is why "*Ratoath Past and Present*" is so vital. Through the wonderful contributions in the book by so many people over such a wide range of areas - social, industrial, historical, religious, educational, sports, agricultural to name but a few -this generation is making a statement about the value we place on our past, the value we place on our heritage, the value we place on those generations who went before us. We, who are fortunate to live in the success story that is today's Ratoath, know that in essence we are reaping a harvest sown by previous generations, generations who had to toil in tougher, more difficult times. Quite frankly, we would not be where we are today without their efforts and their sacrifices.

But there is another key point. Not alone are we acknowledging that we could not have achieved what we have without their efforts, but through this publication we are also making a statement about the kind of Ratoath we are now seeking to build. A Ratoath that embraces change and is progressive yes! But a Ratoath also that walks into the future holding on to the core values that have served us so well and so long -love of place, love of parish, love of community, commitment to enterprise and regeneration, welcome for the stranger. The fact that we as a community have taken the time and energy to produce a publication of the length, width and depth of "*Ratoath Past and Present*" underscores that statement of intent loudly and clearly.

I am particularly proud that we have welcomed and embraced such a substantial number of new residents in Ratoath over recent years. There was a time when welcome for the stranger meant extending a *fáilte* to someone like myself from then distant Leitrim - although my integration was facilitated by marrying into an old and long-established Meath family. We now have people in our midst from all over, and they have helped develop and enrich our community in so many different ways. They also know that they are extremely welcome among us, be it in the many superb sports clubs here or in the extremely welcoming Parish Church. I would hope that one of the values of "*Ratoath Past and Present*" would be to provide those who have newly made their home here with a deeper sense of the roots of this special place that we all now share together. Even the Dubs among us, rightly proud as they are of their own team, may come in time to pay homage to the Royals! Indeed, their children will most likely go one step further.

I hope the publication will also be a source of great interest and pride to the many people from Ratoath scattered around Ireland and indeed the world who were born here, or spent a significant time in their life here. Several have made delightful and important contributions to the book, underlining how important the place was to them and how they have never forgotten it. This book is for them also. It will serve as another means of binding our great, extended community and family together.

When President McAleese kindly opened our Community Centre in September 2006 she spoke sincerely about how beautiful it was, but also about the challenge facing us. Her moving words are worth repeating:

"The big worry - the big, big worry always is "will you be able to hold on to community? Will you be able to create community; will you be able to embrace everybody, and draw them in, and create not just a bunch of houses, not just a bunch of people who happen to live together"?

I think the publication of "*Ratoath Past and Present*" provides an eloquent reassurance to Uachtaran na hÉireann that we took her words to heart. Ratoath, past and present, is in good hands and we will now, collectively, seek to build a future worthy of the great inheritance that has proudly been handed to us by those who have gone before.

All involved in this wonderful publication can take pride in a magnificent job; we are deeply in their debt.

DERMOT GALLAGHER, Harlockstown.

PREFACE:

Background to the Book

RATOATH HERITAGE GROUP goes back many years to the mid 1980s. It was founded by a group of like-minded locals who came together with a view to working towards the preservation of local historical sites and recording of the history and folklore of the area.

For hundreds of years Ratoath had remained unchanged, a quiet little village nestling in the south-east of County Meath. It was mainly known outside of its own environs to the racing confraternity, through its close proximity to Fairyhouse Racecourse, which lies on the outskirts of the village. Towards the end of the 20th century, when Ireland's "Celtic Tiger" economy was booming, the face of Ratoath began to change both dramatically and with a speed that to some, seemed almost frightening. In the year 2002 Ratoath was quoted by the Central Statistics Office (CSO) as being the "fastest growing village in Ireland", having a population of 5,581 persons and still growing.

It was in this era of change, that the seeds of our "book" were sown during 1999 and took root as a project to mark the new millennium and to record the history of Ratoath. At that time other communities were recording historical facts, sociological changes and local stories as part of local history projects. So why could the Ratoath Heritage Group not do the same? Would there be individuals to work on the project? Who might find the stories interesting? What about photographs? How would it be funded? All the usual doubts emerged as the task was explored and discussed. But still we moved on, fearlessly, without previous writing or publishing experience!

The Ratoath Heritage Group embarked on a journey which has taken over eight years. Originally it was thought that it would have taken a shorter period of time, but as each month (and year) went by, new material or forgotten stories emerged and it became obvious that the route to completion would be long and winding with many diversions along the way. The diversions were enlightening.

Early on one key question emerged. In what style should the historical essays, background to clubs, stories and anecdotes be written? Should it be academic, short story-telling or reporting style? This posed some difficulties, as a variety of styles were emerging in the work being gathered and submitted. It was decided to allow the natural writing style and words of the writers to dominate as this would give a greater authenticity to the work.

Many, many hundreds of hours of research and hard work were undertaken by the members of our group of which I am proud and honoured to be a member. I wish to thank each of them for the part they played and for the absolute dedication with which they undertook their roles, all of which have culminated in the production of this wonderful book, of which we can be justly proud.

I wish to also thank The Heritage Council, our sponsors and contributors. We are most grateful to you all. I believe together we have not only "honoured" our past, but most importantly "preserved" it for future generations.

The Ratoath Heritage Group is privileged to present and share with Ratoath people of all origins the rich written and photographic tapestry, *Ratoath, Past and Present*.

JOE MANNERING
Chairperson, Ratoath Heritage Group

Introduction

IN EUROPE "when history is in movement, places are transformed."[1] Since 1989, the end of the Cold War, the unification of Germany, the fragmentation of the Soviet Union, Czechoslovakia and Yugoslavia, and the current political events in Central and Eastern Europe have contributed to political, social and cultural change across a Continent which has resulted in mass movement of people across national boundaries including those of local communities. Historical pasts, geographical positions and cultural interactions have become emphasised as individuals and communities strive to define their identities. Where have we come from? What have been our historical experiences? What are our stories? While political, social and cultural identities are being negotiated at European and national levels, local communities across the greater European geographical area, including smaller communities such as Ratoath, confront the contradictory, paradoxical and divergent demands experienced in such complex situations.

In a new context local history is especially important for those individuals whose area it describes and the stories it unfolds. This is a first step for the people of Ratoath as it is developing a newer, larger and diverse community. An account of local history and stories provides this new community with a link to the past, creating a new opportunity for learning about the local dimension and greater understanding so that the newly created community is able to move forward together. An awareness of the past history of Ratoath should prepare the young Ratoath people for differences and perspectives, and assist them towards an understanding and appreciation of diversity across the community.

Learning where an area and its people have come from helps to inform those who are currently living in that area – some whose families are there for generations, others who are recent arrivals and who are anxious to know about the area. The matrix of geography, human activities and settlements over the centuries, historical, sociological and anecdotal accounts of Ratoath are so interwoven that there are some overlaps in the submissions. Where it was possible these overlaps were edited. It is hoped that this book will encourage "a dialogue with the past" where formal and informal historical links have existed even when boundaries were being drawn and redrawn at different points in history and alongside this that "planning for the future" will be critically considered.

Anticipated constraints imposed on this study were: lack of formal research into Ratoath; inaccessibility of official documentation or primary source material; the credibility of secondary sources; lack of finance and a dependency on voluntary time, finance and computer capabilities. Few of the anticipated constraints hindered the study except for the time-consuming nature of accessing primary source material. Some of the material was accidentally discovered by individuals when carrying out searches in libraries and through

---

[1] Michel Foucher, *The new faces of Europe* (Strasbourg: Council of Europe, 1995).

contact with members of different families. Perhaps there are some stories that remain to be told in a future publication.

The opening section, **Section One** [*Local History, Appreciation of Heritage, Church Matters, Education*] investigates the historical, archaeological and sociological and religious background to Ratoath. Historical investigations of Ratoath and Rathbeggan outline various developments from Pre-Christian to more modern times. The brief entries from the "Ratoath Diary" enable us to get glimpses of events significant to the people of its time. The essay on the Lagore Crannóg reminds us of its historical and cultural importance in County Meath, some of which may have been forgotten in contemporary times. The more recent archaeological discoveries when developing new roads and buildings serve as a link to the human settlements of the past as the landscape is reorganised in shape and use to serve the current population. A new monument to commemorate those who were buried at the Crickeens marks an appreciation of heritage by the contemporary community. An overview of the Ratoath Heritage Group gives a glimpse into its activities.

The state of education is addressed and the reader will discover the sudden increase which has taken place in the last eight years with regard to the number of students, the demand for places and the expansion of the provision which became necessary to keep pace with the rapidly growing population of young people. The CSO analysis of the 2006 *Census of Population* reports that Ratoath, Co. Meath has the highest proportion of young people aged 0-14 years in the country. 32% of the population is in this age group. Patrick Keenan, a successful scholar from Ratoath and a renowned educator, is celebrated.

Lane and Nolan, authors of *Laois History & Society* state that "*a society's culture, ... is often best reflected in the architectural legacy bequeathed to succeeding generations*" and with this in mind some of the houses, farms and stud farms in the Ratoath area which have been significant in people's lives are highlighted. These provide employment and add to the economic welfare of the area.

The Parish of Ratoath is recalled in detail; the rectors, vicars and priests, the deanery, churches, the graveyard, the parochial house. Every effort was made by those submitting work to verify the authenticity of the information.

In Section Two [*Families and Friends, Stories and Tales Across the Decades, Streetscapes and Landscapes*] the stories collected from individuals and families provide us with insights into life in Ratoath over the last century as we learn about the families, the religious practices, social and economic life on and off farms. Each story serves to emphasise the importance of a sense of place and belonging to each individual, each from its writer's perspective. This section demonstrates the interest Ratoath people have in their community, their sense of humour and willingness to be involved in sharing their own and sometimes quite personal stories.

Section Three provides an overview of the associations and clubs. Life in Ratoath has always been busy and exciting. Sport has played a key role in bringing people of all ages together especially younger people and getting them involved in the wider community. Newer activities and clubs have emerged over the last five years to cater for the growing diversity of community interests.

No book on Ratoath would be complete without a section on the equine activities of the area. These activities provide an extensive social and economic network within the community for breeders, trainers, jockeys and punters. **Section Four** focuses on some of the key areas associated with horses: Point-to-point at Creakenstown, Fairyhouse Racecourse, Old Fairyhouse Stud, Ratoath Jockeys, The Ward Union Staghounds and the Irish Grand National.

Section Five [*Community*] explores some of the developments around Ratoath:

Community development from the early years, the development of the Community Centre and the Official Opening of the new Community Centre by the President of Ireland. The opening of the Venue Theatre with *Dancing at Lunaghsa*, 2006 is fondly recalled. Population trends are presented and a New Urban Living study records social and civil life in Ratoath in 2003. Examples of involvement in contemporary development initiatives are documented.

Section Six [*Photographic Gallery*] provides the reader with an opportunity to browse a selection of archive photographs, old and new which were submitted by individuals and families.

While more stories could be written, in the end compromise was inevitable and the Ratoath Heritage Group had to decide on a final deadline. A new generation will undoubtedly compile their stories and memories in a future publication. As the twenty-first century moves forward the future of Ratoath looks bright for its people as it is transformed before our eyes into an urban-rural area with strong overtones of the countryside wedged between Dublin and the towns of Ashbourne, Dunshaughlin and Dunboyne.

It is a pleasure to commend this publication to its readers to enjoy and treasure.

PAUL HALTON
Ratoath

Maps

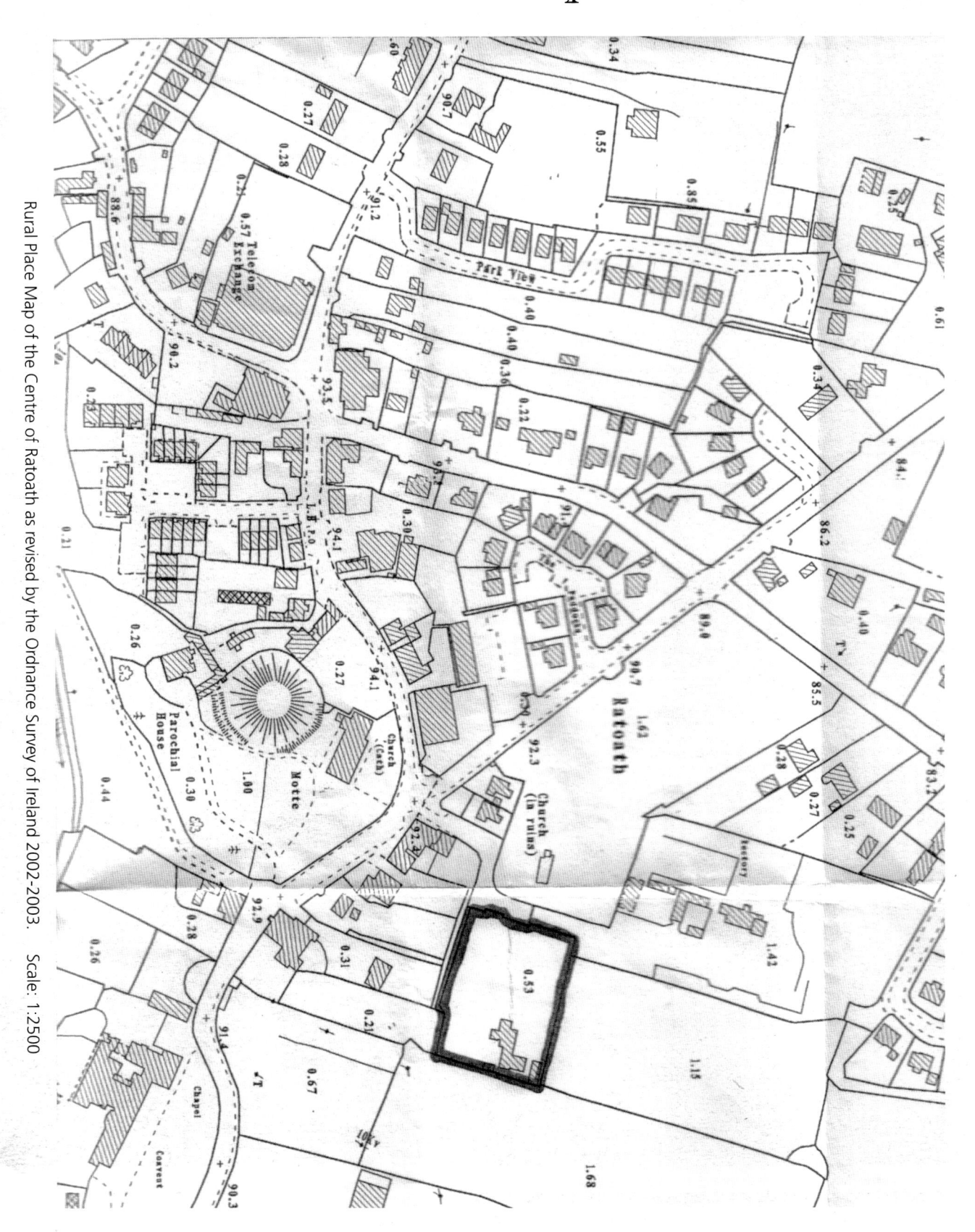

Rural Place Map of the Centre of Ratoath as revised by the Ordnance Survey of Ireland 2002-2003. Scale: 1:2500

Aerial Photograph of Ratoath Village taken in the summer of 1940
Notice the neat rows of cocks of hay in the fields near the centre of the village

AERIAL VIEWS OF RATOATH, 2005 AND 2007.

Photo: Peter Barrow

Photo: Peter Barrow

Map showing centre of Ratoath c 1840

OATH

Quarry

Arch

Manor Ho.
Dispensary

Jamestown

Moulden Br

XXV

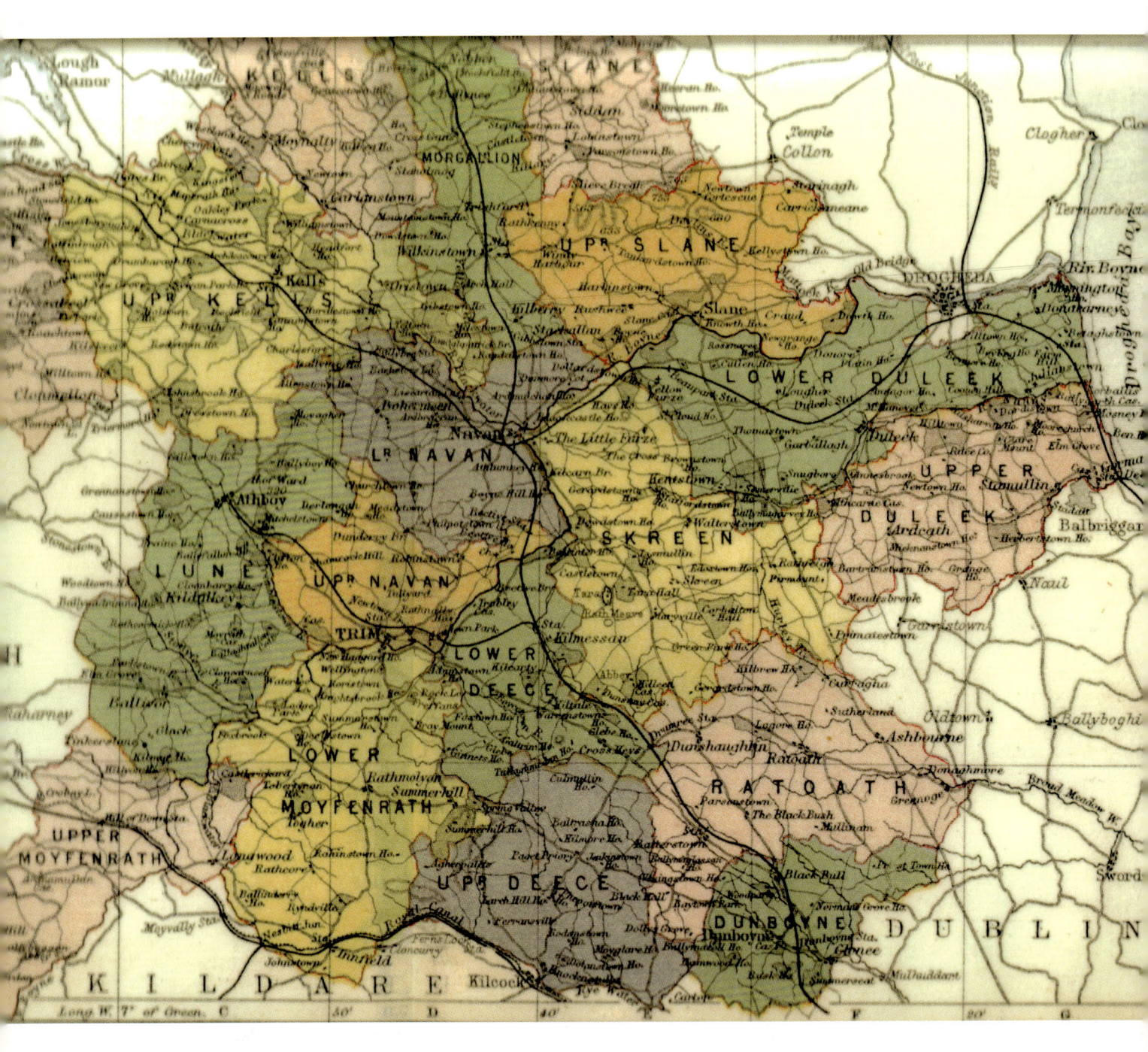

Map of County Meath showing the Barony of Ratoath,
Published by George Philip & Son, London & Liverpool, c 1860.

LOCAL HISTORY

Ratoath – A Historical Perspective

FRANCES MAHER

WE BEGIN with a brief history of Ireland, which is of some importance to the way in which the village of Ratoath and its countryside have evolved.

Colonisation in Ireland
According to ancient Chroniclers there were five successive colonisations in Ireland. How or when these peoples got to Ireland we do not know. Ireland was still under ice at a time when people were moving about in France and even in southern England. The earliest traces of man in Ireland show him, in the later Stone Age, already a tiller of land, possessing pottery, but having no use of metal. Men of this type constructed the megalithic monuments - the cromlechs and the sepulchral barrows, of which the great mounds at Dowth, Knowth and Newgrange are chief examples.

The first colonisation that came to Ireland was that of the Parthalonians. The second, the Nemedians, were much oppressed by the local people, called the Fomorians, who were an ancient sea-faring race. This prehistoric period is in the realm of mythology. The third colony was that of the Firbolg and this begins to get in touch with fact: they were real people. The fourth colony was that of the Tuatha De Danann. These represent gods who in the earlier heroic romances mixed themselves up with the love of wars of heroic mortals, as did the gods of Ancient Greece. There were small bands of people called the Picti, which is Latin, meaning 'the Tattooed'; the Gaels called them Cruithne. The fifth and last colony was the Gaels who were also called the Milesians. The Milesians came from Egypt, through Crete and Spain. They were called Gaels, because their remote ancestor in the days of Moses was called Geodhal Glas.

Their leader was Miled. Soon after he was killed his wife Scota (a Pharoe's daughter, after whom Ireland was in later ages called Scotia) came to Ireland with her remaining living sons. They and their followers fought the De-Danann at Taillte in Meath. *"A quaint tale in the ancient Book of Leinster says that it was left to the Milesian Poet and Judge, Amergin, to divide Eirinn between the two races and that he did. The Milesians were victorious and were given the land above ground. The De-Danann lost and were given the land below ground, giving foundation to the*

---

1   *The Story of the Irish Race.* Author: Seumas MacManus. Publisher: Gramercy; Revised Edition (March 24 1990). ISBN-10: 0517064081. ISBN-13: 978-0517064085

stories of enchanted folk, fairies, living under the Irish hills".[1]

O'Flaherty the Irish scholar of the sixteenth century defines the time of the Milesian invasion as 1,000 BC. The Irish race to-day is often referred to as the Milesian Race.

Early Recording of Important Events

Before the art of writing and the means of duplicating what is written existed, ideas and information could only be transported to other parts of a country by transporting the person who possessed this knowledge. In each family unit there were a few people selected to memorise the happenings in that particular family. They stored knowledge of each generation going back several generations. The training for this task usually took around twelve years. Historians[2], while reproducing the traditional accounts, recognised that they were not trustworthy beyond a point. They fixed that point to be about 320 BC. Archaeology tells us that there is no trace of the Iron Age in Ireland before 350 BC. In Ireland copper and bronze had been in use for more than a thousand years before this; metal work was already highly developed. The Gaels who arrived in Ireland around 320 BC brought the secrets of working iron with them. The reason they were able to conquer the other tribes in Ireland was because they belonged to a Celtic group, which had the first requisite for conquest - superior military equipment. The Celtic-speaking people took over the principal centres of power and ritual in Ireland that were used by the Neolithic farmers and their successors.[3]

The Gaels also brought with them the characteristic Celtic custom of maintaining professional Bards, whose duty it was to record events in rhythm and to preserve earlier records, to compose and to recite. They were also very important because of their ability to transmit the law – that is to say the judgements, which at that time were delivered by the Kings. So it became normal practice that before a King gave judgement, he should consult the living record of what had been decided in previous cases; and thus those proficient in poetry and history became recognised also as authorities upon law and advisers upon judgement.

Early Rulers of Ireland

During the following centuries there were many wars, waged between the rulers of Ireland with one another, for land and booty. About nine centuries before the Christian era, Tigearnmus, Monarch of Ireland of the Race of Heremon was the first to introduce Druidism and the worship of idols to Ireland.

Tuathal Teachtmhar formed the Ancient Kingdom of Meath ('*Mide*' means 'middle') in the second century, AD 103 to AD 160. Fourth in succession to him was Conn of The Hundred Battles who became King of Tara in AD 177. There were several provincial Kings and one High King. The power of these rulers was felt outside of Ireland as the Irish carried out numerous attacks on the shores of Britain, which was occupied at the time by the Romans.

St. Patrick's Mission to Ireland

In the fifth century AD St. Patrick's mission to Ireland was in many ways the most significant event in Irish history. After their conversion the Irish preserved Christianity and learning at a time when both were almost trampled out of existence in the greater parts of

---

2   Gwynn, Stephen. "*The History of Ireland*". 1923, Published by Macmillan, London, 1923. ISBN Misc, pp 3-10, 12, 43-44.
3   "*Timetables of Irish History. An Illustrated Chronological Chart of the History of Ireland from 6000 BC to Present Times*" by Patrick C. Power and Seán Duffy. Published by Worth Press Limited, London. 2001.

Europe. Patrick's work in Ireland lasted twenty-nine years from 432 to 461 A.D.

The Coming of the Danes

One page in the *Annals of the Four Masters* indicates that eight century Ireland was in some respects a leading part of Europe, not a great power, but a country fully abreast of its age. But on the same page of the *Annals* is recorded the beginning of the Viking raids which checked Ireland's peaceful interaction with Europe and grievously threw back the progress of its civilisation. The entry states *"The burning of Rathlin, by the foreigners: and its shrines were broken and plundered."* This refers to the first coming of the Norsemen on the north and east coasts of Ireland. They travelled *"in long clinker-built boats"* that were *"far superior to any other sea-craft in Europe then."*[4]

Ratoath Village

Ratoath anciently called Rathouuthe, (Register from St. Thomas's Abbey) is supposed to have derived that name from a conspicuous mound near the Church, on which Malachy, the first monarch of all Ireland is said to have held a Convention of the States. This would have taken place in the late tenth century. The first part of the word "Rathoath" may be derived from the Gaelic word, "rath", which means a fort or fortification, but this is unlikely, as the place-name probably existed before the Normans erected the "Moat" -unless they built it on top of a rath already in existence. Further studies have shown alternative derivatives for the name of 'Ratoath'.

For instance, the *Ordnance Survey Letters Meath*, by John O'Donovan quoting Nicholas Walsh a native of the village in 1836, states that *"Ratoath, according to the people living in the village, pronounced in English Rath Oath, and in Irish RÁT TÓD, was derived from RiG TÓD (King Thó) a Danish king who lived here. There is a Moat in the town called MOTA RAT TOD from which the locals say the Danes were routed"*[5]. In the churchyard in the village, before the erection of the modern church in 1817, there were the old walls of a building which, according to the locals, served as a vestry to the old church which was originally dedicated to Saint Thomas à Becket and afterwards (not known when) to the Blessed Trinity.

Other significant items reported in the Ordnance Survey include the Moulden Bridge where, on every Easter Monday, they held the Maudlings or Moudlens. The local people said it was a great Pattern (patron) festival, consisting of kicking football, games and revellery.

In Ratoath village, at the meeting of the Dublin and Dunshaughlin Roads, stood a cross which was called the Market Cross. About a ¼ of a mile west of the village on the Dunshaughlin Road stood the Red Cross Tree. There is no tradition of a cross having been here; funerals passing by this tree were carried around it also - the site of this tree was situated on the site of the current roundabout at the entrance to Steeplechase Hill off the Dunshaughlin Road.

There is mention of the name of Mruigtuaithe in the *Book of Armagh*, one of eight places in Meath where St. Patrick founded churches and Eoin MacNeill identifies it as Ratoath. If this is correct it would seem that the second portion of the word comes from the Gaelic word, "tuath" which means a territory belonging to a family or sect. "Mruig" means a graz-

---

[4] *"Timetables of Irish History. An Illustrated Chronological Chart of the History of Ireland from 6000 BC to Present Times"* by Patrick C. Power and Seán Duffy. Published by Worth Press Limited, London. 2001.

[5] *"Ordnance Survey Letters Meath"* by John O'Donovan. 1836.

ing plain. Other attempts at explaining the origins of Ratoath and its name were published in *"Early Irish History and Mythology"* by Thomas F. O'Rahilly[6] in 1946. The in-depth analysis in that publication is beyond the scope of this book.

The Coming of the Norsemen
All the shore area about the River Liffey's estuary was flat, with much slob, but at the point where the Dodder flows in, at a place called the Dubh Linn, or Black Pool, it was here that the Norsemen made their landing place. It was the custom of the Normans to build military structures to ensure their hold over an area. Usually these were made of wood and were known as Mottes and Baileys; a height with a military post on top, which included a Keep, Bailey, Fosse, etc. The Bailey was the land around the Motte, which was flattened and fenced in. The people lived here as though it were a village, protected from the attacks of the native Gaelic population.

Ratoath Motte & Bailey Castle
This was the centre of an important Manor. The Motte consists of a round mound 12m high with a basal diameter of 43m, narrowing to 17-18m at the top. It is overgrown with vegetation, but is surrounded by a deep narrow ditch on the north, south and part of the west sides. There is a crescentric Bailey, 50m by 30m on the east side, through which the drive to the Presbytery was cut.

In the *Royal Society of Antiquaries of Ireland* (30th June 1921), Goddard H. Orphen mentions the Motte and Bailey earthwork erected on a grand scale *(See sketch by Gina Conway[7])*. This was clearly the earthwork of the early thirteenth century castle, the *"site of the manor"* to which reference is made in the Inquisition of 1333. There were no buildings on it then, and we must suppose that, as in many other cases, the original wooden tower and palisades had been destroyed or fell into decay, but had not been replaced with stone.

The street plan of Ratoath largely follows the curve formed by the Motte. West and south of the Motte the village was characterised by a series of long narrow plots of land, perhaps representing a medieval strip pattern similar to that at Newcastle Co. Dublin. On the southwest, the Dunshaughlin road sweeps in a broad curve which suggests an early enclosure. The name is derived from Rath-Tó, "Fort of To," which suggests that there was a settlement on the site prior to the coming of the Normans. However, apart from the place name the only other suggestion of pre-Norman activity is the local tradition of a "cave" in the Motte, which may be a souterrain. *(Editor's comment: During the 1990's, the lands near the centre of Ratoath were gradually rezoned for residential and commercial developments. Consequently, most of the surrounding characteristics described above are no longer in evidence).*

It is likely that it was the second Hugh de Lacy who built the large Motte on a pre-existing prominent site in the village of Ratoath, adjacent to the Catholic Church. The site was well chosen because the summit commanded a view of the Barony of Ratoath.

The Archaeological Inventory of County Meath, published by the OPW in 1987 gives the following information:

Motte: 1657 pp 161

---

[6] "Early Irish History and Mythology", Thomas F. O'Rahilly, Dublin Institute for Advanced Studies [DIAS], published in 1946.

[7] "A brief History of the Parish of Ratoath". Author: Gina Conway former pupil of Ratoath National School. Local History Project completed in 1990. Copies only in local libraries.

Above: Sketch depicts a typical Moate.

Right: Ratoath Motte today, with the Holy Trinity Church in the background

OS 44:4:6 (87.9, 51.4) Hachured 'Moat' OD 300-400) O 0214, 5186
Motte and Bailey: Flat-topped earthen mound (diam. of top 20m, diam. of base 62m, H 11m) with remains of fosse and rectangular bailey to SE. Fragments of font (1571) outside nearby RC church. SMR 44:7

In 1172 King Henry II divided Ireland among his knights and Meath was given to Hugh de Lacy[8]. After the coming of the Normans, Ratoath was retained by Hugh de Lacy as a seigniorial manor and it is recorded that he gave the tithes of Ratoath and Dunshaughlin to the Abbey of St. Thomas, Dublin, prior to 1183 (*See section on St. Thomas' Abbey below*). Eugenius, Bishop of Clonard, confirmed this grant in 1183.

The earliest mention of Ratoath as a Borough is in a Charter of Hugh De Lacy to St. Thomas's Abbey c.1200.[9] (*Ref: Gilbert: 1889, pp.8*). In 1194 the Lordship of Ratoath was granted to his son, also named Hugh. Together with Hugh De Lacy's lands in Ulster and elsewhere, Ratoath was confiscated by King John in the summer of 1210, and was granted by him to Philip of Worcester. Shortly before his death however, King John notified his judiciary that he had restored the Castle of Ratoath to Walter de Lacy as being of his inheritance. In 1241, Walter de Lacy, Lord of Meath, died without a male heir and Meath was consequently partitioned.

The earliest known church building in Ratoath was the Abbey of St. Mary Magdalene,

---

[8] "*Timetables of Irish History. An Illustrated Chronological Chart of the History of Ireland from 6000 BC to Present Times*" by Patrick C. Power and Seán Duffy. Published by Worth Press Limited, London. 2001.
[9] Gwynn, Stephen. "*The History of Ireland*". 1923, Palgrave Macmillan, London, 1923. ISBN Misc ISBN 3.

which was in existence down to the Fourteenth century. Its origin and the time of its suppression are unknown. In 1388 the Abbey owned forty acres of land. The Abbey and lands were attached to the Abbey of St. Thomas in Dublin. A Chantry was founded here for three priests who were to celebrate Mass daily. This Chantry acquired seventeen 'messuages' of land in Ratoath. It is evident from a *Charter of Simon De Rochford* that St. Mary Magdalene's was established before 1224. It is clear from this charter that it had a cemetery and was dependent on the parish church. Dopping, in his visitation of 1682, noted a chapel called St. Mary's near the parish church, which is almost certainly to be identified with the hospital of St. Mary Magdalene. The precise site, however, is unknown. This information is supported by A. Gwynn and R. N. Hadcock, in their publication entitled *"Medieval Religious Houses in Ireland"* and by Mervyn Archdall, A.M. in *"A History of the Abbeys, Priories and Other Religious Houses in Ireland"*, 1873. The Abbey of St. Mary Magdalene was a house of Augustinian Canons and it is suggested by Hugh de Burgo in 1762, that it may have had a hospital maintained by the regular Canons.

St. Thomas' Abbey
In 1177 after the canonisation of St. Thomas à Beckett, Archbishop of Canterbury, a church dedicated to his memory was founded on the western suburb of Dublin on behalf of Henry II, by William Fitz-Alden, the King's representative in Ireland. The church was under the care of the Augustinian Canons of the order of St. Victor. Attending at the opening were Bishops of Meath, Kildare, Waterford and Anglo Norman leaders. In the charter, the foundation of the church and a royal gift of land to it were stated to be intended by Henry II for the spiritual welfare of himself, his sons and his parents.

The Abbey lands of St Thomas' in Dublin extended from Mount Jerome in the south to James' Street in the north of Dublin. The land comprised of 436 statute acres. Nobles visiting Dublin usually stayed at St. Thomas. The Abbey kept 60 poor people, in food, drink and clothing.

Henry II granted to the Abbey tithes of rent in Dublin, fishing rights and tolls from ale. Laurence, Archbishop of Dublin, granted to the Abbey the church, in Kilsallaghan. The Abbey and its grounds were eventually raised to the status of Barony, following decrees granted by Henry's son John. It is worth noting that the freedom of this district from control of the corporation, earned it the title of "Liberties". This area later became known as the Earl of Meath's Liberties. In 1259, the citizens of Dublin were given a water supply by the Abbey.

The general register of the Abbey was placed in the Government Repository in Dublin Castle. The register consisted of transcripts of Documents relative to Churches, Lands, Possessions and rights which the Abbey acquired in various parts of Ireland, during its first century. The Abbey passed together with its revenues to the Earls of Meath.

Elizabeth I in 1569 granted houses and mills in and near the City, the lands of monasteries of Blessed Virgin Mary and St. Thomas's to the Mayor, Bailiffs and citizens of Dublin. The site of the Abbey is now occupied by the modern church of St. Catherine, dated 1760, in Thomas Street, Dublin. The Abbey was dissolved during the reign of Henry VIII.

Although the parish of Ratoath was originally dedicated to St. Thomas à Beckett it was subsequently changed to The Holy Trinity. This may explain the foundation noted by Dean Cogan in 1862 of a Chantry Chapel *"in the parish of St. Thomas with three chapels known as the Roods, St. Mary's and Thomas."* In 1682, Bishop Dopping records the dedication as Holy Trinity, and he notes, that the church was in good repair and although the chancel was unroofed it had a flagon. Parish registers and the altar were railed in; the roof was slated and the windows glazed; it had a clay floor and one bell. The church was situated north of the Motte. Dean Cogan also noted that the site is now represented by a featureless rectangular structure with a tower of 1817 attached.

Castle of Ratoath

In 1223 King Henry III's forces once more took the lands. However, in 1225, Walter de Lacy for the large fine of 3,000 Marks was given rights to the lands of his revolted tenants. The King retained the Castle of Ratour (Ratoath). A year later however, the custody of all Hugh's lands and castles was committed for three years to his brother Walter. Finally, on April 20th 1227, the lands and castles in Walter's custody were restored to Hugh. On August 15th 1227, Hugh was granted a Fair of 13 days at Ratoath. Up to this period the Castle of Ratoath was clearly of some importance and ranked with the Motte castles of Drogheda and Nobber.

The Manor of Ratoath

It is evident that Roger de Clifford II and his Countess sold Ratoath to Queen Eleanor, wife of Edward I. How or when the De Clifford family obtained Ratoath does not appear. It may have been through a grant from Hugh de Lacy, Earl of Ulster, to Roger II, as a reward for services, after the restoration of his lands but it is more probable that it was given by Prince Edward, after Hugh's death. On July 4th 1283 Queen Eleanor's charter granted the Manor of Ratoath to Richard de Burgh, Earl of Ulster. (*See separate article about Ratoath Manor*). In 1317 Ratoath was the scene of an ambush, when the Earl of Ulster attacked the Scots forces under Edward Bruce, but the Earl was defeated and fled to Dublin.

Ratoath in the Mid 17th and 18th Centuries

The seventeenth century brought great changes to Ireland after the warfare of the 1640's. The Rebellion of 1641 by the English Parliament against the power of the King spread to Ireland. The trouble of this decade ended with the brutal campaign of Oliver Cromwell throughout the country. According to the *Civil Survey of the 1640's* the tithes of the long Moorland of Ratoath, belonged to William Eiffe of Raystown as his inheritance in one moiety and the other moiety thereof belonged to one Mr. Dillon of Westmeath in right of his wife. As both of these were Catholics, the Commonwealth confiscated their possessions. The great tithes of Ratoath were left in the possession of Dr. Ambrose Ainger who was a Protestant. The tithes of Lagore, Flemingtown and Ballymore were in the possession of Anthony Dopping, later to become Protestant Bishop of Dublin. The titles of Kilrue, Ballybin, Mooretown, Killegland and Cooksland were in possession of Mr. Henry Bolton, Vicar of Ratoath.

Dr. Michael Plunkett

The Catholic religion was now in a lamentable condition. The wretched mud wall thatched chapels of which the Irish Catholics were then glad to have for their use, were levelled or closed over. In cities and towns, the Catholic clergy were concealed in cellars and garrets. An Elder bush on the Mucky Lane down to the Broadmeadow River was the site where the Penal Mass was said in Ratoath. One of the most famous of Ratoath's former parish priests was Dr. Michael Plunkett. Born in 1653, he was a relation of the Fingal and Dunsany Plunkett family and a cousin of St. Oliver Plunkett, the Primate of Ireland. He must have been educated privately. In fact he became Secretary to Oliver and was ordained by him in 1674. Two years later he was sent to Rome to study and while there acted as Oliver's agent and as agent for the Irish bishops. He returned to Ireland in 1690 and ruled the Diocese of Meath in the absence of a bishop between 1691 and 1713. It is important to note that at this time priests who registered were allowed to remain in their parishes but many priests refused to do so and remained at the peril of their lives. Bishops and regular priests were banished and the government intended that as the registered priests died out and no others were allowed in, that the Catholic religion would disappear. The chapel in Ratoath was then a mud-walled thatched house in the village, surrounded by other houses that screened it from view. Dr. Michael Plunkett was given refuge by the Protestant owner of the Manor House. He was given a secret room to spend the nights in, on the first floor of the Manor. The priest carried out his duties secretly during the day, and at night, used a ladder to get up to his room. This went on for several years and as he got older he had to be carried up this ladder on the back of a loyal servant of the Manor. Dr. Michael died in 1727 aged seventy-five and is buried in Killegland graveyard.[10] A fine monument marking his grave has the following inscription:

> *Jesus, Maria, Joseph, Salvator,*
> *Patrona, Advocate, Salva, Protégé,*
> *Defende Peccatorem, Famulum,*
> *Clientem, sub-hoc Lapide Jacentem,*
> *Michaelem Plunkett,*
> *Pastorem,*
> *He died August 1727.*
> *Aged 75.*
> *Memento Mori.*

Ratoath in the 19th Century

According to Samuel Lewis' *Topographical Dictionary of Ireland 1837*, "Ratoath, the parish (formerly a parliamentary borough) in the Barony of Ratoath, County of Meath and Province of Leinster, 3 miles north west from Ashbourne and 11½ miles from Dublin, contained 1779 inhabitants, of which number 552 were in the Village. In the reign of Henry VI it was classed among the borough towns of Meath. It had an Abbey, dedicated to St. Mary Magdalene, and it sent members to the Irish Parliament which it continued to do until the Act of Union of 1800, when the Borough was disfranchised."

OTHER REFERENCES:
Ríocht na Midhe. Peter Mulvany. 1975, 1988, 1989.
The Medieval Towns of Co. Meath. Royal Society of Antiquaries of Ireland, June 1921.
The Barony of Ratoath; By Adam Maher, & Laurence Kearney, both former pupils of Ratoath School, also Stephen Lane, Colin White, Derek Orr.
A Brief History on the Parish of Ratoath. 1990. Gina Conway.

---

10 Diocese of Meath, Ancient and Modern, By Dean Cogan. 1862.
    Ratoath, By Very Rev. John Cogan. c. 1952.
    Dublin Historical Records, 1952-53 by Rev. Maurice Dufficy.

LOCAL HISTORY

Lagore Crannóg

TONY DARBY

Lagore Crannóg site as seen by Archaeologist Mr Liam Price, M.R.I.A.

> "Lagore Crannóg site is a large and important site of the fortified residence type. As we find a number of Kings of Lagore mentioned in the Annals we would expect our early records to throw some light on its history and in particular to reveal whom these rulers of the fortress were. What position did they occupy in the early political system of the country and for how long was the place a political centre, or local 'capital' of importance"?

Lagore Crannóg is situated where the parishes of Ratoath and Dunshaughlin meet at Lagore Little. This site is one of the historic jewels of the parish.

Today the site is adjacent to the bog land that once surrounded this historic place and there is very little visible evidence of the archaeological excavations that took place there

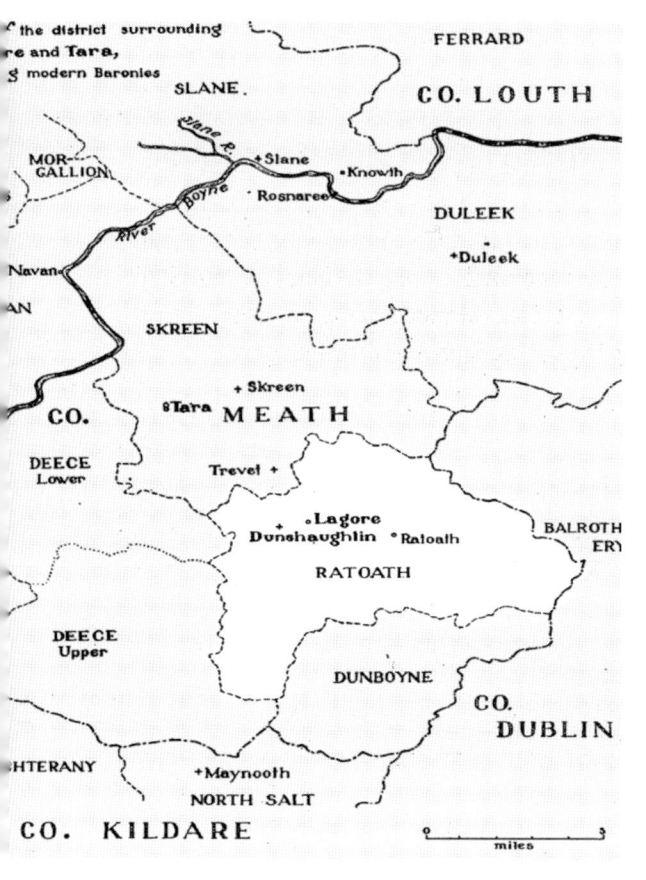

(Left): Lagore is in the parish of Ratoath, Barony of Ratoath, in County Meath, and is five miles away from Tara, the ancient political centre, or "capital", of Ireland.

Lagore Crannóg in 2003

An Artists impression of how Lagore Crannóg might have looked

over the years. Due to the drainage of the Broadmeadow River the lake that surrounded the Crannóg has long since gone. As you can see from a photograph below it would take but a little imagination for one to visualise how life in this part of the world must have been like all those years ago.

Lagore Crannóg Site Description
The site consists of an artificial island approximate 41 meters in circumference and about 2.5-3.0 meters high and fortified by wooden stakes driven into the ground and projecting outwards to protect the dwellings within the settlement from intruders. Access to the island would have been over a roughly constructed timber bridge, or by boat as water surrounded the site on all sides.

Lagore Crannóg first came to the notice of the public as an important historic place in 1839, when Wilde, the archaeologist, took an interest in its history and carried out a number of excavations on the site. He made some interesting discoveries (more about them later). But it was almost a hundred years later when the most significant excavations took place on the site.

In 1934-36 The Harvard Archaeological expedition travelled from The United States to Ireland to carry out an extensive dig on the Crannóg. Some of the finds turned out to be very important, and many of the objects found on the site are on view in the National Museum in Dublin.

In order for the 1934/36 excavations to take place, permission had to be sought from the landowners at that time. Mr. Patrick Rodgers of Ratoath and Mrs. Angelo Murphy of Dunshaughlin owned the property jointly. The Crannóg or artificial island was situated at the eastern end of the lake. (See map)

The Crannóg construction consisted of heavy layers of brushwood and peat interspersed with timbers, sand, clay and straw. During the building of the Crannóg it is thought that a terrible massacre of the workers occurred.

Here is what **Mr. Hencken** stated in his book, when he suggested that a reconstruction of the massacre scene might be as follows:

LOCAL HISTORY
Lagore Crannóg

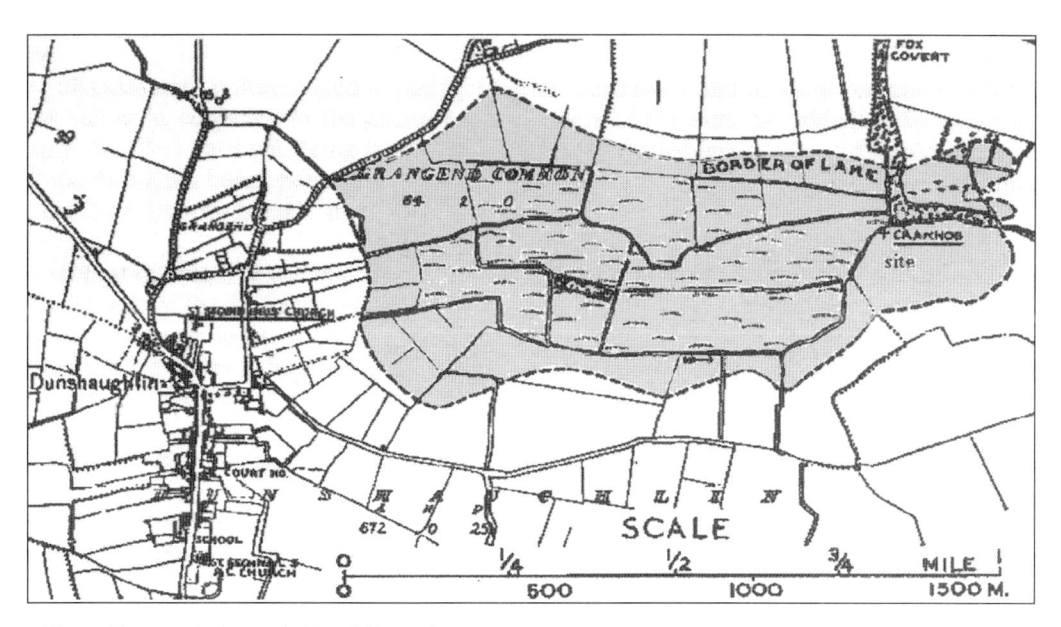

Map of Lagore Lake and site of Crannóg

"A party of workers were building the Crannóg, but had not yet finished laying the foundation layer. Now the party consisted of men, women and children, and some of the women had brought their babies. While at work, the party was massacred with extraordinary ferocity. It appears that the bodies of the victims were cut to pieces and scattered about the site. The strange thing about the massacre was that the backs of the victims' heads were chopped off and left behind, but the rest of the skulls were carried away. The only exception was the body of an infant, which was thrown into the mud more or less intact including the skull. After this horrible episode work was resumed, and the mutilated remains were either allowed to sink down out of sight in the mud or were covered over by continued building."

"In all, some 200 human bones were found on and about the site. Of course human bones scattered about the site raises the question of cannibalism, but the only way one can guess as to whether cannibalism was practised or not is to see whether the bones had been split for the marrow, as was common with animal bones. At Lagore no such evidence was found on the human bones."

"The excavations produced a total of 47,976.25 lbs. of animal bones and in addition to this the following quantities of animal skulls: 608 ox skulls, 173 pig skulls, 153 sheep skulls, 9 horse skulls, 7 dog skulls, 4 red deer skulls, 2 fox skulls, 1 hare skull, 1 otter skull. In addition 938 bird bones were found. a percentage breakdown is as follows: Wild Goose 41.8 %, Wild duck 19.5 %, Domestic Fowl 18.8 %, Raven 7.4 %, (Hooded Crow, Rook, Chough, Barn Owl Buzzard, Sea Eagle, Cormorant, Swan, Heron, Gull, Redthroated Diver, Great Crested Grebe, Coot, Moorhen and Corncrake[1] made up 12.5 %)."

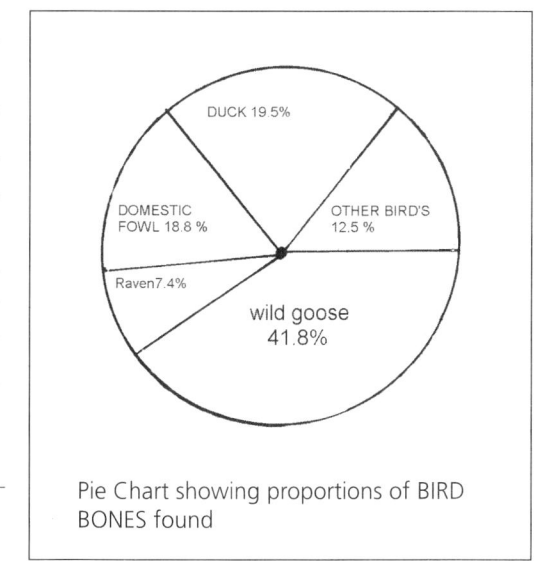

Pie Chart showing proportions of BIRD BONES found

---

[1] Sadly the Corncrake is no longer with us in the Ratoath area. It was last heard in the 1960s.

It is clear that the people that lived at Lagore Crannóg were not vegetarians. It is interesting to note the inclusion of seabirds such as the Chough and the Sea Eagle in the report. One might expect to find them along the seashore and not inland.

The Palisades
We now turn our attention to the construction and appearance of the Crannóg itself. Firstly, there was an outer palisade (fence of wooden stakes) and some time later there were two more palisades added and these would have surrounded the site completely. The significance of the Palisades was to protect the dwellers within the settlement from invaders. The first and earliest, the Pile Palisade, was the original one. The other two, the Post Palisade and the Plank Palisade, belonged to the later refortifications. This proves that two historical destructions of the Crannóg took place.

A report on the construction of the Crannóg by **Mr Hugh Hencken, D. Litt., M.R.I.A., F.S.A.** described the Palisades thus:

> *"The Palisades were differentiated in part by their outward slope and depth of penetration, The Pile Palisade, being the oldest and most subjected to the pressure of the layers of the material added to the Crannóg, sloped outwards most sharply. The Post Palisade being later, on the whole penetrated less deeply and sloped outwards much less. The Plank Palisade, being the latest, penetrated even less and was more or less upright. Also the pile Palisade, being the deepest, was the least destroyed, while the Plank Palisade, being higher up was the most destroyed."*
>
> *"The greatest diameter of the Pile Palisade was 41 metres, and it was made of piles 5-15 cms, in diameter. In places it was stiffened by the inclusion of horizontal timbers placed between the piles. Like the other two Palisades, it was probably analogous to the wall of a rath or stone fort, but how far it may have projected above the original surface is now impossible to say. The Post Palisade was made of oaken post, on the whole a little larger then the piles. Many of them were roughly squared. This Palisade once enclosed an area 36 meters in diameter so far as can be measured. Hence in the second period the occupied area was smaller than in the first. A considerable part of the western edge of the Crannóg had been abandoned, and where undisturbed, was found to be covered with mud."*
>
> *"This area of the site was in a particularly soft part of the lakebed, and may have proved too unstable to be worth enclosing a second time. It should be pointed out, however, that owing to destruction it is impossible to trace the whole course of the Post Palisade. But it occurred in all areas where expected, except where the Crannóg had been disturbed. Post-holes were of little help at Lagore. Though they could occasionally be detected in the thick layers of clay and mud, this condition did not prevail everywhere. The soft nature of the site made it possible to pull out the well-preserved posts even at the time of the excavation. The boggy material of the Crannóg would then close behind them leaving no post-holes."*

Historical Context
The following is based upon the historical account by **Mr Liam Price, M.R.I.A.**

> *"Lagore, the ancient Loch Gabair, is mentioned in Irish historical documents, as the seat of the local kings between 785 and 969 and references to the "island of Lagore" leave no room for doubt that the Crannóg was their residence. But the history of the site began long before 785."*
>
> *"From the genealogies it appears that the kings of Lagore belonged to the family called Clann*

Chernaigh Sotail and that the kings of Deiscert Brega belonged to the same family. Indeed there seems to be no distinction between the kings of Deiscert Brega and the kings of Lagore, and the two titles appear to have been interchangeable. The core of their fluctuating realm consisted substantially of the two modern baronies of Skreen and Ratoath, an area about 23 miles long and 5 to 10 miles wide. But at its greatest extent it included about half of County Dublin and half of Co. Meath. Though their domain, like those of many other provincial kings in Ireland, was very small, it was of more than ordinary importance since it included Tara, and since its rulers were related to the high – kings. Indeed it is clear that in the 7th century one High King of Ireland occupied the Crannóg."

"Now the Clann Chernaigh Sotail were a branch of the Sil Aedha Slane one of the chief ruling families of the Southern Ui Neill. They were descended from Diarmait MacCerbhaill who was high king from 544 to 565. It was in his reign that the legendary cursing of Tara by St Ruadan of Lorrha took place."

(According to legend a criminal named Aedh Guaire fled to Saint Ruadhan seeking protection. The High King of Tara, Diarmait MacCerbhaill, entered the house of St. Ruadhan to arrest the criminal and sentenced him to death. This disrespect of a holy place prompted a battle which was to mark the beginning of the downfall of Tara.)

"This legend is supposed to explain the abandonment of Tara by the high kings, but though this did not happen as early as the reign of Diarmait MacCerbhaill, some change may have taken place at that time. The lands that later belonged to the kings of Lagore belonged to the son of Diarmait MacCerbhaill, the high king Aedh Slane, who died in 604. But there is no evidence to show that he occupied Lagore."

"But Aedh Slane's son, the High King Diarmait Ruanaid, who died in 664, did have his "royal house" on the Crannóg."

Indeed the Rawlin's Manuscripts, B.502 and B.512, contain a most remarkable story connected with Lagore in his reign. This story has a historical basis, and if it is somewhat exaggerated it perhaps serves to depict the life of these lake-dwelling kings. According to this story, in 651 the High King's nephews met their death by being crushed in a mill by a certain Maelodran, son of Dimma Cron. To avenge them Diarmait gathered his under-kings and their armies at Lagore. He offered to spare the Leinstermen if they would deliver Maelodran to him, but they refused. Maelodran then said that he would give himself up and set off alone. On the shore of the lake he encountered the assembled armies, but the kings who led them had gone to feast with Diarmait in his fortress in the lake. Maelodran waited till nightfall. When the rowing to and from the Crannóg had ceased, he took a boat and went over to the Crannóg, where he waited by the door where the king slept.

"Then," continues Kuno Meyer's translation, *"Diarmait went out alone, without the knowledge of anyone, to go to bend his knees. And before the house he met with Maelodran. 'Bring me a wisp,' said Diarmait 'Indeed I will,' said Maelodran. He brings him a handful of nettles. 'Here is my sword,' said Diarmait. Maelodran took it. 'Woe to me! I have been burnt! What is thy name?' said Diarmait. 'Art thou making a stranger of me?' he said 'Here is Maelodran, son of Dimma Cron, Who has slain thy sons and who will strike off thy head now,' seizing his head and Dragging it towards him. 'My full will, O Maelodran!' said Diarmait. ' And from me thine own will! Said Maelodran. After having peace, they both go into the house."* The other kings were then summoned one by one to drink and pledge protection to Maelodran, and this ceremony was finished before morning. Maelodran returned to Leinster with handsome presents from the high- king, and from that day forth was his battle champion.

The next historical reference to Lagore again concerns the Leinstermen. In 676, another nephew of Diarmait, the High-King Finsnechta Fledach, defeated them near Lagore. Perhaps he was defending an important fortress. Diarmait's son, Cernach Sotal, who died in 663, is neither called a king nor is he associated with Lagore, except that he gave his name to the family that ruled there later. Cernach's son Niall (died 701) was neither a king nor is he connected by any historical reference with Lagore, but Niall's son, Conall Grant (died 718), was King of Deiscert Brega, a title that seems to be interchangeable with that of King of Lagore. One of Conall Grant's brothers was the High-King Fogartach (died 723). Fogartach's son, Fergus (died 751), was also King of Deiscert Brega. Maelduin (died 785), the son of Fergus, was the first of the family to be called King of Lagore.

All this implies that at least from 651, when the High-King Diarmait Ruanaid mustered his army there, the Crannog was a place of importance, and that by the eight century it had passed into the hands of local rulers descended from the High Kings.

The next event of major importance in the history of the site occurred in 850 during the Rebellion of Cinaeda Mac Conaing against the High King, when the "Island of Lagore" was burnt "level with its floor." Evidently Tigernach, the King of Lagore at the time, was allied to the High King. But the next year the High King and Tigernach captured Cinaedh and drowned him in the river Nanny near the village of Duleek.

Another destruction of the Crannóg took place in 934 when Amlaibh ua h-Imair, probably Olaf son of Gothfrith, and the Norse King of Dublin, who died in 940, destroyed the "Island of Lagore". This may have brought on the decline of Lagore as a place of importance, for with the death of Beollan Mac Ciarmaic, King of Lagore, in 969 the site disappears altogether from historical record. The Clann Chernaigh Sotail continued to be a family of local prominence for long afterwards, but there is nothing to connect them further with the Crannog. Presumably, the place was abandoned about 1000 A.D.

THE ARCHAEOLOGICAL DATING OF THE CRANNÓG

The occupation layers could be divided into three groups denoting three successive periods, each of which seemed to be associated with different styles of wooden palisades. The disturbance of the site by previous diggings may be blamed for the failure to secure any information on the types of structures that stood within the palisades. These periods are called **Period I, Period II and Period III. Period I** is subdivided into **Ia** and **Ib.** The body of the artificial island itself represents **Period Ia**. This material was all put in place at one time, and objects contained in it, or found under it, cannot be later than the period of construction. **Period Ib** is used to indicate the first occupation upon the island.

Period Ia (earliest construction)
Despite the fact that the site produced objects of Roman date, and even some pre-Roman types, the latest material included in the original foundation below the occupation layers must be used to judge the period when the artificial island was made. A few potsheds were associated with Period I. One of these is a fragment of Roman terra sigillata, which belonged to **Period Ia**. But this can hardly be used to date the Crannóg, since Period I also contained some fragments of much later Continental pottery that could be dated between the 7th and 9th Centuries. Some of these were in **Period Ia**, and indeed one of them was believed to be no earlier then the 8th Century. At the same time the historical reference to the site in 651 indicates that the 8th Century is too late a date.

Period Ib
Period Ib represents the first occupation and contains a few datable objects: a single "Romano – British" shred of a type known from post-Roman sites in Scotland and also known in Ireland from the 5th to the 7th Centuries; a shred of a continental carinated bowl of the 7th - 9th Centuries; a workshop for making glass studs which have Irish parallels of the 7th-8th Centuries; and a bronze object decorated with a snake-like creature resembling those in the 7th Century *Book of Durrow*. This one might be 7th or early 8th Century. Here we see a tendency to the forms of the 7th Century and somewhat later. This helps to substantiate the view that the Crannog was not founded before the 7th Century.

Period II and Period III
The objects found in the Period II and Period III strata do not give satisfactory evidence of date. But here the historical evidence is helpful. Excavation showed that the site had been fortified three times, once when it was first built and twice more later. From the *Annals* we learn that it was burnt "level with its floor" in 850 in the Rebellion of Cinaedh Mac Conaing. Though signs of burning were not marked in the limited areas remaining undisturbed, it is reasonable to suppose that this event marked the end of Period I, and necessitated the refortification at the beginning of Period II.

Again in 934, Olaf, the Norse King of Dublin destroyed the "Island of Lagore". This may well mark the end of Period II, while the third and final refortification that followed marks the beginning of Period III. The only way to approach an archaeological date for the end of Period III, the last phase of the occupation, is to consider the latest objects from the site. These, unfortunately, were not in the stratified deposits but were undoubtedly connected with the site. They include a small brooch later than the Vernacular Style, which ended in the 9th Century; a bronze disc of the 9th or 10th centuries; a few Viking objects (a spear and part of a silver bracelet and four combs) which would date from the 9th or 10th Centuries, a penny of the English King, Edward the Elder (901-925) and two small pins of about 1000 or a little later in which the ring head has become a cap over the head. On the basis of archaeology alone, it could be said that Lagore was abandoned at the close of the 10th Century or at the beginning of the 11th Century. The historical record ends with 969. There is nothing to indicate that the Crannóg was occupied for many decades beyond that date.

THE CULTURE OF LAGORE

Lagore, it seems, represented a large lay establishment, which was almost wholly self-supporting. It shows that a king's residence did not differ from those of other landlords except in size and in the number of different kinds of craftsmen who were employed there. The Crannóg, like other Crannógs and forts, was the centre of an agricultural community, which must have controlled extensive lands in the vicinity of the lake.

Farming
Farming played a big part in the lives of the people of Lagore, as almost 50,000 lbs of animal bones found on the site, tells its own story. And so, what of the farming tools that were found? Among the agricultural tools was a heavy iron plough, and it would suggest that a large team of horses was needed to pull this plough, as the soil was very heavy. Indeed the soil is still heavy to this day. Also some horse bits were found, and of course wheat straw was found in the foundations.

Bronze Workings
Bronze working was carried out on the Crannóg. This is evidenced by the finding of pieces of copper ore, presumably local. Ingot moulds and moulds for bronze rings, a large number of crucibles, a piece of copper or bronze which had spilled during working and waste scraps of sheet bronze were also found.

Iron Workings
Smiths, as well as Bronziers, had workshops on the Crannóg, as large quantities of iron slag were found. It is safe to assume that many of the weapons and tools were made on the Crannóg.

Glass and Glass Moulds
There were a few fragments of glass found, either Roman or of Roman tradition, associated with the earlier history of the Crannóg. They were clearly imported, and may represent imports of broken glass to be used in the making of ornamental studs for bronze ornaments. Moulds for such studs were also found, one of which still contained a stud.

Summary
On archaeological evidence, one would have to say that the Lagore Crannóg was built in the late 7th Century. But according to historical evidence the High King Dairmait Ruanaid was using Lagore as a fortress as early as 651 A.D. Can one conclude that the Crannóg was built long before 651 A.D.?

HOW IMPORTANT WAS LAGORE?
From the genealogies it appears that the Kings of Lagore belonged to the family called Clann Chernaigh Sotail and that the Kings of Deiscert Brega belonged to the same family. Indeed, there seems to be no distinction between the Kings of Deiscert Brega and the Kings of Lagore. Since they were related to the High Kings in Tara, and since the High King lived in Lagore in the 7th Century, we can conclude that Lagore was an important place at that time.

The Demise and Fall of Lagore
The first destruction of Lagore took place in 850 during a rebellion by Cinaeda Mc Conaing against the High King, Tigernach, with the result that the Crannóg was burnt to the ground, but the next year Tigernach had his revenge when he captured Cinaeda and drowned him.

The next destruction of Lagore was in 934 when it was destroyed by Amlaibh ua h-Imair, son of a Norse King of Dublin. This may have brought on the decline of Lagore as a place of importance, for with the death of Beollan mc Ciarmaic, King of Lagore, in 969 the site disappeared altogether from the historical records. And so it seems that Lagore, as a place of importance was no more after the year 1000 A.D.

THE ARCHAEOLOGICAL FINDS

The following description includes the objects from the most recent excavations and also the old finds from the site in the National Museum whose provenance may be verified. This has been done to present as complete a picture as possible of the culture of Lagore. Since the number of stratified objects and the degree of culture change, from period to period, are relatively small, it seems less repetitive to discuss the objects by grouping similar things together. These groups of finds are divided into (1) Stratified Finds; (2) Unstratified Finds; (3) Old Finds are those found on the site before the Harvard excavations in 1934-1936.

Stratified Finds:
These are subdivided as follows:
Pre- Crannóg denotes the few objects that manifestly antedate the site.

Period Ia denotes the material that came to the site when the Crannóg was being built. In this group are the objects from the various layers of brushwood and peat below the first occupation. With them are also included, objects that were immediately under the Brushwood in such a position that they must be connected with the building of the Crannóg, rather than with the objects obviously antedating it.

Period Ib denotes objects belonging to the first occupation.

Period I denotes a small group, which came from an area where the distinction between **Ia** and **Ib** was not clear.

Period II and Period III denote objects of the second and third occupations.
Period Ib-II, II-III and **Ib-III** are classifications used where the layering did not permit more precise designation.

Unstratified Finds: These cannot be fitted into the sequence of building periods defined in the section dealing with the structure of the site, and hence they can only be regarded as belonging to the period of the site as a whole. They comprise of three groups:
Objects found in the lake mud outside the palisades. These had been thrown away or lost by the occupants of the Crannóg, and hence lay outside the stratified area.
Objects found in areas, which had been dug over by previous excavators
Objects from the surface soil. Many of them must have come into that stratigraphical position as a result of previous excavation, including the digging of the "river"

Old finds: These are indicated as such since their origin is not quite as certain as that of the material excavated under supervision. Most of them come from the Petrie collection. Petrie obtained these objects through a dealer named Underwood, but Petrie went to the site with Wilde and verified finds from the boggy soil, and they are what a Crannóg of this period would be expected to yield. There is documentary material in the National Museum that makes it quite clear that the finds are from "Lagore". This is borne out by the fact that there is no other Crannog in the Lagore bog, and indeed there is no indication of any other site in the vicinity. It will also be recalled that the Harvard Expedition found that large parts of the Lagore Crannóg had been previously dug over.

Mr Paddy Ward who lived on the Ratoath – Dunshaughlin Road adjacent to the bog, said that he remembers his father recalling visits to the Crannóg by antiquaries and the digging up of the ancient objects.

OBJECTS FOUND AT LAGORE CRANNOG

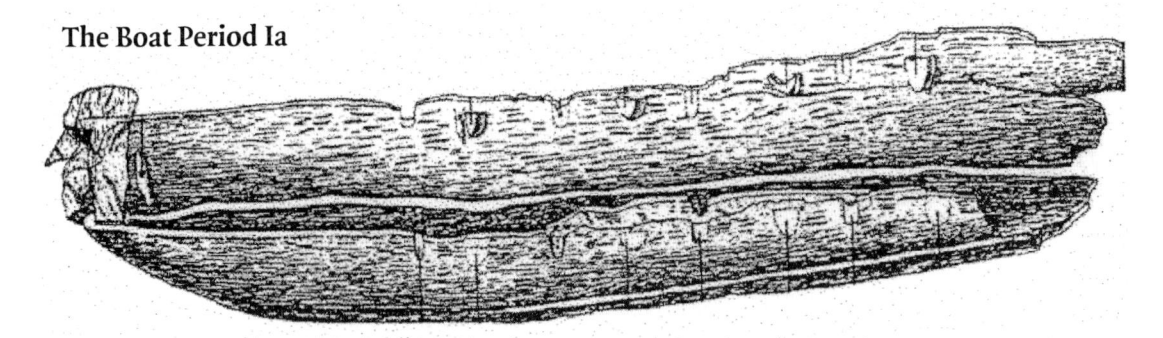

The Boat Period Ia

A large dug out oak boat some 8-10 meters long and 95cms wide was found in the foundations of the site. It was propelled by two sets of oars, but unfortunately when the "river" was being dug much of the bow section was destroyed.

Bronze Dagger

Old Finds: This Dagger was cast all in one piece with an openwork handle.

Lagore Buckle

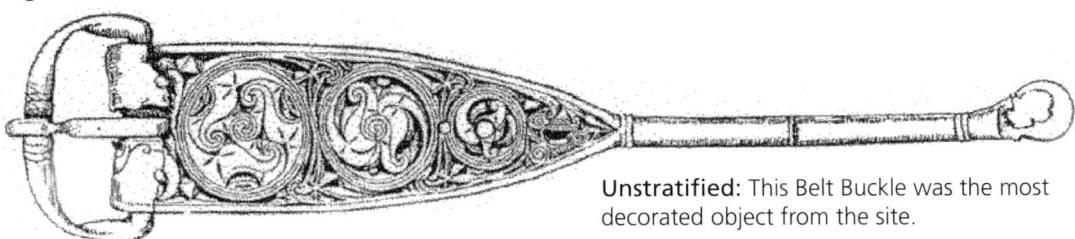

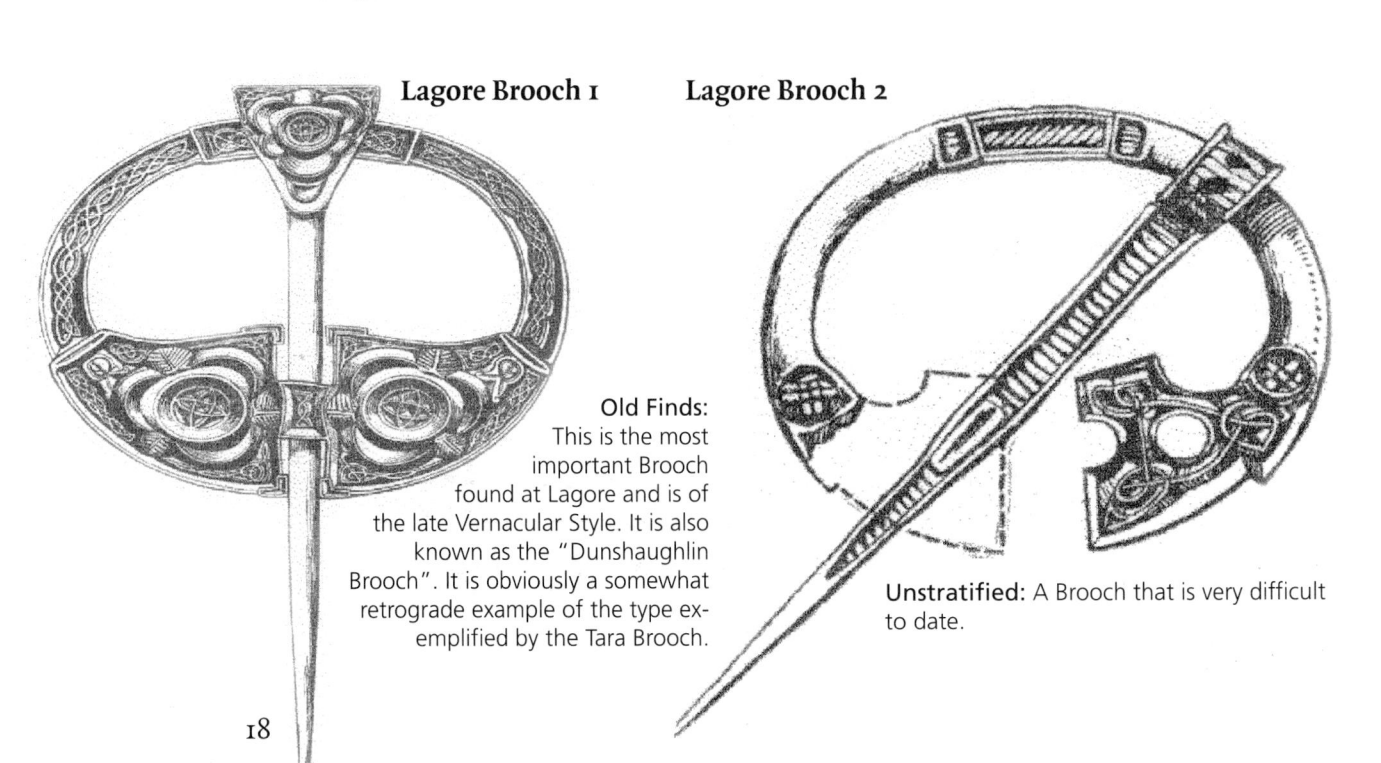

Unstratified: This Belt Buckle was the most decorated object from the site.

Lagore Brooch 1   Lagore Brooch 2

Old Finds: This is the most important Brooch found at Lagore and is of the late Vernacular Style. It is also known as the "Dunshaughlin Brooch". It is obviously a somewhat retrograde example of the type exemplified by the Tara Brooch.

Unstratified: A Brooch that is very difficult to date.

Gold found at Lagore Period Ia

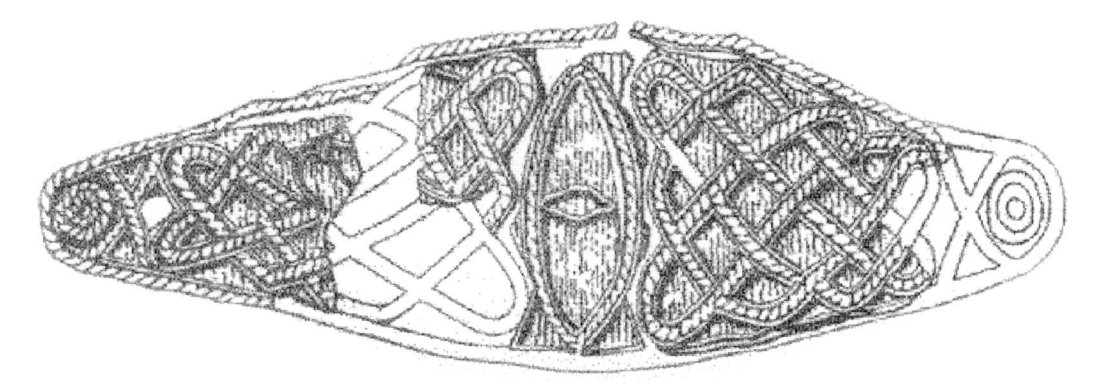

The Gold Ornament shown here is one of two Gold pieces found on the site, the other being part of a Gold Bracelet. The Ornament was found broken in three pieces in the Central Area between layers of Brushwood, and so it is safe to assume that it came into the Crannóg during the building operations.

Prisoners Chains

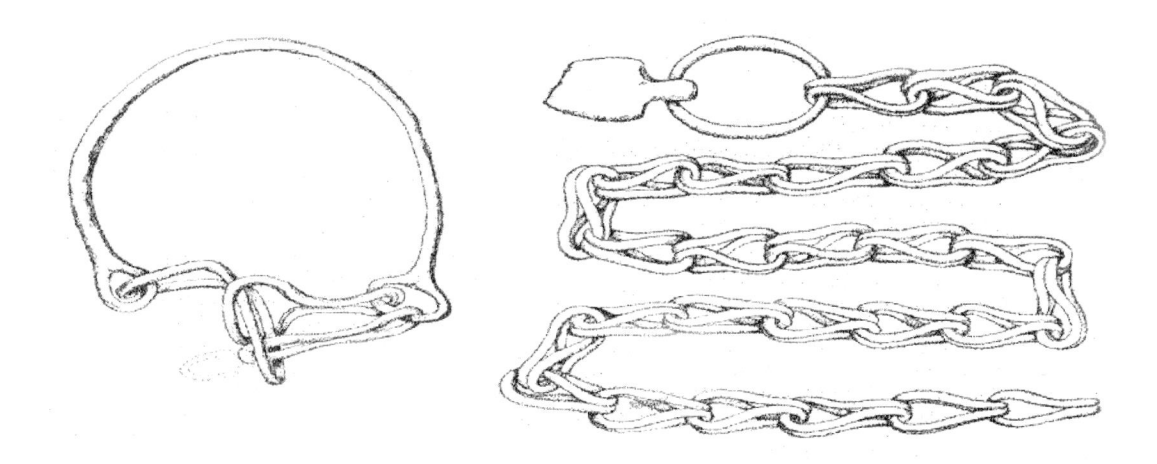

Old Finds: Here we have just some of the chains and leg irons from the site:

Key and Lock Spring

Unstratified: This is a Roman type of key, but not related to the Lock Spring shown here:

Horse Bits Period Ia

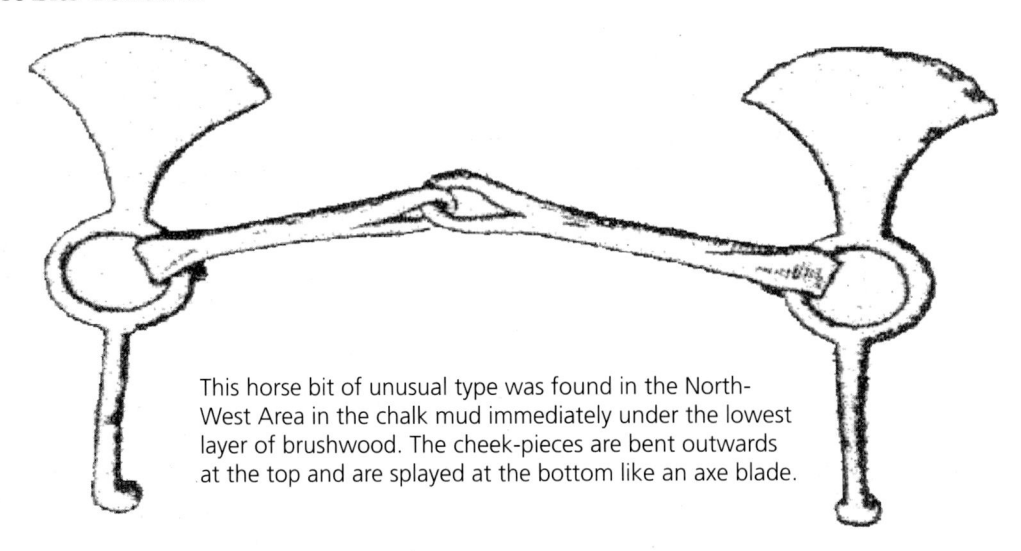

This horse bit of unusual type was found in the North-West Area in the chalk mud immediately under the lowest layer of brushwood. The cheek-pieces are bent outwards at the top and are splayed at the bottom like an axe blade.

Bronze Spear Head

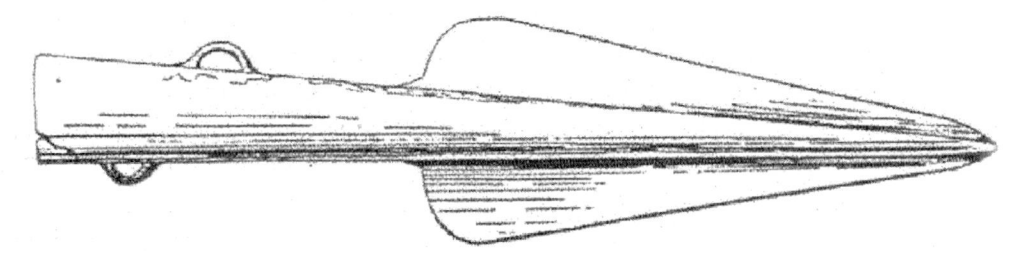

Stratified Finds: This Spear Head was found beside the Skeleton of a Red Deer. It is tempting to speculate that the Red Deer was slain by a hunter as it lay trapped in the mud, and that the hunter was unable to retrieve his prize as it sank down into the mud.

Swords from Lagore

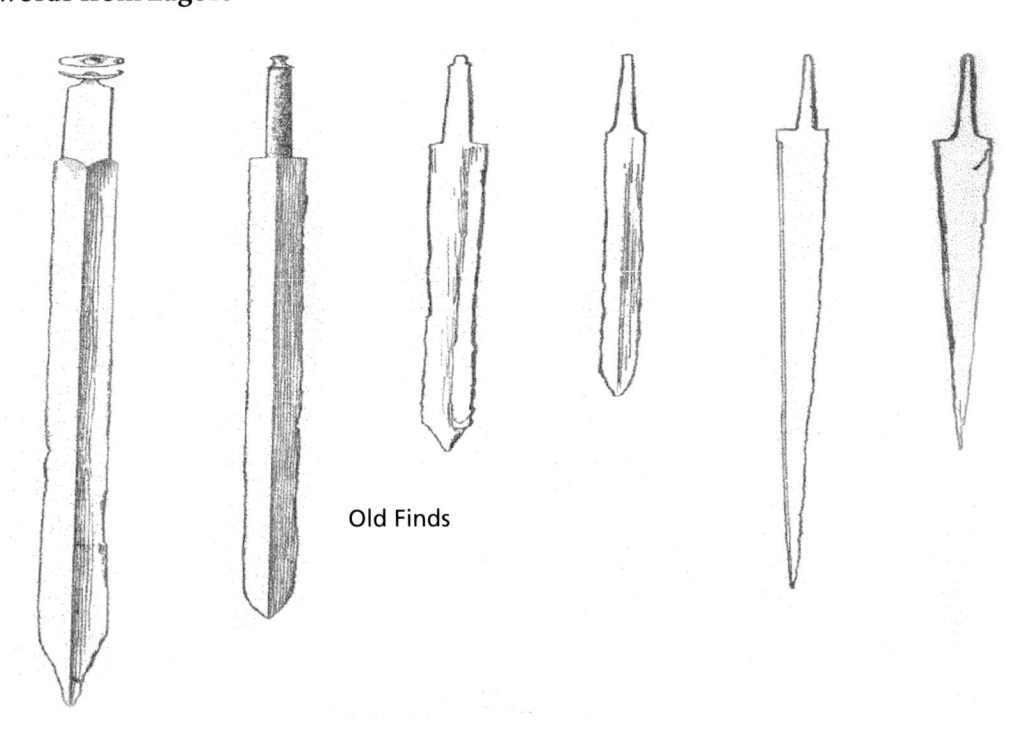

Old Finds

Conclusion – "Lagore what of the future?"

Lagore Crannóg is a very important part of our local history, and as the Irish people of today are becoming more aware of their local history, I am sure we will hear a lot more about the Crannóg at Lagore in the future. There is one important aspect that should be remembered and not overlooked. When one considers that the Harvard Excavation took place almost seventy years ago, and was concentrated on the main site, no excavation of the surrounding area took place. This was due in part to the fact that the pumps that were available at the time were inadequate in keeping the water back. Another interesting fact is that no burial ground was found. Where are the remains of those people from Lagore buried? Are their graves to be found somewhere in the fields nearby?

In 1983 Mr. Ben Lynam, a local farmer, while out walking in the fields near the Crannóg discovered a large stone axe head of ten inches long, which he handed over to the National Museum in Dublin. Mr. D. Sweetman, an Archaeologist with the Office of Public Works, estimated the axe head to be 3,000 to 5,000 years old. In the mid 1960s the skeleton of an Irish elk was discovered at the western end of the lake by a worker who was digging a trench, a point from the antler was saved by Mr Michael Kenny from Dunshaughlin; unfortunately most of the remains of the Elk were destroyed.

Taking these facts into account, I think it is safe to assume that Lagore has a few more secrets yet to be discovered in the years to come. Of course, that is, if the site is recognised and protected as an important national treasure worthy of preservation. Many local people who are proud of our heritage would like to see the Crannóg recognised and protected. However, today this is far from a reality, with large developments encroaching on the Crannóg, this historical site is under serious threat. I think it is fair to say that our heritage is not ours to dispose of as we see fit, for we only have it in trust and must account for it to those who come after us.

The Archaeological Inventory of County Meath, part of the *Archaeological Survey of Ireland* carried out by the OPW and published in 1987, identifies the site of the Crannóg at Lagore as a significant monument of the area. It has been catalogued as follows:

OS 38:15:5 (54.8, 0.7) 'Crannog (site of)
OD 300 – 400 N 8862, 5285

Ratoath Past and Present

47 townlands of Ratoath Parish

Today, the 47 townlands of Ratoath Parish (approximately 11000 statute acres or 4455 hectares) includes ten of the eleven townlands that were once Rathbeggan Parish.

LOCAL HISTORY

Rathbeggan

TONY DARBY

RATHBEGGAN IS LOCATED in the south west corner of Ratoath parish, and in the eighteenth century was a parish in its own right. It was made up of eleven Townlands, depicted in grey on the map opposite: Rathbeggan, Ennistown, Killester, Powderlough, Gormanstown, Mill-land, Wilkinstown, Growtown, Porterstown, Raynestown and Warrenstown.

A Church was established in Rathbeggan by Beccan early in the thirteenth century and was built on the ruins of an ancient Abbey. As to how Rathbeggan got its name we can only speculate, for at that time one would find a small rath or mott adjacent to the church, and with this in mind I am sure it is reasonable to suggest that the name Rathbeggan could have perhaps derived from the name (the Rath of Beccan).

There is little or no record of the early years of the church until 1550 when Rev. John Callen succeeded Rev. John Ledwidge as Church of Ireland Rector. In 1622 when Rev. James Kearns was Rector, a report by Sir Garret Moore to Bishop Ussher suggests that the Church and Chancel at Rathbeggan was in very good condition.

Dr John Bolton of Lagore House was appointed Rector in 1678 and was Rector for the next twenty-one years until 1699 when he was appointed as Dean of Derry, and Jonathan Swift the famous writer, poet and novelist became Rector from 1699. Swift had responsibility for the three parishes of Agher, Laracor and Rathbeggan. It was during Swift's time as Rector that a report in 1733 by Walter Scott suggests that when Jonathan Swift was conducting a Service in Rathbeggan, he had but one person in the congregation and that person was Roger Cox, the clerk. A short time later, Service was discontinued at the church and before the close of Swift's time as Rector there was no Service at Rathbeggan and the church soon fell into disrepair and subsequently into ruin.

It was not until 1817 that the Church at Rathbeggan was rebuilt; the full cost of re-building the church is not known, except to say that £1,000.00 was spent between 1817 and 1823. It was during this time that the Standish family lived in Rathbeggan House.

Rathbeggan House at some time in its history also had Harold K. Allison and his wife Lady Diana and their two children Aileen and Harold in residence.

In 1822 the names of John Standish and James and Arthur Wilson were engraved on the pulpit. It was in the same year 1822 that a storm was responsible for severe damage to the church roof and walls. The church was repaired by some local unskilled workers at the cost of £112, one shilling and two pence. An architect on inspection said that the walls should be taken down, and the estimated cost might be in the region of £200.00. The average cess in the parish was only four or five pence per acre in 1822, but the following year 1823 it was raised to one shilling and five pence and before the year was out, it was again raised to one shilling and six pence.

Nine years later in 1832 the Journal of the House of Lords (Vol. 64) recorded on the 16th July that a petition from Ratoath, for the total abolition of Tithes and Church cess in Ireland, was received[1]. Ratoath represented the Union of Ratoath, Rathbeggan, Kilmoon and Kilbrew. During the 17th, 18th and 19th centuries no more than 3 or 4 families were in attendance at the Church in Rathbeggan.

In 1825 Peter Duncan was Schoolmaster at Rathbeggan and there were between 17 and 22 pupils on the school roll book. He also acted as the parish clerk. From 1859 the Church at Rathbeggan had no Minister and it finally closed in 1864. Only the Standish family were left to attend church, and later that year they were assigned a pew in the church at Ballinaglassan.

After the disestablishment of the Church of Ireland in Ballymaglasson, in 1870, it was demanded by law that the Churches surrender the *Parish Registers* to the Master of the Rolls, unless the Parish provided a fire-proof safe. Because of the enforcement of this law most of the Parishes of Meath had to part with their registers of baptisms, marriages and burials. In 1884 the church at Rathbeggan was finally pulled down and all that remained was the church tower.

Before parting with the registers, a note on one marriage was recorded by Vicar John James. On the 6th April 1839 John Wilkinson of Kilmessan married Sophia Standish of Rathbeggan. Vicar John James conducted the sermon.

Tithes payable in Rathbeggan in 1824

John Standish	John Yourell (Warrenstown)
Edward Bobidge	William Yourell (Bodeen)
Matthew Spring (Powderlough)	Patrick Crowley (Porterstown)
Elias Corbally (Raynestown & Growtown)	Patrick Mc Cann (Powder Lough)
Nicholas & Lawrence Seery (Powderlough)	Sylvester Mc Nally (Bodeen)
Pat Cahill (Wilkinstown)	James Lovely (Rathbeggan & Folistown)
Edward Crehan (Gormanstown)	James Mc Alley (Rathbeggan & Folistown)
Hon. Francis Stanhope (Mill-land)	Rev. James Matthews (Rathbeggan)

In 1824 Rev. James Matthews received £175.00 in lieu of Tithes

Name of Clergy who conducted service at Rathbeggan

No date	John Ledwidge	1678	John Bolton
1550	John Callen	1699	Johathan Swift
1622	James Kearns	1817	Henry Crosby
1630	Adam Ryan	1818	James Matthews
1668	Francis Ussher	1832	John James
1671	James Mandeley		

---

1 From: 'House of Lords Journal Volume 64: 16 July 1832', Journal of the House of Lords: volume 64: 1831-1832, pp. 381-385.
   URL: http://www.british-history.ac.uk/report.aspx?compid=19352#s19 Date accessed: 12 July 2008.

LOCAL HISTORY — Rathbeggan

The present Primary School at Rathbeggan is situated in the townland of Growtown and was built in 1960 by local contractors Christy Martin & Sons, Ratoath. The cost of this new school at the time was £7000.00, and the land was acquired from Mr Tony Crean. Those who worked on the construction of the school included, Sonny Martin, Noel Martin, Danny Hogg (plasterer), Peader Lynam (carpenter), Christy Nulty and Shane Whyte.

LOCAL HISTORY

Townlands in Ratoath Parish

RATOATH HERITAGE GROUP

THE FOLLOWING are the names of the 47 townlands in Ratoath Parish in alphabetical order. These are shown on the outline parish map used in the Rathbeggan article. The meaning of the place names, where known in Irish or English, is shown in the right hand column below.

Balfestown:	Baile an Bhailfigh
Ballybin Minor:	
Ballybin Major:	Baile Binne, Town of the Hill
Ballyhack:	Baile Haic
Ballymore:	Baile Mór, Great Town
Bradystown:	Baile an Bhradaigh
Brownstown:	Baile an Brunaigh
Cabinhill:	Cappach, a hill
Cheeverstown:	Cheevers family
Commons:	Cuimin, an area common to all, where animals grazed
Curkeen:	Coircín a small marsh
Doghtog:	More commonly called and pronounced 'Darthog'
Elgarstown:	From Elgar family
Ennistown:	
Fidorfe:	Fiodh Dorcha, dark wood
Flemingtown:	Family name
Glascarn:	Glas Carn, a green heap
Gormanstown:	
Grange:	Grainseach, a monastic farm
Growtown:	
Gunstown:	Family name
Harlockstown:	Family name
Jamestown:	Baile Sheamais
Killester:	
Kilrue:	Cill Rua, Church of St. Rua

LOCAL HISTORY — Townlands in Ratoath Parish

Lagore Big:	Loch Gabhair, big Lake of the Goat
Lagore Little:	Loch Gabhair, little Lake of the Goat
Legagunnia:	Log an Ghainimh, hollow of the sand
Loughlinstown:	Baile an Lochlain, The Town of the Norsemen
Mooretown:	Baile na Móna, Town of the Bog
Mullinam:	Mullach Laighnean, Lynam's Hill or Summit
Newtown:	Baile Nua
Paddock:	
Peacockstown:	Baile Pheacóig
Porterstown:	
Powderlough:	
Rackenstown:	Family name
Rathbeggan:	
Rathcool:	Rath Cuil, fort of the corner
Ratoath:	Rath Tó, Rath Toadh or Rath of Tóg (Toadh's Fort)
Ratoath Manor:	
Raynestown:	
Raystown:	Family name
Tankardstown:	Family name
Twentypark:	
Warrenstown:	
Wilkinstown:	

Former Lagore House – West view (above) and East view (below)

LOCAL HISTORY

Lagore House

BERYL DONNELLY

Layout of Lagore House and Outhouses

THE LAGORE BUILDINGS comprised of the main house itself as depicted above. Local information suggests that the stone used in the buildings was quarried in the old Fox Covert that was on the estate. The main courtyard which consisted of a double coach house with living quarters above and three dwelling houses, some of which had basement accommodation. The yard itself was in cobble stone, with entrance to the courtyard through a magnificent curved arch which was deep enough to shelter a carriage and horses.

Access to the accommodation above the coach house was by means of a spiral medieval stone stairway. Beneath this stairway was a concealed room with no entrance door, and this room was only discovered as recently as the late 1980's.

Lagore House and Lands

The 1654 *Civil Survey of Meath* shows that a large portion of the area of Big and Little Lagore was owned by Joseph Plunkett, an Irish Papist, who was of Norman stock.

The Bolton Family

We know that most of the lands mentioned in Dr. John Bolton's Will were originally owned by the Plunkett's. Little Lagore was restored to Lt. Col. Christopher Plunkett (20/5/1692) under the provision of the *Treaty of Limerick* and by *Deed*, dated 15/8/1710.

Among the list of names of Vicars in Ratoath is the name of Mr. Henry Bolton who was Vicar in Ratoath and Donaghmore in 1633. His son, Dr. John Bolton, was Dean of Derry from 1699 to 1723.

Nicholas Plunkett transferred the lands at Lagore to Rev. Dr. John Bolton. In 1708 Dr. John Bolton was in possession of the Estate of Little Lagore and in his Will, he stated that he had purchased the property from Nicholas Plunkett. At this time no dwelling existed on the land, all that remained were the ruins of a former stone house and a Mill on the land on the south side of the river.

Dr. John Bolton's daughter Sarah married a member of a celebrated Derry family by the name of Norman.

Family Tree

The following family tree represents details extracted from Dr. John Bolton's Will, dated 1721

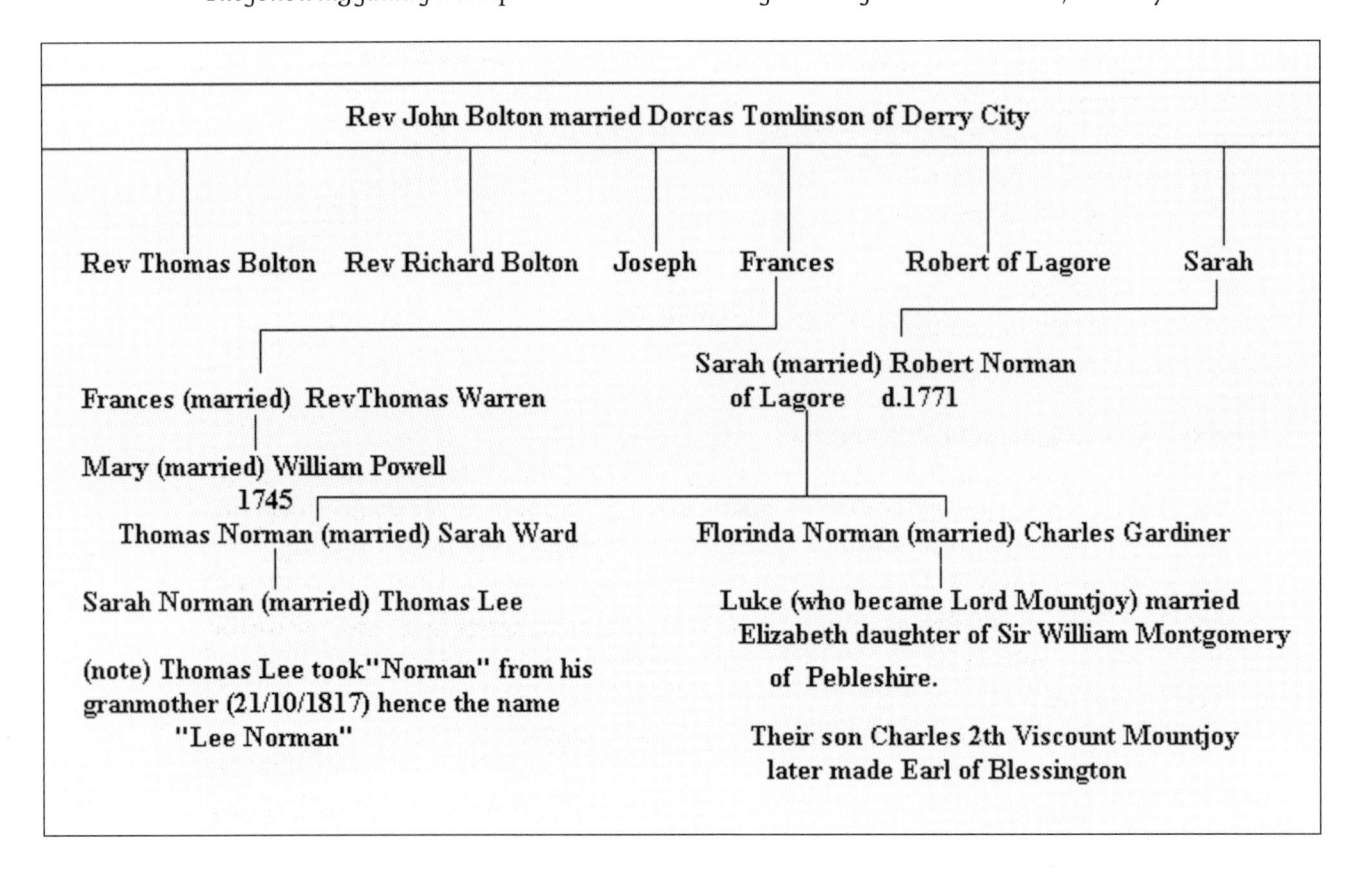

```
            Rev John Bolton married Dorcas Tomlinson of Derry City
                                    |
   ┌───────────────┬──────────────┬──────┬────────┬──────────────┬──────┐
Rev Thomas    Rev Richard     Joseph  Frances  Robert of Lagore  Sarah
  Bolton         Bolton
                                          |
                              Sarah (married) Robert Norman
                                    of Lagore   d.1771

Frances (married) Rev Thomas Warren
        |
Mary (married) William Powell
        1745
Thomas Norman (married) Sarah Ward        Florinda Norman (married) Charles Gardiner
        |                                           |
Sarah Norman (married) Thomas Lee         Luke (who became Lord Mountjoy) married
                                          Elizabeth daughter of Sir William Montgomery
(note) Thomas Lee took "Norman" from his            of Pebleshire.
granmother (21/10/1817) hence the name
         "Lee Norman"                     Their son Charles 2th Viscount Mountjoy
                                          later made Earl of Blessington
```

Lee Norman Crest

By his will, dated 15/2/1721, Dr. John Bolton left all his property to his grandson, Thomas Norman. Dr. John Bolton died at Lagore, Co. Meath around 1721 and included in the property which he left to Thomas Norman were Little Lagore, Ballymore, Elgarstown and Mooretown, Crickstown and several estates in Dunboyne. Norman's Grove in Dunboyne is named after the family. One of the Lord Justices, who tried claims of those who asked to have their lands restored under the *Treaty of Limerick*, was named Bolton. He may have been a relative of Dr. John Bolton. Perhaps this could explain how he got so much property in Leinster. Bolton Street in Dublin is named after the family. Although Dr. John Bolton left the property to Thomas Norman, some of the Bolton family continued to live in Lagore. Thomas Bolton presented Thomas Lee Norman to the Vicarage of Ratoath in 1761 and the Rev. Robert Norman, Vicar of Ratoath, died at Lagore in 1771.

The Representatives of the Executors of the Will of Dr. John Bolton transferred Little Lagore and Mill Land to Patrick Thunder by Deed dated 17/5/1799.

The Thunder Family Crest

The Thunder family came to Ireland about 1300 A.D. and during the 15th and 16th Century they owned much land around Summerhill in County Meath. They were strong Catholics and it is significant that Dr. Patrick Plunkett, Bishop of Meath 1778-1827 always stayed with Mr. Thunder at Lagore from 1800, when he made his annual visit to the parish. There was a private oratory in Lagore House. Patrick Thunder's wife's mother was a Plunkett from Portmarnock and this connection may explain how he came to possess Lagore.

In 1814 Lagore is listed as the residence of Patrick Thunder. In 1854 Michael Thunder is listed in *Griffiths Valuation* as being the owner of House, Office, Stewards and Herds Houses, Gate Lodge and land at Lagore Little, the Ratable Valuation at the time being listed at £606. os. od. The acreage was 515 acres.

At a later date, around 1823, Patrick Thunder, acquired under lease, Cabinhill, Rackenstown, Flemingtown and Brownstown. By the *Land Act of 1859*, lands held under lease for a number of years, could be converted into "Fee" holdings, i.e. it was no longer a tenancy but a "real" property.

The following is a note from "A Ratoath Diary": 1804 –1898.

> 1859 4th January: *"We had a great dinner at Lagore to celebrate the coming of age of Master Patrick Thunder. About 60 sat to dinner. There was plenty of beef, fowl and plumb pudding. Two half barrels of ale along with punch and tea and the dancing kept up till morning".*

Patrick Thunder died in 1827 but the place of his burial is not known. His son Michael succeeded him. Michael was succeeded in turn by his son Patrick. When the present Catholic Church was being built in the 1830's, the Thunder family made a major contribution to the building fund. In residence in Lagore House around the 1920's were Pat and Virgie Thunder, brother and sister, and their aunt Minnie Thunder, who would have been a sister of Patrick Thunder.

Family Vault

A large underground family vault was built by Michael Thunder in 1870 in the grounds of Ratoath Catholic Church. The heading on the vault reads: **Thunder-Haley, 1875-1952**.

The vault is entered from the south side by a series of twelve steps. Above the vault is a large monument with a marble cross on a granite base, within an iron railing. Part of the inscription is on the base of the cross and on a marble inset on the granite base. Among those commemorated on this stone are Michael Thunder who died 1875 and his wife Charlotte who died in 1889; Francis Thunder who died in 1887; Constance Thunder who died in 1898.

> NOTE: *Mr. Stephen Farrell of Navan, being the executor of the late Captain Jack Thunder's will, is currently the holder of the key to the vault of the Thunder family. On Saturday 5th October 2002, Stephen met with the Parish Priest Fr. Gerry Stuart and members of the Local Heritage association at the Thunder vault.*

John Donnelly and Ella Donnelly outside Lagore Lodge in 1929

John Donnelly Snr. the Herd for the Thunder Family outside the herd's House in Lagore Yard in 1930

Mary Donnelly with Nephew Tom Donnelly, Lagore Lodge, 1930

The People Who Worked On the Estate and Their Local Connections
Quite a large number of the staff lived in the main house, while other members of the staff lived in houses belonging to the Estate which were situated on various parts of the estate land.

The Donnelly Family originally came from Tyrone in the 1700's. They lived in Rackenstown, were tenant farmers and the Thunder Family were their landlords. The Great-grandfather, Jack Donnelly, worked and lived on the Thunder Estate in Lagore. He was married to a Catherine Gill from Maynooth. They raised their family there, Paddy, Jack, John, Nan, Brigid and Ellen. John Donnelly worked as a herdsman on the estate. He married Margaret

Rattigan in 1927. She had come to Lagore House as a cook in 1919 to work for Thunders. They set up their home in Lagore Lodge, where Ella, Peter, Jack and Kitty were born. Also living with them at this time was Mary Donnelly who was a sister of Jacks. They lived there until 1939, when they moved to Big Lagore, where Pat Donnelly was born. Brigid later married Jack Eiffe of Ratoath and they went to live in Ratoath Village.

Kate Smith worked in the House in the early 1920's she came from Drumree, also Paddy Gilroy, who was the coachman and later when the motor car came along, he became the chauffeur.

Lagore House was self sufficient up to a certain point. When additional provisions were required, Findlater's of Dublin would have been the main supplier to the Estate.

Local Stories about Lagore House and the Estate
Mrs. Molly Devine of Tankardstown remembers going to Lagore House with her father around 1922. Molly would have been around six years of age at this time. Her father was a clerk with a Firm of Solicitors called Maxwell Weldon of Eden Quay, Dublin. Pat and Virgie Thunder were Wards of Court and Mrs. Divine's father came regularly to the house on business. Some time after this Virgie Thunder went to London with her friend Mrs.Cumerfield. Unfortunately she (Virgie) contacted meningitis and died. She was twenty one years of age. At this time, Captain Jack Thunder was the manager of the estate.

The wall around the Estate, some of which still remains, was built at a cost of 9p. per perch, the height of this wall was between eight and ten feet high, much of which is under the level of the road to day.

A former farm worker recalls a day when digging a hole in which to bury a dead animal, they came upon a curved roof of what appeared to be an underground passage, which incidentally was never investigated. Another story tells of a horse chase which was run on the Estate each year, the winner of this race would become the holder of a golden bridle for that year.

The Bell
Situated in the yard was a bell tower from which was suspended a bell. Each day this bell was rung to summon the workmen for lunch. This bell was later presented to Fr. Joe Foley a native of Dunshaughlin who worked on the missions in Africa, for use in his church there.

A Day in the working life of Lagore House in the early 1900's
Lagore House and Estate were one of two major employers in the area. There was quite a large staff which ran the House and looked after the cooking and many duties of the household and also for the many visiting guests. The estate was self-sufficient. It had its own walled in gardens in which was grown all the fruit and vegetables which were needed to sustain a house of this size and importance. It also had a beautiful rose garden, where there were many plants and shrubs from foreign parts grown there. There were a large number of gardeners involved in the upkeep of these gardens, Luke Ralph senior was the Head Gardener.

The Estate was rich in mature trees, the front lawn had trees of such magnitude that they were referred to as The King and The Queen trees of Lagore. The lawn at the front of the house on which these trees were growing comprised of approximately eighteen acres.

Mrs. Claudia Burgoyne and her son Major Mark Teeling Waters purchased Lagore House and lands from the Thunder family in the 1940's. Major Waters had returned from serving in the Second World War. In 1950, Major Watters had a bottling Plant in Lagore, which was state of the art for it's time.

The Estate had a dairy and it sent milk to the Royal Meath Dairy (Farrell's of the Dairy on the Fairyhouse Road). The milk was tested for TB (tuberculosis) and it was distributed to the hospitals in Dublin.

May Caffrey worked in Lagore House from 1940 to 1948, when Mrs. Burgoyne lived there, with her daughters Claudia and Robin. She recalls details of the former Lagore House as follows:-

> There was a lead staircase leading from the basement to the Stairwell in the Grand Hall. There were white marble fireplaces in all the formal rooms, including the bedrooms. The Dining Room contained a dining room table and two sideboards. A second table that seated eight people was situated in an alcove. Upstairs, one of the bedrooms, the Green Room, as it was called, had a four poster bed in an alcove. When they had guests, the fires in the bedrooms were lit at three o'clock in the afternoon. The main lighting in the house was by gas and great care had to be taken when cleaning the mantles of the lights. Most of the cooking was done on the Aga cooker by part-time cook Maggie Donnelly of the Fairyhouse Road. Molly Mannering also worked in the kitchen. Mrs. Burgoyne was very much involved in the Red Cross Association at local and national level. Consequently there was always a large supply of blankets and medical supplies kept in the house for emergencies.
>
> The wonderful garden of Lagore House was unrecognisable at this time, overgrown with brambles and weeds. You could be torn asunder with briars and weeds when you tried to pick some apples off the trees in the orchard. Working in the yard at this time were, Jerry Keogh and John Henry who looked after the horses. Claudia Borgoyne herself was a great horse woman.
>
> There is a story told of how Claudia went to early Mass in Ratoath, dressed in her riding clothes which included jodhpurs, when she went to receive Communion, the priest refused her, because of her riding apparel.
>
> Between 1933 and 1935 a large number of staff members including gardeners, workmen, butlers, maids were released from their posts as the lifestyle of the Estate was changing.
>
> Bill Donnelly was maintenance man, and he did the painting and general repair to the house and yard, assisted by Billy Lynch, who would always have great stories to tell the staff on a Monday morning.
>
> Findlater's also supplied Mrs. Burgoyne and her household. The order for the week would be taken on a Tuesday by a Mr. Skeehan and the weekly provisions would be delivered on the Thursday.

Lagore remained in the possession of the Thunder Family until they sold it in 1941. Later on Lagore House again changed hands; the new owner was a Mr. Clements who had two daughters, Diane & Daphne. Mrs. Burgoyne moved to St. Mary's Abbey in Trim and Major Waters moved to Lagore Lodge and married a Canadian lady called Doddi. Sheila Brennan worked for Doddi Waters from 1945 to 1956. In 1951 the house was sold to a Captain G.N. Rome M.C.

Disastrous Fire
In August 1952 a disastrous fire brought to a close a large chapter in the life of this great house. The outbreak was first noticed by a former employee of Lagore, the late John Don-

nelly. Every effort was made by several fire brigades and many locals to save the fine building, but to no avail. The result was a ruined burned out shell of a once great house.

Shortly after this period, the ruins and some adjacent lands were purchased by the late Mr. Walsh, father of Ronnie Walsh of Radio fame who presented the Sunday Miscellany Programme for many years on Irish Radio (RTÉ). Mr. Walsh built the present house on the foundations of the old house. The house subsequently passed on to Ronnie Walsh some years later.

In 1956 Michael O'Hare and his wife Agnes became the new owners of Lagore. When Michael moved from Louth he brought two men with him, Paddy Ward and Michael Murphy. Initially, the O'Hare family lived in one of the steward's houses on the farm. The O'Hare family moved into Lagore House in the late 1950's.

A Typical Day at Lagore Lodge
The following are recollections of Sheila Brennan, who worked in Lagore Lodge for Major Waters and his Canadian wife Doddi, from 1949 to 1956:-

A typical day in the Lodge at that time would be to clean out the fireplace in the Sittingroom and re-light with logs. Cups of tea were left in the bedroom for the Major and his wife and the Breakfast table was set. The Lounge was then swept and tidied. Mrs. Waters was a fantastic cook and did most of the cooking. I helped with the preparations and served the courses. Afternoon tea was served and dinner was at eight o'clock.

Nancy Wherrity did the ironing and was there on my day off and also every other Sunday. Mrs. Burgoyne came to visit often when she was in Ireland. Throughout the year, Doddi went to Dublin most days, getting parts for machines, doing business and shopping. The Lodge had its own Generator, so there was lots of hot water available for baths and for washing up and you could have a bath whenever you wanted.

Lagore Lodge in 2000

To the Memory of Lagore

She stood in state amidst the trees for centuries we are told.
She had that welcome look for all in her mantle of fading gold.
She sheltered many on their journey through this life
She was never known to harbour unhappiness or strife.
Many a gallant soldier said farewell in his day
And many a pretty maiden was wooed from her away.
Many a banquet did she hold and many a brilliant ball
And many times she echoed the sound of the Huntsman's call.
But alas to-day, like a ghost she stands gazing at the sky
Holding the secret of what happened on that night.
And how she was doomed to die
'T was sad to think after all her years of service and toil
Not even one was there to quench that thirst from which she did fall.
Farewell now you dear old mansion
You are gone forever more
And memory is all that now remains of you
To the tenants of Lagore.

By the late Mrs. Mary Mooney, Lagore

LOCAL HISTORY

The Thunder Family of Lagore and Ballaly

BERYL DONNELLY and FRANCES MAHER

MICHAEL THUNDER of Lagore / Ballaly, was born at Ballaly (date unknown). He married Ellen O'Rourke and their son Patrick was born in 1770. Patrick married Elizabeth Taaffe of Smarmore Castle, Ardee, Co. Louth in 1798 and he died in 1811. There were five children from this marriage. The eldest son, Michael Thunder of Lagore, born in 1802, married Charlotte Mary Dalton in 1834.

Their son, Patrick Thunder of Lagore, was born on 12th January 1838. He married Mary Anne de Pentheny O'Kelly of Barrettstown, Co. Kildare, in 1871 and he died in December 1912. They had six children.

Patrick, eldest son of Michael de Pentheny-Thunder of Lagore, married Mary Christina O'Sullivan in the 1900's. His younger brother, James William Thomas was born 21st April 1849 and lived in Bellewstown House, Co. Louth. He married Lorna Plowden of Plowden Hall, Shropshire, in 1873. They had eight children, among whom was Bernard William Thunder of Lacken House, Kilkenny, born 1877, who married Mabel Penelope Eckersley, daughter of Engineer Rear Admiral Eckersley. They had seven children of whom Noreen Laura Plowden, born November 1918, married Raymond Horace Andrews. On the 6th May 1946 they had a son Anthony who now lives with his wife Pat in Canterbury, Kent, England. Also among the seven children was Moira Edith Thunder, born 28th December 1916, and married Captain John Spencer Compton on the 29th April 1943. He died on active service in 1944. Their son William (Bill) was born in 1944. He now lives with his wife Tessa in Florida (See photo). Brian Joseph Thunder was born in July 1910 in Kuala Lumpur, Malaysia. He married Margaret Britt-Compton in 1951. They had three daughters, Patricia, Rosamund and Moira. Brian and his wife live in Battle in Hastings. (See photo.)

Patricia and Anthony Andrews who generously provided information on the Thunder Family. Picture taken by John Andrews, September 2003.

There's Thunder in the Sky
There's Thunder Passing By
There's Thunder on the Shore
(Ref. To Ballaly near Malahide)
And there's Thunder in Lagore

(*Right*): Mrs. Pat Andrews, Margaret Thunder and daughter Robbie Thunder. Picture taken by Anthony Andrews in Hastings, January 2004.

(*Below*): Bill Compton, cousin of Anthony Andrews, with his wife Tessa. Bill generously provided us with information on the Thunder family tree.

(*Below right*): Brian Thunder aged 94, July 2003

Note: Mary Anne de Pentheny O'Kelly, *Countess of Holy Roman Empire-* as Heirs (Male & Female forever) of Sir Thomas Arundell, First Baron Arundell of Wardour, born circa 1560, into an ancient Anglo-Norman family. He was a Catholic who at a young age with the consent of Queen Elizabeth and with her letters of recommendation to the Emperor, went as a volunteer in the Imperial Army to fight the Turks.

At the Battle of Gran in Hungary, 1595, he captured a Turkish banner. In recognition of his bravery the Emperor Rudolph II by Imperial Decree bestowed on him the title *Count of The Holy Roman Empire* (14th December 1595). This decreed declared that the title was "Descendible to all and each of the grantee's children, heirs, posterity and descendents of either sex, born or to be born, for ever". In practice under the terms of this Imperial Decree, which was recognized by James I on 4th May 1605, anyone legally descended from Thomas Arundell is therefore a Count or Countess of the Holy Roman Empire and is entitled to a family Coat of Arms.

LOCAL HISTORY

The 1798 Rebellion in Meath

ANN GAUGHAN

THE IRISH REBELLION of 1798 had it's origins in the French Revolution of 1789 which in turn had similarities with the American Revolution of 1776-82. Both of these countries broke away from the long established monarchy system of government and set themselves up as democratic republics.

Throughout the 18th Century, Ireland was controlled by English rulers who were predominantly known as the Protestant landed gentry, who owned most of the land which was let out to tenant farmers. The 1798 Rebellion had been brewing for years, years of oppression and misrule, enormous rents and tithes for the upkeep of the Established Church, all greatly resented by the Catholics. The 18th Century was a time of penal laws: Catholics had no rights, civil or religious. Failure to pay tithes and taxes led to evictions, burning of homesteads, hangings and riots.

Wolfe Tone at that time wanted to break the connections with England. Even though he was a Protestant lawyer, he was one of the main founders of the United Irishmen in 1791. The United Irishmen were founded in Belfast on the principals of a break with the British Crown and civil and religious freedom for all on this island. Their numbers swelled to approximately 500,000 within ten years.

The Yeomanry were created in 1795 by a Government order, thus encouraging local landlords in their capacity as magistrates to form companies of infantry and cavalry from amongst their loyal tenants. These were mainly Orangemen and Protestants but, many were Catholics who were often infiltrated and undermined by Defenders and United Irishmen.

The Defenders were an exclusively Catholic organisation, very active circa 1792/93 and which had it's origins in Armagh, spreading to Louth, Cavan, Meath and Dublin. Defenders recognised each other by a recognised code. The authorities in Dublin became so alarmed with the activities of the Defenders that they put up a reward of £100 for any person who would prosecute them to conviction and this was rampantly enforced in Meath, Louth, Monaghan and Cavan.

To meet the threat of the Defenders in Meath and to protect the Protestant gentry a secret meeting of Meath Protestant gentlemen was called and this resulted in the formation of The Meath Association which was set up by Thomas Butler in 1792. Some of the other leaders were a Mr. Chandler from Moynalty and magistrate Keady Barnes.

The pillaging and plundering by the Orange factions was halted momentarily when the Earl of Bellamount restrained the Cavan Militia and thus the Meath Association found themselves abandoned, but by this time however, the cause of the Defenders had spread to

Ratoath Past and Present

Monument erected in Ratoath during 1998 to commemorate those of all faiths who lost their lives in the 1798 Rebellion. Located at the entrance to the Church and River Walk.

include places like Skryne, Ratoath and on into Dublin.

On March 30th, 1798 the Viceroy, Lord Camden, declared Ireland to be in a state of Rebellion and imposed martial law. Meath, which played a crucial role in the rebellion, had a force of United Irishmen estimated at between ten and twelve thousand. The plan was for the forces of Meath, Kildare and Wicklow to march on the City of Dublin and take out the main government buildings. In Meath the first skirmishes happened at Dunboyne, Ratoath and Clonee, where several soldiers and rebels were killed. The rebel army made their way to the Hill of Tara where they suffered a disastrous defeat at the hands of a Government force of regular army and Yeomen, led by Lord Fingall. This was the first major engagement of the 1798 Rebellion coming as it did a day before the first large action in Meath by Meath rebels. Most of the 1798 action was in Wexford and Enniscorthy. Antrim and Down fought and lost. The remnants of the rebel army in Wexford decided to try to link up with Ulster, not realising that the insurrection there had been crushed several weeks earlier. As the rebels marched into Meath, they had to fight rear guard action as British Army and Yeomen were constantly harassing them. There were numerous skirmishes until the rebel resistance finally ended on 15th July. Meath's role in the 1798 rebellion has been little publicised, however, it did play a prominent part. Circa 800 died in three of the major battles of Tara, Clonard and Knightstown and there were numerous skirmishes between rebels and crown forces, such as at Dunboyne, Ratoath, Clonee and Slane.

Meath is rich in oral tradition about the 1798 Rebellion in the form of stories, poems and ballads, such as Paud O'Donoghue the legendary blacksmith of Curraha, who put the bullying Yeomen to flight. Added to this there are many commemorative monuments and Croppy graves dotted around the county. The Croppies are said to have received their name from the way in which their hair was cut. Other stories tell that the United Irishmen carried corn in their pockets to stave off the hunger when they were on the move. Accordingly, if they were unfortunate to be killed in an unknown place, the spot where they lay would often be identified later on by an isolated tuft of corn.

The Local Connection

Although most of the fighting during 1798 happened in Wexford and in the north east, in

Ratoath, on May 24th 1798, the rebels captured Captain Hamilton Gorges of Kilbrew, M.P. for Meath and Lieut. Elias Corbally of Ratoath, and threatened to hang them. However, they were surprised by the local Yeomen and eleven Angus Highlanders led by Lieut. George Armstrong. In the ensuing skirmish, 35 United Irishmen were killed. The fighting then moved back towards Clonee where at Clonee Bridge, six Highlanders were killed.

According to Dean Cogan, three Wexford men who remained behind the main body were overtaken at Ratoath. They pleaded for a Priest and Lord Fingall (one of the Officers in command) brought Fr. Langan to give them the Last Rites. They were then hanged in the Woods near Ratoath. Folklore has it that these three men were buried at the site of the Red Cross Tree on the Dunshaughlin Road, the site of which is to-day at the junction of the old Ratoath Road and the Woodlands by-pass, to the west of Ratoath Village.

REFERENCES:
"The 1798 Rebellion in Meath" By: Seamus O Loinsigh, published in 1997 by Meath Archaeological & Historic Society.
Dean Cogan: 1826 – 1872. Dioceses of Meath.

LOCAL HISTORY

EXTRACTS FROM A RATOATH DIARY: 1804-1898

FRANCES MAHER

THE FOLLOWING EXTRACTS are taken from a diary, which has been kept in Ratoath since 1804. John Bruen, late of the Post Office in Ratoath, was the last owner of the diary and he gave it to the Parish Priest, Fr. Cogan, about 1965.

The first entry in this diary is:

"John Hade, his book 17th August 1804, Ratoath, Co. Meath."

Later on it says "Nicholas Hade presented this book to Pat Toole September 20th 1840." This diary reads like a parish register of births, deaths and marriages from 1804 to 1898. There is nothing of great significance in the diary but it does show what the writers considered of interest in their time in the village and beyond. It also gives an occasional glimpse of living conditions then.

Entries are brief and seem more of an aid to the memory than a record for posterity.

1828, 9th Mar	– Nicholas Nugent died by football play.
1828, Feb.-May	– Nine people "were converted" in the Chapel of Ratoath.
1839, 6th Jan	– "The big wind came, the greatest that man ever saw."
1841, 3rd Feb	– "A plague rages on the cattle in Lagore, 14 sick in two days."
1841, Jul 21st	– "Mrs Keenan came to Ratoath"
1842, Apr	– "Fish came to the top of the water in the pond and swam on top for a week"
1842, 11th & 12th Nov	– "We took a great take of eels"
1843, 2nd & 3rd Dec.	– "A great destruction on sheep" by dogs on the farms of Mr. Thunder and Mrs. Corbaliss.
1843, Dec. 4th	– "A great combat took place between the Fottrells and the Andersons about timber, by which John and Simon fought several rounds, but the Fottrells captured the timber"

1843, Aug 15th	– "The great Tara meeting took place on 15th August 1843. There were 15 hundred thousand persons attending on the occasion for the purpose of petitioning Parliament for a repeal of the Union"
1844, 30th May	– "O'Connell sentence passed. Was confined to Richmond for 12 months and pay a fine of £2,000 and the others 9 months and £50. Fine and bail for their future conduct"
1845, Jul & Aug	– "A great blight in the potato crop in July and August 1845. Half the crop lost."
1846, Dec.	– The taking down of the hills at Ratoath began and there was famine on the land.
1847, 6th Mar	– "Mary Rooney sailed for America deeply regretted by Pat Anderson.
1847, Apr	– "The soup kitchen was established."
1847, May	– "There was a great want for provisions in May 1847. The wheat went to 32/- a barrel and the beef to 73/- per cwt.
1847, 2nd May	– Pat Cusack went to America.
1847, 15th May	– "Daniel O'Connell died at Genoa in Italy on 15th May 1847 at 35 minutes past 9 o'clock"
1847, 5th Aug	– "O'Connell was buried. The greatest funeral ever was seen. There were 600 priests and 9 bishops."
1847, 15th Sep	– "We had half days rain after the longest drought since the dry summer and the next day the greatest storm since the big wind"
1847, 17th Nov	– "Morrissey levelled the ditches on the 'Cawderless' which were built the month before. He called all the tenants and what did not go, he turned out their cattle"
1847, 19th Dec	– Seven sheep stolen.
1848, May	– The Magranes, Tom Bryan, James McCabe, John Bruton and several others went to America, Pat Magrane went on 6th June and on the 3rd August the Lynams.
1849, Jun	– Mary left Ramsey a broken heart.
1849, Aug	– Kit Foy died of cholera.
1849, Sep	– "The distemper reappeared on the potatoes".
1849, Sep	– "Pat Magrane came from America.
1849, Apr & May	– "James Bryan and his sister, John Timmons and Jane Magrane, Thomas Connor, Alice Reilly, Anne Mayburne, Biddy Connor and John Walsh went to America.
1851, Aug	– "The distemper reappeared on the potato stalks the first week of August but the roots are not too bad yet and it is now the 20th. It's now the 7th September and I fear the potatoes are getting worse."

1851, Dec	– "Mr. Johnson died of typhus fever after one week's illness"
1852, Sep 22	– A certain Pat "was disappointed of his marriage"
1852, Oct	– "A man and woman found dead near Lime kiln, killed I hear reliably".
1852, 21st Oct	– James Keenan went to Australia.
1852, 9th Nov	– "We had a shock of earthquake on the morning of 9th November, a rare occurrence what never was heard before in Ireland and ever since we had continual rain. We had the most rain this year that we had in 50 years. We had a great storm on the morning of the 25th December. It was the greatest since the big wind in 1839.
1852, 27th Dec	– "Went to Dublin and got my tooth stuffed"
1853, 23rd Jan	– Dick Brown came home from America. Two farms were "taken" by neighbours one in 1848 and the other in 1859. The "taker" in 1850 could get no one to plough it.
1856, 5th Jul	– Richard Barnwall defeated in law case "as he claimed the bog of Ratoath." This was the first of a series of court cases between Barnwall and Ratoath people about the bog. There were about a dozen court cases in all between 1856 and 1862. The people claimed a right of way, turbary rights, and the right to cut and take away the grass.
1858, Jul	– "Barnwall said he did not dispute the people's rights but at the same time he wished to make arable land of the bog."
1858, Sept	– John Beggy bought Cairns house for £8. 19. 0.
1858, 20th Oct	– 60 men levelled the ditch around the bog to make a car way.
1860, 9th Jun	– 30 men and boys levelled the sluice across the bog
1860, Nov	– Barnwall succeeded in putting cattle on the bog. "We had Dick Morgan up. There were 32 police looking on, so they bound both parties to the peace. Both parties won some of the court-cases but no entry states the final outcome."
1863, 23rd Mar	– Seven sheep were sheared on Clover Hill and the wool carried away.
1863, Jul	– The Belfry of Ratoath was finished and the bell installed.
1867, 2nd Sept	– "Mr. Kelly came to teach in Gillic's place."
1875, 17th Jan.	– "The priests house finished.
1878, On Feb 14th,	– Thomas Barnwall called all bog owners who wished to sell bog plains, but he bought only one.
1879, 28th Jan	– "Charles Brindley died. Huntsman to the Wards for nearly 40 years.
1883, Apr	– "There was Foot and Mouth distemper and our April fair was stopped." "By August nearly all the Union was affected by Foot and Mouth."
1883, May - Jul	– Will and Eliza Muldoon, Pat Murray, 2 Lynams, Paddy McCabe and

	family, Jim Muldoon, Jim Mcintee went to America. In Feb. 1893 John Moran went to Australia.
1884, Mar	– "Three more families evicted for non payment of rent."
1885, Oct	– Biddy Toole went to a convent in Belgium.
1885, 12th Mar	– Lizzy Toole went to a convent in Belgium. Thomas Toole accompanied her.
1887, 15th Sep	– Jack Anderson went to 'Buenos Ayres' with bulls for Mr. Bobbet, returned on 23 Nov 1895 and returned to 'Buenos Ayres' on 28th March 1896.
1888, May	– "Over 1,000 dairy cattle slaughtered in Dublin on account of the distemper"
1890, 18th Aug	– The potatoes getting very bad with distemper. Thomas Farrell bought, Norman cottage for £450, in 1890.
1891, Jun	– New wall built round chapel yard.
1891, 6th Oct	– "Parnell died, the greatest statesman we had since o'Connell. Died in the bloom of his youth, about 47 years."
1892, Feb.	– "No fast this Lent what I never saw before on account of the influenza"
1892, Apr	– An emergency man assaulted for walking with cattle to the fair green gate.
1893, 22 Sept	– "Kelly the schoolmaster on trial for boycotting and putting the sergeant's son out of the school. Dec.1893 James Doonan schoolmaster came in Kelly's place.
1895, 15th Jun	– Kelly schoolmaster ejected, furniture put out on road!
1895, Sept.	– Labourer's cottage built in Ratoath.
1896, Oct.	– A pump was sunk at the school and the doctor's house built.
1897, 18th Mar	– "Began to build two new houses for the schoolmaster and schoolmistress"
1897, Aug.	– "The master went to live in new house."

Romances

1841 to 1856.	– Nine elopements were recorded from 1841 to 1856. In four cases the girl took money with her. One took £3. 10., another took the price of a cow and another "robbed Tom". Another couple eloped from the Fairyhouse Races in April 1851 even though it was during Lent. One girl eloped with the servant-boy.
In 1841,	– One Nicholas spent from 7th May to 10th "in deep meditation to know whether he would marry the schoolhouse girl or not and went to the priest, and after did not marry, and away on the 11th with Nicholas to Dublin!"

Accidents

1841, 27th Dec. – Brady's Millhouse fell.

1842, 5th Mar – McDonnell's house fell.

1845, 20th Feb. – Thomas Boylan killed with a falling tree.

1859, 4th Jun – A man in the schoolhouse field shot and injured in mistake for a rabbit.

1859, 5th Oct – Bernard Anderson killed by fall from the chapel window.

1865, Jul – M. Reilly died in fall from loft.

1868, 17th Sept. – Mick Brennan's brother killed on new road.

1879, 15th Jul – Leavy's house fell on him and broke his leg.

1886, 28th Jan – John Dory's house burned.

1894, 7th Feb. – Alby Connell's house burned.

Miscellaneous

1840, 5th Oct. – James Brady got a pair of millstones, and in July 1850 he got a new water wheel.

1854, Nov. – "George Smith died. He is the oldest man in the country, 118 years." Other instances of longevity. John Morgan died 27th Jan 1866 "nearly 100 years", and Pat Toole's own mother died 26th June 1876 "aged about 96".

1858, Oct. – "A great comet the greatest that was this 100 years"

1859, 4th Jan. – "We had a great dinner at Lagore to celebrate the coming of age of Master Patrick Thunder. About 60 sat to dinner. There was plenty of beef, fowl and plum pudding. Two half barrels of ale along with punch and tea and the dancing kept up till morning."

1863, 7th Feb. – "James Toole my first son born."

Weather Conditions

Weather conditions are frequently mentioned in relation to crops and the corn mill, here are some samples:

1839, 6th Jan – "The big wind came, the greatest any man ever saw"

1842, 13th Jun – A great thunder storm.

1846, Easter – Easter and six previous weeks all wet.

1847, 15th Sept. – "A half day's rain after the longest drought since the dry summer, and the next day the greatest storm since the big wind"

1848, Aug 27th – Worst floods for 20 years.

1855, Feb. – "We had a fall of snow from 1st to 8th February there were 6 feet in places. It is now the 18th and hard frost yet. Hay is 7/- per cwt, straw 3/6. Snow lasted one month."

LOCAL HISTORY — Extracts From a Ratoath Diary: 1804-1898

1860, Sept. — "This is the wettest season we had these many years. There was never so much bad hay out".

1864, Aug. — "The greatest drought since 1826."

1870, Aug. 27th — "Rain after the greatest drought since 1826. Springs all dry"

1884, Aug — "Driest season for many years, Hay 6/- per cwt. It is now Oct 12th hardly any rain yet. It is now 1st Nov. and Peter did not grind hardly any yet. People drawing water to cattle every day. December 1884 the finest winter ever came.

1885, Feb.16th — Snow after the finest winter we ever had"

1885, 13th Sept.— "Wet, cannot reap or draw in hay"

1887, May. — "Showers of hail, rain, snow and storms"

1887, Aug — "Rain came after the greatest drought since 1826. Springs nearly all dried up. Oct. 13th still dry weather, springs all dry. Nov. 5th we had falls of rain, the first since February. Peter grinding on the 7th. He did not turn the wheel this seven months.

1891, Feb — "The finest winter we ever had, neither rain nor frost."

1891, 19th May — "Harsh frosty weather, potatoes killed".

1892, 16th Sept — "Wet harvest, raining since 1st August, wheat is struck, cutting to-day"

1893, 11th May — "No rain since the first week of March, great growth, whitethorn in blossom.

1893, 9th Aug — "The greatest thunder storm we had this 40 years.

1893, 12th Dec — "Rain just now, Macks can grind after 8 months"

1894, Aug — A great deal of bad hay. Hay cheap. 3/4p per cwt.

1895, 24th May — "Great frost cut all the potatoes over ground. Frost every night."

Prices:
A pair of corduroy trousers cost 6 shillings and 3 old Pence in 1841.
(1 old shilling = 12 old Pence (d) in old money. (240 old pennies (d) in £1 in 1970).

1841, 1st Jan — "Bought a cow on New Year's Day in Warrenstown for £5.-13-9 and she had no milk. Brought her to Ashbourne on 6th January but did not sell her".

In 1845 a pair of trousers cost 12/10 i.e. 9/6 for "stuff", 2/3 for making and 1/- for trimmings.

A pair of men's shoes cost 7/- in 1841, 1843 and 1847.

To sole and heel shoes cost 2/6 in 1843.

A man's hat cost 5/6, a knife 1/6 in 1841 and a "silk neck handkerchief 4/6 in 1844.

1851 — Took the grass of Clover Hill from Mr. Corballis at 45/- an acre.

1860, Beef cost 73/- a cwt in 1860. Mutton 10d and 1/- a lb.

1876	–	Life Insurance policy for £300 for 21 years was £3-13-6, in 1876.
1883	–	Curkeeen bought for £3,300 in 1883.
1884	–	Cost of Simon Fottrell's headstone in 1884 was £9- 1-0.
1890	–	Thomas Farrell bought Norman cottage for £450, in 1890.
1892	–	Cost of building a 9-perch length of wall in 1892 was £50.

1892, Wheat cost 26/- a barrel in 1842, 32/- in 1847, 20/- in 1885 and 22/- in 1892.

1892, Potatoes cost 2/- a cwt in 1892.

Other Notices:

1845, 12th Mar	–	Two arrested for stealing two lambs.
1859, Apr	–	Three men "fined £9. For waylaying and beating two men at the priest house fields."
		"A woman was summoned for stealing turnips. She settled it with £1."
1878, 6th Feb	–	"Pope Pious IX died."

Note: These diary extracts were also published in *Ríocht na Midh* in 1975 in an article by Rev. Peter Mulvany, PP Ardcath and former CC Ratoath.

LOCAL HISTORY

The 'Coderliss' Grounds

NICK KILLIAN

Early Community Development

COMMUNITY DEVELOPMENT has long been a feature of Ratoath over the past 60-70 years. In September 1967, the then parish priest Fr. John Cogan (a unique character in the development of Ratoath), formed *Ratoath Development Ltd.*, a company limited by guarantee and having a share capital. The objective of the Company, as outlined in the Memorandum of Association, was to promote the welfare of persons living in the parish of Ratoath and to promote their education and training. This company was formed to operate the "*Coderliss*" on the Skryne Road, which at that time could only be described as swampy scrubland.

Among the original subscribers to this Company were Dr. Henry Conway; Mrs. Maureen White, Mulhuddart; Thomas Dolan (Postmaster); James Brady, Garage Proprietor; Patrick Donnelly, Lagore Cross, Ratoath (Builder); Andrew Eiffe, Rackenstown (Welfare Officer); Eamonn White, Kilrue (Farmer). The solicitor was Michael Beatty. The Company had 216 original subscribers who purchased shares @ £1 each.

Over the years, this land was developed into a fine, well-maintained amenity for our village, comprising of an 18-hole Pitch and Putt course, a home for both Ratoath GAA and Ratoath Harps Football Club.

Fr. Cogan's vision of the time was farsighted. Ratoath and its environs have benefited over the years and will continue to benefit from his vision of community development for years to come. The rationale was the development of sports facilities for youth and adults in the various codes. The expansion of Ratoath GAA to Brownstown, and the Ratoath Harps to larger facilities on the Skryne Road, is testimony to the men and women, who in the leaner times in the 1960's and 1970's, developed excellent playing facilities and nurtured the sporting talents of thousands of young Ratoath men and women. The vision continues to develop in the new millennium.

Local Place Name

Around Ratoath, the local name '*Coderliss*' has been handed down from generation to generation by word of mouth and has resulted in multiple variations of its spelling. The Gaelic name is '*Cathar Lios*' meaning a Town/City Fort. The Gaelic name '*Lios*' refers to an enclosure where people and their animals retired for security at night or in times of danger. The local name '*Coderliss*' has not been shown as such on any Ordnance Survey maps. Thus, many variations of its spelling continue to be used today. Articles submitted for inclusion

Aerial photograph of Ratoath, taken by Finian Darby in 1989
The borders of the 'Coderliss' grounds are marked on the above picture in red and white.
The red border is the pre 1960s portion and the white border is the additional piece of land that was purchased and added to make up the present day "Coderliss" grounds.

in this book that refer to the 'Coderliss' are published with the spelling submitted by authors.

The earliest written mention of the name, that we could find, was in the Ratoath Diary in 1847 as follows:

> 1847, 17th Nov – "Morrissey levelled the ditches on the 'Cawderless' which were built the month before. He called all the tenants and what did not go, he turned out their cattle"

Many variations of its spelling remain to this day including:
Cawderless, Cowderlois, Coderlios, Coderliss, Codderliss, Codalis.....

LOCAL HISTORY

Ratoath Cemetery

FRANCES MAHER

THE OLD CEMETERY IN RATOATH is set in the peaceful and tranquil grounds of the ruined Church of Ireland church, at the back of the village. Many of the graves predate the church by more than twenty years, which suggest the graveyard was in use in the late 18th century.

Interred in the cemetery are the remains of many of the prominent families and clergy who have served Ratoath and its environs down through the years. Some of these families have gone to great lengths to honour their dead with some highly distinctive and decorative headstones and tombs. Catholics, members of The Church of Ireland, Priests and Rectors are buried here.

Also contained in the graveyard and worthy of note is the unmarked mass grave of the many local victims of the Great Famine of the 1840's.

There are inscriptions on the monuments dating from the early 1700's which are very simple, and which give no clue to the religions of those mentioned e.g. *"Here lies the Body of Anthony Field who departed this life 1709"*.

Old Graveyard

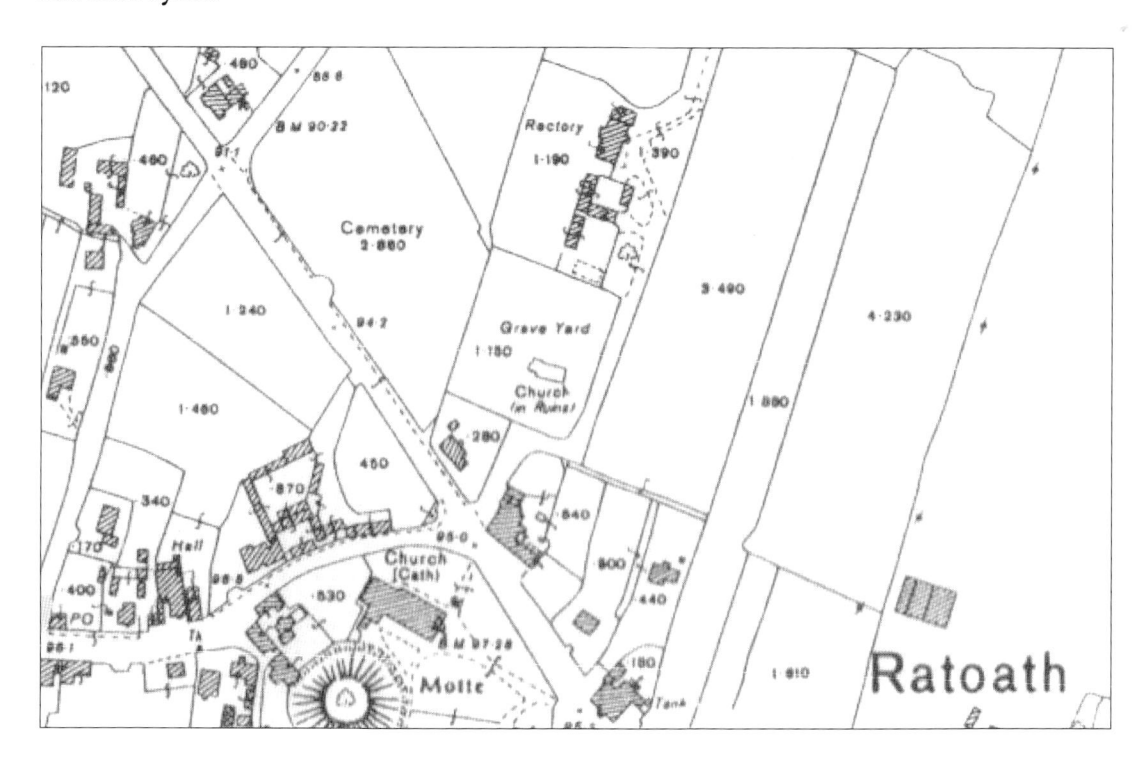

Entrance to old graveyard on Glebe Lane

The entrance to the old graveyard is through an iron gate and stile in the wall. The west side measures 231 ft. approx. and the north side 204 ft approx. The ruins of an old Church of Ireland church and tower stand on an east-west axis on the south side of the graveyard. The nave of the church measures 45 ft. long and 25 ft. wide. The remaining lower parts of the walls stand 6 ft. high. Amid the rubble in the body of the church are pieces of stone with crudely carved crosses. At the West end of the church is a square tower which is approximately 60 ft. high. On the south side of the tower, about 30 ft. up, is a granite tablet with 1817 carved on it. The walls of the tower measure 15ft east to west and 13.5 ft. north to south. There was a door in the south wall of the tower which was blocked up in recent years. A large marble tablet has been inserted into the space. There is a large ornamental monument on the west wall and the north wall had a window and a lean-to building attached to it. Inside the south wall and east of the gate is a cross which was re-erected by Rev. Fr. Mulvany and some men from the parish. Pieces of the cross were found scattered about the graveyard when the area was being cleaned up. The shaft and limbs of the cross are eight-sided and it is fixed into a square base. There is no carving on the cross and it stands 4ft. 10" high. Beside the cross there is a large piece of carved stone and throughout the graveyard there are a number of pieces of windows etc., which belonged to an earlier church. These have been used as grave markers.

The *Ordnance Survey Field Name Book of 1835-36* states that *"The (C of I) church was built in 1817 on the site of an earlier church, dedicated first to St. Thomas À Becket (and later, not known when) to the Trinity"*. Some 19 years before the building of the church (1817) some walls of an earlier building still remained and were believed to have been part of its vestry. A Marble Tablet in the south wall of the tower reads *"Gorges 1728"*, and is dedicated to Richard Gorges of Kilbrew (*Kilbrew being a townland in nearby Curragha*), who had served bravely in Ireland, Flanders and Spain. The plaque had been removed from the old graveyard in Kilbrew. There was also a highly ornamented monument to the Lowther Family dated 1764. The head of the Lowther family was Lord Lansdowne. This monument was later removed to the ancestral home of the Lowther family in Suffolk. There are also monuments dedicated to the following families:

The Field Family dated 1709.
The Crean Family dated 1947.
The Donnelly & Wall Family dated 1932-1963.
The Gaughan Family dated 1940.
The McCormack Family dated 1887-1917.
The Brien Family dated 1924-1940.
The Maynard Family dated 1886.
The Johnston Family dated 1872 -1890. Dedicated to Rev. William Stuart Johnston, second son of Rev. Henry Johnston of Ratoath, who died on 8th May 1872.
The Duffy Family dated 1849-1906.
The Rafferty Family dated 1781-1863.
The Clarke Family dated 1903-1944.

Reference: *The foregoing is an extract from a detailed survey of the Church of the Blessed Trinity and the old Graveyard, Ratoath, completed by Michael J. Kenny, Dunboyne, in 1982.*

Other family names interred in the old Cemetery are as follows:
Bryans of Baltrasna, Ashbourne, Mrs. Linda Williams who died on 6th March 1872.
Mrs. Ester Bates, Baltrasna, died in 1909 and Hester Bates died June 1918 aged 83 years.
Annie Bruen also died in 1904.
Gertrude Clarke died in 1904.
John Bruen died 21st August 1924, aged 78 years.
Members of the Caffrey Family of Ratoath. A stone reads; "This stone and burial place belonged to Patrick Caffery of Ratoath who died from the effects of a fall received in the hunting field 22nd February 1874. Aged 36 years".

The earliest stone that can be found in the Graveyard dates back to 1709. The inscription is faded and is difficult to read.

Another monumental inscription in the Church of Ireland churchyard in Ratoath is as follows:

"Erected to the memory of Rev. Lancelot King Conygham, Rector of Ratoath, by his affectionate widow. He departed this life 7th April 1820 aged 49 years." Beside him is his daughter Julia, who departed this life 18 November 1820 aged 19 years.

Other family names on the headstones of those buried in the Graveyard are as follows:

Mr. Bourns died March 1833 aged 46, his sister Catherine Henshaw, died 1856 and his brother Christopher died 1859.
Eleanor Brady, departed this life Dec. 1802, aged 26.
Members of the Brennan family and Brien family.
Tom Murphy, who died in 1865
A Denis Bryan who died March 1789 aged 52 years and his wife Rose Bryan who died Jan 1789 aged 50 years. Also their sons James and John and several of their children.
There is a stone and burial place erected to Patrick Caulin.

The Church of Ireland Church, (*now a ruin in the old graveyard in Ratoath*) was relatively modern at the time of the survey. The date on the Belfry is 1817, but it must have been erected on a site that was previously a site of worship. The architect was Joseph Welland. The building of the church cost £800. The church had three windows on the south wall. There were no windows on the north wall; there were only plaques commemorating the deceased Rectors of the church.

There were some interesting tablets on the walls to the memory of local gentlemen who distinguished themselves in the wars of Queen Anne and George I. There was a beautiful stained glass window depicting Christ blessing the children, this was moved to Ballymaglasson Church, near Dunboyne, and afterwards erected in the south wall of Dunshaughlin Church of Ireland.

There has been no resident vicar in Ratoath since 1920. Services were held in the church up to 1958. Baptisms were held in the church from 1878 to 1958.

Burials were held in the church from 1879 to 1954. Marriages were held in the church from 1846 to 1945. In 1964 the church building was dismantled and most of the stones remain on site.

In 2002, Ratoath Heritage Group in collaboration with Meath County Council, ESB and John Long, electrician, installed flood lights to illuminate the Church Tower, which helps to highlight this historically significant monument.

The following extracts were taken from a national survey at the end of the 19th Century...

> RATOATH FORMER PARISH CHURCH (C of I). 1817. *All that survives is the tower and the base of the church walls. The former is the usual three-stage structure with pinnacles and a battlemented parapet. MONUMENTS. On the west face of the tower and presumably from the C 18 church, a handsome classical wall monument in the manner of James Gibbs. An inscribed plaque flanked by scrolled consoles and above it a flat aedicule, framing a circular bust niche. The bust, of Jane Lowther †1764, has long since gone. In the churchyard near the tower is a late C 13 or early C 14 sandstone effigial tomb; coffin slab with the figure of a knight wearing a belted round-necked coat and holding a sword, his legs broken off from knee level. Incised Lombardic inscriptions are on the edges of the slab.*

Medieval Signs
From previous information, we know that there was a monastery situated north of the Motte, and also we know that the octagonal Cross uncovered in 1981 by Fr. Mulvany was dated c1200 – 1400 A.D. This cross was made of limestone. The cross is not joined with glue or any such agents, but with a halving joint. The cross is set in a rectangular base with eight sides.

The next evidence of the monastery was the discovery of underground tunnels which were discovered when the church was being knocked down in 1964. A man wanted to build a barn north east of the church and while digging the foundations he uncovered underground Tunnels or passages, these were never explored but instead they were filled in and forgotten about.

The last evidence found of medieval monasteries was "cast iron points". These are used at the moment to mark out a grave near the octagonal cross. These cast iron points were used to cover windows in monasteries.

LOCAL HISTORY

Ratoath Cemetery

Front View of the Octagonal Cross in The Old Graveyard

Side View of the Octagonal Cross in The Old Graveyard

Norman Knight

There is an effigy of a Knight in the graveyard. Norman knights often dedicated tombs or monuments to themselves when they died. This tomb was originally in the Protestant church, but was moved out when the church was demolished. It is reputed to be the twelfth oldest tomb in Ireland. The effigy is situated south of the tower in the old section of the graveyard. The knight's head rests upon a tasselled cushion with remains of foliate decoration in relief upon the edge of the slab at this position. He is armed in mail, over which can be seen a surcoat to the knee, belted at the waist and having a round neck. The coif was apparently thrown back from the head, which has a basin-cut chevalier. The cushion is represented as if it had folds radiating from the head. The hands are positioned one upon the sword grip and the other on the sword below. The sword has a large pommel and a short cross. Some object perhaps part of the strap of the sword mounting appears below the belt and descends down beside the sword. The legs are missing from below the knees. As far as can be seen, despite the worn condition of the stone, the date must be late thirteenth or early fourteenth century.

2006: Main Entrance Gates to Ratoath Cemetery

New Cemetery
Since 1950 the Catholic community have had their own burial ground on portion of an adjoining field, donated by William Farrell, who lived on the Well Road in Ratoath Village. Most Rev. Dr. Kyne, Bishop of Meath, solemnly consecrated the new Cemetery on 5th May 1952.

The first funeral to the New Cemetery was that of Frankie Walsh of Glascarn. Pat Donnelly of Lagore Cross was the altar server for this funeral. The second and third funerals were those of Jane O'Reilly of The Commons lane, mother of Mrs Bridget Carey and Walter Kennedy of Peacockstown.

In 1988 the boundary wall between the Church of Ireland grounds and the Catholic Church Cemetery was demolished, thus making it easier to maintain the entire area as one unit. The people who were involved in taking down the old wall dividing the old and new cemetery were Pud Mahon, Joe Lynch, Imelda Everard and Joe Mannering, all from Ratoath.

The entire grounds of the old and new cemeteries are a credit to the work of the people who look after them and a fitting tribute to all our beloved ones buried there.

LOCAL HISTORY — Ratoath Cemetery

Of interest, on entering the Cemetery through the Main Gate, there is a large white marble Cross erected on a rectangular base which bears the following inscription:

The English and Latin Inscriptions at the base of the Main Cross are as follows:

Three Paters and Aves
And a Glory be to the
FATHER

Indulgence of Five
Years

HAEG CRUX JUXTA
EGGLESIAM RATOATHENSEM
DIU POSITA INDEQUE
TRANSLATA DIE 4TA.. MAII A.D. 1952
HIG ERECTA EST, QUA DIE
CONSEGRATUM EST HOC COEMETERIUM

JOANNE KYNE EPISGOPO JOANNE COGAN
PASTORE

Inscription on the Front of the Main Cross

MISSION
BY THE FATHERS
OF THE S. J.
APRIL 1865

Inscription on the Back of the Main Cross

REFERENCES:
Survey of the Church of the Blessed Trinity and of the Old Graveyard, Ratoath, completed by Michael J. Kenny, Dunboyne, Co. Meath. 1982.
Survey of the Church of the Old Graveyard, Ratoath, completed by Derek Darby, Ratoath, Co. Meath. 1990.

LOCAL HISTORY

Archaeological Excavations and Discoveries in Ratoath in 2004

ANGELA WALLACE

A programme of archaeological monitoring of topsoil stripping was carried out in advance of a large-scale housing development, Steeplechase, in the outskirts of Ratoath, Co. Meath. The area monitored is located to the west of Ratoath, bounded by the Dunshaughlin road to the south and Skryne road to the north. There were no previously recorded archaeological monuments within the area of the development; it does however encroach upon the western boundary of the archaeological constraint area of Ratoath town. It was noted in The Urban Survey of Co. Meath (Bradley, unpublished)[1] that linear strips forming land division north and south of the Dunshaughlin road may reflect medieval burgage plots.

In the course of archaeological monitoring a substantial number of archaeological features were identified on the summit of a low east-west ridge adjacent to the Dunshaughlin road. At the eastern end of the ridge two ring-ditches were identified, a number of linear ditches, burnt pits and kilns. At the western end of the ridge adjacent to an existing farmyard the fragmented remains of three east-west orientated human burials were identified. A portion of a large curving ditch was also visible.

A programme of geophysical survey was carried out in the vicinity of the human remains. The magnetic gradiometry technique was used, this measures and maps patterns of magnetism in the soil. Ancient activity, particularly burning, leaves magnetic traces that show up even today when detected with the right equipment. Buried features such as ditches or pits, when they are filled with burnt or partly burnt materials can show up clearly and give an image of sub-surface archaeology.

The results of this survey appear to confirm the presence of an Early Christian circular enclosure which has been partially truncated by the existing farmyard to the west. On the eastern side of this enclosure a series of linear and curvilinear ditches were identified, they may form part of an outlying field system associated with the Early Christian enclosure, or they may be part of a later medieval or post-medieval field system.

Archaeological excavation on the site commenced in October, 2003. A small burnt

---

[1] "*Urban Archaeological Survey of County Meath*". Author: Bradley, J. Dublin: Archaeological Survey of Ireland. (1984).

(*Above*): Excavation site, October, 2003

Excavators working on the site which shows a Bronze Age Ring Ditch, Bronze Age Barrow and Field Systems

spread was excavated in a seasonally waterlogged area at the base of the east-west ridge and a possible trough was identified but it had been badly damaged by field drains. Burnt spreads such as this were in use over a long period of time and are commonly known as *Fulachta Fiadh*, these sites consist of cooking pits or troughs, surrounded by low mounds of burnt soil and fire-cracked stone resulting from the cleaning out of the cooking pits or troughs. These sites are quite common throughout the country and usually occur adjacent to streams or in marshy areas where water is readily available nearby. It is believed that the troughs were filled with water, which was then heated with hot stones from a nearby hearth; meat was placed in the hot water and cooked in this way. These sites are generally believed to be Bronze Age in date but many have proved to be much later, indicating they were used over a considerable period of time.

The next phase of excavation focused on the eastern summit of the low east-west ridge. The earliest features in this area were two circular ring-ditches. The larger ring-ditch had an internal diameter of c.15m. A smaller ring ditch was located 5.5m to the north and had an internal diameter of c.6m.

The fragmentary remains of one cremation were identified in the fill of the larger ring-ditch. No cremations were identified in the smaller ring-ditch one piece of flint debitage and an unidentified iron object was recovered during the initial clean back of this feature.

A later sub-rectangular enclosure ditch was also identified in this area; unfortunately no closely dateable material was recovered from this feature. A large quantity of animal bone was recovered and also four pieces of worked flint and two iron fragments and a small metal object which may have been a 'fowling arrow'.

Several figure of eight and key-hole shaped kilns were excavated. Kilns were scattered across the site with two on the western side of the field. One was located on the eastern side of the field cutting through a linear ditch, and one was located at the southern end of the

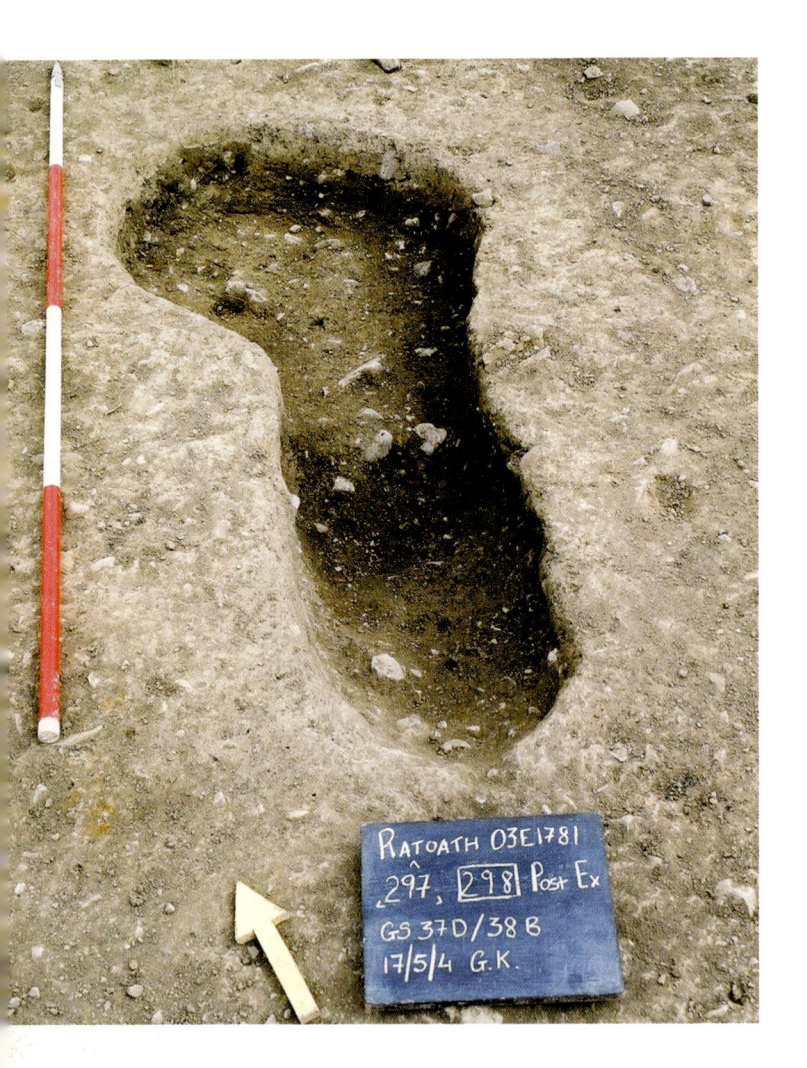

Rotary Quern Stones

(*Left*): Key Hole Kiln – Field 7

field, this one had several small postholes associated, which may indicate the presence of a possible windbreak. Several pits were also excavated in Field 6. These kilns were probably used for corn-drying.

At the base of a figure of eight kiln excavated in Field 7 the intact circular stones of a rotary quern were recovered. These stones would have been used for grinding corn.

The main concentration of archaeological activity in Field 6 appeared to be on the summit of the ridge on the western side of the field. However as excavation progressed a significant number of outlying linear ditches were also identified around the periphery of field 6 to the east, south and north. It would appear that there are at least two different phases of field division apparent in the ditches excavated.

It will not be possible to determine the sequence of ditch phases until further analysis has been carried out. The ditches to the west side of the field may relate to an outlying field system associated with the Early Christian enclosure. The large ditches to the north and south of the field probably represent later medieval or post-medieval land division. Two coins were recovered from the upper fill of a large ditch at the southern end, one of the coins has been too badly corroded to identify any markings but the other coin has markings which appear similar to those found on Irish coins issued during the reign of Charles II, i.e. a halfpenny issued during the years 1681-4.

Excavation is still in progress on the western side of the ridge and more ditches containing a lot of animal bone have been identified. Preliminary investigations commenced within the circular enclosure area in March, 2004 and are ongoing. A silage pit had been built on top of the south-west quadrant of the enclosure, this was demolished and excavation has commenced in this area.

It was feared that the construction of the silage pit had caused a lot of damage to the underlying archaeological deposits. However this was not the case. Preservation appears to be quite good. This area has yielded five finds which are common from Early Christian habitation sites, a portion of a lignite bracelet, three bone pins and a small blue segmented bead. A similar bead was recovered from the excavation at Lagore crannog, which lies approximately 1.5km to the west.

Excavation within the enclosure has been confined to the south-west quadrant to date (2004); it was not possible for this author at the time of writing this article to give an overview of the enclosure as work was only beginning in this area at that time.

A large amount of animal bone was retrieved from the entire site. A zooarchaeologist has examined and identified species such as cattle, pig, deer, horse and wild boar. All the animal bone retrieved from the site were washed and sent to the zooarchaeologist once excavation was completed. This will give a clearer picture of the diet at the time the site was being used. The animal bone will also be examined for butchery markings, which will give an indication if they were butchered on site and what tool types were used for this purpose.

A large volume of soil samples has also been retrieved from various features on the site. These samples are sieved for plant remains which are examined by an archaeobotanist or palaeobotanist. Plant remains can vary in size from microscopic to large wood pieces. Studying the seeds and grains recovered from the site will give an indication about land-use and forms of cultivation as well as diet.

(*Right*): Skeletal remains.

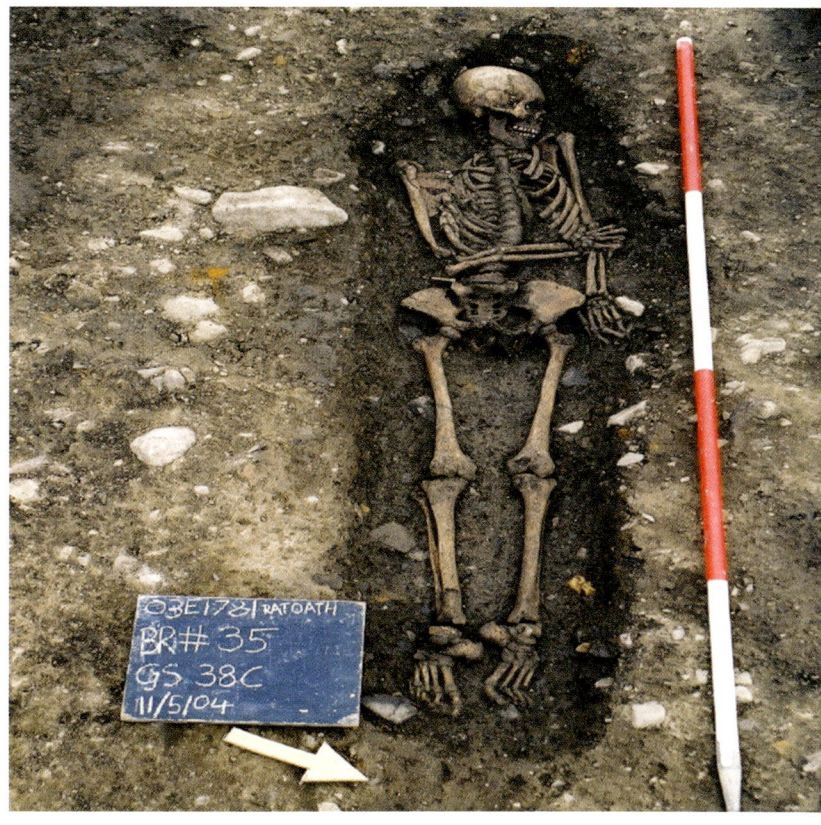

South-west quadrant

Wood, plant fibres and charcoal can tell about building materials and industrial production (and are also used in dendro- and radiocarbon dating techniques). The archaeobotanist will reconstruct the past ecology of the area and this will give an understanding of the role the past society on this site had in selecting and modifying the flora of their surrounding environment.

An osteoarchaeologist will examine the human bone and will give an indication of the gender patterns on the site; the age of the individuals when they died and any illnesses they had which left visible effects on the skeletal remains. The single cremation retrieved from the ring-ditch will also be examined.

Once excavation has been completed, animal and human bone will be washed, dried and repackaged for the various specialists. All the soil samples will be processed through an on site sieving station; the sieved samples will also be dried, sorted and repackaged. Any material such as charcoal, charred grains, and bone fragments which may be suitable for dating will be sent away for radiocarbon analysis. Licences to Alter have to be obtained from the National Museum of Ireland for this. It can often take 4-6 months to process and send all this material to the various specialists.

All the data collected from excavation on the site will be analysed by members of the excavation team, and a preliminary report on all the findings from the excavation will be compiled. Once all the specialist reports have been compiled and samples sent for radiocarbon dating have been analysed a clearer picture of the chronology and environmental conditions on the site becomes available and the final report will be prepared with a detailed discussion of the site. It can often take up to two years from completion of the excavation for all the necessary specialist reports to be compiled and the final report submitted to the Archaeological section of the Department of Environment, Heritage & Local Government and the National Museum of Ireland. Members of the public can access these reports on request.

It is known from historical records that the village of Ratoath was an important centre in the medieval period, the presence of the motte in the centre of the village indicates its importance in Anglo-Norman times. Little is known of prehistoric activity in the village apart from a record of two Bronze Age vessels recovered while digging a drain in 1866. The presence of the burnt spread and two ring-ditches on the excavation may provide further evidence for prehistoric settlement and funerary practices in this area in the Late Bronze/Early Iron Age.

The circular enclosure and possible associated outlying field system also provides evidence for intensive farming activity in the area in the Early Christian period. Prior to the 6th century, the town was located on one of five great highways which led from the royal residence at Tara. Ratoath was located on the Dublin to Tara road, suggesting the possibility of pre-Norman activity in the town. The presence of an Early Christian enclosure confirms pre-Norman activity.

The location of the site is also in close proximity to the nearby townland of Lagore which lent its name to the Dessi Kingdom of Dunshaughlin, whose ruler was referred to as the king of Lagore. This townland, translated as Loch-Gabhair, contained a strongly fortified settlement in the form of a Crannóg. Its inhabitants were 'a race of hardy chieftains, thoroughly Catholic and national, who often measured swords with the Danes' (Cogan 1867, 383)[2]. Earliest reference to activity at Lagore is from 673AD (O'Donovan, 1990 Annals of the Four Masters).

---

[1] "*The Diocese of Meath: Ancient and Modern*". Volume I, II and III. Author: Cogan, A. 1862. Dublin: Joseph Dollard.

The finds from the enclosure to date include a portion of a lignite bracelet, a blue glass bead and three highly polished bone pins, these finds can be closely paralleled with those from excavations at Lagore, suggesting there was contact between the two sites. The considerable quantity of finds and layers of archaeological deposits at Lagore indicates it was a royal residence. The site at Ratoath was unlikely to have had such high status but was nevertheless on an important routeway between Dublin and Tara, and this would have given the inhabitants good opportunities for trade.

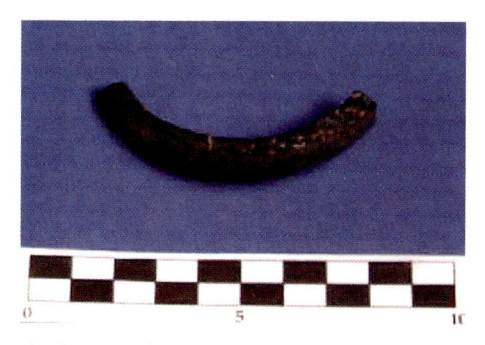

Lignite Bracelet

Small Blue Segmented Glass Bead (similar to one found at Lagore Crannóg)

The increase in large scale developments around Dublin and outlying areas has led to many new and exciting archaeological discoveries in recent years and is providing increasing evidence for settlement, industrial, burial and ritual practices in past times. This site was discovered as part of a programme of archaeological monitoring, in accordance with a planning condition associated with the development. The current legislation encourages the practice of archaeological impact assessments, testing and monitoring in advance of development to ensure that archaeological sites are recorded. Local communities have an important role to play in helping to ensure the heritage of their area is recorded or protected for future generations.

The author would like to acknowledge the support of the developers McGarrell-Reilly for their co-operation and assistance throughout.
Steven Johnston of Arch-Tech Ltd., project manager for the excavation, Agnes Kerrigan, Assistant Director and Claire Ryan, Supervisor, all the digging crew who have worked through some atrocious weather conditions, and also the administrative support staff in the offices of Arch-Tech Ltd.

ANGELA WALLACE, SITE DIRECTOR, FOR ARCH-TECH LTD. APRIL 2004.

REFERENCES:

Hencken, H. 1950. *Lagore Crannog: An Irish Royal Residence of the 7th to 10th Centuries A.D.* PRIA Vol.53 C, 1-247.

McCabe, S. & Johnston, S. 2002. *Archaeological Assessment Report, Ratoath, Co. Meath*, Arch-Tech Ltd. Unpublished report submitted to Archaeological Section, DEHLG and National Museum of Ireland.

O'Donovan, J. 1990 (1856). *The Four Masters, Annals of the Kingdom of Ireland from the Earliest Times to the year 1616.* 3rd Edition. Dublin, De Burca Rare Books.

Wallace, A. 2003. *Archaeological Monitoring Report Licence No.03E1300, Ratoath, Co. Meath.* Unpublished report submitted to DEHLG and National Museum of Ireland.

LOCAL HISTORY

Archaeological discoveries on a new section of the N2 in Counties Meath and Dublin

MARIA FITZGERALD

ARCHAEOLOGICAL INVESTIGATIONS in advance of the N2 Finglas–Ashbourne road scheme revealed approximately 20 new archaeological sites interspersed along the route. Their date range indicates that there was intermittent human activity in the Finglas–Ashbourne area during at least the past 5,000 years. The diverse nature of this activity is reflected by a range of site types, including short-term dispersed occupation pits and features, burnt mound sites, small-scale kiln and industrial sites, and extensive habitation complexes, as well as sites of ritual, burial or ceremonial significance.

The N2 road scheme comprises c. 17 km of dual carriageway extending NNE from the existing N2/M50 junction in Dublin, bypassing the busy and congested town of Ashbourne, Co. Meath, on its western side before rejoining the existing N2 north of the town. The archaeological works for the scheme were carried out on behalf of the National Roads Authority and Meath County Council.

All the sites discussed here were fully excavated during 2004 and 2005 by Cultural Resource Development Services Ltd (CRDS Ltd). Preliminary archaeological investigations for the scheme commenced in 2001, however, with a contribution on archaeology to the Environmental Impact Statement prepared by Valerie J Keeley Ltd. Subsequently, an aerial survey of the route was carried out by Margaret Gowen & Co. Ltd in 2001, and an extensive geophysical survey of the route was carried out by GSB Prospection Ltd in 2002. Cumulatively, these investigations identified a number of existing and new archaeological sites along and adjacent to the route. In order to investigate their potential, and that of the entire route, an extensive programme of test excavations was carried out between August and November 2003 by Judith Carroll Network Archaeology Ltd.

Summary of Archaeological Discoveries
Given the breadth of evidence revealed and the limited length of this paper, it is proposed to present a preliminary overview of the findings and subsequently to discuss some of the more interesting sites and artefacts in greater detail.

Fig 1. Elevated view of deep pits or wells at Site 13b, Muckerstown, Co. Meath (**Hawkeye**)

Prehistoric sites

Most of the new sites revealed were prehistoric in date, or at least had a primary phase of activity during the prehistoric period. With the exception of two burial ring-ditches at Coldwinters, Co. Dublin (Record of Monuments and Places [RMP] No. ME014-015), and Killegland, Co. Meath (ME045-002), comparatively little prehistoric activity had been recorded in the vicinity of the route in advance of the N2 investigations. The earliest site discovered along the route was Site 5, a Neolithic (3200–2800 BC) ritual enclosure at Kilshane, Co. Dublin. Excavation revealed an intriguing ritual and burial site, and a summary of the findings is presented below.

Many of the other prehistoric sites were of Bronze Age date. These included some very large, deep, waterlogged pits or wells of Middle Bronze Age date (Fig. 1) discovered at Muckerstown (Site 13b), Co. Meath. The pits produced an assemblage of unique wooden artefacts that are discussed in greater detail below.

The most ubiquitous prehistoric site type in Ireland is the burnt mound, and five sites of this type were found interspersed along the route in the townlands of Coldwinters (Site 1), Co. Dublin, Ward Lower (Site 7), Co. Dublin, Harlockstown (two sites—Sites 20 and 31), Co. Meath, and Baltrasna (Site 15), Co. Meath. Burnt mounds are largely dated to the Bronze Age, though some earlier and later examples are recorded. They are generally interpreted as cooking sites, but alternative processes that use quantities of hot water—such as saunas, leather preparation, cloth-fulling and cloth-dyeing—have also been proposed.

Other prehistoric sites along the scheme included a small isolated pit at Ward Upper (Site 6), Co. Dublin, which produced c. 600 sherds (representing 24 vessels) of Late Bronze Age pottery (c. 1150–800 BC). The pit may simply have been used for refuse, but given the extent of the pottery assemblage it could also be interpreted as reflecting a more complex ritual deposition in the landscape. Extensive Bronze Age and Iron Age burial and habita-

Ratoath Past and Present

tion complexes were discovered at Harlockstown (Site 19) and Rath (Site 27), Co. Meath, and these sites are also discussed in more detail below.

Early medieval sites
Prior to the N2 investigations, early medieval activity in the Finglas/Ashbourne landscape was represented by ringforts, souterrains and early church sites extensively listed in the RMP (ringforts at Wotton [ME045-022] and Muckerstown [ME045-021], a cropmark enclosure at Killegland [ME045-003], a souterrain at Baltrasna [ME045-026], and early church sites at Donaghmore [ME045-008], Killegland [ME045-004] and Cookstown [ME045-001]). New archaeological sites revealed by the N2 investigations add considerably to this evidence. At the southern end of the scheme, a small, multi-phase cereal-drying kiln and metalworking site (Site 2) was found on a slight rise in the townland of Cherryhound, Co. Dublin. This industrial site had three main phases of activity—a phase of metalworking to the east, followed by phases of kiln activity at the western end of the site. Associated houses and settlements were not discovered but may have been located nearby beyond the road corridor.

At Cookstown, Co. Meath, at the northern end of the scheme, the geophysical survey revealed a circular enclosure (Site 25) located partly within the roadtake but extending under an inhabited farm to the west of the road. Excavation confirmed that this enclosure was an early medieval ringfort (Fig. 2). A ring-pin and the ring portion of a **second pin were recovered from primary ditch fills.**

Fig. 2 Segment of ringfort ditch at Cookstown, Co. Meath - an early medieval farmstead enclosure partly underlying a modern farmstead (**Hawkeye**)

66

The most extensive and significant early medieval settlement complex was uncovered at Raystown (Site 21), Co. Meath. This was a green-field site before the N2 investigations and was first identified during the geophysical survey of 2002. The initial survey was subsequently extended to areas outside the roadtake in order to define the full extent and nature of the archaeological features. Approximately one third of the site was within the area affected by the road scheme and this area was fully excavated during 2004 by CRDS.

Medieval and post-medieval sites

The medieval period is well represented, particularly at the southern end of the road scheme, by upstanding monuments such as Dunsoghly Castle (DU014-00501), Co. Dublin, and Norman mottes at Donaghmore (ME045-007), Co. Meath, and Kilshane (DU014-001) and Newtown (DU014-013), Co. Dublin. Newly discovered medieval sites recorded along the scheme at Cookstown (Site 25), Baltrasna (Site 17/18) and Muckerstown (Site 12/13a), Co. Meath, add to this picture of medieval settlement. Cookstown was a multi-period site with an important phase of medieval rural activity and settlement. The sites at Baltrasna and Muckerstown were interpreted as medieval farmsteads. The evidence at Baltrasna represented the remains of a field system and cobbled laneway from the late medieval period. The site at Muckerstown consisted of the yards, kitchen gardens and infields of a medieval and post-medieval settlement. This site produced about 2,000 sherds of medieval pottery of predominantly local wares, dating from the 13th/14th centuries. The new evidence from the scheme augments the picture of high-status, defensive mottes and castles by revealing dispersed medieval rural settlements and farms.

Kilshane Henge

The earliest and one of the most significant sites from the scheme was a Neolithic ritual enclosure (Fig. 3), 37 m by 27 m, discovered at the southern end of the scheme at Kilshane, Co. Dublin (NGR 311010, 242951; height 81.3 m OD; excavation licence no. 03E1359 ext.; excavation director Dermot Moore). The artefactual evidence from pottery and stone tools indicates that this site had its origins in the Middle Neolithic period (3600–3250 BC), but it also saw intermittent activity during the Late Neolithic and Early and Middle Bronze Age periods.

Fig. 3 Elevated view of irregular henge enclosure at Kilshane Co. Dublin. (**Hawkeye**)

Fig. 4 - Animal bone layer undergoing excavation at Kilshane Neolithic henge, Co. Dublin. (**Hawkeye**)

The enclosing ditch was formed by the excavation of a series of intercutting and overlapping ditch segments. With the exception of some 'cleaned-out' cremation pits and a crouched inhumation burial, all thought to have been of Early Bronze Age date, few features were recorded within the interior. A unique element of this site was the recovery of approximately 300 kg of cattle bone from the base of the ditch segments (Fig. 4). Sherds from globular bowls dating from the Middle Neolithic were also discovered in the ditch fills, sealing the animal bone, and these indicate a similar deposition date. This is also confirmed by a radiocarbon date from the layer immediately above the pot.

This is the largest assemblage of Neolithic animal bone from Ireland to date. Approximately 40 to 50 immature cattle are represented, and these were deposited in the ditch segments in both a disarticulated and an articulated state. In some instances, certain bone types, such as long bones, were grouped together. According to Dr Finbar McCormick (Queen's University, Belfast) the bone was defleshed, but there is little evidence for bone disease or butchery. The bone must have been covered over very soon after its deposition, as there is little evidence for animal gnawing of the bone. Nearly all of the animals were slaughtered at 18 months old, indicating that the event took place in the autumn. The absence of butchery marks on the disarticulated cattle bone and the presence of articulated animals indicate that the bone assemblage is unlikely to represent the remains of feasting. The evidence would suggest that the animals were slaughtered, disarticulated (in most cases), defleshed and deposited in the ditch segments, and that they represent the remains of animal sacrifice.

The upper fills of the ditch, particularly to the east, contained numerous sherds of pottery and a large assemblage of stone tools. The pottery from this layer included 17 Early Bronze Age Food Vessels (2400–1700 BC), sherds of Vase Urns and Encrusted Urns, as well as 12 Middle Bronze Age Cordoned Urns (2000–1400 BC). Although Food Vessels are occasionally recorded in domestic contexts, it is predominantly a funerary ware. The site director, Dermot Moore, suggests that a nearby Early and Middle Bronze Age cemetery may have been cleared out and the contents deposited into the upper fills of the enclosing ditch.

This site appears to be unique, with few obvious Irish parallels. It is comparable to a small group of henges or embanked enclosures, a site type interpreted as being of ritual, ceremonial or burial significance because of the large internal area of the enclosures, the absence of finds from the interiors and the non-defensive nature of the banks. Recorded examples are generally much larger than the Kilshane site, however. The segmented nature of the ditch may also invoke comparisons with the much larger British or European causewayed enclosure sites, interpreted as possible cattle marts or community meeting places. These sites also have limited evidence for internal structural remains but have evidence for the deliberate deposition of pottery, human bone and animal bones in the ditches and in pits. An Early Neolithic causewayed enclosure site was recently discovered at Magheraboy, Co. Sligo (MacDonagh 2005, 17–20), and this site was also interpreted as of ritual significance, with deposits of flint arrowheads, pottery and deliberately broken porcellanite axes.

The Kilshane henge may have served as a community-meeting place for ceremony and/or burial during the Neolithic and Bronze Age periods. Environmental evidence suggests that the landscape was heavily wooded during this period, so the Kilshane site would have been a large clearing in the forest. Did the local community congregate at Kilshane for an event each autumn or at certain other times? Did each family group walk to the site and bring along an animal that they had herded through the forests and countryside? Was it a dispersed community, and from how far did its members travel? There are no known Neolithic sites in the immediate vicinity, but did people come from nearby Neolithic complexes such as Knowth and Newgrange, 32 km to the north-west, or from houses at Coolfore, Co. Louth (Ó Drisceoil 2002), 26 km to the north-east, and Newtown, Co. Meath, 25 km north-east (Gowen & Halpin 1992)—or from much further afield? The cattle bone could be interpreted as a deliberate symbolic deposition, and there may have been games and sports associated with the killing. Were all the animals killed at or near the site, and could they have been offered up in thanks for a good autumn harvest or in appeasement after a bad one? In addition to ceremonial activities, did the community meet to trade and barter animals and tools, and generally exchange ideas and skills? We can only imagine the festival atmosphere at the site, which was certainly an important local focus for community activity.

Prehistoric Harlockstown
An important prehistoric complex was discovered at Harlockstown (Site 19), Co. Meath. This site (NGR 305304, 250560; height 70.82 m OD; excavation licence no. 03E1526 ext.; excavation director David O'Connor) was first identified by geophysical survey, and subsequent excavation revealed a very close correlation between the survey results and the actual site features. Harlockstown was a multi-period and multi-functional site. Primary features comprised an Early Bronze Age circular enclosure (radiocarbon-dated to 1960–1690 BC, Wk-16288; see dating table) cut by a square Iron Age enclosure where extensive metalworking activity took place (Fig. 5). Excavation revealed that the circular enclosure was a burial monument with a cremation pit and two inhumations within the interior. There was no evidence for a mound, but the upcast material from the ditch may have been thrown into the enclosure and the burials inserted into the mound material.

Fig. 5 – Elevated view of prehistoric complex at Harlockstown, Co. Meath, showing Early Bronze Age circular enclosure (left) and square Iron Age enclosure (right) (**studiolab.ie**)

Fig. 6 – Burial with Food Vessel pot in Harlockstown, Co. Meath (CRDS Ltd.)

The inhumed individuals were placed in a crouched position in stone-lined graves and were accompanied by substantially intact decorated pottery vessels known as Food Vessels (Fig. 6). The vessels have been identified as a ribbed bowl and a necked bipartite bowl with a cruciform motif on the base (E Grogan and H Roche, pers. comm.). Both individuals were adults, one of indeterminate sex but more likely female (radiocarbon-dated to 2120–1870 BC, Wk-16290; see dating table) and the second possibly male (L Fibiger, pers. comm.). Food Vessel burials are not unusual in Ireland, with dates generally clustering between 2460 BC and 1980 BC. Such inhumations can be found in unmarked or flat cemeteries, or beneath cairns with either burnt or unburnt remains. The pots were originally referred to as Food Vessels because it was assumed that they contained a food offering for the spirit of the deceased. This has yet to be substantiated by any conclusive evidence from residue analysis, however.

Muckerstown Wooden Artefacts

Two large waterlogged pits or wells, each approximately 2.5 m in depth, were the primary features revealed at Site 13b in Muckerstown, Co. Meath (NGR 307851, 249310; height 70.27 m OD; excavation licence no. 03E1331 ext.; excavation director Caitríona Moore). One of the pits was lined with a wooden panel, possibly wattlework (radiocarbon-dated to 1390–1080 BC, Wk-16818; see Appendix 1 dating table), and both may have been accessed by sloping sides laid with fine metalled surfaces. Their purpose is uncertain and they may simply have functioned as wells, as they were deep enough for the extraction of groundwater. An alternative processing function—such as basketry, tanning, dyeing or flax preparation, which all use watery pits—is also possible. Both pits produced organic materials, including worked wood, but one of the pits produced a unique assemblage of 130 basketry artefacts.

These artefacts have been analysed by Caitríona Moore and Dr Ingelise Stuijts, who

Fig. 7 – Wooden Basketry artefact from Site 13b, Muckerstown, Co. Meath (**CRDS Ltd.**)

found that they were very deliberately constructed composite artefacts, comprising three elements: a bundle of woody twigs, a thicker central spine and a twisted branch or withy looping around the bundle (Fig. 7). They were primarily made from four species: willow, broom, ash and alder.

One of the artefacts has been radiocarbon-dated to the Middle Bronze Age period (1600–1210 BC, Wk-15499; see dating table) and, as such, appears to be a unique artefact type with few Irish or European parallels. Their function is uncertain and they compare most closely with a broom called a besom, familiar from folklife evidence in Ireland. It is certainly intriguing that 130 of these objects were discarded or ritually deposited in this pit. The ritual deposition of artefacts in watery locations is well attested in prehistoric times and the objects may therefore have had a non-functional, symbolic significance (C Moore, pers. comm.).

Prehistoric Rath

An extensive prehistoric complex was discovered at Rath (Site 27), Co. Meath, at the northern end of the scheme, where the new road rejoins the existing N2 (NGR 305049, 254101; height 86 m OD; excavation licence no. 03E1214 ext.; excavation director Holger Schweitzer). The site complex extended over a large area measuring c. 280 m by 100 m, extending northwards from a stream and rising to a hillcrest with panoramic views. The primary features on site included a possible sweat-lodge adjacent to the stream, three ring-ditches on the highest point of the ridge, a metalworking area, a cereal-drying kiln and some deep, waterlogged pits (to the north of the existing N2). This site produced an extraordinary array of high-status finds, including a female buried wearing toe-rings, an unusual copper-alloy La Tène fibula, segmented faience beads and some prehistoric wooden vessels (radiocarbon-dated to 390–190 BC, Wk-16824; see dating table).

Fig. 8 – Sweat-lodge at Rath, Co. Meath: a circle of post-holes within a narrow enclosing ditch (**Hawkeye**)

Sweat-lodge?
Holger Schweitzer, excavation director, interpreted one of the structures as a sweat-lodge. The site was beside the small stream and the building, defined by a circle of large post-holes with a hearth, was located between two of the posts (Illus. 9). The hearth was defined by a double ring of stake-holes and had a flue extending into the interior of the building. The building was surrounded by a curving ditch that may have channelled water from the adjacent stream. The basic principle of such a sweat-lodge or sauna was that stones were heated on a hearth, water poured onto the stones and steam channelled into the lodge via the flue. A trough and a mound of discarded burnt stone were located outside the building.

A disc-headed brooch and fibula were recovered in the vicinity of the building. These dress-fasteners may have been lost during dressing and undressing associated with a sauna. The fibula is of late La Tène type and came from the adjacent terrace leading down to the water. Approximately 30 fibulae are known from Ireland. Preliminary examination of this new fibula indicates that the type is unique in Ireland and is paralleled only by British finds (B Raftery, pers. comm.). The introduction of the fibula brooch to Ireland during the Iron Age is thought to reflect changes in clothing such as the wearing of finer wool and linen garments.

Also from this site, recovered from the fill of a small ring-ditch to the north of the building, were three tiny segmented faience beads. Faience is a glass-like substance that is made from simple elements but can be very difficult to produce. The beads from Rath are of an unusual form; they are made from several discs fused together. They appear to be of European morphology but may have been made locally (A Sheridan, pers. comm.). Irish and British faience dates from the Early Bronze Age period (1900–1500 BC). Unusually, however, the Rath beads have come from a context dated to the Iron Age (740–360 BC, Wk-16317; see dating table). Faience is regarded as a symbol of status but it may also have been worn as a talisman in life and death.

Fig. 9 – Female burial with toe-rings, Rath, Co. Meath (CRDS Ltd.)

The woman with rings on her toes

One of the most spectacular finds from this site was the burial of a woman in the fills of a small ring-ditch at the north of the site (Illus. 10). The woman was found lying on her side in a crouched position with clasped hands placed under her cheek. On her feet were three copper-alloy toe-rings—two plain spiral rings and a third ring decorated with a herring-bone motif. On the right foot, the spiral ring encircled the big toe as well as the tips of the second and possibly the third toe. The decorated toe-ring encircled the fourth toe (Schweitzer 2005, 97, illus. 5). A possible fragment of leather was recorded at her heel. It was not possible to establish the position of the other spiral toe-ring because of the poor preservation of the skeletal remains of the left foot.

The closest parallels for this burial are a small number of high-status Iron Age burials from Britain at sites such as Poundbury Hill (Farwell & Molleson 1993) and Maiden Castle (Wheeler 1943). Most of these burials are male with a toe-ring on one foot, and the rings are interpreted as attachments for leather sandals, which were a sign of sovereignty. However, a burial of a female wearing toe-rings was recently discovered under the floor of a late Iron Age metalworking site at Minehowe, Orkney (Card et al. 2005, 326). Given the paucity of Irish parallels for the woman at Rath, it is tempting to speculate that she was a royal visitor from Britain or at least had very strong cultural connections with that island. The bone has not proved suitable for dating so the burial is dated by comparisons only. Scientists at Bradford University are carrying out isotope analysis on her teeth in order to help build up a picture of her diet, which may yield clues as to her cultural background.

The presence of the fibula and the faience beads indicates that the Rath habitation and burial complex was occupied and used by a high-status wealthy community. Given the exclusively British parallels for the fibula and the burial with toe-rings, it seems possible that this community had strong cultural or trading connections with that island.

Rural Medieval Settlement at Cookstown

Cookstown (Site 25), Co. Meath, located at the northern end of the scheme, was a multi-period site with an important phase of medieval rural activity (NGR 304938, 253010; height 76.27 m OD; excavation licence no. 03E1252 ext.; excavation director Richard Clutterbuck). In addition to the aforementioned early medieval ringfort (Illus. 3), the site also had evidence for extensive prehistoric and medieval phases of activity.

About 30 m east of the ringfort, a row of three medieval structures with infields and kitchen gardens was revealed (Illus. 11). The structures were defined by shallow, enclosing slot-trenches (probably used to hold wooden walls). Richard Clutterbuck, excavation director, has interpreted one of the buildings as a forge. Central to this structure was a shallow subrectangular trench with silty lower fills, which contained large quantities of iron slag. This may have been used as a quenching trough to cool down the molten metal during manufacture. The central area, which was raised, contained four large post-holes that probably held the base posts of a table. Cookstown produced a large assemblage of metal objects, including knives, a pair of scissors, hooks and nails, and it seems likely that some of these were made on site. In addition to large quantities of slag, some copper was also recovered from the forge, and archaeometallurgical analysis is proposed to assess the types of metalworking that took place here.

The row of buildings fronted onto what is interpreted as a medieval laneway. Few medieval rural buildings or settlements have been excavated to date in Ireland, so the results of the excavation and post-excavation research should greatly enhance our understanding of the nature of medieval rural settlement.

Fig. 10 Schematic drawing showing the early medieval ringfort and the row of medieval buildings (Strictures 1-IV) with infoelds and kitchen gardens at Cookstown, Co. Meath. Structure I is the building interpreted as a forge (**Hawkeye**)

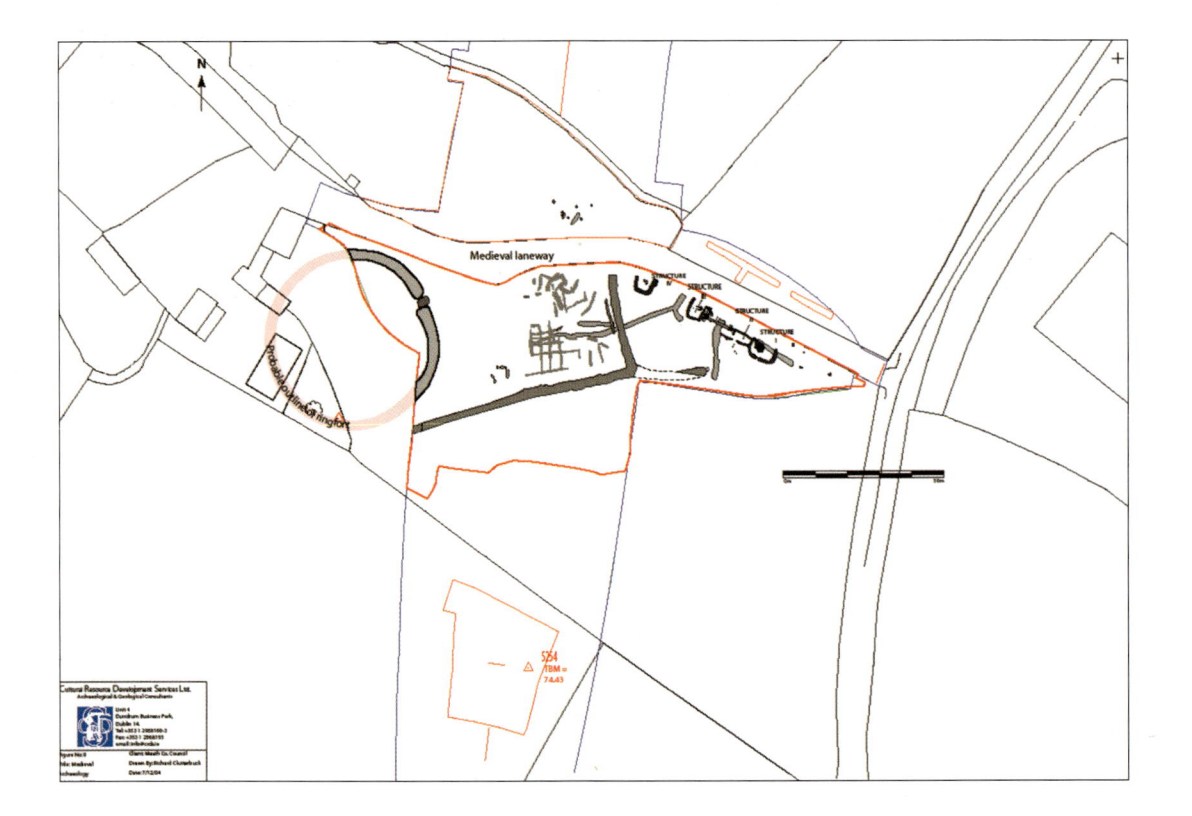

Conclusions

All of the sites discussed above were unknown in advance of the N2 Finglas–Ashbourne road scheme and indicate that human activity in the area was more extensive than previously understood. Additionally, many of these were new site types, not previously recorded or reflected in the RMP for this area, and their discovery has demonstrated that there was greater social diversity and complexity than previously thought. The investigations clearly reveal the potential of future archaeological works to alter our perception and understanding of past societies. It is likely that specialist post-excavation analysis for the N2 project will shed further light on these sites and the activities and ways of life of the people who occupied or visited them. The post-excavation phase of the project is well under way and it is intended to publish the results of the excavations more fully in due course.

Acknowledgements

Thanks to all those involved in the N2 Finglas–Ashbourne Road Scheme, and in particular, at CRDS, senior archaeologist Finola O'Carroll, post-excavation manager Madeleine Murray and site directors Richard Clutterbuck (Sites 24/25 and 26), Donal Fallon (Sites 12/13a, 13c and 17/18), Caitríona Moore (Sites 16 and 13b), Dermot Moore (Site 5), Cara Murray (Sites 14, 15, 20 and 31), Laurence McGowan (Sites 2, 6 and 22/23), David O'Connor (Site 19), Matthew Seaver (Site 21) and Holger Schweitzer (Sites 1, 7 and 27).

REFERENCES

Card, N, Downes, J, Gibson, J & Sharman, P 2005 'Religion and metal working at Mine Howe, Orkney', *Current Archaeology*, Vol. 17, No. 199, 322–7.

Farwell, D E & Molleson, T I 1993 *Excavations at Poundbury 1966–80 Vol. II: the cemeteries*. Dorset Natural History and Archaeology Society Monograph Series No. 11. Dorset Natural History and Archaeology Society, Dorset.

Gowen, M & Halpin, E 1992 'A Neolithic house at Newtown', *Archaeology Ireland*, Vol. 6, No. 2, 156.

Ó Drisceoil, C 2002 'Site 1, Coolfore', in I Bennett (ed.), *Excavations 2000: summary accounts of archaeological excavations in Ireland*, 214–15. Wordwell, Bray.

MacDonagh, M 2005 'Valley bottom and hilltop: 6,000 years of settlement along the route of the N4 Sligo Inner Relief Road', in J O'Sullivan & M Stanley (eds), *Recent Archaeological Discoveries on National Road Schemes 2004*, 9–23. Archaeology and the National Roads Authority Monograph Series No. 2. National Roads Authority, Dublin.

Schweitzer, H 2005 'Iron Age toe-rings from Rath, County Meath, on the N2 Finglas–Ashbourne Road Scheme', in J O'Sullivan & M Stanley (eds), *Recent Archaeological Discoveries on National Road Schemes 2004*, 93–8. Archaeology and the National Roads Authority Monograph Series No. 2. National Roads Authority, Dublin.

Wheeler, R E M 1943 *Maiden Castle, Dorset*. Reports of the Research Committee of the Society of Antiquaries of London, No. 12.

Dating Table

Lab code	Site	Sample/context	Yrs BP	Calibrated date ranges
Wk-15499	Muckerstown, Site 13b	Willow (Salix) artefact from large waterlogged pit/well	2990 ± 40	1520–1310 BC one sigma 1600–1210 BC two sigma
Wk-16279	Muckerstown, Site 13b	Ash (Fraxinus) charcoal from a stone-lined industrial feature	2175 ± 38	360–170 BC one sigma 380–110 BC two sigma
Wk-16280	Muckerstown, Site 13b	Hazel (Corylus) charcoal from drainage feature	1146 ± 52	AD 780–980 one sigma AD 770–1020 two sigma
Wk-16281	Muckerstown, Site 13b	Blackthorn (Prunus spinosa) charcoal from small bowl-shaped pit	1055 ± 68	AD 890–1030 one sigma AD 810–1160 two sigma
Wk-16818	Muckerstown, Site 13b	Brushwood panel of hazel (Corylus) from large waterlogged pit/well	2990 ± 40	1310–1130 BC one sigma 1390–1080 BC two sigma
Wk-16282	Baltrasna, Site 14	Ash (Fraxinus) charcoal from pit	3733 ± 40	2200–2040 BC one sigma 2290–2020 BC two sigma
Wk-16284	Baltrasna, Site 17/18	Blackthorn (Prunus spinosa) charcoal from large pit	2288 ± 35	400–230 BC one sigma 410–200 BC two sigma
Wk-16286	Baltrasna, Site 17/18	Ash (Fraxinus) charcoal from pit	2900 ± 47	1200–1000 BC one sigma 1260–930 BC two sigma
Wk-16288	Harlockstown, Site 19	Alder (Alnus) charcoal from circular enclosure ditch	3515 ± 45	1900–1760 BC one sigma 1960–1690 BC two sigma
Wk-16289	Harlockstown, Site 19	Blackthorn (Prunus spinosa) from small barrow	2057 ± 40	160 BC–AD 120 one sigma 180 BC–AD 30 two sigma
Wk-16290	Harlockstown, Site 19	Human bone (right fibula diaphysis fragment) from articulated burial inside circular enclosure	3599 ± 36	2020–1900 BC one sigma 2120–1870 BC two sigma
Wk-16311	Ballybin/Killegland, Site 22	Alder (Alnus) charcoal layer of kiln	2016 ± 39	60 BC–AD 50 one sigma 160 BC–AD 700 two sigma
Wk-16313	Cookstown, Site 25	Oak (Quercus) and blackthorn (Prunus spinosa) charcoal from fill of inner ring-ditch from a complex of two concentric ring-ditches	2148 ± 47	360–100 BC one sigma 360–50 BC two sigma
Wk-16314	Cookstown, Site 25	Blackthorn (Prunus spinosa) charcoal from fill of inner ring-ditch from a complex of two concentric ring-ditches	2192 ± 40	360–190 BC one sigma 390–160 BC two sigma
Wk-16316	Rath, Site 27	Ash (Fraxinus) vessel from large waterlogged pit	2203 ± 36	360–200 BC one sigma 380–180 BC two sigma
Wk-16317	Rath, Site 27	Oak (Quercus) charcoal from ring-ditch containing faience beads	2353 ± 41	510–380 BC one sigma 740–360 BC two sigma
Wk-16320	Rath, Site 27	Alder (Alnus) charcoal from large waterlogged pit	2190 ± 35	360–190 BC one sigma 380–160 BC two sigma
Wk-16824	Rath, Site 27	Ash (Fraxinus) vessel from large waterlogged pit	2217 ± 36	370–200 BC one sigma 390–190 BC two sigma

LOCAL HISTORY

Through the Eyes of Archaeologists — The Ratoath Pot

RATOATH HERITAGE GROUP

MAKING DISCOVERIES which could be considered significant in the world of archaeology is the dream of many in Ireland. In Meath we are surrounded by fascinating archaeological sites linking us to past peoples and their lives. In recent times many sites have yielded up their treasures as building developments began. The early detection of archaeological sites and their investigation allows monitoring to be carried out prior to construction following strict regulations. It has become evident over the last few years that in some cases the land may have been ploughed but that below the plough level laid untouched settlement features and artifacts for centuries which would not be obvious on the surface. Much has yet to be discovered and much to be documented.

While researching this theme for the book we delved into the ancient past associated with Lagore but also discovered that in the *Journal of the Royal Society of Antiquities of Ireland*, Volume 104, 1974, John Waddell, draws attention to a reference he came across when "*collecting material for a study of Bronze Age cist graves*" which for him must have been very exciting at the time. The reference he discovered revealed the story of an item referred to as the "Ratoath Pot", "*a curious double sepulchral vessel without an internal communication from a stone cist from Ratoath, Co. Meath*". Details of the cist or its actual location were not stated and the pottery vessel was described but not illustrated.

Waddell's attention was drawn by Elizabeth Pirie, Keeper of Archaeology, Leeds City Museum, to a *Report of the Council of the Leeds Philosophical and Literary Society*, 1866-7, p.10 which stated that "Mr. J. Glennon, of Dublin, presented "a double Mortuary Urn, found at Ratoath (sic 1864), Co. Meath, while cutting a drain". No information was given with regard to the exact location of this drain. Collections belonging to the Leeds Philosophical and Literary Society were transferred at some point in time to the Leeds City Museum, but when the building was bombed in 1941 the Ratoath pottery vessel was destroyed. That might have ended the trail but Waddell continued with his search and discovered that someone else had made drawings of the said pot or vessel.

His curiosity aroused, Waddell met with Lily Frances Chitty, renowned Shropshire Archaeologist and Antiquary (1893-1979) who produced a drawing of the Ratoath pot which

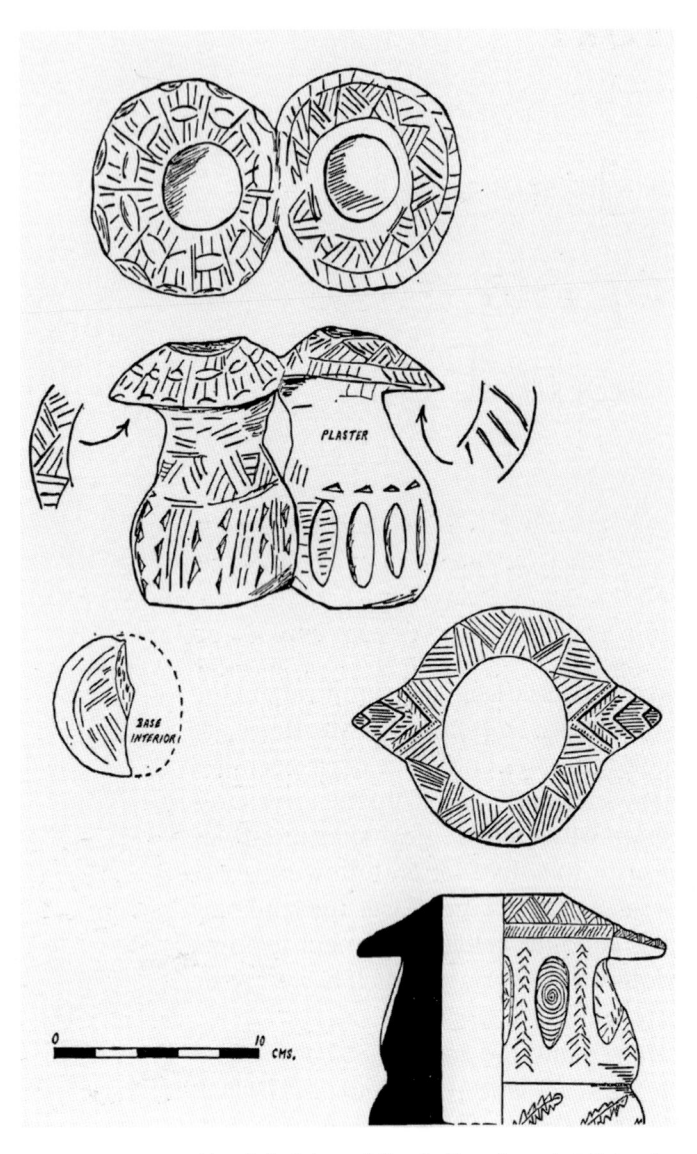

Hand sketches of the Pottery found at Ratoath in 1864. Miss Lily Chitty of Leeds Museum made sketches of the pottery in 1936.

she had sketched on a visit to the museum in 1936, showing a "*double-vessel consisting of two pots joined at rim and body*". It shared a similarity with the Yorkshire Vases from Aqualate Hall, Staffordshire which Lily Frances Chitty had previously written about in Antiquaries Journal Volume 9 (1929). Twin and triplet vessels are known across Europe including Ireland. We are informed that the two parts of the Ratoath Pot "*are of similar form, each consisting of a squat narrow-mouthed cup about 12cm high and each having a projecting rim with a maximum overall diameter of about 10cm*". Waddell states that Miss Chitty "noted that it had been roughly reconstructed "*with linen and plaster; its ornament was partly obscured but had included incised lines and what Miss Chitty noted as rough triangles, excised not impressed, producing a "false-relief" effect; its surface colour was pinkish and grey.*" According to Waddell in 1936 the pot or vessel was identified by a label G7 and written on it was "Ratoath, Co. Meath"; a detached label aptly described it as a "*sepulchral vessel of peculiar form from a stone cist, Ratoath, Co. Meath*". Next his investigations brought him to The National Museum of Ireland where information relating to a similar pot which was sold by the same John Glennon to a T.M. Rayon (Antiquarian) records that it was "*found at Ratoath, Co. Meath in 1864 on removing a ditch...*" and so the mystery continues.

The Ratoath Heritage Group asks how significant these earlier discoveries are in light of the recent discoveries in the Ratoath area over the last six years. The finds at Harlockstown, Clover Hill and Raystown are some that come to mind. This group is excited by the possibilities that more undiscovered settlements and artifacts lie just below the surfaces of unploughed fields close to the expanding village of Ratoath.

The Archaeological Inventory of County Meath catalogues the cist and the vessel as follows:

Cist: 291, pp38
OS 44:4 (NPL) Not Marked. OD 200-300 O 62, 51
Cist: "Double Sepulchral Vessel" said to have been found in a cist.
(JRSAI 1974, 143-5). SMR 44:8

LOCAL HISTORY

Commemorative Monument in Steeplechase, Ratoath

BRÍD NI RINN, SCULPTOR

THE ARCHAEOLOGICAL SURVEY by ARCH-TECH, Archaeological Technology Ltd., of this western part of Ratoath for the proposed residential development by McGarrell Reilly Homes Ltd., discovered that it was a very important site. Evidence of human habitation was found dating from as far back as the Bronze Age. In an ancient enclosure the remains of 54 people were discovered and many more are presumed to lie buried there. Burials took place here up to about 800 AD; pagans being interred in a crouched position and Christians lying flat and facing east. It was decided to preserve this ancient burial ground under a low mound and include a memorial sculpture.

After the initial landscaping by Ronan Mac Diarmada, I was asked to design a recumbent memorial cross, as any upright cross would look too like a modern graveyard. Since it would be seen from all sides it had to be a Greek style cross and this blocky type of Greek cross is often seen in Early Christian sites - there is one in Nobber for instance. Irish granite, I thought, would be a suitable stone because of its light colour and arid durability. The cruciform bronze inlay is based on a design found on the cross-inscribed grave slabs of Clonmacnoise. There is a central roundel with semi-circles delineated at the extremities, outlining another cross within the cross of stone. The triskele central boss is a common motif in Celtic art both Christian and pre-Christian - here it might signify the Blessed Trinity. The portal stones at the eastern entrance, supplied by Walshe's Quarry in Co. Dublin and the bronze plaques, together with the other bronzes were cast in Bronze Art, Dublin. These two bronze plaques in Irish and English show two archaeological finds from the area - the penannular brooch and the copper alloy necklet.

Outline drawing of the specially commissioned Memorial Sculpture designed and erected by Sculptor, Brίd Ni Rinn

ACKNOWLEGEMENTS
Many people helped in this project. In addition to those already mentioned here, a special thanks to local historian Anthony Darby, Caoimhe Ni Shuilleabháin of The Irish Place-names Commission, my friends, sculptress Cliodna Cussen, architect and painter Ann O'Clery, and Pamela and Dalian de Brí, who helped with the Irish translation and also my family.

LOCAL HISTORY

Crickeens Ancient Burial Ground

RATOATH HERITAGE GROUP

THE SPECIALLY CRAFTED Commemorative Monument, installed on the ancient burial grounds at The Crickeens, Ratoath and surrounded by the Steeplechase residential development, is enclosed by a low dry stone wall and cobbled area where it glistens as the sunshine reflects against the granite and the bronze. Approaching it on foot from the Dunshaughlin side, walking towards the east, one enters the enclosure through two tall granite portal stones featuring bronze plaques, one in English and the other in Irish, which commemorate those Christian and pre-Christian people who were interred there. The monument is a wonderful gift to the people of Ratoath which enriches our heritage, past, present and future.

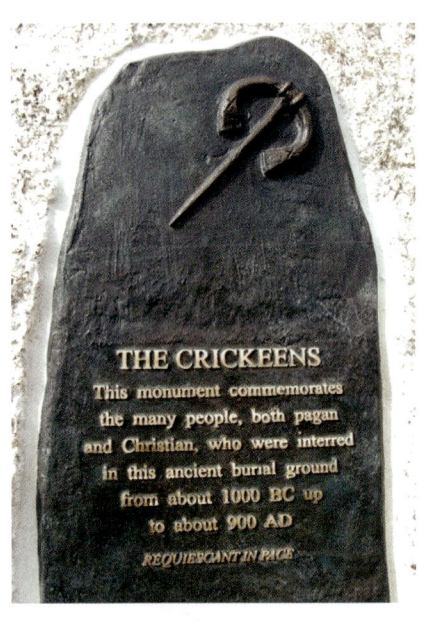

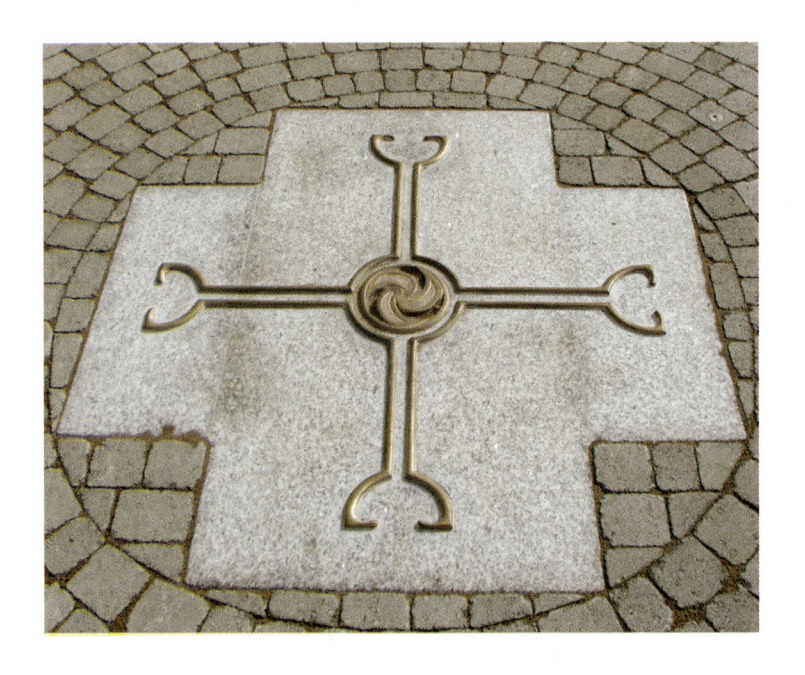

LOCAL HISTORY

Famine, Craftsmen and Mills

CHRIS WARD

The Famine in Ratoath

DURING THE FAMINE the Government sent out questionnaires to the police in order to get detailed information about the crops. The replies are in the National Archives. One set of forms asked the acreage of potatoes planted in 1846 as compared with 1845. In each area fewer potatoes were planted and, although still a considerable acreage was planted as people hoped that it would not get the blight the second year, the reports state that turnips were planted and some oats were sown at Crickenstown, Cookstown, Kilbrew and Ratoath. Below are the questions and answers given by the Police Inspector in the Dunshaughlin District on 25th August 1846. (RLFC 5.22.4. National Archives)

Question 1. Has extent of Potato planted this year equaled that of ordinary years?
Answer   *It has not, nor within a third of (that) planted usually*

Question 2. Has crop been affected by blight and in what proportion?
Answer   *It has entirely, at least to all visible appearances.*

Question 3. Has the early or late crop been chiefly injured and to what extent in each of those crops?
Answer   *The late crop particularly and entirely since it had not attained maturity when the blight affected it and rendered it regrettably unavailable for any purpose.*

Question 4. Has the crop or any portion of it as yet become available for food?
Answer   *The former, that is, the small portion is supplying the farmer at present with a very different food and the rapid decomposition of even this part of the crop is suggesting to him, the obvious propriety of hurrying the portion that is marketable and for sale, which accounts for the low prices in some localities.*
            It has, the early crop is unavailable to the extent and in the manner that I have remarked in my reply to query

Medieval Craftsmen in Ratoath

In the *Dublin Guild Roll 1190-1265* by Connolly & Martin, (Dublin Corporation 1992), we find the following names, these men would mainly have been Normans. Spelling had not become standardised until about the 18th century nor were people bothered about uniformity as it was not seen as important, below are eight different ways to spell Rathoath in the space of seventy-five years.

Henricus Le Mercer de Ratothe
Rogerus de Ratothe
Ricardus Albus de Ratohe
Richman de Ratophethe
Rogerus Norrensis de Rathouethe
Reginaldus de Ratothethe
Nicholas Chepman de Rathoueth
Simon de Rathoueth
Bruning Tannator de Rathoueth
Laurencius Tailliator de Rathouth
Willelmus Palmerus de Rathoueth
Robertus Blundus de Rathouthe

Ricardus filius Reginaldi Palmeri de Rathouth
Willelmus filius Jordani de Rathouth
Johannes le Juvene de Rathoueth
Robertus Hutchet de Rathouethe
Ricardus Palmerus de Rathowethe
Albanus Cyrothecarius de Rathouth
Robertus filius Walteri Palmeri de Rathothe
Willelmus le Neuman de Ratothe
Johannes Tinctor de Rathoueth
Nicolaus de Rathoueth

Mills

The book *Millers and Mills of Ireland about 1850* edited by Hogg was published in Dublin in 2000. He writes that 'the Dublin Slane road traverses Miltown bridge a mile short of Ashbourne and here just to the West the district is known as Miltown, Asbourne (in the town land of Killegland close by had Miltown House but no signs of Milling was found in the immediate local or in the records."

In *Griffiths Valuation 1854*, James Reidy is listed as having 'house, offices, corn-mill and garden' in Rathoath.[1]

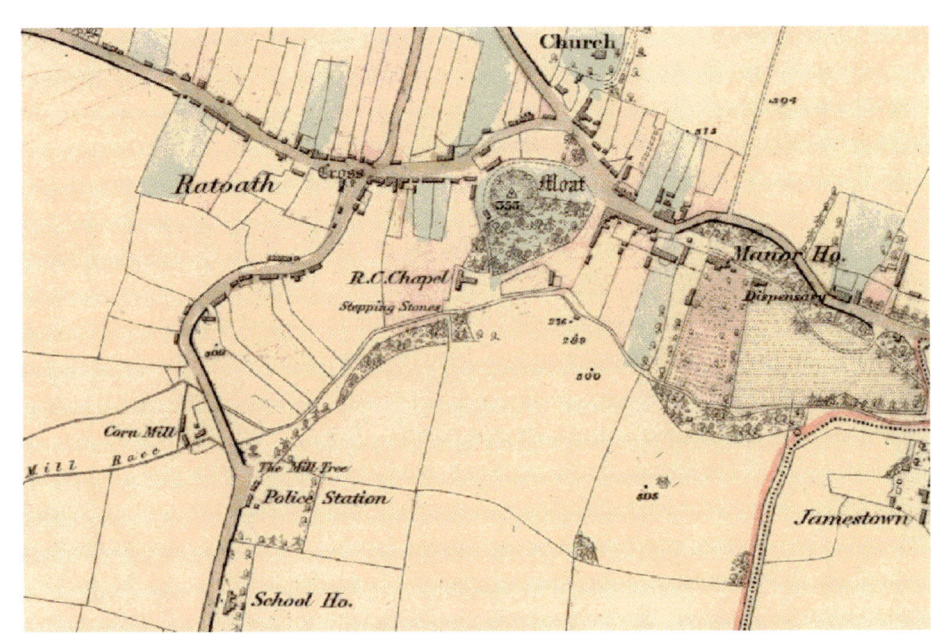

Map of Ratoath village circa 1840 showing the Mill Race, Corn Mill and The Mill Tree
[Courtesy Irish Townland Maps][2]

---

1 On an 1834 map of Ratoath the location of a Mill was identified as being located near the bridge of the Broadmeadow River on the Fairyhouse Road on the opposite side of the road near the entrance to Meadowbank Hill.
2 Map purchased from Irish Townland Maps https://secure.pasthomes.com/mydownloads.php

LOCAL HISTORY

The Cattle Industry in Ratoath

CIARAN BUCKLEY

Introduction

"It was always said that a thousand cattle came into the parish of Ratoath each year after the March fair in Ennistymon." – JOE WARD, *farmer*.[1]

THE CATTLE EXPORT BUSINESS was Ireland's biggest industry between the 1840s and the 1960s. Cattle that had been bred in the west of Ireland were sold east as the year progressed, ending up on the rich grasslands in Meath and Kildare. Ratoath was one of the final stops before the cattle were sold in the Dublin cattle markets and then loaded onto the boats for the English market.

Many of the farmers around Ratoath travelled to the cattle fairs around Ireland buying cattle, which were fed on their farms before being sold to exporters. This article looks at the development of the cattle industry between 1800 and 1960 and examines the way in which it affected one particular farming family, the Duffy's, who lived in Ballybin.

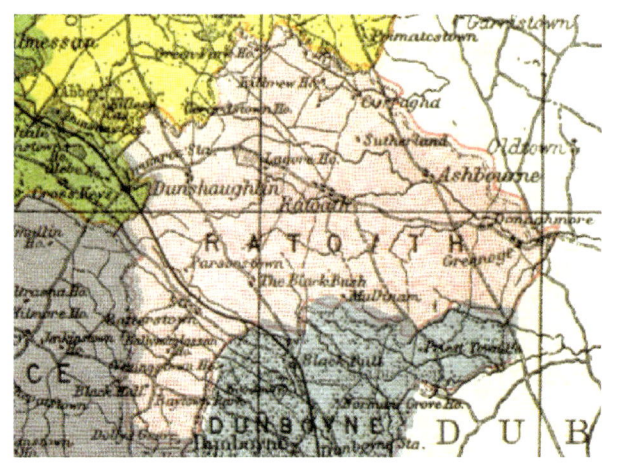

Ballybin

Ballybin is a townland of around 500 acres that lies between Ratoath and Ashbourne, on both sides of the Ballybin road. It belonged to the Marquis of Lansdowne, a direct descendant of Sir William Petty, who came to Ireland as Cromwell's Surgeon General in the 1640s. After Cromwell conquered Ireland, Petty was given the task of surveying Ireland, which was published as the Down Survey in 1652.

Petty also wrote a book called the *Treatise of Ireland* in which he suggested that most of the population of Ireland should be moved to England and that the country should be con-

---

[1] *Strong Farmer – The memoirs of Joe Ward*. Ciaran Buckley and Chris Ward. Published by Liberties Press. 2007 ISBN: 978-1-905484-24-2

verted into a giant cattle farm. The residual population of 200,000 people would look after six million cattle, which would be exported to England.

Although this did not happen at the time, Petty's ideas had a prophetic ring. When the cattle export industry began to develop rapidly in the 19th Century, the population of Ireland began a steep decline, which was only reversed in the 1960s.

The Lansdowne's were one of the most powerful families in the British aristocracy and spent little or no time in Ratoath. They had agents in Ireland who collected the rent from tenant farmers and forwarded it to their main estate in Bowood, which is near Heathrow Airport in England.

Many landlords around Ireland rented tiny farms to subsistence farmers, but Ballybin was leased to commercial farmers who had large landholdings. In 1751 it was leased to a John Grierson and in 1764 it was leased to a man called Matthew Corbally.

In 1780 Ballybin was rented to Thomas Duffy from Carrickmacross in County Monaghan. Three of his sons – George, Peter, and Patrick - divided Ballybin between them. The other brothers also rented farms, including one in Violet Hill, Glasnevin and Rivermount, Finglas. The best known of Thomas's sons was George Duffy, who took part in the 1798 rebellion. He was a fugitive for many years, but managed to avoid capture and hold onto his farm. He was eventually pardoned and lived until 1857. The foundations of his house are still visible at the top of the lane that separates the farm of Patrick Kelly from the Ballybin Duffy's.

Ballybin Duffy's
There are a number of reasons why Thomas Duffy may have moved from Monaghan to Meath. He may have been a regular visitor to the cattle fair in Ratoath and wanted to rent land closer to Dublin, his final market. It is also possible that there was more land available

Duffy's Ballybin (2006)

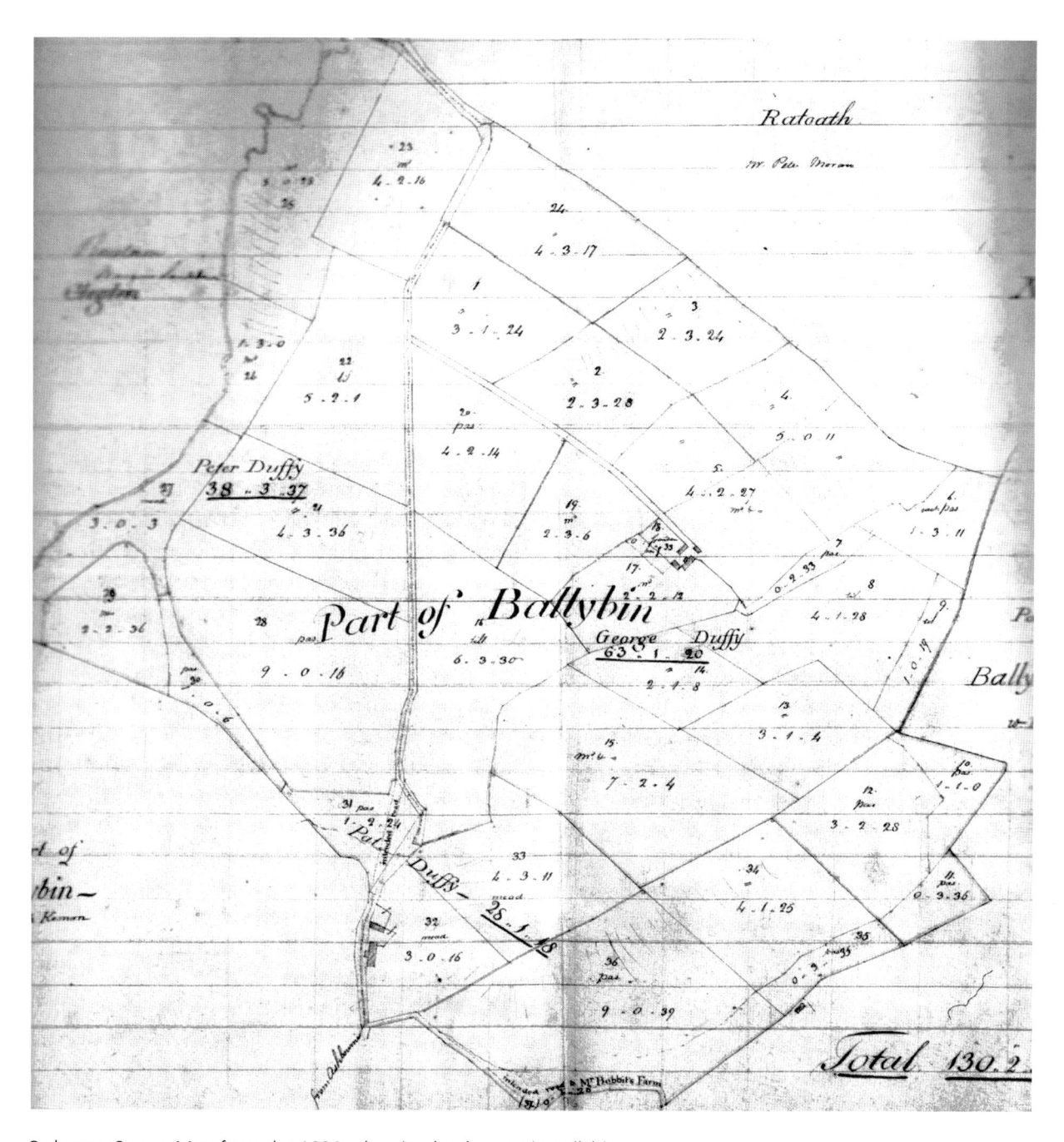

Ordnance Survey Map from the 1820s showing land usage in Ballybin

in Meath than in Monaghan, where farmers had to compete with the flax-growers who were supplying the Ulster linen industry.

In the early years of the 19th Century the Duffy's were involved in mixed farming and a map from the 1820s shows that they had as much land under tillage as they had pasture. Wheat prices were very high in the early 19th Century, because Britain was dependent on Irish wheat imports during the Napoleonic Wars.

The wages paid for harvesting cereal crops were an important source of income for local cottiers, as well as for subsistence farmers from Cavan and Leitrim, who worked as migratory harvest workers in Meath.

Wheat prices began to decline in the 1820s and by the 1840s it was more economic to export cattle than it was to export wheat.

In the 1820s, only 47,000 cattle were exported to England every year. By the end of the Great Famine, more than 200,000 were being exported every year. By 1914, there were more than 835,000 cattle exported in the hold of the boats every year.

Although cattle had begun to displace people before the famine, the failure of the potato crop between 1845 and 1848 accelerated the process. The population of south Meath was stable during the famine, because the population was less dependent upon potatoes than people were in other parts of the country. But the population of Meath went into steady decline after the famine, because cattle grazing was less labour-intensive than tillage and there was less work for labourers.

The unemployed had no choice but to emigrate to England, Canada, Australia and the USA. The growth of the cattle industry hurt the younger sons and daughters of farmers, as well as the children of labourers. It is said that many of George Duffy's children died of disease on emigrant ships on the way to America in the years after the famine.

The shift to cattle also meant that farms became bigger. When George Duffy died without an heir, Lord Lansdowne's agent decided to give it to one of the neighbouring farmers, to increase the size of their holdings. He visited Mat Duffy - George's nephew - on Easter Monday, the day of the Fairyhouse Races. He told him that he was surprised to see him ploughing his fields while there was a race meeting going on, because his neighbours and first cousins had told the agent that he was given to gambling and drink. The agent subsequently divided George's farm between Mat Duffy and his cousins.

Mat Duffy's son Patrick travelled all over Ireland to cattle fairs in Ballinasloe, Athenry, Balla, Ennis and Moate, buying cattle that could be fattened in Meath and then sold in the Cabra cattle markets for export to Liverpool or London. There was huge demand for beef in England, where the population was growing rapidly in the industrial cities. Initially the cattle had to be driven on foot from the fairs to Meath, but once the railways had been built in the final decades of the 19th century, cattle could be loaded onto a train in Balla and unloaded in Clonsilla or Hazelhatch.

Land Reformation Era

This was the golden age of the cattle farmer. In the 1880s the Duffy's built a limestone farmyard, which shows that they were confident that they would never lose their tenancy in Ballybin. In the 1890s they took advantage of a series of government schemes, which allowed them to buy their land from Lord Lansdowne.

Between 1870 and 1909 over 13 million acres of land were purchased from the landlords by 390,000 Irish farmers. The British government financed the transactions, lending money over a 68 year period at an interest rate of 3.25 percent.

Patrick Duffy bought his farm in Ballybin, as well as a number of out-farms in Loughlinstown, Newtown and Legagunnia. Patrick's brother Johnny also bought a farm on the border between Ballybin and Cookstown. This farm still belongs to Johnny Duffy's daughter Statia Duffy, but has been bisected in 2005 by the new N2 motorway.

The redistribution of land was hailed as a great reform, which returned the ownership of Irish land to the people of Ireland. But the unevenness of the distribution created resentment among the majority of the population, who had little economic security and no prospects outside of emigration.

Patrick Duffy had six children, who came of age in the early 1920s, when the Irish state was established. Four of them were able to stay in Ireland, either by inheriting farms or by marrying people involved in the cattle trade. His other two sons – Tim and Patrick - were involved in the Battle of Ashbourne in 1916, the War of Independence and the Civil War. But after the cessation of hostilities they were unable to find work and emigrated to England and Australia.

Early Irish Governments

Although the first Irish governments in the 1920s managed to balance the budget and to encourage a degree of industrial development, the continued reliance on the live cattle export trade meant that unemployment and emigration were still a huge political issue.

It was commonly perceived that the cattle farmers were the cause of these problems, because they had too much land, too much money and too much political power. In addition to being a farmer and a cattle buyer, Patrick Duffy was also a county councillor, which was not unusual. In 1925, farmers had 21 of the 34 seats in the Meath County Council. The county councils were responsible for health, roads and social welfare in the 1920s, which gave them a great deal of influence in terms of jobs and public contracts.

In the early 1930s Fianna Fail won its first election with the slogan "**The bullock for the road, the land for the people.**" The new government refused to hand the land annuities over to the British government and instead used the money to provide the first dole payments in Ireland. In retaliation, the British put a £6 tariff on every bovine animal exported to England. This meant that cattle that were worth £13 were now worth only £7 and cattle that were worth £6 were now worth nothing.

Economic War

The government hoped that the Economic War would bring the cattle export industry to an end and that the big farms could then be carved up among small farmers and cottiers, who would be able to enjoy a life of "frugal comfort." A few big farms near Ratoath were compulsorily purchased by the Land Commission and divided among farming families from Galway and Mayo.

The Economic War was a disaster for all farmers, big and small. Exports fell, unemployment rose and in the late 1930s the Irish government made a settlement with the British which restored normal trading relationships. The Economic War did nothing to break the economic dependency on England and by the early 1960s cattle exports still accounted for 70 percent of Ireland's export trade.

It also did very little to reduce the political influence of farmers. In 1934, 25 of the 35 Meath county councillors were farmers – 12 Fianna Fail councillors and 13 Fine Gael councillors.

Patrick Duffy was quite elderly when the Economic War began and didn't adjust his business and lifestyle to the changed political circumstances. When he died in 1938 he owed money to the banks, who sold Ballybin for a very low price. His youngest son and heir George found himself without a farm and spent the rest of his life in Australia. Patrick's eldest son, Matthew, bought Ballybin back in 1945 and lived there until he died in 1984.

Decline of Cattle Industry in Ratoath

By the late 1960s the cattle fairs were dying out and were replaced by cattle marts, where cattle were sold in an open auction. Farmers considered this a big improvement on the strokes, schemes and haggling that took place at cattle markets. The live cattle export business also went into decline and farmers started selling their cattle to meat factories, where the meat was processed before it was exported. The meat factories were one of the new sources of employment during the 1960s, when the economy grew rapidly during the Seán Lemass era of industrialisation. In the early 1970s the population of Ashbourne began to grow rapidly as people found jobs in Dublin Airport or in the industrial estate in Cookstown, at the end of the Ballybin road.

Most of the adult population who live in Ratoath today (2006) commute to jobs in the computer industry, construction, pharmaceuticals and financial services and very few have any involvement in farming. Some of the large farms in the Ratoath area have been sold during the past 10 years for new housing developments and the remaining farmers have to compete with food that has been imported from countries like Brazil and are dependent upon off-farm jobs and direct payments for their survival. Although the farmers still have significant political influence in national politics, the era of the "strong farmer from County Meath," has passed.

APPRECIATION OF HERITAGE

Ratoath Heritage Group

RATOATH has a rich and varied historical, cultural, sociological and political background. The preservation and promotion of the local heritage is paramount to the work of the Ratoath Heritage Group. Today Ratoath is a thriving and vibrant place taking on a colourful and exciting life. While the streets and surrounding landscapes are shaped to cater for the needs of the community, the Ratoath Heritage Group are conscious of the need to record and in some cases protect the local heritage. Placing a value on heritage in a local community creates a sense of belonging, a sense of responsibility and promotes a quality of living but it does require people to become involved.

The Ratoath Heritage Group is a voluntary organisation. Membership is free and all work is done on a voluntary basis. The Group aims to encourage an interest in and promote a sense of responsibility for our heritage and environment. Our running costs are kept to a minimum and we rely on the generosity of local sponsors, occasional grants from the local authorities and state sponsored organisations to raise the necessary funds to complete projects that we cannot do on a voluntary basis for free.

Projects over the last ten years include:
Conservation of Trees
Graveyard Project
Flood Lighting of Church Tower in Graveyard
Cleaning of the Marian Shrine (The Grotto)
Bi-centennial Memorial 1798
Relocation of the Congressional Cross (twice)
The Lough Lane Project
Participation in Pride of Place Competition
Organisation of local walks during Heritage Week
Heritage Book "**Ratoath Past and Present**"
Development of a Web site (www.ratoathheritage.ie)

New members are welcome as are new ideas for future projects.

Chairperson: Joe Mannering
Secretary: Beryl Donnelly
Assistant Secretary: Frances Maher
Treasurer: Paul Halton

Committee Members: Ann Gaughan, Tony Darby, Maria Dalton, Paddy Dalton, Peter Malone, Vera Malone, Bernie Dolan, Michael Dolan, Daragh O'Neill, Noel Martin, Paul Conroy

APPRECIATION OF HERITAGE

Ratoath Heritage Activities

RATOATH HERITAGE GROUP

The Eucharistic Congress in Ireland in 1932

THE 31ST INTERNATIONAL EUCHARISTIC CONGRESS was held in Dublin, 21-26 June, 1932. This was a major event for Ireland and was hugely significant in terms of asserting the identity of the Republic of Ireland as a leading Catholic nation. The 31st Congress in Dublin commemorated the death of St. Patrick [432 A.D.], the patron saint of Ireland. Thousands of churchmen and visitors came to Dublin from every corner of the world.

As Taoiseach and Minister for Foreign Affairs at that time, Eamon de Valera took a high profile role in the main events of the Eucharistic Congress. He greeted the Pope's special representative, Cardinal Lorenzo Lauri, at Dún Laoghaire Harbour on Monday, 20 June 1932, in person, and he spoke at length on behalf of the Irish Government and State at various formal religious functions and he attended all of the major Masses held during that significant week in Ireland.

Towns and cities around Ireland subsequently erected various monuments to commemorate the success of the 1932 Eucharistic Congress and so Ratoath opted to erect a Congressional Cross at the centre of the village.

Ratoath Congressional Cross

During the period 1992 to 1996, the Ratoath Heritage Group organised the restoration and replacement of a replica of the Congressional Cross on a new site at the R125 Fairyhouse Road junction opposite Ratoath Inn. The people of Ratoath generously contributed to the fund raising efforts. The official blessing of the replica of the 1932 Congressional Cross, was carried out by Fr. Frank McNamara on Sunday 18 June 1996, after 11am Mass.

The cross was originally erected at the same junction in 1932 by Mary Kilmurray and was donated to Ratoath by Fr. Joe Clarke and his sister Annie Gogan to commemorate the Eucharistic Congress of June 1932. After it was accidentally damaged it was removed around 1984.

In 1992, when local people began looking for the original cross, which had been removed over eight years previously from its original spot in the middle of the road at the junction to Fairyhouse, opposite Ryan's shop, they could only get parts of it. The Heritage Group then had a replica of the cross constructed by stone mason Paddy Moss.

A scroll of honour, containing the names of all the local people who contributed to the restoration of the cross, was buried beneath it during the ceremony in June 1996. Even at that time in 1996, it was confidently expected that the site was well chosen and that the

APPRECIATION OF HERITAGE
Ratoath Heritage Activities

Ratoath Congressional Cross pictured in 1935 at its original location at the village centre.
This picture shows Barney Browne in the middle of the road. Gerry White and Liam, Paddy and Con Lynch are pictured to the right of the picture. The Bell tower of the Holy Trinity Church is visible in the background.

Back Wall Plaque on LHS read:
**SECTION OF ORIGINAL CROSS
INSERTED IN WALL
SITE DONATED BY
Fr. J. CLARKE and
ANNIE GOGAN (nee CLARKE)**

Back Wall Plaque on RHS read:
**ERECTED BY
MARY KILMURRAY (nee TOOLE)
IN MEMORY OF
THE EUCHARISTIC CONGRESS,
JUNE 1932.**

**REPLICA OF
CONGRESSIONAL CROSS
ERECTED BY THE PEOPLE OF RATOATH 1993**

cross would not be affected by any developments in the foreseeable future!

However, very soon afterwards a developer obtained planning permission to build a supermarket on the adjoining site. So, scarcely five years after re-erecting the cross, the Heritage Group was approached to remove it to a safe place while construction work took place. The developer generously gave an undertaking, that after the construction work was completed, the replica cross would be returned to a location near the approved site chosen in the early 1990's.

The picture on right shows the replica of the Congressional Cross where it stood from 1992 to 2002 at the centre of the village at the Fairyhouse Road junction until it was removed while the SuperValu Supermarket was being built

Picture below was taken after the Congressional Cross was blessed by Fr. Frank McNamara, PP, in June 1996, and includes L-R: Nick Connor, Noel Eiffe, Pat Donnelly, Molly Talty, May Hessman, Mrs. Nolan, Joe Mannering (back to camera), Betty Colfer, Philomena Eiffe, Molly Maher (with wheelchair), Benny Browne, Mellor Flood, Sonny Martin, A. Another, Jimmy Ralph and Martin Lynch

(*Below left*): Joe Mannering and Paul Halton preparing to move the Congressional Cross to temporary storage while the supermarket site was being developed

(*Below right*): Joe Mannering removing the plaque with the inscription "Erected by Mary Kilmurray (nee Toole) in memory of the Eucharistic Congress June 1932"

Picture above shows stone mason, the late Paddy Moss, supervising the safe removal of the cross in June 2002. Also in the picture are Joe Mannering and Paddy Moss's neighbour who helped to guide the cross and base onto a forklift generously provided by Donnelly Providers. The cross was stored safely at the Parochial House for two years until the erection of the new SuperValu supermarket was completed in 2004.

The Cross is safely secured on a forklift during its removal to a safe storage place at the Parochial House in June 2002.

HISTORY IN THE MAKING – Treasures for the Future

The Buried Scrolls

On Sunday 18th June 1993, at the junction of the Fairyhouse-Dunshaughlin Road at the centre of the then quaint rural village, a sealed canister containing scrolls was buried at the front of the replica of the Congressional Cross where it was attractively and safety situated in an enclosure with a stone-faced wall and wrought iron railings along the bounds of Fr. Clarke's land. Owing to the very rapid pace of development of multiple housing estates around Ratoath, the one-acre garden and Fr. Clarke's old house at the centre of the village were sold for a sum "in excess of one million Irish pounds (punts)" in order to provide shopping and office facilities for the expanding commercial and residential community. As a result of this expansion the Congressional Cross and its hidden treasures, the canister with the scrolls, were removed for safe keeping to the Parish House while construction work was in progress. When the SuperValu complex was completed in 2004 the cross and the scrolls in the sealed canister were repositioned on the pavement outside its front entrance, surrounded by protective bollards facing the busy road junction.

The reinstated replica of the Congressional Cross at its prominent and secure site outside the front entrance to the SuperValu supermarket, since 2004

Blessing and Unveiling of the Ratoath Monument to commemorate the 1798 Rising

Fr. Gerry Stuart and Joe Mannering at the official unveiling of the 1798 Commemorative Monument on 6 December 1998

During 1998, the Ratoath Heritage Group commissioned and erected a monument to commemorate the 1798 Rising. The monument was erected on a raised bed with a natural stone surround, constructed by committee members near the Church gates at the centre of the village. The stone was specially cut and engraved by Paddy Moss and John Lord from The Cottage Garden Centre generously provided and planted the shrubs around the monument. On Sunday, 6 December 1998, Fr. Gerry Stuart blessed the monument and Fr. Joe Deegan and Joe Mannering assisted. The inscription reads as follows:

> ERECTED TO COMMORATE
> THOSE OF ALL FAITHS
> WHO LOST THEIR LIVES
> IN THE 1798 REBELLION
>
> GUID AR SON NA MAIRB UILG
>
> 1798 – 1998
>
> RATOATH

APPRECIATION OF HERITAGE

Ratoath Heritage Activities

Heritage Day Walk

In September 2004 during Heritage Week the Ratoath Heritage Group organised a walk to introduce people to areas of historical interest. This was the first time that such a walk had been organised. Members of the Heritage Group explained the historical background.

Everyone enjoyed the day out in Ratoath and learned much about local history and events.

Meeting in the Community Hall for a post-walk talk by Angela Wallace, Archaeologist and tea for all afterwards.

Visiting the Church and the old graveyard: toddlers, children, teenagers and adults attended.

(*Above left*): Tony Darby explaining the details to an enthusiastic and interested group.

(*Above right*): Outside the Church of the Holy Trinity during the Walk

(*Left*): In the centre of the village, outside McCabe's house the story continues.

95

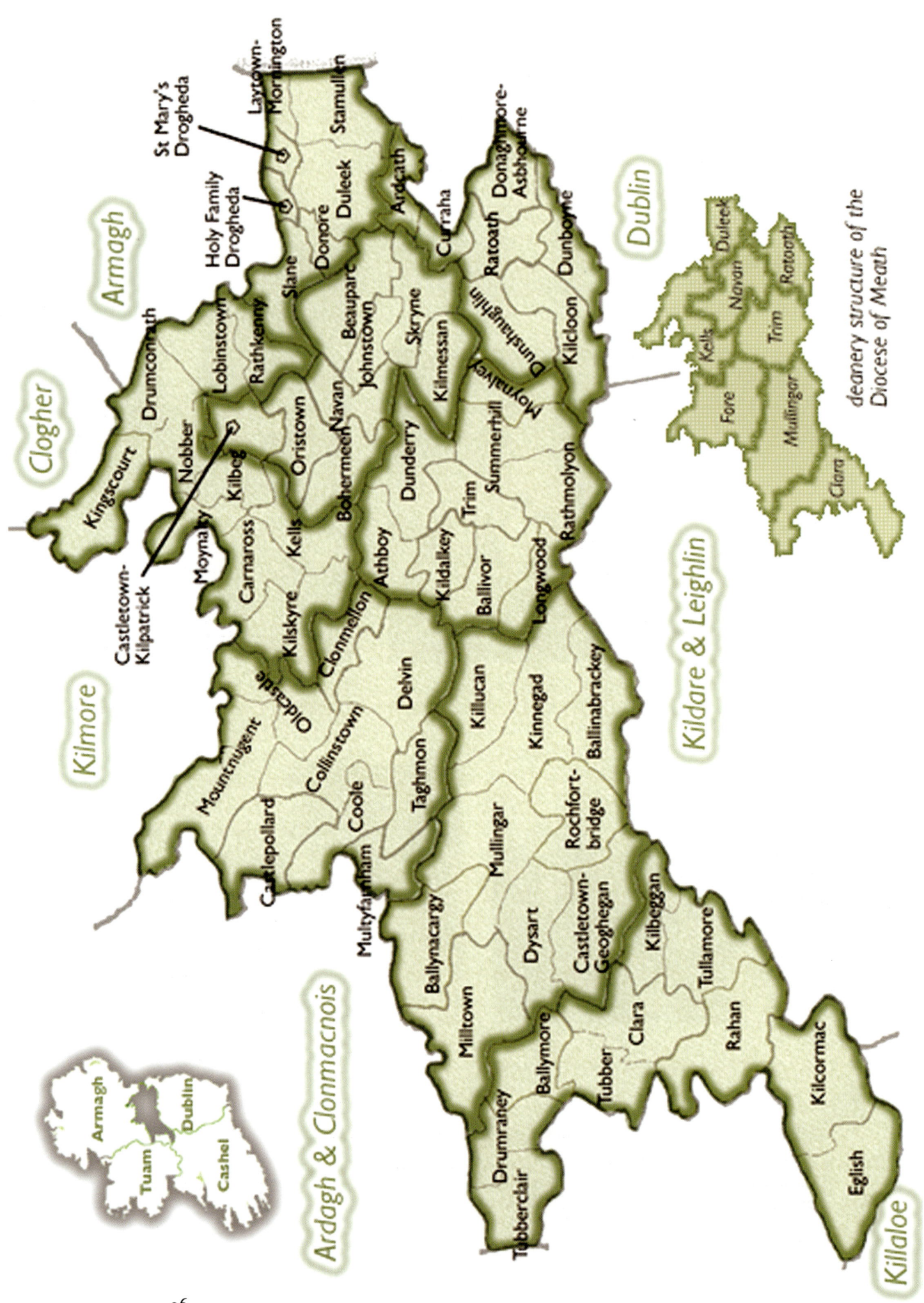

deanery structure of the Diocese of Meath

CHURCH MATTERS

Priests who have served in Ratoath Parish (c. 1405 to 2008)

FRANCES MAHER

RATOATH VILLAGE was the head of the local Deanery of Ratoath. In 1405 Rev. John Mordoun was Vicar in Ratoath, appointed by Henry IV. In 1422, the Rev. William Taillour, Rector of Kilbrew was elected by the priests of the Deanery of Ratoath to collect the Deanery's portion of one hundred and twenty marks, which the clergy of the diocese of Meath had granted as a subsidy to the King who at time was Henry IV.

In 1559 Rev. Patrick Fyne Vicar in Ratoath died. It is noted that he was probably the last Priest prior to the Reformation.[1]

With the Reformation of Henry VIII and with his decree of 1535, churches and monasteries were plundered, shrines were defiled, sacred records were burned or scattered, statues and sacred relics were destroyed. Orders of religious were expelled from hundreds of their houses; churches were taken from the people. Abbots and priests were replaced with ministers of the new religion. "*Even the possession of a manuscript on any subject whatever incurred the penalty of death*".[2]

Henry VIII issued rules that were against religion, Irish Civilisation, Commerce, language, literature and every aspect of Irish life. *Poets and historians were put to death and their books and genealogies burned. Anyone sheltering a priest was to be hanged and his lands confiscated.*[3]

In 1536 a specially assembled parliament in England acknowledged Henry VIII's Supremacy by declaring him "Head of Church and State" under which First Fruits were to be paid to the Established Church instead of to Rome. One twentieth of the Annual Profits of the Church would be due to the Crown of England. Each Diocese had to send a representative to Parliament in Dublin to vote. With the reign of Henry VIII, Bishops in England were chosen in England and not in Rome. Henry VIII also had the right to control the ecclesiastical preferment in Ireland.

---

1 *Diocese of Meath Ancient and Modern*, Volume I, pg. 259-260, Dean Cogan
2 Seumas McManus "The Story of the Irish Race", pg. 265. Revised edition, 1966, The Devin-Adair Company, Old Greenwich, Connecticut. ISBN: 0-517-06408-1
3 Ibid. pg 365-366.

Edward VI and his court advisors intensified the atrocities of Henry VIII from 1547 to 1553. For the next three hundred years, it is not surprising that any church or parish records which happened to be recorded would be kept in secret places and their hiding places revealed to only the most trustworthy because if they got into the wrong hands, the knowledge of their whereabouts would put the person or persons concerned into a dangerous situation.

When Edward VI's sister, Mary I, succeeded him (1553-1558) she devoted herself to the restoration of the Catholic religion, but in the process she had over 300 Protestants put to death. McManus has stated that *"It must be noted that during this time, that of all the people who had reformed to the Protestant religion in Ireland, there is no record of them being persecuted, when the long suffering Irish church was restored"*.[4]

Under Elizabeth's reign it was decreed that all papist Bishops, Archbishops, Deans, Monks, Friars were to leave her Kingdom. It was also stated that *every priest discovered after this date was to be hanged till dead, his head taken off and displayed on a pole in some public place"*[5]. Young men who had vocations had to be shipped off to the continent, where, when they were educated and ordained, they then returned home under threat of death to minister to the faithful.

Historians have noted that *"A report drawn up by Pope Clement IX about Dr. William Plunkett who was Bishop of Meath in 1669 claims that Dr. Plunkett (son of the 9th Baron of Killeen) lay concealed in the woods, on the mountains, and in the cabins of the poor".*

1640: Cromwell arrived in Ireland with an army of c.17,000 Puritans. He carried out a campaign of slaughter throughout the country. During this time thousands of Irish men and women were shipped off to the American colonies and to the West Indies into slavery. These numbers are *estimated* at between thirty and eighty thousand. Most of the inhabitants left in the country were ordered to the west of Ireland as under penalty of death no Irish man, woman or child was to be found east of the river Shannon after 1st May 1654. (A law was issued by parliament)

1685:	James II suspended the Penal Laws in 1685.
1689 – 1702:	William and Mary on the Throne of England, the persecution and plundering of Papists continued.
1704:	Registration of every Priest and in 1710 every registered priest had to present himself at quarterly sessions and take an oath of abjuration under penalty of transportation for life or of being hanged, drawn and quartered if they remained in the country.
C. 1600 – 1727:	Two priests are known to have served in Ratoath Parish. Rev. Richard Nugent who in 1650 was taken by the Cromwellians to Drogheda and hanged outside St. Mary's Gate; and Dr. Michael Plunkett, Vicar General of Meath and P.P. Ratoath for twenty three years. Dr. Michael Plunkett died in 1727 aged 75 years.[6] (See "Ratoath – A Historical Perspective" for more details on his life).
1727 – 1740:	Fr. Patrick Allen, Native of Ratoath, died C. 1740.

---

4 Ibid. pg 366.
5 *Diocese of Meath Ancient and Modern*, Volume II, Dean Cogan
6 *Diocese of Meath Ancient and Modern*, Volume I, Dean Cogan, pg 266-267.

c. 1740:	Fr. Clinch and Fr. Stewart, both of whom are interred in Fr. Allen's grave in Ratoath Churchyard.
1740 – 1789:	Nicholas White, native of Ratoath, died on St. Patrick's Day 1789.
1789 – 1818:	Patrick Langan native of Ardcath, died July 1818.
1818 – 1838:	Richard Carolan, native of Drogheda, died 28th July 1838.
1838 – 1867:	Patrick Sheridan, native of Kilbride, Co. Cavan.

For many years, Fr. Sheridan paid for the education of students for the foreign missions in All Hallows College, an institution in which he was keenly interested and to which he willed the greater part of his property. Fr. Sheridan is buried in Ratoath church. His grave near the pulpit is unmarked (on the west side of the church).

Fr. John Fulham, who succeeded Fr. Sheridan, was already in residence in Ratoath, having been appointed administrator on 12th October 1861. Fr. Fulham, a native of Kildalkey, was born in 1817 and received his early education at Navan. He entered Maynooth in August 1837 and was ordained in January 1843. Prior to his appointment to Ratoath, he served as curate in Johnstown, Bohermeen, Enfield and Tullamore. The elaborate epitaph which adorns his tomb is justified when one reviews the various monuments raised by him during his 32 years in Ratoath. His first act was to provide the parish with a fitting place of residence for its priests. He then completed the church at Ratoath begun by Fr. Carolan. This done, he built the church and schools at Ashbourne. Fr. Fulham enjoyed a considerable reputation as a preacher. *The Tablet* wrote of him *"his charities were widespread and were certainly most unostentatious. Fr. Fulham as parish priest had done everything to beautify the churches of Ratoath and Ashbourne and his parish was a model one"*. He died in October 1892 and was buried, at his own wish, in the grounds of Ratoath Church. A statue of the Sacred Heart marks his resting-place.[7]

On April 17th 1893 Fr. Peter Everard, P.P. Nobber, was transferred to Ratoath. This new pastor was a man of rare culture. As an amateur painter he acquired considerable skill. Added to this, he was a talented musician. He played the violin with skill and he possessed a melodious voice. As a youth he joined the Navan Repeal Band, which consisted of forty players and he was with them at the great Repeal meeting in Tara in 1843.

Fr. Robert F. Kelly succeeded Fr. Everard as Parish Priest in July 1915 and died in 1948.

Fr. John Cogan succeeded Fr. Kelly as Parish Priest in July 1948. Fr. Cogan a native of Ballinlough, Kells, was born in 1899. In September 1924 he was appointed to St. Finian's College in Mullingar and was President of the college there from 1939 until his appointment to Ratoath in 1948. He continued to minister as Parish Priest in Ratoath until his death on 27th July 1984.

Fr. Frank MacNamara succeeded as Parish Priest in September 1984. A native of Clara, Co. Offaly, he had previously been appointed to the staff of St. Finian's College, Mullingar, Co. Westmeath, where he taught until 1984. During this time he was the first director of the Schola Cantorum, which was established there by the Irish Hierarchy in 1970 and he also taught music periodically at Maynooth and at U.C.D. from 1967 until 1984. Fr. McNamara now resides in Multyfarnham, Co. Westmeath (2008).

Fr. Gerry Stuart succeeded as Parish Priest in August 1998. He is a native of Killucan, Co.

---

7 *Diocese of Meath Ancient and Modern*, Volume II, Dean Cogan

Westmeath. On his ordination in 1979 he was appointed to the staff of St. Finian's College and was appointed President of the College in 1988.

Curates:

1861-1870	- Fr. Michael Fox	1935-1936	- Fr. James Carty
1870-1887	- Fr. Francis Meade	1936-1941	- Fr. Edward Meade
1887-1893	- Fr. William Davis	1941-1943	- Fr. Patrick Bartley
1892-1893	- Fr. Thomas Mulvany, Bishop	1943-1948	- Fr. Edward Rispin
1893-1895	- Fr. Peter Conlon	1948-1949	- Fr. Edward Greenan
1895-1896	- Fr. Joseph Masterson	1949-1957	- Fr. James Abbott
1896-1900	- Fr. Patrick Flynn	1957-1958	- Fr. Colm Murtagh.
1900-1906	- Fr. Timothy Brennan	1958-1966	- Fr. William Kirley
1906-1907	- Fr. Francis Callan	1966-1970	- Fr. Gerard Stanley
1906-1915	- Fr. Nicholas Cooney	1970-1983	- Fr. Peter Mulvany
1911-1912	- Fr. John Higgins	1983-1985	- Fr. Malachy Lynam
1912-1912	- Fr. John Harte	1985-1994	- Fr. Gerard McCormack
1912-1915	- Fr. John Hurley	1994-1997	- Fr. Oliver Devine
1914-1915	- Fr. James F. Gilmore	1997-2000	- Fr. Joe Deegan
1915-1927	- Fr. Edward Flynn	1997-2003	- Fr. Paul Crosbie
1927-1931	- Fr. G. Scully	2003-2006	- Fr. Philip Gaffney
1931-1935	- Fr. Philip McGahey	2006-Date	- Fr. Patrick Donnelly

Farewell Presentation to Fr. Oliver Devine in 1997

1997: Fr. Frank McNamara is pictured above making a farewell presentation of a Waterford Crystal lamp, on behalf of Ratoath parishioners, to Fr. Oliver Devine, C.C., on the occasion of his transfer from Ratoath to take up a new appointment in Drogheda.
Fr. Oliver later became Parish Priest of Balivor and Kildalkey.
Left to Right: Pictured with Fr. Frank McNamara and Fr. Oliver Devine were Noel Eiffe and Joe Mannering who organised the presentation on behalf of the parish.

CHURCH MATTERS

Vicars appointed to the Deanery of Ratoath

FRANCES MAHER

AFTER THE REFORMATION, church government was very unsettled, the tithes that belonged to the different parishes were granted, in whole or in part, by the Crown to laymen, just as confiscated lands were granted. In most cases the grantees were Protestant. These men had the right to nominate the Vicar. The great tithes of Ratoath were in the possession of Dr. Ambrose Ainger, by patent from the crown and worth £20.00. In 1580, the Rev. George Watsonne succeeded John Hele who had been appointed by Queen Elizabeth I [1558-1603]. He died in 1582 and in turn was succeeded by John Fleming who in turn was transferred to Slane in 1601. There was no Vicar appointed until 1603.

Next to be appointed was Nicholas Smyth, who married a lady, called Jane Cooke from Dunshaughlin and he was then moved to Oldcastle. After Nicholas Smyth, Henry Bolton was appointed Vicar in 1633 and he in turn was moved to Rathfeigh.

Rev. Noah Webb was appointed Vicar in 1675, and the following year was moved to Dunshaughlin. The Rev. Charles Newburgh was installed on the 9th May 1676 and in 1678 he was transferred to Dundalk.

The next Vicar to be appointed was Rev. John Bolton, but he became Dean of Derry and in 1720 Richard Bolton became Vicar. He died in 1761 and is buried in Cruicetown (near Nobber). The Rev. Thomas Lee Norman succeeded from that year; he stayed in Ratoath until 1794. Lancelot King Conyngham was his successor and he left in 1820 when Robert Norman was installed as Vicar on October 28th. He died on 6th November 1844. There are no records to indicate where all the services were held from 1406 to 1817, but the Rev. Robert Norman was probably the first to have held a service in the church (date on church stone is 1817).[1]

Next to be appointed was Rev. Henry Johnston who was installed on 23rd November 1844 and he retired in 1885. He was succeeded by the Rev. John Healy and in 1887 was succeeded by Rev. Houlin Monsarratt who resided in Ratoath for six years and died in 1905. He was succeeded by the last Rector in Ratoath, Rev. William Foster Legge, who was installed on December 9th 1903 and he died in 1932, aged 72.

---

[1] "*A Topographical Dictionary of Ireland*". Author Samuel Lewis. In two volumes. Published by S. Lewis & Co. 87, Aldersgate Street, London. 1837.

According to Samuel Lewis's Topographical Dictionary of Ireland, 1837[2],

"Ratoath, the parish (formerly a Parliamentary Borough) in the Barony of Ratoath, County of Meath and province of Leinster, 3 miles N.W. from Ashbourne and 11 ½ miles from Dublin, containing 1779 inhabitants, of which number 552 are in the village. In the reign of Henry V1 it was classed among the borough towns of Meath, and has attained such importance as to give its name to the hundred in which it is situated. It also had an Abbey, dedicated to St. Mary Magdalene, and it sent members to the Irish Parliament, which it continued to do till the Union of 1800, when the borough was disfranchised".[3]

"The village contained 96 houses, but retains nothing of its former importance. The manufacture of sacking and the weaving of linen are carried on to a small extent and fairs, chiefly for cattle and pigs, are held on 18th April, 1st, June and 20th November for which, though authorised by patent, no toll has been lately demanded. The village also has a dispensary. A constabulary police force is stationed here, and a manorial court was formerly held, but within the last few years has been discontinued".[4]

Samuel Lewis went on to state that "the Parish comprises 8,207 ¾ statute acres, as applotted under the tithe act. The land is generally of good quality and in a state of profitable cultivation; rather more than half is under tillage, producing favourable crops; the remainder, with the exception of a moderate portion of bog, is in meadow and pasture. Stone of good quality is quarried for building and for repairing the roads. The principal seats are "The Manor House", (where manorial courts were held until 1830) of Mr. J.L. Corballis, pleasantly situated in the town, and Lagore, of Michael Thunder, a handsome residence in a richly wooded demesne, abounding with stately timber".[5]

"The living accommodation is a Rectory and Vicarage, in the dioceses of Meath, called The Glebe House, which was situated close to the Church. Built in 1813, at an expense of £2,200 of which £100 was a gift and £800 a loan from the late Board of First Fruits, and the remainder was defrayed by the then incumbent. The Glebe comprises of 6 ½ acres, valued at £19.10 per annum. The gross income from the whole benefice amounts to £788. 7s. 3p. per annum. [6]

The Rectory is partly impropriety in T.L. Norman and J.L. Corballis, and the Vicar of Athlone; and partly united to the vicarage, which by act of Council in 1682, was united to the rectories and vicarages of Greenogue, Killegland, Creekstown, and Donaghmore, and to the chapelry of Cookstown, together forming the union of Ratoath, in the alternate patronage of the Crown and the family of Norman. The Tithes amount to £515, of which, £55 is payable to T.L. Norman, £62.10s to the Vicar of Athlone, and the remainder to the vicar of Ratoath.[7]

In the Roman Catholic divisions this parish is the head of a union, comprising also of the Parishes of Cookstown, Killegland, and Rathbeggan. There are chapels at Ratoath and Killegland. About 240 children are taught in a parochial and a national school, of which the former is aided by a donation of £10 per annum from the incumbent. The Rath from which the parish takes its name has been planted; several old coins have been found near it. There are no remains of either the abbey of St. Mary Magdalene or of a chantry for three priests, which formerly existed here".[8]

---

2 Ibid
3 Ibid
4 Ibid
5 Ibid
6 Ibid
7 Ibid
8 "The Parish of Kilbeg". Jack Fitzsimons, 1974. The Leinster Leader. Royal Society of Antiquaries of Ireland, 63 Merrion Square, Dublin 2.

Parish Sense
The word 'parish' is used in three really distinct senses:[9]
(1) To signify the total area and population under the jurisdiction of a single cleric the parish priest.
(2) The civil or ancient parish.
(3) Each of the two or three amalgamations that have been re-amalgamated, or canonically united, to form a parish of sense no (1).

Final note: The remains of a stone structure were discovered in Woodlands near the Lough Lane, Ratoath, during the late 1990's. Perhaps future studies will reveal its origins.

References
"Survey of the Church of the Old Graveyard, Ratoath". Derek Darby, Ratoath, Co. Meath. 1990. Unpublished

---

[9] *"The Parish of Kilbeg"*. Jack Fitzsimons, 1974. The Leinster Leader. Royal Society of Antiquaries of Ireland, 63 Merrion Square, Dublin 2.

CHURCH MATTERS

Priests Native to the Parish of Ratoath[1]

RATOATH HERITAGE GROUP

- **Rev. John Martin**, died P.P. Ballivor.

- **Rev. John Martin**, died C.C., Ballynacargy, Co. Westmeath.

- **Rev. Nicholas McGrane**, Professor St. Patrick's College, Navan, died P.P., Coole.

- **Rev. Thomas Plunkett**, born 1822, educated at Gillic's Academy and St. Finian's College, which was then in Navan [1802 to 1908]. He entered Maynooth in August 1840, joined the Vincentians; ordained 1847; was engaged in missionary work at Phibsboro and Sheffield, died 21st August 1861.

- **Rev. Joseph Clarke**, born in 1912, ordained in 1938, Chaplain of the Irish Army from 1938 to 1969, PP Glasson, Athlone from 1969 to 1978, PP Kilcloon from 1978 to 1991. Retired to live in Ratoath from 1991 to 1997, died 25th April 1997.

- **Rev. Daniel Louis Meagher, S.J.**, a native of Ratoath, was born on 18th August 1911. Was educated at Ratoath NS, the Marist College in Dundalk and St. Finian's College, Mullingar. Entered the Jesuit Novitiate at Emo on 14th September 1931, then studied for a time a U.C.D., Tullabeg College and Milltown Park where he was ordained on 31 July 1944. Taught in the Crescent College in Limerick, then in 1950, set out to join Jesuit Mission in Northern Rhodesia (as it was called at that time) where he was appointed Regional Superior of the Irish Province. Developed rheumatoid arthritis and was admitted to Mater Hospital in Nairobi where he died on 14 April 1980. His body was flown to Zambia for burial.

- **Rev. Patrick Meagher, S.J.**, a native of Ratoath and brother of Fr. Daniel. He was born on 11th April 1917 and was educated at Ratoath NS and St. Finian's College, Mullingar, and he entereed the Jesuit Novitiate at Emo in September 1935. His education con-

---

1 *A Short History of The Parishes of The Diocese of Meath 1867-1937*, Rev. John Brady, 1937.
Ratoath Parish Website.

tinued at UCD, Tullabeg College and Milltown Park where he was ordained on 29th July 1948. He taught at Mungret College and Gonzaga College and was appointed Provincial Secretary. In 1975 he moved to Manresa Retreat House, Dollymount, Dublin.

- **Rev. Thomas Meagher**, a third brother, born on 11th February 1919. Educated at Ratoath NS and St. Finian's College and entered the Holy Ghost Novitiate in September 1937. Studied at UCD and Kimmage and was ordained on 15th July 1945. Undertook mission work in Kenya and became Secretary to Archbishop McCarthy in Nairobi and Vicar of the Diocese. He retired in 1980 and was appointed spiritual director to the assumption Sisters at Thika in the Diocese of Nairobi.

- **Mgr. Michael McNulty**. Born 1900, ordained in All Hallows in June 1931, having prepared for priesthood in China to within a year of ordination. Unfortunately, his health broke and he was obliged to return home. Two years later he entered All Hallows and was ordained for Capetown, South Africa. He went to Capetown in October 1931 and his first appointment was as a school chaplain. He became P.P. of the Parish of Woodstock in Capetown and remained there for 20 years. Following his pastorate there he transferred as P.P. to the parish of Widaboom also in Capetown and spent a further 20 years ministering there. In 1956 he was made a Domestic Prelate by Pope Pius XII with title of Monsignor. In 1970 he retired and returned to live in the parish with his nephew Mr. Sweeney. He died in 1978 and is buried in the graveyard adjoining Ashbourne church.

- **Rev. William Kelly**, born 1933, was educated at Ratoath NS and St. Finian's College. Ordained on 16th June 1957, at All Hallows for Salford Diocese.

- **Rev. Raphael Kelly**, brother of Fr. William, also born in Ratoath, educated at local NS and St. Finian's. Was ordained on 4th June 1966, at Lugano in Switzerland and served for many years in the Diocese of Guaranda, Ecuador, died in 2000.

- **Rev. Patrick Browne**, born on 4 August 1948. Educated at Ratoath NS and O'Connell's Schools, Mungret College and All Hallows. Was ordained on 16th June 1974, at All Hallows for Westminster archdiocese. Appointed to Edmonton parish in London, then to Cathedral House in London where he was appointed Cardinal Hume's Secretary and became P.P., Kentish Town in 1989. He is currently Parish Priest of Holy Apostles, Pimlico, London and Director of Vocations to the Permanent Deaconate in Westminster Dioceses. (See separate article by Canon Pat Browne in this book).

- **Rev. Daniel Eiffe**, born in Ratoath on 8 October 1950. Educated at Ratoath NS, MSC House of Studies, Carrig-na-Mhar, Cork and UCG. Ordained on 4th June 1977 in St. Theresa's, Mount Merrion, Dublin. Appointed to a parish in the Sudan in 1989. (See separate article in this book).

- **Rev. Derek Darby** was ordained to the priesthood in Ratoath on 11th June 2001. Currently serving in Ashbourne Parish.

CHURCH MATTERS

Recording Local Church History:
Dean Cogan (1826-1872)

FRANCES MAHER

We are fortunate that the local church history of Ratoath has been recorded. It is fitting that we include a brief biography of one of the key figures who was involved in research during the late 1800s and whose work is of historical significance. Dean Cogan was born in Slane in 1826. He was educated at a local school and later at the Seminary in Navan. He was ordained a Priest in Maynooth on 25th May 1850. Dean Cogan began writing articles for the "Tablet" in 1856 and wrote the first Post-Reformation History of the Catholic Church.

He met Rev. Dr. Matthew Kelly D.D. of Maynooth who spoke of the invaluable wealth of knowledge that could be got from each Diocese in Ireland and encouraged him to compile a history of the Irish Church. Dean Cogan concurred with his remarks and travelled through every parish in the Diocese of Meath. His ensuing works include:

The Bishops of Meath.
The Abbeys of Meath.
The Abbeys of Meath founded after the Norman invasion.
The Chantries of Meath.

He succeeded in his work by means of recording the inscriptions on tomes, registers, lists of the dead, family papers, inscriptions on chalices etc., together with the Presentation lists of Parish Priests by James II in 1704, also papers and diaries of the late Dr. Michael Plunkett. Dean Cogan's significant work was an important historical record of Christianity in Ireland and the history of the Roman Catholic Diocese of Meath and was entitled *The Diocese of Meath* and published in two volumes (1862, 1867). Subsequently Dean Cogan officiated in Johnstown, Beauparc, Dunboyne and Navan parishes and spent most of his life ministering in these parishes. The last ten years of his life were spent as Professor and Dean in the old St. Finian's College in Mullingar. He died on 28th December in 1872 and is buried in Slane.

Continuing the Work of Cogan
Fr. John Brady, who continued Dean Cogan's work from 1867, was born in Dunboyne and educated in Belvedere College and in Maynooth. On the 5th June 1932 he was ordained Priest and subsequently from 1933 to 1936 worked in the parish of Crayford and assisted in the church of St. John Vianney in the Archdioceses of Southwark, England. Fr. Brady also worked as Diocesan Catechist from June 1935 to 1936, and became Diocesan Historian on 2nd January 1936.

CHURCH MATTERS

The Church of the Most Holy Trinity

RATOATH HERITAGE GROUP

RATOATH PARISH lies in the south-eastern end of the diocese of Meath and shares its boundaries with Curragha, Skryne, Dunshaughlin, Kilcloon, Dunboyne, and Donaghmore-Ashbourne. Ratoath has one church dedicated to the Most Holy Trinity.

"Many authors recount of a consultation in Ireland, when St. Thomas of Canterbury was sentenced by King Henry VIII, degraded and forbidden to be honoured as a saint, how the people met near a chapel which had been formerly dedicated to the same St. Thomas, being by the King's appointment to elect as the Patron and one coveted to choose St. Peter and St. Paul. At length, by advice of one of the best judgement, they elected the Blessed Trinity for their Patron, saying: **If the King for other respects would also degrade or depose St. Peter and St. Paul, yet if any would maintain their state against him, none could more forcibly than the Blessed Trinity.** *The owld Justice Plunkett of Donsoghly was present at this consultation."*[1]

Derek Darby states in his essay The Towering Guardians that

"When the Protestant form of worship was introduced into the church, the Catholics who remained refused to attend, even under the threat of fines, loss of property and banishment. For close on a century they had no civil rights and legally were not presumed to exist.

It was the time of the Mass-rock and we can just guess how they managed to hear Mass and receive the sacraments. Tradition has it that Mass in Ratoath during these troubled times was said under an elder tree on Hessman's Lane, which is the small lane leading down to the little foot bridge over the Broadmeadow River. One of the many regulations was that if a priest received anything on the occasion of a baptism or marriage, he had to hand it over in whole or in part to the Protestant clergyman. Even up to the 1820's there is a record of annual settlements being made to a Rev. Mr. Dobbyn."

However, the Catholics did hold out and decided around 1760 to erect a place of worship of their own. The present church of Ratoath replaces a Mass-house of the 1760's, the site

---

1   A short history of The Parishes of The Diocese of Meath. 1867 -1937 by Rev. John Brady

Original location of the Stepping Stones

of which is still pointed out at a place called "The Stepping Stones". The Authorities were prepared to tolerate such "chapels" provided they were erected in some remote place. Like all the chapels of the period, it was in constant need of repair. At his visitation in July 1797, Dr. Plunkett offered "*congratulations on the improved state of the house of God.*" Of the nature of this building we know nothing beyond the brief information contained in a passing reference in an account of a meeting "*held in Ratoath chapel of the Ratoath, Skreen and Dunboyne Independent Club*" on 27th January 1829. It states "*notwithstanding the unfavourable state of the weather, the chapel was crowded to excess at an early hour, and the galleries exhibited all the female rank, beauty and fashion of the surrounding neighbourhood.*" At least three galleries would have been necessary to accommodate such a galaxy. It must have been a well-constructed building, as it had a choir gallery.[2]

It is said that the wall around the priest's garden was built with the stones from this old building. There was a marble slab with an inscription on one of the walls similar to a foundation stone, which was found by the late Fr. Cogan and is currently held in the grounds of Ratoath Church. The following is a picture of this earliest stone that came from the old chapel located at the Stepping Stones. Not all the words on the inscription are clear.

It reads as follows:
"*Chappel built by the Parish of Ratoath and Union. Dr. Cheevers, President, Mr. White P.P. An. Dom. 1760*".

This chapel is clearly marked on the 1834 Map of Ratoath.

---

2   *A short history of The Parishes of The Diocese of Meath. 1867 -1937* by Rev. John Brady

Fr. Nicholas White was Parish Priest from 1740 to 1789.

When the Penal Laws began to be relaxed, the Catholic Community moved their church to the present site which until then must have been just a village green. A belated lease of the property was granted on 1st May 1879 by a Mr. Corballis to the diocesan trustees for 999 years. Having provided his children with schools, Fr. Richard Carolan, P.P. since 1818, directed his attention to the need of a proper church. We know from his memorial monument, that the church was *"Begun under his auspices."* Tradition gives the date of erection *"about 1836"*.

The four walls of the church were erected 1836-1838 in Fr. Carolan's time and nothing further was done following his death in 1838 until Fr. John Fulham was appointed parish priest in 1869. In the intervening years a bequest of £100.00 was given by Miss Catherine Bonynge of Ratoath towards the completion of the new church.

Fr. Fulham re-built the front of the church and the belfry in cut stone in 1868. He extended the church on the back and added on the apse and sacristy in 1874. While doing this work, he lodged in a house in the village and in the same year he built the present parochial house. He is buried in the church grounds under a statue of the Sacred Heart.

Extensive repairs were carried out by Fr. Kelly during 1923-26. They included a new heating system, pitch pine ceiling, windows, chancel arch and altar rails. In the intervening years some renovation work was carried out on the church.

On the 4th July 1982, due to an increase of population, the combined parish of Ratoath-Ashbourne was split and Ratoath became a parish in its own right.

In the late 1980's it was decided that a major renovation was necessary. Arthur Lardner, Architect drew up plans and work was carried out by local builder, Pat Donnelly. The unique gold leaf décor on the interior wall of the church at the back of the altar was painstakingly restored to its former splendour on the advice of the officials of the Office of Public Works. The Church was re-dedicated by Most Rev. Michael Smith on 20th October 1991. The total cost of the project was £250,000.

In 2001 the church roof was re-slated. During 2002-2003 the exterior plaster work was removed and the walls were re-plastered. On some areas of the left hand side of the interior of the church, the plaster was removed and the areas re-plastered. Parts of the windows were repaired as deemed necessary. The entire interior of the church was re-decorated. New amplification and speakers were installed. The grounds next to the church were paved with granite paving stones. New kerbs were installed around the lawn areas on both approach avenues to the church and the driveways themselves were newly tarmacadamed.

Chalices and Ciboria

The sacred vessels used to this day are:
>A silver chalice inscribed *"Ratoath me fiere fecit."*
>A silver chalice inscribed *"Luke Eife Ratoath 1843"*
>A silver chalice inscribed *"Ratoath me fieri fecit 1865"*
>A gilt chalice inscribed *"The gift of Mrs Thunder Lagore to the church of Ratoath 1865"*
>A silver ciborium with inscription *"Donum Michaelis Thunder ad Ratoath 1865"*
>A silver ciborium with inscription *"Donum Patricii et Margaritae Rogers et familia ad Ratoath 1914"*

Mass was concelebrated on 20th October 1991 for the re-dedication of the Holy Trinity Church led by chief celebrant Most Rev. Michael Smith.
Pictured (L-R): Fr. John Kerrane PP Dunshaughlin,
Fr. Colm Murtagh PP Kildalkey, Fr. Peter Mulrany PP Ardcath, Fr. Patrick Dillon PP Kilcloon (later Ballinabrackey),
Fr. Andrew Rispin PP Dunboyne, Rev. Michael Smith, Bishop of Meath, Fr. Joe Clarke PP Kilcloon, Fr. Gerry Stanley PP Rathkenny, Fr. Joseph Garvey PP Curragha, Fr. Martin Bourke PP Ashbourne (later PP Clara), Fr. Tom Gilroy CC Dunboyne.

The Archaeological Inventory of County Meath published by the OPW gives the following information regarding 'Holy Trinity Church' in the old graveyard and the Font:

Church Site: 1489, pp144
OS 44:4:6 (88.9, 53.0) 'Holy Trinity Church'. OD 300-400 O 0223, 5201
Church (site): Dopping's Visitation Book 1682-5 refers to church (RMAHS 1971, 37-8). Nineteenth-century church remains on site. Late thirteenth century or early fourteenth century effigy (Hunt 1974, 213) and seventeenth cross in graveyard.
SMR 44:6. 15-04-1985

Font: 1572, pp 152
OS 44:4:6 (88.5, 51.6) Not marked. OD 300-400 O 0219, 5188
Font: Octagonal font (diam. 0.44m, H 0.2m) with biconical stem outside RC church and close to motte (1657).
SMR 44:7   28-8-1985

CHURCH MATTERS

The Church of the Most Holy Trinity

Extract from "Drogheda Independent" of Saturday, August 1st, 1925

On Monday last, [27th July 1925] His Lordship the Most Reverend Dr. Gaughran, Bishop of Meath, held his triennial visitation for Confirmation in Ratoath. Addressing the people His Lordship said "You have actually built a new Church; £5,637 has already been expended on your Church repairs and in addition two new contracts for the erection of new organ gallery and for painting the Church are now in hands. The cost of these two contracts will be £1,077. You were asked to put your shoulder to the wheel and you did it. God will not be in your debt. He will give you a rich reward for what you have done for the beauty of His House."

Ref: *A short history of The Parishes of The Diocese of Meath. 1867 -1937 by Rev. John Brady.*

Harvest Celebrations at the Church of the Most Holy Trinity
October 2007

III

CHURCH MATTERS

Holy Trinity Church Remembers

RATOATH HERITAGE GROUP

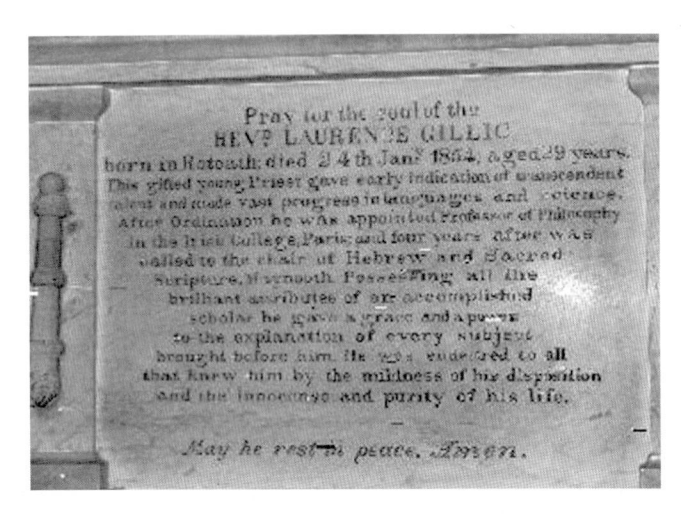

Rev. Laurence Gillic was born in Ratoath in 1825 and was appointed to The Irish College, Paris, as Professor of Philosophy after his ordination to the priesthood and four years later he returned to Maynooth. Sadly he died at the young age of 29 years. This plaque to his memory can be seen in Holy Trinity Church, Ratoath.

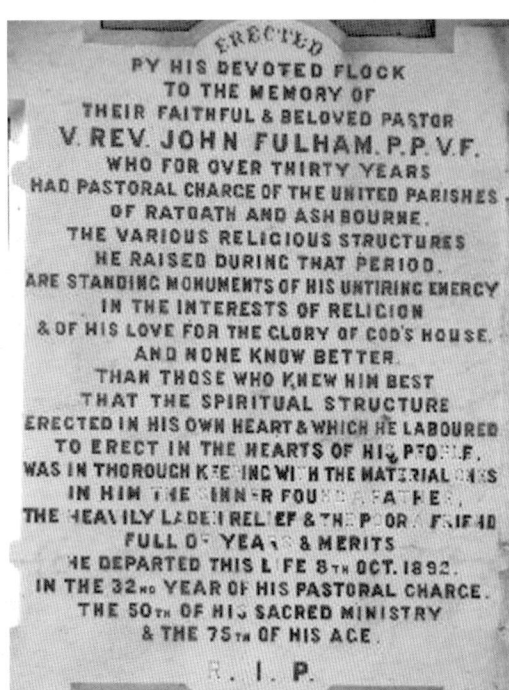

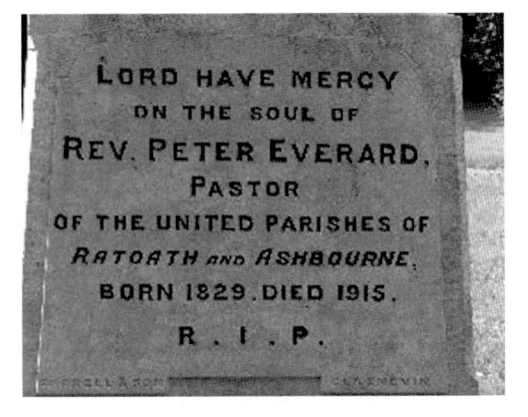

Rev. Peter Everard, Pastor, of the United Parishes of Ratoath and Ashbourne, who died in 1915

(Left): A headstone to the memory of Rev. John Fulham, P.P., who died on 8th October 1892, is situated in the grounds of the Holy Trinity Church, Ratoath.

CHURCH MATTERS

Holy Trinity Church Remembers

Rev. Robert F. Kelly P.P. Ratoath and Ashbourne, who died in 1948

The picture below was taken circa 1932 or 1933 during the annual procession of the Blessed Sacrament around the centre of Ratoath. The picture shows a large procession, on its way from Holy Trinity Church, approaching the Barrack Cross. Notice the Church of Ireland church to the left of the picture which was then in regular use. The procession was led by Fr. Robert F. Kelly P.P. with Fr. Philip McGahey C.C. Ratoath and Fr. Farrell from Skryne.

CHURCH MATTERS

Ratoath Parochial House

RATOATH HERITAGE GROUP

J H. Corballis Esq., Ratoath Manor, gave the site of Ratoath Church and Parochial House on lease of 999 years to Dr. Nulty, Bishop of Meath, on 1st May 1870. Fr. Fulham built the parochial house in 1874 with a loan of £1,000 from the Board of Works. When Fr. Fulham came to Ratoath in 1861, Fr. Sheridan was in residence at the old parochial house on the parish farm with c. 11 acres at Tankardstown. Accordingly, he purchased a house in the village and lived there until 1874. Fr. Sheridan's house had been built in 1842 with material from the old Mass house. Previously, the priests

Photo taken circa mid 20th Century
(Note: one of the many gardens, cultivated by the Ralph Family, outside the walls of the Parochial House and along the north side of the Broadmeadow River – today we call this area the River Walk)

had lived in a house in the village and afterwards in a house on the site of the sanctuary of the present church.

Ratoath parochial house had some repairs carried out to both its interior and exterior in 1948-49 and electricity was first switched on for Christmas 1948. In 1954 the yard was concreted and the avenue tarmacadamed. Central heating was installed in 1969 and the house was linked to the mains water supply in 1972. In 1985 Fr. Frank McNamara carried out major renovations and refurbishing to the floors, walls, roof, etc., the architect was Mr. Arthur Lardner and the builder was Mr. Patrick Donnelly, Lagore Cross.

Under the guidance of Fr. Gerry Stuart, repairs, rebuilding and renovations in 2005-6 have resulted in further improvements; the renovation of adjoining stone buildings into a new Parish Resource centre was completed.

(Left): Renovated stone buildings. (Photo taken August 2007)

(Bottom left): Main Entrance to the Parochial House with original features: redbrick detail around the main door and oratory stained glass window and horizontal brickwork across the centre of the building on all sides.

(Bottom right): Curving pathway leading from the Parochial House to Holy Trinity Church, Ratoath

CHURCH MATTERS

Family Surnames in Ratoath Parish in 1950's and 1960's

Acton	Crean	Gleeson	McAuley	O'Neill
Andrews	Cullen	Glynn	McCabe	O'Reilly
Baggally	Cunney	Gogan	McCann	O'Sullivan
Barker	Curley	Gorman	McCarthy	Parkinson
Blake	Cusack	Guiney	McCormack	Rafferty
Boshell	Daley	Halton	McDermott	Ralph
Boylan	Darby	Henry	McGowan	Reilly
Brady	Dolan	Hessman	McGrane	Reynolds
Brennan	Dollard	Hickey	McGrath	Roche
Brien	Donnelly	Horgan	McIntyre	Rogers
Brindley	Donohue	Hughes	McKeown	Rooney
Browne	Doolan	Johnson	McLoughlin	Rowe
Bruen	Dooley	Kavanagh	McNabb	Ryan
Bruton	Doonan	Keague	Meagher	Sherry
Byrne	Doran	Kehoe	Monahan,	Shevlin
Caffrey	Dowd	Kelly	Mooney	Smith
Cannon	Dowling	Kennedy	Moore	Smyth
Carberry	Duffy	Kenny	Morgan	Staunton
Carey	Eiffe	Keogh	Muldoon	Taaffe
Casey	Elliott	Kerrigan	Mulvany	Talty
Caul	Ennis	King	Murphy	Toole
Clarke	Everard	Kinsella	Murray	Tyler
Cleary	Farrell	Lambe	Nash	Walls
Clifford	Fitzpatrick	Lloyd	Naughton	Walsh
Clifton	Flanagan	Lynam	Newman	Wherity
Clince	Flood	Lynch	Nolan	Wheeler
Colfer	Foley	Lynskey	Nulty	White
Conmey	Fortune	Lyons	O'Brien	Whyte
Connor	Fox	Madden	O'Connell	Wilkinson
Conway	Gannon	Maher	O'Connor	Woods
Cooke	Gardiner	Mahon	O'Dwyer	
Corcoran	Gaughan	Mannering	O'Hare	
Costello	Geraghty	Martin	O'Keeffe	
Cowley	Gillic	McAndrew	O'Mahony	

CHURCH MATTERS

Father John Cogan (1898-1984)

FRANCES MAHER

FR. JOHN COGAN was born in Ballinlough, Carnaross, Parish of Kilskyre, near Oldcastle, Co. Meath, on 29th June 1898. He was educated in St. Finian's College, Mullingar, Co. Westmeath.

Fr. Cogan studied for the priesthood during a sensitive time in our country's history. His sympathy was with the Nationalist Cause and in 1920 his brother Commandant Seamus Cogan was killed by the Black and Tans in Oldcastle; a street in the town is named after him.

Ordained in Maynooth on 17th June 1923, he gained his Higher Diploma from the National University, Maynooth, after which he began teaching there. Later he taught in St. Finian's College, becoming Vice-President in 1933 and President in 1939. Stories abound of Fr. Cogan's ability to feed students during the War Years. Fr. Cogan was appointed Parish Priest of Ratoath and Ashbourne in 1948 following the death of the then Parish Priest, Fr. Kelly, and he continued as Parish Priest up until his death, making him one of the longest serving Parish Priests in the Dioceses.

His achievements in Ratoath and Ashbourne are many and he leaves behind ample memorials to a life's work. He built three new National Schools, one each in Ratoath, Ashbourne and Rathbeggan, and along with Fr. Mulvany was responsible for the building of the new St. Declan's School in Ashbourne. His foresight in the purchase of seven acres behind Ratoath School gave ample room for future development and extension of the sporting facilities. The purchase of the land for the new Cemetery and the careful attention in the laying out of the Cemetery were among his finest achievements. His work also included the building of the Marian Shrine in 1954, the extension to the existing Hall, the extension to the Church and many other projects. The purchase

Fr. John Cogan who was Parish Priest of Ratoath & Ashbourne from 1948 until his death in 1984

Headstone over Fr. Cogan's resting place in Ratoath Church grounds.

of the Coderliss Grounds and the setting up of the Ratoath Development Company gave the village a much needed sports amenity. His last public function was to open a modernised Community Centre in Ratoath on Friday 6th March 1984.

Father Cogan published a book entitled "*Ratoath*"[1] which covered the history of Ratoath both as a Parish and a Barony and it covered the various townlands and families that lived in the parish during the 1960's. It is an invaluable reference book, without which an enormous wealth of historical events and data would have been lost to posterity.

---

[1] "*Ratoath*" Author: Very Rev. John Cogan, P.P. Published by Drogheda Independent Co. Ltd. c. mid 1960's.

CHURCH MATTERS

Fr. Frank McNamara

RATOATH HERITAGE GROUP

REV. FR. FRANK MCNAMARA succeeded Fr. John Cogan as Parish Priest in September 1984. Fr. McNamara originally came from Clara, Co. Offaly. He had previously been appointed to the staff of St. Finian's College, Mullingar, Co. Westmeath, where he taught until 1984. During this time he was the first Director of the Schola Cantorum, which was established there by the Irish Hierarchy in 1970. He also taught music periodically at Maynooth and at U.C.D. from 1967 until 1984. Fr. McNamara returned to his native Offaly in recent years and was appointed to the Parish of Tullamore. Currently Fr. McNamara resides in Multyfarnham, Co. Westmeath (2008).

CHURCH MATTERS

Fr. Gerry Stuart
– Celebrating his Silver Jubilee

RATOATH HERITAGE GROUP

BAPTISMAL RECORDS in Killucan parish list the milestones in Gerard Stuart's journey of Christian faith – Baptism in 1954, First Communion in 1961, Confirmation in 1966 and Ordination to the Priesthood on 20 June 1979.

Since his Ordination, Fr. Gerry has worked tirelessly as teacher and as President of St. Finian's College, Mullingar until his arrival here in Ratoath in 1996 where he continues his work with the same energy and commitment. School documents in Mullingar and parish registers here in Ratoath record Fr. Gerry's involvement in the spiritual journey of many families and individuals. Framed pictures, wedding-albums and family photos in many homes around the parish record his work and spiritual support and guidance to parishioners of Ratoath.

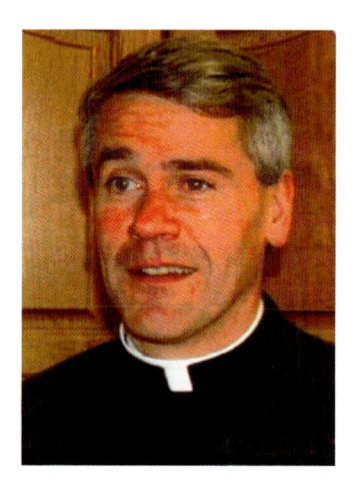

Fr. Gerry's Silver Jubilee was a cause for celebration by the parishioners of Ratoath. We were delighted that some of those who were present at Fr. Gerry's Ordination and First Mass in 1979 were able to come to Ratoath and join with the parishioners for this very special occasion.

In particular, the parish community welcomed Fr Gerry's family and colleagues who joined us in thanking God for the life, health and friendship of our parish priest. The Celebration of the Eucharist was held at Holy Trinity Church, Ratoath on Sunday 27 June 2004.

CHURCH MATTERS

Silver Jubilee Mass for Fr. Gerry Stuart
Ratoath, 27 June 2004

DERMOT GALLAGHER

It is an enormous privilege to be asked to speak at this wonderful occasion in the life of Fr. Gerry Stuart. No words of mine could do full justice to the huge achievements of Fr. Gerry in his 25 years of dynamic and committed priesthood, but as a proud parishioner, I am obligated to try.

When Fr. Gerry began his journey of priesthood 25 years ago in 1979, Ireland and indeed Ratoath were very different places. Ireland's membership of the European Economic Community, as it was then, was only six years old - although, interestingly, in that year also we had the Presidency of Europe, under the Taoiseachship of Jack Lynch. Emigration was still the lot of many of our young people, unemployment was high and the Celtic Tiger was but a distant dot in the future, unimagined by any of us. Ratoath was still essentially a small, rural parish, not fundamentally different in character to what it had been 20 or 30 years before.

Kerry won the All-Ireland that year - the reign of Sean Boylan had not yet begun. In my native Leitrim, we dreamed our dreams of Sam Maguire - in that respect, at least, nothing much has changed!

1979 was also the year of the extraordinary visit to Ireland of His Holiness, the Pope. It is an interesting coincidence that this week we had news that the Irish Bishops might be inviting him for a return visit this year, and what a huge development that would be.

But the most important event of all in the life of the young Gerry Stuart that year was his ordination to priesthood. That day, he took solemn pledges to serve his God and his people. Today is testimony to how fully he has discharged both.

It is for others who knew him better in his other ministries to extol the manner in which he conducted those. Even at a distance, most of us heard great things about his fine work as President of St. Finian's College in Mullingar. His passion for education fitted him perfectly for that post. While he rightly won much praise for his work in overseeing the extensive, historic renovation of the structure of the building there, his real achievement was the way that he placed at the heart of that fine institution a commitment to the welfare of the students in his care, focusing on the formation of the whole person - academic, human and spiritual.

For us here in Ratoath, that was all by repute. What I wanted to speak personally about today is the extraordinary impact he has had in our parish in the six years he has been among us. These have been the years of the Celtic Tiger. The years of huge change in Ireland, and in Ratoath. With a pace and a breadth that not even the keenest commentator could have predicted, Ireland has witnessed an unprecedented transformation, which has played itself out in economic, social and personal terms.

Ratoath has been an accurate microcosm of that wider process of change. The quiet rural space that I referred to earlier has been turned in the briefest time into one of the fastest growing communities in the region.

I use the word "community" deliberately and intentionally because that is where Fr. Gerry comes in. Too often, and sadly, the experience in other areas faced with such rapid change was the fracturing of community, the turning of close-knit, small neighbourhoods into a sprawling collection of households, each effectively isolated islands, cut off from each other in every sense. Strangers in their own place. And with all the consequences that go with that in terms of the social, communal and indeed religious fabric.

Fr. Gerry has helped ensure that, remarkably, Ratoath has been spared that fate. Instead, with skills that would do justice to the highest-paid change management guru, he has helped guide and shepherd this place and this people through the rapids of change so that today, many miles downstream, Ratoath is still demonstrably a community - different to what it was before but, a real, living, vibrant community.

But there's more. Not alone has he prevented something negative happening, but he has actually helped turn the huge process of change and upheaval into a positive and harnessed it for good. He has transformed the complexity of the changes that have taken place in this parish - physically, psychologically, structurally and spiritually - into an energy and a vitality that has enormous power, a power that we all feed from and live from.

Fr. Gerry, I still don't quite know how you pulled it off. But just look around this Church today, this Church which you have itself transformed. Just look around this parish. The buzz is palpable. The energy, the sense of connectedness and belonging. And that is true of all ages. The young men and women, the children, the older among us. We are all clearly part of the Christian family that you lead so profoundly well. And we naturally think here also of those who have passed away during the last six years, and who were ministered to so caringly and so sensitively by you and colleagues. In particular, you deserve enormous credit for the way you have knit together the newer arrivals with the blow-ins like myself from previous generations and, of course, with the real natives, like my wife, and the other venerable clans of old Ratoath.

If I dare speak for anybody here today, I think it is for those of us who came from outside, but who today can say with total sincerity - "Ratoath is home; Ratoath is where we feel at home". For that, Fr. Gerry, a huge amount of the credit goes to you. And I know that you would wish me to pay the warmest tribute to your exceptionally fine colleague priests, past and present.

Of course, lest the Pope might be called on to do a canonisation if he comes later in the year, Fr. Gerry displays the odd hint of mere mortality. Three that I know about, in no particular order, are Manchester United, Westmeath football team and horses. Any man partial to that trinity cannot be accused of lacking humanity. But my attitude is that if they keep him fresh for the challenges of pastorhood in our parish, then we should encourage his little distractions. Except when Meath play Westmeath!

Fr. Gerry Stuart, you are a credit to your family, to your county, to your adopted home of Ratoath and, most of all, to yourself. We hear a lot of talk about difficult times for the priesthood and for the Church. But as long as there are priests like you to bear witness with such integrity, energy, courage and commitment to your vocation, then the priesthood and the Church can surely look to the future with real hope.

We wish you every joy as you celebrate this very special milestone in your life. And from a selfish point of view, we wish you very many more happy and fruitful years as our Parish Priest here in Ratoath. Oh yes, and all the best to Westmeath in this year's campaign, to Manchester United next season, and to the horses whenever they catch your fancy. In the case of Westmeath and Man United, you might be short of sense but you're not short of the courage of your convictions. And overall, my final advice to you, and I know the whole congregation shares this, is that you might forget about Man. United, Westmeath and horses and accept that salvation and eternal reward are the best bet!

We all salute a great teacher, a great priest and friend and an outstanding Leader of people.

CHURCH MATTERS

Ordination of Fr. Derek Darby

BY PAUL HALTON

Sunday the 11th June 2001 was a historic day when local man Derek Darby was ordained to the priesthood in Ratoath. Fr. Derek is the son of Pat and Bróna Darby and brother of Rhona Munch and Aideen Darby of the Dunshaughlin Road. He became the first person to be ordained in the Church of the Most Holy Trinity Ratoath since it was built in 1836. The whole village and surrounding areas were decked in bunting and flags of every colour; Papal flags, Football Team colours, and messages of good wishes were draped on every building and across all the streets.

Derek was ordained by Most Rev. Michael Smith, Bishop of Meath, in a ceremony attended by 40 priests, including Fr. Gerry Stuart P.P. and Rev. Paul Crosby C.C. Ratoath Parish, friends, family and members of the local community. As Derek arrived at the Church a guard of honour was formed by the local Soccer, G.A.A. Martial Arts, Athletic, Riding Club and Scouts Clubs and also by the children who had celebrated their First Holy Communion in 2001. Before and after the ordination ceremony, the Kentstown Accordion Band created a festival atmosphere in the Church Grounds. The Ratoath Church Choir provided the sacred music and Fr. Derek's sister Rhona took part in the readings, and his sister Aideen sung The Psalm. His aunt Gwen Lynam also sang during the ceremony.

The Ceremony: This was very moving and took the form of Mass:
- **Anointing of the young Priest's Hands** – this follows the ancient tradition of the king being anointed for the service of the Lord.
- **Presentation with the young priest's Chalice and Paten** – this is the same chalice and paten, which Fr. Derek used for his First Mass on the following evening.
- **Promise of Obedience** – Fr. Derek made a commitment of respect and obedience in serving the Bishop in his ministry Investiture- Fr. Derek wore his new alb and chasuble, the vestments a priest wears when celebrating Mass.
- **Invocation of the Saints** – in a very ancient prayer, the Church called on the saints to bless Fr. Derek and to intercede on his behalf.

CHURCH MATTERS

Ordination of Fr. Derek Darby

Ratoath Choir Members rehearsing before the Ordination of Derek Darby to the Priesthood, June 2001

- **Laying on of Hands and Prayer of Consecration** – at this point, the Bishop laid his hands on the candidate and invoked the Holy Spirit.

Fr. Derek celebrated his first Mass in Ratoath on Monday 12th June 2001 at which more than 800 people attended. The church was unable to contain the entire congregation and the ceremony was relayed by speakers outside for those unable to enter the church.

Individual invitations to his first Mass and Parish Function at Fairyhouse Racecourse were issued to all Ratoath parishioners. The celebration which followed was attended by over 1400 people and it probably was the biggest local event ever held in the parish. This special occasion brought together the older families and newer families who have made Ratoath their home. A presentation was made to Fr. Derek of a crystal desk-set, a watch and a cheque. Following his ordination Fr. Derek was appointed to St. Mary's, Navan.

Fr. Derek with his parents, Pat and Bróna Darby

*This tree was planted by parishioners
in Ratoath Church grounds
on New Year's Eve 1999
to celebrate the transition to the new millennium*

CHURCH MATTERS — Remembrance Trees

*This tree was planted by parishioners
in Ratoath Church grounds
to mark the appointment of
Fr. Gerry Stuart as Parish Priest
on 1st September 1998*

EDUCATION

Folklore Collection

COMPILED BY RATOATH HERITAGE GROUP

In 1935 the Irish Folklore Commission (Coimisiún Béaloideasa Éireann) was set up by the Irish Government to study and collect information on the folklore and traditions of Ireland. It eventually finished its work in 1971. Its role was superseded by the Department of Irish Folklore in University College Dublin (UCD), which continues to serve as a repository of the Irish Folklore Collection.

The Folklore Commission operated under the Department of Education. It aimed to collect, preserve and classify all aspects of Irish folk tradition in a systematic manner and it aimed to make its findings available to researchers.

The Schools' Collection Scheme
Although the Schools' Collection Scheme in 1937-38 was voluntary it nevertheless resulted in about a half a million manuscript pages of folklore. It was an ambitious countrywide scheme, whereby Primary School pupils, aged 11-14, were encouraged to collect stories and lore under specially-prepared guidelines. Instructions as to how the scheme was to be carried out were issued to the principal teachers of each primary school. The School's Collection is now considered to be '*a monument to the initiative of the Irish Folklore Commission, the co-operation of the Department of Education, the dedication of Irish National Teachers and the scholarship of the children in the National Schools at that time.*' The original manuscripts are kept at UCD.

Folklore Topics
The main topics on which information was gathered were: Settlement and Dwelling; Livelihood and Household Support; Communications and Trade; The Community; Human Life; Nature; Folk Medicine; Time; Principles and Rules of Popular Belief and Practice; Mythological Tradition; Historical Tradition; Religious Tradition; Popular 'Oral Literature'; and Sports and Pastimes. The information was gathered in English, with the exception of a few Irish words and phrases.

Folklore from Ratoath and District
With the kind permission of the Department of Irish Folklore, UCD, we are delighted to include the following fourteen stories about Ratoath and District. These very interesting stories were written by pupils of Ratoath National School in 1936, as their contribution to the Schools' Collection Scheme. Copies of the original handwritten stories are shown on one side of each page. Some of the photocopies of the originals were not easy to see clearly and therefore we show each story in typed format, line by line, on the opposite side. We pub-

EDUCATION

lish these stories without comment as they ably speak for themselves! Note that most but not all of the stories have the name of the pupil who wrote them, together with their age and class.

The following transcripts have been typed up using the original handwritten manuscripts.

Topic 1: **Hidden Treasure**
Pupil's Name: Cissie Everard, Class: VI
Age: 13 years

Hidden Treasure
The only stories I have heard of the above in the Parish of Ratoath are:-
Sometime about the rebellion of '98 there was a fight with the military at Lagore House.

A good deal of valuable Silver and Cash was in the house at the time and the butler taking fright gathered all in an apron and going down late at night through the large beech trees in front of the Halldoor he scooped a hole at the foot of one large tree and covered up the treasure. During the night he was badly wounded and died before he could tell the exact location. It is said the treasure was never discovered although after the big storm in February 1903 several persons searched for traces round the roots of large torn up trees.

Topic 2: **St. Mary's Convent**
Name: Lucy Caffrey
Age: 14 years
Address: Raystown, Ratoath, Co. Meath

Outstanding at my residence, Raystown, opposite my house there is a field called "The Millers". It is very interesting to walk to the end of it. You can trace the remains of ruins of houses which were formerly the residence of nuns and priests according to old Irish tales. People say it was Cromwell demolished them. I myself often admire the beautiful situated houses they were, with nice little entrances leading to the doorways.

At the back of the monastery there was an immense graveyard in which the nuns and priests were buried. You can still see the graves with flat stones on top. There were many different kinds of gardens and lawns such as fruit gardens, flower gardens and every kinds of trees growing in which there were lots of nice fruit such as plums in which they were six trees; there are some of them there still and they are very rich; and plentiful people come from many parts to pluck them.

There is also a bush in that field called "The Lone Bush". There is also supposed to have been a soldier buried there; many people saw the vision of him pointing a gun towards them. On one occasion a man died with the fright; this happened many years ago in the time of the "Battle of the Rath".

No one ever attempted to cut this tree; it is still to be seen in the centre of the field.

Topic 5:   Weather Lore

Weather Lore

Locally it is said – when the crows fly high and fall down into the rookery on the Moate in the village it is a sign of rain, also if the swans or wild geese are seen passing over towards the bog.

The most rain comes from the West here, and an old saying amongst the haymakers in the Summer is watch the "Curlew".

Topic 4:   Epidemic

Epidemic

About 90 years ago there was an Epidemic of Small Pox in the district which caused many deaths.

In one family alone there were 13 adults died between May and November.

Mr. Bruen's father had the illness but recovered; though he bore the marks on his face to his death.

N.B. (All the foregoing stories were related by John Bruen, Post Master, Ratoath)

EDUCATION
Folklore Collection

Topic 5: Storms

Severe Weather
The most severe wind storm remembered by anyone in the locality is the great wind of 1903, in February.

Hundreds of trees were blown down across Lagore and Ballymore, which part of the parish was wooded, and the roads were blocked by trees for several days afterwards.

Nearly every house in the village was damaged, some of them being completely unroofed.

An old travelling man known as "Paddy the Farmer" was found dead on the Lagore road by one of the villagers, Frank Fortune.

It was stated he died from exposure.

A cross was cut on an oak tree under which he was found.

Topic 6: Schools

Schools
There is a field known as "the school house Field" on the old road from Lagore to Cabinhill (called the Crushand) where there was a school in olden times. There was also a "hedge school" held in the house of Noah Birch. (Ned Gargan's old house, now demolished).

On the site of the present school was the famous Mr. Gillic's Accademy where boys came from all over Ireland.

Mr. Gillic's son, The Revd. – Gillic was a very learned young man having being raised to the Dunboyne chair in Maynooth College.

He died young and a plaque to his memory can be seen in Ratoath Catholic Church.

131

Ratoath Past and Present

Topic 7: Old Crafts (a)

Crafts:-
In the village several old crafts were carried on nearly all of which have now died out.
There were two forges, Gillic's now Foley's and Rourkes now Madden's. The latter is now converted into a shop.

Weaving
Weaving was carried on in the house occupied by the relatives of the late John Moore. The weavers were Robert and - Toole.

Tannery
There was also a Tannery in Ratoath.
There were two carpenter's Shops. Patrick Anderson's and Nicholas Murray.

Topic 7: Old Crafts (b)

Name   =   Kathleen Eiffe
Age   =   10 years
Address   =   Ratoath, Co. Meath

At one time there were two bakeries; one of them was owned by Eiffe's and the other by Gargan's. Eiffe's was where Costelo's shop is now and Gargan's is where the Post Office is now. There were also weavers by the name of Toole's. They lived on the school road somewhere about where Johney Madden's is now. There were also two trades of Nailers. One of them was James Nolan; he lived somewhere about Keogh's and the other was a Patrick Kane; he lived on the school.

EDUCATION

Topic 8: Nailer's Forge

Nailer's Forges

Writer   Katie Sherry
Class   VI
Age   14 years

Patrick Keane on the road above the school and _____ Nolan next where the butcher's shop is now, carried on the business of Nailers.

Lime was burned in Kilns in several places; one Kiln in ruins at Lagore in the lime kiln field. There was also an old building locally known as the Pigeon House in the field above the school which was probably a lime kiln. Mc Guley's carried on baking; this was where Mr. Costello has the shop now and also did Gargan's in the room in which the post-office is now. Shoemaking was also a trade in the ...

Topic 9a: Penal Days

Ratoath and District in the Penal days

Written by:-   Teresa Sherry
Class:-   VI
Age:-   13 years

During the Penal times Priest hunting was very rife around here. It was of course impossible for a priest to appear in public and great punishment was meted out to those who associated with them. At that time there lived in the Manor House of Ratoath a Protestant Gentleman (named Fitzpatrick) and in an upper room or attic he kept the Rev. Michael Plunkett P.P. As the priest was very old and feeble, a young man (James Ramsay) remained each night in the Shrubs and Laurels surrounding the house and, when the priest was required to attend anyone, he raised a ladder, which he kept in readiness for the purpose, to the small attic window and carrying the old decrepit priest on his back down the ladder brought him out on his errand of mercy. This young man was a close relation of Bruins where he lived and where all messages for the priest were sent and prayers said by congregations when possible. The house is standing and ...

Topic 9b: Penal Days

Written by = John Fitzpatrick
Class = VI
Age = 13 years

The Woodlands is a field situated on the School Road outside the Village of Ratoath. Long ago there was a Monastery there. During the Penal times it was destroyed and anything of value was taken. But the Nuns got all the Gold and Silver and melted it down on pans and hid it. There is a lot of hills in the field; it is said they are the remains of the Monastery. The field is owned by Mr. Corballas, Ratoath.

Topic 10a: Priest Hunting

Written by = Teresa Sherry
Class = VII
Age = 13 years

Long years ago there was a monastery in a place called the woodlands Ratoath; there were two priests living in it. There was a tree which was called the Red Cross Tree growing beside the monastery. The Danes were around about that time and hearing about the priests they went to them and asked them to give up the Catholic Religion but the priests would not consent.

And in order to make the priests suffer they tortured them and hanged them out of the tree and buried them under it. In later years the people have kept the custom in carrying the coffin around the tree before being buried.

This custom has recently ceased because the tree decayed and fell but the remains of the graves are to be seen yet.

Topic 10b: Priest Hunting
Name = Lillie Moore
Age = 14 years
Address = Tankardstown, Ratoath, Co. Meath

The most ancient Residence I know is the Manor House, it is situated just outside the village of Ratoath. It is a very large and beautiful building; it is a three-story house, on the third there is an old chapel in which the priests used to say mass in secret and hide from the priest-hunters in the Penal days. Outside there are two beautiful lawns and on them are many uncommon shrubs and plants which present owner Mr. Corbalis brought home when he was a captain in the British War. At the back of the house there is a big wood and in the wood flows a beautiful river.

Topic 11: Ratoath Moate
Name = Kathleen Sherry
Age = 13 years
Address = Ratoath, Co. Meath

In the vicinity of Ratoath there is an ancient place called Moate, and at the back of it a river flows near which the Danes fought many a battle.

There was an old Danish Queen who lived there; she died in a very short time and she was buried in the Moate.

Ratoath got its name by this old lady named Tógh. At the back of the Moate there is a metal slab, and it is said that if anybody move this slab they would die in a very short time.

EDUCATION

Patrick Keenan

A Successful Scholar of the Nineteenth Century

FRANCES MAHER

THE MOST DISTINGUISHED pupil of Ratoath School was Patrick Keenan. The site of the house where the family lived was, according to local information, opposite the school car park, on the Fairyhouse Road. As his name is not in the Baptism Register of the parish, we must assume that the family came here when Patrick was a young boy. There is a tradition that the family came from the Dunsany direction, but there is no mention of his name on the register there either. There is no doubt that Patrick began his educational career in the local school where Mr. Gillic taught at that time. The next mention of him is as a monitor (teacher) in the Central Model School in Dublin. He began his teaching career in Belfast and after a few years in that city, passed the examination for inspector. It is said that one of his first appointments was to inspect the school of his former teacher Mr. Gillic and that he asked to be excused. Soon afterwards, he was made Headmaster of the Central Model School itself, which was the most important school in Ireland. The fact that he was a man of outstanding ability was apparent in 1871, when, on the death of the Resident Commissioner of Education, Sir Alexander McDonnell, the one time monitor from Ratoath was appointed his successor. He appears to have been a born organiser and diplomat. His new office was an exacting one, but he managed to win the esteem of all parties. He improved the status of the teachers and re-organised the whole system. As a result, he was appointed to carry out a similar scheme in Malta.[1] In recognition of his services here, he was made a Knight Commander of the Order of St. Michael and St. George, a Companion of the Bath and a Privy Councillor. Such an accumulation of honours for an Irish Catholic in those days was singularly rare. His bust stands in the central position of the main hall of the Department of Education & Science,

---

[1] Dr. George Cassar, University of Malta, writing "History teaching in Malta" refers to the view held by Patrick Keenan in the late 19th century when investigating the situation of education in Malta that History should be one of the compulsory subjects in the Matriculation Examination (Keenan, 1880, p.108).

Marlborough Street, Dublin. It was the gift of the National teachers of Ireland, as a token of gratitude for his work on their behalf. The inscription on the plinth of the bust reads:

The Right Honourable
Sir Patrick Joseph Keenan
K. C. M. C. – C. E. – L.L.D.
(1826 – 1894)

Filled Various Offices in the Service of
The Commissioners of National Education.

Was Resident Commissioner from 1871 to
1894

The Authorities at the time would not allow it to be stated that it was the gift of the National Teachers of Ireland. Eventually, in 1961, the I.N.T.O. sought permission to have the omission rectified. Their request was granted.

Note: When researching we also discovered the following about Patrick Keenan:

(a) Sir Patrick Joseph Keenan's son, Sir Norbert Michael Keenan, was born on 30th January 1864 in Dublin. He was educated at Downside School, Somerset, England and Trinity College, Dublin. Sir Norbert Michael Keenan read law at King's Inn, Dublin, and the Middle Temple, London. He became a barrister in both England and Ireland. In time he became a prominent figure in both the legal and political life of Australia and was considered by many to be an able speaker with a high sense of honour. Like his father, he too was knighted (1948). He died on 24th April 1954.

(b) Sir Patrick Keenan spent his whole life in the service of Irish education and it has been said that for 30 years he had never taken a holiday.

EDUCATION

Ratoath National School

FRANCES MAHER

We do not have any historical records of "hedge-schools" in Ratoath, but rather those that came after them. However, one of the stories in the folklore collection included in this publication recounts that *"there is a field known as 'the school house Field' on the old road from Lagore to Cabinhill (called the Crushand) where there was a school in olden times. There was also a 'hedge school' held in the house of Noah Birch. (Ned Gargan's old house, now demolished)"*.

During the 16th Century, Patrick Plunkett the 7th Baron of Dunsany, who died in 1601, is reputed to have been educated in Ratoath. Mary Rose Carty and Malachy Lynch in their book entitled *"The Story of Dunsany Castle"*[1] state that *"Patrick was left a minor and his wardship was granted by Privy Seal, 1565, to Sir Christopher Barnewall"*.[2] They go on to state that *"Patrick was educated in the grammar school at Ratoath under the direction of a master named Staghens. He became renowned as a person of learning and set a standard for learned men. He was one of the Masters of the Guild of the Virgin Mary of Killeen."*[3]

More than 200 years later, in the 1780's, Dr. Patrick Plunkett visited Ratoath, where he found three Catholic schools in operation. Of the three schools mentioned by Dr. Plunkett, one of them must have been in Ratoath, the second in Killegland or Cookstown, but no one has indicated the locality of the third. There is a tradition that there was a school at the western end of the Bog Road in Powderlough. The *Second Education Report (1826)* describes three schools which may have been their successors. Two of these schools were kept by Thomas and Catherine Gillic, the parents of a distinguished Maynooth Professor. Their joint school was built on a site donated by Catherine Keogh, wife of John Keogh, in 1823 and was opened on 26th April 1824. This site has been in use ever since. John Keogh, of Catholic Emancipation fame, had an estate in Ratoath, but he lived in Mt. Jerome, Dublin.

At the time of erection, the 1824 school must have been a fine building. It cost £370. Of which the Kildare Place Society advanced £110. The balance was raised by Parish subscriptions. In 1825 the Society for Promoting the Education of the Poor of Ireland granted £50 to Fr. Carolan "towards building an addition." The school was managed by a committee of 15, which paid Mr. & Mrs Gillic £10 each. An additional £16 towards each teacher's salary was contributed by the pupils. At a later period, Mr. Gillic received boarders to his school, or academy, as it was called, who paid from £12 to £15 per annum. When the Assistant Commissioner of Education came to Ratoath on inspection in May 1856, he found the state

---

[1] Dunsany, 2000: Carty, Mary-Rose and Lynch, Malachy - *"The Story of Dunsany Castle"*. ISBN (978)-0-95173821-4.
[2] ibid
[3] ibid

EDUCATION

Ratoath National School

(Above): The two old semi-detached School Houses that were built in 1897 and demolished in the early 1990's

Ratoath National School, 1950

of instruction satisfactory, but added: "*the sleeping accommodation of the boarders is very bad. The Bedrooms are small and dirty, besides being badly lighted and ventilated. They are also shamefully over crowded, as is obvious that when four beds are placed in a room twelve feet by eight and a half, for three boys, the health and comfort of the children must suffer.*"

The third school was held in a thatched house given by James Corballis, Esq., who also paid the master £10 per annum. It ceased to exist soon after 1824.

Fr. Everard built the Teachers' residences in 1897 with a loan of £500 from the Board of Works. Fr. Everard bequeathed £300 for the repayment of this loan. These buildings are now gone but were located where the staff car park is at present.

In 1911, Fr. Everard organised the building of Ratoath National School, still in use today, which was constructed by a builder called Cromer, to replace that built by Fr. Carolan. It was built and furnished at Fr. Everard's own expense and cost almost £3,000. It was his princely gift to the Parish of Ratoath. The school is accordingly dedicated to him.

In 1929-30 the interior of the school was decorated and the exterior renovated. Similar work was carried out in 1949-50. In 1956 an additional half-acre was acquired from Miss Kate Dowling.

In 1959 there were 166 pupils at Ratoath School. In 1965 the figure dropped to 137 owing to the opening of Rathbeggan School. In 1959, 1962 and 1965 new extensions were added. Central heating and toilets were installed and an improved playground was provided at a cost of £15,000. In 1972 a field of approximately 7 acres was purchased for £8,000 from Mr. Larry Halton to accommodate yet another extension, which was completed and opened in 1978.

Ratoath National School, 1997

In 1997 due to the rapidly increasing population in the parish with its new housing developments of Mruigtuaithe, Clonkeen, Meadowbank Hill, The Old Mill and Fairyhouse Lodge, an additional extension had to be built. The school comprised of Classrooms, Computer Room, Prefabs, Library, General Purpose Room, Special Needs facilities, Wheelchair

Ratoath National School, 1997

facilities and ramps. In 2003, the number of pupils was approximately 860. There were 35 teachers in the school. Maurice Kearney had been a Teaching Principal since 1974. Deputy Principal was Ms. Audrey McCarthy. Again proposals had been sanctioned for the refurbishment and extension of the school and the building of a new 16 classroom Primary School on part of the existing school grounds.

In 2005 a new two-storey school was built on the same campus. This enabled the primary school accommodation to be split into a Junior and Senior school to cater for the rapidly expanding population of children in and around Ratoath. Subsequently, a number of extra pre-fabricated classrooms were required on the primary school campus in 2007 to accommodate new arrivals to the area.

Good News for Ratoath Schools [September 2008]

The following announcement was published in the Parish Bulletin of Holy Trinity Church, Ratoath on Sunday 28 September 2008.[4]

> "All in our parish have welcomed the news that Ratoath Junior National School and Ratoath Senior National School have been given the go ahead for their extensions. The Minister for Education and Science, Mr. Batt O'Keeffe T.D., has given approval for a 10 classroom extension, 3 special education tuition rooms, as well as an extension to the G.P. room for Ratoath Junior National School.
>
> A 4 class room extension and 4 special education tuition rooms have been granted for Ratoath Senior National School. He has also approved the redevelopment of the car park in the school grounds. When completed, the site on the Fairyhouse Road will cater for 1,000 pupils in the very best of facilities. All projects will now go to tender immediately and to construction in the New Year [2009]. While we have waited for a few years to hear this good news, much thanks must be expressed to the principals of the schools and their teaching staff and to the Boards of Management of both schools who have worked tirelessly on behalf of the pupils, teachers and parents to see this project reach this stage. We thank too the parents association for their support and assistance at all

---

4 http://www.ratoathparish.ie/parish-bulletin web page accessed on Sunday 28 September 2008.

EDUCATION   Ratoath National School

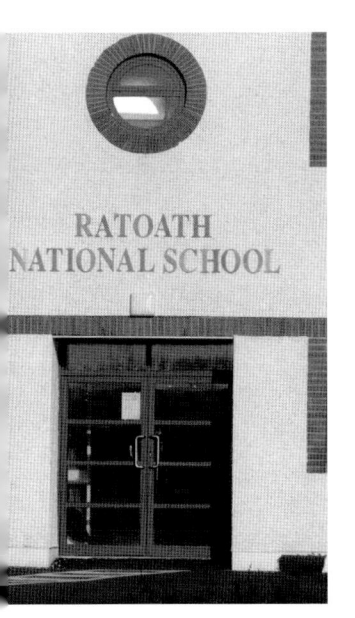

(Above left): Entrance to the new Ratoath   The two-story addition to Ratoath National School, 2005
National School built in 2005

times in helping us to progress the work to this point. We would also like to express our sincere thanks to our local public representatives for their constant representation on our behalf. In particular, we wish to thank Minister Mary Wallace T.D. who opened many doors for us with the Department, accompanied us on our many visits to the Planning and Building Unit of the Department in Tullamore and who kept in contact with the Department on an almost weekly basis"

Photographs from Earlier School Years

Ratoath Girls School, circa early 1920's

141

Ratoath National School, boys 1947

Back row, left to right: Mary Donnelly, Netta Flanagan, Mary Ryan, Patricia McLoughlin, Betty McLoughlin, Babs Mulvany, Rita Donnelly, Norah Carey and Philomena Eiffe.
Third Row, left to right: Mona Donnelly, Stephanie Conway, Kathleen McAndrew, Margo McLoughlin, Gretta Gillic, F. McAndrew, Brigid Mannering, Ita Mannering, Mona Brennan, Maura Moore and Ida Brennan.
Second Row, left to right: Bill Eiffe, Jimmy Maher, Johnnie Carey, Michael McAndrew, Tony Everard, Peter Carey, Pat Donnelly and Patrick Toole.
Front Row, left to right: Brian Everard, Tony Toole, Michael Maher, Joe White, Liam Gorman, Nicholas Kavanagh, Kevin Elliott, Nicholas Keogh and Michael McLoughlin.

Ratoath Senior Girls Class, circa 1930's.

Front Row L-R: Gretta Brady, Babs Sheridan, Eileen Ralph, Una Toole, May Fitzpatrick, Bridie Moore
2nd Row L-R: Bridie Lambe, Nancy Gorman, Ester Moore, Kathy Brennan, May Sherry, Bridget Boshell, May Dolan
3rd Row L-R: May Nulty, Molly Nulty, Peggy McCarthy, Annie Sherry, Ita Ralph, Catherine (Tally) McGrane, Teresa Reilly

EDUCATION　　　　　　　　　　　　　　　　　　　Ratoath National School

Ratoath Boys School, circa 1936

Front Row L-R: Brendan Ralph, Luke Rafferty, Jimmy Brady,
2nd Row L-R: Sean Fitzpatrick, Andy Eiffe, Joe Elliott, Joe Farrell, Paddy Nolan
3rd Row L-R: Christy Lambe, Johnnie Smith, Gerry Keogh, Frank Bryan, Jim Cowley

Ratoath Boys School, circa 1930 (Below)

Front Row L-R: Tom Cowley, Phil Brady, Frank Bryan?, Jimmy Ralph, Jem Cowley, Eddie Smith, Dessie Donnelly, Brendan Ralph, Joe Elliott, George Elliott, Jimmy Reilly, Paddy Everard, Desmond Toole, Bud Casey, Billy Woods, Peter Brennan, Oliver Doran
2nd Row L-R: Donal Moore, Batty Donoghue, Kevin Reilly, Paddy Dolan, Noel Casey, Pat Donnelly, Richie McGrane, Jimmy Woods
3rd Row L-R: Sean Everard?, Mickey Brien?, Billy Nolan, Jim Brindley, Johnny Madden, Jimmy Donnelly, Jimmy Lambe, Tommy Dolan, Mickie Elliott?, Christy Foley, Dinny McCarthy, Jack Casey, Joe Gorman, Joe Moore, Luke Dunne, Jimmy Reilly, Raymond Brady, ? Johnny Murray
4th Row L-R: Joe Murray, Johnny McCarthy, Paddy Meagher, Hughie McCarthy

Church Choir, circa 1958

Front Row: Gerry Geraghty, Pat Browne, Benny Browne, Kathleen Walls, Sean Lynskey, Joan Kinsella, Olive Flood
Back Row: Fr. John Cogan, Ellen Wherity, Mary O'Hare, Frances Kinsella, Seamus Gaughan, Anne Maher, Josie Donnelly, Ollie White, Mary Gannon, Jane Gannon, Anne Lynskey, Fr. William Kirley, Maura Walls, Pat Walls

Recollections on School in the 1940's

In the 1940's children walked miles to school. At the time Mrs. Staunton taught Junior Infants, Infants and First Class. Mrs. Dowling taught 2nd Class. Mr. McEntaggart taught 3rd and 4th Class. Mr. J.J. Kelly taught 5th, 6th and 7th Class. — GERARD RALPH

EDUCATION

An Introduction to Ratoath School 2001

Fr. Everard Memorial National School Ratoath – A School Tour
"Welcome to our school, tá fáilte romhat."

TAIDH McNAMARA, Teacher

As you enter the school grounds you can't help but notice the wildlife garden. This feature is not only attractive, but also an important learning tool. The children discover and investigate their natural environment. The school has won many major awards in this area, winning the E.S.B. Environmental Award All-Ireland Champion, to mention but one. You will notice that there are both composting schemes and can recycling schemes run in the school. The pupils, together with their teachers very successfully manage these schemes. The school promotes recycling throughout the school. The grounds are extensive; the pitches are also used by the many clubs who enjoy these facilities. The yards and pitches are much needed places of recreation for the pupils; they are used for the wide and varied sports activities taught in the school.

The very positive atmosphere in the school is apparent as you go around the classes. As Bryan Mac Mahon the Kerry writer/ teacher would say *"the blessed rapport"* between pupils and teachers is intact. The children get a wide variety of opportunities to develop. They are encouraged to be confident and celebrate their achievements.

The school is outward looking, forging links with schools in Finland, Denmark, Wales, and Ireland. The School has also taken part in many cultural exchanges. Meiko from Japan and Elisa Pettinlli from Italy, both gave us valuable insights into their culture. Our own culture is actively promoted in all its forms throughout the school and in extra-curricular activities. There are Irish evening classes for adults; the emphasis is on basic skills. So why not come along and "**Labhair Gaeilge Linn.**"

The School has benefited massively from the active interest and contributions of the Parents' Association. The classrooms are well equipped and have the latest modern technology. There is an Information Technology room so vital in providing pupils' I.T. skills. Parents have also been very generous with their time in so many ways; a Paired Reading Scheme and yard supervision are among some of the practical ways parents provide support. *Míle Buíochas* to all those who help out in so many ways.

The School Government is a body of pupils elected by their peers. It has an important role to play. It provides pupils with a platform to learn many valuable organisational skills and to make their voice heard. The government organise many events throughout the year including fun day, copper trail, sale of work, and talent competitions to name but a few. Much of the money collected has been sent to Fr. Joe to help in the marvellous work he is doing in Africa.

There are many extra-curricular activities available. The School Choir works hard all year, they provide musical accompaniment for Holy Communion and Confirmation services. Other activities include Gaeilge, Ballet, French, Speech and Drama, Art, Story-telling, Chess, Irish Dancing, Music, Gardening, G.A.A., Soccer, Athletics, Choir, Irish Music and many more.

EDUCATION

Salmon of Knowledge Sculpture

RATOATH HERITAGE GROUP

IN MAY 2008 a standing stone sculpture entitled "Ratoath Salmon" was unveiled at Ratoath Senior School by the Cathaoirleach of Meath County Council, Councillor Nick Killian, to celebrate the process of education. The beautiful Celtic inspired work which stands 2 meters high has been permanently installed in the forecourt of the school. The story of the *"Salmon of Knowledge"* is one which is familiar to all of us. This work was commissioned by the school through the Per Cent for Art Scheme[1].

The Wexford based artist Daniel Cullen is well-known for depicting Celtic, Christian and Pre-Christian mythical tales through his large 'standing stone' sculptures, built by hand using stoneware architectural clay.

Artist Daniel Cullen, School Principal Maurice Kearney Ratoath Senior National School and three members of the School Drama Group in May 2008

---

[1] The Per Cent for Art Scheme was established in Ireland by the Office of Public Works during 1978. It remains a funding mechanism to support the commissioning of works of public art, whereby one per cent of the overall cost of a construction project, such as the extension of Ratoath National School in 2005, is ring-fenced and allocated for an art project, like the *Salmon of Knowledge Sculpture*.

Ratoath Past and Present

Ratoath Senior National School Celebrates All-Ireland Drama Competition Winners

Ratoath Senior National School Drama Group won the 2008 All Ireland Drama Competition with their dramatisation of *"The Salmon of Knowledge"*.

Above: Ratoath Senior National School Drama Group pictured here in May 2008 with Daniel Cullen's "Ratoath Salmon".

EDUCATION

RATHBEGGAN National School

FRANCES MAHER

For years the people in the Rathbeggan area had complained that they were being neglected as some children had to travel distances of from three to five miles to the nearest school.

As a first step towards securing a school, it was necessary to convince the Department of Education of the need for one. A site comprising one acre was purchased from Mr. Crean. The Contractor was Mr. C. Martin. A survey of population, potential pupils, etc had to be made and eventually sanction was given for the erection of a two-room school for 64 pupils. The school was opened on 1st April 1961, with about 50 pupils in attendance.

The average number increased gradually, until it reached the 90 mark. To provide accommodation for this number, either a third room had to be built or temporary measures taken. In view of the usual delays in building contracts, the latter course was taken. A very comfortable pre-fabricated structure measuring 29ft. by 10ft. was provided in 1964.

In 1972 a third classroom was added to the original structure. The builder was Mr. Patrick Donnelly, Lagore Cross, Ratoath.

Mr. Boland was the first Principal, succeeded by Mr. Brendan Bric, and then Mr. Michael o'Carroll. In 1981 work began on an extension to the existing building, as the average attendance had now risen to 165. A P.E. hall, 3 large classrooms, a remedial classroom, staffroom, office, extra toilets etc., were added. The architect was Mr. Edward Smith and the builders were Alright Construction Ltd., of Skryne. Work began in 1981 and concluded in 1982. The school re-opened on 4th October 1982. The total cost of this renovation was £232,416.

In 1975 there were 78 pupils in the Rathbeggan School. In 2003, there were seven classrooms in the school. The number of pupils was 168.

Ms. Miriam Toole was Teaching Principal from 1982 to December 2002 when she retired. Mr. Kieran Rushe became the new Teaching Principal. Currently there are 190 pupils (2008), 11 teachers, including 2 resource teachers and one part-time learning support teacher.

Rathbeggan National School Award

2007: Rathbeggan National School students displaying their Pride of Place Award and Certificates pictured with their Principal, Mr. Kieran Rushe, Ms. Catherine Clinton (Science Co-ordinator) and Chairman of Meath County Council, Nick Killian, who presented the awards on behalf of Meath County Council in November 2007

EDUCATION

St. Paul's National School Ratoath

MORAG McGOWAN (School Principal)

St. Paul's National School was established in Ratoath in September 2005 in response to the growing demand for school places in the area. It was originally to be based in Tankardstown on parish land but the site was considered too dangerous, and access too difficult. A local landowner stepped in and offered land to the parish, on which to site the school, in Jamestown.

Parents and teachers worked hard during the summer to get everything organised. So, even though the temporary building wasn't ready for the 1st September 2005; the school, with Ms. Morag McGowan and Ms. Elizabeth Ward and 29 very excited children, was ready for action. With a new uniform and a school crest designed by one of our parents we flew the flag of St. Paul's for our first month, in the Hall of Ratoath Junior National School.

When we moved down to our temporary buildings we had two classrooms and a hall, a playground and some grass area. In 2006 we had enlarged the playground and reseeded the grass area as a play area. We had grown to five full-time teachers, including the Principal, one part-time teacher, two special needs Assistants and 102 children.

In 2007 we grew even more with ten full-time teachers, including the Principal, one part-time teacher, two special needs assistants and 184 children. We look set to continue to grow into the future and we will soon begin work on our permanent 24 classroom school, on our current site.

The School crest was designed by one of the parents.

The *background colour*, Azure blue, signifies "Strength & Loyalty."
The *shield* signifies "Protection & Faithful Service"
The *two horses* signify "Readiness for Duty"
Significant to the Deed – due to Fairyhouse
Recognising that there are now two National Schools in Ratoath
The *Cross* depicts a Bishop's Cross
The *Chevron* signifies "Protection"
The *colour Red* signifies "Strength & Magnanimity"

Ratoath Past and Present

September 2005: The first pupils of St. Paul's National School with their teachers Ms. Morag McGowan and Ms. Elizabeth Ward.

October 2007: Staff and pupils of St. Paul's National School, Ratoath.

EDUCATION

Ratoath College

MÁIRE NI BHRÓITHE, PRINCIPAL

RATOATH COLLEGE opened its doors on August 29th 2005 in Fairyhouse Racecourse. The school had no permanent accommodation and thanks to the generosity of Fairyhouse racecourse a home was found for the 66 first pupils and the 7 staff. For two years the students were taught in the corporate suite, using the jockey's weigh room as an art room and the vast grounds of the racecourse as their playing pitches. On Wednesday afternoons the school moved to Dunshaughlin Community College where used their practical facilities for subjects such as Science, Woodwork and Home Economics. During their time on the racecourse, the school had many well known visitors including Dr Garret Fitzgerald, Senator Fergal Quinn, Mary Davies CEO of the Special Olympics, John Lonergan Governor of Mountjoy Prison, Gay Byrne and Charlie Bird from RTÉ.

On June 1st 2007 the students, teachers and their families walked with the Garda band to their new home in Jamestown Ratoath. They planted an oak tree which had first been planted in Fairyhouse and buried a time capsule full of memories of their time in Fairyhouse. This time capsule will be opened in 2028.

Students of Ratoath College celebrating their last day of school at Fairyhouse Racecourse on June 1st 2007

Ratoath Past and Present

On August 29th 2007 (two years to the day that the school originally opened) 311 students and 44 staff members entered the new premises in Jamestown. They are full of hope for a bright future for this school. Their new premises is a state of the art building with 6 technology rooms, 5 science labs, 3 computer labs, up to date Information and Communications Technology (ICT) facilities throughout the school and some interesting architectural features. The building is built for 900 pupils and over the coming years pupil numbers will increase to fill the building.

New First Years of Ratoath College at Jamestown on August 20th 2007
(Photo: Courtesy Seamus Farrelly)

FAMILY AND FRIENDS

The Barker Family

PATRICIA BARKER

MY HUSBAND Jimmy and I live on the Fairyhouse Road. We have three daughters Veronica, Deirdre and Siobhan who have all left home at this stage. We live next door to the cottage previously owned by my parents Tom and Catherine McLoughlin. They lived in the village originally and moved to the cottage in 1938. I was born there - brought into the world by Nurse O'Mahony who lived on the Curragha Road (adjacent to the present day Foxbrook Estate) and who went about her duties on a high black bike. My father was a very kind jovial man who liked nothing better than a pint and a chat about the horses. He attended Fairyhouse races as long as his legs would carry him there. My mother was a very hospitable woman and the kettle would go on as soon as one stepped through the door. There were four of us in family - Eileen, Sheila, Tommy and myself. Eileen died in 1964 and Tommy in 2006.

My husband's parents Kit and Brigid moved to Curkeen on the Bog Road in the early 1930's along with their two eldest children Paddy and Joan. Christy, Jimmy, Sean and Alice were born there. The family later moved to Dunboyne where Nellie, Peter, Tommy, Oliver, Joe, Ann, Brendan, Dermot and Breda duly arrived. Sean went on to become a successful jockey - the highlight of his career being the winning of the *Queen Mother Champion Chase* at Cheltenham 1975 on a horse called *Lough Inagh* trained by Jim Dreaper. Sadly both Brendan and Sean have both passed away.

On reflection my childhood although not in any way privileged was nonetheless a happy one and the freedom we had would be envied by many youngsters to-day.

FAMILY AND FRIENDS

The Brady Family

CHRISTOPHER JOHNNY BRADY

My GRANNY Therese Foley was a McGoldrick from Dunshaughlin she was an only child and she had two Uncles who owned the Post Office in Dunshaughlin. Unfortunately they were struck down with TB therefore she was the end of the line.

Theresa married Christy Foley from Dunshaughlin and they settled in Ratoath around 1905 on the site that is now Brady's Garage. They had 7 healthy children and at least 3 others that died at birth. They ran a shop in the village, had stables, farm sheds and a few acres of land in the Reask (on Skryne Road). Christy was a Farrier so when you went to him you could get farm fresh milk, get a horse shod, a home produced bacon or a leg of lamb. I suppose a convenience store in its day. They claimed to have had the second car in Ratoath after the Rogers family.

Their children's names were Maud, Vera, Tommy, Sheila, Christy and Brenda. Maud never married and ran a shop in Ratoath up until her health failed. She died in the nursing home in Ratoath in 1978. For her hobbies she made butter and won All-Ireland Gold medals for her efforts. She also made the tea at Kilmoon Hall for over twenty years. Kilmoon in those days was a place where many a happy couple met.

All of Christy and Therese's other children married and had children of their own and between them they had 19 children (my brothers and cousins). I never met Christy, my Grandad, he died in 1960 but they named me after him, I now have a son Christopher, so he at least the forth in a row. Therese died in 1977. My mother Sheila is the last remaining of Christy and Therese Foley's children and Sheila is in the good hands of Silver Stream nursing home where she celebrated her 91st Birthday on 2nd January 2008. Sheila like all her brothers and sisters was born in the house over the shop.

My father Jim Brady was born in 1909 in County Cavan and left school at 11 years of age. His older brothers, Andrew and John Pat, were active members of the IRA and fought against the Black 'n Tans. Jim was one of five boys and five girls; he left home at an early age. He successfully tendered for a contract to plaster Longford Court House. This he did almost 80 years ago, after that he was never seen in Cavan again except on the occasional visit.

Most of Jim's working life was in England or working for English Companies abroad. His travels took him to places such as, Entebbe, Khartoum, Cairo, Beirut, and Belgrade. He worked on a dam over the river Nile at Lake Victoria. Today, electricity produced at that Dam (Owen Falls) is still a major contributor for Kenya, Nigeria and Uganda. In 1955/56 the British were expelled from Aden and Jim, Sheila and baby Michael were on the first plane out, stopping off at Belgrade for refueling. This was an opportunity for President Tito's PR to kick in and take photos of him offering refuge to the English. Who was first down the steps (you guessed it) *'Paddy'!* ... to be photographed ... (poor Tito)?

Jim and his brother John Pat built 56 houses in the 1930's for Meath County Council. These houses can be seen on Fairyhouse Road, Ballybin, Dunshaughlin and Dunboyne. They took digs in Foleys house in Ratoath where Jim met Sheila, but being a cute Cavan man he did not pop the question for another 7 or 8 years! Jim and Sheila had 4 boys and during their travels baby's popped out all over the place, such as in Aden, The Middle East, Dublin, England and England again. Indeed when Michael was born in Aden there was a party for three days and people came from miles around. A white baby was rare but one with red hair rarer still!

Jim & Sheila built a petrol station garage and home in Ratoath Village in 1962. The second day after opening he had to stay home from Sheila's Bridesmaid's wedding, her niece to mind his business. The day's takings were £3-10-6 or THREE POUNDS TEN SHILLINGS AND SIXPENCE.

A Memory: Ratoath National School in the sixties had four teachers and about 120 children, no mains water, no buses and the only two families that traveled to school by car were the Farrells of Harlockstown & Meaghers who were earlier owners of the public house now known as "The Auld Stand".

Jim & Sheila Brady's 40th Wedding Anniversary

FAMILY AND FRIENDS

Christy and Kathleen Martin – The Bungalow, Ratoath

NOEL AND SONNY MARTIN

CHRISTY MARTIN was born in 1902 and reared at the Riggins, Dunshaughlin. He married Kathleen O'Connor of Greenpark, Dunshaughlin, in 1934, whose mother was Bridgid Robinson who herself was born and reared in the village where the entrance to the Venue Theatre now stands. Kathleen had attended Ratoath National School. She was a noted Handball player and a Camogie player who played many times for Meath.

Christy and Kathleen had five children: Rita, Noel, Moira, Sonny and Nuala. Rita went to England to train as an SRN Nurse. She came back and trained in Holles Street as a midwife and later she became a district midwife. Many mothers in Ratoath say 'Rita delivered my children'. Moira and Nuala worked in Ratoath Post Office. Noel and Sonny followed their father into the Building and Joinery Business.

In the late 1920-1930 Christy was an appointed contractor to the Government and carried out work for the Justice Department, Education Department and The Irish Land Commission. He also worked on the Court Houses in Dunshaughlin and Kells. In 1935 he constructed Land Commission houses at Ennistown, Porterstown Ratoath, Lagore, Mooretown and Greenpark, Dunshaughlin. Land Commission houses continued to be built through the war years (1939-1945) right up to the mid 1960's. Other contracts included Clarke's pub bought by John Gogan in 1947 (now the Ratoath Inn). In 1948, Christy raised the roof from what was then a single storey building to make it a two-storey as it is today without ever taking off a slate or a gutter or disturbing the business in any way. The work was carried out with a series of jacks.

Christy & Kathleen Martin on their wedding day in 1934. Also in the photograph is the best man Kathleen's brother, Richard O'Connor

In 1948, Fr. Cogan came to Ratoath and he immediately engaged Christy to carry out construction work, as there was a lot of parish work to be done. One of the first things was to develop a new cemetery so Christy started building a new wall and entrance. The Mission Cross that stands as a focal point in the cemetery was safely removed from the main entrance path at the Church and erected in the cemetery instead.

The Parochial Hall: The Parochial Hall as it was then called was in bad repair. An extension and tearooms were added and a full maple floor fitted. Afterwards was considered to be one of the best dance floors in the country.

The Church: Christy, his sons and staff embarked on a major refurbishment of the Church, which included the addition of a second set of altar rails and the segregation side rails. Three quarters of the Church had large black flags just laid on soil and that area had to be excavated to a depth of 2ft (or 600mm) and a new maple floor laid. The Church was also fitted with new oak seats. It was discovered that there was a bad infestation of woodworm in the ceiling and to beat this 15mm of timber was removed from all sides of the large king trusses in the ceiling and the entire area then treated.

The Marian Shrine

In 1953, Christy Martin set about designing and building a shrine for the Marian Year in 1954. John Crane from Roscommon prepared the mosaic work. The actual craftsman who worked on the mosaic was Romeo Bitali. There was great joy in the Parish in anticipation of the new and colourful shrine. The I.C.A. of the time ran a Supper Dance to raise funds and it was very successful. The figure of the Little Flower on one side was donated by Eamon White, Kilrue, and the depiction of the Pope on the other side was donated by Hilda Rogers. The blessing of the Shrine in the Marian year, 1954, was an occasion many people will remember. The Shrine was erected on a site donated by the Rogers family on the site which originally was that of the weighing scales.

Grotto – During construction in 1954.
R-L: Christy Martin Senior, Romeo Bitali, Fr. John Cogan P.P., Declan Crane (Son of John Crane) and John Crane.

Augustinian Nursing Home (now Silver Stream Nursing Home): In 1950 the Augustinian Sisters came to Ratoath Manor. One Saturday afternoon my father, Christy and myself (Noel) went down to repair a floorboard. From there we continued to do repair work throughout the building. The Manor House was in bad repair. The front of the Nursing Home where the lawn now is was full of dense shrubbery and an old stone wall surrounding the site that was half broken down was removed and a new wall, railings and two entrance gates were constructed. Also erected were the Shrine to the Sacred Heart and the Shrine to the Blessed Virgin that remains to this day in the courtyard. A three-acre garden was walled in. The produce from the garden meant that the Nuns were self-sufficient. We renovated the main house and put extensions to the rear and were constantly employed there for 12 years.

School Works: Rathbeggan School was built in 1960 by Christy Martin. Rathbeggan was an 'out post' in the parish at that time and the location of the school was questioned by some. After three years the foresight of Fr. Cogan proved all the sceptics wrong and since then the school has continued to develop. In the past 60 years the Martin family also completed schools in Rolestown, Stillorgan and Bray, and carried out remedial work on the schools at Batterstown and Ratoath.

As Ratoath and Ashbourne were one Parish in the 1960's Ashbourne Church was renovated and a new gallery was installed. Also the old school was modernised and tearooms were added to what is now the Community Hall in Ashbourne.

Martin Family Home
The Martin family home was built on a site on the Well Road in 1927. It was the first timber framed and timber-clad house in Meath. It had three bedrooms, running water and a bathroom. Our father Christy died 7th December 1964 aged 62 and mother died in October 1966.

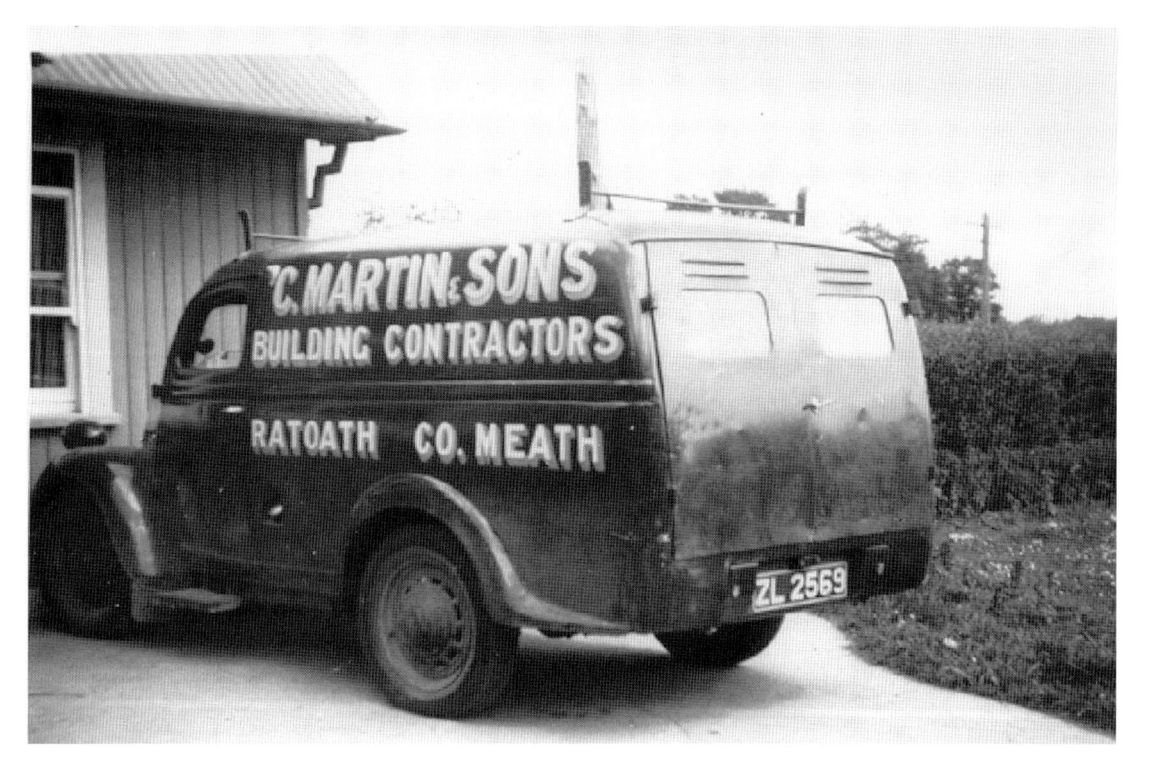

Martin's Van circa 1950s

The home place became the family home of Sonny and Florence Martin. One day in February 1969 during a storm an E.S.B. fault occurred in the village and the house and contents were burnt to the ground. Items lost in the fire were £70 cash and a new set of football jerseys, the property of Ratoath Harps. It was a terrible loss at the time. Just think how far the Harps have come since then! A year later a new bungalow was built on the same site.

After the death of our father we concentrated mainly on the Joinery Works for over 30 years to our retirement in September 1998. The business then went to Thomas O'Connor, my cousin's son, who worked with me for over 20 years. The Joinery Business still runs very successfully in the Ashbourne Industrial Estate.

The picture on the right (Courtesy: *The Irish Times*) shows Christy Martin (Senior) driving his Hudson Super Six car, registration number ZE 1521, on the bend in front of the Manor House, 16th December 1952.

FAMILY AND FRIENDS

Conway Family Fairyhouse Road

NOEL CONWAY

My great-grandfather Laurence Dowling was born in 1817. I am not sure if he was from Ratoath. His major claim to fame in our family is that he married late in life to Anne Waters from Dunboyne who was thirty-six years his junior. He fathered their youngest child also Laurence (Larry) the only boy in 1894 when he was seventy-seven years of age and his wife was forty-one years of age. They lived on the Fairyhouse Road where they raised five children one of whom was my grandmother Roseanna. The house was demolished only a few years ago, to make way for the entrance to Seagrave Park. In latter years, locals would know this as Larry Halton's house.

My grand-aunt Alice married Tim Guiney from Kerry, they lived in the house and worked the farm, which is now Seagrave Park up to the late 1950s when they sold it and moved to Maynooth.

My grandmother Roseanna was born and reared in the house on the Fairyhouse Road. As a teenager, she went to work as a domestic servant for the O'Connor Donn in Kerry where she met her future husband Patrick Keane who was a member of the R.I.C. They married in Ratoath 1917 and returned to the Ratoath in 1967 to celebrate their 50th wedding anniversary. They lived in Ratoath at some time in their married life as my mother Aileen attended Ratoath National School. An interesting point here is that her sister Catherine was at the time involved in the War of Independence as a courier for Michael Collins.

Catherine, known as Ciss, worked as a priest's housekeeper in Donore for a Fr. Flynn. This was a perfect cover for her to carry messages and orders to the North Dublin and East Meath area. The Black and Tans suspected her and raided the house on the Fairyhouse Road on several occasions. The stories in the family are that she hid firearms behind the wainscoting and they were never discovered. On one occasion when the Tans searched the house she hid the important letters she was carrying in the blankets of my grandmother's new born baby, luckily the officer in charge would not let them search the baby. When Fr. Flynn, her employer, died he bequeathed her a piece of ground at the back of Ratoath National School, years later she donated this land to the parish and this allowed the school to begin its first expansion in the early 1960s. Ciss died in 1975 and is buried in Ratoath. She is the only local person that I know of who was buried with full military honours.

My mother's uncle Larry who was born in 1894 lived next door to us on Glascarn Lane. To Larry his house was his castle even though it had no electricity, hardly any natural light, only one room, thick mud walls and a tin roof. Larry referred to himself as Larry Doolan as he thought the name Dowling was too grand! When he was a child Larry had an accident or fall which caused him to have one leg 6 inches shorter than the other; as kids we always

The house where Tim & Alice Guiney lived. It was later owned by Larry Halton and was demolished in 2004 to make way for the entrance to the new Seagrave Park development.

thought he was cranky; maybe this was the reason. His social life was his nightly walk with his severe limp to the village hot spot at that time which was Maud Foleys shop (pre Molly Talty days). He stood at the counter for a couple of hours, chatted, and gossiped with Maud or whoever would come into the shop. He never worked that I know of and he died in 1973.

My grand aunt Elizabeth married Peter Lynch a master stonemason from Skryne. He used to regale us with stories of Corbalton Hall where he worked as a young man in the 1920s. I am sure he would be delighted to see the restoration job done by Pat McDonagh.

FAMILY AND FRIENDS

Costello's Family Grocery Shop

MAY RYAN (NÉE COSTELLO)

JAMES COSTELLO'S family grocery shop, near the entrance gates to the grounds of the Holy Trinity Church (opposite Ryan's pub) was one of the main business establishments in Ratoath during the 1940's and 1950's. This was formerly a licensed premises owned by James and Kate McAuley. In the 1920's the Government revoked the license.

On the death of James, Kate's niece Julia Yourell came to live with her. Julia, who was born at Blackbull, Dunboyne, stayed with her aunt for a number of years.

On the death of Kate, Julia bought the house and started a grocery business. In 1936, she married John Costello of Brittas Bay, Co. Wicklow, and together they ran a thriving family grocery business for about 30 years. They had one daughter May.

Both John and Julia always took an active part in all parish activities and were involved in the many changes that took place in the parish over the years. In 1970 they retired from business and went to live in Dublin. They are both buried in the local cemetery.

Right: James and Kate McAuley with Julia Yourell.

FAMILY AND FRIENDS

The Dolan Family

PADDY DOLAN

BOTH MY PARENTS were from Co. Meath. My mother, Alice Smyth, was born in Ratoath in 1885 and my father, Patrick Dolan, was born in 1888 in Dunderry. My father came to live in Ratoath when he was just a boy. He worked for Fr. Everard in the Parochial House in the 1900's.

On the 26th November 1913 my parents were married. Sometime after that my father worked as a Chauffeur to the Rogers family. Our family lived in Rogers' yard in an old cottage where the Ratoath Pharmacy is situated today.

The stables in Rogers' yard were always jammed full of stunning horses, particularly when the Easter meetings at Fairyhouse came around each year. Some of these horses ran in the Irish Grand National. On race day, their owners walked them up the Bridle Path to Fairyhouse and some of them came back champions! As a young boy in 1938-39, I remember having the pleasure of sitting on one of the champion horses that came back to the yard; it was either *Shaun Peel* or *Clare County*. These were great horses at the time.

My parents had five children namely Bernard (Benny), Thomas (Tommy), May, Alice and Patrick (me). Benny (1915 - 1974) won a scholarship to St. Finian's College, Mullingar. He captained a winning team for the College in the All-Ireland College's Championship Final and later played football with Skryne Senior team and hurling with Ratoath. Benny worked as a representative of the Irish Life Insurance company. He often walked Jack Browne's greyhound around the Crushen (road from Lagore X to the High Crossroads on the Skryne Road).

Tommy Dolan (1918 - 2000) played Gaelic Football for Ratoath and throughout his live was an avid follower of Gaelic games. He was the Secretary of the GAA Club for many years. Tommy married Bridie White of Ashbourne in 1957. They have three sons Brian, Martin and Philip. Philip played hurling and was a fine goalkeeper *"saving our bacon"* in the goals many a time. Tommy was the local Postmaster in Ratoath for over 20 years until his retirement in 1989. He has three grandchildren Kevin, Andrew and Bevan.

May (1917 – 1974) played Camogie and with the help of Ann Gorman set up Ratoath Camogie Club. When she was working and living in Dublin she came home for the weekends unless Ratoath were playing Ashbourne during the week then she would cycle from Dublin to play with the team and then cycle back into Dublin again. On one occasion Joe White asked my mother *"How is May?"* She replied *"Fine"*. My mother wondered why he asked. Then Joe went on to say *"Well May got a right cut to the head last night."* When May came home the following Saturday with a new hair style my mother immediately knew why!

My sister Alice (1924 - 1999) stayed at home to help my mother in the house. She too was a keen follower of GAA, playing Camogie along side May and watching my brothers and I playing hurling in Ratoath.

I was born in Ratoath in February 1922. In 1950 I set up a butcher's shop and ran it until my retirement in 2000. My passion in sport is hurling and athletics. I competed in long

Paddy & Alice Dolan (Senior)

Left to right: The Dolan Family - Tommy, Alice, Paddy, May and Benny

distance cross country running and played hurling for Ratoath in numerous positions throughout my hurling career. As an active member of the Ratoath Club I trained many hurling Ratoath teams, one of which was the winning senior hurling team that beat Dunboyne in the 1963 Meath final and was Chairperson and Treasurer of Ratoath Club for many years.

In the 4th September 1960 I married Margaret (Gretta) O'Brien from Baltrasna, Ashbourne. We had five children Claire, Margaret, Paul, Miriam and Padraig. Claire is Postmistress of Ratoath Post Office and was also a keen Camogie player like her Aunt May. Claire played for Kilbride Camogie Club and her daughter Mairead is keeping the family tradition alive by playing for Kilmessan Camogie Club and Ratoath Ladies Football Club. She represented Ratoath and Meath in the Community Games Under-14 Long Puck for 3 years in a row. Her other keen interests include Ratoath Scouts, and competing in Show Jumping, Hunter Trials and One-Day Eventing.

Margaret is married and living in Westmeath. She also played Camogie for Kilbride. Paul now runs the butcher shop in Ratoath and he played hurling for Ratoath for many years and won a junior medal in 1999. Miriam is married and is working and living in Navan. She was a Scout Leader to the local, 9th Meath Ratoath Scout unit. Padraig, formerly a postman, now works on garden maintenance. He is married and living locally. He also played hurling for Ratoath at a young age. Today Gretta and I live on the Fairyhouse Road in Ratoath and we have six grandchildren Mairead, Rebecca, Patrick, Oisin, Heather-Mai and Jane.

FAMILY AND FRIENDS

Donnelly Family, Fairyhouse Road

ANNE DONNELLY

JACK DONNELLY and Maggie Keogh married in the 1940's. They lived in Ratoath village for a few years before moving up the Fairyhouse Road. They had one daughter, Anne, and four sons, Paddy, Tony, Christopher and Dick. Christopher and Tony died tragically in car accidents in 1973 and 1982 respectively.

Jack lived beside his brother Dick, his wife Chris and family. Anthony and Aggie Donoghue and family were their neighbours on the other side. Jack died in 1982 and Maggie died in 1989.

Donnelly-Kilcline Family Wedding on 22nd August 1970

L-R: Richard (Dick), Jack & Maggie Donnelly, Tony Donnelly (groom,) Patricia Donnelly (bride, nee Kilcline), Mary, James & Josephine Kilcline.

FAMILY AND FRIENDS

Donohoe Family

AGGIE DONOHOE

We left Belmullet, Co. Mayo, in 1953 to come to Co. Meath. With us were my husband Anthony's father and mother, David and Catherine, and our five children – David, Mary, Willie, Tony, and Kathleen who was only six weeks old. We came with two other families: the Barretts who went to live in Navan and the Healys who went to live in Balrath, between Slane and Ashbourne. We had five more children after coming to Ratoath: Alice, Patrick, Vincent, Ger and Breda.

I left behind in Mayo my mother, two sisters and two brothers. It was a big change from Mayo to Meath in the 1950's but we soon made friends and got to know the Careys, Stauntons and Walshes, who came here a few years before us. Our nearest neighbours were May and Joe Geraghty and a family of Careys who lived in an old house across from where David Donoghue lives now. Their names were Johnnie, Katie, Mary and James. None of them married. Further up towards Ratoath lived Maggie and Jack Donnelly and family (plus George, the dog), Chris, Dick Donnelly and family and Peg and Kevin White and their family.

Why We Moved from Mayo
In Mayo we all lived on small farms which were self-supporting to a certain degree but from May to December each year the men, including my husband, went to England to seek work and the women remained at home looking after the farm and the family. When the Land Commission asked families to move to Meath and Kildare in the 1940's and early 1950's a lot of families from Mayo agreed to move, including us. We exchanged our house and farm in Belmullet for a house and 27 acres of land here in Meath.

Once we moved here we started growing corn, wheat and sugar beet, for sale. Anthony also got seasonal work in Carlow pulling sugar beet for a few years. We always had a few cows, calves and hens. Eventually we expanded into dairying which meant that Anthony could remain at home and we made a living on the farm. Alfie Toole did the threshing (trashing) of the corn for us and he would always get a few men to help. It was a great day out for the children but a very busy one for the adults!

The Fairyhouse Road was so quiet and much narrower in the 1950's than it is today. There was very little traffic. The children safely played games and rode bikes on the roads and most of them walked or cycled to school.

FAMILY AND FRIENDS

Doran Family, Tankardstown

DORAN FAMILY

OLIVER DORAN was born in 1920. He and Ita Nulty were married in the Holy Trinity Church in Ratoath by the late Fr. Rispin on 11th September 1947. They had eight children, all of whom are residing in Ireland. They built a new home in the early 1950s at Kilbride Road, Tankardstown. Oliver worked for some time on dairy farms before moving on to work at Glascarn Stud farm. Afterwards he worked in the building industry in the Dublin area for many years.

Ita Doran (nee Nulty) was born in 1921. She worked for many years as a cook in the Meath region using basic recipes for traditional dishes and home baking, handed down from her mother, which she further developed and passed on to the next generation.

Oliver's father, Michael Doran, was an only child and he was born and reared in Ballymore Eustace, Co. Kildare. Michael worked with horses in Kildare and later at Slane Castle. He later moved to work at Glascarn Stud farm. He married local girl Rose Brennan. They had four children and they all attended the local National school in Ratoath.

Ita's father, Christy Nulty, was born and reared in Kilrue with his brothers and sisters. He worked on a local farm for a time. He then moved to Moyglare farm, now called Moyglare Manor, outside Maynooth. He married Christina Manning from Kilbride. They lived at Moyglare, for some years, where they had six children. They moved back to Ratoath, where all the children attended the local National school.

Micheál and Oliver have worked on the maintenance of Fairyhouse racecourse since their teenage years: Micheál for 39 years and Oliver for 34 years. In 2004 Fairyhouse changed its style of fences on the racecourse from the "Irish Type" to the "Cheltenham Type".

Micheál and Oliver Doran pictured at the final trimming of the "Irish Type" fences on the Fairyhouse Racecourse in 2004.

Doran Family 2007
Seated L-R: Ita, Micheál, Christina and Oliver Snr.
Standing L-R: Christy, Evelyn, Gerry, Rosemary, Oliver and Pauline

FAMILY AND FRIENDS

History of the Eiffe Family

NOEL EIFFE JUNIOR

THE EIFFE'S are one of the older families in Ratoath. The family can document their history in Ireland as far back as 1326. The name, which originated in Germany, can also be found spelt as Eiffen or Eife. The Family coat of arms consists of 'On a blue shield a chopped branch of an oak tree with two leaves and 3 acorns atop the shield; a five barred silver helmet of a duke or marquis with blue and gold mantling. Standing Erect from the helmet is the above oak branch.'

The Eiffe family name has a long association with the Port of Hamburg and was once associated with a Shipping Firm of *Eiffe & Co.* which represented ship owners from Central America to the Far East. This company was taken over in the 1980s.

The following entry is inserted in the 12th Century Bible held by the Eiffe Family of Hamburg:- '*Our predecessors came from Heleben and was a farmer, he had two sons one went to England and the other Johann Gottlies Eiffel went to Hamburg.*' (No match can be found for this location, Heleben, but it may be a misspelling of Hemleben, which is located west of Leipzig).

All the Eiffe's in Ireland and England are believed to be descendant from this individual. In a record from *The Keeper of Public Records* in Ireland there is listed in 1542 a Morgan Eiffe, who arrived in Ireland via London.

In 1641, at the height of the Cromwellian War, the following entry was made in the Survey of Meath: *William Eiffe is listed as having his lands valued as £20 confiscated by the Commonwealth.*

Old gravestones can be found in the old graveyards of Ratoath and Donaghmore that list the last resting place of many of the Eiffe's.

Between 1848 and 1851 the following are listed as emigrating to the United States of America: John, Patrick, James, Thomas & Thos; all with the exception of Thomas landing in New York. Thomas was disembarked in Boston.

Some of their descendants settled in upstate New York; purchased some land and cultivated hops for the brewing industry. Family ties are still maintained and a direct descendant of James Eiffe, a Syracuse School Teacher, Michael Eiffe, has been instrumental in gathering information on the American line of the family tree.

A younger Brother of James Eiffe, Michael, emigrated to Australia in the 1850s from whom the Australian and New Zealand branch of the family is descendant. There are two locations in Ratoath that will always be associated with the Eiffe family. One is the Barrack House, the family home of Dan and Sarah Eiffe. This house is located at the Skryne Road and Curragha Road junction and it was the original Village RIC Station before Irish independence. The other location was the original Eiffe Family home at Lee Valley Ratoath. The building which stood until 2001 consisted of a two storey farm house. The bottom walls consisted of stone; with mud wall comprising the remaining ten feet. A thatch roof adorned the building before it was replaced with tin in the 1960s.

Another great, character was Andy Eiffe late of Rackenstown Ratoath. Andy who was well known all over the County was one of the driving forces behind the purchase of the Brownstown GAA pitches. It would be a tragic irony that this complex would later be called after his eldest son John (Sean) who was killed in the line of duty while serving as a member of An Garda Siochana. A younger brother of Andy, Noel, emigrated to Australia in the 1950s. Noel was credited with training the Australian GAA team and officiated at the first international match in 1968 when an Australian Selection played the Meath Team.

William (Bill) Eiffe one of the younger brothers of Andy & Noel achieved the distinction of winning both a Junior Football & Hurling All Ireland Medal for Meath.

The Eiffe Family in Ratoath is still growing in number with relations now extending out to 4th or 5th cousins.

FAMILY AND FRIENDS

Family of Sarah and Dan Eiffe, Barrack House

EIFFE FAMILY

Back Row L-R: Michael, Dan, Vincent, Paul, Gerard, Hubert. **Middle Row L-R:** Anne, Jacinta, Madeleine, Marie, Sheila, Gabrielle. **Front Row L-R:** Ursula, Angela, Martina.

Above: Sarah and Dan Eiffe
Left: Dan and Sarah Eiffe on their wedding day, c. 1940's

FAMILY AND FRIENDS

Everard Family, Bradystown

PAUL EVERARD

ON THE 8TH MARCH 1886 James Everard married Anne Tallon in Dunshaughlin. Their home was Bradystown, Ratoath. His brother Pat, after spending many years in America, came home to buy 'The Villa' in Dunshaughlin.

James and Anne had five children: Patrick (1887), James (1889), Thomas (1891), Mary (1893) and Joseph (1895). James died in 1900 leaving Anne a widow with five children under 14; this is evidenced through the census of 1901. In 1918, two of these children died, Joseph aged 23 and Thomas aged 27. One died from meningitis and the other died from the worldwide flu epidemic that affected Ireland.

Patrick the eldest son was heavily involved in the founding and development of Ratoath Hurling Club. Patrick married Mary Fox from Skryne on 6th April 1921. They had eight children: Patrick, Anne, James, Patricia, Mary, Thomas, Joseph and Eileen. Patrick Senior died in 1936 aged 49.

Anne married Michael Rooney and lives in Glasnevin, Patricia married Brendan McEn-

James & Anne Everard married in 1886 and their children L-R Patrick, Mary, Joseph, Thomas and James, circa 1900

Right: Patrick & Mary Everard (nee Fox) and their Children L-R Mary, Anne, Patricia and Tommy, circa 1933

taggert and lived in Dunshaughlin, Mary married Tom Cross from Kildare and Eileen married Jimmy Millar from Laois. Of the boys, during World War II James joined the 1st Battalion of the Queens Own Cameron Highlanders in the British Army and died in battle against the Japanese in Burma on 11th June 1944 aged 21. His grave is in Kohima war cemetery in India. (See James Everard)

Following in his father's footsteps Patrick became heavily involved in the GAA, being both Ratoath and Meath hurling Board Chairman for many years. Joe who still lives in Bradystown was an active GAA member representing Ratoath at both hurling and football. Joe married Margaret Ryan and has three children Patrick, Noel and MaryAnn - all of whom still live in Ratoath.

Tommy was also an active GAA member, representing Ratoath at all levels and he played hurling for Meath Junior Hurlers. Tommy married Imelda Ryan (also from Ratoath) in 1960. They had eight children Paul, Martin, Thomas, Mary, James, Anne, Deborah and Siobhan. Tommy died on 12th April 2006.

Paul & Thomas Everard, 1986

Thomas (in the photo with Paul) died in 1987 aged 22, while he was a passenger on the ship 'The Herald of Free Enterprise' which capsized in Zeebrugge harbour in Belgium on 6th March 1987. 189 people lost their lives Thomas being the only Irish person. Deborah died shortly after her birth. Paul has represented Ratoath GAA at all levels for many years playing and coaching. All the rest of the children live locally with the exception of Ann who lives in Louth.

FAMILY AND FRIENDS

The Everards – Rackenstown

EVERARD FAMILY

THE EVERARDS of Rackenstown were farmers. They travelled by pony and trap to the Market in Dublin to sell hay, straw and corn. Jim Everard was one of nine children born to Margaret Casey and Thomas Everard. Jim carried on farming after he married Lydia Hickey of Greenogue in 1939. They had five children. Jim died in 1988, aged 82 years and Lydia died in 2005, aged 93 years.

Jim and Lydia Everard on their wedding day in 1939. Fr. Rispin is standing behind Lydia Everard. The photograph was taken outside Lydia's home in Greenogue.

FAMILY AND FRIENDS

Foley Family, Lagore Road

IRENE FOLEY

I CAME FROM BERLIN, Germany, in May 1949, to work as *Au Pair* for Mr. and Mrs. Col. Mainwaring of "*The Manor*" Ratoath which is now the Nursing Home.

In August 1949 I met Christy Foley in Maud's shop. We got married the 29th April 1951 and lived first in Dublin with Christy's sister Vera and her family, later moving to Ratoath in 1952 to live with Christy's parents. Christy built our house at Lagore Road and we moved into it in December 1952. Barbara was the only child born in the house. The other 6 children were all born in Dublin. Christy used to shoe horses for Dan Moore, among them were well known horses such as the twice Gold Cup winner *L'Escargot* and *Flying Wild*. He also shod horses for Archie Cooke in his yard at the centre of the village where The Paddocks is today.

FAMILY AND FRIENDS

Gerry Keogh & Family

GERRY KEOGH

GERRY KEOGH was born on the 23rd May 1924 at the Reask, Dunshauglin, to Jim Keogh and Catherine (Katie) nee Nixon, Berlstown, Tara, the eldest of six children, Christie, Jack, Jude, May and Rita. On coming home from school we gathered sticks and carried water half a mile from Farrell's well. Our neighbours were Chrissie & Tom Murphy and their children Amy, Oliver & Brendan. Tom Murphy died in 1932 the time of the big snow and they could not get him out of the house to bury him. McEntaggarts made a coffin, a plain box and they brought it to the Reask. They dragged the coffin across ditches and fields and eventually interred Tom in Ringelstown, Kilmessan, which was his wish. The Murphy children were very young at that time and Chrissie Murphy worked for Mrs. Haughey (Charlie Haughey's mother) at the Riggins, Dunshaughlin. Charlie Haughey went to Cushinstown School, and left The Riggins at the age of 9 or 10 when the Haugheys moved to Donnacarney.

I attended school in Curragha because Oliver Murphy, the next door neighbour, went there. The first day we "mitched" and never got to school, spending the day in the Reask. Jackie White's sister came along with apples which we then roasted over an open fire. When I came home from school they asked me about my day. I had to make up a lot of lies. The next day the same thing happened but my mother and father knew that I was telling lies. They said something had to happen so that was the end of my days at the school in Curragha. I was then sent to school in Ratoath. The headmaster was Ted Gannon, a relation to Teddy Gannon, Fairyhouse. When it came to First Holy Communion, a dilemma emerged as I lived in one parish and attended school in another parish. The parish priests of both parishes refused to let me make First Holy Communion in their parish. This went on for a year. My mother and father were going back and fort between the parishes. Eventually in frustration my father said *"at the end of the day if you want to give him his Communion give it to him and if you don't it doesn't make any differ"*. So one day Fr. Smith arrived at the house on a horse and provided a solution to the problem. My mother brought me to Currgaha on a Saturday morning, Fr. Smith heard my confession on the steps of the Parochial House and I got my Communion the next day. My father said at this stage that this could not happen when it came to Confirmation. There was no problem I got my Confirmation in Ratoath. I stayed in school until I was thirteen. In 1938 or 1939 I attended the Technical School in Dunshaughlin, situated in The Workhouse. The Headmaster was Mr. Ciaran O'Connell and I told him I was 14 when I was in fact 13. I was awarded a scholarship to an Agricultural College in Cavan, but, was unable to avail of it and so I started to work around home.

In the early 1930's we acquired a Land Commissioned farm with 25 or 26 acres just across the road from our home at Halltown Cross. My father lived there from the late 1800's. He was involved with the IRA in 1916 and his house was used as a safe house where guns were kept under the floorboards. At that time there was no sign posts and the army would always come to our house looking for directions and he always said that he slept with the revolver under his pillow. My father and I were both cyclists. On Sundays my father and I would cycle to Mass in Ratoath and then race home on the bikes. I would have been 15 or 16 years old. Around that time I joined Kentstown Cycling Club and continued racing up until 1946 or 1947. When I went to Dublin to work I gave up cycling for a while and played hurling with Ratoath, football with Donaghmore and hurling with St. Laurence O'Tooles, Dublin.

In 1950 I married Mary Doyle from Wexford in a church on South Circular Road, Dublin. One evening when we were walking in the Phoenix Park with our first child, Gerry, there was a cycle race on and I told Mary that I would be able to go as fast as those fellows. She said to me not to be ridiculous. So I got out the bike and trained all through the winter until racing time, in April or May of the following year 1955, and started to race again. After four or five races I was winning. I was 27 or 28 years old by then and I raced until 1959. My achievements as a cyclist include winning the 100 mile Championship of Ireland in 1955, the Rás 3 Day Event, Coming 14th in the Rás Talton as a member of the Dublin team, winning the Ring of Kerry Race, winning The 50 Mile Championship of Ireland, coming 2nd Second in the 100 Mile Championship three times, winning the Tralee to Cork mountain stage of the Rás in 1955 (142 miles over the mountains), two Tours of Wicklow, two Tours of Tyrone, two Tours of Louth and two Tours of Meath. I won every race the game had to offer except the Rás Talton, finishing 2nd in the Rás Talton overall in 1957. Frank Ward won it that year, both of us racing for the Dublin Team. I gave up cycling in 1959, I rode the 59th Rás and I said at that stage I had never had any bad falls so it was time to finish. At this stage I had four children and went on have a further four to complete the family of eight; four boys and four girls, two sets of twins Gerry, John, Geraldine, Valerie, Tony, Rita, Eugene & Pauline.

I started to ride in the Veterans in the 1960's, winning everything it had to offer, did a few charity runs including the ISPCC Mizen Head to Malin Head, raising £35,000, taking the Charity Ride for Stuarts Hospital in Palmerstown, raising £17,000, the biggest amount of money that had ever been raised for Stuarts Hospital. In 1983 I took part in the San Francisco to New York - 36 days, 3,500 miles for James Hospital Leukaemia Research, raising 100,000 US$. Seamus Egan's daughter Susan had died from leukaemia at the age of 7 and my own grandson Edward Gannon died in 1999 from leukaemia. Seamus Egan travelled with me. I was in the Blarney Stone pub in Pittsburgh on my 60th birthday, they had a pot on the stage, two foot wide and it was full of money for the charity. We travelled into Chicago and there was a police man there who was originally from Tipperary who apologised for not having anything organised for us, he was not given enough notice. He said he would organise something for us and as we headed off the next morning I said to Seamus that's the last we will hear of him! About two months afterwards I got a phone call from this man saying "*I will be in Dublin on Thursday*". So we met him in the Clare Street Hotel and he presented us with a cheque for 17,000 US$. After that I gave back a little by organizing cycling events. I retired from AIB in 1988 and opened the bike shop in Ratoath, at the back of Molly's shop and was there for 16 years.

The Generosity of Others
We stayed in the Soda Springs Hotel in Nevada, on the way to Salt Lake City, got up in the morning, paid our bill and left. The owner of the hotel discovered we were gone and followed us for over 50 miles to give us our money back as she said our stay was "*on the house*".

Some Childhood Memories
There was an old lady who travelled from house to house with a basket selling medals,

laces and safety pins. She always lit a little fire on the side of the road, to heat water in a tommy can. Coming home from school one day I remember picking up a stone, throwing it at the little woman and hitting the tommy can which was full of tea and turning it over. I picked up the can, brought it home and my mother made a pot of tea and I returned with it to the woman on the side of the road at Cabinhill.

    A fella used to call to our house, we called him Humpty Dumpty. He travelled around in an ass and cart selling mugs, jugs and bits and pieces. Another man with no legs travelled in a box with two sticks. Shows were held in the Codliss. Pictures (films) and the strongest man in Ireland were the key attractions. We rode the bikes everywhere, to Swords, the Naul and Garristown. I am still living in Blanchardstown and still "tricking around" with the bikes.

Note: *This information was recorded on the 15th June 2007*

FAMILY AND FRIENDS

Could the Gorman Family be the oldest Family in Ballybin?

GERALDINE CLARKE (NÉE GORMAN)

JAMES GORMAN and Bridget (nee Stafford) came to live in Ballybin around 1910. Both working for the Duffy's, they lived in a house attached to the land of Matthew Duffy for whom James worked as a farmhand. They had many children; Matthew, Jay, Paddy, Frank, Joe, Liz, Jenny, Nancy, and Molly, as well as Kathleen who died quite young. These children settled either in or not far from Ballybin, and to this day the next generation continue to reside in the surrounding areas.

Matthew lived at Coolquay, The Ward, and had two children; Elsie and Jenny. Jay also lived in the same area and his family were Kit, Jimmy, Paddy, Bridget Martina and Lil. Paddy lived in Ballybin, and also worked for Matthew Duffy jnr. He married Theresa Reilly and they had a son and daughter Aidan and Mary, who now live on the Fairyhouse Road near the Racecourse.

Frank with his wife and four sons Frank, Jimmy, Liam and Matthew also lived in Ballybin. Frank worked for Leonard Meagher who had a pub-grocery and petrol pumps where the Auld Stand is today. Frank had a motor bike and when people heard him coming on the road they referred to him as *"the bee in the bottle"*. Jimmy lives on the Fairyhouse Road and Matthew lives in Ashbourne. Frank Jim and Matty all played hurling for Ratoath. It was common to see the Gormans and the Wheelers having a practice early on Sundays prior to a match. Between the two families there were 5 players from the team.

Joe lived in Ballybin and was married to Teasie Byrne who came from Mountrath and worked for Doctor Harry Conway. They had five sons and one daughter John, James, David, Geraldine, Dermot and Martin who to this day all live around the area. Joe was a good hurler and his sons played for Ratoath, John was probably the better known family member having played well into his forties.

Jenny married John Morgan who was a bus driver on the route from Garristown to Dublin and they lived at the Rath Cross. They had six children; Kit, Colm, John, Jim, Maureen and Nell. They all emigrated and live in Canada, Australia. Jenny was a top class cyclist. Nancy married Ben Lynam and lived in Lagore. They had six children Ann, Bronagh, Sylvia, Olive, Gwen and Ken. Bronagh is now Bronagh Darby. Sylvia lives in Ashbourne. Nancy played Camogie for Meath for several years.

Liz was married to Jack Ryan and lived in Lagore. They had four girls; Melia, Ann, Mary and Margaret. Melia is now Melia Everard and lives in Glascairn and Margaret is married to Matty McCabe and lives in the village. Molly married John Ryan and also lived in Lagore; they had two daughters Claire and Irene. So the Gormans have been around Ratoath for almost 100 years and are certainly the oldest family in Ballybin. Gormans have always been involved with hurling and three generations have now played for Ratoath.

FAMILY AND FRIENDS

John Caul, Fairyhouse

ANNE BYRNE

JOHN CAUL OF BALLYBIN, Fairyhouse, was born in Naul, Co. Dublin, in 1875. His family were millers. He had one brother, who died as a child and two sisters. One sister, Bridget (known as Bea.) married John Gogan of Dunshaughlin. They ran the Public House and Grocery store in Dunshaughlin, which is still there to this day. John's other sister Celia (known as Sis) married a John Fitzpatrick of Paceland, Dunboyne.

In 1909, John's Uncle Pat Kelly of Ballybin, Fairyhouse, died. At the time of his death Pat Kelly owned Fairyhouse Racecourse and surrounding farmland. John then inherited the farm. When John arrived at Ballybin a Mr. Gadwell of Drogheda was the Manager of the Racecourse. John was appointed 'local manager' and he also farmed there. When Mr. Gadwell retired John became General Manager at the course.

John married Julia Monks of Coolquay, The Ward, on the 21st April 1915. John took great

Julia Caul

John Caul 1875–1964

pride in Fairyhouse and the Races. At that time the races were only run on one day, Easter Monday. The Irish Grand National was a great celebration in those days. The preparation for The Races went on for weeks leading up to Easter. 'Caul's Yard' got a coat of whitewash and paint. In fact Ratoath village was a hive of activity before the big meeting. Once the prayers of Holy Week and Easter Sunday were over it was time to go to the Races, hail rain or shine. Julia Caul spent weeks cooking and cleaning in preparation for the inevitable arrival of visitors on the big day. John Caul retired as Manager of Fairyhouse Racecourse in 1948. On his death in April 1964, a tree situated outside the 'Old Weigh room' was dedicated to his memory. Unfortunately this tree was cut down during the refurbishment of the enclosure ("The New Fairyhouse") in 1999.

The first regulation fence is also known as 'Caul's Regulation'. John and Julia Caul were very much part of Fairyhouse and Ratoath village. Mrs. Caul died on 7th Oct. 1973 and is buried with John in the local Cemetery. They had one daughter, Julia who married Michael Clarke.

Obituary

JOHN GAUL of Fairyhouse, died on Thursday morning at his residence beside the racecourse enclosure. Very few of the thousands of race goers who enjoyed their days racing knew him. Yet three generations owe a great deal to the care and affection with which he tended everything in connection with Fairyhouse. When John Caul came to Fairyhouse over fifty years ago, the Grand Stand was in course of completion. Until then, the only stand was one put up by a local carpenter with planks for the day.

Mr. Joseph O'Reilly, making his report as Chairman to his fellow Stewards on the completion of the stand in 1909 spoke in the highest terms of the attention and care that John Caul took of all the interests placed in his charge. For the next fifty years his devotion to Fairyhouse never diminished. Some two weeks before the meeting when he was already in failing health, he was asked for permission to make some improvements in one of the public car parks which were his property. This was readily granted as anything that tended to the success of the meeting always received his instant co-operation.

John Caul took the keenest interest in all the doings of the Stewards of the meeting, who were his personal friends. In many cases he has known four generations of their families. It would be a fitting tribute to his memory if the tree which now stands outside the winning unsaddling enclosure, and under which Arkle stood to be unsaddled last Easter Monday, should be allowed to stand as a tribute to his memory.

Mr. John Caul, Fairyhouse, Ratoath, Co. Meath, who has died, was well known in Irish racing circles for more than 50 years. He was an extensive farmer and owned part of the land over which the Fairyhouse races are run. One of the jumps on the course of the Irish Grand National - Caul's Regulation - was called after him. Mr. Caul was for some years the manager at Fairyhouse. His wife and a married daughter, Mrs. Julia Clarke, survive him.

FAMILY AND FRIENDS

Kennedys of Peackockstown

FRANCES MAHER & JOE MANNERING

MR. PATRICK KENNEDY SENIOR lived in Peackockstown House which was built in the 1840's. Around 1918 Patrick started school in Ratoath at the age of 4. His classmates were Johnny McCarthy, Larry Dowling, members of the Doran and Lynch families, Christy Smith, Mattie Lambe, Patsy Sherry, Johnny Sherry, Jim Doolin, John Robinson, Bennie Dolan, Johnny Gogan, Tommy Gogan, Kevin Delaney, George Parr, Willie Delaney, Pauline Kennedy, Lilly Kennedy, Maude Kennedy, Jimmy Mannering, Fr. Joe Clarke, Annie Clarke (Gogan), and Paddy Toole.

Many families in Dunshaughlin sent their children to school in Ratoath at this time because the school had a very good reputation. There were four classrooms in the school, 2 main classrooms and 2 other classrooms that were partitioned from these two rooms by sliding doors. The teachers were Mr. & Mrs. James Doonan, Mrs. Staunton and Mrs. O'Brien from Curragha.

Patrick Kennedy's parents Mr. & Mrs. Walter Kennedy cutting a cake on their 50th Wedding Anniversary, November 1950

Kennedy Family photograph includes: Johnny Duffy, Stacia Duffy, Mrs. Johnny Duffy, Walter Kennedy Snr. Patrick Duffy, Babs Rooney, Patrick Duffy, Ballybin and Una Martin

Large Family Group includes Mr. & Mrs. Walter Kennedy Senior (mid picture). Pa Kennedy is at the extreme right at the back. Mrs. Maisie Kennedy is holding Walter Kennedy Jnr. (as a babe in arms, second from right).

Patrick told of memories that his father, who was born in 1876, had told him about "Paddy the Paper", who around 1883 brought the papers from Dublin on a Sunday by bicycle. Paddy would leave the papers under a stone on his way to Dunshaughlin and later in the day on his way back collected the money due. This man Paddy would get two old pence for each Sunday newspaper he sold, that was one penny extra, for cycling from Dublin.

His father also remembered the Doctor's house being built (now called The Grange) and that old Tom McGrane, who was Fr. McGrane's father worked on the building of the house and how Tom McGrane used to run Patrick's father off the site when he played there as a child.

Patrick himself told of starting work at seven in the morning ploughing with horses on the farm. Cows were milked by hand. They had their own potatoes and made their own butter. In those days the locals travelled by bicycle to the odd dance in Swords. These were farmers' dances. Ronnie Quigley Senior had a hackney car and brought people to dances. Patrick Kennedy also remembers the big snow storm of 1932. The snow was up to the telegraph wires, lasting for six weeks and no one could travel the Kilbride Road.

FAMILY AND FRIENDS

Keogh Family, Rackenstown

MARIA KEOGH

WE HAVE SEEN RATOATH expand and grow over the past twenty years, both in housing developments and in population. During this time many new people from other parts of Ireland have chosen the little picturesque village of Rackenstown as their home. Giving its name to a County Meath village, townland and a parish, Rackenstown has many generations of Meath families; families who have been living in the Parish for over one hundred years or more. One such family is the Keogh family which has grown to four generations since it started off in Rackenstown over 80 years ago.

Firstly let us speak of Rackenstown townland itself. The original Rackenstown House was not situated on the site where the present dwelling is built. It was a small stone built house, the ruins of which still stand further down the yard near the present family home. It was owned by the `Rahan family` over 300 years ago thus giving the name to the townland as it was then. The Rahan family name was an English translation of the *Clán of Raicin* from Offaly or Westmeath. As a result, the place-name of *Baile Raicin* or `Rackenstown` emerged. Rackenstown House, as it is today, was built circa 1841. It was owned by the

Rackenstown House in 2008

Charles & Elizabeth Keogh in 1927   Nicholas and Kathleen Keogh on their wedding Day in 1968

Thunder family and was part of their estate. In 1926, shortly after the reclamation of lands by the Irish Government and after the formation of what was known as the `Saorstát`, the matter of dividing up lands on estates was undertaken; either vesting the land or selling it off to interested parties. The Land Commission was authorised to vest the land they acquired and distribute untenanted land 'pari passu'.

In March 1927, one representative in Dáil Éireann, a Mr. Everett asked Mr. Hogan, the Minister for Lands and Agriculture, "*whether the Land Commission proposes allotting the townlands of Rackenstown, on the Thunder Estate, Lagore, Dunshaughlin, County Meath, and if same will be divided among local landless men and uneconomic holders.*"[1]

The Minister replied "*The untenanted lands on the estate of Reps. of Patrick Thunder, deceased (Rec. No. S. 1504), Co. Meath, have been divided among the herd and small holders in the district with the exception of one parcel in the townland of Rackenstown, the allocation of which is at present under consideration.*"[2] Therefore, Thunder's estate, which was over 4000 acres, was divided up into many farms except for the lands of Rackenstown House and the farm on which the house now stands. This was first purchased by the Everett Family but later sold to the Keogh family.

It was this farm and house collectively known as Rackenstown House that was purchased by a Charles Keogh from Curragha in 1926. He then married Elizabeth Dowling, originally from Cushenstown, Garristown, Co. Dublin and they went on to have six children; two boys, Colm and Nicholas and four girls, Ann, Lil, Tina and May. This was a well planned house when it was first built. It had, and still has, a concealed tunnel under the house which runs the whole way to Kilbrew House in Curragha, over three miles away. The

---

1   Dáil Éireann – Volume 18 – 11 March, 1927. Ceisteanna – Questions. Oral Answers. – Land Act Operations.
2   Ibid

tunnel would have been used in troubled times to escape underground to safety. Although the tunnel still exists it has been sealed off for many years. The house itself is built of stone and solid pine. It has the original shutters in each lower window which are working perfectly. The property has its own spring well in working order. In fact when Guinness's staff from the Hop Store in James' Street, Dublin, came out to Charles Keogh, to deliver brewed grains for cattle feed, they brought empty bottles in order to take home to Dublin some spring water from this natural well! Although the house has changed somewhat physically over the years, and Charles and Elizabeth have since deceased, it has many happy stories to tell and has seen four generations of Keoghs grow up there.

Charles died in 1958 and his son Nicholas was chosen to run the farm and lands. At that time Colm was working for C.I.E., Tina and Ann were both working as nurses; May was running her Aunt Liz's bar, which, although now under new ownership, is still Dowling's of Crossmacol. Lil worked as a Sales Representative / Demonstrator for Brother Ireland, the Knitting and Sewing Company. Some of the six children in the Keogh family home had moved on and married. Nicholas, who was at the time living at home married Kathleen and had three children Stephen, Nicholas Junior and Maria. Lil who was also still living at home at that time, and Elizabeth, her mother moved to Lagore Little to live in a new bungalow there. Nicholas and Kathleen reared their three children in Rackenstown House and ran their farm of dairy, sheep and horses.

Nicholas Senior, like his father Charles, had a great interest in horses. He too reared and trained horses and was successful in producing a fine racing mare, *Rahan Bridge*, named after the original Rahan family. His father had a racehorse called *Unknown Batchelor*. This horse was ridden by Lawsey Geraghty a very good friend of the late Charles Keogh and, in line with tradition, Nicholas would love to see his grandson, Barry Geraghty, ride one of his racehorses first across the line to keep up old memories.

Stephen completed a Manufacturing Technology degree and is an engineer working and living near Dundalk with his wife Jeanette. Maria completed a diploma in Food Science in Letterkenny and is a Garda. She has built her own house near Rackenstown House as has Nicholas Junior. He is married to Susan and they have two children: Charlie and Sarah. In line with tradition and his love of farming and animals, Nicholas Junior decided to go to Warrenstown College and train in Farm Practice and Procedure. It was his choice to take over the operational running and general upkeep of the farm on the retirement of his father Nicholas. Even now in 2007 his young son Charlie and daughter Sarah are showing a great love for the countryside and for animals and they are showing potential to become the next generation of young budding Keogh farmers to run the Rackenstown Farm.

FAMILY AND FRIENDS

The Mahon Family

MAHON FAMILY

OUR MOTHER Winnie Mahon (née Walsh) moved from Sligo with all her family to Glascarn as a teenager. Our father, Michael Mahon, who was never known by any other name but Pud, was born and reared in Primatestown, Ashbourne, Co. Meath.

When Pud and Winnie got married they lived in a house on the Curragha Road. They moved from there into a house in Ratoath village and then into a house on the Fairyhouse Road while they waited for their own house to be built. They had eight children, namely Eileen, Marian, Angela, Ger, Kathleen, Michael, Noreen and Kevin.

Pud worked in Dardis & Dunnes Grain Store in Ashbourne, where Dunnes Stores Supermarket now stands. From there he went to work in Hendrons in Broadstone, Dublin, as a van driver. Most of the time around Ratoath, if there wasn't machinery on the back of the van, it was full with children. On Sunday mornings if the weather was good, children from the Fairyhouse Road and Glascarn Lane would drop in to see if Pud was going to the seaside. Nearly every Sunday, Pud would load up the back of the van and head for the beach. Even before he had a car, he would hire a minibus to take the family and their friends to the zoo or the cinema.

Everyone knew that the local children were safe with Pud, Winnie and their family. Pud and Winnie made sure there were loads of sandwiches and soft drinks and nobody went hungry. The only difficulty which occurred was once when the car was parked out too far on the beach in Bettystown and the tide came in. That was not a good day!

There was also great excitement when the Mahon's got their first television, the second on the road. The local children would assemble in the living room to watch anything that was on. Unfortunately, if we didn't behave ourselves none of the children was allowed watch television.

Shopping in Ratoath was a very different experience to that of today. Kelly's traveling shop came around to the houses every Thursday and had everything from flour to soft drinks and the most delicious penny toffees, some with nuts. A coalman from Drogheda delivered coal in the area every week. A sheet of newspaper stuck in the hedge outside the house was a signal to the coalman to call. There was very little traffic on the roads. On Christmas mornings the ritual was that we would get our toys and go down the road and meet the Cullen children half way to their house, at about 5 o'clock in the morning, and play on the road for hours until Pud came looking for us.

Unusual Designs
Our mother, Winnie made most of our clothes. When she saw an unusual outfit on someone she arrived home and started cutting out a paper pattern to figure out how it had been made. This meant that we were in the height of fashion all the time. There are some great memories of hot pants, ponchos, flared trousers and snazzy tops. Even sitting behind

someone at Mass, who was wearing an Aran jumper with an unusual design, usually meant that Winnie was figuring out the stitches and before long the pattern was knitted into a jumper or cardigan for one of us. From embroidery to painting and wallpaper, curtains to loose covers, she could turn her hand to anything. The girls' First Holy Communion dresses were handmade, as were our wedding dresses, bridesmaids' dresses and Winnie's own outfit. This was not only for our family but for anybody who asked her.

People from the area who were getting married would come to Winnie to ask her to make all the outfits. It was not uncommon to see yards of lace, ribbon and other material all over the living room. Children could not bring even a cup of tea into the living room for fear of spilling it and ruining the wedding outfits! This was a real hardship because the only television in the house was in the living room. And even if you did get to watch television, every time the sewing machine was used, the television would go all fuzzy.

Self sufficiency from the Land

Winnie always kept a few pigs, two cows and a calf or two. The pigs were kept until early December when they were sold, and the money used for Christmas to make sure we all had presents and that there was plenty of good food to eat. Having the cows meant that we never bought milk or butter. The cows were milked by hand every morning and evening. The milk for the house was put aside and the remainder was put through a separator to separate the cream from the milk. The surplus milk was then fed to the calves. The cream was kept until Saturday when all the cream was put into a churn and mixed to make butter. The butter was salted and put into pads. Some of the butter was kept for the house and

Mahon Family, Fairyhouse Road, c.1970
L-R seated: Angela, Pud, Winnie, Marion. **Back:** Noeleen, Geraldine, Kevin, Kathleen

the rest was either sold or given to neighbours. The buttermilk left in the churn was used to bake bread.

We never bought any vegetables. An acre of land behind the house was always planted in potatoes. The rows were opened by a tractor and the seed potatoes dropped into the drills by hand. When the time came to dig out the potatoes Winnie used a garden fork. She dug a few drills at a time. When we came home from school in the autumn, we picked the potatoes that she had dug and put them in a pit that was made up by digging a shallow trench in the field. Lime was spread on the ground around the pit. When the potatoes were all picked and stacked in the pit in the correct triangular shape, the pit was covered with straw, lime, clay and the old potato stalks. This ensured that no rain could get in, the rats were kept out and the potatoes were protected from frost.

Some of the land was closed off for making hay. When the hay was cut in the summer time, it was turned by hand, dried out by the heat of the sun and stacked into hay cocks (stacks). In later years, the hay was baled. The cocks of hay, and later the bales, were stored over the winter in the hayshed.

Pud came from a family of Farriers. At any one time there could be horses to be shod or donkeys' feet to be dressed. The farrier work was all done in the farmyard by Pud.

Voluntary Activities in the Community
Pud was one of the people who started the Sunday night Bingo in Ratoath. He was the Bingo caller. Sunday evenings were spent putting out the chairs in the Community Hall and checking that all the numbers were in the machine. The Bingo is still running on Sunday nights and now takes place in the GAA Clubhouse, Brownstown.

The annual Wheel of Fortune before Christmas was also a great day for all the community. Pud delivered the turkeys and hams to the winners. On one occasion, he was asked to deliver a turkey to someone in Cabra, Dublin. Unfortunately the winner had forgotten to put their address on the ticket and after driving around for four hours, and being in and out of nearly every house in Cabra, his patience was really tested when the winner of the turkey could not be found!

Pud was a great organiser for charities or to get things done, e.g. concerts or shows for different organisations and charity groups. He often put on concerts in the nursing home and this involved making up our own plays and acting in them. The concerts included Irish dancing and singing. If anyone got an idea about something to entertain the patients, it was done. The concerts were followed by tea, soft drinks and biscuits provided by the Augustinian Sisters in the nursing home.

When we were growing up Ratoath was very different to what it is today and we didn't have much luxury. Nevertheless, as children we never got into trouble. Everyone knew who their neighbour was and if the children were out playing they were safe, because everyone looked out for each other.

FAMILY AND FRIENDS

The Mannering Family

JOE MANNERING

MY GRANDFATHER, James Mannering, lived in Pullwee Street, Ratoath, with his brother Michael "Dorcan" Mannering. In 1901 James married Elizabeth O'Reilly from Slane. They had six children, four boys, John, Michael, Patrick and James, and two girls, Molly and Elizabeth (Lizzie). Their home was in Tankardstown.

Jack Mannering (my father) married Alice Coleman from Colemans Cross, Mulhuddart, in 1930. Jack worked in Collinstown Airport (now known as Dublin Airport) as a construction worker for eight years and then went to work in Fairyhouse Racecourse. He was the first man to build "Birch Fences" in Fairyhouse and afterwards built similar fences in Wexford and Roscommon Race Courses.

Jack and Alice had thirteen children, seven boys and six girls. Sadly one daughter died at birth and a son died following an accident at a very young age. They raised their children at The Paddock, Kilbride Road, Ratoath. My father grew his own vegetables in our back garden and my mother cycled to the fruit and vegetable markets in Dublin each week to sell the produce to make ends meet. My father died in 1966 and my mother in 1984. To date they have 56 grandchildren and 40 great-grandchildren.

Picture above shows Jack and Alice Mannering with family members at the wedding of their eldest daughter, Josie, to Mr. Charlie Deens on 23rd August 1958.

FAMILY AND FRIENDS

Mary Wallace

ANN GAUGHAN

IN 1971, the Wallace family sold their farm in Dunboyne and moved to a new farm on the Fairyhouse Road beside the Racecourse. Mary Wallace was 11 years old then. The Wallace children had attended Dunboyne National School before moving to Ratoath National School. Later Mary attended Loretto Convent, Balbriggan, and she went to the College of Commerce in Rathmines before taking up a job in Blanchardstown Hospital. Mary's father, Tommy Wallace, was a member of Meath County Council from 1967 and her mother, Rosemary, was very much involved in local women's organisations, particularly the I.C.A.

When Mary was just 22 years of age her father Tommy died suddenly while attending a race meeting in Fairyhouse, and as a result Mary was catapulted into politics when she was co-opted to his seat on Meath County Council. In February 1982 Mary became a member of Meath County Council; she was elected to Seanad Éireann in 1987 and to Dáil Éireann in 1989.

While TD for Ratoath Mary became Minister of State in the Department of Justice from 1997 to 2002 and again Minister of State in the Department of Agriculture & Food from 2006 to May 2008. She was appointed Minister of State at the Department of Health & Children with responsibility for Health Promotion and Food Safety on 13 May 2008. Because of her farming background she enjoyed representing the people of rural Co. Meath on issues such as rural dwellings for local people and the many issues that arise for farm families.

When Mary became a Minister of State for the first time in 1997, she vacated her seat on Meath County Council which she had held for 15 years, during which time she had served on the North Eastern Health Board and the Meath Vocational Educational Committee, and chaired the Meath County Agriculture Committee. Also, prior to becoming a Minister of State, Mary had served on, and chaired, the Joint Oireachtas All Party Committee on Women's Rights 1995-97 (Vice-chairperson from 1989-92). She was also Chairperson of Fianna Fail National Women's Committee 1992-94 and Chairperson of the National Steering Committee on Violence Against Women 1998-2002. Most recently Mary has chaired the All Party Oireachtas Patient Focus Support Group.

By 2007 the Wallace family had served 40 years as public representatives in the Ratoath and wider Dunshaughlin area. Mary works in a very busy constituency which has been impacted substantially by the increase in population. She welcomes the wonderful contribution which the many new residents in Meath East, especially over the past 10 years, are making to the community and sporting life. As a TD for Ratoath, Mary has been directly involved in assisting and supporting many changes in the community, in particular the new school building which her son Tom now attends. The school is one of 4 primary schools in Ratoath Parish. When Mary herself went to Ratoath School there were just four classrooms in the entire school.

In June 2005 when school children took their summer holidays there were two schools

The Wallace Family: Tommy and Rosemary with children Thomas, Ann, John and Mary

in Ratoath. In September 2005, three months later, there were five schools including the new Ratoath College post primary school. Testament in itself of her on-going hard work and the several trips to the School Building Section of the Department of Education in Tullamore to ensure that schools were provided for the increased population not just the three new schools in Ratoath but new schools and school extensions throughout her entire constituency.

Mary believes passionately that her work throughout Meath East, to encourage expansion of education and community facilities, is paramount in catering for both existing and new residents and she is always happy to support the many community and sporting groups working in these areas to continue to develop these facilities. Up until 2002, Meath was a 5-seat constituency. Due to the population increase it is now changed to two 3-seat constituencies of Meath East and Meath West. Ratoath is in Meath East and is one the fastest growing villages in Ireland from a population of 600 in 1990 to 9,600 in 2008.

Mary has one sister, Ann and two brothers, Thomas and John. On 28 Sept. 1994 she married Ratoath man Declan Gannon and their son Tom Gannon was born on 28 Sept. 1995. Declan, Mary and Tom live on the Fairyhouse Road and Mary's office is based next door to the family home.

As elected representative Mary devotes a lot of personal time and attention to the concerns of groups and individuals in this very busy constituency. The parish which only had one bus per day to Dublin in the early 1990's now has buses every 15 minutes from 7am for daily commuters to and from Dublin and a bus service every hour to Dublin Airport, D.C.U. and Navan the N2 motorway was opened in May 2006 and greatly assists many residents in their daily commute to Dublin. The new Community Centre and sporting facilities are wonderful assets for a thriving and appreciative community. On the heritage side Mary's next local project is the development of the Manor Wood Forest and River Walk amenities. There will always be projects to be worked upon and to be improved and whether it is at local or national level it is always good to have our own representative in Government.

FAMILY AND FRIENDS

The McCarthy Family

MARY DINNENY (NÉE MCCARTHY)

THE MCCARTHY FAMILY was originally from Buttevant, Co. Cork. My grandparents had a butcher's shop on the Pullwee Street (Lagore Road) in Ratoath. My father John McCarthy (now deceased) was born on 26th January 1917 and lived in Ratoath all his life. There were seven in his family, all now deceased except for one brother who lives in Dunshaughlin. My father attended the Primary School in Ratoath and Technical School in Navan. He then worked in Fairyhouse Racecourse and became Foreman there some years later. He remained there for sixty-two years. I remember my father getting up at 6am on race meeting mornings and not getting home until 10 pm. Easter Monday and Tuesday were especially busy but he absolutely loved his job.

Rose O'Shea, my mother, came from Co. Roscommon. She met my father in 1945 in Fairyhouse and two years later they got married on 31st May 1947. She came to live in my father's home place on the Glascarn Lane where she still resides to this day. I was born two years later and they called me Mary Elizabeth. Four and a half years later my sister, Rosaleen Margaret, was born. Both of us went to Primary School in Ratoath. I sat my Primary Cert exam in Fairyhouse Racecourse as the school was under repair at the time (1963) and then I attended Dunshaughlin Technical School as it was called at that time.

I worked in Dublin at the drapery business for a number of years, something that I always wanted to do. Some years later I met Tom Dinneny from Killeshandra, Co. Cavan and we married in 1977. Tom's father was Michael Dinneny who played for the Cavan football team in the thirties and he won two All-Ireland medals. Tom and I built a house on the Glascarn Lane beside the entrance to Cairn Manor and we still reside there. My sister, Rosaleen, got married two years after me to Tom Nolan from Batterstown where she now lives and has two in family.

In 1963 there were a total of eight houses on the Fairyhouse Road from the top of Glascarn Lane to the School. There was only one bus a day to and from Dublin. The only time you would see a double decker bus was on Easter Monday at the racecourse! There have been lots of changes in Ratoath since I was a child!

Pictured left to right:
John & Rose McCarthy with their daughters Mary and Rosaleen.

FAMILY AND FRIENDS

The Moore Family

MOORE FAMILY

SR. ESTER MOORE of the Barrack Road, Ratoath, entered the French Sisters of Charity of St. Vincent De Paul in her early 20's and has devoted her life to the service of those with special needs for over 60 years. Sr. Ester is the daughter of the late Ester and John Moore and the other members of her family were brothers Nicholas, Thomas, Joe, Patrick, Chris, John and Donald and her sisters Mary and Bridie.

(Above): The Early Days: Sr. Ester Moore with her mother, Mrs. Ester Moore and Moore Family.

(Above): Sr. Ester Moore, 2006

(Left): Senior Citizens' Party in 1969

Mrs. Ester Moore, aged 93 and then the second oldest person in the Ratoath area, pictured with friends at a Senior Citizens' party in February 1969.

Front Row L-R: Fr. John Cogan, P.P., Mrs. Ester Moore, Ann Browne and Breege Monahan (joint treasurers.)
Centre Row L-R: Dr. H. Conway, Mrs. McGowan and Mrs. Martin (Secretary). **Back Row L-R:** Fr. Stanley C.C., Sean McGowan and Sonny Martin (Treasurer).

FAMILY AND FRIENDS

O'Brien Family, Tankardstown

RUAIDRÍ AGUS BLATHÍN O'NÉILL

IT IS IMPORTANT to note that there are two houses on the Kilbride Road known as No 1 and No 2 Glascarn. These two dwellings were built in 1923 A.D. They were a bequest from the British Soldier's and Sailor's Land Trust for services rendered in the Sudan, Boer and World War I battlefields.

The recipients of the two houses were Patrick O'Brien and Nicholas O'Reilly, each receiving one acre. Patrick O'Brien, originally from Castleknock, Dublin, married Alice Fortune from Ratoath Village. Occasionally he quipped "*I married misfortune!*"

Tragedy struck when Alice's beloved younger brother "Kit" (Christopher) lost his life at the Second Battle of Yprés, France, on 25th April 1916, aged 20.

He was the son of Edward and Mary Fortune. He was a personal friend of the Meath poet Francis Ledwidge. Despite having survived harsh service in Gallipoli and Serbia, Led-

(Right):
Private Christy (Kit) Fortune who died at Yprés, France, on 25 April 1916, aged 20

(Below):
In Memory of Private C Fortune in the perpetual care of the Commonwealth War Graves Commission

FAMILY AND FRIENDS — The O'Brien Family

O'Brien Family, Tankardstown, pictured outside their home in the mid 1930's
L-R: Ed, Alice (Mother), Frank, Pad, Mick and Molly. (Notice Molly's doll on hedge behind her!)

widge was also killed while serving in Flanders, at Boezinge, on 31st July 1917 during the Third Battle of Ypres.

Christopher Fortune served in the 8th Battalion of the Royal Irish Fusiliers in the rank of private (Service No. 21060). His death is recorded as one of the Commonwealth War Dead. Christopher, or Kit as he is known to his family and friends, was interred at Vermelles British Cemetery, France. *May he rest in Peace*

Grave/Memorial Reference: Sp. Memorial 5.

Vermelles is a village located about 10 kilometres to the north-west of Lens. Over 2134 First World War personnel are commemorated at Vermelles British Cemetery, of these 198 are unidentified and there are six special memorials erected to soldiers from the United Kingdom known to be buried among them.

Pat and Alice had eight children, namely Pad, Ed, Molly (O'Neill), Carmel, Christy, Frank, Mick and James. Their house today is happily occupied by their grandson Roddy O'Neill with his wife Bonnie and their children. In recent years the Fortune home on the Dunshaughlin Road, Ratoath, was demolished and replaced by the new apartment block called Fortune Court.

Buíochas Le Día

FAMILY AND FRIENDS

O'Neill Family, Pullwee Street

MARY O'NEILL

MICHAEL O'NEILL arrived in Ratoath in the 1940's. He came from his mother's home place of Dunshaughlin where he had served his time to his uncle Paddy Blake, as a butcher. He had been brought up in Finglas. Michael's father Thomas O'Neill, an American citizen, having come back to Ireland and married Julia Blake. Michael came to Ratoath to work for Tom Everard, on Tom's retirement he opened his own butchers in 1946. He met Molly O'Brien during this time. Molly was a native of Ratoath, her mother being from the Fortune family.

John and Mary Fortune lived in one of the first two Parnell Cottages built in Meath, located in Pullwee Street where Fortune Court is today. They had seven children, Jack, Frank, Neddy, Michael (Mun), Kit, Alice and Bridget. Kit died in World War I in France in 1917 at the age of 18 years. Alice was to marry Patrick O' Brien from Castleknock a British soldier and lived in Alice's home place in Pullwee Street till they were allocated one of two British soldier houses built in Tankardstown in the 1920's. Molly, their daughter, was about eight years of age when they left Pullwee Street for their new home in Tankardstown.

Molly O'Brien had 5 brothers, Pad, Ed, Mick, Frank and Jim. A brother, Christopher and sister, Carmel, died as a result of childhood illnesses. Molly trained as a nurse in Navan and

Mickey and Molly O'Neill with friends on their wedding day, Fr. Eddie Rispin CC Ratoath is seated in the front row.

Sir Patrick Dunne's hospital. She nursed in England during the war but returned to mind her ailing widowed father. She met Michael O'Neill during this time. It was on an Easter Monday in Foleys' shop (now Brady's Garage) where she was a firm friend of the family, in particular with Sheila Brady (nee Foley). Molly and Michael (Mickey) married in 1946.

Eight children were to follow between 1947 and 1959: Roderick, Fiacra, Paddy, Brian, Mary, Daragh, Sheila and Dominic. When they first married they lived in Tankardstown, then with Roderick and Molly's youngest brother, Jim O'Brien. The O'Neill family came to Pullwee Street to live in Clarke's house that stands on the entrance of Streamstown where Rita and Paddy Martin were later to live and the Yellow Well (Pullwee) was located. They built their own home in 1954, calling the house *Knock Marian* as Molly put a stone from Knock in the foundation and 1954 being the Marian year. Mary O'Neill lives there today with her family.

Michael O'Neill (Mickey) extended his business by opening a grocery shop where Mick Nash's used to be – beside his relocated butchers, where Katy's and Tony Darby's now stand. He also opened a butcher' shops in Ashbourne which Jim O'Brien helped run, along with having a small business which was still running in Finglas. He was a great enthusiast of all sport. His first cousin, Micheal O'Brien, was an outstanding Meath football player, but horse racing was his passion.

Molly and Mickey suffered a great blow when Molly lost her brother Frank, her only brother to have married, when he fell to his death on a building site in England in 1964, aged 41 years. Frank O'Brien is survived by his widow Sheila and his only child Mary. But more tragedy was to follow. In 1967, they were to loose their son Paddy, aged 18 years. In 1969 saw Fiacra also taken in a car accident die age of 20 years. They were not quite a year apart when born. But Molly's greatest loss was losing Micky seven months later on Easter Monday 1969, on the same day they met. He was 53 years old. She found comfort in good and true friends over the years to follow. Fr Pat Brown making her feel special at his first mass, introducing her to Cardinal Basil Hume, when he came to Ratoath to meet Pat's family and his friends. Fr. Dan Eiffe always called and was here for her funeral. Molly loved her family above all else like all mothers do but some of her heart had already left with the two boys and Micky before she got to join them on 23rd June 1991 aged 75 years.

O Neill's Butchers' 1963 also in the photograph is Alfie Mahon's Morris. The red VW beetle is Pat Donnelly's.

FAMILY AND FRIENDS

The Rafferty Family

JOAN KING (NÉE RAFFERTY)

JOHN AND ANNE RAFFERTY had eight children, John (Jackie), Edward (Neddie), Anthony (Tony), William, Kathleen (Dolly), Anne (Nan), Bridie and Daisy.

Jackie, Neddie and Willie served in the British Army, based at Catterick in England. Both Jackie and Neddie were injured in Dunkirk and returned home after a period of recuperation. No news of Willie ever reached home and he was presumed missing in action. Jackie married Rosie Keogh from Ratoath and they resided in the house down the lane by the side of the church in Ratoath, overlooking the Broadmeadow River (area now referred to as the River Walk).

Neddie married Mary Bruton from Bodeen and they lived in Brutons homeplace.

Anthony married Mary Brennan from Cushenstown and they raised four children in

John Rafferty (Centre) with two of his children Anthony (Tony) and Kathleen (Dolly) in 1925

Catterick, January 1930
Edward (Neddie) Rafferty is 4th from the left at the back standing.
John (Jackie) Rafferty is 3rd from the left seated.

FAMILY AND FRIENDS　　　　　　　　　　　　　　　　　The Rafferty Family

the homestead at Cabinhill. Kathleen (Dolly) was married to Thomas McClorey whose family hailed from Co. Down. Nan married Willie Henry from Greenogue and they had nine children some of whom still reside in the Ratoath/Ashbourne area. Bridie emigrated to England and was wed to Tom Whittaker, they had one daughter, Patricia. Sadly, Daisy died at an early age.

(Above): Anne (Nan) Henry (nee Rafferty) 1931

(Right): Anthony (Tony) Rafferty with his niece, Patricia Whittaker, with a cock of hay on a horse-drawn hay bogie in the 1940s

(Below left): Private John (Jackie) Rafferty

(Below centre): Kathleen (Dolly) seated left Anne (Nan) standing and Bridie Rafferty

(Below right): Anthony (Tony) Rafferty on his wedding day with his bride Mary (nee Brennan) Also in the photograph is best man Jim Everard and bridesmaid Lydia Everard.

FAMILY AND FRIENDS

Richard and Christina Donnelly

The Commons, Fairyhouse Road

MARY O'SULLIVAN (NÉE DONNELLY)

RICHARD (DICK) DONNELLY was born on 25 July 1902 and was brought up in the stone cottage beside Dessie Tooles in what is known as The Strand. He had two brothers, Jack and Paddy, and five sisters, Alice, Judy and Nannie and twins Kitty and Mary.

Christina (Chris) Kelly, originally from Kimmage in Dublin, was born on 25 December 1905. Her mother died shortly after her birth and following the death of her father in 1909 when she was four years old she moved to Kilbrew, Curragha where she was reared by her aunt Nannie Cleary.

Dick Donnelly and Chris Kelly met at a crossroads dance in Curragha and married in 1932 in the Curragha parish church. They temporarily lived in Blackhall Place, Dublin and then moved to Jack Sherlock's house in Ratoath, which is now the site of the Supervalu Supermarket. Their eldest daughter Mary was born in the Rotunda Hospital in 1938 while they lived in Jack Sherlock's and the couple then moved to their long-term home at The Commons, Fairyhouse Road. The rest of the family Mona, Alice, Josie and Mick (the Briar) were born at The Commons.

Dick Donnelly worked all his life on John Caul's farm at Fairyhouse. He took pride in his work and could often be seen furrowing in *"the bridge field"* with Billy and Paddy – the Caul's workhorses. He loved the races at Fairyhouse - especially the Easter Festival. John Caul allowed him the use of the land at Easter and he would make a few bob charging punters for parking. Dick was awarded for 50 years unbroken service with a gold medal by the management of Fairyhouse Racecourse and a day out to the Spring Show at the RDS.

Chris was passionate about the horses and besides the local race meetings at Fairyhouse she travelled whenever she could to race meetings in Punchestown, Bellewstown and once a year to the Galway Festival. She had favourite jockeys and among them were Dougie Smith, Aubrey Brabson, Pat Taffe and Tommy Carberry. She placed a bet almost every day and her pastime in the evening was bingo. Chris attended all the local and surrounding bingo halls from Ratoath to Dunderry and from Kilbride to Drogheda. She was a very popular level-headed lady and was called upon in all local emergencies especially delivering newborn babies (all of Winnie and Pud Mahon's children) and the laying out of the deceased of Ratoath.

Gaelic games were big in the Donnelly house. Dick played hurling and would cycle to Croke Park with his buddies Jack Donnelly, Mickey Walls, Paddy Ward, Billy Lynch, Tottie Reilly, Blocker Blake and the Darby Gillic to see Meath play football. His love for sport and

Dick and Christina's Wedding
Standing Christina and Dick and
Seated Nancy Brady and Mickey Walls

referees together with his 'calm temperament' was passed on to his son Mick (the Briar) Donnelly. Mick won a Junior County medal for football with Ratoath in 1970 and he also played soccer for 21 years with Ratoath Harps. The Harps had their first ever win against Offaly in the late 1960's and Mick contributed to that win by scoring two of their three goals.

The local national school – Fr Everard Memorial School – was founded in 1911 and Dick Donnelly was one of its first pupils. Evidence of this was seen by his granddaughter Mary (daughter of Mick) in the first school roll book. Unfortunately most of these old records were destroyed in a fire in the school. He left the school in 1916 when he was fourteen to go to work in Cauls. Four generations of the Donnelly family have attended this school – Dick himself, all his children Mary, Mona, Alice, Josie and Mick, all of Mick's children Darren, Gemma, Triona, Mary and Cathal and Dick's great grandchildren Daniel and Conor O'Sullivan (grandchildren of Dick's eldest daughter Mary whose son Roy O'Sullivan moved from Birmingham to Dublin in 1991 and then settled in Ratoath in 1998).

Three of Dick and Chris' children still live in County Meath. Alice moved to Duleek and reared her six children there, Josie settled in Slane with her five children and Mick married Mary Reilly from Halltown, Skryne and they live in the family home on the Fairyhouse Road. Mary and Mona moved to Birmingham and reared their families there.

Dick left work in 1976 due to ill-health after serving 62 years with Caul's farm Fairyhouse. He passed away on the 19 May 1977 aged 75 years. A story is told that, while he was being waked at home, his longtime friend John (Darby) Gillic came to pay his last respects. Darby placed a baby power in the coffin with Dick and whispered to his friend "*have one on the other side on me*". They are both probably having one together now on the "other side". True friends!

Chris lived on for another fourteen years and passed away on 18 February 1991. She was one of the original punters and gamblers of Ratoath and was loved by all who knew her. She revelled in all that was County Meath; be it Easter as Fairyhouse, local football or County football, she lapped it all up. She was a familiar figure on the Fairyhouse Road cycling to the village and was seen regularly having chats and chinwags along the way with her good friends Maggie Donnelly, Winnie Mahon, Mrs. Woods, May Hessman and Molly Talty to name but a few.

FAMILY AND FRIENDS

Roche Family

JOHN & MARY ROCHE

WE MET at a dance in the old hall in Ratoath. We went out together for five years and travelled to dances everywhere within reach, on our bicycles, including carnivals in Kilmoon and Donaghmore where dances continued on to 3 a.m. We danced in the local hall also; dancing to many bands such as the Del Rio Swing Band which was managed by local man, the late John Eiffe. Admission was normally a half a crown. We got married in the early 1950's and had one son, P.J. Times were hard then. When we married I earned five pounds and six pence per week for milking cows for the late Harry Everard. That was for Sunday and Monday. As the years went by life improved. We are living in Glascarn over fifty years and now in 2007, we are both in our late seventies and still enjoying life, T.G.

FAMILY AND FRIENDS

Rooney Family, Glascarn

BERNIE DOLAN (NÉE ROONEY)

GLASCARN, Ratoath, was home to Christopher Rooney originally from Bodeen and his wife Christina Rooney (nee Reilly) who came from Fairyhouse, Ratoath. They had one daughter and five sons. Christy was Farm manager for Colm Donnelly of Glascarn Estate. He was very heavily involved in the Ratoath G.A.A. He died in 1987 at the age of 57 years. In his memory, the local G.A.A. Club host The Christy Rooney Memorial Cup annually. His sons have carried on the tradition of involvement with the Club. His eldest son Dermot guided the Ratoath Under-14 football team to a very successful 2007 season by winning the Division One Championship and the Division One League, and the team went on to represent Meath in the 2007 Féile. To this day all the Rooney family continue to live in Ratoath.

FAMILY AND FRIENDS

Rory & Petra Conway

RORY CONWAY

I WAS BORN and reared in Ratoath where my father was the local GP. My mother was a very sound hard-working North of England woman. Although I wasn't active in sport like my father and the rest of the family I shared their love of sport and people. I trained abroad in various places until my mother told me the pub was up for sale in 1977.

Petra and I got married in 1980 and we then ran the pub 'Rory's' for the next 20 years until we sold it. People living in Ratoath now would hardly believe how rural a village it was then. There were two 'country' (single decker) buses to Dublin during the week. Because we were newly married Jem Brien kindly agreed to do stand in barman on a Sunday morning. He drew his friends, Farmer Mulvaney, Christy Mulvaney and Frankie Gorman to name a few. Petra was two years in the pub before The Farmer asked her to pull a pint of Guinness. She had arrived.

The year of the big snow in 1984 brings back happy memories of Mrs. Pauline Byrne, Skryne Road, giving milk to anyone who could slide down to her house. We never knew John Long was a mean scrabble player. Everyone commented on the lovely atmosphere in the village during the week long cold spell.

James (Blackie) McGrane who has a superb mind finished off the Irish Times giant Christmas simplex crossword for us. Who else but Blackie would know that the singular of 'Magi' was 'Magus'? Mick Ryan (publican) and all his family were not only our competitors but also very supportive neighbours. Gerry and I had a path worn from his pub to mine with all the times we 'borrowed' stuff. Bailey Everard was the only one who got away with calling me 'old guy'. There were two great Jim Bradys in the village, Jim from the Garage and Jim from the Fairyhouse Road. Mark organised the 'Battle of the Bands'. It was the forerunner of 'Witness'.

Petra and I were very privileged to know a lot very mannerly young people and their parents. Willie & Theresa Donohoe did their bit to keep us fit by organising the Terry Fox Run/Walk. We love returning to our friends in Ratoath especially to the annual Mass in honour of Sarah Browne. Even though I won't mention them by name we lost some other very dear friends tragically and we always remember them in our prayers. Fr Gerry McCormack is remembered with kindness as bringing a new breath of fresh air to Ratoath. In my opinion Fr Gerry Stuart and his team bring continued hope, help and understanding to the community

The icing on the cake for us was celebrating 'BobbyJo' winning the Irish Grand National with the Carberry family - Tommy the trainer, Paul the jockey, Pamela the wife and mother. What a week the whole village had. The champagne flowed like Guinness. Nobody begrudged the hangover.

Petra and I now have a B&B in Laytown, called Highfield House, where we have a special welcome for our friends. Instead of walking behind the counter we walk the beach.

Note: *Rory first published his story in the "Village Voice" on Thursday 7 April 2005, pp 18, in an article entitled "What Happened to...Rory and Petra Conway"*

FAMILY AND FRIENDS

Walls Family in Ratoath

ROSE O'NEILL (NÉE WALLS)

Paddy and Mary Walls

THE WALLS FAMILY is in Ratoath over 100 years. The first member of the family, Paddy, was born Wall in 1860 but died named Walls (who knows when or how the 's' came to be added to the name). Paddy arrived in Ratoath and lodged in John (Darby) Gillick's house. This was the house where Maud Foley's family subsequently lived and it is now owned by Brady's Garage on Main Street.

Mary Mullen (later to become Mary Walls) was born in Collon, Co. Louth, in 1875. Mary's family were tenant farmers, they were evicted and then moved to Skryne. Mary worked as a cook in Park House, Skryne Road, owned by the Rogers family at that time (around 1900). Paddy Walls worked with horses for Frank Rogers over in Glascarn Lane, the stud farm now owned by Colm Donnelly.

Second and Third Generations
On 9th October 1901 Paddy Walls married Mary Mullen and they had five children: Tommy, Michael (known as Mickey), Paddy, Johnny, and Mary, who died at 14 years of age. The death of her only daughter had a profound effect on Mary and the rest of the family.

Mickey married Nan Doran of Glascarn. Tommy married Molly Carroll from Garristown. Paddy married Molly Flood from Oldcastle and Johnny married Kitty Connell from Ratoath. Johnny had six children (his granddaughter, Orla Brennan, plays international women's rugby for Ireland). Paddy had two children; Tommy had one child, and Mickey had eight children: Rose, Anne, Molly, Michael, Frank, Martin, Anthony (Bobby) and Lena

Mickey worked with horses in Dan Moore's (now Tattersalls) Stables for most of his life, and was groom to Flying Wild, the grey mare owned by Raymond Guest, the American Ambassador to Ireland (1965-68). Mickey's son-in-law, Johnny Lumley, was groom to Arkle and Flying Bolt at Tom Draper's Stables. All of Mickey's family stayed in Ratoath, except Rose, who lives in Kilkenny. Anne is married to Johnny Ryan and they own the "Near Buy" supermarket in the centre of the village.

Tommy worked for many years as gardener and driver for the Augustinian nuns, who owned the nursing home, formerly the Manor House, which is now owned and run by the Silver Stream Healthcare Group since 2002. Johnny worked at Woodpark Stud, Dunboyne, now owned by Sheik Maktoum. Remarkably, not one of the Walls emigrated permanently, although some worked in England for a while.

Through the generations
The Walls family has always been very involved in the GAA in Ratoath, in both hurling and football, and this love of sport has continued with the Lumley's and the Ryan's. Paddy and his sons spent their lives working with horses and, while not so many of subsequent gen-

erations did, they maintained their interest by their involvement in racing syndicates. The younger Walls family members continue this love by participating in the hunt and hunter trials - full circle!

Paddy loved gardening. His garden was full of raspberries, blackcurrants, gooseberries, and flowers, and this love he passed on to his children, grandchildren and great grandchildren. Grandfather Paddy's house in the village on Irish Street is occupied by grandson Tommy Walls and his family.

Paddy died aged 79 in 1939, and Mary died aged 94 in 1969 and they could never have imagined their great grandchildren travelling the world as they do. It is certain that Paddy and Mary would be very proud of all their descendants.

(Above): Orla Brennan Rugby player for Ireland, 2007

FAMILY AND FRIENDS

The White Family, Fairyhouse Road

PATRICK (SHANE) WHITE

PATRICK AND CATHERINE White originally lived opposite Ryan's Pub, where the Shrine to the Sacred Heart is situated today. Paddy was born in Ballybin and Catherine (nee Murray), lived on Main Street where her family ran the Post Office for many years on the site of Johnny Ryan's Near Buy Supermarket. They also operated the first Taxi Service in Ratoath. Patrick died in 1973 and Catherine in 1988. They had five children, Joseph, Mary (Amy), Olive, Shane and Joseph who died in 1950 aged 11.

FAMILY AND FRIENDS

White Family, Kilrue

THE WHITE FAMILY

JOHN AND ANNA MARIA WHITE (nee Flynn) were married in Dunshaughlin around 1905. They had eight children, as well as two surviving stepchildren from John's first marriage. John White died on 21 January 1925 and Anna-Maria White died on 6 Feb 1965.

Eamon, the youngest, was born in 1919. He was best known for his farming and business interests. He gained a scholarship to UCD to study Horticultural Science, but returned home to run the family farm following the tragic death of his brother Ignatius (Natty), who died as a result of a tractor accident on the farm on 28 March 1941. Over the next thirty years he built a farming business which included tillage, beef production, poultry, pigs and sheep, as well as a construction business for poultry/pig-housing systems.

Joe White, Christmas 1980

During a trip to Canada in the late 1950s he saw the facilities farmers there had for storing and drying grain and his farm at Kilrue was one of the earliest farms in the country to construct grain storage/drying facilities. In the mid 1960s he visited Holland and was impressed by the quality of the housing design and environmental control in intensive livestock buildings. In partnership with an overseas company over the next ten years he successfully built modular high-specification housing units across Ireland.

Eamon was active in the Irish Grassland Association and served as national president of the organisation. He was also involved in local community initiatives, including The Ratoath Development Association and St. Vincent de Paul Society. He had a keen interest in flat racing and was a frequent visitor to the Curragh. Eamon died on 2 August 1990.

His brother Joe, who also worked on the farm at Kilrue, had a lifelong interest in both horse racing and greyhounds. Two of his dogs, "Lady go Lovely" and "Mullinahob", enjoyed moderate success and managed to put some silver on the dresser at Kilrue! Joe died on 2 September 1989.

Their sister Esther nursed in England and later returned to Ratoath, where she married Jimmy Brindley and lived at Mullinam. Esther died in October 1988.

Kathy married Tony Kinsella from Church Street, Dublin. They lived for a few years in Ardee before moving to settle in Sutton, where they both were active in local politics. Katty was the last of the family to die, aged 95 in 2006.

Monica White married Tim Carberry, from Garristown, and is the matriarch of the "Carberry Clan". Her son Tommy named one of his horses "Joe White" after his uncle, but unfortunately Joe did not live to see it run and win the Topham Trophy at Aintree, ridden by his grandnephew Paul Carberry.

Maisie married Paddy (Pa) Kennedy and they farmed at Peacockstown. She was very involved in breeding greyhounds and some of these she passed to her brother Joe when they were old enough to be trained. Maisie was also a gifted baker and her gifts of Christmas Cakes & Puddings were much welcomed each year by her sisters and brothers.

Pat, the eldest of the family, was also big into horses and greyhounds and was known as "Pat the Slipper". He managed the greyhound track in Enniscorthy for a time, where he met his wife-to-be Gretta Brennan. Gretta, although born in Carnew, was reared in Enniscorthy and after their marriage they moved to Galway City, where Pat initially managed the greyhound track before becoming the area representative for D.E. Williams. No matter where Pat was he always made the annual pilgrimage home at Easter for the races at Fairyhouse. One of his sons, Padraig, continued the family love of horse racing and owned a number of horses, including "Royal Appointment", the winner of the Kerry, Munster and Connaught Nationals.

Members of the White family celebrating Suzanne's First Holy Communion at Ashbourne Church in 1986. Pictured L-R were:
Eamon White, Pa and Maisie Kennedy (nee White), Ester Brindley (nee White), Maria Delaney, Brian White, Nance and Jack Hyland, Mary White, Anne White (nee Hyland) with Peter, Suzanne and David White in front.

FAMILY AND FRIENDS

The Woods Family

PAT WOODS

PAT WOODS is married to Anne and at time of writing (2007) their two sons Colm and Shane were aged 14 and 12 respectively. Pat's father, James, died in 2003 at the age of 81. His uncle Paddy lives in Killsallaghan, Co. Dublin and his sister Kathleen lives in Dunsany, Co. Meath, and she has 5 children.

Pat's earliest childhood memories are of playing games of hurling on the Fairyhouse Road with the Walls brothers. Pat recalls that the first television on the Fairyhouse Road was in Benny and Alice Dolan's house. Every Monday evening the house was full of children who gathered for the "Western" films which were very popular. Other memories include playing football as a child in Sonny Carey's field when "you were not supposed to!"

Despite all the rapid changes around them in recent years the Fairyhouse and Ratoath people still enjoy one another's company.

FAMILY AND FRIENDS

Irish Nun is War Heroine

Germany and the French Republic Honoured Her

RATOATH HERITAGE GROUP

"War nurse with opposing armies...personally honoured by Kaiser Wilheim for services rendered to wounded men of the German forces... decorated by the President of the French Republic ... Irish nun in a convent in France for half a century....."

THESE ARE BUT SOME of the highlights in the remarkable life of Soeur (Sister) Margaruite Corballis of Co. Meath, whose death was announced from Pan, Pyrenees, in France. Her death at the age of 68 removes a nun of great nobility, greatness and courage according to sources of the time.

Margaruite was the third daughter of the late James Henry Corballis, of Ratoath, Co.Meath, Ireland and was only eighteen when she entered the French order of the Sisters of Charity in Pau, Pyrenees. The late Soeur Margaruite was sister of Mr. James Corbaliss and also of Mr. Frederick Corbaliss, who was a private Chamberlain to the late Pope Pius XI. She was aunt of Captain J.C. Corbaliss of Rosanagh, Co.Wicklow.

Amid Heavy Fighting

During the European War of 1914-1918 [World War I] she was a nurse in the Strasbourg district during some of the heavier fighting, and her skilled hospital work among the wounded French troops brought many high and memorable tributes. When a section of the German Army forced its way through the French lines, Soeur Margaruite was captured at the hospital base.

Such efficiency and skill did she display in her nursing work that the Germans soon placed her in charge of a hospital base in the Rhine. For her services among the wounded, she was strikingly honoured by receiving a letter from the Kaiser.

At the end of the war she was able to return to Strasbourg and on French soil another honour was bestowed on her. President Millerand, President of the French Republic, came specially from Paris to decorate her with the Legion of Honour for her services as a nurse among the French troops.

FAMILY AND FRIENDS

In Memory of James Everard

— Queen's Own Cameron Highlanders

RATOATH HERITAGE GROUP

JAMES EVERARD, the son of Patrick and Mary Everard, of Ratoath, Co. Meath, served in the Queen's Own Cameron Highlanders in the rank of private (service no. 6985970). His death is recorded as one of the Commonwealth War Dead. At the age of 21 he died in service on 11th June 1944 (World War II) and is buried in Kohima War Cemetery, Nagaland State, India (grave/memorial reference: 5.K.9), some 200 kilometres from the Indo-Burmese border (now known as the Indo-Myanmar border).

Kohima is best reached by air from Calcutta to Dimapur or from Delhi to Dimapur via Gauhati in Assam State and then by a winding road up the mountains. Kohima is 74 kilometres from Dimapur. It can also be reached by road from Gauhati - a long and difficult journey. An inner line permit is required to visit Nagaland and sometimes special permission needs to be obtained from the State Governor. Kohima War Cemetery is situated on the left of the Imphal-Diampur road (Highway 39) close to the centre of the town. The cemetery is completely terraced with terrace levels ranging from 3 – 5 metres high.

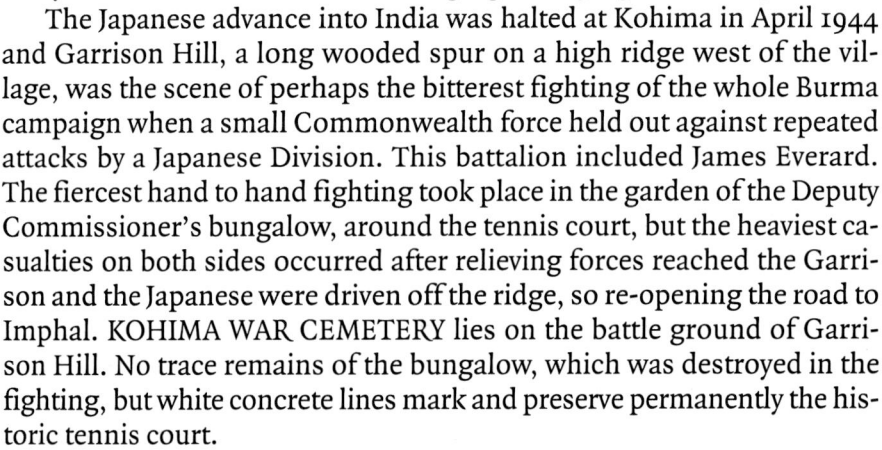

The Japanese advance into India was halted at Kohima in April 1944 and Garrison Hill, a long wooded spur on a high ridge west of the village, was the scene of perhaps the bitterest fighting of the whole Burma campaign when a small Commonwealth force held out against repeated attacks by a Japanese Division. This battalion included James Everard. The fiercest hand to hand fighting took place in the garden of the Deputy Commissioner's bungalow, around the tennis court, but the heaviest casualties on both sides occurred after relieving forces reached the Garrison and the Japanese were driven off the ridge, so re-opening the road to Imphal. KOHIMA WAR CEMETERY lies on the battle ground of Garrison Hill. No trace remains of the bungalow, which was destroyed in the fighting, but white concrete lines mark and preserve permanently the historic tennis court.

The cemetery now contains 1,420 Commonwealth burials of the World War II including the remains of James Everard from Ratoath. At the highest point in the cemetery stands the KOHIMA CREMATION MEMORIAL commemorating 917 Hindu and Sikh soldiers whose remains were cremated in accordance with their faith. At the lower end of the cemetery, near the entrance, is a memorial to the 2nd Division. It bears the inscription: *"When you go home tell them of us and say, For your tomorrow, We gave our today."*

Reference: Everard Family & Commonwealth Graves Commission, 2007.

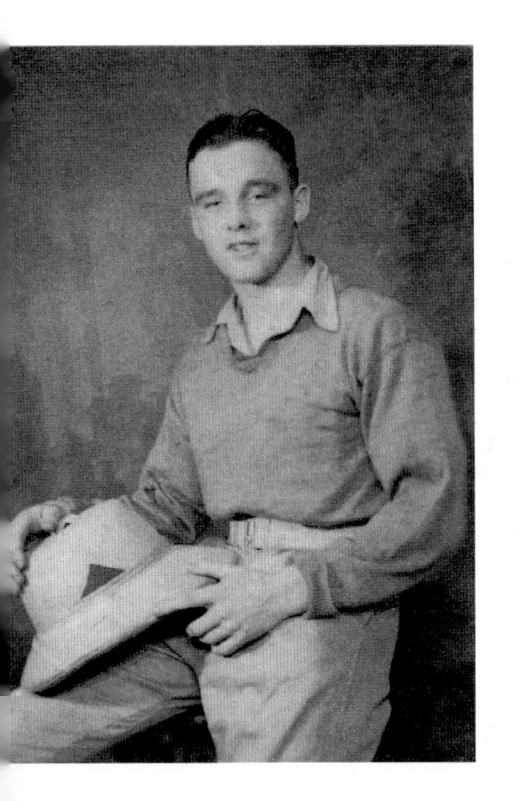

FAMILY AND FRIENDS

From Wilkinstown to the Padma Shri and other Stories

GREGORY PEPPARD

NOT TO BE CONFUSED with the village of Wilkinstown/Dunshaughlin, the Townland of Wilkinstown consisted of a farm of about 140 acres located in the Barony of Rathbeggan about 2.5 kilometers south west of the village of Ratoath. What connection can there be between this quiet rural setting in Co. Meath and the chaotic maelstrom of the Calcutta streets?

In this biographical genealogy we find how a Loreto Nun has her roots in the farming community of Meath. S M Cyril Mooney has given her life to the education of the poorest of Kolkata (Calcutta) in India and, although her school in Sealdah teaches the children of the better off families, in the late 1970's she threw the doors open to the street children of Calcutta. These children were allowed come in of their own accord and became known as rainbows as they came and went as rainbows are prone to do. And so the rainbow school programme was born. In 2007, S M Cyril Mooney was awarded the 'Padma Shri' award by the government of India. But let us start at the beginning.

An Administration Bond[1] dated 1798 showing that William Cahill of Wilkinstown died intestate gives us a point at which to begin this story. Parish records[2] confirm this with an entry for William Cahill dying on May 24th 1798 and interestingly a Thomas Cahill of the same address dying on April 17th 1798 just over a month earlier. However, the full circumstances of their demise and how they are related to the later Cahills has not yet been fully ascertained.

It is known, however, that twenty eight years later, on the 26th November 1826, Patrick Cahill signed a lease agreement with Thomas Lee Norman for the Wilkinstown property. Patrick Cahill demised the leasehold to his son John Cahill who is one of the parties in a Marriage Agreement[3]. He was the father of one known daughter, Bridget (Binnie), who had been married to Bernard Monaghan by whom she had four children, unfortunately he died and she was left to run the farm with very young children and an aging father. James Barry a gentleman farmer from Wicklow stepped into the breach and agreed to marry Bridget, but what about her first family. Well James was not without means and owned another the valuable farm of Johnstown Kilpeddar in Wicklow and so a marriage agreement was drawn up which provided for Bridget's father and children. Her father remaining on the farm, while the children were to receive a monetary inheritance at the age of eighteen in the

---

1   National Archives of Ireland, Administration Bonds, Diocese of Meath, T2427
2   Dunshaughlin Parish Records. NLI Pos. 4177
3   Registry of Deeds, Henrietta St. Cahill/Barry Deed, 1869, Book 38, No.215 Wilkinstown, Rathbeggan, Co. Meath.

case of the sons and the daughters at twenty one or younger if they got married. This Marriage Agreement came to fruition with the couple getting married on 28th August 1870. And indeed the Land Valuation cancellation books recorded James Barry as the registered occupier the same year.

This secured the farm and the newly married couple had two daughters Anne and Mary Josephine, Anne died quite young and Mary was sent to board in the Dominican Convent School in Wicklow.

Unfortunately marital bliss was short lived and three years later we find James and Bridget legally separated. This document4 dated the 15th August 1873 records James Barry the first party, Bridget the second party and a James Case, a butcher living in Dublin, as the third party. The agreement allows James Barry to retain the Farm but he is required pay Bridget an annuity of £40 sterling. If James defaults on this payment Bridget can go to the farm and remove goods to the value of the default plus extra for distress, *'as a landlord would do with his tenant.'* This last sentence speaks loud as to the actual situation between them.

Mary Josephine Barry

Mary was placed as a boarder in the Dominican Convent School in Wicklow and received a polished education studying subjects such as Botany. She is said to have been very ladylike and well read though rather aloof. She lived with her aunt Mary Barry in Johnstown.

Mary Josephine Barry and Patrick Mooney

Mary Barry's Botany exam results, 1891
(Dominican Convent, Wicklow)

Patrick Mooney

Patrick Mooney was born and grew up on the farm of Trudder, Newtownmountkennedy, Co. Wicklow, which was a freehold farm that has been in the Mooney family since at least 1796 and passed on from father to son without interruption to this day. It has been said that Patrick Mooney was described as more of a gardener than a farmer and he also had a reputation locally as a bonesetter. He made crutches and aids for people with incapacitating injuries.

---

4   Registry of Deeds, Henrietta St. Dublin, Barry to Barry Deed, 1873, B? No. 72

Mary Barry and Patrick Mooney were married on the 1st February 1902 in the little Catholic chapel of Kilquade and settled on the Barry farm of Johnstown, Kilpeddar Co. Wicklow where they had four children: William Barry, Frances, Kevin and Hubert. When Mary's father James Barry died on the 2nd March 1906 they moved to Wilkinstown farm in Co. Meath. Patrick Mooney died on the 2nd December 1932 and Mary died almost eighteen years later on 28th July 1950 and the farm passed on to the two younger sons Kevin and Hubert.

Wilkinstown Timeline
The following Diagram is a timeline showing how the farm of Wilkinstown was passed on through the Cahill, Monaghan, Barry and Mooney families.

WILKINSTOWN FARM

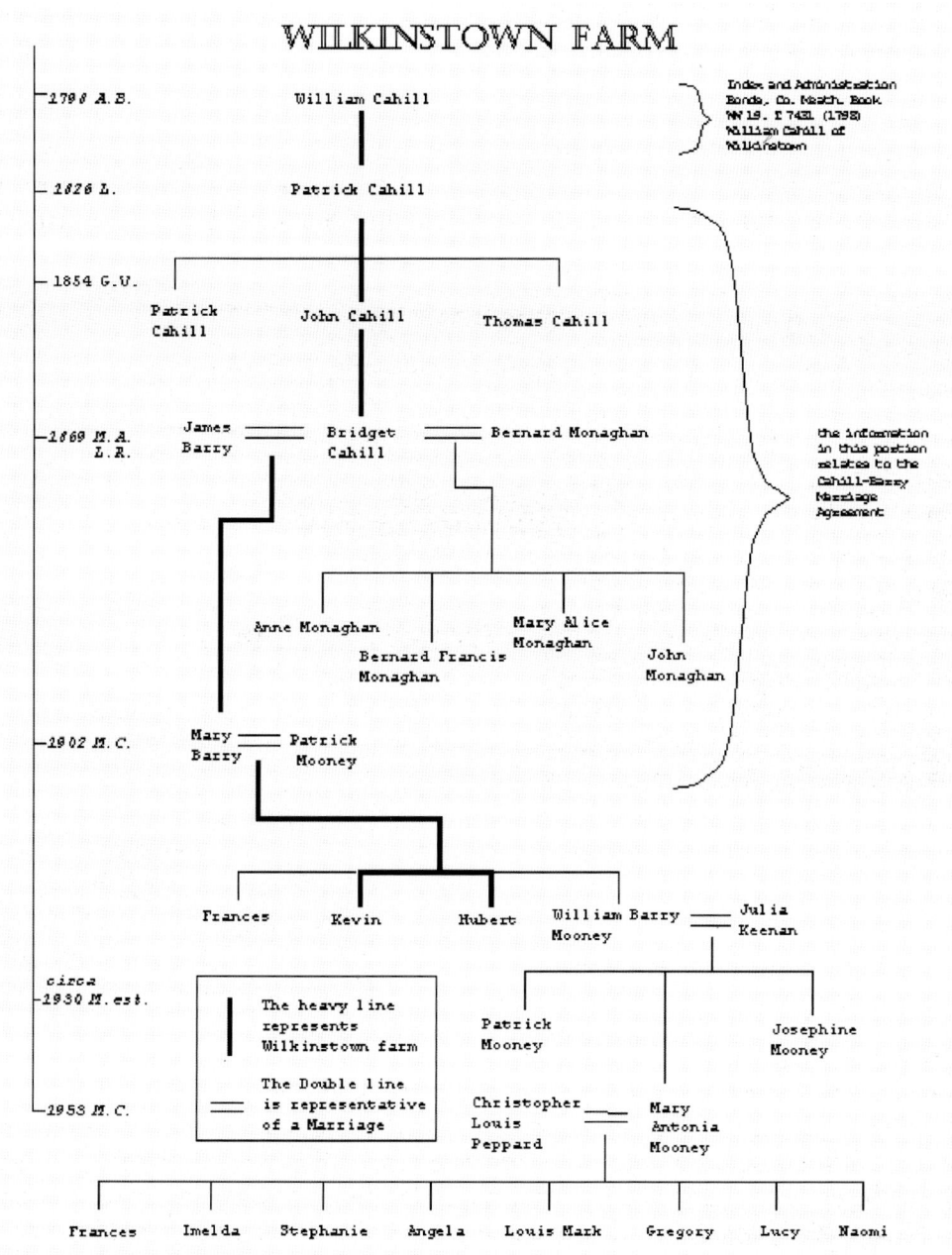

- 1798 A.B. — William Cahill — Index and Administration Bonds, Co. Meath. Book WN 19. F 7431 (1798) William Cahill of Wilkinstown
- 1826 L. — Patrick Cahill
- 1854 G.V. — Patrick Cahill, John Cahill, Thomas Cahill
- 1869 M.A. / L.R. — James Barry = Bridget Cahill = Bernard Monaghan — the information in this position relates to the Cahill-Barry Marriage Agreement
  - Anne Monaghan, Bernard Francis Monaghan, Mary Alice Monaghan, John Monaghan
- 1902 M.C. — Mary Barry = Patrick Mooney
  - Frances, Kevin, Hubert, William Barry Mooney = Julia Keenan
- circa 1930 M. est. — Patrick Mooney, Josephine Mooney
  - The heavy line represents Wilkinstown farm
  - The Double line is representative of a Marriage
- 1953 M.C. — Christopher Louis Peppard = Mary Antonia Mooney
  - Frances, Imelda, Stephanie, Angela, Louis Mark, Gregory, Lucy, Naomi

Abbreviations on timeline: A.B. = Administration Bond; M.A. = Marriage Agreement; M. est. = Marriage date estimated; L. = Lease; L.R. = Land Registration; M.C. = Marriage Certificate; G.V. = Griffiths Valuation

William Barry Mooney

Sr. Cyril's father William "Willie", the first child of Patrick and Mary Mooney, was born 27 December 1902 at Johnstown, Kilpeddar Co. Wicklow. He started his education in a little school in the Glen of the Downs, now long gone, and then in 1912 entered the National School in Kilcoole[5]. William grew up in his former years at Kilpeddar but later on moved to Wilkinstown and is mentioned in a letter dated 1927 to be living on the family farm of Wilkinstown, Rathbeggan, Co. Meath, as shown above in a letter of recommendation from John Wilkinson of Rathbeggan House.

William Mooney was an irregular during the Civil War and was arrested and interned in Maryborough (Portlaoise) which broke his connection with the Wilkinstown farm and his mother. After his release from detention William married Julia Keenan of Calary who had managed a dairy in Talbot St. Dublin and the couple moved to Scotland where, for a couple of years, he managed the orphanage farm at Smyllum Park, Lanark run by the French Sisters of Charity.

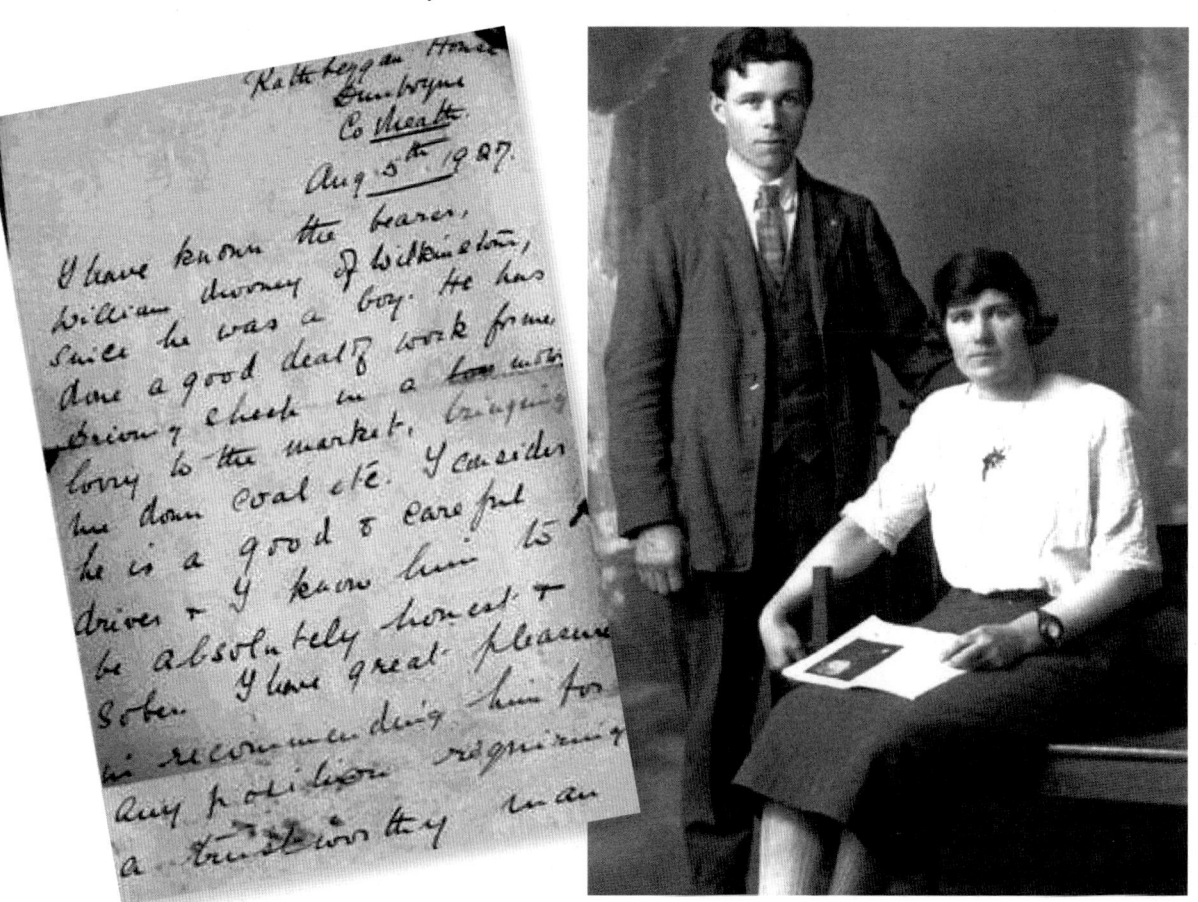

Julia Keenan

Julia was the youngest daughter of William Keenan of Calary, County Wicklow and Mary Kavanagh daughter of Thomas Kavanagh the local blacksmith in Kilmacanogue.

Born about 1898[6], in her early teens Julia Keenan became an active member of *Cumann na Mban* and like her daughter, Sr. Cyril Mooney, received a medal of recognition from a national president for her efforts, albeit for a very different reason. This does show, however, the strength of character in both these extraordinary women.

---

5   Kilcoole, Co. Wicklow, *School Registers from 1861*. Compiled by G.H. O'Reilly. Irish Genealogical Sources. No. 16, 1999
6   Based on her age in the *Census of Ireland 1901*.

On their return to Ireland a year later William Mooney was employed as groundsman on the Curragh and then as groundsman in Woodbrook, Shanganagh, Bray where they lived in an old coastguard station where their first two children, Patrick and Mary Antonia were born. This house was so close to the sea that Julia often described her fear during storms as the waves lashed against the windows and indeed since then the old building has collapsed into the brine.

William Mooney spoke very little about his involvement in the troubles and declined to accept his medal mainly due to his disillusion with the futility of the Civil War. Times were not easy in the thirties and through the emergency. William Mooney at least had work. And after Woodbrook, William was employed as a foreman by a Civil engineer and public works contractor called C. S. Downey and the Mooney family moved to live in Bray where Josephine Mooney (later to become S M Cyril IVBM) was born on the 21 July 1936.

Working under Downey, William Mooney was involved in many large projects such as Foynes Airport, Lough Swilly Bridge, Ballybough Flats, Monkstown Farm county council housing scheme, Poulaphuca Dam and Wolfe Tone Square, Bray. He was highly regarded by both his employers and his men alike. He died in 1972.

Sister Cyril Mooney IVBM

Josephine (now known as Sister Cyril Mooney) was the youngest of William and Julia Mooney's three children; the eldest, her brother Pat, became a fire chief in the Bray Fire Brigade and her older sister, May, married Louis C. Peppard a Dublin architect who, with his business partner Hugo Duffy, designed some notable churches and other buildings in the Dublin area and beyond.

This Postcard depicts the P&O Passenger Liner, 'Chusan,' that sailed from Southampton to India in 1956. Sr. Cyril Mooney was a passenger.

Ratoath Past and Present

When Josie was about 13 years old she came home from school one day and announced to her mother that she was going to be a nun. Her mother advised her to be patient and to complete her education and then see how she felt about it. When she got her Leaving Certificate in 1953, her call to the religious life was as strong as ever and she entered Loreto Convent Bray and took Sr. Cyril as her religious title.

What her mother said four years earlier was not quite accurate; although Josie had indeed finished her schooling, her education was far from over. In a postcard (pictured below) sent to her sister May she writes to say that they have just boarded 'Chusan' at Southampton on 29 September 1956 bound for India leaving at precisely 2 a.m. The trip would go the long way around by the Cape of Good Hope due to the developing Suez Canal Crisis, with Egypt nationalising the canal on 26 July 1956, and she finally arrived in India on 10 October 1956.

Sr. Cyril continued her education studying Zoology in Lucknow, India, and obtained her PhD. in Endocrinology. At this time she ran the inter college there and taught science. In 1964 Sr. Cyril was involved in child-to-child outreach programmes where students were sent out on Saturdays to villages in the locality to impart what they had learned to village children who had little or no schooling. Reminiscent of the hedge schools in Ireland years ago, much of the teaching was done outdoors with bowls of sand on which they could write in the place of slates and chalk, this mutually beneficial system reinforced what the better off children were learning by having them teach and also developed in them a strong social conscience and of course the village children were being given an education which the may never have otherwise got.

In 1973, S M Cyril moved to Calcutta and worked at Loreto House. Again she took children to teach in the villages, and in 1979 she was transferred to Loreto Sealdah where she changed the school from a mainly paying school for better off children to one with half of its pupils from poor backgrounds. It was here she initiated the Barefoot Teacher Training, Hidder Domestic Child Labour Programme, Rainbow Educational Programme and, as in Lucknow, the Child-to-child Village Programme, and the Shikshalaya Prakalpa which is an initiative to educate all Calcutta's Children.

She also created a system of Value Education which has been used in about 50 government schools where it has been developed into a course on Human Rights. The Rainbow Homes is another programme created by S M Cyril, which takes in girls from the streets and uses the large schools from 2pm to 8am the following morning – a period each day when these premises would otherwise be vacant.

S M Cyril Mooney is and has been involved in many associations, resource groups and committees relating to teaching, education, science and human rights. She is the Secretary of the Calcutta Archdiocesan Council for Education, President of Heads of A.I. Schools Association in Calcutta. She is also a member of the Advisory Committee to the Government of India on a campaign called 'Every Child' to educate all Children and Adolescents who live and work on the streets. She is Convenor of both the West Bengal State and Kolkata Resource Groups for Education of Deprived Urban Children. She was nominated as a member of the governing body of the State Council of Educational Research and Training in West Bengal.

S M Cyril has been accorded many awards for her work, she received the NOMA award from UNESCO in 1997 (an award for spreading education and literacy among the poor). She has been awarded the telegraph award seven times Social Service four times and also Hall of Fame, Creative Excellence, and Best School. The Loreto Day School, Sealdah, Kolkata became the beneficiary of the Earhart Birthday Centennial Committee Award which was presented in 1988 to Linda Finch, a well known aviator who retraced the famous flight of Amelia Earhart, Sister Cyril also won the 'Better Calcutta Contest' ten times, for Outstanding Performance, Creative Excellence, Social Excellence, and Special Involvement. In 2002 at Toronto she received the International Christian Stewardship Award. From CINI (Child In Need Institute) she received the Friend of CINI Award, The ladies Study Circle made her 'Woman of the Year'. She received the Alexander Award for Excellence in Science in 2007 and the Padma Shri the same year.

The Padma Shri

One of the highest accolades the Indian Government can bestow on a civilian, the '**Padma Shri**' was accorded to Sister Cyril Mooney in 2007. She received this award for 'Education and Social Work of a High Order'. Sister Cyril is the only Irish person ever to have been given this medal, as she stated while giving a talk in her home town of Bray, and that she accepted the award on behalf of the entire Loreto Order. The Ratoath Parish Website[7] published an article titled 'Missionary Nun honoured in home town' (Bray, Co. Wicklow) where Sister Cyril was born and grew up but Ratoath was the home of her forbears and she along with her brother and sister have childhood memories of visiting the Farm at Wilkinstown.

S M Cyril Mooney with her Padma Shri Award that was presented to her by the Government of India in 2007. Pictured alongside her is her Nephew Gregory Peppard

OTHER STORIES

Dogfight over Wilkinstown

On the 22nd August 1942 May and Pat Mooney were visiting their grandmother in Wilkinstown when they heard the sound of airplanes overhead. May recollects standing in the farmyard and hearing debris rattling down on the corrugated iron roof of the barn. Pat went up to Ratoath Village to see the downed spitfire which crashed into a field beside the village. The unfortunate pilot was badly injured in the arm and was brought into the Presbytery nearby but the poor man did not survive.

---

7   http://www.ratoathparish.ie/index.php?option=com_cifeed&task=newsarticle&artid=4083 . Viewed 21/12/2007

(for further details of this event read *Ratoath Spitfire Crash* by Tony Darby in the section *Stories and Tales across the Decades*).

The Meath Hounds
This picture was on a Christmas card sent to Wilkinstown farm. The Meath hunt would regularly traverse the lands of Wilkinstown and the children would wait at gates for coins and sweets to be thrown to them by the huntsmen and women as they galloped through and would conduct hopeful searches of the ditches where the riders had crossed hoping change had jingled from their pockets.

Shortcut to Fairyhouse
Staying on an equestrian theme, the location of Wilkinstown adjacent to Fairyhouse Racecourse meant that it was often used as a shortcut to the races, especially at Easter during the Irish Grand National. At a time when bicycles were much more used as a mode of transport than today, people coming to Fairyhouse races would shortcut through the farm leaving their bicycles in the yard and the kids would be allowed turn a few pennies for minding the bikes.

Moore's Biplane
The children also remember talk of the airplane owned by the Moore Family of the Old Fairyhouse Stud. In the picture below we see the airplane with the Moore's and Sr. Cyril's Aunt, Frances Mooney, on the right.

Conclusion
This article has told the story of S M Cyril Mooney in the context of her forbearers who lived in Wilkinstown, Ratoath, Co. Meath and while it must be understood that there are others who share the same ancestry, this is her story.

FAMILY AND FRIENDS

My Roots in Ratoath

CANON PAT BROWNE

I HAVE SUNG with The Academy of St Martin in the Fields Choir in the Royal Festival Hall in London – one of the world's most famous concert halls. Other 'gigs' with them have included the Barbican and the Cathedral of San Tiago in Compostela. I do this in my spare time from being a parish priest and a director for men called to the Permanent Diaconate – something that is just about to take off in Ireland. I am a priest of the Westminster Diocese here in London, a Canon of Westminster Cathedral and Dean for the 10 parishes in London's West End and City. Both pursuits (singing and priesthood) started in Ratoath many moons ago.

I remember the very first day I started school as a five-year-old when JJ Kelly the headmaster called me over in the playground. He was walking in the playground with his son and he asked me to sing them a song there and then. It went on from there. At the age of eight I pestered him to join the adult choir that sang in the church. For a long time he said I was too young but persistence broke him down.

He had us singing the Hallelujah Chorus from the 'Messiah', many 4 part motets and lots of Gregorian Chant, not always to the delight of that part of the Sunday congregation which much preferred a 'quick Mass'. People like Michael Maher, Nicky Sherry, Tony Darby, Mary and Olivia O'Hare, Frances Kinsella, Anne Maher, Lizzie Mannering, Katie Darby, Ter McCann and my mother were all part of this choir. I was by far the youngest! (With one or two exceptions). Many years before, JJ had staged a production of the Gilbert and Sullivan 'Mikado' up at Fairyhouse. My father (Jack) played Nanki Poo and my mother (Lucy) played Yum Yum. This was probably about 1946 or 47. They married about a year later! And I came along within 10 months of that. They obviously enjoyed playing the young romantic couple.

Mr Kelly then decided to teach me the piano. I practised in his house during school lunchtime and his wife Jerry listened, to make sure I was doing it. I was always jealous of one of the other kids whose parents had got him a piano to practise on. He didn't have to give up lunch-breaks!

Anyway, JJ put me in for my first exam. 1 got a distinction. JJ got a heart attack and had to give up teaching piano and that was the end of my piano career. But the singing was always there. And it was with great delight that when I came to Westminster Cathedral where they have a professional choir, I was able to sing from memory, word and note perfect, so much of their Gregorian chant repertoire. My job there for the next eight years was to be the Precentor, that is the priest liaison-person who worked with the choir and congregation in all the main liturgies. I sang the Gospel there when Pope John Paul visited the UK and again in St Peters in Rome when he beatified English and Welsh martyrs.

I remain forever grateful to Mr. Kelly for introducing me to music. It is so much a part of my life.

Molly O'Neill, the Lord have mercy on her, would have always thought that I was destined to be a priest. As a child when asked 'what do you want to be when you grow up'? I would have answered, along with other things, a priest. Jack and Lucy, my parents were certainly a great influence. Though not well off themselves they had a great concern for the poor and gave generously when they could, teaching us to do the same. That we 'said our prayers' morning and night, was a must, and we were taught to do it from an early age. Family Rosaries were attempted now and then, usually after a parish mission when Lucy would have heard a fiery sermon on *'the family that prays together, stays together.'* But they were not a success and usually ended up with one of us kids kicking or thumping another, fits of giggles, chewing sweets, and eventually Jack with verbal gusto gave up on it. But he was a very loyal man of the church. I remember one night there was the most almighty storm. As he would have put it, 'you wouldn't put out an old bucket'. We kids were all tucked up in bed. There was a knock on the door and it was an old traveller woman, soaked to the skin. He brought her in and invited her to spend the night by the fire out of the rain and cold.

Father Cogan too was a great influence. No, it wasn't his charisma for preaching. In fact he had the most awful stammer and it was agony sometimes listening to him. Neither was it his warmth of personality. He had been known to give the odd altar server a good box in the ear for misbehaviour in his younger days. But after we served his weekday morning Mass, we would go and get his morning paper. By the time we returned he would have taken off his vestments and would be kneeling on the *prie-dieu* (or kneeler as I called it then), saying his prayers of thanksgiving after Mass. He always did this. He looked so calm and peaceful - and faithful. I think in retrospect that was what impressed me most. It was an insight into the spirituality of this otherwise somewhat gruff, earthy, distant character and in contrast it *was* gentle and mysterious.

I left school when I was 14 and did various jobs. It was when I was working in Meagher's Pub, now the 'The Auld Stand' that Father Gerry Stanley came to the parish. He was a young, lean, black-haired priest. We got to know each other. He told me stories of his work in Peru, where he had been for the past number of years. I was fascinated and one day found myself blurting out to him *'maybe I should think about being a priest?'* He was very wise and suggested I think about it seriously and pray about it for the next year and see if I still felt the same.

I did a retreat some months later and when in confession talked to the priest about it. He asked me about myself and when he heard my story he told me to forget it as I had no education or money. Anyway I didn't. I came home from the pub one night and broke the news to my father and mother. They were absolutely stunned and didn't know what to say. So they didn't say anything and I went to bed. The next night though when I got home, they had talked about it. My father asked me who did I think I was. Was this another of my hair-brained ideas? And we had a terrible row. It wasn't that they had no respect for the priesthood. They had such a respect that no son of theirs could be good enough for it. And they were afraid for me.

I was going on nineteen and the following September, I found myself in a Jesuit College doing a catching up course, taking me up to Leaving Certificate standard so I could go into a major seminary, which I did one year later. Six years later I was ordained in All Hallows College, Dublin, for the Diocese of Westminster where I have been working as a priest ever since.

I am now in my thirty fourth year of Priesthood. I look back with much warmth to my roots in Ratoath and with respect for its people. I just pray the kids growing up there today get passed on to them the faith and the security of person-hood that my family and the community there gave me as I grew up. The place had a soul and growing up there I was able to discover mine. I give thanks for that. (See photograph, in Photographic Gallery, of Cardinal Basil Hume when he visited The Most Holy Trinity Church in Ratoath to concelebrate Mass with Fr. Pat Browne, who was then Cardinal Hume's Private Secretary).

Footnote: Canon Pat Browne sent his story from Westminster Diocese on 20th March 2008

FAMILY AND FRIENDS

Goodbye Ireland – A brief memoir

DAN EIFFE, 2007

Thirty years have passed since I set off from Dublin Airport for Africa. I had never been out of Ireland before and as I looked down on the beaches of Malahide and Portmarnock, my heart sank with trepidation. I would not be home for three years and knew nothing of the country or life that was in store for me. Years ago, to be away for 40 years was the order of missionary work. Then, Africa was known as "The White Man's Grave." Many never returned or saw their families again. Archbishop Shanahan of Nigeria and Bishop McCarthy of Kenya were two missionary giants whose incredible debuts into Africa turned them into household names for decades that followed. Inspired by these earlier missioners, I set off hoping to follow in their footsteps as an ordained Missionary of The Sacred Heart.

There was one major difference in outlook from the missioners who had served previously. I was brought up on liberation theology which essentially defined salvation in a different way. Salvation was not only concerned with the life hereafter but, to reach that life, mankind first needs to be liberated from poverty and oppression so that, valuing its dignity, mankind may come to realise the love of God.

Vatican II was a major influence on the Church in this period, particularly in 1963 when Pope Paul's encyclical *Populorum Progressio* came out, dealing with the development of peoples. The emphasis of the church shifted from a narrow sacramental role to that of securing each persons individual dignity and their right to enjoy justice, liberty and freedom from poverty. We were trained in what was considered a very radical approach and much of the material we worked from had been banned in several countries. One writer in particular whom we studied was Paulo Freveres, whose approach of concidentisation of people had rebellious tendencies. His books *Pedagogy of the Oppressed* and *Culturisation of Freedom* were a prominent part of our syllabus and had a profound effect on me. I cannot emphasis enough how it shapes a young man at thirteen years old to take him and put him into that environment and then into seminary at eighteen years of age. The radical social teaching we received at that time meant that sending us into South Africa or Sudan was like placing us back in Ireland during the Penal Days. The reaction of myself and priests like me to the oppression and injustice that was dealt out to our parishioners and those around us should have been expected.

How things have changed since the days when the role of the missionary priest was to save black babies from their dark past and introduce them to western "Civilisation". My generation went abroad to fight apartheid and injustice- to fight for human rights. I could not indicate on my work permit that I was a Catholic Priest but rather a Development Worker because the apartheid system knew us as the 'Roman Danger'. The main opposition to the apartheid regime in South Africa was the Church. The African National Congress (ANC) was then in exile while some of their leaders were detained in Robben Island where Nelson Mandela was incarcerated at the time.

Welcome to South Africa
I was sent to Venda which is the most northerly point of the Transvaal next to the then Rhodesian and Mozambican border. I found the Venda language more difficult to learn than the Irish with which I had struggled for many years back home. In some of the Venda villages high up on the mountains they never saw a white person. I was given my little half ton Toyota pick-up and sent off into the villages. I spent most of my days flying around the bush in a cloud of dust, visiting villages, performing the sacraments and working with the catechists who were my assistants. I was young, energetic and worked so hard.

I was so exhausted on Holy Thursday that I lay down on bed fully dressed. At around 2 am, I heard Father Paddy fall. He had suffered a heart attack. I dragged him up and proceeded to give him the last rites and to hear his confession. The sisters came and found me, passed out; lying on the floor with the holy stole around my neck. The story went all over South Africa and I was constantly asked *"What did Paddy confess to you that made you pass out?"*

Our work was extremely dangerous as we were working a lot with black youth and challenging the apartheid system. The Bureau of State Security, (BOSS), were notoriously cruel. I arrived in RSA, (Republic of South Africa) in the year in which the famous black consciousness leader, Steve Biko was killed. The then government was very brutal with their opponents. We would sometimes be picked up and warned by security to toe the line, (as they saw the so called "Line").

I was lucky but some of my fellow priests were not so lucky. South Africa, to the north, is separated from Zimbabwe (known as Rhodesia before 1978) by the Limpopo River. This was a strategic area. The Church employed social workers, who were often picked up and detained in Johannesburg etc., and these were regularly tortured and some even put to death. Upon release, some of them had to be smuggled out of the country. As a priest I was in a good position to disguise them as priests and to drive them through police checkpoints and let them off into the bush at night. I hoped they would make it across the river Limpopo. If one escaped the security nets, one had to contend with the crocodiles as they bounced across on the rocks in the Limpopo. I never knew if any of them made it. (See the film "Cry Freedom").

Some of our own church rules were out of touch with the reality facing us on the ground. For example, most men had many wives. You needed the paramount chiefs on your side to be able to operate. These were often polygamous. Only one wife, the first one, was recognised by the church. In one village in my parish, the chief, Rambuda, had 45 wives, all Catholic. In fact his family alone constituted the whole church. There were hundreds of his children. I could not say Mass there as I would only have been allowed to give communion to the first wife and would have to send the rest away. Even with the Catholic Acuminate (new Christians) it was ruled you should only baptise the first wife. On the other hand, if the husband did agree to send his second or third wife away they would be accepted as loose women in the community which for the husband would be demeaning. These were very poor people and did not have many choices. Their concept of polygamy had nothing to do with bigamy. A woman was married because there was a need to marry and be married. Men were not married. It was women who were married. Since marriage took place because of need and not because of love, (which is the western way), it tended to last. Unlike love, need did not fade away. Divorce did not exist. In any case, a woman was married to the clan.

The famous comedian, Spike Milligan, came to visit me because he wanted to make a series of documentaries for the BBC on topics such as polygamy, death and witchcraft etc, contrasting the very traditional Venda way of life with the western way of life. For example, how could the chief cohabit with 45 wives all peacefully working together, while we in the West sometimes fail with one wife? Spike asked me *'Does Rome agree with what you are doing here?'* I replied simply, "*I am doing my best in the circumstances and if the Pope or the Cardinals in Rome want to come here and do my job they are most welcome to provide better solutions.*" (as the BBC camera was rolling and I did not want to be excommunicated!). These issues covered contraception, etc. On hearing that I was one of a family of 15 people asked, "How many wives does your father have?" My father, Dan, loved that story.

I started some small agricultural projects to help the poor with food production. This well-meaning enterprise earned me a rebuke from my conservative bishop who, in reaction, wrote to remind me that I did not come to Africa to do this kind of work but rather to evangelise. As part of my priestly role, I became an undertaker as well as wardrobe mistress, providing bridal dresses donated by friends from Ireland and burying the dead.

I will never forget one day having to identify a dead body from the mortuary of a local hospital which had no electricity. I had to search through 45 bodies. I ran in and out for a breather as a drunken guy pulled them out for me to examine one by one. I was not sure I got the right corpse. I had a coffin on my little pick-up and we put the woman's body in and proceeded to a remote village, 40 kms. away, for the burial ceremony. On the way a storm arose and I skidded down a valley, across a river and up a slippery hill. The coffin fell out and I had to drag it up the hill in the mud and rain and put it back into the pick-up. I will never forget how bizarre this was and I hummed to myself the song *'If Ma could see me now'* but not doing, as the song says, "*smoking my cigarette, drinking my wine!*" The custom was to cut pieces off the dead body in the house, (where I could see them!) and bury them later, around the mud houses to protect themselves from the wrath of ancestors. This is crucial in African religion where ancestor worship prevails. Well, I certainly did not let them open that coffin again and I made sure she was really buried. (Since I was not so sure I had the right corpse anyhow and I wanted to get out of there alive!).

By 1987, I was using three different languages in my parish. I understood Venda and therefore heard confessions and said Mass etc. I simply knew how to read the other two. In one church where I used to say Mass, the only man who could translate my English sermon was always drunk. God knows what he did to my carefully prepared sermon. I often wondered. In between I had a study break. In London University I did an MA on South African History and Politics etc. During those times, I got wonderful support from the people of Ratoath on whom I could always count. I went back to visit Venda 20 years after my time working there and found the area unrecognisable, having opened up with roads, a university, hotels etc. I hope we in some way helped, in particular to dismantle apartheid.

My Home and My Heart Sudan
There is a saying in the Horn and East Africa that when you drink the waters of the Nile you never turn back and leave and that's what happened to me. The Nile, both White and Blue, flow through Sudan and out through Egypt.

A small background is required here to understand the context within which I write on Sudan. Sudan is the largest country in Africa, 31 times bigger than Ireland. Basically, it is divided into the North and South. The northern ruling elite, based in the capital Khartoum has, from ancient times, exploited the Southerners. They enslaved them in the 17th and 18th Century and when Sudan gained independence from Britain and Egypt in 1956, the Southerners, largely uneducated, were sold out to the Northerners who until the peace agreement, two years ago, continued to fight and exploit them. Since Independence, there has only been a 16 year long lull in the war. Since 1983, two and a half million people have died and over two million internally displaced out of a total of eight to ten million Southerners. Most civil wars in Africa have no good cause but the war in Sudan was genocidal and the rest of the world neglected it until recently.

I got heavily involved, particularly with the US administration, in this just cause in the most remote and underdeveloped area of Africa. I had to testify to Congress a few times concerning the situation in Southern Sudan. I found great scope and challenge here. I had enormous resources of aid which I could use to support the people and their cause. Above all, I was freed from the narrow confines of church law and thus able to do things which I believed were right in the circumstances. The Sudan Peoples Liberation Movement/Army (SPLM/A) was the poorest liberation movement in the world. They were fighting on behalf of the Southerners. They also had no experience of how to promote their cause internationally and what they were fighting for. The war was normally referred to as the forgotten tragedy - The Forgotten War.

A Brief on Activities
I was plunged into the middle of this civil war in the jungles of South Sudan and fought in the struggles against oppression for South Sudanese. I went to Juba, the capital of Southern Sudan, then under government control. I brought relief aid to 300,000 displaced people who had fled the war. The town was cut off, except by air and surrounded by the Sudan Peoples Liberation Army (SPLA) while the GOS (Government of Sudan) held it as a garrison town. It was shelled regularly by the SPLA and the only supplies that came in were by air when pilots risked being shot out from the sky. There, I met my Sudanese wife, Nouna. We were so badly shelled that sometimes I had to lie on top of our children to protect them before I got them out to Nairobi in Kenya. Terrified, I prayed that they would not be shot on take off. God listened to my prayers. In 1991, I left the town, my nerves in shreds. I then went into rural areas where I headed the organisation called "Norwegian Peoples Aid".

My life was in constant danger even in Nairobi because of my involvement in the war. I came out of Juba in mid 1991 and continued to work as an aid worker and political activist among the SPLM/A in the bush/rural areas of the South. My work entailed providing all forms of relief aid, food, shelter and medication which we moved into remote areas where people were cut off from all supplies. We built bush hospitals, clinics, etc. In 1988, I convinced GOAL to come to the South (Juba) which they later had to evacuate, but they joined me again in 1992 and in 1998; same with CONCERN in 1992.

In 1991, the liberation movement (SPLM) split and one group of 25,000 armed men attacked the others. Many thousands were killed. I was the only white man there and I filmed dreadful scenes which were shown all over the world. The breakaway group lost support because of the atrocities they committed. They later reconciled and they are now all party members of the new government of Southern Sudan. In essence, I became the envoy for the Southern cause backed by the media and western nations. From 1987 to 2003, I worked as a humanitarian aid worker with a political mandate, in particular as Field Director for Norwegian Peoples Aid. Through our work, we managed to support the Sudan Peoples Liberation Movement which led the struggle for the Southern Sudanese Africans mainly Nilotics and some Bantu ethnic groups against their northern aggressors.

I realised relief aid no matter how much we got, would not solve this war so I openly supported the liberation fighters known as the SPLM. The solution to this war had to be political as its roots were political not humanitarian. At the same time I provided humanitarian assistance. The SPLM have now become the Government of South Sudan having won a peace agreement in January 2005.

Briefing the World

By organising and briefing the world's TV, radio and print media including CNN, BBC, NBC, Reuters, AFP etc. (most of the world's press came through me) I was able to expose to the world what was happening over the years. My organisation worked independently of the UN, which the government very much controlled. It was essential to use the media to reach influential leaders in order to address the situation of the forgotten war, to expose the suffering, injustices and to appeal for intervention. At the peak of the war, it was very dangerous for all of us there. The UN, UNICEF and aid agencies had to evacuate regularly and I was often left behind alone. On one occasion in 1998, a rebel commander captured three priests and three elderly Sacred Heart nuns and held them in an underground hole threatening to execute them. He claimed they undermined him by helping the local people during the famine. It was a terrifying experience for them. I was in Nairobi and I flew in to Sudan and negotiated with him for 3 days. Thank God, he agreed to let them go and he was arrested by local forces.

Exposure of the war resulted in enormous quantities of relief being sent through Kenya for South Sudan. In 1998, we had a huge famine where over two million people faced starvation. In March 1998, I was very angered when a UNICEF statement announced that the famine in Southern Sudan was not too bad and that people were not dying. This spurred me on to address the press in Nairobi regarding the crisis. I chartered a plane with 24 representatives of international media houses based in East Africa which dropped us into the heart of the famine. We came out three days later and the press went wild. This resulted in the biggest airlift of humanitarian aid ever out of Lokichoggio, northern Kenya into Sudan. Within three weeks, an average of 60 flights of relief per day dropped relief into Sudan and International NGOs such as Goal and Concern who had left the area were able to return once more.

Many readers will have seen pictures of this famine on your screens. I was called to the US Congress to testify alongside the Director of UNICEF and World Food Programme New York in July 1998. There I presented media reports etc. The situation was rescued and less than 100,000 died, though still too many. The power of the media helped us to save many lives.

Besides humanitarian assistance, I worked with the SPLM in developing their capacity in the war and managed to convince some leaders to support and even arm them as this war was one of genocide. I addressed the US congressional committee twice in Washington. By talking to congressmen, senators and ambassadors etc. and inviting them to come with me to Sudan where I would brief them, they agreed to support our cause to stop the slavery, bombing and killings.

September 11th 2001 and its Impact on Sudan

It is incredible to think that some good could come out of something as evil and tragic as the events of September 11th 2001 in New York and Washington. We would have no peace agreement in Sudan had those terror attacks not occurred. In 1998 I addressed the Congressional Affairs committee and spoke about the three levels of Sudanese terror. One was internal and directed at the peoples of the South of Sudan. The Second was regional and directed at Kenya and Uganda and encouraged terror in East Africa. The third and the one that was to prove to be of the greatest concern to the Americans was International. The Sudanese government had terrorist training camps on its soil and Osama Bin Laden had been resident in Sudan between 1990 and 1996. As well as owning and controlling a construction company here he had established a base. We spoke of the world as being a global village where what happened in one part could have a direct knock on effect elsewhere, no matter how far away.

I was standing on the steps of Capitol Hill, where I was due to address a hearing on Sudan, that morning on September 11. I just stood there in disbelief. I thought this was the most secure place on earth having just come from a war zone in order to seek support for peace. I now found myself in the midst of another potential attack. Nina Shea of Freedom House told me about what had happened to the Twin Towers and about the attacks that were expected in Washington. Running down the hill we heard a huge explosion and smoke appeared over the skyline. It was from the impact of the plane hitting the Pentagon, which was just below us on the opposite side of the Pontiac River. Prior to this I had been successful in getting Congressman Payne to persuade Bill Clinton to just mention Sudan. Now things had changed, the Global village was in operation and in a tragic way Bin Laden had put the Sudanese government and their support of terrorism onto the frontline. My friends the rebels who had been fighting this despotic regime for decades now became respectable freedom fighters and people with whom the West could do business.

Liberation
Throughout this time, the Northern Sudanese government was after me and I was scared for my life and the lives of my wife and sons living in Nairobi. In 1994, the liberation movement was nearly finished and pushed out of Sudan. I managed to get them the material support to push the enemy forces back. They succeeded in so doing, and in 1997, regained control of over 800,000 sq kms. of the South. In 1994, the liberation movement was pushed back south to within 15 kms. of the Ugandan border. All aid groups, the churches and the UN abandoned the area. Half a million people fled. My compound was bombed a few times daily. On one occasion a tank shell, 100 mm, landed on top of our dwelling and I was partially buried. A journalist who was with me was badly hurt.

The President of Uganda, Yoweri Museveni, called me from the South to Gulu town. He feared that if we lost the front to the Islamic fundamentalist government, they would, in time, invade him too. Our liberation SPLM movement was our only defence. I told the president that I came to Africa as a simple little priest and here I was begging a President for military supplies to support a military campaign. (from Father Dan to what I became known as, Commander Dan!) After a four hour meeting, the President agreed to help us by giving SPLM the artillery plus other materials they needed.

He responded immediately and the enemy was pushed back. The war turned around and the SPLM regained control of the South over the next 2 years and of course later won a peace agreement. In the scheme of things it is hoped that a separate and independent Southern Sudan state will come into being in four years time. I argued that all of this was done for self-defence. There was no UN there, no NATO or African Union. We had a moral obligation to defend ourselves. We were not the aggressors. The Northern Islamic government were wiping out the Southern population much more than in Darfur today.

BBC TV, Sky TV and NBC each made a documentary with me at the height of the crisis in the field when it looked as if we were finished. The fact that I was the only white man left behind got a lot of publicity which resulted in my organisation receiving many millions of dollars. In 1998, I was very honoured to become the only non-Norwegian to be awarded the **Norwegian Golden Pin Award** for my work in Southern Sudan.

John Garang de Mabior was the SPLM/A leader who was killed one year ago in a helicopter crash after being sworn in as the first Vice-president of the Government of National Unity. Earlier, he had become the President of the Government of South Sudan. He and I had been very close for 18 years and had struggled together for the cause. Now, having finally won, he was killed in very curious circumstances. I was devastated by his death. He was to us what Mandela was to South Africa.

Reflections

Some 29 years ago, I chose for my ordination card the Gospel passage "*I have come to bring the good news to the poor.*" Through a media house I founded a newspaper – *Sudan Mirror*, and *Radio Nile*. I believe that is what I am doing, bringing the good news. I am currently the Director of Sudan Development Trust which is the publisher of the newspaper and proprietor of the radio station. Apart from offering training, we use our media to promote peace and justice in Sudan. My three current partners/donors are Trocaire, Pax Christi-Netherlands and Christian Aid-British. These three have all agreed to give me grants for my work. *Sudan Mirror* is regarded by the Sudanese society as the mainstream newspaper having accompanied them through the struggle. The threat to the South from the Northern government still exists. The Islamic government still wants to control the South so I shall continue working in Sudan to maintain peace.

I feel sad when I go back to Ireland and read negative press about the Church. I have seen first hand what great things have been, and are still being achieved by so many great priests and nuns. I feel sobered when I realise how many of them I knew who have given their all and are now dead. The President of Ireland, Mary Mc Aleese, visited Southern Sudan three years ago (2004) and said she was so proud to visit the Irish because we came as missionaries with love, not to colonise or to exploit. I noticed tears in the eyes of some of the very old nuns and priests to whom she spoke. Nobody had ever spoken to them like that before. I am now more at home in Africa than in Ratoath and sometimes I feel like a stranger. Maybe someday if I retire there I will rediscover my old home.

STORIES AND TALES ACROSS THE DECADES

Victorian Doctor

CHRIS WARD[1]

Dr. O'Reilly practiced in Ratoath from about 1830 to 1870. The only written reference, I have seen to him was in a book, "*Victorian Doctor: Being the Life of Sir William Wilde*",[2] the father of Oscar Wilde, but he was obviously a very famous character in his day.

But back to Dr. O'Reilly; Sir William says in his book that he was a student in the Coombe Hospital with a "wild, redheaded fellow from Ratoath called O'Reilly". The reference in the book says that he (Wilde), O'Reilly and another student had enough money to buy a corpse from a "body snatcher" or if you wish a "Resectionist". They were pulling their purchase up a laneway at night to the Hospital, when to their horror they saw the Master of the Coombe coming towards them. O'Reilly said "this fellow is so drunk we are pulling him home to put him to bed". The Master said it was disgraceful that one of his students should get into such a condition and he passed by without saying more. A person who bought a human body at that time got a very heavy sentence if he was caught. The reason for that penalty was that the people who sold the bodies to the doctors for experimentation often killed their victims by choking.

Dr. O'Reilly and the Ward family were friends, so when my father and his brothers went twice a year for medical examination, the doctor left them in the waiting room till all the other people were attended to and then asked them in to his drawing room for a chat. He liked my Uncle John best of the brothers. One day while in his house the doctor took down a small ornament; offering it to him he said "*would you like that?*" John said "*No*". He then sent his man to the yard to bring in a bantam cock; He asked him would he like the cock. John said "*No*". He then got a mug from the kitchen and when this was offered to him John said "*Yes*".

"*Well*" said O'Reilly, "*you are an old oddity the same as myself*". On another occasion he was looking at John who was a very serious boy and a bit stout. The doctor said to him "*you will make a great slob of a Bishop*". He was very near the mark. He became a priest!

Dr. O'Reilly found that people thought that when he gave them a clear bottle of medicine that it did them no good. They would say "*that bottle of water you gave me was no use*" So he used to colour the medicine with harmless liquid and that did the trick, A man would come to the dispensary asking for the green bottle that cured Pat K., as he had the same complaint. A woman would ask for "*the pink bottle you gave to Mrs. o. It did her great good*".

---

[1] This article was submitted by Chris Ward whose father Joseph Ward (1909-2000), Clonee, submitted the original article to the *Dunboyne News*, Vol. 2, No 27, 1973. The article is reproduced here courtesy of the *Dunboyne News*.

[2] Wilson TG. *Victorian Doctor: Being the Life of Sir William Wilde*. New York, LB Fisher, 1946

After examining the patient he would say "*I will give you the pink bottle*". Of course it was not the same medicine as he gave to Mrs. O. as the woman had different complaints but he coloured it pink! As each patient came out of the dispensary and into the waiting room, on their way out, they took a pull out of the bottle watched by the people on their way in.

One day a man who had gone home with his bottle rushed back in 20 minutes, burst into the dispensary and said "*Doctor, I started to drink the bottle as I went down the avenue and by the time I got to the Moulden Bridge I had it all taken. Will you give me another bottle?*" The doctor turning on him said "*You old fool. If you are dead in the morning don't send for me*", the man replied "*I won't, doctor I won't*". He gave him another bottle.

STORIES AND TALES ACROSS THE DECADES

The Royal Meath Dairy

MAEVE GALLAGHER (NÉE FARRELL)

IT COULD BE SAID that "the milk of human kindness" is sometimes challenged – though never soured given our traditional ties and friendship – during the many, mighty Gaelic matches fought between Meath and Dublin. On those rare occasions when we find ourselves on the losing side, we have only ourselves to blame because the forebears of those "Dubs" were reared on the best of Meath milk, produced here in our own parish. This came from the Royal Meath Dairy which supplied the people of the City of Dublin with fresh milk for over a generation.

"The Dairy", as it was commonly known, was established by my father, James (Jim) Farrell, and by his brother, Tom, in Folistown on the Fairyhouse Road in the early 1900s. Folistown is the last farm on the Fairyhouse Road in the parish of Ratoath.

The Royal Meath Dairy continued until the mid 1940s when the two brothers decided to move into the beef and tillage areas. This was motivated also by Jim marrying Peggy Buckley of Salestown, Dunboyne and moving to Harlockstown at the other end of the parish. However, even to this day older parishioners will still stop and share with me their reminisinces of *"The Dairy"* and *"what great men your father and uncle were."*

Tom passed away in Folistown in September 1978 and Jim in Harlockstown in September of the following year.

James Farrell

Left: The Summer Milking Parlour

Milk Lorries used by the Royal Meath Dairies

STORIES AND TALES ACROSS THE DECADES

Farm work and other Recollections of Ratoath

DINNY MCCARTHY

I WAS BORN on 8th February 1918 in Ratoath to Michael and Margaret McCarthy. I was one of seven children. My parents ran a grocery and butcher's shop in the village in an old house where Matty McCabe's house is at present. I went with five of my family to Ratoath National School until I was 14 years old. There were four teachers, two for the girls and two for the boys. Mr. & Mrs. Doonan taught us. I remember at about age 12 our teacher Mr. Doonan got sick and a Mr. Murphy from Cork took his place. It was from bad to worse! One day the late Paddy Brennan, another fellow and I were seated in the same desk. Murphy caught us talking. As he came at us I shoved Paddy Brennan out of the seat. Murphy headed for the door to block us. So we went for the window. We played 'ducks and drakes' for half an hour. In the end he told us to sit down. We were very lucky lads! As teenagers growing up there was nothing to do. Hurling and Camogie were all we had. The Community Hall was always closed. The people of the parish built it as a Town Hall and the Committee that ran it handed the keys to the Parish Priest and he designated it as a Parochial Hall. He turned the key and would let nobody in, except once a year when he held a 3 x 15 Card Game.

Fair Days in Ratoath: A Fair Day was held twice a year in April and November. In fact I was there on the last day a Fair was held in Ratoath. The cattle for sale were queuing for miles along the roads. There were pigs in creels, chickens, ducks and drakes. I saw the 'Runner 'Monkey', Mr Sheridan selling his apples, oranges, 'Peggy Legs', sandwiches and minerals. He would butter the bread with his fingers! Tom Bell was selling weanling calves and he sat on a big stone outside Monaghan's pub (Ryan's pub now). Christy Walsh was his salesman and Tom himself collected the money.

My Parents: Michael & Margaret McCarthy

The Post: John Bruen and his sister Mary Jane ran the local Post Office and Bill Conway was the local postman. Fr. Kelly P.P. and Barney Anderson often called in to the post office to collect their post. Inevitably various discussions arose and memorable stories and yarns exchanged during these visits!

The Forge: The two blacksmiths in Ratoath were Christy Foley and John Madden. They shod the farmer's hunt horses. Often we would stand at the open door of the forge and watch the sparks flying when the blacksmiths hammered the shoes. There was a well at Lagore Cross that was called the "*Guban's Well*". It was located in a little paddock on O'Hare's land.

Stables: Pat Rogers had stables and a yard in the centre of the village. He had a windmill to draw water from the Broadmeadow River into the yard. Supplying horses to the British Army during the First World War he was the biggest farmer around. Pat owned Big Lagore, Tankardstown, Paddocks, Glascairn, Balfstown and Brownstown. He built Park House on the Skryne Road. The Moorehead family now live there. Pat Rogers' son, Frank, went to live in Paddocks, Kilbride Road. His son, Charlie, went to Balfstown to set up racing stables. He trained all of Miss Doherty Paget's horses during the World War II. His son, George, moved to Brownstown, where he also became an expert on horses. Most of the local farmers supplied Pat Rogers with hay, straw and grain to feed the horses in the yards. Paddy Hessman was the Weighbridge man. He checked in everything.

Cars: There were three Ford Model T cars in the village. Jim and Tom Clarke of the pub owned one and they provided a hackney service. Christy Foley used his car for visiting the farms to shoe horses.

Racing: I remember the early Fairyhouse Races. The tea tents were lined along the ditch, straight down from the stands. I saw people using the ditch as a toilet. The ditch ran down to a watering hole. The people who made the tea would go down to the watering hole to fill the kettle! On Sunday nights before the races, I saw the people who sold apples and oranges arriving to set up their stalls. Their children slept on top of the boxes of oranges and apples and they sold their contents the next day!

1932: My first job was helping my uncle on Mrs. Little's farm in Curragha. Using a crosscut saw, we cut up timber that fell in the Big Snow of 1932. Mrs Little had her land set for grazing to Mr. Chisell. I helped him take cattle off the train at Clonsilla Station and we walked them from there to Curragha. On other occasions we took cattle from Curragha to the Dublin Cattle Market, all in one day for 16 shillings in old money (16/-). There were several big farmers in Ratoath. Their children had racehorses and hunt horses. They played hockey on the Pigeon House field in Jamestown farm and later they played in Glascarn in a field owned by Jim and Patricia Barker, Kilbride. The medium-sized farmers tilled some of their land to grow potatoes and turnips and also had cattle and sheep. The small farmers grew all their own food and kept chickens, pigs and ducks, using everything they produced.

1933: I went to a job picking stones and thinning turnips earning one shilling a drill, each a half-mile long. I could only do two drills a day!

1934: I got a full time job, seven days a week, for 14/- working with Mr. Brindly, Mullinam. There were no half days and no holidays. In before 7 o'clock in the morning, with breakfast eaten, to milk cows. I wouldn't get home until 7 o'clock at night. I stayed for nine months. After that I went to work with Clarke's in Cabin Hill and was paid 8/- a week and 3 meals a day.

1935: I then went to work with Farrells of the Royal Meath Dairy. I was paid 22/6 and a small can of milk. I milked cows, made hay, thinned turnips and did general work for the next four years.

1937: I married Josephine Nulty, Paddocks, Kilbride Road, in 1937.

1939: Next I went to work for Mr. Kennedy Senior of Peacockstown on a farm he owned in Hammondtown, Ashbourne, for £1 a week. We had a free house, free firing, free grass for a cow and calf and a ton of potatoes at the end of each year. The Second World War broke out.

1941: Mr. Kennedy's son, Patrick, took over the running of the two farms in 1941. We had to start tilling the land. With two horses, we ploughed, harrowed, sowed, mowed, reaped and harvested all the crops. A man down the road showed us how to work the horses. We had four horses and all the machinery we needed. Mr. Patrick Kennedy, Junior, and I worked very hard.

1947: My uncle asked me to move to Dunshaughlin with my wife and six children. We agreed and settled into Dunshaughlin where another boy was born. From then on the seven children, Josephine and I remained here in Dunshaughlin.

Christina Nulty

McCarthy Family:
Mrs. McCarthy with children Johnny, Denis, Hugh, Peggy and Susan

STORIES AND TALES ACROSS THE DECADES

Ratoath Boys' Annual Bicycle Race, 1927

BERYL DONNELLY

MICHAEL ELLIOT recalls the Ratoath Boys' Annual Bicycle Race which took place in 1927 when he was ten years old. The race itself was organised by Joe Clarke and it was for boys under the age of sixteen and was not confined to the boys of Ratoath.

Over sixty boys took part and they included the Murrays and McEntaggarts from Dunshaughlin one of whom was the red hot favourite to win the race which started at the high crossroads on the Skryne Road. Because Michael Elliot was just ten years old he was allowed a half minute start ahead of the rest of the field. The race course was eleven miles in total, starting at the high crossroads, down the Skryne Road into the village, then over the Dunshaughlin Road, turning right at Lagore Cross and down the Crusheen Road. When two circuits were completed the race finished at the Post Office which was situated where the SuperValu car park is today.

In his own words Michael remarked *"I had a small bicycle in comparison to the other boys taking part and I peddled like hell until I crossed the finishing line in first place. My prize was a ten shilling note and a medal with a gold centre".*

STORIES AND TALES ACROSS THE DECADES

Working with Iona Airways and Aer Lingus

MICHAEL ELLIOT

We lived in the Coderliss until 1930 when we moved to the Kilbride Road. I worked from 1933 to 1936 for Iona National Airways and Flying School which had been founded by Hugh Cahill at Kildonan Aerodrome, north of Finglas, County Dublin. I was fifteen years old when I started work. On Sunday mornings my job was to refuel the aeroplanes for the day's flying. After Iona Airways went out of business I applied for a job in 1939 at Aer Lingus but they wrote back to me stating that all jobs were being shelved because of World War II and the Irish Army had taken over the airport.

I worked locally in Ratoath during the World War II years until 1946 when I received a letter from Aer Lingus to report for work at 9 o'clock on a certain Monday morning at Collinstown. At that time in 1946 Aer Lingus were flying the DH86 which was a double wing aircraft. Later the Dakota aircraft came into operation – they could carry more people and fly further. I retired in 1981 after 35 years of service.

Summertime in late 1920's. Pictured is one of the old dwelling houses in the Coderliss (now Pitch and Putt grounds), with summer flowers in full bloom in the well managed garden.

Footnote: These two stories were recounted by Michael Elliot in August 2008, to his niece Beryl Donnelly. Michael now in his early nineties lives in Clonsilla, County Dublin. He enjoys good health and is kept busy looking after his garden and socialising!

STORIES AND TALES ACROSS THE DECADES

Entertainment in Ratoath during the 1930's and 1940's

NICK SHERRY

IMAGINE A VILLAGE with no electricity, no running water, no television, a couple of people with battery radios, no cars, except for the Priest and Doctor, no white bread, no coal or most other essentials. This was the village of Ratoath in the late thirty's and early forty's during the war years when I was growing up.

There was very little entertainment in the 1930's and 1940's apart from travelling shows and Duffy's Circus once a year. "The Fit Ups" were shows that would set up in the "Codalis" a piece of waste land which is now the Pitch and Putt course. The travelling show would stay for four to six weeks. The shows were put on in a tent with wooden sides, wooden floors and a canvas roof and held up to 200 people. They staged plays like "*Murder in the Red Barn*" and "*The White Sister.*" We gazed spellbound at those plays. People came by bicycle from all the villages around to see the shows. Films were also shown three nights a week. Cowboy films with famous actors of the time such as Tom Mix, Gene Autry; Horror films such as The Scorpions, The Mummy's Hand; Adventure films such as Tarzan, Robinson Crusoe; Comedy films with famous comedians such as Abbot & Costello, Laurel & Hardy and George Formby – boy we were hooked! Admission was 4-6 old pennies for children.

One-man Shows
Sometimes entertainers would come to the village and put on one-man shows e.g. the Man with the Dancing Doll as remembered in the poem below. Another was "Butty" Sugrue (his real name was Michael Sugrue) and he was considered Ireland's strongest man. A large crowd gathered outside the church gate after last Mass on a Sunday to see him perform and we pushed our way through the crowd to the front. A large circle formed and in the circle stood a man stripped to his waist, his muscles rippled under his bronzed skin. "*Who is he*"? We asked a man. "*That's the strongest man in the world*", he said. "*Where does he come from*"? We asked. "*He comes from Co. Kerry*", he replied. In the centre of the Circle was a large wooden cart wheel. Around the rim was a thick band of steel, the centre was also made of steel. I heard them say it weighed 16 stone. The man stooped and catching hold of the wheel, he lifted it to his chest. Beads of sweat stood out on his forehead as he gave a great heave to lift the huge wheel above his head and rested the rim on his chin, he then took his hands away and everyone clapped with amazement.

His next trick was to lay a sack on the ground, and from another bag he emptied broken glass on to the sack, spreading out the glass. The Great Man then said in a loud strong voice "*Ladies and Gentlemen, I am going to lie on my back on the broken glass. I will place this door on my chest and I want three of the heaviest men to stand on the door*". Three big men stood on the door that lay on his chest. We didn't want to look as we thought blood would run down the road when the men stepped off. When he got up, there was no blood at all except for bits of glass stuck in his skin. When it was all over he went around with his cap and he got a good lot of pennies and six-penny pieces. We hoped he would come back the following year.

Horse Races
Sport took up most of our spare time with hurling, cross country paper chase and of course getting ready for races at Creakenstown point to point and at Fairyhouse. This usually involved putting up furze jumps to make the course. We would jump over these jumps hour after hour – we must have been very fit! The point to point at Creakenstown was always a great occasion; from early morning crowds would arrive by bicycle or they would walk long distances to the races. Red and white buses arrived from Dublin carrying people longing for a day out in the countryside and all kinds of lorries were used to transport the horses. Clouds of dust would rise from the roads as the huge crowds travelled to and from the races.

My First Day at the Races
It was every boy's dream to go to the Creakenstown races and I was no exception. On one occasion I asked my mother if I could go. *"You are too young"* she said. *"But Noel and Kevin said they would mind me"*, I replied. *"Oh that's all right so"*, she said. I then said to her that the lads had told me that if we put a shilling on jockey Ted Kelly in three races that we would make a lot of money. She almost had a fit! I was lucky that my older brothers were there and they gave me a half crown. When we arrived at the course there were a lot of people already there. Large women in white coats were calling out *"race cards – a shillin' – race cards"* in an accent I had not heard before. *"Tuppence each the apples 'n oranges"* another was shouting. So we bought our race card and an apple. We went down to the bookies to bet on jockey Ted Kelly. We won the first two races but lost the next two. We walked home tired but happy at the end of my first day at the races. We were all broke!

THE MAN WITH THE DANCING DOLL[1]

Slane on "The Fifteenth" seemed the same,
The same old friends you'd meet,
Though there were strangers also there,
Thronging the Village Street,
But where was the figure I used to see
I couldn't find at all,
On street, or square, or anywhere,
The man with the dancing doll.

He used to sit with his marionette
Making it caper and dance,
From under the shade of his wide-brimmed hat
You'd catch his sharp-eyed glance.
A shabby figure, though neat and clean,
Neither short nor tall,
Whatever you gave it drew a smile
From the man with the dancing doll.

He called at your home and asked for "help,"
Was grateful for what he got,
Resumed the journey that never was done
And never repined at his lot,
Paying his share of the age-old debt,
Incurred by Adam's "fall"

And never asking the how or why,
The man with the dancing doll.

But now he's at rest where the weary feet
Arrive at the end of the road,
Where God Himself comes forth to greet
And remove the pilgrim's load.
When Emperors, Kings and Lords must die,
And dynasties must fall,
There couldn't be an exception made
For the man with the dancing doll.

Yes! Emperors and Kings have died,
Some plummeted down to hell
Because of their lust and avarice
To the note of their "passing" bell.
But no such evil was charged on his scroll,
He went at his Maker's Call,
As one who had paid, in the full, his toll,
The man with the dancing doll.

PHILIP GAMMONS
Ladyrath, Wilkinstown, Navan, Co. Meath

---

1 "Meath of the Pastures". Jim Gammons. A collection of verse by his late father Philip Gammons. Book launched at a commemoration of Francis Ledwidge, World War 1 poet, in Slane, Co. Meath on Sunday 30th July 2006.

STORIES AND TALES ACROSS THE DECADES

Threshing in the Parish of Ratoath – "The Threshing in the 1940's".

GERARD RALPH

JACK WADE, a driver from Drogheda direction, drove the Threshing Mill and Farrell's hired him. Owen Osbornes came to do the threshing on the Fairgreen opposite the Convent (now the location of the Corballis Apartments and Shopping Centre). For weeks beforehand, trees were cut down in order to provide fuel for burning in the steam engine. The driver, feeder, two cutters and other followers were paid by the farmer and he could pick whom he liked from the local men who turned up hoping to get hired to earn a few days' pay. Threshing corn was an annual farming community activity across the countryside in the autumn which also relied on the assistance of family and neighbours.

STORIES AND TALES ACROSS THE DECADES

Fair Days in Ratoath

NOEL EIFFE

UP TO FIFTY YEARS AGO the local fair was a most important event in every part of Ireland outside Dublin. Later the fairs were replaced by the more efficient cattle marts, established on the outskirts of large towns. In his book entitled "Fair Day"[1], Patrick Logan records the establishment of the fairs and markets in Ireland in the 15th century. The parliament ordered that:

> "Richard, Duke of York [Lord Lieutenant 1447-60] and his heirs forever, Lords of the Manor of Ratoath in the liberty of Meath, that they in the town of Ratoath, parcel of the same manor, may have their market in the said town to be held on Monday from week to week, and also that the said Duke and his heirs may have a fair to be held in the said town twice in the year, one on the vigil, day and morrow of St. John the Baptist and the other on the feast of the Innocents at Christmas and on the following two days."

It was also decided that citizens of Dublin, Drogheda and other towns were free to trade in Ratoath. At that time, the Duke appears to have been trying to reassert some claims to Irish lands.

There were three fair days a year in Ratoath, 18th April, 1st June and 20th November. These fairs were listed in the Fairs of Ireland in Old Moor's Almanac. The children had a day off school and a man by the name of Johnnie Clarke would cut most of the children a stick with which to drive the cattle if so needed. Johnnie owned and lived in the Ratoath Inn, and was the father of the late Mrs. Annie Gogan and Fr. Joe Clarke. Kit Walsh of Garristown was the main dealer at the fairs. Cattle and suck pigs were on sale. There was a gentleman, named Peter Yourell, who was a great judge of cattle and rarely would anyone buy an animal without first consulting him. The fairs ceased in Ratoath around 1948. The late Fr. Cogan P.P. made a great effort to revive them but with the advent of the cattle mart, the fair days were finished.

Making the Deal on Fair Day
Fairs were a great social occasion with people coming from all over the county and some from adjoining counties. The long main streets of villages were thronged with animals and with those who wanted to sell, to buy or just to see. The buyer would spend time examining the animal, taking his time and then make a bid, always less than the asking price. The seller might not know the true value of the animal so there was always a margin allowed for

---

[1] *Fair Day - The Story of Irish Fair Days and Markets*. Author: Patrick Logan. Published by Appletree Press Ltd, Belfast 1986. ISBN: 0-86281-146-5

bargaining. Bargaining would begin, voices raised loudly for all to hear, the seller refusing to sell, the buyer refusing to raise his offer. Often the buyer would make some derogatory comment about the look or lineage of the animal, very insulting to the seller. And so this theatrical event would continue, drawing more people around to view the spectacle. Sometimes the seller would send the potential bidder away declaring for all to hear that "*my cattle are worth more than that and I will not deal with the likes of you!!*" The genuine buyer on the other hand would pretend to leave and the audience would plead with him to stay, "*Divide the difference*" someone would plead, "*Go on he'll give them to you for that*". And so it would go back and fort, pleading and encouraging with much spitting on hands and slapping on hands until the deal was done and both sides satisfied that they had got the best deal!

The Village Weighbridge
A weighbridge was situated where the Marian Year Shrine stands and its main use was to weigh the horse drawn loads of hay that were required to feed the horses stabled in Rogers' Yard, the site is where Pat Donnelly's shopping centre and the houses in The Paddocks are now located.

STORIES AND TALES ACROSS THE DECADES

Drama Class in Ratoath 1936 – *The Merchant of Venice*

RATOATH HERITAGE GROUP

IN MAY 1936 Ratoath Dramatic Class produced "The Merchant of Venice" in the pavilion at Fairyhouse. On the night the pavilion was crowded with a very appreciative audience. According to a report in The Irish Times on the 28 May 1936 there was a large number of clergy present.

The theatrical producer was Mr. O'Sullivan and following the performance he complimented the troupe on their energetic and professional production and stated that he hoped the excellent standards established by the Dramatic Class on that night would be followed in the future. It was his hope "*that Shakespeare's plays would find once more a place on the stage in every town in Ireland*".

The Chairman of the County Councils' General Council, Mr. Condon, was so impressed by the production that he described it as "*a triumph of courage, intelligence and good taste*". Father Kelly, Parish Priest was very proud of the success of the local Ratoath Dramatic Class and also thankful to those who played a significant role in helping to make the evening a success.

Present with his orchestra was Mr. Patrick Delaney, R.I.A.M., and also in attendance was Mr. William Reidy, R.I.A.M.

1936: Local Drama Group presenting the play "Merchant of Venice" at Fairyhouse Racecourse.
Pictured in stage costume are: **Back Row, L-R:** Miss Reilly, Bernie Moore, Maude Foley, Nan Donnelly and Sheila Foley. **Front Row, L-R:** May Sherry, Dan Eiffe, Paddy Sherry, Fr. Kelly, Mr. Reilly, John Sherry and Tommy Foley

STORIES AND TALES ACROSS THE DECADES

Coming to Meath and Working in Park House

MARY KATE GAUGHAN

Introduction

WE CAME TO MEATH from County Mayo on the 24th March 1943. It was a good move for us even though we were broken hearted leaving Mayo. As broken hearted as we were, it was worse for the family and relations left behind, at that time moving to Meath was like moving to another country. Some years previously the Land Commission had changed the river bed which adjoined our farm in Mayo and as a result when the first heavy rains came the land flooded and with it went all our crops and our home was dangerously close to have been taken. Our compensation was a farm in County Meath. My grandmother at the time was 96 and one of her nieces wanted to keep her but my parents would not leave her behind. I still remember our neighbours and friends crying as they watched my father pull the door closed for the last time and head for our new life in Meath. When we arrived in Meath that afternoon the shops were shut and we hadn't even any bread, but thankfully we were blessed with good neighbours. When we arrived, my Mom ran up the road and the first house she saw was Jack Ryan's. She walked in and Liz, Jack's wife was after baking two big cakes of wheaten bread and after telling her the story Liz wrapped a tea towel around one of them and we had our first meal in Meath. Liz was formerly Liz Gorman from Ballybin and she and Jack had four daughters Mella (who later married Tommy Everard and now lives on the Glascarn Lane), Mary, Anne and Margaret (now Mrs Mattie McCabe). We became lifelong friends with Jack and Liz may they rest in peace. Our other neighbours were The Boshells family, Mr and Mrs Andy Toole, and Mick and Lotty Byrne.

Starting Life in Ratoath
My father and mother were delighted with the green fields and when the lorry arrived with the cattle, they weren't too long until they had the cattle put into their new home. My grandmother died later that year and she was buried in the old graveyard in Ratoath. We were getting used to County Meath, I remember one of the hardest things to get used to was the firewood, because in Mayo it was turf, turf, and more turf, mainly due to the fact that there was loads of it, and we cut our own. Turf was so easy to light and with one big fire you could boil, roast, bake and grill and we found the wood hard to get used to, however we did eventually get the upper hand of it and boil, roast, bake and grill for many years. My sisters, Philomena and Bridgie and my brother John started school in Ratoath and life started to fall into place. Other families came to Meath from Mayo around the same time, Jack Staunton and his family and the Carey family. All the men worked together sharing horses, ploughs and harrows.

Trashing Day
There would be big gatherings on trashing days and every man got dinner and tea and a few bottles of Guinness. During one trashing day after I was married, I was out in the Poplar House helping mam get the meals ready. It was dinner time and I was heading for the yard when I heard shouting and then I saw the blaze - the straw was on fire. It had been a scorching dry day and a spark from the engine ignited the straw, my parents lost everything. It was an awful loss but it could have been a lot worse, God was looking after us, my brother Anthony was almost trapped in a shed and just made it out in time. As always, the neighbours were great and my parents did get over it. Our neighbours in the Bog Road were just as good to us as the ones we had left behind in Mayo. Many of those neighbours as well as my parents have long since passed away, may the light of heaven shine on them.

Tilling the Land
The spring work had started right away when we arrived in Meath and Michael my brother who was the ploughman and was very interested in farming. He now lives in Yorkshire and is a great grandfather. Anthony was the cattleman and still lives in Poplar House today with his wife Ann and family. John our youngest brother immigrated to the States. Shortly after we came to Meath my brother Michael went to work in Ballymore House for a family called Kineghan's. He was a ploughman there for 2 or 3 years and that time a young man came to work there named Paul Flynn (may he rest in peace) who was better known to those who remember him in later years as Paul Flynn of the road. At that time, Paul was a regular visitor to our house and mam would wash his clothes and patch his work clothes. Paul was quite a stunner in those days. Michael and himself would cycle to Dublin some weekends and when he dressed up you would stand to look at him. He used to wear this navy blazer and light grey trousers with a snow-white shirt and the shoes were always shining. I still remember his raven black hair with deep waves.

Grandmother
In May my grandmother began to fail, she missed Mayo and the cosy house and fireside we left behind. Popular House was lovely, it was new and it was lovely but it was different it wasn't home as she knew it, but she was with her family and that was where she wanted to be. So every day we got her up and dressed and she would sit in by the fire in her old chair and smoke the clay pipe. She would call me when it went out and I would have to light it for her and I don't know how I managed not to get hooked on tobacco.

Working at Park House
The month of June came and the weather was beautiful and things seemed to be going smoothly. I was at that time doing a line with my now husband Anthony Gaughan. I met him the day we arrived in Meath and we got some thing going between us that was nice. His mam and dad worked together in Scotland when they were in their teens and the fact that they were already 3 years in County Meath before us they were able to pass on good advice and help. One day, the 13th of June, a knock came to the front door and this lady asked could she come in. It was the late Hilda Rogers' Mam put on the kettle she didn't ask 'will you have a cup of tea', she just produced it. She took down two small china cups. She poured out the tea and she buttered two scones I still remember her words "Sit over now at the table Hilda". Hilda was after hearing that there were girls in this new family and as they had no housemaid for a few weeks she asked mam would she let me work for her mother. Mam asked how soon and she said would she let me start tomorrow. I started work in Park House on the 14th of June 1943. It was a lovely house to work in. At that time there was just Mrs. Rogers and Hilda. The housekeeper was in her seventies. Mary Cuddy was her name, she started there as a nanny, she reared the whole family; 3 boys and 3 Girls; George,

Anthony and Mary Kate Gaughan on their wedding day in Ratoath in 1946

Frank and Charlie, Hilda, Violet and Gladys. (Mary Cuddy would be a great grand-aunt of Dick Donnelly in St. Oliver's) then, when all the family left, Mary was kept on as a housekeeper and companion for Mrs Rogers. Her husband Pat was dead many years before I went there.

I was always treated with great respect. Mary and I got on like she was my nana, she was a lady in every way; she had snow white hair tied in a bun, she had a collection of beautiful combs and when I left to get married she gave me one of them. The family were all in the equestrian business and Hilda left every morning in her mini for Balstown. She was secretary for Charlie her brother. Most of the horses stabled in Balstown were belonging to Dorothy Paget. Balstown gave great employment locally.

Park House where I worked was big into entertaining and during these times there would be local women brought in to help out e.g. Maggie Donnelly (Dick Donnelly's mother), Rosie Keogh and Mollie Donnelly another sister, who were all nieces of Mary Cuddy. They were wonderful girls to work with. When I think back there was never any 'crossness' or no one was bitchy. We all worked in harmony. The food was first class and we all got the same, my job at the parties was to wait on table. Rosie or Maggie brought in the food and put it on the sideboard. One of the men would carve. I would stand on his right hand side and he would put the sliced meat or Turkey on a big platter. There would be huge dishes of three or four vegetables, all home grown. Mollie always stood at the sideboard ready to hand out whatever was called for. When all plates were full and when they started to eat we would leave the room. It would be well over an hour before dessert would be called for. Those meals lasted around two hours and the coffee would be served in the drawing room.

World War II Years
During the war years petrol was scarce. Mrs. Rogers had a pony and trap and it was used quite a lot. There was a workman there by the name of Dick Clarke who took care of the garden, fruit trees, vegetables, lawns and the glasshouse. He grew tomatoes, cucumbers, courgettes and early lettuces. There was a cow kept which not only provided the milk but each year produced a calf. The cow and pony were kept in that field where Park House Estate is now. This cow was wonderful for the rich milk she gave and you could lift big dollops of cream off the crocks. We churned once a week and I made up the butter in pound weights (lb). It was left in the pantry on a marble slab and my memory of it is that it never got soft. I made a lot of cakes and scones all with this beautiful butter. I often think now how we would use up to about one lb of butter a day, for just four of us. Mrs. Rogers lived to her nineties, Mary Cuddy I think went in to her late 80's, and Hilda lived to a ripe old age. When you think of all the talk there is nowadays about cholesterol, it makes you wonder!

Hilda
Hilda was a nun in the Sacred Heart Order for about 12 years, she went in I think when she was sixteen. Once when she was very sick during my stay there, (I think she developed pneumonia) and there was a night nurse there for three weeks, her mother asked me to do the day time care i.e. bringing her meals, washing her or just sitting and reading to her. Rosie Keogh took over and did my work during this period. Anyway, as Hilda was getting stronger and could sit up in bed, she would tell me stories of her years in the convent. When she was about ten years there, she wanted to leave. She told me of her unhappiness as she was trying to pluck up courage to talk to the Mother Superior and also break it to her parents. Her eldest sister Violet was a reverend mother also in the Sacred Heart Order in England. Hilda had prayed for the strength to talk to someone and one day as she was getting the alter ready for mass she fell going up the steps and broke the bottle of wine. She had to go to the office to talk to the head nun and tell her what happened and to say she was so sorry. The nun who was writing at the time lifted her head and looked her straight in the face and said "Better to break them bottles of wine than break one of our golden rules" and Hilda felt she was back again to square one. It took another 2 years before she got the courage to ask someone for help. Many times during those years she said she hit rock bottom. She was a very young girl and she had never known any other life. She said that during her time in the convent she longed for the outside life, to run through the fields, to talk to girls her own age, simple things like that. I could write pages of the stories she told me. Her request to leave had to go to Rome and the process was slow but eventually she came home. Once home however, at the beginning things were almost as bad as the convent, she felt so ashamed, she found it impossible to mix and there was no help from the church. When she entered the convent her father gave the Sacred Heart Order, what they called at that time, a fortune (or dowry), much the same as a girl getting married. But when she left she was let home with this long black coat, her hair was very short and in such bad condition she thought it was going to fall out. One day she hit rock bottom she got a stick and she broke every blessed picture in the house. That was the turning point in her life and she started to change. She did eventually go back to the church.

At that time, I presume she (Hilda) would have been starting her job, she was very good hearted, and my wages were £2.50 per month (old money). I started with £2.00. She was always bringing me gifts of clothes and things I could never afford to buy myself. For example, she brought me silk underwear, silk stockings, fancy gloves, a pure leather bag and when I was leaving to get married she gave me a beautiful roll of pure wool lemon material.

(Mrs. Mannering, who was an aunt in law of Joe Mannering and who lived in a cottage outside the village on the Dunshaughlin road, made my wedding suit - a jacket with a pleated skirt and a line of casual skirts). When I was leaving Hilda was very upset and she said I was an answer to a prayer.

Sewing Class
Mrs. Rogers had a sewing class every Monday afternoon making gowns for Holles Street Hospital. The material for the gowns would come out cut and then this group of women came in around 2.30 p.m. and started sewing them, they would then get them parcelled up and sent off. I understand there were several of these groups around the country; it was to help the Dublin poor. Some of the women I remember were Mrs. Meagher who lived in what is now "The Auld Stand", Mrs. Frank Rogers, Janet McCabe and Dr. Mary McCabe. There was high tea for everyone at 5.30 p.m.

Going to Sunday Mass by Horse Trap
During my time in Roger's, I learned to harness the pony and get him rigged on to the trap and I would often drive Mrs. Rogers to mass. She went to mass every morning and I would then go back up and collect her. However, in the fine weather she might feel like going out for an hour and we would head off down the Skryne road. One particular day, I remember, she said to me we would go to Dunsany I had never been there and as we travelled along she told me stories about some of the people that she knew there, I never forgot the beauty of the trees and the fields. There was no worry about cars and I don't remember meeting any throughout the whole journey.

Fuel Scarcity at Park House
There was a scarcity of fuel. I remember one time we had used up all the turf and Hilda was waiting for a load; there wasn't even a bit of turf mould left. It was a Sunday evening and my Sunday off; I was dressed to go out and went in to say I was leaving. The room she was sitting in got no evening sun even though it was summer. She looked cold so I went back out and up that field where the new houses are now. I picked two armfuls of dried sticks out of the ditch. I came back with a huge bundle; the fireplace was set with crushed paper. I broke them outside the back door and came in, put them on the grate, and set a match. I saw the tears slide down her cheeks as she caught my hand and she said I hope you will never want for anything and I never have. I don't mean money that didn't matter too much, but we had so many good things in our life.

Leaving to Get Married
I left Park House in April 1946 and married in June 1946. I met Mary Cuddy at mass on most Sundays and on seeing me she would always cry and would always say, "I miss you a cushla". I had never been back to Park House after I left but Hilda did come up to visit us and they were not able to get any girl for months after I left. She thought I might know of any girl that would work for them. However, around that time there were big changes and girls leaving school were going to technical schools or secondary schools. Another big change was married women, having reared their families, were going back to work. Women were getting more liberal and even the fear of being seen in a pub was going and we started to wear lipstick and put on make-up and there was whispers about the birth control pill. After our babies were born you couldn't go out anywhere, not even to your parents' home without being churched. The first Sunday you went to mass after the birth you went to the altar rails after the mass and the Priest prayed and blessed you. I could never understand why we had to be cleansed after all that pain and when one time I questioned it with a Priest the answer he gave me put me off. I never got it done again. The old tough church rules slowly began to die away. I remember the great feeling of not having to wear a hat to mass

as for so many years, even if you were just passing a church and wanted to go inside to pray, you put a hanky over your head if you didn't have a hat with you. The other rule I hated was the fasting from midnight, especially if you were pregnant. I still remember cycling to mass on a cold wet Sunday and feeling faint with pure hunger. I do think that we live now in the most wonderful time, we have everything so easy, washing machine, dish washer and our homes are heated. When we were married there was no running water, no toilets, only the very rich had those luxuries.

Conclusion

People talk now about the good old days. They were not good. There was a lot of slavery about then. I thank God that I have lived to see all this and I see all our family with nice homes, good jobs and all our grandchildren getting on with their lives and I pray that the road they travel may not be too rough, that they will always have a love for their parents and for all the people they meet on that road and above all that they will never lose the Faith.

From Mayo to Meath in 1943 – A Report

"Eight families, including one of 17 members, who had lived near Belmullet, Mayo, migrated to new homes in the Kilcock area of Meath. Among them was Mrs. Kate Healy (95), of Srahnaplaia, Barnalea, Belmullet, who had never been outside Mayo before. The migrants were Michael Carey, Carrowmore, Belmullet, his wife, his wife's aunt, aged 82, and 14 children – the largest family migrated so far. Patrick King, Srahnaplaia, his wife, his wife's mother, Mrs K. Healy, and six children; Edward Murray, Derreens, his wife and five children; Anthony Tighe, Carrowmore, his wife three children; John Heraghty, Carrowmore, and his family of five, including his mother; Michael Munnelly, Carrowmore, and his mother and sister; and Michael Donoghue, Carrowmore, his wife and four children, who are to live in Duleek."

The above was a report first published in The Meath Chronicle in 1943. Ref: pp161. One Hundred Years of Life and Times in North Leinster - A Meath Chronicle Publication. 1997.

Footnote: Sadly, since this article was written, Anthony Gaughan, Anthony King and Michael King have all passed away. *May they rest in peace.*

STORIES AND TALES ACROSS THE DECADES

Spitfire Crash at Ratoath

TONY DARBY

Sunday August 23rd 1942 and the people of Ratoath village were at 8 o'clock Mass in the local Catholic Church. The priest had just delivered his Sunday morning sermon when the peace and quite of the morning was suddenly shattered by the sound of gunfire. My mother who was eighteen years old at that time was in the congregation. She recalled "the roar of aircraft engines and the sound of spent cartridge shells falling on the roof of the Church". The priest hesitated for a moment and then continued on. When Mass had finished and people were leaving the Church, they were informed that a plane had come down less then a mile from the village in an area known locally as the Fairgreen [which lies to the north of the Ashbourne Road almost opposite the present nursing home].

At 8.30am, when the first local people[1] reached the stricken aircraft they found the pilot

Site of the Ratoath Spitfire Crash on 23rd August 1942
(Crash site is marked by a white circle on this aerial photograph of Ratoath taken by Finian Darby in 1989)

badly wounded and still strapped in his seat. There was confusion as to what to do next as nobody seemed to be in charge of this emergency. After some time the local maternity nurse, Miss O'Mahoney, who lived nearby and Dr. Henry Conway, the local doctor, arrived on the scene and went to the aid of the stricken pilot. Sadly their efforts were in vain, for later that day the pilot, Flight Officer Bolesaw Josef Sawiak of Squadron 315, was pronounced dead.

For Flight Officer Sawiak that Sunday morning started much the same as any other day as he and his comrades waited for the call that would see them in action against the German Luftwaffe.

At 07.57 am the sirens went off and two Polish pilots, Flight Officer Josef Sawiak and Sergeant Lisowski, who were based at Woodvale in Lancashire on the west coast of England, were scrambled under the code name Black 1 and Black 2. Their mission was to intercept a German Junker 88D-1 that had been detected on radar, flying low above the sea and along the Irish coastline, its destination was the shipyard in Belfast.

Sergeant Lisowski had a mishap on take-off and had to get a replacement plane. Meanwhile Flight Officer Josef Sawiak, flying a Supermarine Spitfire Vb, identity BL959, with markings PK-T, went on alone to engage the German Junker. Lisowski was by now flying eight minutes behind Josef Sawiak.

The Junker 88D-1 had a crew of four and was well armed with three MG 15 machine guns of 7.92 calibre. As the Spitfire came into view the pilot of the Junker banked hard left, and that action took the plane over neutral Ireland, but Josef Sawiak followed and an aerial battle between the two aircraft ensued.

The aerial dogfight continued across Garristown in North Co. Dublin. Colm Donnelly, an eyewitness at that time, said that *"the German plane was flying so low it was just about skim-*

Flight Officer Bolesaw Josef Sawiak

Woodvale RAF base, Lancashire, in 1942. Bolesaw Josef Sawiak is pictured standing in line, third from the right

---

1 The following local people are understood to have made their way to the scene of the crash: Peter Yourell, Paddy Corrigan, Eddie Nulty, Nicholas Sherry, Maud Foley, Paddy Yourell, Darby Gillic, Peter Gillic and Dan Eiffe.

The site of the August 1942 Spitfire Crash near Ratoath (this picture was taken in 2005)

Charlie Fitzsimons, Baldarragh, The Naul, Co. Dublin, is pictured here holding a spent cartridge shell that was found at the site of the Spitfire crash in Ratoath.

ming the top of the trees, as for the Spitfire it tried in vain to get beneath the German plane". It was at about this time that Flight Officer Josef Sawiak was hit in the left arm and although mortally wounded he continued to attack the German plane. As the planes approached the village of Ratoath Spitfire pilot Sawiak was beginning to weaken from loss of blood and had to take the plane down. He made a crash landing in a field close to Ratoath fox covert, by this time he had inflicted serious damage to the German Aircraft.

A squadron of Spitfires from the RAF airfield in Ballyhalbert, Co. Down, joined Sergeant Lisowski coming in from the east. The German plane turned south as the Spitfires took up the battle with the stricken aircraft.

Sergeant Lisowski in his Flight Report stated that one of the pilots from Ballyhalbert said that he had seen the Spitfire pilot Sawiak go down, and also he thought that Sawiak might have taken out the rear gunner of the German plane.

At Tramore in County Waterford, the German Junker 88D-1 was finally forced down. The four German crewmen (Lt. Paul Stormer, HPTM Gothfrised Bernd, OFW Karl Hund and UFFZ Josef Reiser.) survived the ordeal and were taken away by the Military Police.

The body of Flight Officer Josef Sawiak was returned to Lancashire, where his body was interred with full military honours in Our Lady of Compassion cemetery in Formby, Lancashire, England.

Josef Sawiak was accredited with victory over the Junker 88D-1. As for his Spitfire it was taken away by the Irish military.

Footnote: I would like to acknowledge the contribution of Anna Weglowska from Poland in researching this article.

STORIES AND TALES ACROSS THE DECADES

The Emergency Harvest in 1946

& the Memories of Anthony and Mary Kate Gaughan

ANN GAUGHAN

IN 2001, RTÉ television broadcast a documentary that included two Ratoath people who gave their account of the 1946 Emergency Harvest. They were Anthony and Mary Kate Gaughan of Porterstown Lane. The programme began with an outline of the cause, i.e. the continuous rains of 1946, resulting in a severe problem for the farmers. There were frequent reports in the newspapers. Typical headings were similar to those printed in the Irish Press of Thursday the 29th of August "Big Rainstorm hits the Harvest" and in the Evening Herald on the 5th of September. Government Ministers began calling for voluntary harvest help for the now critical conditions. Indeed the government realised that it was not just a problem for the farmers but it was a threat to the food supply for all the people of Ireland. World War II had just ended and there was no prospect of importing food because nobody had food to sell. So there was a real danger of, or getting close to, starvation. Eamon De Valera feared bread rationing. Grain, and particularly wheat, in certain fields was over ripe and there was very little time to save it. Only about 4/5 weeks to save from disaster. There was a genuine fear among the people as it was only 100 years since the famine and the people were still haunted by the amount of lives lost in the famine and there was a fear of history repeating itself and so, when a break appeared in the weather the Taoiseach of the time, Eamon De Valera made a nation-wide appeal in the media for volunteers to help save the harvest.

The Minister for Agriculture Dr. James Ryan appealed for an all out harvest drive, and the Department put notices in the papers looking for volunteers and transport in all areas. The people rallied around and the volunteer rush was unprecedented. All areas answered the call. The volunteers gathered at various centres around the country and there was an air of excitement and an air of urgency. In the newspapers on September 17th the Archbishops called for prayer for the harvest, i.e. their graces Most Reverend Dr. D'Alton of Armagh; Most Reverend Dr. McQuaid of Dublin; Most Reverend Dr. Walsh of Tuam; and Most Reverend Dr. Kinane of Cashel.

The Red Cross prepared the food that was donated and young mothers volunteered to make sandwiches. The Volunteers were given their packed lunch and also two free cigarettes. They climbed aboard one of the many modes of transport from bread vans to army lorries, which took them out to the countryside to one of the many farms in need of help.

Mary Gaughan said that it meant the complete saving of the harvest and that *"there was no earthly way we would have got it off the fields but for them (the volunteers) on that scale"*.

Mary says, "You never thought that this could happen because you didn't believe that it could happen." She went on to say, "*We were very immature, very immature, we thought that the like was not for ourselves, you know. Nothing could happen, nothing bad could happen to us. We'd make the world. We'd change the world. We were married that year. Then we were landed into this bad harvest, into the worry of not being able to survive our first year together. Then when the word came that there would be volunteers coming out, it was a great joy because we knew that, if the weather took up within the week, we would get the harvest at least off the field.*"

Anthony says, "*We would have lost it. We would have completely lost it because when they come, it only took a week to do it like, whereas if they hadn't come we would only be getting little bits of it done, it would be gone like, it would be no good cutting, it wouldn't be worth cutting. We were lucky enough they came out and they were great lads. They didn't mind going in with the scythes or anything. They went in and they were better than ourselves. Matter of fact now they really were. I still can picture them coming off the lorry in pairs. Sure they were running up the field to get to work. It was marvellous you know, but they were delighted to come out. I'm sorry that I didn't keep their names. They were great, they were wonderful lads, and all they wanted was a good feed and that was it.*"

Many of these volunteers, especially those from Dublin, had never been to a farm before and they hadn't a clue how to stack or anything like that, they had to be shown. It was an experience for them. The three words they had to learn were "*gather, bind and stack.*" Many of the volunteers, not knowing what to wear, arrived in suits and unsuitable shoes but they soon learned. At the end of the day, the work was being done and that was the main thing. They were doing what they came to do. There was a great sense of adventure and even romances blossomed.

Anthony Gaughan also recalls with fondness, "*They were marvellous workers. A few of them weren't as good of course, but they did their best,*" he laughed. "*They turned the head to the ground,*" he laughed, "*but we couldn't say nothing like. It wouldn't be fair; they were so good you know. We'd have to go back and turn the sheaves of corn back up, and then there was little sheaves made. What did they call the sheaves?*" He asked Mary, "*the volunteer sheaf's*", she said, "*they were little tiny ones,*" he went on to say, "*they did their best now, they did their very best, but we would go back in the evening and we would put about six of them together to make a sheaf.*"

The country girls were great, they had maybe just gone up to Dublin to go to college or to work and they were delighted to get back out into the countryside again. They had no problem with the work. The town girls on the other hand added amounts of amusement to the whole scene; indeed there was often a competition between the town girls and the country girls as to which of them really could do the best. The home-made bread went down a treat with the volunteers at lunch-time; a lot of them had never tasted anything like it before. The chat going home in the evening among the volunteers was often about who got what food that day, some did very well with beautiful hot dinners whilst some only got maybe ham and tomatoes and they weren't impressed. There were some great stories told and the singsongs on the way home were great.

Mary Gaughan recalls a story about a lad called Jimmy. "*Jimmy never saw an egg being laid nor he didn't have a clue where they came from. I used to have him bringing in the few eggs out of the hen house and he couldn't believe 'cause he'd lifted up a hen this day. She was just laying an egg and he couldn't believe,*" she laughed, "*he said he'd never eat an egg again in his life,*" but I said, "*where did you think the eggs came from?*" "*I don't know,*" he said, "*my mother always bought them in the shop,*" she laughed, as she recalled his words.

Nothing was to distract these volunteers from the work at hand. Even the All Ireland final of that year, between Kerry and Roscommon, was put back to ensure that there would be no obstacles in the way and that there would be nothing to stop the people helping with the harvest. It was all hands on deck. There was even a sense of patriotism about the whole thing, especially with De Valera coming out in the media to make the appeal. It was not long after the war and there was still a sense of patriotism in the air. When it was all over there were no major celebrations or big fuss. People just thanked the volunteers and their neighbours or whatever for their loyalty. There was of course a sense of relief, but apart from that, everyone just went back to work and everything just returned to normal.

Mary Gaughan recalled a sense of emptiness when the harvest workers left, and she says, "*When you are living in the country, at times there is not much happening in it. This was something very, very, you know, interesting. Here we had those city lads and country lads all mixed up together, it was fun, it was fun, it was fun!*"

Reference: Above information was compiled from a 2001 RTÉ Television documentary entitled "Emergency Harvest"

Footnote: Sadly, since this article was written, Anthony Gaughan has passed away. *May he rest in Peace.*

STORIES AND TALES ACROSS THE DECADES

Memories of a Lifetime

FRANK MAHER, 2001

Like so many others in the country, my Grandfather Martin Maher emigrated from County Clare in 1847. Many of his family had died from starvation as a result of the Potato Famine that ravaged the countryside. With him on the boat to England were his sister Ellen, a Mrs. Griffin, and her two children. Her husband had died of starvation, and she was trying to find a better life for herself and her two children. My Grandfather settled in Bolton, a small town in Lancashire. He married and raised a family one of whom was my father Jim. My father and mother married in 1899 and had five sons and three daughters.

I remember the 1914-1918 War very well, food was rationed; there were no sweets or chocolate. I remember the Zeppelins coming over the houses. They looked like huge cigars with lights under them. In 1922 I started my apprenticeship as an Electrician. I worked in factories, shops, and hospitals, warehouses and was involved in the installation of the first artificial silk mills in Bolton, near Manchester. My family were very much involved with music and opera. I joined the St. Mary's Amateur Grand Opera Society in 1927 and took part in *The Lily of Killarney*, *Faust* and *Il Travatore*. In 1931 I joined the St. Edmunds Dramatic Society and there I met my future wife Molly Naughton. In 1936 Molly and I were married.

My wife Molly's father came from Limerick and her mother came from Beaufort in Kerry. In 1939 the Second World War started. I joined the A.R.P. (Air Raid Protection). As an electrician I would have to go out during the Bomb Raids to make fallen electrical wires safe. Over these years our children Jim, Michael, and Christopher were born. Molly's parents, the Naughtons, returned to Ireland in 1939 and settled in Irish Street, Ratoath.

Maher Family returns to Ireland
In 1945 almost 100 years from the time that my Grandfather had left Ireland, we decided to come back to Ireland. We built a bungalow in Ratoath and our daughter Anne was born there. Ratoath at this time was a very quiet place. Mr. Madden senior lived opposite us, on Irish Street. He had a forge and an anvil, and he shod horses outside his home. Mrs. Madden senior ran a small grocery shop. Their son John repaired radios and TV sets.

Leonard Meagher had a public house opposite the Church and a grocery and small hardware shop at the back of the pub. The Costello family had a fine grocery shop near the Augustinian convent while Mick Nash and his wife ran a grocery shop near the village cross. At the back of Mick Nash's shop was a boot and shoe repair shop run by Tommy Smith. Foleys had a shop which sold groceries and milk. There were no milk deliveries to the houses at that time. On one of the walls in Foley's shop there was a hand-painted picture of Charlie the Bull, a bull belonging to Major Watters who lived in the Lodge opposite Lagore House. His mother, Mrs. Borgenine, had painted this picture. Across from Foleys was a

The Maher Family celebration of their parent's 50th Wedding Anniversary, July 1986 In Ratoath Community Centre
Front: L-R: Anne Brady, Molly and Frank Maher, Monica Maher **Back: L-R:** Michael and Frances Maher, Pat Brady, Chris Maher, Liliana and Jim Maher

shop run by Peter Talty and beside this was the Community Hall, where pictures were shown once a week. Close by were two other small buildings one of which was a butchers shop run by the Dolan Family.

There was no public water system in Ratoath at this time and drinking water had to be got from a public pump that was situated in front of what is now Ryan's supermarket. I worked with an Electrical Firm in Dublin and cycled into Dublin on Monday morning, stayed in digs while I worked in town and then cycled home on a Friday night.

After some time I decided to set up my own business and work for myself. Rural electrification was just being introduced in the country areas at this time. The poles to carry the electrical cables were being put up around Ratoath and its outskirts. The local farmers were very anxious to get connected up to the rural electrification scheme. Electricians came from other areas to work on these new installations. Many people were quite scared of electricity at first. Since 1945, many changes have taken place in Ratoath. The once small quiet rural village has grown to a large extent. Some changes do enhance the area, others unfortunately do not. Sadly our beloved son Michael died in October 1998.

I am now (in 2001) ninety three years old and my wife, Molly, is ninety one. We have seen many changes in our long lives. Thank God, we are both very healthy, considering our age. We have lived and survived two World Wars. We have seen the advancement of medicine, flying, television, mobile phones, washing machines, central heating and modern technology.

I take a walk every day, unless the weather is very bad. On the 8th July 2001 Molly and I celebrated our 65th Wedding Anniversary together with our children and their spouses, our twenty one grandchildren and eleven great grandchildren. Thank God for a good life.

Footnote: *Since we received this article from Frank Maher, sadly his wife Molly died on 30th July 2002 and Frank himself died in December 2005. May they rest in Peace.*

STORIES AND TALES ACROSS THE DECADES

Life in Ratoath

JIMMY RALPH

My grandfather, Luke Ralph lived in Ratoath Village; in the house next to the Church Grounds. The house at one time belonged to Major Corbaliss but my grandfather bought it from him for the sum of £50.00.

My father, also Luke, was Head Gardener in Thunder's Estate (where the O'Hare Family now lives) in Lagore. When Mrs. Minnie Thunder died, he decided he would never work for anyone again. He tilled the garden and grew vegetables and flowers, and as the family grew up and were able to help with the work of cultivating, he sold his produce. My mother reared hens and sold eggs for food and settings. The combined produce led to a small shop, selling garden produce, eggs and groceries. Eileen, Ita and I made deliveries on bicycles as far away as Skryne, Nutstown and Ballymadun. Then as the garden was tilled more extensively, there was a surplus of produce and my father took this surplus produce into the

The Ralph Family
Front row: Alex, Luke and Margaret (parents), Margaret, Anthony and Gerard
Middle row: Rosie and Pauline. Back row: Ita, Brendan, Jimmy and Eileen.

Patricia Nulty with Luke Ralph Senior as he selected Lupins from his market garden.

Dublin Market on a bicycle. This was in the late thirties. This continued for years, during which time I rode with him, and occasionally my mother rode into the market also.

Demand for our produce continued to grow and we rented Rosie Keogh's garden. This garden was down the lane from the back Chapel gate and was known as the Pound. It is now a green area situated adjacent to the newly built Churchview Apartments. In this garden, which we rented for over 20 years, we grew double white narcissi and Ester Reed Summer Chrysanthemums for cut flowers and bedding plants. By this time we were renting Mary Moore's garden (behind DeLacy Court, beside the Cemetery). This house and garden have gone completely now. We also rented Darby's Garden on the Dunshaughlin Road. Along the way we acquired a van and often went two and three times per day into the market.

In 1954, following the construction of the Marian Shrine, the Ralph family planted a hedge behind the shrine. In 1956 we bought the house and 2 acres of land from Kate Dowling, situated beside the School. Gerard specialised in wedding bouquets and flowers and we all helped to make thousands of holly wreaths for the Christmas trade. The business had expanded so much that we were now employing several local youths.

We did quite a bit of landscaping as well in Louth, Meath, Dublin and Kildare. One of our more unusual jobs was to create a bog scene in the Round Room in the Mansion House in Dublin for the film "*Darby O'Gill and the Little People.*"

When the sale of outdoor flowers began to decline, due to the importation of foreign blooms, we erected glasshouses in Ratoath Village and at Fairyhouse Road, and these were worked until I retired in 2000.

STORIES AND TALES ACROSS THE DECADES

Early Memories of Ratoath

NICK KILLIAN

The Crows were busy

I WAS BORN IN 1949 and one of my pleasant memories was coming to Ratoath to visit my relations. My first memory of Ratoath is of crows, yes crows, daffodils and black railings. Every Easter my parents came to stay in Ballybin with my aunt and uncle, Sonnie and Christina O'Connor. The annual visit to Ratoath was to attend Fairyhouse Races, at that time a one-day event held on Easter Monday.

The bus journey from Dublin for me as a young child was a great adventure, heading out from Bus Áras, out past Glasnevin cemetery, by Merville Dairies on the Finglas Road and winding its way to Ballybin along narrow country roads, passing the White House public house, with grass growing in the middle of the road. The first sight on stepping off the bus, at the turn for Ballybin before you came to Ratoath village, was the crows busy nest-building on the large ash trees at Dr. McNabb's house on the corner of the Ballybin/Ashbourne Road.

On Easter Monday, Dad and Mam, me on my Dad's shoulders and Auntie Chris [my uncle Sonnie would be working at the races] walked along with all of the local people. Through Jamestown farm up past Keague's (now Everard's) and along the Bridle Path, we crossed the Glascarn Lane to Cunny's Lane onto the outside area of Fairyhouse Racecourse. Thousands would be on the outside, as people were not able to afford to pay into the reserved stands. There was all the fun of the fair, the 3 card trick men, the shouts of the bookies and the smell of Mc Ardle's ale from the drinking tents. The Grand National winner was met with loud cheers and I always remember the rush to the bookies to collect the winnings.

Living in Ratoath

In 1974, my wife Anne and I were lucky enough to be given a site by my Aunt and Uncle. Six children later, we are still living in Ratoath. I have been fortunate to have had the opportunity of living in a small rural community on the edge of the Meath /Dublin border. As Ratoath grows today into a diverse community, its expansion has given the residents, both old and new, the opportunity to propose a different role and identity for Ratoath into a modern rural village in County Meath; albeit edging even closer to urban Dublin or vice a versa depending on your point of view.

During the last 32 years I have been privileged to work with like-minded committed people in Ratoath in the development of community facilities for our village, with my own involvement primarily being with the Community Centre since 1979. My other interest is Education and I had the honour of serving as Chair of Ratoath National School Parents Association and its Board of Management. I now serve as Chair of Ratoath College and look forward to moving into the new College in September 2007 at Jamestown. Little did I know that the very fields I walked with my parents and relations going to Fairyhouse Races would one day host a second level school!

One thing that has not changed is the crows. They are still living and building nests at Ballybin!

STORIES AND TALES ACROSS THE DECADES

The Poteen Maker of Glascarn

NOEL CONWAY

During the period, 1950's/1960's, our family grew up on a small farm on Glascarn Lane. This farm is now all of Fairyhouse Lodge. I spent many of my younger days chasing cattle around those fields. Even though our farm was small in present day terms, the work was intensive and very hard. My dad, Michael Conway, was never a full-time farmer; his day job was as a sales rep for Lenehan's of Capel Street, Dublin, which, at that time was the leading supplier of small machinery around the country. This meant that my mother Aileen was the farmer during the day with the help of my three brothers and one sister. When we were young we reared pigs intensively; we could never understand how our city cousins would complain about the smell as we were so used to it.

At that time there were only eight houses from one end of Glascarn Lane to the other, now (2007) there are fifty one homes there. Many of those original eight families are still there but one family that is no more is the Cunny family. They owned the farm opposite our house and lived in the house where Martin Everard now lives. It was a Land Commission farm and I remember Winnie, Beezey and Paddy though my Dad also knew their parents Paddy Senior and Mrs. Cunny.

The custom at that time was that if a cow was calving you always called in help from some of your neighbours just in case of difficulty. One night around midnight, my Dad got the call from Cunny's that a cow was calving and could he come and help. He got out of bed and went over to Cunny's hayshed. He noticed that the cow was not in any distress but there was no sign of Paddy. Not being familiar with the shed he called out and began to search around. He came across a passageway through the hay that led into a small room. Paddy was sitting down and was a bit surprised that my Dad had found his way into his secret room in the shed. The room contained all the equipment for making poteen and Paddy was in the process of preparing a new batch. He was disappointed that his secret was out but he convinced my Dad to sit down and have a drink. A couple of hours later my Dad got home, covered in muck, dirt and cuts from the number of times he fell on the way. I think that was the only time ever that he was not able to go to work the next day!

STORIES AND TALES ACROSS THE DECADES

Memories of the Augustinian Convent and Nursing Home, Ratoath

SISTER CLEMENT (BRÍD DORAN)

Ratoath and its surrounding areas hold so many special memories for me. May 1972, having made Final Vows and completed my training as a nurse I was appointed to the Augustinian Convent and Nursing Home, Ratoath. Sister Margaret Reilly was the sister-in-charge at that time! Having arrived at Dublin Airport on the 12th May, Tommy Walls was there to meet me as the sisters weren't driving cars in those days, though that was soon to change and many a driving lesson Tommy Walls and Paddy Farrell (who also worked at the nursing home) gave me, often risking their lives down the Skryne Road. I remember once driving Tess Lambe home from work and I had to drive back through the main road and Dunshaughlin, as I didn't know how to get into reverse!

Back to that journey from the airport, – through Swords and on past Donaghmore Church. This was Tommy's route from the airport, one which I continued to use until this year. On that same journey we had a very interesting conversation about horses. He pointed out Tom Dreaper's stables to me as we went past, the home of Arkle and where Paddy Murray, Nicky Connor and Johnny Lumley worked for so many years. Then I heard about Tommy Carberry, just making a name for himself at that time. Tommy pointed out Doctor Conway's house to me - later to become Doctor Michael Browne's house. I remember saying to Tommy, "is Ratoath a big place"? So, before going to the convent I had a tour of the village and Holy Trinity Church. Father Cogan was the Parish Priest and Father Peter Mulvaney was the Curate. Then, as if by association of ideas, Tommy said, "that shop over there, where the convent buys all their groceries, that's Meagher's and there are three priests in the family. And now guess what? The postman Jack Browne - his son worked there, and now he is 'IN' to be a priest." Tommy was as proud of Pat as if he was his own son.

By a strange coincidence, as I write these memories of Ratoath, Father Pat Browne is here in Archbishop's House with me, a very committed and dedicated priest. God works in mysterious ways! Up the village he pointed out Maude Foley's shop and Brady's garage, Molly Talty's shop, Dolan's the Butchers and the Post Office which was then opposite Tony Darby's butcher's shop. Then we went round by the Convent and Mary Moore's shop as it was always called. Mick Ryan's pub was just across from the convent gate and Tommy told me Mick was related to one of our Sisters. So he *was always good to us.*

In the nursing home in those days we had Morning Prayer at 6.30am and we went on duty at 7.00am. We combined prayer with work. Days off were non-existent and the five Sisters were involved in every aspect of care. Our workers were as committed as we were, and,

Sacred Heart Shrine built by the Augustinian Sisters

looking back now I hope they have happy memories as I have. Team spirit wasn't talked about in those days, but we had it and we affirmed each other as we worked together. Mrs McCabe, Mrs O' Connor (Ballybin), Tess Lambe, Mary Woods, Bridget Brennan, Nellie Connor, Vonnie Cullen, Tina Gorman and Judy Cassidy. Andy Eiffe was a regular helper when it came to form filling.

Even then I enjoyed getting involved in the life of the parish, especially with the young people Anna Cullen, Geraldine Mahon, Kathleen Colfer and Mary Naughton - some of the young people then - and myself organised a sale of work for Ratoath School. Sister Luke helped us and we made £50 selling soap - a fortune in 1974. Maurice Kearney was very appreciative of our efforts.

These are just a few Snippets from those early years. In the last eight years that I have been back in Ratoath, there were many changes - all for the better. As a community of sisters we became more involved in the parish and more people got involved in the running of the nursing home in the same committed way. Sixty local people are now employed there. We opened a Youth Centre with the help of Father Gerry Stuart and Father Paul Crosbie. November 1997 was a special day for the sisters at Ratoath when twelve lay people from the area were welcomed as "Friends of St Augustine" into the Augustinian Family of Lay Associates. This group of twelve had been meeting regularly in the convent chapel to pray for Vocations. After a special ceremony of initiation I proudly led them over in procession along with all the guests to the newly renovated centre in the convent grounds. Originally a storehouse, now it is a fine conference-cum-prayer-room. It is used for prayer groups and youth groups always with the one Augustinian ideal "one mind and one heart on our way to God".

I could write a book on Ratoath. Happy years! But that's it for now.

Note: Sister Clement sent this to us from Westminster Diocese on 18th October 2000 and continues to keep in touch with her friends in Ratoath.

STORIES AND TALES ACROSS THE DECADES

Sisters of Saint Augustine

MADELEINE O'NEILL[1]

THESE SISTERS have dedicated their lives to the care of the mentally ill and for the past fifteen years have been doing excellent work in their Private Nursing Home down in Ratoath, County Meath. So far, this is their only house in Ireland but they are well known in England, particularly in Sussex, and in Belgium where the Order originated. The Sisters of St. Augustine of the Mercy of Jesus were founded by Canon Maes at Bruges one hundred and twenty-five years ago to undertake nursing in its various branches but with special emphasis on the care of people suffering from mental diseases. The English Bishops having heard about their work in the mental hospitals which they had established in Belgium invited the Congregation to open a branch in England and the first house there was opened an 1870 by Elizabeth Van Pae, Mother Mary Raphael. This convent called St. George's Retreat, near Burgess Hill in Sussex is now the Mother House and Novitiate of the Order which has been separated from the Belgian Congregation since 1887.

The Sisters of St. Augustine arrived in Ireland in April, 1951, having bought the historic old home of the Corballis family, Ratoath Manor, surrounded by quiet County Meath fields and beside the dozey little village of Ratoath. They had to spend almost two years getting the house into repair, adding a harmonious wing on each side, converting a stable into a serene and beautiful oak-paneled chapel before it was ready to open as the first Augustinian Nursing Home in Ireland in November, 1952, with accommodation for 50 ladies whose ages at present range from about 21 to 95. The majority are chronic cases who have been here since the home opened, old ladies whose minds have become slightly unhinged by senility, many of them are bedridden and completely helpless, needing constant unremitting care.

Others, especially the younger ones, are not noticeably ill at all; they like to help with the running of the house, and enjoy all the normal pleasures such as television, film shows—the Nursing Home has its own very fine concert hall and there are film shows and concerts every weekend — picnics, parties, and shopping for new clothes. Sometimes they invite one of the Sisters to come along and help them choose a new hat or a new spring suit. "We are delighted to see them taking an interest in their appearance and in clothes. It shows that they are feeling well," said Sister Mary Peter, the Superioress, who seemed to me a person of infinite understanding and kindness. Looking round at the elegant furnishings, glass chandeliers and tasteful colour schemes, I wasn't surprised to hear that there was a long waiting list of people anxious to get into this Nursing Home — the atmosphere is like that of a Grade A hotel.

---

1   The article was published in the *Irish Press* in March 1967

"It is important that the patients have bright cheerful colours and nice things around them, we do everything we can to make it seem like a real home—and we also try to keep the fees as low as possible." Sister Mary Peter told me. There are small wards with five or six beds for those who are bedridden and need constant vigilance, a few very pretty little single rooms and several double and treble bedrooms, ail done in different colour schemes, apple blossom, celadon green, daffodil yellow, etc., and most of them looking out on great rolling acres of green fields. "Is the heart of the country a good setting for a Nursing Home of this nature? Do the patients like the extreme quietness of the country or do they find it hard to get used to at the beginning?" I asked. "On the contrary, we find this an ideal setting for our work. Patients suffering from nervous disorders react splendidly to the calmness and serenity of the country. We sometimes get cases that have given a lot of trouble in other Hospitals and yet when they come down here the quiet atmosphere seems to soothe them and we find that they cause us no trouble at all."

STORIES AND TALES ACROSS THE DECADES

Remembering Confirmation Days in Ratoath

PEGGY FLOOD, GERARD RALPH, LORNA FLOOD

Confirmation Day for Ratoath and Ashbourne Girls and Boys in Ratoath in 1949

We were unable to obtain all the names of the girls and boys in this picture as many of them came from Ashbourne for their Confirmation Day in Ratoath in 1949. Missing names are represented by "???" in the following list:

Girls to Left of picture
Front Row L-R: ???, ???, ???, ???, ???, ???, ???, Biddy Mannering,
2nd Row L-R: Moira Martin, Mona Brennan, Sheila Moore, Maura Moore, Mary Donnelly (Next to Fr. Cogan),
3rd Row L-R: Betty McLoughlin, Nancy Byrne, Ita Mannering, ???, ???, Ida Brennan, Babs Mulvany, Patricia McLoughlin and Margaret Duffy,
Back Row L-R: May Costello, ? Walls, ???, Joanie Flanagan, ???, ???, Joan Kavanagh, Peg Reilly.
Boys to Right of picture
Front Row L-R: Michael McLoughlin, Kit Morgan (Ashbourne), ? Fitzsimons (Ashbourne),
? Newman (Ashbourne), Barney Kearns (Ashbourne)
2nd Row L-R: Fr. John Cogan (Centre), ???, N. Chapman, ???, Joe White, ???, ???,
3rd Row L-R: Patrick Toole, Colm Reilly, Christy (Sonny) Martin, Nicholas Keogh, Angelo Mulvany, M. Counan, Seamus (Blackie) McGrane
Back Row L-R: K. Byrne, Kieran Brady, Bill Eiffe, Tony Everard, Jimmy Maher, Hughie Ward (Ashbourne), Patsy McCabe

STORIES AND TALES

Remembering Confirmation Days in Ratoath

Three Ratoath people recall their Confirmation day memories, Peggy Flood confirmed in 1934, her granddaughter Lorna Flood confirmed some 66 years later and Gerard Ralph recalls his day in 1946. The changing times are well illustrated by these stories.

My Confirmation Day - by *Peggy Flood*

I was confirmed in 1934 in the Church of the Most Holy Trinity in Ratoath by Bishop Mulvaney. It was a beautiful May Day. Bishop Mulvaney asked some of us a question from *The Catechism*. Only those allocated number one were asked questions. I wore a blue satin dress with a frill on the hem made by Molly Everard of Rackenstown. To complete the outfit I wore a wreath and veil. The wreath featured Lily of the Valley flowers made from wax. My shoes were black patent leather and my father had to cycle to Dublin to buy them. I took Ann as my Confirmation name. Following the ceremony my mother gave me a shilling. I went to Peter Talty's sweet shop to buy acid drops, Killarney toffee and fizz bags. We returned home, I changed my clothes and went out to play. My father did not attend my Confirmation, as he was working.

My Confirmation Day – by *Gerard Ralph*

On Confirmation Day in May 1946, my brothers Alec, Anthony and I were confirmed together. Although I was only 9 years of age, I had got the necessary "1" and therefore could receive my Confirmation. We were confirmed by the Bishop of Meath, who was then Archbishop Elect of Armagh and he later became Cardinal Dalton.

My Confirmation Day - by *Lorna Flood* *(daughter of Mark & Kathleen Flood)*

On the 24th March 2000 I made my Confirmation in the Church of the Most Holy Trinity in Ratoath. Bishop Smyth confirmed me. I took Donna as my Confirmation name. My sponsor was Aunt Mary. Caoimhe Carey, my cousin, also made her Confirmation. My outfit, bought in Miss Selfridges, was a blue sleeveless jacket, navy trousers and white top with blue sleeves and navy sandals. My mother, father, brother Keith, Granny Flood, Grandfather and Grandmother Naughton, my aunts and cousins went to the County Club, Dunshaughlin, Co. Meath, for lunch. After that I went to the Tallaght Shopping Complex and did some shopping. I received a considerable amount of money as presents.

STORIES AND TALES ACROSS THE DECADES

The Ratoath Inn

LEO AND ROSE McGIRL

LEO AND ROSE MCGIRL bought the Ratoath Inn in 1972. Soon afterwards they built a lounge at the back. Music sessions were held there for many years on weekend nights. During that time all the staff were locals and their help was very much appreciated by the McGirls.

The property was sold to the Brazil Family in 1990.

Right: Rose and Leo McGirl pictured outside the Ratoath Inn on the occasion of the official opening of the new Lounge by "The Dubliners" in 1976

Bottom left: Leo and Rose McGirl at the bar in the Ratoath Inn with Steve and Maureen Baker

Bottom right: Annie Gogan behind the bar in Clarke's Pub in the 1960s (now the Ratoath Inn)

STORIES AND TALES ACROSS THE DECADES

The Humours of Peacockstown, Ratoath

JOHN SHEAHAN

In 1976, we moved from Raheny to Peacockstown – a change of lifestyle from suburban bustle to rural tranquillity. Our neighbours in Raheny thought we were emigrating. "Away down the country," they said, but we loved it from that first May morning in 1976 when we woke to the singing of the birds.

We felt that we were on holidays, and it was exciting to think that life was going to feel like that from then on, and so it has been.

We made our way to Sullivan's shop and were welcomed by Terry and her mother, and what a delightful shop it was, where you could buy anything from a flitch of bacon to a bicycle tyre to a pair of wellingtons.

Sheahan Family, Peacockstown

Mary and John Sheahan with their children

The postman, Bobby, had been the trumpet player with Royal Blues Showband, and like myself was a city boy. On his first morning delivering, he was reprimanded by some of the old neighbours for not picking up their newspapers and coal and groceries from Sullivan's as his predecessor George had done for years. He too was learning old rural ways. He often took the time to have a cup of tea, and play a few tunes with me, and then take our son, Fiachra and some of the new neighbour's boys in the van with him to help with his deliveries.

One morning a musician friend from Galway was hitching out to visit me. He was delivered by Bobby with the morning post. Such was the casual way of life then, when we seemed to have more time to share.

Our children thrived in the atmosphere of the countryside. They all acquired wellingtons and were soon familiar with the wildlife in the hedges and ditches for miles around. They settled in so well, that during games between Dublin and Meath, we had an identity crisis in the family.

Peacockstown has proved to be a great place to burn the midnight oil with neighbours, old friends and fellow musicians. The atmosphere has been a source of inspiration for me. Among my musical compositions over the years is a piece I called 'The Humours of Peacockstown', which was used by RTÉ as a signature tune for their Folk on Sunday programmes.

The move to the countryside has been an adventure we never once regretted. We have been blessed with wonderful friends in Peacockstown, and look forward to many more years of peace and tranquillity in County Meath.

John Sheahan, October 2008

Above: The Dubliners: 1975-1979. L-R: Jim McCann, Barney McKenna, Luke Kelly, John Sheahan.
The band played at the opening of a new lounge at the Ratoath Inn in 1976.
(*Photo*: Courtesy John Sheahan)

STORIES AND TALES ACROSS THE DECADES

Newcomers to Ratoath… "21st Century Blow-Ins"

MARIA & PADDY DALTON

IN THE YEAR 2000, having lived most of our lives in North Dublin, we decided to move house. Our daughter Regina, having married a Meath man, was very happily settled in Ratoath, and whilst visiting them we noticed a new housing development at Jamestown Park. Regina suggested we take a look and up to that moment in time, it had never crossed our minds to move out of the Dublin area. However, our first grandchild, Jack, was then 8 months old and I have no doubt that anyone who has crossed that bridge will agree, becoming a grandparent is one of the most joyous and satisfying of life's experiences.

We viewed the showhouse, with which I fell in love, and it didn't take me long to envisage living in Ratoath. At this stage the main focus for me was to be near my only daughter and her family. I should mention that we also have one son, Andrew (now 25 years old), who was quite happy to move with us. All other aspects of the move, i.e. no local friends, new estate, new neighbours, access to facilities, etc., etc., took second place to being near my family. I felt that, in time, I would overcome any problems and if some remained unresolved, it would be worth that endurance to be living near to my family.

Paddy, at this stage, was most apprehensive of making the move. He had serious concerns that at our age we might not settle, would find it hard to make new friends, not "fit in" with the mostly "young" families in the area and be overcome by loneliness. Following much discussion we decided to give it a go and in April 2001 we moved to Jamestown Park.

At the outset, it felt very strange to be living in a place where we knew absolutely nobody. Nevertheless, as the weeks and months went by, we gradually got to know people and it was a very "nice" feeling to go into Johnny Ryan's shop for a newspaper, any of the three "locals" for a drink or to Mass on Sunday mornings and *always* be warmly greeted. I know I very quickly felt I belonged and really enjoyed going for walks around the village. Despite feeling lonely initially, Paddy very soon made two new friends …. Fr. Paul Crosbie and Joe Mannering, both of whom made him feel so warmly welcome and gave very generously of their time to chat to him and listen to his anxieties. It was primarily their friendship that Paddy credits with helping him to overcome his doubts and fears and to settle happily in Ratoath.

In examining the broader picture, it now amazes me how quickly we integrated, it almost happened without us even noticing, and certainly did not take any great effort on our part. The local services and amenities are now utilised fully by us and our son, who now also has a large circle of friends in Meath and he also does all of his socialising in Meath. We all very seldom set foot in Dublin now!

Through getting involved in local groups, such as the Heritage Group, we have learned

Paddy Dalton with Fr. Paul Crosbie and Joe Mannering in the grounds of Ratoath Church after the Silver Jubilee Mass for Fr. Gerry Stuart, PP, on Sunday 27 June 2004

2007: Maria and Paddy Dalton pictured in their home in Ratoath with their grandchildren from left: Kate, Grace, Jack and Ryan Doherty.

quite a lot about the area and made many more new friends. We are very fortunate to live only a short walking distance from the village and yet be so close to the countryside. We also feel lucky to be part of the whole "new community" who have settled in Ratoath in the past few years. I feel the fact that so many people were all "new" to the area in such a few short years helped us to bond with and look out for each other. I have at times considered how the older established Ratoath community might have felt "being invaded" or even "taken over" by us newly settled residents, but, a large number of them were once just like us when they were resettled here, many years ago, from the West of Ireland. Perhaps this is one of the reasons which helped us to feel accepted and settle so well – but if so, another phenomenon which I feel in no small way shares the accolade is "Ratoath Parish" under the guidance and stewardship of the Parish Priest, Fr. Gerry Stuart. With the involvement of so many members of our community, I believe Ratoath Parish is truly at the heart of the wonderful community spirit that exists in Ratoath today.

From my very early days attending church, I felt "at home" and that "I belonged" and it was there too that Paddy met his first two friends (Fr. Paul and Joe). We are both very happy to live among and be part of such a lovely community and of course to be only a "stone's throw" from our now larger family of four beautiful grandchildren, Jack, Grace, Ryan and Kate, is the icing on the cake.

STREETSCAPES AND LANDSCAPES

A Journey through Ratoath in the 1950s
– No longer a Village

PATRICK SHERRY

THE DOCTOR'S HOUSE is on the right and on the left is Corballis Manor House. Mr. Corballis was a big landowner then, owning the 'Fair Green' opposite and the 'Woodlands' behind the house now owned by the Darby family. Mr. Corballis brought my brother and I as boys to wash his car (one of only three in the village!) for which we got six old pence. We also went shooting with him on the bog of Dunshaughlin. There was plenty of game in those days - geese, pheasant, snipe and duck. We carried the game and rabbits home for him, he was a crack shot and rarely missed. Our payment was a couple of rabbits - he kept the game himself. On one occasion we hid a goose under a bush but when we went back later we found only feathers and a fox in the next field licking his lips!

Back to our journey through the old village. On the left was McAuley's pub (now a bookie's shop) and opposite was Monaghan's Pub (now Ryan's). Next is the second lane, leading down to the river where there is a wooden bridge and 'stepping stones' so that people can cross over. Next on the right lives Mrs. Balfe, who rings the Angelus and the Mass bells. On the left is the church where most Sundays I served first Mass and sang in the choir at the second mass. All of my family sang in the choir but my late brother John was the star singer as he won medals for singing at the Feis Ceoil.

Now we are at the junction of two roads, one leading to Skryne and the other up the centre of the village. There is a huge weighing scales at the junction (where the Marian Shrine is now) for weighing cattle, etc., at the annual 'Fair' which was held in those days. Three men came from Dublin on horses and carts in those early days, one known as the 'Run-a-monkey' who would sell fruit and cakes from his stand at Monaghan's Pub. Another man known as 'Ray-Ray' came with herrings on a Friday. Tom O'Neill came in the nineteen twenties with bread loaded in huge baskets on a flat dray.

Leaving Meagher's Pub and the Protestant Church on the right, we pass Moore's house on the right and come to the cross roads near the present cemetery. You turn right for Curragha and it was on this road we had our 'hurley field' owned by Bill Duffy. This was the centre of all G.A.A. games. Like all villages or towns in Ireland, the G.A.A. games were the main pastime we had. To the left lived the well-known Farrell family, big landowners who donated the present land to the parish for a cemetery.

As we go through this junction the well-known Eiffe family live on the right. Further down on the left are the Rogers family, also landowners and involved in the horse business. On the right is 'The Codulas', a piece of common land now home to the Pitch and Putt Club.

We go back again to the church and go through the main village, with Foley's Forge on the left and Rogers' stables and paddocks on the right where scores of hunting horses were stabled. On this side also was Keoghs house and they ran the first Taxi service in the village, followed latterly by Jimmy Clarke with an early model T Ford! Further on the right was Talty's shop where we bought our pennyworth of sweets.[1] On the left is the third lane (Hessman's Lane) which leads to the river. In the early days there was a windmill bringing water from the river to Rogers' Yard. On the left lived the Ralph family, the first family ever to grow flowers for marketing.

On the right stands what we called the 'Town Hall' since replaced. Concerts and card games were held here, but in Father Kelly's time dancing was banned for whatever reason, best known to himself! Even when we won the 1940 hurling championship he refused the hall for a dance to present the medals. The medals were presented in a farmer's loft in Ballymore. Years after my brother John and I discovered our medals were Junior *Football* medals! I reckon the football champions got our Junior *Hurling* medals but nobody complained at the time! I did write to the Meath Chronicle in latter years, relating the facts but got no response.

Further down on the left live the Walls family. All the brothers played for Ratoath hurlers, except for Johnny. The Walls also managed to win the gardening award from the County Council for many years.

Opposite lived the Anderson family, whose orchard we robbed every year, I'm ashamed to say! On the left after Walls was Madden's forge, then Rose Lynch, and opposite the Reilly family. Next on the left were the Toole family who were big landowners and were also involved with Ratoath hurling. The river 'Broadmeadow' crossed under the road just there.

In my young days lived the 'Macs of the Mill' and there was then a huge mill wheel (long out of use) well back from the river, which suggests that the river had been much wider in the previous century. Next was the 'Macs' lane leading down to the wooden bridge previously mentioned. One of the 'Macs of the Mill' (McNulty) lived near where Jimmy Ralph and family live'.

And, so to the place of most memories, the school. I went there in 1922, aged five. The school was built in 1911 and was more or less a new building. We had a very strict school

---

1 Molly Talty's shop and house at the centre of Ratoath Village were demolished in 2005 to facilitate the expansion and redevelopment of the Ratoath Community Centre which reopened in April 2006.

teacher, Mr Doonan, In spite of this he was widely recognised as the best teacher in Ireland and pupils came from other parishes to his school.

This reminds me of another incident which happened in the lane at the end of the school field. Christy Smith and I were on manoeuvres with the L.D.F. during the war, and we held a position awaiting the army. Our turn came to take a short sleep in the lane during the night. As we slept, the army came through, tanks and armoured cars and all. They marched our group (those who were awake!) to Fairyhouse as prisoners of War! When we woke up and realised what had happened, we made our way forlornly home and met up with Jack Bruen of the Post Office, who called us deserters and other choice names. I laugh heartily when I think of this now, but at the time it was very embarrassing! Once a year we went happily from school to the 'Point to Point' in Mullinam. Horses were everywhere in and around Ratoath, so we were reared on 'mare's milk' as it were.

Back again to the 'Cross' and going towards Lagore, Jack Bruen's Post Office and land was on the left. Jack was a wizard with the wireless at that time and I remember sitting on the wall with a crowd listening to the first radio broadcast of what I now think was the 1926 Hurling Final. Opposite Bruen's was Murray's who we called to often as they had a gramophone, and Barney Brown who lived there played his fiddle.

Next was McCabes and as Peter was my godfather I borrowed his bicycle to go to see Meath and Kildare play in the semi-final in 1928. The Canal End in Croke Park was a mud bank at that time and I saw very little of the game! I do remember Paul Doyle of Kildare scoring from every angle and the ball was the old heavy leather type. I also remember it was sixpence in to Croke Park and three pence for the bike.

Next came the three McGrane houses on the right. Tom and his wife were first and Father Nicholas was their only son. Mrs. McGrane was called upon by neighbours to help in every emergency. Next was Kit McGrane and there hangs a story. Someone told the teachers that a group of us had cut underneath a plank so that Kit would fall into the river and that she actually did. We were lined up on a Monday morning - we got six of the cane on each hand. We had to drag Kit up the next day to confirm that nothing like this had happened. Mr. Doonan gave us a shilling each - a penny for each belt of the cane.

And now to Dick McGrane the postman, who was also in charge of the L.D.F. if memory serves me. In the twenties we lived in a thatched house next to the O'Brien's and beside McGrane's. (All these houses are now long gone). I remember my Mother bringing my late brother John and I over to the well in the Woodlands as a lorry load of soldiers were firing off guns at the 'Cross'. We stayed there until they left. I was five years old at that time so it could be 1922 Civil War times.

Next on the left lived 'Gran' Fortune and we were there often as she had a gramophone too! The 'Dorkin Mannering' was great at ferreting rabbits which were our staple diet at the time. Next was our second home where the Darby families live. Opposite the 'Dorkins' was

Ratoath Hurlers, 1940:
L-R: Paddy Sherry, Tom Foley and John Sherry

another Toole family in a two-story house, long since gone. On now to Johnny Clarke's house which still stands today as far as I know. Next is Lynch's where Christy Smith lived. Further on lived Jack Eiffe and family, and before them on the same site lived McCarthys; hence we called the wood there 'McCarthy's Wood'.

We now go round the bend and on the left was the 'Red Cross Tree' where old people told us people were hanged (including a priest). It could have been a hanging tree for people on the run after the 1798 rebellion. At that time people were hanged for stealing a sheep or even a lamb. In my young days every coffin was carried out and around the Red Cross Tree and then to the church. Next was the Loch Lane which lead to the Bog Road and so to Lagore Cross, left turn is to Ballymore and right to Crusheen Road. Just before Lagore crossroads on the right hand side stood the lovely house where Stephen and Molly Blake lived. The Beech Wood and the Oak Grove were situated further along the Lagore Road but these were long gone by the time the O'Hare family came there. The Thunder family lived in Lagore House and in my youth the old people told me that the Corballis family donated the site and the Thunders built the present church. The Thunders are buried in lead coffins in the church grounds; the only lay people buried there.

Blake's Cottage, Dunshaughlin Road

My happiest memories of Ratoath are of the hurling team even if we only won one championship and as the late Andy Eiffe, a great GAA man said to me 'You won that by default!' as Kildalkey who beat us in the 1939 final failed to turn out for the 1940 final!

Ratoath folk were always very clannish. I remember my first game at sixteen, when the late 'Darby' Gillic floored a defender who was giving me a hard time, and was sent off. When I was in St. Finian's College, Mullingar, you had your name on your hurley stick and mine was taken out by somebody and broken. The late Benny Dolan found out who it was and flattened him! The three shillings for a new hurley stick was handed over to me immediately!

We ran a tournament to raise parish funds – two semi-finals and a final, which went to a replay. Forty pounds was taken in at the gate – a princely sum then as wages were about £2 a week! Sadly we lost the replay. I still have my 1940 medal, it is a prized possession.

I bought a grave in 1971 in Ratoath so that when Gabriel blows his horn I will know exactly where I am. I have set out my memories of Ratoath in the old days because, in the words of the old song: 'Fond memories bring the light of other days around me'.

Footnotes: *Patrick Sherry also recounted that in 1941 the LDF (Local Defence Force) had to stand guard at farm entrances during the Foot and Mouth outbreak of that year. Patrick also composed the theme song for a concert about Ratoath Village in Fr. Bartley's time.*

Since writing his memoirs Patrick Sherry passed away on 23rd April 2004, aged 87.
May he rest in Peace.

STREETSCAPES AND LANDSCAPES

Ratoath Song from 1940s

PARTICK SHERRY

On your way from Dublin City travelling down to Navan town
There lies a little village on your right as you go down.
It's not too far from Tara where the Irish Kings once ruled
And on your way to Fairyhouse its in Clarke's your thirst you'll cool.

Chorus
It's the prettiest little village in the whole of Ireland's crown
And I wonder if you'll guess the name of this little Irish town?
Dunshaughlin and Dunboyne are near but it's far in front of both
If you travel over Ireland's ground you'll never whack Ratoath.

Our curate he is so big and tall an Irishman so true
That very soon he'll reach the moon to light his Kerry blue.
He's the master of the drama and he leaves not one alone
He teases every single sole from Drogheda to Athlone.

Of course we have a hurling team their colours white and blue
But don't confuse with Cavan or we'll have to change the hue!
We'll hurl any team you know from Trim to Knocknagow
And we'll knock the stuffing out of them in a ruction or a row.

We can't leave out the L.D.F. or the Red Cross marching near
They swing along with their marching song with rifles and their gear.
There's not a group to match them as they're marching by the moat
And Ireland's proud to hear their step, those Soldiers from Ratoath.

1940's: Members of the Ratoath Local Defense Force (L.D.F.) marching past Everard's House, opposite the Church of the Most Holy Trinity at the centre of Ratoath village

STREETSCAPES AND LANDSCAPES

Growing up on the Dunshaughlin Road in the late 1950's

TONY DARBY

Growing up in Ratoath in the late fifties and sixties was a marvellous experience. Life was simple, so uncomplicated and so rich in the small things that people long for nowadays. For instance, the wonderful friendship and caring that people had for one another, on our road, was something special. In the following article I will give a little insight into the families that lived on the Dunshaughlin Road, what everyday life was like, what kind of working day they had and how they spent their leisure time.

The Sherry Family
I was born in my parent's home on the Dunshaughlin Road, Ratoath. This road was known as Pullwee Street to the locals. The name itself is derived from the Irish name, *poll bhuí*, a yellow hole or well. This well was located on the boundary between the Streamstown Development and O'Neill's family home and it was some fifty metres in from the roadway.

My home was a small modest cottage set on one Irish acre of land. My father Kevin, was a native of Dunshaughlin, but came with his family to live on a small farm in Mooretown (a town land at the edge of Ratoath parish) when he was twelve years old. My mother Kathleen ("Katie", nee Sherry) was born in the house where I was born. The house was constructed in 1910 and in its early days was the home of my grandparents Patrick & Mary Sherry.

Mary Sherry   Paddy Sherry

Mary & Patrick Conway

My great grandparents Mary & Patrick Conway were married on the 6th August 1878 in the local parish church. In those early years they lived in a thatched house on five acres of land (beside what is now Parkview Estate). Mary (Murray, her maiden name) was the postmistress in Murray's Post Office. In those days the horse drawn mail car was the only mode of transport to get the mail to and from the village. Mary's husband, Patrick, was a Sergeant in the R.I.C. police; unfortunately he died a young man at a little over forty years of age.

The story goes that one night Patrick was sent out to investigate some illegal activity that was taking place after dark. What happened that night is to this day unclear. Clearly the injuries he sustained in that altercation brought about his untimely death. As a result my grandmother was never to see her father, as she was born some weeks after his death. In Ireland in those days when one lost a parent before one was born one would inherit a gift of healing or 'a cure' as it was known locally. My grandmother was no exception and she inherited the cure for thrush. On my summer holidays to my grandparent's farm I saw many people come to the farm with their children to have them cured of this ailment. The

Patrick & Mary Conway

visits seemed to be worthwhile because as we returned home from Mass on a Sunday morning people would stop and thank her for the time she had given them and their children. I think it only proper to say that my grandmother never asked for or was she given anything in reward for this service, as that was the custom at that time.

My grandparents, Patrick and Mary Sherry, had ten children, four boys, John, Paddy, Nicholas and Joe (who died when he was a young boy) and six girls, May, Annie, Kathleen, Theresa, Enda and Nellie. My grandmother Mary (nee Conway) continued to live with her mother until she married my grandfather Patrick Sherry, and for some time after that they lived in the old homestead before moving down the road to the house where I was born. In later years they moved to a farm within Ratoath Parish in the Townland of Mooretown.

A Close Call

My uncle Paddy recalls that in the early hours of a midsummer's morning my grandfather's sleep was interrupted by the sound of many feet scurrying by his bedroom window. He looked out the window to find the field at the back of the house being searched from top to bottom by the Black and Tans. Needless to say some very anxious moments were to follow as the 'Tans' (as they were commonly known) checked out every nook and cranny of the field. After some time they decided to move on, leaving behind them a flattened meadow with hay of little value. Their departure was timely considering that they failed to discover a military uniform belonging to my grandfather which was hidden in a hole high up in the trunk of a tree. If they had found the uniform it would surely have brought an end to his life.

The Pump

Life on the road was simple in my early years with most of the men working locally in whatever jobs were available at the time. The women looked after the children, making meals, washing and so on. One very important aspect of life was the lack of running water in the houses along the road. The men had to draw the water from **The Pump** outside Jack Browne's house (Now Johnny and Ann Ryan's shop). The metal cover over the well where the old pump was situated is to this day visible in the parking lot in front of Ryan's shop. The water was drawn in all sorts of utensils, from buckets to churns, large and small. Tom Brennan had the cutest churn of all, it was small with the handle on top and its profile was that of the larger and better-known creamery churn. It held approximately two gallons of water. Another local resident would take home water on a small hand drawn cart with two small metal wheels and in it would stand two large churns full of water. The rumble of the wheels could be heard coming from a very long way off. The water was not only for the house, but also for the farm animals that were housed in the sheds nearby.

My outstanding memory of *The Pump* is that of coming home on a winter's night after serving as an altar boy in the church, and with little or no light to guide me on my way (no street lighting in those days!). I was always happy to get as far as The Pump because it was there that the men would have a chat as they took their turn to get water. On those nights as I approached I could see the glow and smell the smoke of many cigarettes and pipes as the men stood around The Pump. With a little luck I might have some company on the remainder of my journey home – a further three hundred metres along the darkest passage of the road.

Kevin & Katie Darby

Of course there is no denying that at times things were pretty tough in those early days. I remember my mother as a truly remarkable woman and how she kept going from dawn to dusk knitting, mending, patching, and so on, and rearing four sons. My mother was a very religious woman and insisted on the rosary being recited each and every night. What a task she had rounding up her sons for that half hour, after pleading with my brother Pat and myself to hold our positions while she went looking for Paul only to find on her return that Pat and I had done a disappearing act.

On one occasion, when the timber in the great woods of Lagore was sold, the owners decided to sell the branches of the trees to the locals for £3.00 per tree. My father and Billy Lynch purchased **a couple of trees** and they brought the timber home in a horse drawn cart. It was my first visit to Lagore and Michael Lynch (Skipper) introduced me to the wonderful orchard that was part of Lagore at that time.

During the 1950's in Ratoath, firewood was scarce and most nights you would find a number of men in the woods on the lookout for some timber for their fires. On my father's return he would cut the timber into small manageable lengths to fit the

Kevin Darby

Katie Darby

fire grate. And so, with the timber cut and the pigs and hens fed, eggs collected, and the fowl locked up for the night (the cunning old fox was always on the lookout for a stray hen or duck), it was time for the neighbours to make an appearance.

The Gathering

Mickey Brennan from next door would pay us a visit and fill us in on all the news of the day. On arranged nights my father would go with him to check out his rabbit traps. But on most other nights Mickey and my father would sit around the fire and talk about times long gone, and given the chance, they had no difficulty in solving the problems of the world, as they saw them. After some time they would be joined by more of the neighbours: Mickey Muldoon, Christy (Burke) Smith, Christy Foley, Tom Clince, John McCann, Paddy Lynam, Johnny Madden and Frank Maher. These were just some of the friends that would frequent our house at that time. The parish Curate was also included among the visitors.

Ghost Stories

A great pastime in our house was story telling. When one of the neighbours mentioned a new ghost, or a spirit sighting in the locality, the men would gather around the fireside in such a tight circle that the tips of their caps would almost touch and so that not a word would be lost in the telling of the story. My father had a great interest in ghost stories, as I could tell by the look in his eyes when the stories were told of banshee sightings at Judy's Hole on the Lagore Lane, or the stories of a large black dog on Ballymore Hill, or a little old lady sitting on a gate at the entrance to a local wood, or of course the well known Jack O Lantern sightings at Germ's Lane. All of the stories had a local connection, and as I had a good knowledge of the locality, I knew where these events had taken place and I can say without a moment hesitation that I spent many a sleepless night after I had gone to bed thinking about the banshee at Lagore and all the other weird things that went about their business in the middle of the night. As I lay in the bed I would conjure up all kinds of images in my mind of banshees and ghosts among the shadows in the far corner of my bedroom.

Barbers

My father was one of two barbers on our road, Mickey Brady being the other. Dad's special haircut was the "short back and sides" for the price of one shilling and six pence (1s 6d). So on Saturday nights we had a large number of visitors to the house. He continued this work for many years and during that time he never changed his style of cutting. However, one day he discovered that a mother who had brought her son for a hair cut had great difficulty in getting him through the gateway (for he hung on to the gate for dear life with both hands and feet and refused to budge). Fashion had changed and the youth of the day (early 1960's) no longer wanted short back and sides! Some time after that incident my Dad decided to call it a day.

The Great Outdoors

In the springtime each year, I can remember so well, the sound of the garden forks in the vegetable plots as Mick Flood, Tom Brennan, Joe Lynch, Jimmy Mannering and my Dad prepared the ground for the vegetables. He would also paint the outside of the house with whitewash so that it looked good in the eyes of the people going to Fairyhouse Races on Easter Monday. In the summertime my father would plant and tend the garden, make the hay and clip the hedges.

As for the children, the summer was a time for being outdoors and having fun. So off we went to McGrane's land (now Sommerville estate) and the Broadmeadow River, where we would dam the river (the water was crystal clear in those days) and spend the rest of the summer swimming, playing games and having a wonderful time by the riverside. In the evening when it was time for bed I would go to sleep to the sound of the corncrake in the meadow at the back of our house.

Pets
Jackdaws were great favourites as pets in the late 1950s and most of the boys on our road had one at some time in their early school years. I had one called Jack. Often as I rambled home from school across the Woodlands, Jack would meet me half way and take on anyone or anything that might be a threat to my safety. When he died I was truly devastated!

On one occasion my mother sent me with a message to a house in Lagore. The lady of the house invited me in for a cup of tea and some of her home baked cakes and as I took a seat at the table the family pet Jackdaw flew in and took up a position on top of the dresser in the kitchen. The pet Jackdaw had a look in his eye that I did not like and I said to myself *'I might be in a little bit of trouble here'*! At that moment the lady of the house put a couple of buns on a plate and filled out a cup of tea. As I put the milk in the tea cup the Jackdaw landed on the table and started to walk up and down the table in front of me. I could see that the hackles on the back of his neck were standing up and that is a very bad sign! The next move was mine and as I reached over my hand to get a bun, he dashed towards the plate and took up position between the plate and myself. No way would this jackdaw let me take a bun from the plate until the lady of the house intervened with the sweeping brush and escorted the bird out through the doorway!

Musical Memories
There was always music in our house; in the early days it was Tottie Reilly on the fiddle, and my Dad playing his accordion with some of his friends. As we got older two of my brothers Pat, Paul and myself, got our chance to play and as we became teenagers, we were 'hooked', as they say, on the famous groups of our time and wanted to play their music.

The Craftsmen
Front: L-R Dickie Donoughue, Tony Darby, Paul Darby
Back: L-R Chris Maher, Jim Tobin, Pat Darby
(Photographer: Michaël Maher)

We set about forming a group and after much work and practice, (poor Mother! how did she put up with us?), *The Craftsmen* were formed. We had Pat on drums, Paul and I on guitars, Dickie Donoughue on bass, Chris Maher on keyboards and Jim Tobin as lead singer.

STREETSCAPES AND LANDSCAPES — Growing up on the Dunshaughlin Road in the late 1950's

My only regret is that my youngest brother Finian was too young to play at that time, because in the years that followed, he was to become the finest musician in our family.

As the band became popular, we thought we should have a manager and we approached Nicholas Keogh, a local man from Rackenstown, to see if he was interested in the job. Nicholas said that he would take up the offer; we were very fortunate to get him, for he was a very good manager. Roddy O'Neill and Shane White joined the group some time later. Eventually, as our popularity grew, two forty-eight-seater buses would depart from Ratoath village at weekends with the band and their fans on their way to gigs around the country!

Finian Darby

Local Meeting Places
There were certain houses on the road that were meeting places at different times for the youngsters. The first was the old Post Office, the home of Jack & Mary Bruen. Today the site of their home has become the car park for the present day SuperValu supermarket.

(1) Jack & Mary Bruen's Post Office
The former Post Office had a thatch roof and it stood some twenty paces back from the roadway. It was a long bungalow with the living quarters on the left side and the Post Office to the right. An old red hay barn stood to the west of the site. It was here that we as youngsters were to see our first TV pictures. What an occasion that first day was - such excitement! I can see it still, Robin Hood on his horse with his long bow in his hand and he riding out of the snow (I think the 'snow' was permanent on Jack's TV!).

The assembly in the Post Office on a typical afternoon, after school, was about 20 chil-

Jack Bruen with his dog 'Ace'. (Photograph by Moira Martin)

dren inside and outside the counter, with Jack on the switch board and Ace, his dog, lying prostrate in the doorway. Ace was a big dog, a very big dog! I believe the breed came from Newfoundland.

At different times through the years Nan Moore, Carmel Mullen, Moira and Nuala Martin, worked with Jack in the Post Office. To gain entry to the Post Office one had to step over Ace in the doorway and that in itself was some achievement. On one occasion a local woman arrived to the Post Office. She was about to step over Ace, who was lying down and blocking the doorway, when he suddenly decided it was time to get up. (Roddy O'Neill, who was outside the Post Office at that moment, vividly recalled the rest of the story). The result was that Ace was last seen with the unfortunate woman on his back travelling at speed out the Dunshaughlin Road only to return some time later in an exhausted state!!

The Show
Bobbie McDonnell and his show came to the village once every couple of years and he would set up his tent in Jack Bruen's garden (where Gerry and Ann McKeever now have their home) This was a big event for the street. Young and old would make their way to the show to see what was on offer. I recall being disappointed twice on the same night. The first was when the strong man (who was the highlight of the show) gave a demonstration of his agility on the horizontal bar. This of course did not please us youngsters as his demonstration fell far short of our expectations. As we sat on those hard seats in Bobby's tent, it was unanimous that we could better this performance ourselves in the branches of the trees in Desmond Toole's wood!

The second disappointment occurred when the show came to a close. Bobbie insisted that we had to leave by the side entrance where the doorway opened out onto a ditch full of nettles. As Bobbie had no outside light and we wore short pants, try guessing as to what happened next (I think Bobby did not like our lack of enthusiasm for his strong man act).

Dyser Morgan's bicycle shop stood on this same site in my early days. The shop was made of wood and in time it became the first clubhouse of St. Andrew's Athletic Club.

(2) Mickey Brady's House

The next great meeting place on the Dunshaughlin Road was the home of Mickey Brady. Brady's house was the last house outside the village (beside what is now called Brownstown Estate). It has to be said from the outset that Mickey was one of the most tolerant and fascinating gentleman that one is likely to meet in a lifetime. He was a tall fit man who wore a hat and was a great shot with a .22 rifle. He had some great stories to tell about his fishing, shooting and trapping days and we listened with great interest to every word that he had to say.

The number of young people that would congregate at the Brady household was truly astonishing! On one occasion I remember twenty-two youngsters setting out from Brady's house on a lovely summer's day to spend the afternoon in Lagore Fox covert. They brought bows, arrows and catapults (all homemade) with them. On arrival at the fox covert, camp was set up and some of the boys climbed to the top of the oak and beech trees while the rest had a great time running through the woods in pursuit of everything and anything that moved in the undergrowth. I can recall the names of the young men who were there on that day as follows: The Brady

Mickey Brady

STREETSCAPES AND LANDSCAPES   Growing up on the Dunshaughlin Road in the late 1950's

brothers, Ciaran (Key), Pat (Packen), Noel and Kevin. Tony (Sammy) Morgan, Tony Toole, Neill Taaffe, Pat (Dinky) Donnelly, Nicholas Keogh, Mellor Flood, Dan Eiffe, Nicholas (Nicky) Sherry, Eugene Eiffe, Tommy and Larry Mooney, Michael (Skipper) Lynch, Ken Brennan, the Maher brothers Jimmy, Michael and Chris, Brian Everard and myself.

Mike Brady

Pat (Packen) Brady

Noel Brady

As time went by, more lads joined the group, including Nicholas (Borris) Kavanagh, the Corrigan brothers Leo and Anthony, Brendan Lynch, Gerry (Gerarldo) Keague, Leonard Brennan, Joe Mannering and my brother Pat.

Ratoath's first soccer team, 1962
Front L-R Kevin Brady, Gerry Keague, Brendan Lynch Ciaran Brady, Leonard Brennan,
Back L-R Chris Maher, Nicholas Keogh, Leo Corrigan, Ken Brennan, Joe Mannering, Tony Morgan

One day as we sat on the grass in front of Brady's house it was decided to form two teams to play soccer. Soccer had not yet come to the village, so this was something new. A field had to be found for the game and we were fortunate to have a farmer with a kind soul, (Johnny Gogan), who allowed the games to be played in his field, (the field is where Brownstown Estate is now). The year was 1962. The first game had neither shape nor make about it and the vocal exchanges could be heard at the parish church in the village. And so Ratoath had its first game of soccer. To help with our fitness, we would train in Desmond Toole's wood on the opposite side of the road from the pitch. The iron bar that was suspended between two trees for the teams to work out on was removed in 2005 when many mature trees were felled to make way for a new roundabout.

Anne and Johnny Gogan

(3) Mickey & Molly O'Neill's House

The third meeting house on the road was the home of Mickey and Molly O'Neill. Molly was from the Tankerstown Road at the end of the village. Mickey had one of the butchers' shops in the village. They had eight children, Roddy, Fiacra, Paddy, Brian, Daragh, Dominic, Mary and Sheila. The hospitality in this house was second to none, with many young people from all roads in the village congregating there in the evenings. Football, donkey racing, motor scrambling and many other activities took place there. They had many animals as pets, including, dogs, donkeys, jackdaws, a badger, a fox, guinea pigs, ducks, sheep, geese and lots more.

I recall my father and I standing by our gate one night when a fox passed through from the Woodlands. He was a beautiful animal, big and strong. As he made his way up the road in the direction of O'Neill's house my father turned to me and said "I hope he has the good sense and pass O'Neill's Gate." As you might have guessed the fox turned in through the gate. For a moment there was silence and then the whole place erupted. Out of the gate came the fox with six dogs in hot pursuit and at the head of the pack was Spikel the Irish terrier. The fox came back down the road at high speed and he passed through the gate into the woodlands. But Spikel in his haste got stuck in the gate and held up the rest of the pack. The fox made good his escape to the sound of laughter from my father and me.

Fiacra and Paddy O'Neill

STREETSCAPES AND LANDSCAPES   Growing up on the Dunshaughlin Road in the late 1950's

The O'Neill Family
Front L-R: Daragh, Molly, (baby Dominic), Mickey, and Sheila. Back L-R: Roddy, Mary, Brian, Paddy & Fiacra

Some of the youngsters that frequented the O'Neill household in those days were Michael (Spider) Eiffe; the Browne brothers – Pat, Benny and Noel; Joe Walls; Christy (Sonny) Martin; Tommy (the Fish) Wheeler; Joe Lynch; Paul and Pat Darby.

Tragedy hit this family in 1967. Paddy had just turned eighteen years old when he lost his life in a car accident outside the village at the Moulden Bridge. (A small memorial stands on the site of the accident).

The following year, 1968, Fiacra (twenty one years old) also lost his life in a road accident near Blanchardstown, Co. Dublin. The following year, 1969, Mickey, aged 53, lost his fight for life after a short illness. Molly died in 1991.

Jim O'Brien (brother of Molly O'Neill) lived with the family most of his life. Jim was a butcher in the village and a good hurler.

Jim O'Brien

The Parnell Cottages
On the opposite side of the road from O'Neill's house stood the two Parnell cottages (Fortune Court is now built on the site). In the early years the Fortune family lived there at the east end. They were later followed by the Nulty family, Biddy, Christy, Eddie and Mary and also Mick (Mun) Fortune. The Mun was by all accounts a hurler of great skill and brought

Parnell Cottages which were demolished to make way for Fortune Court

many honours to the road. But it was Eddie who was to go one better and in 1963 brought a senior hurling medal to the house for the first time.

Christy spent his early years working in Clarke's pub, bottling and labelling Guinness, and later he went to work on building sites. Mary married Paddy Walsh from Glascarn Lane. They now live in Brownstown.

Michael (Mun) Fortune   Eddie (Britt) Nulty   Christy Nulty

Jimmy & Betty Mannering
In the other Parnell cottage lived Jimmy and Betty Mannering. Betty had a thriving dress making business and had some very influential people in the parish as clients. Jimmy would spend a lot of his time in the garden planting vegetables and saving the hay. They had no children. I remember a few incidences with Jimmy as I grew up.

Jimmy had a great dislike of the corncrake that frequented his garden, as it kept him awake most of the night with its creaking sound. This was too much for Jimmy to take. So one night while I was down in the woodlands at the back of our house, I heard a vocal outburst coming from Jimmy's garden and I thought a row was taking place. I peered through a hole in the hedge to find Jimmy in hot pursuit of the corncrake, and raised high above his head was the household brush, but of course the corncrake came to no harm as Jimmy had great difficulty in locating the bird in the long meadow grass and he soon gave up the chase.

Billy & Mary Lynch

Across the road from our house lived Billy and Mary Lynch. They had five children four girls and one boy, namely: Peggy, Kit, Judy, Alice and Michael (the Skipper).

Mary (Mamie) Lynch

Billy Lynch

Michael (Skipper) Lynch

Local Horsemen

Christy Smith was a relative of the Lynch family and he lived with them until he got married. Christy was involved in the G.A.A. and played for the local team in his younger days. He had a great love of horses and after some years he set up his own bookmaker's office at the rear of Molly Talty's shop (where Gerry Keogh had his bicycle shop before it too was demolished in 2005 when the present Ratoath Community Centre was constructed). Information on race horses was accessible in the village from the very famous and well-known racing stables of Dan Moore and Tom Dreaper as to how the horses were doing on the gallops. The result was that the locals became experts in the art of picking the winners.

Christy Smith, Bookmaker

Some of the jockeys that went to school in the village in those days went on to scale the heights in National Hunt racing both in Ireland and in England. One such man was Liam McLoughlin, the most courageous jockey I ever had the pleasure to see. He had some outstanding successes. First and foremost it is not widely known that Liam was the jockey to ride Arkle when the horse won his first race. That was at Navan in the early 1960s. After that he went on to win an Irish Grand National on Keforo in 1962. In that same season he was to ride into the history books as the only jockey to ride the same horse (Keforo) to victory in the Irish Grand National, the Leopardstown Chase, The Thyestes Chase and The Maloney Cup and all in the same year. That record still stands to this day.

McLoughlin Brothers

Liam McLoughlin's brother Peter (my best pal at school) was also a jockey with the Dreaper Stable and he had many winners including the Leopardstown Chase

Paddy Woods **was another great jockey from the Dreaper Stable and a Ratoath sports**

Peter & Liam McLoughlin

man in every way, playing for the local G.A.A. club and also setting up St. Andrew's Athletic Club. Paddy had many winners including the Irish Grand National.

Dick and Annie McGrane

Dick and Annie McGrane

Dick and Annie McGrane had nine children: John, Sonny, Ritchie, Seamus, Christy, Mona, Sheila, Kathleen & Nora. Dick was a military man and fought in World War I at the Battle of The Somme in July-November 1916. He had lady luck on his side as he somehow survived that cruel and terrible battle. (Dick was born in 1900). Their daughter Nora now lives in Huntershill, Sydney, Australia where she has been a nun for over fifty years.

Many years later four of their sons followed him into military service.

Dick McGrane was a postman in Ratoath village and he owned the land through which the Broadmeadow River flowed. It was there that we as children spent our summers, swim-

STREETSCAPES AND LANDSCAPES Growing up on the Dunshaughlin Road in the late 1950's

Sr. Nora McGrane

Seamus (Blackie) McGrane

Mona McGrane

ming and having fun. In the 1990's the lands were sold to developers and the Riverwalk Court Apartments and shops were built there in 2003 followed by the Summerville housing estate in 2005-2006.

Paddy & Rita Martin
Paddy and Rita Martin lived in a two storey house next to O'Neill's. (the site is now the entrance to the Streamstown development). Rita was a nurse but most of her time was spent working with Paddy building up their horticultural business. Paddy was a member of the hurling team that won the 1963 senior hurling championship. It was also in this house that Fr Joe Clarke was born in 1912.

Christy & Irene Foley
The Foley Family lived on the opposite side of the road from us. They had seven children four boys and three girls: Henry, Dermot, David, Gerry, Barbara, Sandra and Irene.

Christy was the village blacksmith and one of his clientele was none other then D.L. Moore, the famous horse trainer, jockey and grandfather of Paul Carberry who won the English Grand National in 1999.

Christy Foley

Irene Foley

Christy was an amateur jockey and rider of Magic Hero, owned and trained by his brother Tommy, and the great competition in the Farmer's Race between Harry Everard's horse Ellen's Tang (a horse broken by my grandfather and ridden and looked after by my father). Christy played football & hurling for the local club and in later years he played for Kilbride Football Club.

Tom & Kathleen Brennan
Tom and Kathleen Brennan lived next door to us. They had six children: Phyllis, Rita, Ida, Mona, Vera and Ken. Mickey, a brother of Tom, also lived with them. The Brennan house was a hive of activity as Mickey was one of the bicycle repairmen in the village. He was also

Mickey Brennan    Phyllis Brennan    Mona Brennan

a rabbit trapper and an excellent shot with a rifle. He told stories of his hunting trips with Pa Donnelly and how they camped out in the woods for days, until they had enough rabbits to make the trip on bicycles to the Dublin market to sell them for five shillings each (32 cent at today's prices). In the autumn he would work on the threshing mill where his job was to help feed the mill with corn. The threshing mill would call to each of the farmers in the area who had corn to thresh. Tom's son, Ken, had a great interest in sport. He also played Gaelic football and soccer, and made a name for himself in the boxing ring. Nowadays he concentrates on Pitch & Putt at the local club. All the Brennan girls got married, moved away from home. In the summer months they made many trips home.

Ida Brennan

(Below): The Brennan Family L-R: Sheila, Kathleen, Tom, Vera, Rita, baby Michael Hall and Ken

Jack & Brigid Eiffe

There were eleven children in the Eiffe family: Andy, John, Noel, Jim, Bill, Eugene and Dan, and the girls Kathleen, Ita, Philomena and Anne. The Eiffe family is one of the oldest families in Ratoath, with the name coming up in parish records as far back as the 1640's. According to a civil survey at that time, William Eiffe of Raystown held the titles (ownership) of the long Mooreland of Ratoath. In 1854 Luke Eiffe had a bakery on the main street. In my time the Eiffes were farmers and great sportsmen, with every one of them at one time or another playing for the local G.A.A. club. Bill was outstanding as a player and played for the county in football and hurling and won many medals.

My memories of the Eiffe family were as great neighbours and a very religious family. On a number of visits to their house in my young days, Jack invited me to partake in the family rosary. The rosary in the Eiffe household was of a very long duration, as the trimmings that Jack had at the end of the five decades were on a par with what went before. So when we finally reached the end, I had to be helped to my feet as I wore only short pants and my knees were locked having been in contact with the concrete floor for so long.

Anne Eiffe was a great favourite with my mother and she would visit our house regularly. My brother Pat and I were always delighted to see her as she was in our age bracket, but Anne would make sure that we were always on our best behaviour and free from any mischievous ideas.

(Below): **The Eiffe family** Front L-R Dan, Andy, Jack, Brigid, Kathleen, Anne, Eugene Back L-R Noel, Jim, Ita, Philomena, Bill and John

Pat & Agnes McCabe

The McCabe family lived next to Jack Browne. There were three children in the family, two boys, Patsy, Matty and their sister Anna. Pat had land down at Germ's lane, which he farmed. He also had a truck and did some contracting work; in those days it was difficult to find a truck available for hire, so Pat was a busy man. But it was on the sports field that

Right:
Pat & Agnes McCabe's Home at the centre of the Village

the McCabes were to make their names. Pat and his brother Peter set the wheels in motion in the early days with some great hurling for the local club.

Matty and Patsy scaled the pinnacle of hurling in Co. Meath. In July 1963 Ratoath, for the first time in their long history, brought home the senior hurling championship cup. What a day that was, seeing Matty lift the cup above his head and hear the roar of the crowd. I think every able-bodied person in the village was at the match that day. Rumour has it that a local shopkeeper, thinking that we were about to lose the game, absconded with minutes remaining on the clock. She returned to her shop in the village to tell her customers that the team had lost. But what a surprise they got, for in those dying minutes of the match, Patsy McCabe got the ball some thirty yards out from the Dunboyne goal posts. He made some progress towards the goal, and, with a mighty pass, he found Tommy Mahon who in turn found the roof of the net, and as they say, the rest is history! Before moving on from the McCabe family I think it is worth mentioning that Matty McCabe was one of the finest hurlers to play for the club and a great team captain.

Jack & Lucy Browne

Jack & Lucy's house was the first house on the road, situated at the crossroads in the centre of the village. It was in this house that the Murray family ran the Ratoath Post Office. Jack Browne's mother's family, the Murrays, owned the Post Office at that time.

Lucy and Jack Browne

Jack & Lucy Browne's Home (Murray's Post Office). Later it was replaced by Johnny & Anne Ryan's NearBuy Shop

296

STREETSCAPES AND LANDSCAPES   Growing up on the Dunshaughlin Road in the late 1950's

Jack was our postman and he had a very large area to cover each day. Our postal district was much larger in those days. On the longest part of his run he had to cross open fields with his bicycle in order to deliver the post. The first crossing, after he delivered the post to Lagore House, was to cross open fields and the Broadmeadow River to reach the cul-de-sac which in turn would take him to Mooretown. Having delivered the post to Bert Mooney in Wilkinstown, (and Bert lived at the end of a long lane) Jack would once again cross the open fields to reach Porterstown Lane so that he could continue his daily postal deliveries. Jack was the only one in the village who could repair a watch or clock. He also found time for a little fishing with his friends. There were five boys and two girls in the Browne family, Pat (now a Canon in the Diocese of Westminster, London), Benny, Noel, Dermot, Aidan, Ann and Miriam. Jack and Lucy were beautiful singers, as were all members of the family.

Flood Family

Mick and Peggy had two boys, Mellor and Mark and three girls, Beryl, Olive and Pauline. Mick was involved with horses all his life and loved sport. Mick was the man who was responsible for the village being wart free as he had the cure for their removal, which involved the use of ivy, and, if my memory serves me right, there was no serious problem with warts on our road as ivy was in plentiful supply!

Peggy Flood

Mick Flood

Olive and Beryl Flood

Mark, Pauline and Mellor Flood

Mick and Peggy also kept a beautiful vegetable and flower garden. Mellor was in my opinion a very classy soccer player, with a great turn of speed and, if playing today, I have no doubt that he would be playing at the highest level. He was also a player on the 1963 senior hurling winning side. Mark was a very good soccer player and is now involved in the running of the Ratoath Harps Club.

Joe Lynch as Lord Mayor with family members
Front: Martina, Noel, Margaret, Marian. Back: Martin, Peggy, Joe, Bernie

Joe & Peggy Lynch

Joe & Peggy had nine children three boys and six girls, Ann, Joe-Joe, Marian, Martin, Bernie, Una, Margaret, Martina and Noel. The Lynch family were splendid neighbours. Joe was the first Lord Mayor in the village and raised the largest amount of cash to help with the construction of the former Community Centre. He was involved in most community activities in the parish and was a great loss when he died at the age of 62.

Their son Joe-Joe in the early years played in goal for the Ratoath Harps. He was also involved in the setting up of Lagore & District Gun Club.

Ann Lynch

Joe Lynch

Casey Family

The Casey Family had for many years lived in the family home at Fox Lodge farm before moving down to live on Pullwee Street. The Casey family home was where Joe and Mary Lynch now live. Mrs. Casey and her two sons Bill and Jimmy moved into this home in the late 1940s. Jimmy went to America in the early 1960's and Bill remained in the family home until his death a few years ago.

Bill Casey

Great Sporting Moments

Veronica and Daragh O'Neill

The involvement in sport of all kinds on the street was indeed great with some outstanding achievements. The first that springs to mind is the day in 1995 when Daragh O'Neill and his wife Veronica brought home the trophy after winning the All Ireland mixed doubles in Pitch and Putt. But Daragh was not satisfied with only one All Ireland title. He went on to take yet another trophy as the *"worst dressed man"* in Ireland which was organised by a well known radio station.

On the playing fields, the winning of the 1963 senior hurling championship for the first time was exciting as eight of the team came from Pullwee Street. It is worth noting that in the 1960s seven young men from the street played for the county team. In horse racing, jockey Danny McCann lived on the street for much of his racing years. Danny's claim to fame is that he came second in the Aintree Grand National in 1947.

The Red Cross Tree

The Red Cross tree was located at the end of Pullwee Street where the roundabout at the entrance to Steeplechase is now situated. The story of the tree is that during the 1798 rebellion it was the scene of the hanging of three Wexford men, on their way north from the battle at Vinegar Hill in Co. Wexford. As they approached Ratoath, they fell behind the main body of men and became isolated. They were then set upon and captured by Lord Fingal and his men. They begged for a Priest and Lord Fingal[1] asked Fr. Langan to come and give them the Last Rites and they were then hanged on the Red Cross Tree. Folklore has it that these three men were buried at the site of the Red Cross Tree.

An unusual aspect of the tree was that as funerals from the village made their way to the graveyard, the men who were carrying the coffin would make a detour down Pullwee Street and around the Red Cross tree and then return to the village. Why this was the case I am unsure. Some people say that a priest was among those hanged on the tree. I can state with certainty that my uncle was involved with carrying the coffin which turned out to be the last to make the journey around the tree in 1933 when he was sixteen years old.

Killeen Castle, former home of Lord Fingal

---

[1] An interesting footnote on Lord Fingal, the 8th Earl of Fingal, was that as Captain of the Skryne Cavalry he led his Yeomanry, on 26th May 1798, to Battle against the rebels on the Hill of Tara in which many local people lost their lives.

STREETSCAPES AND LANDSCAPES

Well Road and Main Street

NOEL MARTIN AND BERYL DONNELLY

Martin's Family Home

In 1888 Christy Martin Senior's Great Grandfather, a journeyman carpenter, came to work in Maynooth College. Later on he moved to Carton House Estate. The family saved all the money they could and some time later they bought a piece of land at the Riggins, Dunshaughlin. His son Christy was born there in 1904.

Many years later, in 1927 he built a house in Ratoath on the Well Road. This was a wooden structure, it had an A.B. cooker installed which was hopper fed. The house was very modern for it's time, consisting of indoor plumbing. Christy died in 1964, and Mrs Martin died in 1966. Their house was destroyed by fire in 1967 and a new bungalow was built a year later. Today Sonny and Florrie Martin live there with their family.

"Norman Cottage"

The Farrell brothers lived in "Norman Cottage." There were seven brothers in the Family. One brother lived in Halltown. They owned all the land on the right hand side of the Skryne Road, between the Barrack Cross and the High Cross, Cabinhill. At this time the Land Commission divided the Rogers land in Lagore. Some of the tenants did not take the land or the houses. So the Farrell brothers took this land and paid rent and rates and stocked it.

They employed seven men in Norman Cottage, some of whom were Mickey, Jimmy and Bill Muldoon, Dan Eiffe and John McGrane. In the early days Molly Blake was

Norman Cottage, Barrack Cross
Home to Noel and Mary Martin on the Well Road

their housekeeper. Every day, two buckets of potatoes were cooked for the dinner. In the sitting room there was a large trunk containing an enormous amount of money which was used for everyday expenses. The Farrell brothers all died within a span of seven years. The house then passed to Paddy Toole and was later sold in 1963 to Jack and Bridget Eiffe. The present owners are Noel and Mary Martin who bought it in 1976.

MAIN STREET

The Post Office
This house was originally the home of Paddy and Nanny Smith and their son Johnny.

When the Smith family passed on, the Whelan family who were from Wexford, bought it in the 1950's and it was bought by Tommy Dolan in the early eighties. This building began to be used as The Post Office when the old Post Master John Bruen died. The site of the Old Post Office was in John Bruen's house on Pullwee Street (now called the Dunshaughlin Road).

The site of this former Post Office is now the car park of the SuperValu Supermarket. Today Ratoath Post Office is situated on the Main Street in the Village and Claire Dolan, a niece of Tommy Dolan, runs it.

Robinsons's House
This house was built by Dick Robinson, who lived there with his wife and daughter Nan and sons, Sonny and John. One of the sons became a Christian Brother in Castletown, Co. Laois. Nan married Paddy Moore in the early Forties and they lived there until they both passed away. Today their house is the site of the Ratoath Medical Centre, owned by Dr. Michael Burke, who occupies the ground floor. On the second floor is a physiotherapy practice run by Rory O'Neill.

There were two out buildings, one of which was originally a dwelling house occupied by the Robinson Family around 1848. This building in its time was a turf store. Paddy Moore sold the turf in the 1940's. Paddy Dolan ran his butcher's shop there from 1949-1961. Next door Nan Moore ran an ice-cream parlour. The ice-cream was sold to the patrons who had to pass the shop on the way to the local Hall.

Talty's House
This was originally a bakery. Molly Talty came to live there in the 1920's. She ran a sweet and ice-cream shop. This was also a great house for card sessions. After Molly, Bartle Bermingham ran a greengrocer shop here and Gerry Keogh's bicycle repair shop was at the rear of the premises. For more than a quarter of a century, Molly never missed the July Race Meeting in Galway. She died

Molly Talty with her good friend and neighbour May Hessmann

Molly Talty seated outside her shop and home on Main Street

on the first day of the July meeting in 2002. It was fitting that at the end of her funeral Mass, which was attended by a large number of her friends, Fr Paul Cosbie and John Long sang "*Galway Bay*" accompanied by the organist, and they were joined in song by the congregation, as her cortege left the Church. '*Ar deis Dé go raibh a anam dilis.*'

Ratoath Hall

The Hall was known as Oliver Plunkett Hall. It was built on Rogers' land as a social Club for their workers. Card games and rings were played in it. The Parish Priest, Fr. Kelly, closed the Hall for many years, and it was not until Fr. Cogan came to the Village in 1948 that the Hall was re-opened. Down through the years many great nights were had there, with dancing, Shows, Boxing Tournaments, Film Shows, etc. Among the bands that played there were, Maurice Lynch, The Del Rio, The Arcadians and many more. The floor, which was put in by the late Christy Martin and members of his family, was made from Maple and was regarded by the dancers who graced it as being one of the best dancing floors for miles around.

Some of the shows that were performed in the Hall were 'The Mikado' and 'The Children of Fatima'. Among the Films which were shown in the Hall by Fr. Cogan and John Bruen were, 'Hop along Cassidy', 'Dick Barton Special Agent', 'Laurel & Hardy' and 'George Formby'. Card games, mainly Three Fifteens, were held in the Hall and they were run by the G.A.A. The site of the Old Hall was the site of a new local Community Centre and today this too has been replaced by the most modern Community Centre in Ireland. – Refer to separate article entitled "Ratoath Community Centre: The Early Years".

Everard's House

This house dates back to the time of the Bianconi Stage Coach. It probably was the place where the Stage Coach stopped. Bill Duffy lived here in the 1940's. After his death the house and land were owned by Harry Everard who lived there. The housekeeper was Nan McKeown. Sean Everard, Harry's nephew, owned the house after Harry's death. Sean lived there until his death in 1965.

The porch and hall door were removed and the front entrance was moved to the back of the house. Vet. Paul Kelly, his wife and family lived there until moving to a house outside the village. Shops and apartments have replaced this historical building since 2000 at the front and the vetinary practice still operates in its original space.

The building adjacent to the Everard's house was a shop which sold groceries, papers and sweets run by Mick Nash and his wife Sadie. Today this is Katie's Diner. Next door Mickey O'Neill built a state of the art butcher's shop in the 1950's. From there Tony Darby runs his butcher's shop. At the rear of the buildings, Tommy Smith had a Cobbler's Shop. A new development of townhouses has been built in 2007 at the bottom of the garden at the back and the Cobbler's Shop is long gone.

STREETSCAPES AND LANDSCAPES

Skryne, Cabinhill Road

NOEL EIFFE

AS YOU APPROACH Ratoath from Cabinhill, the last house in Ratoath parish where it meets the parish of Skryne was formerly the home of Jack Flanagan and is now owned by the Keane family. Also in Cabinhill are the Brennan, Byrne, Mulvany, Walsh, Bryan, Kelly, Hartnett, Brown, Mullins, Cooke, McCullagh, McSweeney, Madden, Morrissey, Sweeney, McDermott, Monaghan and Rafferty families who are landowners as are Maura Woods and Sean Woods.

Twentypark is the next townland on the Skryne Road home to the Crowley, Brennan, Peters, Kelly-Hallsgrove, Muldoon and Delaney families. Pauline Byrne owns Twentypark House and farm. Her son James and his family live in a bungalow on the land. Twentypark house was built in 1911 by a builder named Cromer who also built the Fr. Everard National School in Ratoath the same year. The then owner of Twentypark House was Simon Toole who passed it on to his nephew Patrick Toole. Patrick's brother, Desmond Toole, owned the farm where the Steeplechase development now stands. Around 1920 a cottage was built on the farm and it was occupied by James Muldoon and his family. There was a considerable amount of woodland and firewood on both farms and during the emergency years of World War II many houses in the locality were heated by the firewood from both properties. Twentypark house changed hands in 1964 to the Byrne family who are the present owners.

Patrick McCabe lives just off the Skryne Road. The Colreavey family live on the Skryne Road and the Lahart family have a bungalow on land known as the 'Smooth and Iron' because of the shape of the plot of land.

The Sheephole is nearby on the right-hand side and is owned by the Toole family of the Strand who own the farm on which it is located. In the past local farmers dipped their sheep here during the summer season to protect against parasites.

To the right as one travels towards the village is the Steeplechase housing development with its many new families living in houses, townhouses and apartments arranged around beautiful landscaped parklands.

The 'Coderliss', where the GAA, Ratoath Harps and Pitch & Putt sports grounds are situated, was formerly a commons. Quite a few families lived there in the past including the Elliot, Fitzpatrick, Carr, Kelleher, Clarke and Bonus families. In the past these common grounds were also a venue for travelling shows and for showing films, if one was lucky enough to have the four old pence to pay to see them! The last resident to live there was Mick Nash who passed away in 1983. Mick originally came from Co. Clare and he ran a sweet and grocery shop at the centre of the village where Tony Darby and family run a Butcher's shop today. His house is now the Pitch & Putt Clubhouse, with renovations. These sports grounds are owned by Ratoath Development Ltd., formed on 29 September 1967. (See separate article entitled 'Coderliss' Grounds).

Park House is situated opposite the 'Coderliss' grounds. Nearby on the same side, Noel & Anne Ryan and family live at Pine Hill. Philomena and Jim Eiffe live next door to the Ryans. Further up the Skryne Road towards the village is a small housing development called Norman Grove.

STREETSCAPES AND LANDSCAPES

Park House

SHEILA MOOREHEAD

Park House, Skryne Road, Ratoath

PARK HOUSE, a stately home surrounded by large gardens, is off the Skryne Road and was owned by the Rogers family in the 1940's. Today the main house is owned and occupied by their descendents Gerry and Karen Moorhead. Mrs. Sheila Moorhead, Gerry's mother, resides also at Park House.

STREETSCAPES AND LANDSCAPES

Royal Irish Constabulary Barracks, Ratoath

PAUL HALTON

THE OLD Royal Irish Constabulary Barracks, which is at the crossroads of the Skryne and Curraha Roads was built around 1840 and was occupied by the R.I.C. for some time. They vacated it in 1906. The family of the present owner Michael Eiffe occupied it in 1910 and shortly afterwards bought it from the owners, the Corbaliss family. It has been owned by the Eiffe family since then.

The *1901 Census - Other Townlands in south-eastern Meath*[1] recorded the following information about those serving at Ratoath R.I.C. Barrack House. The census information included ID Number, Number in Townland, Household Number, Firstname, Lastname, Position, Religion, Literacy, Age, Gender, Occupation, Status and Birthplace.

499	Ratoath R.I.C.	1 1 J M	sergeant	RC R+W	45	male	married	Dublin
500	Ratoath R.I.C.	2 2 R K	constable	RC R+W	50	male farmer's son	married	Leitrim
501	Ratoath R.I.C.	3 3 J B	constable	RC R+W	48	male farmer's son	married	Carlow
502	Ratoath R.I.C.	4 4 T M	constable	RC R+W	40	male farmer's son	not married	Queen's County

It is interesting to note that the names of those serving in the Royal Irish Constabulary were merely initialed in the census returns of 1901.

---

1 http://www.rootsweb.ancestry.com/~irlmea2/Census/townlands2.htm web site accessed on 16 September 2008. This site is a member of Ireland Genealogical Projects, IGP TM

Barrack House, Ratoath, as it stands today (2008)

STREETSCAPES AND LANDSCAPES

Cabinhill Townland

PEGGY BYRNE

CABINHILL TOWNLAND is approximately two and a half kilometres from the village of Ratoath. Not a lot is known about the origin of the name Cabinhill but rumour has it that in years gone by there were many small cabins built in the area on the hill. Cabinhill extends from the High Cross to the Reask Lane, taking in the area that borders with Bodeen, its approximate acreage being about 206 acres.

In the 1950's there were about twelve residences inhabited by about 50 people. Since then people tended to have smaller families, and more houses were built in the area. There is currently about 22 houses and the population is about 72 people occupying them. Many are from the Ratoath area. All those years ago Cabinhill was a very different place to live. There were no cars and everyone walked or rode bikes wherever they went. The first person to own his own car was Jimmy Monaghan. I think it was a Ford Prefect. It was a delight to get a lift to Mass on a Sunday morning in it, if you were lucky! The only time there was any traffic on the roads was when the races were on at Fairyhouse. All the children would sit by the roadside and take the numbers of the passing cars.

Usually we would play football and hurling on the road without fear or danger. The homes were very modest but everyone knew everyone else and helped each other. We had very little money but times were good and everyone seemed to be happy and more contented than they are nowadays.

Joe Keeffe: One of the characters who lived in Cabinhill who we remember with affection was Joe Keeffe or "Holy Joe" as the children fondly referred to him. Joe lived alone in a one-roomed mud walled house with a thatched roof, one small window and a divider door. The walls inside were totally covered with holy pictures; hence the name 'Holy Joe'. Joe always walked wherever he went and in wintertime he always wore a big cloak. He was a very pious quiet spoken man and was very well respected especially by the local children to whom he loved to talk and tell stories. He always kept a supply of barley sugar sticks for them which encouraged their return.

Joe often spoke of his two nephews whom he visited from time to time and was very proud of them. He did odd jobs for the local farmers and he often wrote in the 'Irelands Own' magazine. On one occasion he was said to have written *"The Meath farmers would grub their Turnips but were less inclined to grub their Workers"*. Joe was apparently the first person in Cabinhill to purchase a battery operated wireless. He was a very dry humoured witty person, always ready with a joke for everyone. Joe did not end his life in Cabinhill; he went to live with his relatives to be cared for when he could no longer maintain independence in his own home.

Dick Byrne: He was another old gentleman who lived in an old tin roofed house in Cabinhill. He was a widower and never had any children. His only relative was his nephew, Jimmy Byrne. Dick died around 1946.

The Monaghan Family: Johnnie Monaghan lived alone in another old thatched house. He was a bachelor and was a brother to Jimmy Monaghan. He also had two sisters, one who lived at the Bush, which is where Johnnie ended his days. Jimmy and Mary Monaghan, a well respected couple, ran a dairy farm and were very hard workers. They had three children, Jerry, Bridget and Patrick. Their daughter Bridget Geraghty is the mother of the well known jockey Barry Geraghty. Both Mary and Jimmy have been dead for many years.

The Elliott Family: Elizabeth and Jack Elliott reared a large family, many of whom went to Dublin and England to get work. The Elliott household was very welcoming. There always seemed to be someone "dropping in for a cuppa and a chat" and if anyone needed help e.g. when sick, they could rely on Mrs. Elliott and all would be well. If anyone had chickens or turkeys with the "Pip" Mrs. Elliott would be sent for to put things right. Jack Elliott worked in Cauls of Fairyhouse for years and after his wife died he went to England to live with his daughter. He lived to the ripe old age of 90+ and was buried in England.

The Reilly Family: Jimmy Reilly originated from Curragha. Sadie (nee Gargan) came from Swords. Jimmy and Sadie Reilly came to Cabinhill in 1949. They had 13 children but sadly four were to die. Of the 13 Joe, Gerrard, Rose, Paul, Ann, Dermott, Rita, Martin and Charlie survived. All the family except for Martin married and moved out. Sadie, Jimmy, and Martin then moved to Ashbourne 16 years ago where they currently reside.

The Bissett Family came to live in Cabinhill circa 1948-1950. This was another large family who after a few years moved to live at Oberstown, Skryne. The Johnson Family were the next family to inhabit Bissetts house, followed by Angelo and Brenda (nee Hickey) Mulvaney who had a large family and lived in Cabinhill for many years. When the family married and moved out, Angelo and Brenda went to live in the village of Ratoath where they still reside.

The Flanagan Family: John Flanagan lived in Bodeen before getting married to Annette (nee O'Brien) from the Dunshaughlin area. They reared eight children, four boys and four girls, Dick, Teddy, Johnnie, Jimmy, Chrissy, Noeleen, Ann, and Joan. Unfortunately their mother, Annette, did not enjoy good health and sadly she died at quite a young age. All the family emigrated to England and Australia except for one son who currently resides in Kerry. John lived to be 90 years and died in a nursing home in Dunshaughlin.

The Byrne Family: James Byrne was the only son of John and Bridget (nee Fitzharris). James was born in 1905. He lived in Cabinhill all his life. He often spoke of making his First Holy Communion in 1911, the year Ratoath School was built. James, known locally as Jimmy, married Margaret (nee Brassington) in 1938. He was then a small dairy farmer and also kept pigs and hens, etc. When the farm was no longer viable James worked for the Meath County Council. James and Margaret had a family of eight, Ann, Jack, Peggy, Eileen, Billy, James, Vincent, and Michael. He was a very strict father but fair and he loved his children and enjoyed telling them ghost stories and stories about the Black & Tans and Banshees. At 9 p.m. each night he insisted on us saying the rosary on our knees on a cold floor. He also insisted on us saying The Angelus at 12 noon and 6 p.m. If in the house, you were expected to drop what you were doing and stand to attention. James had a great interest in politics and always supported Fianna Fáil which is how he met Margaret through canvassing for an election. Margaret was a good camogie player and she played for Ashbourne before her marriage. She was the eldest of three girls of William and Mary (nee Byrne) Brassington originally from Garristown.

Margaret and James were married for twenty years when James sadly died in 1958 at the age of 53 years. Margaret lived to be 80 years old and died in 1986. Jack the eldest son was born in 1941, the only year that the Irish Grand National was cancelled because of Foot and Mouth Disease. He died in 2006 at the age of 65. Billy, who was born in 1945, sadly died suddenly in 2005 at the age of 59 years old.

James and Margaret Byrne on their Wedding Day in 1938 with Margaret's mother and James' father.

(Left): Margaret Byrne with her daughter Peggy

James has a great sense of responsibility towards his family. Each year he would till the two fields behind the house and always grew his own potatoes and vegetables. He would cut a tree down on his land in the Reask to ensure we had fire wood for the winter. Every Saturday evening he collected all the shoes to clean them for Sunday Mass and in the winter he lined the wellies up for washing. As Christmas approached each year he made holly wreaths to sell to get some extra money for Christmas.

Margaret (Maggie) was also a great parent and a lovely gentle person. She baked bread every day, and scones and apple pies at weekends. She would take the cream from the milk and every week she would churn to make butter. Remembering that old churn; it was hard work. We all gave a hand. Maggie rode her bike to the village every day regardless of the weather. She enjoyed a chat with the shopkeepers. She arrived home with two bags of groceries on the handlebars of her bike and often had one of the smaller children on the carrier. Maggie loved her bicycle and continued to ride it until she was about 75 years old when she became too frail.

Peggy trained to be a nurse in England. She married Ken Brennan and has got three children, Tracey, Karl and Rosy. Peggy continued to nurse in Ireland and has dedicated the past 25 years to caring for autistic children. Peggy is the only member of the family to still live in Cabinhill. Eileen also trained to be a nurse in England. She went on to do midwifery and renal dialysis. She spent the last 25 years as a district nurse training student nurses and other health professionals. Eileen has now retired and is currently living in Longford.

Billy Byrne pictured in 'The Courtyard Bistro', Ratoath in 2005

The Lambe Family: Pat Lambe, an old gentleman, lived up in the field in Halltown. He was the herdsman for the Halltown Estate. Pat was a widower and lived alone after his family married and moved away. He had access to grazing for his own stock at Halltown and provided the local people with milk. Pat walked wherever he went with his dog Shep. Sadly he died in 1955.

Jim Lambe, son of Pat, married to Tess, lived in the village of Ratoath. Jim was the local barber. Most of the Cabinhill men went to him to have their hair cut. The Lambe family moved to Cabinhill in September 1954. Sadly Jim died in May 1954, four months prior to the move. Tess moved with the two young children, Mary and Paul. She reared them single handedly. Mary trained to be a nurse, got married and has two children. She lives next door to her mother who lives in Cabinhill with her son Paul.

Right: Pat Lambe

Left: Jim and Tess Lambe on their Wedding Day on 29th Nov. 1950 in St. Paul's Church, Arran Quay, Dublin.

The Mulvaney Family: Angelo and May (nee Morgan) lived in Cabinhill with their three children, Peggy, Michael and Ann. Peggy and Ann married and lived in Dublin. Michael married and remained in the homeplace. Angelo died at the age of 52 years in 1962 and May lived to be 80 years and died in 1996.

May and Angelo Mulvaney, Cabinhill. Circa 1950's

The activities of the Cabinhill children in the 1950/60's – some memories

As children in Cabinhill we all played football and hurling together using cardigans or coats as goal posts. We went up the fields to make a dam and paddle, none of us could swim. Looking back it was a miracle that none of us came to any harm. We jumped ditches, pretending we were horses and fished for tadpoles with jam jars. We rode on the back of the bogies when the hay was being drawn in. Frequently we rode bicycles designed for one, but often had a passenger on the carrier and another person on the handlebars as well.

The Cabinhill children at the High Cross of Cabinhill in 1955.
Back L-R: Anne Byrne, Michael Mc Loughlin, Peggy Mulvaney,
Margo Mc Loughlin and Jack Byrne.
Front Row L-R: Liam Woods, Peter Mc Loughlin, Anne Mulvaney Chiddy Morgan and Michael Mulvany.

We had lots of innocent fun. As we got older all the children from the neighbourhood i.e. Lagore, Bodeen and Cabinhill, would meet in the evenings, sit on the side of the roads on the bank, and on Flemingtown Bridge chatting and laughing a lot. We were so innocent and naive. The highlight of the week was going to the ceilidh on Sunday afternoon and then graduating to the carnival in Dunshaughlin and Kilmoon on Sunday nights when we got older. We travelled on our bicycles in a group and never came to any harm.

When the Mission came to Ratoath we were expected to attend. When the Missioner gave his Sermon he scared us to death and it seemed to us that we were destined to be condemned to eternal damnation if we did anything wrong. Most of the time we didn't understand what he was talking about anyway.

STREETSCAPES AND LANDSCAPES — Cabinhill Townland

John & Jimmy Flanagan 1959

Mrs. Flanagan with Grandchildren

Byrne Family

Mary Brassington (née Byrne)

Mother of Margaret (Maggie), Kathleen (Kitty) and Mary (Mollie), Grandmother of Nora (Mollie's Daughter).
Also Grandmother of Maggie's children, Anne (Nan), Jack, Margaret (Peggy), Eileen, William (Billy the Butcher), James (Jem), Michael and Vincent.

STREETSCAPES AND LANDSCAPES

Kilbride Road

JOE MANNERING

THE ELLIOT FAMILY is one of the longest established families in the Ratoath area. Joe and Mary Elliot's children are Michael, Peggy, Kevin and Eric. Eric, his wife and family now live in the home place on the Kilbride Road.

Tankardstown Yard: Frank Rogers owned Tankardstown Yard and he kept brood mares and cattle there. Johnny Walls and his family lived in Tankardstown House and twelve men worked in the yard. Later Donnelly's of Garristown, fruit growers, bought it from the Rogers family and Joe Morris lived in the house from then on. Across the road, Joe Fox lived in a nice tin roofed house until he had a new house built. The tin roofed house is still there. Oliver and Ita Doran live further along the road and they have seven children. On the other side of the road the old Mannering home was situated. James and Elizabeth lived there with their family of six children. Next along the road is the Nulty home where Thomas and his wife and two children live. Next door, Ronnie Quigley and his wife Mary (nee Nulty) live in a new bungalow.

Rathcoole Lane: Up to 1960, there was only one house on the Rathcoole lane (Brennan's lane) and today there are fifteen houses on the lane.

The next house was owned by the late Larry Newman. Michael Lysaght and his wife Maria and family live there now. Larry's niece built a house in his garden and Mrs. Marie O'Brien and family now occupy it. The next two houses are owned by another O'Brien family and by the O'Reilly family respectively. These houses were always known as British Army houses. Presently the O'Neill family occupy the O'Brien family home. Charlie Reilly and his wife Beannie and daughter Mary live in the Reilly home place. Pad and Ned O'Brien and Larry Newman rode their bikes to Croke Park every Sunday to watch hurling and football between the 1930's and 1950's. They also worked in Fairyhouse racecourse.

That brings us on to Paddock House. Frank Rodgers and his wife Mary, who also owned Tankardstown, Glascarn and Paddock townlands owned the Paddock House. Again that was a stud yard, employing about twelve local people. Dr. O'Callaghan is the present owner. Ann and Norman Colfer have also built a house on Paddock land.

That brings us up to the late Pierce Glynn house where Maureen lives with her son Ben. The Manning family lived in that house for many years before Pierce Glynn. Eoin Hackett and his wife Marie and their five children live nearby.

That brings us to the Mannering family – Jack and Alice had thirteen children. There are two homes now on that site, the Mannering family lives in one and Sean O'Neill and his wife Geraldine and four children live in the other. That brings us to the Kennedy's of Peacockstown. This family goes back five generation of names called Patrick or Walter. Patrick Senior, now deceased, lived there with his son Walter, and his wife Ita, and their son

Patrick. And so the family tradition continues. Also living nearby Patrick senior's is daughter Frances with her husband and children. Next along the road, Bill Acheson lives with his wife and family. We go on then to the late Bobby Doran's lane where he lived with his wife Alice in a cottage and now his nephew Jerry and his wife Pauline and their 2 girls live in a new bungalow beside the old house.

Peacockstown Estate: There are a total of eleven houses in the Peacockstown Estate.

The next group of houses are occupied by Frank Caulfied and his wife and family; Andy Peat and his wife and family; Seamus Hennessey and his wife and family. Tom Nulty's home is next and his son Anthony lives in another house nearby. We then have the Ryan family. Billy Marlow, his wife and family live opposite them. Across the road there is Barbara Brennan and her family. The Hickey family used to live in the next house. The Duggan family is next and beside them Charlie Sommerfield lives with his wife and family. Next to Sommerfield's resides Tom Martin and his wife and family. That brings us to O'Sullivan's Shop and the O'Sullivan family. We then come to Cheeverstown where Noel White and his wife and family live and next to them are Eoin O'Sullivan and his wife and family. Finally we have reached the farthest end of the parish, Balfestown Stud. Presently, there is nobody living at Balfestown Stud. (See more details about Balfestown Stud on Page 450)

Betty Mannering, Dressmaker, congratulating Michael Kauntz and Eva Dreaper at their wedding reception. c. 1970's

STREETSCAPES AND LANDSCAPES

Irish Street to Fairyhouse Racecourse

FRANCES MAHER

IN THIS ARTICLE we recall the homes and businesses that were situated on Irish Street and the Fairyhouse Road in the mid 1950's and we endeavour to trace the changes that have occurred to these properties since then. We begin at the centre of the village. The first building on Irish Street on the left hand side was Clarke's Public House which was run by John Gogan and Annie Gogan (nee Clarke) for many years. In 1972 Leo and Rose McGirl bought it and since then it is known as the Ratoath Inn. The property was sold to the Brazil family in 1990.

The Walls family lived in the second house on Irish Street for several generations and it is now occupied by Tommy and Bernie Walls and their daughter Laura. The next house on this road was that of the Madden family. Mr. Madden senior had a forge at these premises and horses were shod there. Mrs. Madden ran a grocery shop and their son John, although without formal education, became an expert in the field of electronics and was considered very much ahead of his time. In the late 1970's, John married Elizabeth Shaffrey who was parochial housekeeper in Ratoath at the time.

Sheila Naughton and Elizabeth Madden, 1999

1956: Adjoining houses on Irish Street, now the homes of the Naughton and Maher Families

On the opposite side of the road there used to be two thatched houses; the first was owned by Ally Martin and the second by Jack Sherlock. In circa 2001-2002 the SuperValu supermarket was built on the site where these two houses once stood. Frank and Molly Maher and their family, Jimmy, Michael, Christopher and Anne resided in the next bungalow called Shamrock Lodge. Today, it is the home of Packen and Anne Brady and their family.

Following on, on the right hand side, there were originally two single storey thatched buildings that were used as workshops by the Anderson family, Barney, Christopher and Paddy. A two-storey house known as Shamrock House was also owned by the Anderson family who were carpenters by profession. When they went off to America they sold their property to Mr. and Mrs. Thomas Naughton who in turn re-built them. Sheila and Pat Naughton and their family occupied one of the newly re-built two storey homes and Michael and Frances Maher and their family afterwards occupied the other.

The next was a cottage occupied by Ellen Reilly. This building was later demolished and the site was developed in the early 1990's into the Mruigtuaithe housing estate. Opposite this, a Mrs. Donnelly occupied a small cottage. The cottage was re-sold and enlarged over the years and is now occupied by Mick and Mary Tallant and their sons Stuart, David and Philip.

The next house on the right hand side was owned by the Fitzpatrick family who later sold it to Mr. and Mrs. Christopher Smith. On the left hand side stood the home of Mr. and Mrs. Patrick White and their family, Shane, Olive and Amy. The next house, with farm buildings, was called 'The Strand', and was owned by Desmond and Julia Toole and their family, Anne, Una and James.

The School Road in the 1950's (continuation of Irish Street)
The next house on the right hand side was formerly called The Mill House and was later known as '*Mac's of the Mill*'. Dick Mac and his sister Fanny lived there. The house was later sold to Paddy and Anne O'Connor who owned it until the late 1990's. Today, it is the site of Tesco Express and River Walk Apartments.

Up the hill, on the left hand side, was the home of Jimmy and Nancy Ralph who have recently sold it and moved to the Curragha Road. This house was formerly rented to the Casey family, sold to a Miss Kate Dowling, who in turn sold it to James Ralph in 1956.

Moving up the road, still on the left hand side, were the two school houses that were built in 1897 (*See picture in article on Ratoath National School*). They were occupied in the 1950s by James Kelly and Sean McGowan and were demolished in the early 1990's to make room for a new car park for the expanding national school.

On the opposite side of the road from the school buildings in the 1950's were the remains of a dwelling house that local people say was once the home of the Keenan family (refer to the article on James Keenan in this book).

Fairyhouse Road in the 1950's
Next property on the right side of the Fairyhouse Road was the home of Tim and Mrs. Guiney. It was sold in the late 1950's to Tom Mulligan and Laurence Halton and it was demolished in the early 2000's to make way for Seagrave Park housing development.

The next house after that belonged to Willie Dowd and his wife Biddy. The house now belongs to the Mills family. Next we have the former home of the Dolan family, now the home of the Mc Allister family.

Opposite that, on the left hand side of the road, was the home of the Morgan family. Mr. and Mrs. Alex Ralph reside there today. Mr. and Mrs. Tom McLoughlin were the former owners of the next house. Dave and Angela McHugh now live there. The next house on the left hand side was the home of Pud and Mrs. Mahon and their family.

Mr. and Mrs. Jimmy Woods lived in the next house on the left hand side and it is now the home of Michael and Veronica O'Riordan and their family. Also on the left hand side is the home of Michael Walls and family.

On the same side of the road, just past Glascarn Lane, was the home of Mary and Peter Moore and Kevin and Peg (nee Moore) White and their family.

The Moore Family, Mary and Peter with their daughters Lil and Peg outside their home on the Fairyhouse Road in the early 1940's

STREETSCAPES AND LANDSCAPES — Irish Street to Fairyhouse Racecourse

Staying on the left hand side of the road, the next house was that of Mr. and Mrs. Dick Donnelly and their family. Next after that was the home of Mr. and Mrs. Jack Donnelly. This has now been replaced by the new Carraig Na Gabhna housing development.

The home of Mr. and Mrs. Davey Donohoe, their son Anthony, his wife Aggie and their family, was next along the Fairyhouse Road. On the right hand side of the road there were the ruins of a house, which had been occupied in the past by John Carey, Kate Collins and a Mary Carey. Next door to this was the home of Joe and May Geraghty and their family.

Our journey so far has taken us from Irish Street, at the centre of the village, along the School Road, as far as the Commons Lane.

In the 1950's, there were two houses on the Commons Lane. Michael Carey and his wife Bridget together with their fourteen children and Bridget's mother, Jane O'Reilly, resided in the first house on the Lane. Today this house is occupied by Johnnie Carey.

The second house on the Commons Lane was occupied by Jack Staunton, his wife Ellen and their six children. Today it is occupied by John and Kathleen Staunton.

Returning to the Fairyhouse Road, the next home after the Commons Lane was that of the Reilly family. This particular home is in the townland of Ballybin Minor. The last house on the Fairyhouse Road, just before Fairyhouse Racecourse, was the home of Mr. and Mrs. Paddy Walls and their family.

(*Above*); Michael and Bridget Carey, Commons Lane in Mid-1950s

(*Above right*): The picture on the right, was taken on 24 March 1943, and shows the Carey family in prayer and blessing their new home with holy water on the Commons Lane.
L-R Back: Bridget and Michael, Mary, Jane and Bridget
L-R Front: Tom, Johnny, Peter, Elisabeth and Margaret
(The photograph was generously provided to us by the Carey Family)

"*IN AINM AN ATHAR*"—When the Mayo migrants arrived at their new homes, yesterday, their first action before they entered them was to sprinkle holy water on the doorways invoking God's blessing on the house. Here is Mrs. Bridget Carey, who travelled with her husband and fourteen children, performing the ceremony.

STREETSCAPES AND LANDSCAPES

Curkeen House

MIRIAM TOOLE

Front of Curkeen House

CURKEEN HOUSE was built circa 1867 by Patrick Toole, grandfather of the present owner, also named Patrick Toole. Curkeen and its surrounding land was acquired after the Rising of the United Irishmen in 1798 by the O'Toole brothers who had left Wicklow to come to Meath to fight with their close allies, the O'Byrnes. They were defeated in a battle near Dunshaughlin and so never returned to Glendalough.

The first branch of the family lived at The Commons on the Bog Road. The first owner of Curkeen lived first in a small farmhouse over the fields behind the present house. While living there Patrick and his brothers built the present Curkeen House.

Details of a diary reveal that the house cost in the region of £980 – a lot of money in those days, and 84 loads of stones were drawn from the quarry in Curraha! Various extras have been added to the house since it was first built although the original structure still stands and it now home to the 4th generation of the family.

STREETSCAPES AND LANDSCAPES

Darthogue (Doghtog)

JOAN AND FRANK DEERING

THERE HAS BEEN a house in Darthogue for hundreds of years with the current house being built in 1898 by Michael McCabe. At that time the farm was used to breed race horses. The McCabes lived here until 1964, followed by the Horgans for four years. Frank and Joan Deering moved to Darthogue in 1968 with three young children and their fourth child was born in 1971.

Since then dairying and tillage have been main enterprises of the farm. Arriving here from a farm in Co. Dublin a milking-parlour was erected and a paddock-grazing system was introduced, both very modern concepts at that time. The milk produced has always been for liquid consumption and of the highest quality and in 1991 Frank and Joan were proud winners of the All-Ireland Upjohn Quality Milk Awards.

Pictured above (*right*): Frank and Joan Deering with their children, Anne, Paul, Catherine and Marie, holding the cup having won the All-Ireland Upjohn Quality Milk Awards, 1991. To the back are Pat O'Neill, CEO Avonmore, Seamus Kirk, Minister of State Department of Agriculture and Food, and Edwin Teehan, General Manager Animal Health, Upjohn Ireland.

The staff have been mostly local. They included apprentices training for farm-management and the long serving Micky Muldoon of Twenty Park who milked and tended the cattle with dedication for 18 years till his retirement. The farm continues as a family farm with Paul in charge.

STREETSCAPES AND LANDSCAPES

Glebe House and Glebe Gardens

MARY ANNE HALTON

BUILT IN 1813, as a Rectory of the Church of Ireland *"at an expense of £2,200 of which £100 was a gift and £800 a loan from the late Board of First Fruits, and the remainder was defrayed by the then incumbent. The Glebe comprised of 6 ½ acres, valued at £19.10 per annum. The gross income from the whole benefice amounted to £788 - 7s - 3p per annum"*. [Read Ratoath: A Historical Perspective by Frances Maher.]

On the retirement of Rector Rev. Legge, Glebe House was bought by the McKeever family. Since then, over the last thirty years, Glebe House with its gardens, has been home to the Lardner family and currently the Heslin Family. Arthur and Moira Lardner built a smaller home, Glebewood, on the lands adjoining Glebe House. The main house and gardens, known as Glebelands, became home to Leo and Carmel Heslin, and their family. During this period of time the historic gardens of Glebe House continued to be developed in turn by both the Lardners and Heslins. Lardners created their Lutyens influenced gardens at Glebewood. *"Indigenous trees have been supplemented with the addition of blue cedar, pine, cones, conifers, acers and larch."* [Gardens of Meath]

The gardens originally listed in the *Gardens of Meath* were acknowledged as *"prize-winning gardens with almost 200 hundred years between them. Glebelands from 1813 and Glebewood from 1990."* For a number of years garden lovers and experts were privileged to be able to visit these significant Irish gardens and personally meet the owners who so enthusiastically welcomed everyone and shared their love and knowledge of gardening and plant management throughout the ever-changing seasons. Sadly, the creators of the gardens, Arthur and Moira Lardner, and Leo and Carmel Heslin, died too soon. Their resting place is in the adjoining cemetery just over the wall from their much loved homes and gardens.

STREETSCAPES AND LANDSCAPES

Ratoath Manor

RATOATH HERITAGE GROUP

On entering Ratoath Village from the Ashbourne side, one cannot help but be impressed by the fine building on the left hand side which is called "The Manor". According to Christine Casey and Alister Rowan in their book entitled *The Buildings of Ireland North Leinster*, The Manor House is a long seven bay 2-storey house of late 18th Century appearance, roughcast, with a central ionic door case and windows with exposed sash boxes. The ground floor windows are set in segmental headed relieving arches, inside, is late Georgian joinery with thinly applied mouldings. There are more recent additions to the side and at the rear of the Manor. This was the seat of J.I. Corballis in 1836. Of interest is a note from the Department of Folklore U.C.D., dated around 1930's, by Teresa Sherry of Ratoath who at the time would have been about thirteen. In her article on *Ratoath and District in the Penal Days* she refers to a Protestant gentleman by the name of Fitzpatrick who had hidden Rev. Michael Plunkett in an upper room of the Manor House in Ratoath.

Prior to Mr. Corballis the property is said to have been occupied by a Mr. Peard, who was an architect at the building of the Bank of Ireland, College Green. The Corballis family was very successful in the Bakery business in Dublin and bought the property from the Lowther

> Name : Lillie Moore
> Age : 14 years
> Address : Tankardstown, Ratoath. Co Meath
>
> The most ancient Residence I know is the Manor House, it is situated just outside the village of Ratoath. It is a very large and beautiful building it is a three-story house, on the third there is an old chaple in which the priests used to say mass in secret and hide from the priest-hunters in the Penal days. Outside there are two beautiful lawns and on them are many uncommon shrubs and plants which present owner Mr Corbalis brought home when he was a captain in the British War. At the back of the house there is a big wood and in the wood flows a beautiful river.

The above hand-written note by Lillie Moore from Tankardstown, aged 14, circa 1930's, while in Ratoath National School, and is reproduced here with the kind permission of the Department of Folklore, UCD, Belfield, Dublin.

family about 1820. According the Ratoath Parish Register James Corballis was witness to a marriage around 1828. This James Corballis may have built the "Manor". In 1854 according to Griffith's Valuation James and Mary Corballis were listed as minors. It was this James Corballis who granted a lease of the site for the Catholic Church and parochial house to Dr. Nulty in 1870. Miss Emily Corballis left a "charity" for "*the maintenance of public worship in the R.C. Chapel of Ratoath, for the repair and maintenance of interior or of grounds of said Chapel*".

According to the booklet published for the Pro-Cathedral in Dublin many of the benefactors who subscribed to the building of this fine edifice, were allowed to be interred in the Crypt of the Pro Cathedral when they died. On the back of the Tabernacle in the Pro-Cathedral is the following inscription:-

"*Pray for James and Mary Corballis of Ratoath and their relatives, interred in the vaults beneath*".

The Corballis family are buried in the old part of the Ratoath cemetery to the left of the church tower and there are inscriptions on the tombstones commemorating the family members interred there. However, the name of James Corballis who died in 1940's is not inscribed on the tombstone.

John Farrell of Norman Cottage, Well Road, became the owner after the Corballis family for the period 1946 to 1948. A Colonel Mainwaring became the owner in 1948 and occupied it with his daughter Dianne and son Robin until circa 1951. During this time he built a section of the west wing (on the village side).

Noel Martin recalls that after the World War II years, when basic foodstuffs were in short supply, he and his friends often played around the manor as children and Lucy Browne (nee Caffrey) who worked there for the Mainwaring family would give them bread and jam which was a rare luxury in those days.

The Augustinian order of Sisters bought the "Manor" and about eighteen acres in 1951 for the purpose of establishing a nursing home. Shortly afterwards the Martin Brothers were building the wall around the new cemetery when Fr. Cogan asked them to come and see Rev. Mother Peter of the Augustinian Order who required some repair work to be undertaken on the building. The Martin Brothers agreed to work on the renovations of the Manor. The main reconstruction of the building continued over a period of about a year.

One of the first jobs they carried out necessitated opening up a doorway into a room which had remained unused for many years. On entering into the room they observed a wooden altar in the centre of the room. The window was a lancet type and in the right hand corner of the room they found a wash-hand basin stand. The Martin Brothers continued to work on and off around the Manor House for almost 18 years. Among the various jobs undertaken was the construction of a small oratory in the original building.

The Augustinian nuns re-built, extended and modernised the building into much of which it is today. The east-wing was built by Brennan Brothers of Dublin and the west-wing was built after that in 1960. In the late 1980's the present convent chapel was constructed. The "Manor" was re-sold in 2002 to a Company by the name of Silver Stream Healthcare which continues to run it as a Nursing Home, caring for the elderly and infirm.

STREETSCAPES AND LANDSCAPES

Strand House

ANNE KEOGH

JAMES TOOLE, born in 1777, was one of the three brothers who settled in Ratoath after the 1798 rebellion. The tombstones in Glendalough, Co. Wicklow, bear the same Toole names that have been handed down through the generations: - James, Patrick, Thomas, etc. James died in 1827 and is buried in the old cemetery in Ratoath.

As early as 1851, this branch of the family rented the 'grass of Clover Hill' from the landlord, Lord Corballis, for a yearly rent of forty-five shillings per acre. On January 11th 1868, a lease for twenty-one years of the lands of Clover Hill and Twenty Park was drawn up between the brothers Thomas and Patrick Toole and Lord James Henry Corballis.

Patrick Toole, son of the aforementioned Patrick, bought these lands through the Irish Land Commission later. This Patrick Toole, who died in 1949, was the father of Desmond Toole, the last resident of the Strand House. The present Strand House was built in 1868 and entries in a family diary record that "*Pat Toole and his family moved into the house when the plastering was finished in 1871*". The remains of the previous residence are located in the yard of the present Strand House.

In 1946, Desmond Toole married Julia Rose Muldoon who owned the premises known as 'Ryan's Pub' opposite the Church.

Julia died in 1981, twenty-two years before Desmond.

Desmond and his son James farmed Clover Hill until 2001. Desmond died in 2003. Over two hundred years later, the Toole family names are still carried on as the present James Toole who farms 'Clover Hill Farm' in Lagore has two sons, Patrick and Peter.

Strand House (2007) located next to the roundabout on the Fairyhouse Road

Above: Desmond & Julia Toole

ASSOCIATIONS AND CLUBS

Ratoath Active Age

MAUREEN BUTLER & ANNE BRADY

RATOATH ACTIVE AGE GROUP was formed in June 1991 by a small group of local people, including Fr. Gerry McCormack who worked in the parish at that time. The club received a cheque for £1,000 from the National Telethon held that year and this enabled them to purchase essential start-up equipment, e.g. tables, a boiler and some bowling equipment.

Active meaningful participation in life and the activities available to us as we age means something different to each individual. The Active Age Group meet Friday mornings in the Community Centre. Everyone enjoys a cup of tea and a chat and can join in a variety of activities depending on individual interests e.g. bowls and adapted games, yoga exercises, card games and bingo before having lunch. The group consists of people who have lived all their lives in Ratoath, together with people who have just moved into the area in recent years. All are welcome!

Ratoath Active Age Ladies pictured planting a tree at Ratoath National School in 1993.
L-R: Molly Devine, Maureen Glynn, Betty Colfer, Mary Hunter, Vonnie Cullen and Lucy Browne

Ratoath Past and Present

In 1993 the group were invited to Áras an Uachtaráin to meet the then President, Mary Robinson. That was a very special and enjoyable day for everyone! Over the years members of the Active Age have travelled to Malahide Castle, Musical Shows, the National Botanic Gardens and many more places, too numerous to mention.

The club is always keen to learn new skills and have enjoyed over the years:
Painting Classes, Colour Me Beautiful Demonstration, Odlums Cookery Demonstration
Gardening, Crafts .... and many more events

The Active Age Group was delighted to raise the sum of £2000 for Church Funds in 1998 through a cake and plant sale together with a raffle for a beautiful hand knitted blanket which was the result of a lot of hard work from the group. An annual get together in Tattersalls is held and it receives enthusiastic support from a wide area around Ratoath.

Members of the Active Age Group outside Áras an Uachtaráin

Fr. Paul Crosbie enjoying one of the Active Age Christmas Gatherings in the Ratoath Community Centre, c. 2000.
Pictured with Fr. Paul were Aggie Donohoe, Peggy Flood, Lizzy Madden and Molly Devine

ASSOCIATIONS AND CLUBS　　　　　　　　　　　　　　　　　Ratoath Active Age

President of Ireland, Mary Robinson, chatting with members of Ratoath Active Age Group, including Anne Brady, Vonnie Cullen, Eileen McDermott, Betty Colfer, Molly Devine and Tiny Brennan

Left to Right
Frank Maher, Seán Duffy, Molly Maher
One of our oldest members was Mr Frank Maher who celebrated his 97th birthday in 2005. Sadly both Frank and his wife passed away before this book was published. May they rest in peace.

The Ratoath Active Age club is still going strong and we look forward to welcoming new members and enjoying more trips and most of all "being active"!

ASSOCIATIONS AND CLUBS

Ratoath Irish Countrywomen's Association (ICA)

ANNE RYAN

A PATCHWORK QUILT is an interesting and beautiful object. All those colours, all different shapes and sizes, old and new pieces blended together, edged and backed in a single coloured fabric to make one complete mosaic, giving strength, unity, warmth and pleasure. Likewise, would I describe Ratoath ICA.

In 1974 Ratoath was a very different village to what it is today. It was a small close-knit community and somewhat insular, understandable, seeing as it was nestled between the bigger villages of Ashbourne and Dunshaughlin and with a bus going from Ratoath to Dublin on Mondays and Wednesdays. So for newcomers moving into the area it could be a daunting and lonely experience.

One such was Marie Reilly of Fairyhouse Road. Marie's youngest child, Carol, had just started school and with a little time on her hands Marie had a look around the area and discovered that there was no club or association catering for women. Being the dynamic lady that she was, Marie contacted the Meath ICA Federation President, Dorothy Gillette, with a view to starting a guild in Ratoath. Dorothy agreed ot come to the village to it set up provided there were enough women interested. Marie then enlisted the help of the late Aileen Conway and together they trudged the highways and byways of Ratoath bringing the good news to all ladies of Ratoath.

So it came about that on the first Tuesday in October 1974 Ratoath ICA was founded. Our first President was Florrie Martin. Over the years we have had many and varied activities. Drama Groups, Public Speaking Courses, Painting, Dressmaking, Cookery, Embroidery, Shell Craft and Quilting are among some of our interests.

Celebrations at Ratoath ICA: For Ratoath ICA the millennium year (2000) was of great importance as the guild celebrated 25 years of active engagement in the local community.

We were the first organisation in our area to extend the hand of friendship to our counterparts across the border. In 1999 we welcomed a group of ladies from Saintfield, Co. Down W.I. (Women's Institute) to our village. We hosted them in our homes and entertained them royally as only ladies from Meath could do. The following year a reciprocal visit was paid by us. We were warmly welcomed and entertained lavishly. We still have contact with some of these ladies.

Fast forward to the present day and let us take a look at how we have evolved. Our current President is Caroline Power. We have a vibrant Book Club, an enthusiastic Theatre Going Group, an ardent Arts and Crafts Group and a fun-loving Bevy of Travellers who

Ratoath ICA 25th Birthday Party 2000 [Tattersalls]
Front L-R: Anne Ryan, Joan Butler, Margaret Oates, Kathleen Keogh, Barbara Murray, Linda Wallace, Patsy Gilmore;
Middle Row: Maura O'Flaherty, Nancy Ralph, Maureen Woods, Gretta Kelly, Angela Wheeler, May Woods, Jean Keogh, Teresa Gorman, Eileen McDermott;
Back Row: Meda O'Callaghan, Maureen Butler, Mary Kelly, Aggie Donohoe, Veronica Cullen, Mary Harvey, Kathleen Staunton and Caroline Power.

have visited London, Paris, Prague and Krakow. Just for light entertainment we have a Scrabble Club and a Card Club.

Each year we do one major project to help and support our local community. Some of our projects to date have dealt with Autism and Suicide Awareness and out upcoming project in October 2008 will deal with Alzheimer's disease.

Within the ICA we welcome all ages, professions, stay-at-home mums, working mums, single women and widowed women. We are non-political, inter-denominational and non-sectarian. The single most important aspect of our ICA is that we have fun and friendship. We meet on the first Tuesday of every month at 8.15pm in the Community Centre. A warm and genuine welcome awaits you.

Ratoath I.C.A. on a visit to Cork in 1996
Front L-R Kathleen Staunton, Anne Ryan, Barbara Murray, Maureen Woods, Joan Butler.
Back L-R Jean Keogh, Kathleen Flood, Maureen Butler, Angela Wheeler, Caroline Power, Peg Gorry.

Ratoath I.C.A. 2008
Standing L-R: Anne Ryan, Barbara Murray, Greta Kelly, Maureen Butler.
Front L-R: Joan Butler, Vivian Curran, Caroline Power, Maureen Hughes.

ASSOCIATIONS AND CLUBS

The Pioneer Association

RATOATH HERITAGE GROUP

THE PIONEER ASSOCIATION was founded by Father James Cullen, S.J., and a curate in Co. Wexford. His method was to invite people with no personal problem with the use of alcohol to go further and be "pioneers; to commit themselves to daily prayer and to deny themselves even the most innocent use of alcohol for the rest of their lives.

The Association was founded in December 1898 in St. Francis Xavier Church, Gardiner St. Dublin. Within 20 years there were 260,000 Pioneers in the country and the Association had become an institution in Irish life. It was known as the P.T.A.A. - the Pioneer Total Abstinence Association.

Members of Ratoath PTAA in 1979 celebrating its Golden Jubilee in the local Community Hall. Seated in the centre of the picture is Rev. B. McGuckian, S.J., Central Director of the PTAA in Ireland who presented Gold & Silver emblems and Certificates to qualifying members. Some members included in the photograph below are: Babs Mulvaney, Eugene Eiffe, Sean Kirwan, Matty McCabe, Andy Peake and Mrs Jimmy Reilly.

1979. PTAA event in Ratoath Community Centre entitled Renewal, Action and Youth. RAY-1.
RAY-1 event in Ratoath Community Centre in 1979 Picture includes Sonny Martin, Margaret Dolan, Rev. B. McGuckian, Clare Dolan, Mairead Looney, Marie Deering, Therese Maher, Ann Deering and Brendan Reilly.

PTAA RAY-2
Congress was held in Warrenstown Agricultural College

The PTAA was founded in Ratoath in 1910 and affiliated to the national body on 14 November of that year. Unfortunately, the Register of names from 1910 - 1929 is not to be found. The Ratoath branch was re-affiliated in 1929 and this 'new' register contains names of people in the parish who were already Pioneers. Catherine Donnelly became a Pioneer in 1906, but there is no record of where she joined. Her name appears in the 1929 Register. Mary Donnelly joined the Association in 1910, Luke Ralph in 1919, Annie Sheridan in 1920, Annie Farrell in 1921, Kate Sheridan in 1924, Mary Everard, Bridget Gillic and Mrs. McAuley joined in 1925.

1928 saw an increase in members, with Mrs. Bridget Eiffe, Margaret Donnelly, Mary Elliott, Kevin Ward, Mary Woods, Pat Walls, J. Ryan, Bridget Sheridan and John Brady joining the ranks. At this stage M. Blake is listed as a promoter - obviously having joined at an earlier stage although there is no record. William Robinson is the first entry in the 1929 Register with Rev. C. Scully C.C. as Spiritual Director. Rev. P. Mc Galley, C.C, followed him in 1932. The Working Council in 1929 was: Margaret Rogers, President and Mary Bruen, Vice-President. William Robinson was Treasurer and John Bruen was Secretary.

The Council included Thomas Gannon, Porterstown, Mary Everard, Rackenstown, James Doonan, Ratoath, Mary Blake, Lagore, John Ward, Harlockstown, Michael Gannon, Luke Ralph, Patrick Sherry, Dan Eiffe, Mrs. Thomas McGrane, Harry Everard and Mr. W. O'Doherty.

Like the PTAA in other parts of the country, the fortunes of the Ratoath branch waxed and waned over the years. In 1929 there were 134 members, by 1933 there were 248. In 1950 Fr. J. Abbott admitted 18 new members. There was an upsurge of Pioneers members in the parish in the 1970's and 1980's. In 1972 Renewal, Action and Youth - RAY - was launched by the PTAA. This led to renewed interest in the PTAA among young people. RAY members promised to abstain from alcohol until they were 18 years old. During that time they learned the effects that the excessive consumption of alcohol had on peoples' lives. Seminars, Socials, Talent Competitions and Quizzes all became popular. Junior Pioneers from Ratoath participated in Talent contests, quizzes, etc. The photograph below was taken at a Congress held in Warrenstown College. The main speaker was Rev. A. Farrell, then P.P. of Trim.

In 1979 Ratoath PTAA held its Golden Jubilee celebrations with a party in the local hall. Rev. B. McGuckian, Central Director attended and presented gold and silver emblems and certificates to local members.

Today, as in many parts of Ireland, the PTAA in Ratoath is experiencing a 'wane'. Perhaps there are those among the newcomers to the parish who would be interested in reviving it!

ASSOCIATIONS AND CLUBS

Ratoath Badminton Club

FIONA SIMPSON

RATOATH BADMINTON CLUB was founded in 1984, when the Community Centre was built in Ratoath. From small beginnings, the Club went on to win trophies in various Divisions in both Dublin and Meath leagues, fielding three teams most years.

Three of our members, Mary Connolly, Barry Watters and Ciara Herd, subsequently went on to represent Meath at Inter County Level.

After a break of over three years due to the redevelopment of the Community Centre, Ratoath Badminton Club resumed activities in September 2008 in the new Sports Hall at Ratoath College in Jamestown. Already nearly sixty enthusiastic players of all levels and ages have joined. We are entering a number of teams in the Meath league and hope they will bring home some silverware!

We are seeking coaches and local volunteers to help with the running of the club as we endeavor to establish the sport once more in the expanding Ratoath community.

The Club is presently open to adult badminton players at all levels including beginners and experienced players. We hope to extend the club to include juvenile members so that we can attract the youth of Ratoath to the sport, but this will be dependent on acquiring Ratoath College hall for a second night on an on-going basis

October 2008: Mixed doubles Badminton game being played at the new Sports Hall, Ratoath College, Jamestown

October 2008: Members of Ratoath Badminton Club pictured in the Sports Hall, Ratoath College, Jamestown

ASSOCIATIONS AND CLUBS

Ratoath Bridge Club

MAUREEN BUTLER

BRIDGE IS TRULY a millennium game. It spans the bridge of time with worldwide membership from international level to your local club. No matter where you go today, you will find a Bridge Club to join, meet new people and make new friends. You are always made welcome. With the range of home entertainment all at the touch of a button the temptation to sit in front of the box is growing. Don't. Put on the glad rags and go out and meet your friends for an enjoyable game of bridge.

Ratoath Bridge Club developed from a group of local people who began taking lessons from Mary Tallant in June 1989. The venue was the Ratoath Inn, courtesy of Leo and Rose McGirl the proprietors at that time. These were joined by other players from the surrounding areas and regular weekly tournaments soon got under way growing from five tables initially to the large club that it is today.

Peter Ryan was elected as our first President with Mary Tallant and Mary Corcoran holding the positions of Secretary and Treasurer respectively. Other committee members included Deirdre Corcoran Rita Henderson and Frank Mason was Vice-President. The Millennium Year President of Ratoath Bridge Club was Frank Deering.

Ratoath Bridge Club has frequently contributed to worthy causes in the community such as the Active Age Group and Ratoath National School by running fund raising tournaments.

After a number of years the club moved to Tattersalls but remained there only a short while before moving again to Ratoath National School. Today Ratoath Bridge Club play each Thursday night in the GAA Clubhouse, Brownstown. BRIDGE is one of the best social outlets in the world today. New members are always welcome.

ASSOCIATIONS AND CLUBS

Ratoath Garden Club

IRENE HAYES & PATRICIA SMITH

Ratoath Garden Club (RGC) was formed in the village over fifteen years ago (c. 1993) by Pasty Dervan, Margaret Everard and Eileen Creagh and later assisted by Ann McKeever, Marie Rooney and Colin Bryant. The club aims to promote interest in gardening throughout the Ratoath, Ashbourne and Dunshlaughlin area.

Club meetings are generally held in the Ratoath Community Centre on the last Monday of every month from September to May, and sometimes this may change but notices are put up locally and on the Parish bulletin. We are always delighted to welcome new members. Meetings are designed to be Fun and Informative, catering for both the novice gardener and the more experienced members who are always happy to pass on their expertise.

Each month a different guest speaker attends, presenting lectures or demonstrations on specific topics. Some of our recent guest speakers were Carl Dacus (Royal Horticultural Society of Ireland - RHSI), who spoke on "The Plantsman's Garden" and Paul Maher (Botanic Gardens) who spoke about "Tender Plants at Home in Ireland". For our May 2008 meeting we went locally to Warrenstown College to see a demonstration given by Yvonne Ferguson on "Summer Bedding in a Production Environment."

ASSOCIATIONS AND CLUBS   Ratoath Garden Club

Usually at RGC meetings, there are opportunities to get advice about your garden queries either from the guest speaker or from some of the very knowledgeable gardeners within the Club. We also have an information corner about ongoing garden activities and each month we cover a specific garden topic depending on the time of year; some recent examples were "Good Seed Growing" and "Propagation Made Easy."

Each year we have a garden tour in early June, the day includes three garden visits and dinner. We were very fortunate in 2008 with the beautiful weather and three most amazing gardens. The day ended with a beautiful meal in the Glenview Hotel, Delgany, Co. Wicklow.

Other activities that are included in the Garden Club Programme are Plant Sales, Quiz Nights and Garden Visits. Indeed one year the club was invited to contribute plants to an herbaceous border in Altamont Gardens in memory of Corrina North and subsequently to a wonderful garden party.

One of the highlights of the gardening year is our December Party. In 2008 our Guest Speaker, Carol Bone (AOIFA - Association of Irish Floral Artists), will demonstrate floral art and decoration for Christmas as seen in Farmleigh House. This will be held at the GAA Clubhouse, Sean Eiffe Park, on December 8th 2008 – keep this date in your diaries!

Ratoath Garden Club members enjoying a Guided Tour of Wrenswood Gardens in Wicklow, June 2008

ASSOCIATIONS AND CLUBS

Ratoath Foróige Club – The Early Years

GRETTA JUDGE

THE RATOATH FORÓIGE CLUB began in October 2004. With the help of ten dedicated voluntary leaders and the enthusiasm of the members the club has grown from strength to strength. The club is part of the Foroige national voluntary youth organisation, and the leaders were all given training in child protection etc. before embarking with the club. The fundamental purpose of Foroige is to involve young people consciously and actively in their own development and the development of society; this philosophy is carried out every week in the clubs activities. The members run the club themselves; one of their first activities is to form a committee consisting of a Chairperson, secretary, treasurer and public relations officer. From here on the club is run democratically by the members, with assistance from the adult leaders, advising and supervising them. We currently meet every Wednesday evening in the national school at 8pm and the members have an evening full of activities or demonstrations planned. The club is thoroughly enjoyed by the young members and leaders alike. The leaders would like to take this opportunity to acknowledge the excellent work done by the members and at this stage pass you over to them for their view of the club.

Our first year, 2004/2005

The club started in October 2004, in the national school. There were thirty members and around eight or nine leaders. We went on trips and did fundraising, some of our trips included visiting leisureplex, Carlingford adventure centre, and going bowling. However, as the leaders are always saying we get nothing for nothing, so before we could go on a trip we had to fundraise. We went bag packing in Tesco in Ashbourne to raise money for ice skating in Smithfield. We raised enough money and it was almost as much fun fundraising as it was skating. The club is a great way to meet new friends and to keep in contact with people. (*Gavin Quigley*)

First Impressions

When I first came to the club I thought it was well structured and a lot of fun. The team-building games like the farmer and the carrot are great fun. (*Jason Mc Evoy*)

Ice skating in Smithfield

This was the first trip we members organised for ourselves. We assigned the necessary jobs, such as booking Smithfield, arranging a bus, collection times and not forgetting the all important parent consent forms. On the night we met at the school, handed over consent forms and after the roll call we all got on the bus. We were all laughing and singing and having great craic on the bus journey (even the bus driver). We spent about an hour on the ice, while some people took to the ice gracefully others, well; let's just say they had some difficulty. The enjoyment lasted throughout the night and it all went according to plan. We even stopped in Katys for chips on the way home. (*Danielle O'Rourke* and *Kristin Mc Donald*)

Our environmental project, Bat Box making.

We invited a man to the club to give us a lesson on building bat boxes. He arrived with tones of wood and nails and instructed us on how to make bat boxes. He also told us how bats are good for the environment and keep lots of bugs away because they eat them. They eat at night so they don't have to compete with the birds and they don't like drafts so the entrance to their box is very small. He told us the best place to put the boxes, I can't remember where I put mine, but it's outside somewhere.
(*Karl Madden*)

Drugs Talk

Billy and Colm are the Gardai who gave us the drugs talk. They told us about the uses and side-effects of drugs, also about peer pressure and the consequences if you use or are caught in possession of them. They answered all our questions and brought in drugs they had recovered. We had an opportunity to examine them in detail (we also found out why cannabis is called 'shit' much to the girls' disgust) and learned what they look like. It was a great night, we were very grateful for them giving their time to talk to us. (*Connor Haynes*)

Our Community project: Painting a mural in the village.

This was a big project, and it took a lot of planning on our behalf and the leaders. It took two days to complete the mural on the hoarding around the building site of the new community centre. The first day we had to undercoat it with a blue base paint. The Community Centre Committee sponsored the paints, brushes and rollers for us to use. On the second day an artist came to sketch the outline of the characters for us to paint. A reporter from the Meath Echo interviewed us and took some pictures of us when we finished. All together it took about eight hours and was well worth it because we saw out masterpiece displayed for a few months and got very positive feedback form the community about the work. We then won an award from the presidents' young citizen programme (best of all was the gift vouchers we received) (*Eve Brannon and Jennifer Watters*).

Our end of year trip Carlingford Adventure Centre
One night in Forage we all decided to organize a trip for all of the club members. We decided to go to Carlingford, but we needed to fundraise (yet again). We did a church gate collection and we also used some the money we had accumulated in the club. After lots of organising we set for Carling ford at 7.30am on one Saturday morning in June. We were all very tired, but after a quick stop for sweets everyone was a bit more excited. We went canoeing, rock climbing and abseiling. We had lots of fun even though the water was freezing and the suits were not very flattering to say the least. The instructors were really nice and helped those of us who were a little scared. It was one of the best trips ever: we can't wait to go again this year. (*Emma Quigley and Louise Geraghty*)

Year Two in the Club

This year in our Foróige Club we have been very busy, we have done many activities. Some of the activities we have participated in will be explained by the new members to the club. This year the club has been very popular, we have eleven people on the waiting list along with the thirty or more already in the club. We have a lot to tell you about, hope you enjoy. (*Eric Lawless*)

Trip to Templemore Garda Training Centre

Due to one of our club leaders being a Garda he arranged for us to visit the training center in Templemore and provided transport. The experience was great and it gave us an insight into garda life, we got the see a *fine* guard (our chauffeur) tour guide. Everyone enjoyed it and it was an unforgettable outing, possibly a few new recruits in the making. (*Danielle O'Rourke* and *Kristyn Mc Donald*)

Mid term break

For our mid-term break we went on a trip to the pictures, this was the first time for many of the new members to plan an event. We went to see the hilarious film Big Momma's House. Kiera organised the bus, Shane booked the cinema and Charlotte got us a discount for the food in TGI's because there were so many of us in the group. When we arrived at Blanchardstown we went on a little shopping spree for goodies and then off to see the picture. We had a great night, the food was lovely and we really enjoyed our night out with the Foróige Club. (*Shane Willams*).

First Aid

On the 1st March we had a first aid class; the instructor demonstrated how to handle a crisis. He explained about pressures points, how to make slings and the easiest way to put someone into the recovery position. Thankfully you don't need too much strength to do this as the leaders can be quite hard to move. It was a very useful night and we learnt the value of keeping calm and just doing your best. (*Sarah Mason*).

Self defence

We had a busy month during March, on the 22nd we had a self defense session. It was a mixture of kick-boxing, tae-chi and jujitsu. We got to use the boxing gloves and pads; we did different patterns of kicking and punching and even got to flex our muscles on the leaders. I thought it was a good night as we learned different moves and had a chance to sample different types of self defense, and had an excuse to be tough on the leaders! (*Aoife Madden*).

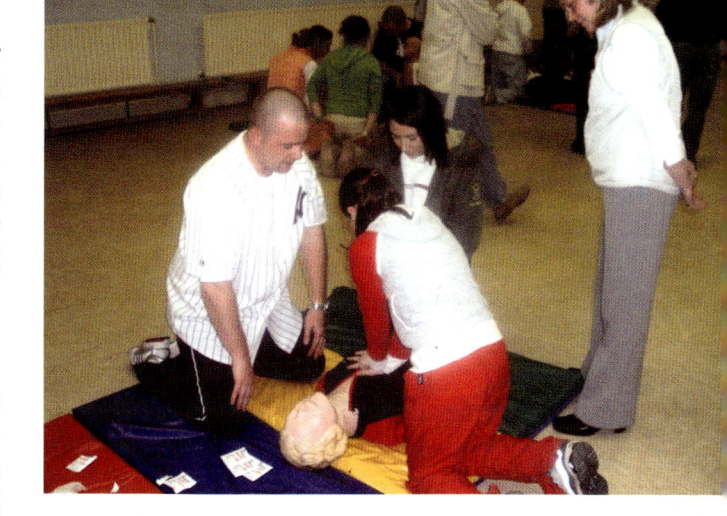

Conclusion

Our year to date has been very good we have all very much enjoyed it and there is more to come. Still to look forward to, is our cultural project, an inter-county disco, where we get to meet all the eleven clubs in Meath and make new friends. But best of all our end of year trip to Carlingford on the 27th of May and moving into the new premises in the community centre. All the members would like to say a great big thanks to the leaders for their time and effort they put into the club, we love our Wednesday nights and hope they will go on for many years to come. (*Claire Lawless*).

ASSOCIATIONS AND CLUBS

9th Meath Ratoath Scout Group

JOHN AND JULIA LONG

THE SCOUTING TRADITION in Ratoath began in 1977. A number of enthusiastic local adults decided that the young boys of Ratoath would benefit from Scouting. Over the years Ratoath Scout Group has accumulated a great deal of experience and expertise. As a member of Scouting Ireland the Aims of the Ratoath Scout Group have been clearly defined. While scouting is primarily about Fun and Friendship, it must also have parameters of control and direction of purpose.

In the **Beaver Scouts** Section, children learn about themselves, nature, helping others and finding fun in accordance with the Beaver Scout theme "Helping Other People".

The **Cubs Scouts** sections offer unrivalled fun, learning and Adventure. We take part in a weekly meeting and we also go on hikes and weekend camps.

The **Scouts** and **Venture Scouts** Sections have an important role to play in setting the agenda for the Group. The philosophy is essentially learning thorough doing and being motivated to undertake the 'doing' because it is fun. In both the Scout Troop and Venturer Unit, the Members have the opportunity to undertake specialised development training...training that will stand to them in their journey through life.

The following pictures were generously provided by John and Julia Long.

Below: Picture shows 9th Meath Ratoath Cubs at Lough Dan, Co Wicklow in 1981

Above: Ratoath Cubs pictured at the 9th Meath outing to Lough Dan, Co. Wicklow in 1981

Left: Picture taken in Ratoath Community Hall, mid-1980's.
Included in the picture to the right are:
Ann Wallace, Joan Bolger, Kevin Bowers, Shane Long, David Duffy, Neil Kelly

Pictured below: at the Cub Fun Day outing in 1986 were: (l-r) Joan Bolger, Anne Duffy, Chris Maher and Mary Clarke

Below: Ratoath Cubs at Summer Camp in Ballyconnell, Co. Cavan, in 1989.

343

ASSOCIATIONS AND CLUBS

Ratoath Athletic Club

RONNIE QUIGLEY & PHIL BATESON

PREVIOUSLY KNOWN as Oliver Plunkett Athletic Club, Ratoath Athletic Club was established in 1974. Officers at that time were: *Chairman:* John Gorman; *Vice-Chairman:* Charlie Reilly; *Secretary:* Willie McLoughlin; *Treasurer:* Paddy Everard and *Club Captain:* Tommy Clusker. One of the founder members of the club, Ronnie Quigley, was a successful athlete at Leinster and national level. He is currently chairman of the club and involved in the Athletic Association of Ireland both at Leinster and national level. In spite of having only a small pool of athletes, Ratoath Athletic Club quickly became one of the strongest clubs in the county and went on to win in Meath, Leinster and also at All-Ireland level.

One of the most successful athletes in the early days was Brian Eiffe, who dominated the 100m and 200m in Leinster during the late 1970's as a juvenile. He went on to set records which stood for many years on the schools circuit, was National Novice Champion and was selected to run for Ireland in the Tailteann Games. In 1981, Tommy McLoughlin was not only Junior Meath cross-country champion but was Intermediate and Senior champion as well. He went on to win medals at Leinster level at cross-country and on the track at 3000m and 5000m and was selected to run for the Irish national team as well as the Irish Schools team.

The most successful female athlete to come out of Ratoath was Aideen Darby, who, as a juvenile, was Leinster Champion at shot putt, discus and javelin and went on to win All-Ireland medals in all three events. Colm Keogh has had a fine career with the club and has won sprint titles at county and Leinster level. He was a member of the Meath Senior team who won the National League title in 1993 and is currently involved with coaching sprinters in the club.

As well as athletes, many people have dedicated themselves to helping with the administration of the club. Many of these have been parents of juvenile athletes and without them it would have been impossible to achieve anything. It would not be possible to name everyone involved but special thanks to John Gorman, Lilly Mulvaney, Tommy Boshell, Martin Mc Loughlin (RIP), Sean Sweeney, Nicolas Killeen, Vincent Donnelly and Dermot Reilly.

Until recently, the club traditionally held road races around the village every year. In 1984 the club took part in major fund raising to help build the Community Centre. One of the events organised was a sponsored run from Galway to Ratoath. Ratoath Athletic Club, formerly a B.L.E. club, was affiliated to the Athletic Association of Ireland when it was set up in 1999.

Ratoath Athletic Club trained for many years at Ratoath National School, which ensured that the club was central to the community and accessible to local children. When this was no longer available, it was thanks to the generosity of Ratoath GAA and Cushenstown A.C. that the club was able to keep going. Both of these clubs offered their facilities to the athletic club for training for a period of six years. In 2000, an exciting new development took place with the acquisition of land for a new athletics track at the Jamestown Sports Campus in Ratoath. This facility has been developed in conjunction Ratoath Community Centre and has re-

Aideen Darby throws the Shot Putt at the Meath County Final in 1990.
Photo Courtesy of 'The Meath Chronicle'

ceived funding from the National Lottery and Meath County Council. The new track opened for use in October 2008. Finally Ratoath Athletic Club has a place to call home.

During the summer season the focus is on Track and Field competition. Athletes take part in the Meath County Championships, the Leinster Championships and hopefully qualify for the National Finals. The Senior Men's relay 4x100, 4x200 and 4x400 teams have been very successful in recent years at both Leinster and National level.

During the winter season it is cross-country running, also at County, Leinster and National Finals under the guidance of former Irish International middle distance runner, Gerry Finnegan and former World Masters Cross Country Champion, Tom O'Connor.

Coaching in the club alongside Gerry and Tom are Colm Keogh, Tom Boshell and Phil Bateson, who was also the Club Secretary in 2008.

Ratoath Athletic Club 2008:

Club Secretary:	Phil Bateson	Club Chairman:	Ronnie Quigley
Club Treasurer:	Colm Keogh	Coach:	Gerry Finnegan
PRO:	Tom Wallace	Child Officer:	Vincent Donnelly

Training times are Tuesday night 7-8pm Friday night from 7.00 - 8 .00 and Sunday from 12 - 1pm at **Jamestown Sports Campus**. Adults Meet and Train Wednesday 7-8 at **Jamestown Sports Campus**. Indoor winter training is held in the adjacent Ratoath College Sports Hall on Tuesday nights 7-8pm.

Young athletes from Ratoath at the Leinster Championships, Kilkenny 1997

There are currently (October 2008) around 180 members in Ratoath Athletic Club. Ranging in age from 6 years upwards, the club caters for boys and girls, men and women. The club runs a "Little Athletics" group for 6-10 year olds. As well as games and fitness for younger athletes the club members train in the full range of track and field sports from sprinting and middle distance running, hurdles and jumps, shot putt, javelin and discus. This diverse range of activities gives an opportunity for people with different talents to achieve their full potential. An adult "Meet and Train" has also been set up and at the moment meets on Wednesday nights.

The club would welcome new coaches and "helpers" and especially anybody who has recently moved into the area with an interest/experience in any facet of athletics, who would be interested in getting involved even for one hour per week.

The picture below shows members of the Ratoath Athletic Club participating in a training session following the opening of their new training grounds at Jamestown Sports Campus in October 2008

ASSOCIATIONS AND CLUBS

First Soccer Games in Ratoath

TONY DARBY

RATOATH'S FIRST GAME of competitive soccer was played by a few lads from Brownstown against farm hands from Clifton's farm (now Jamestown Estate) in the summer of 1962. The players did not have any sports gear whatsoever to tog out in, but, nevertheless both teams enjoyed the kick about.

Two weeks later a game was arranged between the lads from Brownstown and the farm hands from White's farm in Kilrue. The build up to this game drew a lot of interest from people not directly involved in the game itself, and as the time of the game drew near, some allegations about the ability of some of the players from Brownstown to play the game, were made by players from another sporting code.

The game was arranged to be played in the G.A.A. field known as "*The Hurley field*" on the road to Curragha. When the two teams assembled in the field for the game, the Brownstown lads noticed that the team from White's farm had not only additional players not associated with the farm, but players from outside of the parish. The lads from Brownstown questioned the inclusion of the additional players and the answer they got did not please them, so they decided to with- draw from the game. After some heated argument, it was decided that the game should go ahead.

The pitch was in good shape, but a little long for a game of soccer, so it had to be shortened, and this was achieved by placing two piles of coats to represent the goal posts. We also had the problem of a large concentration of cow pads adjacent to the road end goal.

The Brownstown team had no official football kit and had to make do with all-white gear that included some white t-shirts, low neck see-through string vests, white shirts and one player with no shirt. As the hot summer sunshine had not yet arrived, his white skin blended in nicely with the team colours. As for their opponents, they had multiple colours in their kit and were better togged out.

The boys from Brownstown were a little on the tired side having had a hard night at the carnival in Dunshaughlin on the previous Friday night. So the game plan was a blanket defence, and to try and get the ball to their teenagers, Tony Darby and Mellor Flood formed a two-man attack with the intention of surprising the White's Eleven on the break.

The game had just started when a bout of "*fist-de-cuff*" (a local name for a row) started near the touchline at the road end of the pitch and it soon spread throughout the playing field with scuffles on and off the pitch, and so, when tempers finely cooled down, the game got underway. Midway through the first half, a tackle on a Brownstown player, Mellor Flood, resulted in the player being unable to continue and a substitute was brought on as a replacement.

Scoring chances were few and far between and the exchanges between the players continued to be over-robust with some very dangerous tackles going in. With only minutes remaining in the first half, the deadlock was finally broken when Nicky Sherry found his nephew Tony Darby with a fine through ball, but the striker still had a lot of work to do. With Joe Everard and Sean Plunkett from the White's Eleven bearing down on him, but with a change of speed and a little side-step, plus a little help from one of the aforementioned cow pads, he was through and fired a low hard shot to the right of goalkeeper, Willie Reilly, from the Moulden Bridge, to put the boys from Brownstown one up going into the break.

In the second half the White's Eleven stepped up their game to try and get back into the contest, but try as they might the Brownstown defence stood solid with six-foot one inch goalkeeper, Tony Morgan, in outstanding form, and at the back Brendan Lynch, brothers Ciaran, Kevin and Pat Brady, with great support from Chris and Jimmy Maher formed a solid defence. In midfield John Clince and Nicky Sherry were having the game of their lives with a continuous supply of good quality ball to the front men Joe Mannering and Tony Darby. As the game reached its conclusion, a fine ball from John Clince found Joe Mannering on the right wing and Joe sent a measured pass to the inrushing striker, Tony Darby, who hit the ball with such force from two yards out, that he would surely have burst the net. That is of course if the goal had a net!

The game finished with the score Brownstown...2 White's Eleven...0.

The referee on the day was Mun Fortune from Pullwee Street.

Brownstown Boys 1962

Back Row L-R:
Kevin Brady, Gerry Keague, Brendan Lynch, Ciaran Brady, Leonard Brennan.
Front Row L-R:
Joe Mannering, Nicholas Keogh, Chris Maher, Leo Corrigan, Ken Brennan

ASSOCIATIONS AND CLUBS — First Soccer Games in Ratoath

The full Brownstown Panel in 1962 included:

Tony Morgan	John Clince	Pat and Tony Darby
Brendan Lynch	Gerry Keague	Mellor Flood
Jimmy, Michael & Chris Maher	Nicholas Kavanagh	Leonard Brennan
Kevin, Ciaran and Pat Brady	Nicholas Keogh	Leo Corrigan
Nicky Sherry	Tommy Mooney	Ken Brennan
	Joe Mannering	

Brownstown Boys 1962. Team A
Back Row L-R: Nick Keogh, Frank Brady (with Hat) John Clince, Tony Morgan, Michael Maher and Ciaran Brady.
Middle Row L-R: Kevin Brady, Anthony Corrigan, Jack Gaffney.
Front Row L-R: Joe Mannering, Pat Darby, Gerry Keague, Ken Brennan, Dan Corrigan.

Ratoath Harps Committee, January 1968

Chairman & Manager
Christy (Sonny) Martin

President
Anthony (Sammy) Morgan

Treasurer
Pat (Packen) Brady

Secretary
Roderick (Roddy) O Neill

Club Captain
Benny Browne

349

Ratoath Harps first team – A.U.L. League Division 3, 25 August 1968

1. Fiacra O Neill

2. Benny Brown

3. Pat Brady

4. Steven Pryle

5. Mick Walls

6. Mick Donnelly

7. Paul Darby

8. Noel Brown

9. Pat Cantwell

10. Paddy Reilly

11. Tommy Wheeler

ASSOCIATIONS AND CLUBS

Ratoath Harps

BRIAN CONWAY, DARAGH O NEILL,
JIMMY COLFER, MICK TALLANT

The Early Years

FROM THE SUMMER of 1962 onwards, local challenge games were organised in Ratoath on a sporadic basis. The "Ban" was in force, it was to remain for almost another decade and knowledge of the game was fairly limited. The onset of television and 'Match of the Day' coupled with the tremendous exposure arising from England's staging, and ultimate victory in the 1966 World Cup, created a new and unprecedented interest in the game. Following a meeting in Johnny Gogan's bar (now Ratoath Inn) which was attended by Mellor Flood, Benny Brown, Tony Morgan, Roddy O Neill and Sonny Martin, it was decided to enter a Five-a-Side indoor tournament in Navan. Beechmount Ballroom was the "entertainment Mecca" of county Meath and hosted the tournament which catered for both men and women. The top prizes were transistor radios, which were all the rage at the time. Ratoath made the final under the name of "Chelsea Greyhounds"! However, they were out of luck in the decider, and didn't manage to get tuned in and had to settle for second place. Chelsea Greyhounds Team: Fiacre O Neill, Paddy O Neill, Ollie Reilly, Mellor Flood, Joey Walls and P.J. (Paddy) Reilly, who won a minor All-Ireland (GAA) title with Meath in 1957, along with Mickey (Spider) Eiffe.

In 1967 Ratoath Soccer Football Club was formed and the following Committee was charged with the task of nurturing the club: Christy (Sonny) Martin, Patrick (Pakin) Brady, Anthony Morgan, Benny Brown, Mellor Flood and Roddy O Neill. Honorary members were John Bruen, Johnny Gogan and Eamonn White, three men who provided pitches and to whom Ratoath Harps will be forever indebted.

Benny Browne (above left) a founder member of Ratoath Harps discusses old times with another long time member Daragh O Neill

Ratoath Harps Managers from the early years
L-R: Sonny Martin, Patrick (Packen) Brady, Kevin Brady, Roddy O Neill

Sonny Martin remembers *"We formed a soccer team to cater for the lads who weren't good enough to get a game of Gaelic football. We had a huge amount of players who were not going to make top class GAA players and they wanted to play some type of game"*. Sonny continued *"our original idea was to give the lads a game of soccer and perhaps some of them would graduate onto the football (GAA) team"*. However, the continuation of the weekly game fanned the spark which the Five-a-Side Tournament ignited and the first string in the "Harp" was firmly in place.

Making Progress
Ratoath successfully applied to the **Athletic Union League (AUL)** in 1968 where they were to spend two seasons. Home was located on the Lagore Road, with the aid of Jack Bruen and the extraordinary efforts of Roddy O Neill, who were major motivators for the club during its first five years. Roddy takes up the story, *"Resistance to a soccer club was strong. You see, soccer was a foreign game and Kilbride were then the Kingpins in Meath GAA circles."*

Ratoath Soccer Team 1968
Back Row L-R: Michael Walls, Steven Pryle, Mick Donnelly, Andy Bell, Paddy Reilly, Ollie Reilly, Pat Brady.
Front Row L-R: Michael Garrigan, Fiacra O Neill, Pat Cantwell, Benny Brown, Tom Cantwell.

Faced with a challenge, the founders of the club responded and stuck to the task, Roddy continues "Ashbourne had joined the AUL the previous season ('67/'68) and Jimmy Feeley gave us some pointers". "Our knowledge of the game was very limited. Basically what we saw on the television, but we didn't really know the rules. We used to ask the referee to explain his decisions when he penalised us and explanations were generally very helpful".

Even in those times top class officials took charge of games. "Once we had John Carpenter refereeing our match. On the previous Wednesday night he had taken charge of a European Inter-Cities Fairs Cup match. Then he had to deal with us!" Roddy continues, "The team talks before the game were something else. The main instruction was 'Remember lads, you cannot handle the ball'. Players frequently sought help and advice on where to stand as we weren't familiar with centre half or centre forward positions."

The first game on 25th August 1968 was against Marino Corinthians and brought a 1-6 defeat. The team was Fiacra O Neill, Benny Browne, Pat (Pakin) Brady, Stephen Pryle, Mickey Walls, Mickey (Briar) Donnelly, Pat Cantwell, Paul Darby, Terry Summerville, Noel (Scaff) Browne and Tom (Fish) Wheeler. Pat Cantwell scored.

Out of Time
Tom "Cub" Walsh from Straffan Co. Kildare, a leading GAA inter-county footballer, played with Ratoath Harps, but for his efforts, he was dropped from the Kildare panel because he played soccer. The Club's first competitive win was achieved wearing Ratoath GAA jerseys. They were left without gear following a serious fire, which gutted Sonny Martin's (manager) house, on Friday, 31st January 1969. However, the GAA Club rescued the soccer team.

Competitive Harps
Ratoath Harps' first competitive point was against the Wicklow team, Blessington, when Mick Donnelly scored in a 1-1 home game on the 24th November 1968. Mellor Flood's broken leg, sustained in a pre-season friendly, was a major blow to the Club. The first win was in Offaly with a 3-1 victory over Dillonites (now Tullamore Town) with goals from Mick (Briar) Donnelly (2) and Tony Kane (1). Roddy's involvement with the club ended in 1973 at which stage they were competing in the Leinster Junior League where they had two stints (1970/'74 and 1977/'82).

The North County Dublin League accommodated the Harps for two seasons, 1975/1977. Another Ratoath club, Rovers, also competed in the North County Dublin League. Ratoath Harps were officially recognised as and from 1970 following the admittance of Finn Harps to the League of Ireland, which prompted the addition of "Harps" to the club name. The club also moved to a new home during this period. The new location was at Kilrue Lane on the land of another club benefactor, Eamonn White.

The club's final season in the Leinster Junior League in 1982 was the best. They achieved a second placing in Division 3B. The following season saw an ambitious move to intermediate football in the Leinster Senior League.

The club's third and final home venue was at the Coderliss, the present home grounds off the Skryne Road, where a good relationship was built up with the local GAA Club. The two clubs benefited from a harmonious sharing of the rent for the use of the facilities.

The Harps and the Rovers
In 1972, a second team was formed in Ratoath called Ratoath Rovers, who played in the North County Dublin League. As is usual in small communities a strong rivalry existed between both teams. When Ratoath Harps joined the North County Dublin League a few years later, many intense local derbies were played. In later years, in order to strengthen soccer in Ratoath, the two clubs combined and called themselves Ratoath Community, which reverted back to Ratoath Harps later.

Ratoath Harps (Kilrue 1972)
Back Row L to R: Nicky Somers, Kevin White, Jimmy Colfer, Joe Lynch, Anthony Reilly, Mick Folan, Joe Mannering, Daragh O Neill,
Front Row L to R: David Foley, Mick Brady, Joey Brown, Mellor Flood, Eddie Nulty, Noel Brown, Joey Healy, Frank Reilly

The main person behind the Rovers was Willie Reilly (Chairman) who was ably assisted by his committee: - Frank (Plum) Reilly, Alan (Pa) Donnelly, John Looney and Mervyn Ennis.

English Tour 1972

The club's early ambitions reflected a pedigree which would carry them through some lean spells. That ambition was clearly evident when they embarked on a brief tour of the U.K. in April 1972, scarcely five years old. Stephen Pryle from Skryne, a brother of David Pryle, who less than a decade later would be involved with the inaugural Mid-Meath League, was one of many Irishmen working in London for a firm called J&E Hall. Stephen made contact with the fledgling Irish soccer club and the idea of a mini-tour across the Irish Sea was born. Following brief discussions the idea took off and 24 enthusiasts coughed up the £10 fare. The intrepid travelers set off from Dún Laoghaire en-route to Holyhead and the train journey to London. Roddy O Neill offered £5 to anyone who scored a hat-trick and Mellor Flood almost won it in the second game against J&E Hall.

The schedule was quite hectic with the squad departing on Friday and returning on Monday. In between they played three games the statistics of which are:-

DATE	VENUE	DETAILS				RATOATH SCORERS
1/4/72	Bexley	Dartford Heath	4 v 1		Ratoath Harps	Kit Doran
2/4/72	Dartford	J&E Hall	1 v 4		Ratoath Harps	Mellor Flood (2), Ivan Elvin, Joe Healy
3/4/72	Dartford	Inter Fico	1 v 1		Ratoath Harps	Owen Sullivan

The squad on tour was: Roddy O Neill, Kit Doran, Joe Healy, Joe Healy (Jnr.), Jimmy Colfer, Tom Ford, Jim Gorman, Martin Walls, Mellor Flood, Ivan Elvin, Stephen Pryle, J. Lynch, P.

ASSOCIATIONS AND CLUBS — Ratoath Harps

O'Sullivan, G. O'Sullivan, D. O'Sullivan, F. Walls, C. Daly, P. Cantwell, P. Kavanagh, T. Wheeler, P. Reilly, G. Monaghan, Declan Brennan and R. Brennan. 1960's pop star, Marianne Faithful, attended one of the games, while the squad also took the opportunity to socialise and make the most of the short time they had in London.

Ratoath Harps English Touring Team 1972
Back Row L-R: Jimmy Colfer, Ivan Elvin, Pat Kavanagh, Joe Lynch, Raymond Brennan, Owen Sullivan, Stephen Pryle
Front Row L-R: Christy Doran, Tommy Wheeler, Joe Healy, Mellor Flood, Paddy Reilly, Pat Cantwell

St. Patrick's Day Cup
The last game on the Lagore Road pitch produced a record 13-2 win against old rivals Duleek, while the first game as Ratoath Harps brought defeat by the Garda team. Honours were few and far between although a Shield was won in the North Co. Dublin League and an annual tournament for the St. Patrick's Day Cup, between Ratoath and Duleek, gave the trophy cabinet something to support.

Ratoath Harps on St Patrick's Day, 1978
Back Row L-R: Noel Conway, Michael Brady, Paddy Kenny, Terry Brady, Brian Conway Mark Flood, Martin Dolan.
Front Row L-R: Christy Doran, Daragh O Neill, Mellor Flood, Dessie Brady, Paddy Monaghan.

An Ambitious Move

During Johnny Flanagan's reign as Chairman, Ratoath Harps successfully applied to the Leinster Senior League and became one of a handful of Meath Clubs which have, or still do, play Intermediate Football, which is a grade below Senior (League of Ireland) Football. The Club spent two seasons (1982/'83 and '83/84) at Intermediate Level. While success on the field eluded them they learned a tremendous amount about what was required to run a successful club and the experience gained was invaluable. Johnny takes up the story, "*Robbie Cooke had moved into the area and was a very experienced player at League of Ireland level. The enthusiasm which existed, coupled with Robbie's experience, prompted us to make the move*". Robbie adopted the player-manager's role while Johnny was the assistant.

The first game was on 22nd August 1982 when Mellor Flood scored as the Harps went down (1-2) to Cherrywood Athletic. The squad on duty that day was: Niall Fitzgerald, Kieran Gaughan, Daragh O Neill, Mick Walls, Paul Myers, Dessie Brady, Michael Regan, Tommy Ennis, David Brennan, Mellor Floor, Noel Carey and David Gorman.

The following month, September 1982, TEK United were beaten with goals by Robbie Cooke and Noel Carey while in October the club played in the FAI Cup, but were beaten by three goals in Dalkey. Paul McGrath wasn't eligible to play for Dalkey as he had signed for St. Patrick's Athletic and would later sign for Manchester United.

Parkvilla were regular opponents and during the first season, the two Meath clubs played out two draws (2-2 and 3-3) with Mark Flood (two), Robbie Cooke, Daragh O Neill and Owen Power scoring. The following season only one victory was recorded. The club did well against TEK United. However, by the end of the season, a change was needed and the club decided to move again, this time to the rapidly expanding Meath & District League. Some of the notable clubs Ratoath played against were: Ashtown United (now Ashtown Villa); St. Patrick's, Bray (Bray Wanderers).

Leinster Senior League Team 1982/83
Back Row L-R: M Butterly, Anthony Gaughan, K Kelly, Mark Flood, Niall Fitzgerald, David Gorman, Robbie Cooke, Paul Myers, Christopher Brady, Johnny Flanagan.
Front Row L-R: Tommy Ennis, Daragh O Neill, Mellor Flood, Kieran Gaughan, Noel Carey.

Ratoath Harps 1983/84
Back Row L-R: Seamus Murphy, Barry Walsh, Paddy Cully, Martin Mooney, Tommy Reilly, Martin Rothwell, Declan Brennan.
Front Row L-R: Daragh O Neill, Noel Conway, Jimmy Colfer, Gerry Reilly, Brian Mulvaney, Paul Murphy, Declan Reilly.

Meath & District League (MDL)

The club's first season in the Meath & District League (1984/85) failed to yield any trophies, but brought some memorable games in the form of local derby clashes against Dunshaughlin, Skryne Rangers, Castle Celtic and Kentstown Rovers. Ratoath finished fifth behind champions Spiders from Navan. The Navan side went through the campaign unbeaten in what was the first of the most competitive second division title races in the short history of the league. Ratoath Harps, in conjunction with the Meath and District League, embarked upon a joint fund raising venture with an agreement that the MDL would continue with the weekly forecast cards from the end of the 1984-1985 season. Such was the success of the venture that Ratoath completed major development work at Ratoath Park while the MDL's fund raising enabled them to purchase 25 acres of land outside Navan in 1988.

LEAGUE WINNERS 1986
Back L to R: Terry Brady, Martin Everard, Paul Elliott, Dermot Rooney, Paul Everard, Mervyn Ennis, Mark Flood, Packie Dowdall, Declan Brennan
Front L to R: Frank Reilly, Alan Donnelly, Martin Reilly, Noel Carey, Brian Conway, Tony Hartnett, David Gorman

Ratoath had started the weekly forecast cards a couple of season's earlier following discussions between Declan Brennan and Mark Flood. Ratoath continued to raise substantial amounts through the cards for a couple of seasons. The second division title ended in Ratoath in the 1985/86 season with four points to spare ahead of Dunboyne who were in their first season in the MDL (with two teams) after moving from the AUL. Brian Conway's hat trick was the highlight of the clinching game against Newtown United and the Leagues assistant secretary Conall Collier presented the cup in Newtown Club following the match.

Cup Winners 1988
Back L to R: Paul Donnelly, Martin Mooney, Alan McGrath, Mark Folan, Christopher Brady, Brian McCann, Gary Donnelly.
Front L to R: Brian Conway, Daragh O Neill (Captain), Alan (Pa) Donnelly, Noel Conway, Cecil Brennan, Patsy Kelly, (Children: Cormac O Neill and Matt Conway)

The club has enjoyed reasonable success in the meantime with glory achieved in the inaugural reserve cup against Oldcastle (1987/88) while the first team finished second in Div.1 in 1988/89 and runner-up in the Reilly Cup a season later.

Ratoath Harps 1987/88
Back Row L-R: Paddy Monaghan, (Assistant Manager) Mick Davis, Ger Cooke, Val Cassidy, Mark Flood, Jim Rattigan, Paul Everard, Dermot Gorman, Domo Close (Manager)
Front Row L-R: Stan Gibney, Paul Elliott, Brian Conway, Mervin Ennis, Alan Donnelly, Noel Carey, Cecil Brennan.

ASSOCIATIONS AND CLUBS — Ratoath Harps

1988 feast of football to celebrate Twenty Years of Soccer
In 1988 Ratoath Harps invited players from the early days to revisit the past with an exhibition match. The veterans are pictured below...

Veterans Team 1988
Back Row L-R: Ray King, Raymond Brennan, Ivan Elvin, Shane White, Sam Conroy, Joe (Joe) Lynch, Owen Sullivan
Front Row L-R: Tony Darby, Mellor Flood, Paddy Reilly, Jimmy Colfer, Tom Cantwell, Christy Doran.

Back L to R: Mick Folan, Chris Maher, Christo Ennis, Anthony Reilly, Daragh O Neill, Nick Somers, Mick Walls.
Front L to R: Benny Browne, Aidan Browne, Tony O Toole, Frank Reilly, Mick Donnelly, Padraig Gaughan, Eddie Nulty, Mick O Toole.
Children L to R: Paddy O Neill, Keith Walls and Siobhan O Neill.

Ratoath Harps (before a match in Trim) 1991
Back Row L-R: Cecil Brennan, Mick Flood, Mark Flood, Tommy Reilly, Declan Brennan, Patrick Naughton, Michael Davis, Mellor Flood, Christopher Brady, Mick Donnelly, Philip Foster, Martin Mannering, Johnny Flanagan, Ken Donnelly.
Front Row L-R: Barry Walsh, Dermot Gorman, Ger Cook, David Gorman, John Mc McCormack, Paul Murphy, Ivor Reilly, (Child: Lorna Flood).

The most satisfying successful win was in the Fiacra O Neill Memorial Shield (91/92) when Westmeath side Ennel Court United were beaten in Ratoath. The club sponsored the Shield to commemorate Fiacra O Neill one of the founder members. Goals from Cecil Brennan and Noel Conway secured the trophy while Daragh O Neill came on as a substitute and almost scored a third goal. In an emotional presentation Daragh, who captained the side, referred to his late brother Fiacra. Brian Conway also served on the MDL committee for a number of seasons and was in the selection of the Oscar Traynor Trophy team. The league regularly staged finals in Ratoath.

FIACRA O NEILL SHIELD WINNERS 1992
Back L to R: Bobby Walls (Manager) Mark Flood, Noel Conway, Cecil Brennan, John Looney, Daragh O Neill, Alan (Pa) Donnelly, Ger Cooke, Johnny Flanagan (Manager) Mellor Flood.
Front: Barry Walsh, Ken Gill, Vincent Moore, Karl Brennan, David Gorman, Dermot Gorman.

ASSOCIATIONS AND CLUBS — Ratoath Harps

Fiacra O Neill Shield won by Ratoath Harps 1991/92
L-R: Benny Browne (Ref of the Year 1993) Johnny Flanagan (Manager) Daragh O Neill (Capt) Mark Flood (Chairman Ratoath Harps)

Schoolboy football was also catered for with five teams in action in the north eastern counties schoolboy's league. Indeed, in 1991, the schoolboy's league played a u-17 friendly against Queens Park Rangers in Ratoath, while for the opening of the park in 1986, Derry City visited. Ratoath were now firmly established as one of the leading clubs in the Meath & District League.

Northern Visitors - Derry City

The biggest day in the club's history was undoubtedly Sunday, 20th July, 1986. That was the occasion of the League of Ireland newcomers, and former Irish League side, Derry City's visit to Ratoath Park.

The Burmah-Castrol challenge between Ratoath Harps and Derry City drew a large crowd to the ground with the grandstand, which was built for the game and packed to capacity. The driving forces behind the ambitious plan for the official opening of the grounds were Brian Conway and Christopher (Johnny) Brady. Guest players strengthened the Ratoath team, which was managed by Turlough O'Connor, and included Martin Rogers (Parkvilla) and John Swift (Shamrock Rovers), a son of a well-known Meath & District League referee.

Derry City players were heralded as the "*Saviours of League of Ireland Football*" and had just completed a first season in senior competition. Noel King was the Manager, but Derry City's Board had brought in Jim McLaughlin as General Manager and his first duties with the club coincided with the visit to Ratoath. Brian Conway and Johnny Brady pulled off a remarkable coup by staging the match and Derry City attracted a good sized crowd to the venue. Overall the game was a huge success and gave Ratoath Harps a high profile. For that game the "shared" facilities with the GAA were used, but a subsequent divergence of views left Ratoath Harps out in the cold and without the use of changing facilities. With the benefit of hindsight, that episode was a blessing in disguise. The club reacted positively, installed temporary facilities and embarked upon an ambitious building plan which produced a fine clubhouse and further enhanced the image of this progressive club.

Ratoath Harps Selection v Derry City
Back Row L-R: Ronnie Murphy (Bohs) Aidan Gorman(OMP), Mervyn Ennis (Ratoath Harps), Robbie Cooke (Ratoath Harps), Dessie Quinlan (Drogheda), John Byrne (Bohs), Jim Grace (St. Pats), Turlough O Connor (Bohs), John Swift (Shamrock Rovers),
Front Row L-R: Clem McAuley (Trim Celtic), Paul Elliott (Ratoath Harps), Martin Rodgers (Parkvilla), Gino Lawless (Bohs), Alan O Reilly (St. Pats), Tom Duff (Athlone Town)

Ratoath Ladies Soccer

Throughout the years there has been very strong support from the ladies involved with the club. At various stages there has been very successful ladies soccer teams in Ratoath through the efforts of Jimmy Reilly (early years), Alan (Pa) Donnelly, John Looney and Mervyn Ennis. This gives Ratoath Harps an extra dimension as a social club as well as a soccer club.

One of the great all-rounders, involved in Ratoath Harps through the years, has been Jimmy Reilly. After an active career in GAA circles, he turned his attention to soccer and was involved with under age, adult and ladies soccer throughout the years. This talented man has also trained winners of donkey derbies, greyhound classics as well as winning soccer teams.

Schoolboy Football

Schoolboy Football began in Ratoath in 1972 when Len Tiernan, Lee Valley, started an under-13 team under the name of **Ratoath Hibernians**. The team played in the Dublin and District schoolboy league. At that time Ratoath was looked upon as being very far out in the country, so all our 'home games' were played in the Phoenix Park. The first league game was away to Lucan Celtic where we were taught a valuable lesson and beaten 7-1. However, one week later, we recorded full points against Kilbarrack, 3-2, with goals from Paddy Monahan, Brian Conway and a late winner from Anthony Gaughan.

Jimmy Reilly and Gerry Monaghan

Unfortunately, Len Tiernan had to move to England at the beginning of our second season, due to work commitments. The team had gained great experience in the two years, but, with no guidance, the team fell apart. Dessie Brady and Brian Dolan, although young at the time, at 15 years old, gave great help and assistance to Len Tiernan in running the team.

There was no schoolboy team in Ratoath again until 1983 when Anthony Gaughan took up the task. With help from Paddy Monahan and John Flanagan, the team was again entered in the Dublin and District League under the name of Ratoath Harps, with some success.

With the help of Frank Dwyer, Bob Duff and Brian Conway, teams were entered in different leagues including the Drogheda schoolboys summer league and the Meath schoolboys League for the following few seasons. In 1989, for the first time, parents and non-players started to become involved. Later that year a group of Ratoath parents got together and formed a schoolboys section to cater for the youth of the area. A Committee was established consisting of Mick Tallant (Chairman), Pat Geoghegan (Secretary), Tommy Sheridan, John Hendrick and Nick Killian.

Two teams were entered in the Drogheda Independent Summer League at under-nine and under-eleven level. Within two years nine Ratoath Harps players were included on the Meath representative panel for the Kennedy Cup, one of Irelands top schoolboy competitions. This squad was managed by the late Jim Cashin and acquitted themselves well at U.C.D. that year. Jim Cashin took over as Chairman in 1990 and maintained that position until his death in 1998. Jim was and still is a big loss to the club. Tommy Sheridan took over as Chairman until 2000, when the schoolboy and adult clubs amalgamated. It is with the help of the above, their committees and the parents who were willing to help, that the schoolboys section has progressed from strength to strength since 1989 when it consisted of just two teams to the present day (2007) where we can boast 28 schoolboy teams.

Tommy Sheridan in the Cup Final with the Under-9 Squad in 1990
Back L-R: Simon Crawford, Stephen Moore, Paul Hendrick, Nigel Crawford, Hugh Geoghegan, Gavin Donnelly, Colm Rooney, Michael Mc Hale, Tommy Sheridan, (Manager)
Front L-R: Willy Smith, Niall Geoghegan, Conor Killian, Paddy Mc Hale, Paddy Cummins, Dave Tallant.

Mick Tallant and Liam Creagh with the Under-12 Cup finalists in 1992-93
Back L-R: Mick Tallant (Manager) Oisin O Donovan, Colm Rooney, Conor Killian, Gavin Donnelly, Richard Donnelly, Gareth Lynch, Bobby Lake, Liam Creagh, (Assistant Manager)
Front Row L-R: Sean Killian, Barry O Shea, Jonathon Drake, Dave Tallant, Noel O Malley, Willy Creagh

Jim Cashin and Martin Meaney with the Under-14 team that won the Cup in 1992-93
Back L-R: Jim Cashin (Manager) Conor O Donovan, Leonard Brown, Preston Sheridan, Conor O Donoghue, Shane McCann, Martin Meaney (Assistant Manager)
Front Row L-R: John Moore, David Sullivan, Diarmuid Byrne, Ian Cashin, Alan Rafferty, Brian Duffy, Tony Farrell and Jonathan O Brien.

Drogheda Independent Summer League

Year	Grade	Achievement	Manager
1989-90	Under 9	Cup Finalists	Tommy Sheridan
1990-91	Under 10	Cup Winners	Tommy Sheridan
1991-92	Under 11	Cup Finalists	Tommy Sheridan

Meath and District Schoolboy League

Year	Grade	Achievement	Manager
1990-91	Under 10	League Runners Up	Tommy Sheridan
	Under 10	Cup Finalists	Tommy Sheridan
	Under 12	League Runners Up	Jim Cashin
	Under 12	Cup Winners	Jim Cashin

	Under 10	Shield Winners	John Hendrick
	Under 11	Shield Finalists	Mick Tallant
1992-93	Under 10	League Champions	John Hendrick
	Under 12	Cup Finalists	Mick Tallant
	Under 14	League Champions	Jim Cashin
	Under 14	Cup Winners	Jim Cashin
	Under 14	Senior Cup Winners	Jim Cashin

North Eastern Counties

1995-96	Under 12	Senior Cup Winners	Tommy Sheridan
1995-96	Under 18	League Cup Finalists	Noel Farrelly
1997-98	Under 18	League Cup Winners	Mick Tallant
	Under 18	Shield Finalists	Mick Tallant

North Dublin Schoolboy League

1995-96	Under 13	League Champions	John Hendrick
1997-98	Under 8	League Champions	Mark Flood
	Under 14	League Champions	Jim Flinter
1998-99	Under 8	League Runners Up	Pat Naughton

Senior Club

Year	Achievement	Manager
1976	North Dublin Co. Shield Winners	Willie Reilly
1981-82	Leinster Junior League Runners Up	Shay Murphy
1982	Meath Chronicle Cup Winners	Shay Murphy
1983	Meath Chronicle Cup Winners	Robbie Cooke & Jim Colfer

Meath & District League Senior (Division 1 from 1990)

1985-86	MDL Division Two Champions (Only League Title)	Declan Brennan / Jimmy Colfer
1987-88	MDL Cup Winners	Tommy Reilly / Brian Mc Cann
1989-90	Reilly Cup Runners Up	John Flannagan and Bobby Walls
1991-92	Fiachra O Neill Shield Winners	John Flannagan and Bobby Walls
1997-98	MDL Premier Reserve Champions	Mark Flood and Donal Coyne
1997-98	MDL Premier Reserve Winners	Mark Flood and Donal Coyne
1997-98	Fiachra O Neill Shield Winners	Mark Flood and Donal Coyne
1998-99	MDL Excel Print Cup Winners	Martin Gillett & Frank Bohan
1999-2000	MDL Division 1 Runners Up	Noel Farrelly
2006-2007	L.S.L. Major 1 Champions	Gay Goucher & Vinny Macken
2006-2007	Polikoff Cup Runners Up	Gay Goucher & Vinny Macken

Note: In 1990 Division 1 became Premier and Division 2 became Division 1

Martin Meaney and Noel Farrell with the Under-18 team in 1996 Final
Back L-R: Martin Meaney (Manager) Brian Duffy, Anthony Rafferty, Aaron O Neill, Jonathan O Brien, Conor Killian, Noel Farrell (Manager)
Front Row L-R: Eugean Mc Keever, Trevor O Shea, Dave Tallant, Tony Farrell, John Moore, Conor O Donovan, Oisin O Donovan.

Violet Moore and Pauline Cashin with the Jim Cashin Cup in 1999.

As a fitting memorial to Jim Cashin's dedication to the development of the game of soccer in the Ratoath area during his lifetime, the Jim Cashin Cup is presented annually to the winners of the Under-12 Inter-Leagues Competitions which are run nationally by the Schoolboys Football Association of Ireland (SFAI). (Ref: http://www.sfai.ie/inter_leagues.htm)

Ratoath Harps continued in the **Meath & District League** until season 2000-2001 when it was decided to move back to the Leinster Senior League in an effort to attract new players who were moving into the locality. Ratoath initially struggled in this new environment, despite the best efforts of several coaches, as the necessary influx of players did not materialise.

ASSOCIATIONS AND CLUBS — Ratoath Harps

Leinster Senior League 2003
Back L to R: Luke Robinson, Matt Conway, Derek Boyle, Paddy Cummins, Ciaran Rothwell
Front L to R: Willie Creagh, Paul Hendrick, Luke McMahon, Alan Farrelly, Steven Creagh, Jason Smith

Ratoath Harps 2003
Back Row L-R: Willie Creagh, Blaine McAuley, Rob Flinter, Luke Robinson, Ritchie Lombard, Dave O Neill, Neil Cummins, Orin Harney, Killian O Callaghan, Mick Tallant
Front Row L-R: Barry Breen, Steven Fox, Dave Tallant, Maurice Reid, Niall O Shea, Matt Conway, Philip Tallant, Steve Creagh

Season 2005-2006

As season 2005-2006 approached adult football was at its lowest ebb for years but a chance meeting between committee member Mark Flood and current first team manager Gay Goucher started a change for the better. Gay and his right hand man Vinny Macken introduced some new players and higher standards, to the club and immediate improvements were noticed. Good runs in Cup competitions and a battle for promotion ensued, but unfortunately there was no silverware at the end of their first season.

Leinster Senior League 2005-2006
Back L-R: Colm Currie, Matt Conway, Derek Kavanagh, Barry Maguire, Gary Duff (Player of the Year), Gareth Wilson, Brendan Arthur, Robbie Kelly, Danny Lonergan, Gay Goucher.
Front L-R: Brian Conway, Keith Byrne, David Hempenstall, Jordan Lancaster (Top scorer), Marcus Cowzer, Damien Lynch, Graham Kavanagh, Vinny Macken.

Season 2006-2007 started with high hopes and initial performances augured well. Good runs in the Leinster and F.A.I. Junior Cups were topped with a Polikoff Cup Final appearance, which unfortunately resulted in a defeat by St. Pats. The Harps got over this defeat in the best possible way by winning the Leinster Senior League Major 1 title and bringing long awaited silverware to the trophy cabinet. Darren and Michael Gilchrist took over the second team in the Saturday Leinster Senior League Premier 2 division and had a great season, just missing promotion.

Leinster Senior League MAJOR 1 LEAGUE WINNERS 2006-2007
Back L to R: Colm Currie, Ciaran Rothwell, Robbie Burke, Danny Lonergan, Damien O Neill, Derek Kavanagh, Gary Duff, Robbie Kelly, Joey Burke.
Front L to R: Vincent Macken, Dave Geraghty, Ritchie O Brien, Jordan Lancaster, Gareth Wilson(Captain) Marcus Cowzer, Graham Kavanagh, Matt Conway.

ASSOCIATIONS AND CLUBS — Ratoath Harps

Increasing Growth in Club Membership

Coinciding with the return to the Leinster Senior League was a major housing boom which resulted in the population of Ratoath increasing at an alarming rate. As with all voluntary bodies in the area this increase in population put enormous pressure on Ratoath Harps; but every cloud has a silver lining. As the number of teams increased to over thirty we discovered, within our Club, members of the highest calibre who have brought Ratoath Harps to a level, on and off the pitch, which was unforeseen several years ago. In almost forty years of existence the Club has been fortunate to have top class Chairmen in position at all stages, but special mention must go to the outgoing chairman, Martin Edmonds. The increasing growth in membership and profile of the club has not happened by accident and Martin has been instrumental in bringing it to the level it now occupies as one of the top clubs in Meath and surrounding areas.

RATOATH HARPS CLUB OFFICIALS 2006-2007

Chairman:	Martin Edmonds
Vice Chairman:	Shane Kavanagh
Secretary:	Brian Conway
Assistant Secretaries:	Joy Tyrrell, Joan O'Sullivan
P.R.O.:	GaryO'Connor
Club Registrar:	Gerry Doody
Facilities Manager:	Jimmy Colfer
Chief Groundsman:	Daragh O Neill
Commercial Manager:	Donal Coyne
Football Committee:	Jimmy Colfer, Brian Conway, Paul Conroy, Dave Cullen
Social Committee:	Hazel O'Connor, Joan O'Sullivan
Lottery Committee:	Martin Woods, Jim Connor, Joan O'Sullivan, Alan Donnelly
Development Committee:	Martin Edmonds, Brian Conway, Jim Connor, Paul Harris, Donal Coyne, Gerry Doody, Danny Keenan
Audit Committee:	Martin Edmonds, Martin Woods, Paul Harris, Gary Donnelly
Managers' Forum Committee Representatives:	Paul Conroy, Mark Flood, Gerry Doody
Children's Officer:	Dave Cullen
Director of Coaching:	Dave Cullen
Chairman, Managers' Forum:	Shane Kavanagh

New Grounds

The Ratoath Harps Club made a major decision in 2002 to purchase 5 acres of land from Bill Eiffe. This is situated behind the Pitch and Putt course on the Skryne Road. The site has been developed to a very high standard and today it boasts a fully lit all-weather training area, a full size flood-lit pitch and two grass training areas. Due to the rapid population growth in Ratoath, the Harps have continued to plan ahead by securing an additional area of land for two more pitches, known as Clover Hill, which is located adjacent to the Steeplechase Estate.

The Ratoath Harps regularly publish a free newssheet called *The Harp* to provide updates on fixtures and results. In addition they have developed a comprehensive web site:
www.ratoathharps.com

ASSOCIATIONS AND CLUBS

History of Ratoath G.A.A.

RAY MURPHY

Introduction

On the 1st November 1884, when seven men sat down in Hayes's Hotel in the County of Tipperary to put together their ideas on the formal foundation of the G.A.A., little did they realise what they were about to put in motion?

But one of their basic ideas was very simple. You played for your school, your parish, and your club. If you were good enough, you played for your county. Ratoath men did it in the past and continue to do it today. Love it or loath it, there's scarcely an Irishman or woman who isn't touched in some way by Gaelic games. Over three quarters of a million people are members of the G.A.A. and numbers continue to rise. The club, the county, is talked about in pubs and clubs throughout the land. And the history of the games goes back a long way.

Games of hurling are documented in the thirteenth century. **Caid**, the forerunner of football, is referred to in the Statutes of Galway, written in 1527. The passion and the rivalry are especially noticeable in Meath v Dublin matches, or in Munster hurling finals.

Ratoath GAA Club at the start of the 21st Century

So let us start with the present day. Who are we and what are our objectives?. The face of Ratoath has changed dramatically in the last ten years (1996-2006). A small rural parish of some seven hundred families in the 1980's has grown in leaps and bounds to incorporate large housing developments and new names and faces. In 1995/96, seeing this trend, and being acutely aware of the shortcoming in facilities in the parish, the club undertook it's largest ever development plans. Some twenty-seven acres of land were purchased on the Dunshaughlin road, adjacent to Brownstown, for use as new playing fields.

The developer started work on the Sean Eiffe Park in February 2003 and the official opening was in June 2004. At the end of 2005 work was ongoing at the back field, developing two main pitches and a juvenile pitch. These pitches will be floodlit.

On the playing fields, teams are participating in both hurling and football. Every official county competition, for which we are eligible, has a team from Ratoath involved. Blitz competitions, tournaments and indoor events have teams from Ratoath. Development of the games continues, hand in hand with facilities development. With the aid of Leinster Council grants, (following plans submitted by the club), national schools in Ratoath and Rathbeggan have been equipped with the gear required to facilitate hurling and football.

Ladies football has been resurrected, following a lapse of some years. We had a Camogie team in a tournament in Gormanstown early in 2002. Camogie continues to go from strength to strength and in 2003 the u12 girls won the Meath Championship, and also in 2003 we had our 1st junior team since the late 1950's. Local children are taken to play for county panels, to take part in training schedules and football and hurling classes.

A club crest was introduced in 2001, designed with the help of pupils in both national schools. There has been a huge uptake on tracksuits, in the blue and gold of Ratoath, which were also invoked in the current year.

And the youngsters, the lifeblood of any club, are always striving to make a name for themselves. The Under Ten footballers won the Foran Cup, defeating Seneschalstown in the semi-final and Walterstown in the final, in the autumn of 2001. Read their names - new faces and new names playing hand in hand with the descendants of older Ratoath families.

Back row: R O'Byrne, P Kennedy, F McGorman, P O'Neill, A Gillespie, J Lysaght, F Coyne, C Fogarty, A Crowe, O Browne and A Smyth.
Front: K Gorman, C Nugent, G Reilly, B O'Brien, G Eiffe, M Daly and G Rooney in centre. J McGowan (with football), R Crehan, B McMahon, C McCullough, C Rooney, P Flood,
R Giles, D Cunningham and D Cummins. Pictured with D Gorman, J McMahon, D Rooney, D Reilly and S McMahon.

Pictured above are the Meath Community Games champions 2002. This is the Ratoath u-10 football team and the players are as follows, at back L to R, P. Flood, C. Nugent, K. Gorman, C. O'Neill, W. Doyle, B. O'Brien, A. Gillespie, M. Daly, R. Giles and D. Cummins. At front are G. Reilly, J. Wallace, P. Dowd, C. Mc-Cullough, B. McMahon, J. McGowan, E. Wallace, C. Rooney, P. Lennon and S. O'Connell. Pictured with D. Reilly, T. Wallace, D. Rooney and D. Gorman.

Again, and following in the footsteps of former Ratoath players, five local lads became the holders of All-Ireland medals. Keelan Fahy, Diarmuid Brennan, Donal Kirwan, Mark Reilly and Kenneth Fitzmaurice were members of the Meath hurling panel who defeated Carlow in the 2001 Under 16 All Ireland B Final. They are rising to join the likes of Bill Eiffe who won a Leinster Junior Hurling medal in 1961, and Leinster and All-Ireland Junior Football medals in 1962, a National Hurling League medal in '63. Bill also played senior football with the county from 1957-1959. Stan Gibney won a Leinster Senior Football medal in 1986 and was a member of the Meath senior panel during 1984 to '86.

Mattie McCabe has Minor, Junior and Senior County Hurling medals. Mattie, John Harty, Frank Walls, Tommy Wheeler and Bill Eiffe, each received All-Ireland Junior Hurling medals in 1970. Interestingly enough, Mattie has an unusual medal, a Gaelic Weekly medal, which he won playing with Meath. The Gaelic Weekly was a magazine that covered Gaelic games in the '50's and '60's. They were the sponsors of a Senior Football Tournament, which Meath won three times in a row. Meath were allowed keep this cup and it's now the trophy for the I.F.C. winners.

In the recent past Ger McCullough, played with the Meath Minors who reached the All Ireland final in 2002, but the team was beaten by Derry. Since then Ger has played with the Meath Under-21's in 2004 and 2005. Ger is currently on the Meath Junior team and reached the All-Ireland final against Cork, where unfortunately they were beaten 0-10 to 1-4. Diarmuid Brennan won the Keogh Cup (Leinster) with Meath in 2004 and with the Meath Senior team in 2005. He was also on the Meath Under-21 team that defeated Kerry 1-17 to 0-16 in the All-Ireland B series in 2005.

Along with the above, Sean Wheeler, Pat Donnelly, Paddy Martin, Pudser Toole and Tony Darby all represented the county, in hurling, during the decades.

The Meath Under-16 panel is pictured below (full name is given for Ratoath lads). **Back row:** D. Gorman, K. Fitzmaurice, R. Bowe, C. Flaherty, E. Harrington, P. Kenna, C. King, D. Brennan, M. Lynch, B. Regan, E. Keogh, D. Kirwan, R. Gilsenan, and R. Feeney. **Front row:** M. Reilly, M. Burke, P. Fagan, L. Mulligan, K. Fahy, J. Meyler, P. Donoghue, C. Delaney, A. Ennis and J. Quinn.

Hurling and the Early Years
The Ratoath Club itself has a long history indeed. Formed as a hurling club, it is known that a team existed in 1903, which played under the name of Ratoath Erin's Hope Hurling Club. Some sources indicate that a team existed prior to this date, and that a club team was playing in the late 1880's.

Jim Gilligan and Patsy McLoughlin (who did a history of the Dunshaughlin club in 1984) came across a record of two games between both clubs in 1887. In the early years of the G.A.A, clubs came and went from season to season. There were few official competitions, and local tournaments were the order of the day. These early years of the association were turbulent years, and the political climate was fairly rough, to say the least. In 1886 when the first county committee meeting was held, only fifteen clubs were affiliated. In 1889, Meath did not recognise Central Council, and were unable to contest the All-Ireland. Many clubs simply did their own thing. The landlords and the clergy, and Bishop Nulty of Meath were opposed to the organisation. In 1891, there were only four counties under the auspices of Central Council. When in April of 1902 the county committee held a meeting to reform, in the county, only the affiliated clubs were invited. Those (five only) clubs were Rathkenny, Castletown, Navan, Julianstown and Athboy. A major drive was then mounted in the county and I suspect that Ratoath came on board (i.e. affiliated a team) in the following year (1903). But I have no doubt that we were playing, as a team and a club, a long time before this.

In the 1880's the then manager of Fairyhouse Racecourse, one John Caul, and Bill Duffy a local farmer and prominent figure in the racing world at that time, were founding members of the hurling club. Duffy utilized his racing colours, (which were green with a yellow, over the shoulder sash), as the first strip used by the club. This was not unusual as many teams, in this era, played in local racing colours. It's in this strip that Ratoath hurlers took to the field. Incidentally, Duffy lived in the house, still occupied, which fronts the Veterinary Clinic in the village centre. Bill Duffy died in 1943. And it was around this house that the early hurling teams of Ratoath were nurtured. Paddy Everard (Snr.) would have been working hand in hand with Duffy and Caul in these early years. Paddy Everard Snr. died in 1936.

Pictured below are left to right:
John Caul, Bill Duffy (photo taken in 1918) and Paddy Everard Senior.

The following (overleaf) is the oldest photo that I have come across. The caption reads, "*Ratoath Senior Hurling Team, Erin's Hope Hurling Club, 1906.*" As far as I can see this is also inscribed on the players sash. This snap, was taken in 1906, but I don't know where it was taken. The picture is a photocopy from some book, which I have been unable to trace. Any information from readers would be most welcome. I have tried to name the faces but the names mentioned to me cannot be confirmed and are contradicted a lot of the time.

Ratoath Senior Hurling Team, Erin's Hope Hurling Club, 1906.

The year, 1912, saw Ratoath's first success on the hurling fields. A senior league title was captured in that year, and a junior hurling championship in 1929. On 29th March 1930 a Ratoath team beat Kildalkey to win the Junior Hurling Championship. The date is very early in the year and I suspect that this was the 1929 final. A local paper carried a report, showing Ratoath 4-2 up to 0-1 at half time. It failed to show the final score. Also it only mentions fourteen players. This team was listed as Paddy, Andy, Jim and Tom Everard, John Donnelly, Patsy McCabe, Frank Gorman. Pat Tugwell, John (Darby) Gillic, Billy (Squirrel) Lynch, Stephen (Blocker) Blake, Micky Walls, Thomas Walls, and Mick (Mun) Fortune.

Junior Hurling Championship titles were again attained in 1931 and in 1940. Thphotograph on the following page is another of the earliest photos of a Ratoath team, which I have discovered. Paddy Everard tells me that this was taken in 1935, (he's fairly sure about this) on the Curragha rd. The snap was taken at a tournament in aid of parochial building funds. This would explain the presence of the then P.P., Fr. Kelly. Ratoath played Skryne in the final.

In the same year (1935) Meath County Board purchased, from the Land Commission, lands in Navan, on which now stands Pairc Tailteann. The purchase price was £700.00.

In 1938 Ratoath met Kildalkey in the Junior Hurling Championship Final. Paddy Everard told me that they were *'hammered off the field'*. After that hurling almost became extinct, in the parish, in '38/'39. There was no team in Ratoath. This was not so unusual in the early years of the G.A.A. Players moved about the county, seeking work on the land, and strong teams aged and disbanded. You must also remember these were tough economic years in Ireland with massive emigration, and high unemployment.

Paddy Everard recalls going to see a game between Dunshaughlin and Oberstown, (Skryne) and counting at least fifteen Ratoath men between the two teams. A meeting was called in the hall with half a dozen interested parties. All at the meeting contributed a shilling each (5p in real money). Jimmy Woods cycled to the County Board in Navan, paid the fee and affiliated a team from Ratoath. We were back on the road.

The photo shows **from the left** in front row: Dan Eiffe, Tommy Foley, unknown young lad, Paddy (Hanaway) Walls, Benny Dolan, Fr. Kelly and right behind him is Patsy Sherry Jnr.
Behind them are Mick (Mun) Fortune, Mickey Walls, Matty Lambe and Jack Donnelly.
The **next row** has Johnny Brady and Joe Ryan (both in civvies) Kevin Smith, Paddy Toole, Billy Lynch and Tom (The Bailey) Everard, and Jimmy Monaghan (with headgear!)

At the back are Frank Brady and Christy Foley Snr. (both with hats), unknown man in cap, Paddy Dolan, another unknown man in cap again, Kevin Mooney, Paddy Muldoon (with cap), Tommy Dolan, Christy Foley Jnr, John Sherry (big man in centre), Christy Smith (behind unknown young man). Then Jack Browne and Tommy Clarke (both with collar and tie). Dick Donnelly, Tommy Moore, Joe Gorman and finally Paddy Sherry Snr. We think we have most of the names correct.

Ratoath met Kildalkey in the Junior Hurling Championship in 1942, drew the final and lost the replay. Ratoath played a Minor Hurling Championship final in 1953 against Trim in Navan. Ratoath, who were amalgamated with Kilmessan, won, and Trim objected saying that we had played an over age player. I've spoken to the man and he says they (Trim) were right; he was a month over age. He was suspended for a year, which was a very severe penalty for a young lad. Trim was awarded the game. Later he met a Trim player who slagged him over the loss of a medal, and who commented laughingly that they (Trim) had played 'three wrong wans'. Joking, maybe we'll never know! One of the Ratoath minors (and genuinely a minor) was a married man.

Saint Patrick's
St. Patrick's, known locally as St Pat's, was a team formed by Ratoath Club players (who were then playing Junior) and players from other Junior Teams about the county. St. Pats started up in the late forties. There were only about three Senior Clubs in the county at this time. These amalgamations were allowed to facilitate the best junior players to play at senior level, and to make a decent senior competition. The County Hurling Board proper was only formed in 1946. During these years Ratoath paired up with players from clubs such as Kiltale, Batterstown and Drumree. Skryne men and priests from Warrenstown also joined with us during this era.

Playing as St. Pat's, Ratoath men won Senior Hurling Championship honours in 1953 and '54, beating Trim on both occasions. The O'Growney Cup was won in 1955 and '56. St Pat's team also won an O'Growney Cup in the 1950's.

Back row, B. Smith, P. Gorman, T. Dolan, N. Eiffe, B. Eiffe, T. Kane, P. McCabe, P. Dolan, D. Smith, A N Other, B. Delaney, N. Smith, M. Deviney and M. Kane.
Front Row. P, Kelly, S, O'Brien, R, Brennan, T, Everard, B, Kelly, M, Regan, B, Byrne, T (Junks) Mulligan and P, Kane.

The Blue and Gold and Other Matters

The club strip changed sometime during the early period (in the twenties and thirties) and Ratoath wore a blue jersey, which had a laced neck front and white collar. Paddy Woods says that these were the club colours up to the early fifties. Other people that I have spoken to confirm this fact. He also recalls cycling back to Ratoath in the early fifties (after attending an All-Ireland final) in the company of several clubmen. They were chatting about the game and the smashing jerseys that Tipperary had worn on the day. (Tipperary contested the All-Ireland in 1949, '50 and '51, and won them all).

Within a few years Ratoath were wearing the blue and gold. Personally, Paddy says that he still regrets the clubs decision to change. A green jersey with two buttons at the neck, and with a white collar, was also worn. This was a long sleeved woollen jersey. It's reported that this material was extremely itchy and hairy, and often smelled of wool and sweat, despite best efforts at washing.

Playing gear was not as plentiful as it is today. There was no such thing as golf classics or corporate sponsorship. Paddy Dolan recalled that, in later years, they ran card games and card drives in the hall to raise funds. Participants paid half a crown (12½ p) to enter. On a good night the Club would make £10.00. A dance in the local hall was also a popular fundraiser. Dermot O'Brien (a popular accordion player for you youngsters who never heard of him, he died in 2007) was booked in one night in 1957. A thunderstorm knocked out the electricity, so he packed his bags, went back to Navan, and returned the following week. Seamus (Blackie) McGrain remembers his father Dick repairing and hand-stitching sliotars, many, many, years ago.

Incidentally Paddy Dolan received an award from Meath County Board in 2000 for long and distinguished services rendered throughout the years. Social and recreational outlets were somewhat restricted. Gaelic games played a huge part in the lives of ordinary people, and a hurling tradition ran very strongly in many local families. Team spirit and club loyalty was the order of the day. For most, like in other counties, there was little else. People walked or cycled to games throughout the country. Transport was a scarce enough utility. Many people recall Paddy Woods (with his elbow sticking out the window), in his 'Baby' Ford, making several trips to and from Warrenstown, or Patsy McCabe on his white racing bike, heading for a game.

Another activity participated in was boxing. Many of the non-players, and some players, were involved with the Boxing Club in Dunshaughlin. A Fr. Joe Foley, who played for Ratoath, was involved with this club. A formidable boxer in his day, Fr Joe taught skills, dare I say, which possibly came in handy on the pitch!

The '50's and '60's were the golden era of hurling in Ratoath. We won the Junior Hurling Championship in 1957 against Batterstown and the following year saw the team promoted to the senior ranks for the first time. The intermediate grade did not exist.

The rendezvous points for players and followers alike were Molly Talty's and Maude Foley's shops. Peter Donnelly tells me that there no drinking sessions after games, but that the team and supporters gathered about this vicinity to discuss the games. Fifty years ago this was the heart of the village, with only scattered dwellings and farms outside of this area. Peter also says that one of the teams, in the fifties had fifteen pioneers and fourteen non-smokers. How times have changed!

But the efforts and successes of the fifties were not to be wasted. Within a few years (1960) the first Senior Hurling Championship final was contested against Trim. But it was not to be, as Trim were victorious on the day. Ratoath met neighbours Dunboyne in the 1963 Senior Hurling Championship after beating Athboy in the semi. This was a huge day for both villages. Dunboyne was considered favourites on this occasion, and it had been many a year since they had reached this stage in this competition. Likewise for Ratoath, this was a great day, and the pride of the parish was at stake. Down by 11 or more points during the second half, Ratoath battled on to emerge victorious by a score of 9-3 to 6-11 (30 points to 29 points). Neither club has won a Senior Hurling Championship since. The score in itself is probably a record, which may still stand?

The team on the day included Tony Darby (goalie), Joe Everard, Peter Donnelly, and Tommy (The Wolf) Troy (**back line**). Sean Wheeler (0-1), Bill Eiffe and Paddy Martin (halfbacks). Patsy McCabe and Pudser Toole at midfield. **At half forward** Mattie McCabe (2-1), Frankie Gorman and Tommy Mahon (2-1). **Full forwards** Eamonn (Mellor) Flood, Pat Donnelly (5 goals) and Dick Ryan. This was a senior hurling championship, a magnificent achievement. Two of the lads, Mellor Flood, and Tony Darby were just seventeen years old. A presentation dinner dance was held in the County Club, in honour of this team, in 1989.

Senior Hurling Championships were lost in 1967 to Athboy, score 1-11 to 1-6. Losing to Athboy was no disgrace as they had won the Senior Hurling Championship in '66, beat us in '67, and won again in '68. In '69 Kilmessan beat Athboy in the semi and we met them in the final. Kilmessan came out winners.

A Junior Hurling League (yes, we had a junior team as well) was won in '68 (played in '69) with a win over Killyon 4-4 to 0-4. A newspaper cutting shows Pat Donnelly (2-0), Michael Mulvanney and Jem Toole, a goal each. Two points from Tommy Wheeler, and a point each from Paul Darby and Tommy Mahon. Also mentioned in the report are John Harty, "who played a terrific game" Noel Eiffe and John Gorman. The early seventies got off to a good start. The M.H.C. of '69 (which was played in early 1970) saw Ratoath beat Kilmessan. Three players from Dunboyne assisted the Ratoath lads that year.

The photo shows, Paddy Dolan (club chairman), Paddy Martin, Tommy Mahon, John Eiffe, Kevin Darby (at back), Jimmy Gorman, Pat Donnelly, Tony Troy, Bill Eiffe, Tommy Dolan, Mick Ennis, Joe Everard, Eddie (The Brit) Nulty and Tom Wheeler.
At the front are Frankie Gorman, Pat (Pudser) Toole, Eamonn Flood, Dick Ryan, Mattie McCabe (Capt.), Tony Darby, Peter Donnelly, and Sean Wheeler.

The 1969/70 minor winners are pictured below. The team was:

Back row. Peter Moran, Pat Gregan, Noel Browne, John Browne, John Gorman, Tony Conmey, Tommy Reilly, Francis Reilly, Martin Madden and Anthony Conway. **Front row,** Danny Gaughan, Anthony (Bobby) Walls, Maurice Cullen, Ray Brennan, captain Paul Darby, Declan Brennan, Jim Lynskey, Jem Toole, and Pauric Gaughan.

A Junior Hurling League was also won this year. (1970)

The Silverware

Pictured below with the silverware are back row, Tommy Wheeler, John Harty, Colm Cromwell (Meath Co. Board.) Mick Donnelly, Jimmy Woods and missing from picture, Tommy Dolan. At front are Charlie Reilly, Paddy Everard, Bill Eiffe, and Tom Wheeler. This photo was taken in 1970 and the trophies are as follows, the Junior Hurling Leinster and All-Ireland trophies, the County Meath Junior Football Championships trophy, the County Meath Junior Hurling League trophy and the Minor Hurling trophy ('69). Ratoath of course won the last three, with Ratoath men, mentioned earlier, on the Meath panel for the other two trophies.

In September of 1981 Ratoath contested the Intermediate Hurling Championship against Kilskyre. They had beaten Athboy, Kilskyre, Gael Colmcilles and Longwood to reach the final. In a pre-match report the *Meath Chronicle* listed the panel as follows. Ken Sullivan, Jim Flaherty, Noel (Scaf) Browne, Mellor Flood, Michael Walls, brothers David (Rasher), Dermot and John Gorman (Capt.), brothers Pauric, Anthony and Ciaran Gaughan, Dessie and Michael Brady (more brothers), Stan Gibney, Pat Merlehan, Pat Donnelly, Joe Dervan, Brendan Aylward, Andy Kenny, Michael Mooney, John Eiffe, Michael (Briar) Donnelly and Tony Conmey.

The game was played in Trim, and some of the more unfamiliar names were lads from Donaghmore who were playing with Ratoath. A guy from Kilskyre, George Baugh (who played Senior County Hurling for Meath) scored two quick goals early in the game. Ratoath who was the better team threw away the match with '*a rake of wides*' says Jim Flaherty. Kilskyre won by three or four points. Jim and Frank Walls won Leinster Junior Hurling medals with Meath in 1972.

This report also mentions Alice Eiffe whom; it seems, like many a good Ratoath woman today, was the lady who washed the kit. Stan Gibney broke his leg in a challenge against Donaghmore in the weeks prior to the game, and was out for the match.

The photo of this team was taken after the first round game against Kilskyre.

At back L. to R: P. Dolan, M. Mooney, D. Brady, B. Aylward, P. Donnelly, S. Gibney, T. Conmey, K. O'Sullivan, P. Merlehan, M. Walls, P. Gaughan and T. Campbell. **In front:** J. Flaherty, N. Browne, J. Dervan, D. Gorman, J. Gorman, D. Gorman, E. Flood, M. Brady and A. Kenny.

In 1983 we met Dunshaughlin in the final of the Intermediate Hurling Club in Trim. A youthful Ratoath team were the favourites, against, what were called 'the league of nations, and an aging team' led by Capt. Ollie O'Neill. (Yes, the same Ollie that busses and referees many of you youngsters today). We were beaten 1-5 to 0-6 points. In the Centenary Year (1984) this game was celebrated by Tadgh Ó Dushlaine (Delaney), a native Irish speaker and Dunshaughlin supporter, who penned a tune to the air of 'The Boys of Kilmichael', the final verse which reads,

> On Sunday the 9th of October
> Ratoath came to Trim in great joy
> For they thought that the contest was over
> And the boys of Dunshaughlin destroyed.
> But we waited determined and fearless
> Most eager to enter the fray
> When the final whistle was sounded
> By two points we'd carried the day.

That Ratoath team was C. Noone, T. Conmey, M. Walls, G. Doran, D. Brady, P. Gaughan, E. (Mellor) Flood, A. Gaughan, J. Gorman (0-5), J. Wallace, M. Fitzgerald, K. Gaughan, N. Browne, S. Gibney (0-1) M. Donnelly, P. Donnelly and M. Brady. Also on the panel were M. Gaughan, G. Gorman and T. Gleeson.

The club remained at Intermediate for a few years, but lost a lot of players through emigration and reverted back to junior again.

In 1984 Ratoath beat Navan O'Mahoneys in the final of the Under-16 hurling. The opponents in the semi were Kilmessan. The game was won by a couple of points. The panel was as follows, Paul and Philip Dolan, Paddy Ward, Fintan Gaughan, Brian and Mark Condron, Peter Taffe, Seamus and Sean Cullen, Patsy (Ned) McCabe, Martin Mulvanney, Brian and Peter McCabe, Andy Toole, Paul McCann, Mick Brazil, Martin Eiffe, Joey McLoughlin and John McCormack and Kevin Moroney. Two years later this panel contested the Minor Final against Wolfe Tones, and they were beaten by 2 points.

In 1988 we beat Killyon in Navan in the semi of the Junior Hurling Championship. We met Kilmessan in the final, and won, final score 1-9 to 2-3. Ciaran Mooney was team captain.

Back row: Sean Cullen, Paddy Dolan, Gerry Gorman, Noel Eiffe, Philip Dolan, Andrew Toole, Ciaran Mooney, Conor Noone, Peter Hartnett, Paul Dolan, (0-1) Patsy (Ned) McCabe, (0-1) Frank Kelly, (0-2) Tony Conmey, Pauric Gaughan. **At the front** are Mick Barron, (1-0) Alan Donnelly, Peter Taffe, Kevin Moroney, John Gorman, (0-5) Stan Gibney, Brian McCabe, and Sean Lynch.

In 1993 we lost the semi of the J.H.C. to Boardsmill.

An injury time point, from Paul Kirwan, won a Junior Hurling Championship, in '99 against Dunboyne. Ratoath pointed nine times in the second half as against only one point from the opposition. The result on the day was 2-12 to 3-8.

The photo below shows at back, Aidan Hickey (0-2), Sean O'Grady, Noel O'Malley, Ger Lynch (0-3), Paul Kirwan (0-3), Austin McMahon (1-1), and Barry Crowley (0-1). **Front are** John Kirwan (0-1), Sean Ryan, Paul Dolan, Philip Dolan, David Lumley, Paddy Cummins, David Eiffe and Damien Ryan (1-1). **The rest of the panel included** W. Smith, M. O'Neill, G. Maher, D. Willis, S. McIntyre, C. Killian, F. O'Neill, S. Killian and A. Everard, Smith, Maher and O'Neill came on as subs.

We were in form again in 2000, when we beat St Pat's by nine points or so in the J.H.L final.

Homeless Club, Playing Fields and Other Pitches
In the early years, the foundling club used lands at Fairyhouse Racecourse, no doubt helped by John Caul's connections. Shortly afterwards they had the use of Bill Duffy's and later Harry Everard's lands (the same land) on the Curragha Road, from the mid-1910's up to the '60's as playing pitches. This land, known as *'the hurley field,'* was the Santry Stadium of Ratoath for nearly fifty years. All events of any consequence were held on this land. But this was also a working farm and the field was not always available. Also during the late sixties, and into the very early seventies Mick O'Hare loaned land on the Dunshaughlin Rd, lands near Tony Darby's present house on several occasions. A field right beside Ben Ward's house (called Beech Wood), and still known as Beech Wood by the O'Hare family, was also in use in the seventies. A pitch was also in use on land, near what was then Reilly's house on the Kilbride Road, just beyond Moulden Bridge during the fifties. Incidentally, this field was close to some lands, which the club considered buying prior to the Brownstown deal. Lands were also used on occasion opposite the Nursing Home during the '30's, and near Joe Everard's house on the Bog Road.

The lands currently being used by ourselves on the Skryne road, (which were originally commonage), were formally leased to the various clubs by the late seventies or early eighties. There were several houses on this land in earlier years occupied by the Elliott, Clarke, Nash and Carr families. I suspect that the ruins of some of these houses, or a rough roadway, lie below the pitch surface, and this might explain the 'bad patch' we have between the midfield and the top goals. Andy Eiffe signed the agreement on behalf of the club on the 16th of October 1981; Patrick Donnelly signed on behalf of Ratoath Development, and this document is witnessed by Patrick McDermott, farmer of Cabinhill Ratoath. This was the first pitch which Ratoath could call its own.

Old Friends
Pictured here are some of the men, sadly no longer with us, and who gave great service to the club in years gone by.

Tommy Dolan who led the way to many a far away game, and sometimes got us lost, and who shed tears of joy, with the odd old win. Tommy served in practically all positions at club level, over the years, and loved travelling to a game on a fine evening. He enjoyed just sitting in the car, in later years watching the lads training.

Andy Eiffe, tireless worker, a great man to get in the few bob, and a great all round organiser, also served the club very well for nigh on fifty years. Andy also served in all officer positions within the club. He would be as proud and as 'pleased as punch' with the new development.

Paddy Hickey, the cool and level headed Paddy, who held his peace, at the usual flare up at a committee meeting, would then drag on the cigarette, and silenced all with his few level-headed sentences.

Gentleman Tom Wheeler, a great pal of Paddy's, gave sterling service on the field of play over the years.

Sean Eiffe, probably one of the finest players the club has ever seen, as a juvenile and in later years as an adult. Alas taken from us all before we were ready.
In his memory the new G.A.A. facilities at Brownstown were named Sean Eiffe Park.

The Fifties and Football

Football started to come to the fore, spurred on, no doubt by the County's fortune on the playing fields. Meath who had contested, (and lost) their first All-Ireland as far back as 1895 (against Tipperary, would you believe) started to become a force to be reckoned with. In the early years of the Association, the County Team was represented by the senior county winners, and in '95 this was a club called Pierce Mahoneys from Navan.

They beat Cavan in '49, lost to Mayo and Cavan in '51 and '52. Plenty of Ratoath hurlers were playing their football with neighbouring parishes and clubs. It was only natural, therefore, that there was a demand for local football. So in 1953/54 football was introduced into the club. (Some sources say that the football club was only registered in 1957). The men involved in this start-up were probably most of the men pictured below. This is a picture of the 'committee' taken in what was known as the 'Tea Rooms' attached to the old Community Hall. I'm led to believe that this snap was taken at a dance in the hall, in 1956/57. The Community Centre stands on the same site.

Back: Paddy Woods, Charlie (Chucker) Reilly, Christy Smith, Peter Donnelly, Andy Eiffe, and Ray Brennan.
Front: Jem Eiffe, Noel Eiffe, and Paddy Everard, Tommy Dolan and Tommy Everard.

Paddy Everard was also chairman of the county hurling board from '63 to '66, and a Meath football selector from 1967 to '69. These were the days of Bertie Cunningham, Peter Moore, Jack Quinn, Mattie Kerrigan and 'Red' Pat Collier.

The Final that Never Was
In 1955 the newspapers carried the headline, "*Ratoath will meet Nobber in Junior Final*" But it never happened. Ratoath met Oldcastle in the semi final of the Junior Football Championship and Oldcastle won. Ratoath objected at County Board level, and a replay was ordered. We beat Oldcastle in the replay 3-4 to 1-5, and were set to meet Nobber in the final. The opposition, in the meantime, appealed to Leinster Council which ordered a third replay of the semi-final. In the dying minutes of the game the Ratoath goalie (who was then fifteen or sixteen years old, and who went on to have a distinguished career with the club) let the ball slip through his fingers into the back of the net. We were beaten, and never did reach that final.

Junior Football Championship 'A' was won in 1961, and as was the case in those years, the winners went on to play the Junior Football Championship 'B' winners, who happened to be Walterstown. I have seen a newspaper cutting from the Drogheda Independent, which reported the match. The game was played in the month of December. The report commends Ratoath who had "*beaten all opposition,*" and had the team down as hot favourites. It also reported that the weather conditions were '*deplorable*'. The paper named the team as follows. Johnny Carey, Patrick (Pudser) Toole, Peter Donnelly, Sean Plunkett, Bill, Jim and John Eiffe, Joe Everard and Patsy McCabe, Pat Donnelly Peter Carey, Mattie McCabe (0-1). Charlie(Chucker) Reilly, Ray Brennan, Noel Eiffe and Tommy Everard. Mattie's point was our only score. Walterstown scored 0-10.

This photo shows the Junior 'A' winning panel. **At back are** P. Carey, P. Dolan, P. McCabe, P. Toole, A. Hessman, P. Donnelly, M. Ennis, T. Everard, J. Eiffe, S. Plunkett and T. Dolan. **At front are** M. McCabe, L. McLoughlin, J. Eiffe, P. Donnelly, J. Carey, S. Wheeler, C. Reilly, J. Everard and B. Eiffe. Seated in front is M. Walls.

Seven-a-side Football
Seven-a-side Football Tournaments were very popular during the sixties. All the local clubs organised these events, and teams often took part several times a week in different competitions.

Teams played all about the County and went as far as Celbridge and Maynooth. Wristwatches were often presented to the competition winners.

These events were very popular and attracted large numbers of supporters. The games were taken very seriously and have been described to me, as "*... they were hard battles*" On one occasion, in 1960, Skryne were beating Ratoath in a Dunshaughlin tournament final when the referee blew the whistle early. At least that's the line the Ratoath followers took. (The match was being played in a field owned by Murray's, which was located just after you turn right for the existing Dunshaughlin pitch, after crossing the Navan Road).

As the referee, a man called Delaney (a Laois man, and working as a guard in Athboy) left the field, the Ratoath supporters followed. The referee took fright and ran and the crowd followed. It's reported that Paddy Moore locked the gate, which the referee had to scamper over. Bill was chased down into the village and was found hiding in Mrs. Togher's house in Dunshaughlin, close to Murray's pub (now Cathy Ned's). I can't get a straight answer as to what happened next, (they just look at me and laugh), but I hear that the local constabulary had to be called. Peace was restored ... eventually! Also I hear that a mighty row blew up in the convent grounds in Maynooth, when we were playing Dunboyne in a similar tournament. Don't know who won the game, but I hear that we won the row.

Pictured below is one of Ratoath's winning teams from that era 1963, pictured in Enfield, and not one of them, I'm assured, was involved in the Dunshaughlin or Maynooth incidents.

Back: Joe Everard, Patsy McCabe, Pudser Toole, Pat Donnelly, and Mattie McCabe.
Front: Tony Darby, Mellor Flood, Peter Donnelly, Charlie Reilly and Bill Eiffe.

In 1970 Ratoath went on to beat Cortown (2-8 to 0-6) in the Junior Football Championship 'A' final in Navan, and then met Navan O'Mahoneys the 'B' winners. Ratoath beat them in Trim and pulled off the double.

The photo shows this panel and **at back are:** Mickey Walls, P. McCabe, T. Conmey, T. Wheeler, M. Donnelly, P. Donnelly, J. Carey, A. Conway, J. Gorman, Martin Walls, N. Eiffe, J. Browne and M. McCabe. **In front are:** J. Harty, P. Gaughan, J. Toole, T. Reilly, B. Eiffe (Captain), F. Reilly, E. Flood, R. Brennan, F. Walls and S. Lynskey. Anyone know who the child is?

Wins and trophies were becoming scarce, and the next significant trophy was a Meath Football Championship (MFC) won in 1977, beating Kells 2-8 to 0-7. In '79 we met Moynalty in the semi final, drew the match, and beat them in the replay 1-12 to 0-5. Sean Eiffe scored 1-5 in this game. We eventually met Navan De La Salles (O'Mahoneys) in the final and won this Minor Trophy again (1-8 to 2-4). On both occasions Ratoath were amalgamated with Donaghmore. The '79 team is pictured below.

Back row L. to R. Sean Eiffe (0-1), David Kearns, Dermot Browne, Noel Beggy, Dermot Rooney, Brian Burke, Padraig Furlong and John Duffy (0-5). **At front are:** Team Captain Declan Tormey (1-1), John Eiffe, Jim Smith (0-1), Stephen McInerney, Stan Gibney, Paudie Long and Paul Everard.

Sean Eiffe, John Duffy and Stan Gibney were Meath minors the same year.

In 1980 we lost the Junior Football League Final, following a replay, to Moynalvy. The semi was against Skryne and we played them twice to reach the final. The game was played in Dunshaughlin and we were beaten by a few points in the final replay.

A Ratoath team from 1980, pictured in Skryne.

At back are: Stan Gibney, Sean Eiffe, Brian McCann, Stephen O'Connor, Paul Everard, Terry Brady, Brian Burke, Dermot (Bruno) Browne and Pat Donnelly. **At front are:** David Gorman, Martin (Rat) Reilly, Brian (Pro) Conway, Dermot Gorman, Noel (Scaf) Browne, Anthony (Rubber) Gaughan, Dessie Brady, and Pauric Gaughan.

Legends and Other Stories

Tommy Dolan bought himself a brand new bike. His pride and joy. Within days, there it was, gone! The Guards were summoned. Neither a sight nor a sound of the bike. A couple of days later, Molly Talty was doing a bit of cleaning, polishing and dusting, as you would. And there under the bed, yep you've guessed it, was Tommy's bike.

More Stories

Local street leagues were all the rage at one time. A famous battle took place between Pullwee St. and Lee Valley in 1950/51. Peter (Larkin) Cleary, Jim, John, and Noel Eiffe, Mick Brady among others represented Pullwee St, under player/manager Andy (Eiffe). Pullwee St. were hot favorites, and certainly seemed the stronger team. Nicholas and Sean Connor, Jimmy Gough, Christy Foley, Paddy Woods, Tommy Morgan and Vincent McCauley were some of the players representing Lee Valley. And no, I haven't mixed up the areas. Mickey Walls was the ref. Lee Valley won by a point.

Ratoath were Intermediate Level from 1981-89, without winning a Junior final? This is a strange one; the club at the time proposed that we (Ratoath) would be a better team if we were playing at a higher level, and delegated two stalwart officers to go to the County Board seeking promotion. They made such a case at the County Board, that the Board capitulated and promoted Ratoath. There's many a player got 'stick' over this on the field. Now there's one for you!

East Meath League

The E.M.L. commenced in 1981 and lasted for about five years. At times up to seventeen clubs were participating. Clubs from the areas roughly between Slane and Kilcloon and from Donaghmore to Colmcilles were involved. Most of the clubs were in the Intermediate Grade. Our own Andy Eiffe, Dave Donoghue and Jim Brady were very involved in the organisation. George Glynn (Donaghmore) was Chairman of the Committee and Tony Byrne (St. Pauls) was the Secretary of the group. Competitions ran from mid April to the end of July. Ratoath lost the semi's of this competition in '82 and '83 to St. Mary's and Duleek, lost the final to Mary's in 1984 and beat Dunshaughlin in '85 in the final 2-12 to 1-10. Stan Gibney was Team Captain and received the Man of the Match Award.

In '82 we won the Spring Football League Division 2 against Dunboyne 0-9 to 7 points. That panel was, Joe Lynch, Aidan Conway, Dermot Rooney, Noel Colfer, Declan Brennan, Paul Everard, Anthony Gaughan, Dessie Brady (0-5), Sean Eiffe, Martin Reilly, Mickey Walls (0-1) Brian McCann (0-1), Ray Brennan, Tommy Reilly (0-2), Brian Conway, Brian Burke and Dermot Browne. A fellow called Sean Boylan was playing center back for the opposition, but I hear he was substituted during the game. Also in 1982 Navan O'Mahoneys beat us in the Under-21 Football Championship Final (by 2 points.).

In 1985 we won the Division 2 Winter League. *On the team were:*

Back L. to R. P. Gaughan, P. Everard, J. Gibney, T. Brady, M. Mockler, D. Rooney, P. Donnelly, M. Ennis, T. Reilly, Dessie Brady and S. Eiffe.
Front: N. Browne. N. Carey, B. Wallace, M. Reilly, David Brady, S. Gibney, B. Conway, M. Gaughan, K. Gaughan, M. Gleeson and A. Donnelly.

Ratoath were associated with St Martins (football) at minor level from about 1982/83, and this amalgamation lasted some ten years.

Ratoath won the M.F.C in '87 when amalgamated with Martins. Navan De Le Salle were beaten in the quarter final, St Cutberts in the semi (1-14 to 2-5) and Slane were beaten in the final, 5pts to 4. Eight of the nine points were scored from frees. This was a very good Slane team with five of their panel playing minor for the county team. No player from our combination was involved at county level.

The 1987 Ratoath Football Team

Back. J. Gilligan, D. Rooney, D. Kealy (0-3), P. Kealy, L. Eiffe, P. Dolan, D. Melia, S. Farrell (0-1), L. McMahon, T. Rooney, D. Donnelly, N. Foley, P. Farrell and D. Donoghue.
Front. K. Stoney, C. Byrne, S. Clare (0-1), B. Kealy, P. Galvin, A. Foley (Capt.), B. Rooney, J. Davis, P. O'Rourke, D. White, M. Walsh, D. Maher.

We were beaten in the semi in this competition in 1988 by Duleek, and lost the final in 1989 (against Duleek again) also with St. Martins. The '89 final was played three times. The first game was abandoned at half time, as the father of one of the Duleek players collapsed and sadly died at the game. The second meeting ended in a draw (2-3 to 0-9) and the third meeting ended with a Duleek win, 2-6 to 1-6. For the record some of the Ratoath lads in the '89 final were Robert Ennis, Ciarán Byrne, Peter McCabe, Terry Rooney, Donal Coyne, Barry Donnelly, Pierce Fahy, Robert McGuinness and Shane O'Neill. On the subs bench were John Dollard, Ivor Reilly and David Moroney. Incidentally, a sub for St Martins/Ratoath at this game was a young fellow called Evan Kelly.

In 1992 we contested the Junior 'A' Football Championship Final against Gael Colmcille. We beat Enfield in the quarterfinal (1-12 to 1-9), beat St. Vincents in the semi (2-4 to 0-9), and unluckily the final was lost 2-9 to 2-6. Terry Rooney was man of the match on final day. We beat St. Bridget's in the Division 4 Junior Football League Final also in 1992 (1-9 to 0-10). Again in '92 we contested the Under-21 Division 2 Final against Kilcloon at Dunshaughlin, and lost this game by a point.

In 1993 we met Parnells in the Meath Football Final at Walterstown. This was after meeting St. Pats of Stamullen twice in the semi before beating them, 11pts to 10. Familiar names on the panel include Fiachra Lynch, Conor Donovan, Declan Sweeney, Ciaran O'Malley, Mark Carbury (Team Captain on the day, and who also broke his hand during the game) Keith Walls, Graham Clarke, Fergal Rooney, Andrew Everard, John Kirwan, Brian White, Paul Donnelly and Conor Donoghue. Among the subs were Derek Walsh, David Eiffe, Simon Donnelly, David Lumley, Damien Mannering, Neill Kelly, Paul Kavanagh, and Ray McCullough. Despite being five points up with ten minutes to go, Parnells won by six points.

The 1992 Under-21 Ratoath Football Team

Back. John Reynolds, Neill Kelly, Shane O'Neill, Terry Rooney, David Moroney, Robert Ennis, Philip Byrne, Fergal Rooney, Paddy O'Grady, Peter McCabe and Donal Coyne.
Front. Marty Mannering, Clive Lumley, Stephen Rafferty, Davy Lumley, Simon Donnelly, Ivor Reilly, Mark Carbury, Stephen Reeves, Neill McGoldrick.

In 1997 we beat Clonard in the 'A' football league, score 1-10 to 0-10. The panel that year was as follows, B. Kelly, F. Rooney P. McCole, S. Donnelly, B. Duffy, A. Rice, L. Browne, B. Rooney, D. Ryan, K. Mulpeter, M. Carbury, C. O'Malley, D. Lumley, O. McWilliams, P. Dolan, M. Foley, G. Clarke, G. Lynch, A. Hickey, C. Lumley, A. Everard, D. Eiffe and T. Rooney. Ger Lynch scored 0-7 on the day and points from Terry Rooney and teams captain Anthony Rice. Graham Clarke got another point and the killer goal.

Captain Anthony Rice congratulates his teammates.

Also in '97, we became divisional winners over Kilbride 1-13 to 1-3, battled through the quarterfinal (Martry 3-7 to 1-9), the semi final (Meath Hill 3-14 to 0-7) and contested the u-21 league final proper. This time the opposition was Drumconrath, under coach Tommy Dowd. The 1st game at Rathkenny ended in a draw (2-6 to 1-9). The replay saw the teams in Pairc Tailteann. The opposition took an early lead scoring 0-4 without reply, and Ratoath were two points behind at the break. It was tit for tat throughout the second half, and Drumconrath equalised early in injury time. The fact that eight minutes extra time was played in the second half, during which the opponents scored the winning point, still raises the hackles on many a player and supporter to this day. In a nutshell we were robbed. Final score 1-9 to 1-8.

The team that year was Paddy Coyne (0-1), Ciaran O'Malley (1-2), Conor O'Donovan, Conor Donoghue, Owen McWilliams, Damien Ryan, Graham Clarke, Paul Flaherty, Davy Lumley, John Kirwan (0-3 & Capt.) and Paul Kirwan, Andrew (Boxer) Everard, Leonard Browne, Sean Killian, Barry Crowley, Cormac Meaney, Paul Browne, Noel Everard, Donal O'Grady, Terry Maher, Ger Lynch (0-2) and Aidan Hickey.

The Girls and Ladies of Ratoath

Needless to say the girls and ladies of Ratoath were not standing idly by while their men folk enjoyed themselves. Camogie was very popular during the thirties and into the fifties. A former player, in later years, May Dolan, was the boss, and organised training and games throughout the county. The girls regularly played in Ashbourne and Kentstown, and attracted quite a large following. I cannot find any record of, and I haven't heard, of any competitions won over the years by any of these Camogie Teams. The girls played in navy gymslips, which for the most part were made by a Mrs. Kennedy who lived on the Fairyhouse Road. A white blouse was also worn. It was the uniform of the time. Mun Fortune also gave a hand at training. All these sessions took part in the '*Hurley field*' i.e. the lands on the Curragha road, or on the roads about the village. Paddy (Friday) Moore had an open backed lorry, and, apart from cycling this was the principal means of transport for the teams. Didn't Paddy have a great job?

Mary (Nulty) Walshe recalls playing in Oldcastle on one occasion, meeting the Ratoath lads there (who had played in Kilmessan) and going to a céile later that evening in 1949. What cars there were, were left behind and both teams hopped on board Paddy's lorry for the trip home. And sure why wouldn't they. Below is a picture of the Ratoath Camogie team, taken about 1939. The house on the left, in the photo, was Paddy Dolan's parent's house. This site is now occupied by the pharmacy. It's probable that Fr. Bartley, who was the local curate at this time, took this snap. The team folded up, during the middle fifties, through emigration and marriage. Now just how many camogie players married hurlers is anybody's guess.

More Yarns – Camogie and Football

I hear that the Camogie lassies invited a team from Crossakeel to Ratoath for a challenge, on one occasion. Being the good hostesses, they enquired from the P.P., Fr. Kelly, if they could use the hall for refreshments. Certainly, was the response, but no dancing. Anyway, it wasn't long before the inevitable happened. Jimmy Woods and Tommy (Totty) Reilly arrived with the music, accordion, and fiddle. The word got back to the P.P. (doesn't it always), who reckoned he had to do his pastoral duties. They were all chucked out!

Ladies football was started in the early 1990's, and by 1994 the ladies had won the Division-3 League beating Dunsany. On promotion to Division 2 they promptly beat Moy-

The photo shows **from left**, Maud Foley, Peggy Flood, Cathy Brennan, Brigid (Bridie) Kiernan, Nancy Brady, Brenda Foley, Molly Mannering, Peig White, Mary Moore, Alice Dolan, Lizzie Mannering, Tiny Smith, Shiela Farrell, Lil Coyle and May Dolan. Other exponents of the game over these and later years were, Shiela and Eileen McLoughlin, Ella Donnelly, Tiny Brennan, Nancy Smith, Nancy Gorman, Maura Flanagan, Winnie Staunton, Marie and Aloque Brennan, Ger and Nuala O'Brien, Bernie Kenny, Ter and Katie Sherry. **Others involved were** Sheila Foley, Mary (Moll) O'Brien and Nan Rafferty.

lough in the final in '95. Also in '95 they drew the semi-final of the championship against Summerhill. They were beaten in the replay.

In 1996 they met Summerhill again in the Junior A Championship Final, and beat them 2-6 to 0-8.

1996 Ladies Football Team

Back: Kerri Walsh, Deirdre McGrath, Barbara Kelly, Caitriona Lynam, Edel Daly, Margaret O'Connor, Orla Brennan, Mary Maguire, Christine Poleon, Elaine Kavanagh, and Pauline McGrath. **Front:** Lisa Donnelly, Alison Kelly, Claire Donnelly, Charlene McAuley, Roisín Grogan (Capt.) Patricia Moran, Rita O'Reilly, Evelyn O'Connor, Laura Morrissey and Leona Gilchrist. Missing from photo is Geraldine Kavanagh.

Below are the Ratoath Under-12 girls who were Meath Community Games champions for 2002. There are three sets of twins in the team, namely the Adams, Woods and McCann girls. Must be something in the water!

The photo shows, at back, N. Francis, M. Halpin, M. Power, S. O'Sullivan, S. Adams, M. Walsh, A. Reilly and S. O'Gorman. **Middle row has** A. Reilly, C. Flood, A. Lowe, R. Quinn, A. Burke, N. Mercer and S. Dowd. **At front are** A. and L. McCann, R. Adams, C. Ryan, L. Woods, K. Walsh and F. Woods.

Juvenile Teams

Literally hundreds of children have passed through the Club over the years. Some went right through the ranks and played for many years at adult level, and some have represented their county. Again they have played with their schools and colleges and have achieved many honours for themselves.

I have seen a newspaper cutting, which reported on the final of the Curran Cup (Under-14 football) in 1975. Ratoath beat Castletown 3-8 to 2-7. It also says that we lost the final of this competition in '72 to St. Marys and to Castletown in 1974. The team is listed as Martin Everard, James Meagher, Dermot Rooney, Frankie Welsh, Noel Carey, John Eiffe, Dermot Reilly, Paul Everard, Noel Farrell, Dermot Gorman, Sean Eiffe (Capt.), Kieran Smith, Anthony Gunn, Dermot Browne and Padraigh Redmond.

In the nineties Ratoath teams had good successes on the playing fields. Juvenile hurling was seriously resurrected in the early nineties, with Street Leagues, which were played in the school field. Johnny Ryan encouraged by Ben Ward did a sponsorship job. In '92 we lost the Under-11 Hurling Championship Final when the referee disallowed a goal (a winning score). One of our players (who had been substituted) hadn't reached the sideline when the goal was scored, or so said the referee. There is many a mentor around today who remembers this episode very well indeed. And they are still mad over it. Ciaran Mooney or Pauric Gaughan will tell you all about it! But they persevered and in 1993 this competition was won. Both the 1992 and 1993 games were against Boardsmill.

Pictured below is the Under-14 team who were beaten in the final of the Curran cup in 1985.

Back: I. Corbett, P. McCabe, C. Byrne, S. Keogh, T. Rooney, R. Mc Guinness, and B. Donnelly. Middle. S. O'Neill, S. Fay, P. Fahy, D. Coyne, D. Moroney, S. Reeves, P. Ward.
Front: B. Burke, M. Foley, C. Lumley, D. Carey, R. Ennis, F. Galvin, I. Reilly and D. Rafferty. Pictured with D. Rooney, M. Mannering and D. Donoghue.

The 1993 team is pictured below:

Roidín Crowley, David Moore, J.B. Maher, Toirleach O'Neill. Fiachra Gaughan, Eric Murphy, Ciarán Flinter, Leo Lynch, Stephen Gaughan, Austin McMahon, James McIntyre and Lisa Donnelly. **At front are** Chris Kenny, Danny and Jamie O'Connor, Una Kenny, Enda Murphy, Patrick Bryan, John Crehan, Stephen O'Reilly and Carol Morrissey.

"Waiting for the medals".
Players, mentors and supporters in the school field in the early '90's.

The Under-15 Football League was won in '92. (4-4 to 0-7). The opponents were St. Michael's and the game was played in Kilberry.

Back: Michael O'Neill, Ronan Donnelly, Aidan Hickey, John Kirwan (1-0), Kevin Murphy, Leonard Browne (1-0), Mark McCann, Ray Fahy, Conor O'Donovan and Paul Kavanagh (0-1).
Front: Jonathan O'Brien (1-0), Damien Ryan, Cormac Meaney, Conor Donoghue (Capt. 1-3), David Eiffe, Alan Rafferty, Damien Mannering and Sean O'Grady.

The Under-14 Divisional Football League was won in 1993 against Ardcath (4-8 to 0-8). This game was played in Pairc Tailteann, which was a terrific occasion for a young team, with Niall Geoghegan as team captain. We reached the finals again in '94 and '95, and beat Clanna Gael and St. Pats. Very nice, three Under-14 titles in a row.

Captain Niall Geoghegan (scored 1-3) in 1993 making his after match speech was surrounded by the following in the photograph below: Paul Hendricks, Stephen Fox, Hugh Geoghegan (1-1), Conor Killian, Paddy Coyne (1-3), Paul Kirwan, Nigel Crawford, and Willie Smith (part hidden). Also on this panel were J. Everard, D. Goodman, O. Donovan, T. Murphy, P. Keane, R. Fahy (1-1), N Geoghegan, D. Tallant, W. Creagh, C. Greer-Murphy, B. Crowley, and C. Murrihy.

For the record the '94 team (that beat Clanna Gael) was Conor and Sean Killian, Gavin Donnelly, Oisin Donovan, Niall and Hugh Geoghegan, Colm Rooney, John Everard, Paul Flaherty, Jonathan Drake, Tommy O'Reilly, Willie Smith, David Carney, Sean Clarke, Barry Crowley, Sean Ryan, Noel O'Malley, Ciaran Murrihy, Fergal Moran, John Ward, Colm Ward and Leo Lynch.

We lost the Under-13 Football League Final in 1994 in terrible conditions in Dunshaughlin. In 1995 after winning the Under-14 Football League we were defeated in the Division 2 Championship Final by Drumconrath/ Meath Hill in Donore. We contested the Under-15 league final against Syddan in 1996 and won this trophy.

Under-15 Football Team 1996

Back: L. Lynch, S. Clarke, D. Carney, G. Donnelly, P. Flaherty, E. Murphy, N. O'Malley, T. Maher and T. O'Neill. **Front:** G. Maher, K. McMahon, B. Crowley, S. Killian, E. McKeever, D. Hayes and S. Ryan.

We contested the Under-14 Championship again in 1998, against Castletown, drew the final in Bective, and lost the replay. The team that lined out was, R. Gallagher, S. O'Reilly, O. Horan, P. Kelly, K. Fahy, C. Murphy, T. McGuane (Capt.), G. McCullough, R. Madden, D. Kirwan, P. Hobbs, J. O'Hare, C. Brady, S. Gorman and J. Hickey. The subs were C. Kelly, K. Fitzmaurice, J. Carroll, V. McIntyre, D. Brennan, J. Geaney, J. Greer-Murphy, K. Carney, M. Reilly, P. Colreavy, R. Wallace, J. Everard and D. Shanny. I remember that Jamie Geaney had played throughout the competition, but couldn't field on the day because he had his appendix removed in the days before the game. In 1999 Ratoath represented the county in the Under-14 Leinster Hurling Féile in Co Laois, after beating Kiltale in the semi and the favourites, Boardsmill (2-2 to 0-7), in the County Final.

Conclusion

We started with a young team and we end with a young team. This photo was taken only God knows when and where. Look at the players, youngsters aged from six or seven to thirteen or fourteen. Not unusual perhaps, for a juvenile team in a small village in those years. See the old fashioned hurleys, the knee length breeches and the knee-high socks. It may not be a Ratoath team at all, but the strip would seem to match the early period, and I think it deserves publishing. The only thing I know for certain is that this photo came from a Mrs. McCauley's house in Dunboyne, following her death. The name Jack Eiffe was written on the reverse of the snap. It would be great to get some more info on this photo.

It has been difficult to try and capture one hundred years of the history of a Football and Hurling Club in a few short pages! How do you do justice to their trials and tribulations? It is equally difficult to put to words, the efforts of a handful of people in their quest for silverware. How do you quantify the hours of training, the sore hands, the sprains and the aches and the tired muscles? The games lost because of injury to key players. That miserable, last minute point or the missed free that cost the match.

Many of the people shown in photographs or mentioned in this article are deceased. Some lived to a ripe old age and some were taken tragically, as young men and women in their prime. Those that you knew, celebrate their lives, remember them as they were, and think of them now and then. Dozens of trainers, mentors, and coaches have passed through the club over the decades. Likewise club secretaries, treasurers and committee members have all contributed their talents. A few appear in photos, or are mentioned in this article, but the Club is about footballers and hurlers, and it's on those people that I have concentrated.

In researching this article, I have met and spoken to many people. I have seen their eyes light up, and hazy memories return, when a particular game is recalled. The stories of the full back on the opposing team whom *"sent me home with seven stitches"*, or that *'bowsie'* of a corner-forward. But their memories still bring a smile and a laugh. A great wealth of material and photography is in private hands throughout the parish. It needs collection, copying and documentation. Only a small proportion is published here, and it gives some insight, I hope, into the people and the families caught up in the history of Ratoath G.A.A. In particular, special thanks are due to Paddy Everard, Alice Eiffe, Angela Wheeler, Helen Hickey, and Lorraine Eiffe. Thanks also to Kevin and Tony Darby, Mattie McCabe, Bill Eiffe, Pat, Peter, Ella and Beryl Donnelly. Paddy and Paul Dolan, Dave Donoghue, Michael (Skipper) Lynch, Michael Barron, Pauric and Danny Gaughan, Kevin and Peig White, Dermot Rooney, Dessie Brady, Ben Ward, Paddy Woods, Frances Maher and Mary Walsh.

Also thanks to Ann and Ciaran O'Malley, John Gorman, Danny McCann, Ray Brennan, Colm Cromwell and Paddy O'Dwyer, to Ratoath Heritage for their marvelous idea and to my wife and family for their unending patience and support.

Thanks are also due to everyone who contributed to this article. To those who supplied the snaps, newspaper cuttings and answered the telephone queries. Those of you who found the time to meet, and to talk. Those of you who named the faces and told the stories, and to all whom helped in any way. On behalf of Ratoath G.A.A. thank you very much indeed.

ASSOCIATIONS AND CLUBS

Ratoath Rugby Club

DAVID MARRINAN

Ratoath Rugby Football Club (RFC) was established on November 9, 2004 and it was accredited by the IRFU on January 7, 2005.

Presenting Denis Hickie, Malcolm O Kelly and Maura Coulter with Life Memberships of Ratoath RFC at the inaugural awards dinner were: (Left to Right) Tom Devaney, General Manager Marriott Hotel Ashbourne; David Marrinan, Hon. Secretary; Denis Hickie, Ireland and B&I Lions; Brent Pope, RTÉ; Tony Murphy, VP; Malcolm O'Kelly, Ireland and B&I Lions; Doug Gibson; Richard Whitty; Maura Coulter, Ireland Women's international; Stephen McKenna; Derek Gillen, President.

Ratoath RFC was founded in Derek Gillen's kitchen on November 9, 2004 after he was approached by neighbour, Donal O'Brien, with Cllr. Nick Killian and asked if he thought forming a Rugby Club would be feasible. With close friends and neighbours with a love of the game living in the area, among them fellow ex St. Mary's College RFC senior players, Ratoath had all the talent and expertise needed.

Present at the first meeting were Mark Coatsworth, Alan Nield-Crabbe, Derek Gillen, Dominic Kenna, Stephen McKenna, David Marrinan, Tony Murphy and Richard Whitty. The members of this group had a vast amount of experience playing the game between them and equally important, they had an impressive array of skills – including printing, finance, design, construction, organisation and IT (Information Technology) – all of which would be used in getting the fledgling club off the ground.

The Club completed the necessary paperwork and sent a cheque to the Leinster Branch of the IRFU and on January 7, 2005, Ratoath RFC was affiliated to the Leinster Branch, becoming the youngest Rugby Club in Ireland. The following week the website www.ratoathrugby.ie was launched as the first point of contact to the outside world.

In the design of the playing gear the club chose to keep with the blue and yellow colours of the local GAA club as these were seen as the 'village colours' and to reflect the equestrian tradition of the area the strip design was modelled on racing silks worn by the jockeys on Fairyhouse Racecourse – because of this the kit is jokingly referred to as 'the silks'.

To tap into the increasing popularity of Rugby in the area, the club brought Irish international players Maura Coulter – soon after to be invited to join the committee – Denis Hickie and Malcolm O'Kelly to two local schools, Ratoath and Rathbeggan, and subsequently signed up over 150 children to the club. The committee, with the help of Mary Wallace TD and Cllr. Nick Killian, searched for somewhere to train and play. After several offers came to nothing, Ratoath RFC was offered 5 acres on the Curragha Road as a temporary training ground, with a view to securing a permanent base there in the future.

At the time of writing, committee members have come and gone. Mark Coatsworth, Alan Nield-Crabbe and Stephen McKenna have left and been replaced by Maura Coulter, Dave Moore, Doug Gibson, Joan O'Sullivan and Rob Kevelighan.

The field has been transformed into a club with a full-sized pitch, floodlit training area, dressing rooms, toilets, committee room and parking for 50 cars. The club is fielding teams from U-7 to U-16 and is adding an older age group every year. It has a coaching team of 20 and employs a part-time Youth Development Officer to bring the Club to the local schools.

The first major fundraiser, a gala ball held on April 14, 2007 to award life memberships to Irish internationals Maura Coulter, Denis Hickie and Malcolm O'Kelly, raised over €20,000. The event was attended by the players with RTÉ's Brent Pope as Master of Ceremonies.

Ratoath RFC[1] is located in the fastest-growing area in the country and, with the talent at our disposal and the continuing support from coaches, parents and players; the committee believes the club will grow into one of the strongest clubs in the region and a social hot-spot in the village of Ratoath.

Committee 2007: Maura Coulter (Director of Rugby), Doug Gibson, Derek Gillen (President), Dominic Kenna (Hon. Treasurer), Rob Kevelighan, David Marrinan (Hon. Secretary), Dave Moore, Tony Murphy (VP), Joan O'Sullivan (Child Welfare) and Richard Whitty.

Ratoath R.F.C., Mt. Pleasant, Curragha Rd., Ratoath, Co Meath.
E-mail: info@ratoathrugby.ie
Web Site: www.ratoathrugby.ie

---

[1] Towards the end of 2008, Ratoath Community Centre Board of Management announced that Ratoath Rugby Football Club, was selected as the Anchor tenant for the football pitch in the new Ratoath Sports Campus in Jamestown that will also accommodate Ratoath Tennis Club and Ratoath Athletic Club.

ASSOCIATIONS AND CLUBS — Ratoath Rugby Club

Young Rugby Players at the Ratoath Rugby Grounds, Curragha Road

Let's scrum together for a photograph!

Trophy in Hand: Young Ratoath Rugby Club Team

ASSOCIATIONS AND CLUBS

Lagore & District Gun Club

TONY DARBY

When I was first approached to write something about Lagore & District Gun Club my mind went back to the days long before the gun club was formed. In those days it was very common to find a shotgun or a rifle in most houses, as shooting and hunting were very popular pastimes and also a mechanism to providing food for the table.

When the cold frosty weather of winter had finally set in, one had only to look towards the western sky in the evenings to see the duck and geese with that familiar V shape as they migrated in from overseas to the bogs and wetlands of Ireland. It was time for the shooting man and his dog to get ready, and on a Sunday morning after Mass, he would set off with his dog, his gun and a packed lunch to see where the trail would take him.

On my shooting trips a very popular run was, where I would cross the woodlands at the rear of my parent's house on Pullwee Street, onto the Lough Lane, and from there I would follow the Broadmeadow River to the Green Hills bridge, then turn southwest to Lagore bog and on to Ballymurphy Fox covert. On the return trip I would take in the Crannóg and Lagore fox covert.

The landscape had a much different look about it then, with many woods and bog lands to be found. The wild game was in plentiful supply, but at times very hard to locate as there was thick cover everywhere and the wild fowl always seemed to know that I was coming and seemed to congregate in large numbers in the middle of the bog and out of shotgun range!

1976 saw the formation of Lagore & District Gun Club. It all started when a rumour reached the village that the Land Commission was about to rent out the shooting rights of the Big Lagore bog to an outside Gun Club. The Land Commission had for many years rented out the shooting rights of the bog to a Bank official from Dublin city, by the name of Mr. Gargan. Mr. Gargan had a dislike of anybody shooting on his patch. So he hired a Mr. McAuley as gamekeeper and I can say he carried out his duty with great authority. The result was that as soon as one was about to set foot on the bog, Mr. McAuley was on hand to send you away. The outcome of all this was that the duck and the geese were on the bog in their thousands, but we could do no more than stand at the edge of the bog and dream of what we might achieve if only allowed on the bog.

When the late John Smith suggested that we should form a Gun Club and make a bid for the shooting rights *"but only as a Gun Club would we have first choice to the bog"* we jumped at the opportunity. A meeting of all game-shooting men in the locality was called by Michael Mooney with a view to forming a Gun Club. The people who attended the first meeting came from Ratoath, Dunshaughlin, Ashbourne and Curragha. It was decided to call the club Lagore & District Gun Club.

The first Committee and club members were as follows:

John Smith, Brian Everard, Nicolas Keogh, Terry Brennan, Gerry Caffrey, Patsy Carty, Kieran

Gun Club members at the millennium clay shoot in 2000
From L-R: Gary Donnelly, Ken Molloy, Rory O'Rourke, Fergal Keogh, Martin Donnelly, Gerry Donnelly, Ivan O Neill, Niall Tonge, Patsy Carty, Ken Donnelly, Declan Woods, Eamon Tonge, Brian Donnelly, Gerry Caffery, Ronan Donnelly, Anthony Darby Jnr, Padraig Dolan and Michael Mulvaney

Brady, David (The H) Foley, Michael Mulvaney, Con Colfer, Tony Darby, Pat Darby, John Dollard, Brian Donnelly, Joe Donnelly, Martin Donnelly, Michael Eagan, John Hunt, Derek Kenny, Charlie Keogh. Adrian Leonard, Ken Lynam, Joe Lynch, Paddy Lynch, Michael Mc Donald, Leo Mc Girl, Matt Marmion, Jerry Monaghan, Michael Mooney, Jack Mc Guinness, Rory O'Rourke, Tony Powers, Joe O Reilly, Fred Roberts, Michael Ryan, Bob Slattery, Declan Smith, Eamon Tonge, Tommy Walsh, Liam Woods, Padraig Gaughan, Christo Ennis, Iggie Mc Ivinney & Stan Phillips.

In 2000, with great excitement I made my way to the Club's first clay shoot of the new millennium and to see how things were progressing within the club. I have to say that I found everything in excellent order. The location for the shoot was on Colm Donnelly's land. The site was just off a laneway known locally as Bob Fox's lane. The scene was a hive of activity with a wonderful turnout of club members from far and near. The shoot got off to a great start with some excellent displays of marksmanship at all the traps and with very attractive prizes on show one had to shoot well to win.

I also got the opportunity to meet some shooting pals from the early days of the club including Michael Mulvaney, Brian And Martin Donnelly, Rory O'Rourke, Patsy Carty, Eamon Tonge, Gerry Caffrey and many more. **In 2002,** the club members were celebrating their twenty-fifth year as a gun club.

The names of the club members and officials for the year 2002 were as follows:
Michael Barron, Kieran Brady, Thomas Brennan, Dermot Byrne, Gerard Caffery, Noel

Carey, John Carroll, Noel Carroll, Patsy Carty, Thomas Clince, Anthony Darby (Jnr), Padraig Dolan, Gerry Donnelly, Ken Donnelly, Martin Donnelly (Snr), Martin Donnelly (Jnr), Ronan Donnelly, Ronald Duff, Martin Edmonds, Noel Eiffe, Declan Fitzgerald, James Flinter, Robert Flinter, Mark Flood, Padraig Gaughan, Stephen Gaughan, Shay Graves, Thomas Hackett, Dr. Seamus Keenan, Fergal Keogh, Shane Long, Joe Joe Lynch, John Mannering, Patrick McAuley, Adrian McCullagh, Peter McCullagh, Francis McGee, Leo McGirl, Seamus McNerney, Ken Molly, Michael Mulvaney, Patrick Naughton, Ivan O'Neill, Michael O'Neill, Rory O'Rourke, Stan Phillips, Roy Plunkett, Richard Quigley, John Reidy, Fr. Declan Smith, Gabriel Sullivan, Eamon Tonge, Niall Tonge, Mark Usher, Declan Walker, Ed M Wheeler, Declan Woods, James Hayes, Seamus Power, Fergal Power, and Brian Donnelly.

The landscape which the Gun Club shoots has changed in many aspects over the last ten years. With many new houses bring erected in and around the villages and with Insurance costs at an all time high there is an even greater emphasis on safety. Nevertheless it is wonderful to see the club in such excellent shape.

ASSOCIATIONS AND CLUBS

Ratoath Pitch and Putt Club

BRÓNA DARBY

BACK IN 1970, Jack Keogh, Patsy and Mattie McCabe and Noel Ryan met in the old parish hall with the late Eamonn White and Andy Eiffe to discuss the possibility of a Pitch and Putt course at the "Codalis". This fine sports field is situated just ¼ mile from the centre of the village of Ratoath, on the Skryne Road. In 1972 the first committee was formed, consisting of Jack Keogh, Patsy and Mattie McCabe, Noel Ryan and Martin Lynch.

Over the years the committee was helped by volunteers in developing the course to form 9 holes and eventually 18 holes. People outside the Club gave great support in those early years, with people like the late Phil Byrne giving machinery any time it was required and likewise the late Dan and Sara Eiffe – supplying electricity at no cost to the Club. A clubhouse was needed and finance was raised by a raffle for a Colour Television or £260. It was a mighty prize in those days! Lines were sold for (2/-) 10p in today's money. The Wood clubhouse was built and electricity and water were linked up. In recent years, FÁS workers and students have assisted the Club with the routine maintenance of the course.

Many of the people who were attracted to the game of Pitch and Putt have distinguished themselves in other sports and it provides them with an outlet for their competitive instincts. There is also a great horse racing connection in the Club, led by Paddy Woods who was chairman for a time. Paddy was a successful jockey, riding two winners of the Irish Grand National in Fairyhouse in the 1960's. One of the greatest National Hunt Jockeys, Tommy Carberry, was one of the Club's first sponsors and to date we still play for the Carberry Cup.

Looking back on the early years it is hard to believe the Club has come such a long way with membership of 75-80 adults and 50-60 juveniles who compete at all levels of competition. In the early years membership was £3.00 and it cost 5/- or 25p to have each member registered with the P.P.U.I.

The First open was held in 1977. In the early 1980's, as the complex included the GAA ground and the Pitch & Putt course, the soccer club found themselves without a pitch. Eventually, agreement was reached and the Pitch & Putt Club gave up their first 9 holes and rearranged other holes and were given the late Michael Nash's Cottage fondly called the garden. Work again had to start on the new part of the course and clubhouse.

Did You Know ...?
- Ken Morgan holds course record on present course: 43
- Sonny Martin holds course record on old course: 43
- Daragh O Neill won National Mixed Foursomes in 1995 with his wife Veronica
- Three Ratoath members appeared on the front page of Backspin
- Martin Lynch took Sonny Martin to the 19th green in the Club Matchplay
- David H. Foley claims he won 1st competition with Francis (Plum) Reilly Cup
- The Spanish Juvenile Girls Golf Champion joined our Juvenile Section in 1997
- Noel Ryan won the first Club Matchplay beating Paddy Monaghan.

(Reproduced from Ratoath Pitch & Putt Silver Jubilee booklet, 1972-1997)

Winners of the First Ratoath Team of Four Competition
L-R: Aidie O Rourke, Celia Gleeson, Lilly Rutledge, Kay Turney. Peter Ryan (President) is in the centre presenting the Cup to the winners

Front L-R: Lilly Mulvaney, Bróna Darby, R. Martin
Back L-R: K. Brennan, Veronica O Neill, Daragh O Neill, Pat Darby

Pictured right: Left to Right: T. Brady, B. Fox, C. Brennan

ASSOCIATIONS AND CLUBS — Ratoath Pitch and Putt Club

L-R: R. Martin, Peggy Flood and P. Smith from the County Board

L-R: Lilly Mulvaney, Bróna Darby, Martin Lynch, B. McCabe, B. Fox

Winners of the First Ratoath Team of Four Competition
L-R: Celia Gleeson, Aidie O Rourke, Lilly Rutledge, Kay Turney
Pictured in the background is President Peter Ryan

Ratoath Past and Present

L-R: Veronica O Neill, P. McCabe, Daragh O Neill at prize-giving event in the Pitch & Putt Club House.

Front L-R: T. Darby, B. Fox, D. O Neill,
2nd Row L-R: S. Brady, J. Gannon, M. Lynch, P. Flood, R. Martin
3rd Row L-R: K. Darby, I. Foley, L. Mulvaney, V O Neill, B. Darby, M. McCabe, B. Donnelly
Back L-R: S. Martin, C. Farrell, T. Gorman, E. Gorman

Below: Pitch & Putt Ladies Group

ASSOCIATIONS AND CLUBS
Ratoath Pitch and Putt Club

Pitch & Putt 21st Birthday Celebration 1994
L-R: Ken Brennan, Brian McCabe, Peggy Brennan, Sean Coyne, Phil Conroy, Patsy McCabe, Aidan O'Brien, Ger Kelly, Johnny Ryan, Pat Darby, Peggy Flood

Ratoath Pitch & Putt 1999
Front Row L-R Veronica O Neill, Pauline Byrne, Rosemary Wallace, Alice Eiffe, Patricia Woods, Peggy Flood, Martin Lynch, Cyril Brennan, Noel Martin, Tommy Dolan and Bróna Darby.
Next Row Beryl Donnelly, Lillie Mulvaney, Irene Foley, Rose McGirl, Nuala Lougheran, Paddy Woods, Joe Mannering, Raymond Brennan, Marie O'Neill, Frances Maher and Margaret McCabe.
Next Row Ken Brennan, Kevin Brady, Elaine Gorman, Kevin O'Farrell, Una Brennan, Kevin Darby, Theresa Donoghue, Mary Martin, Theresa Gorman and Sonny Martin.
Back Row Fr Paul Crosby, Pat Donnelly, Vincent Swan and Noel Ryan.

ASSOCIATIONS AND CLUBS

The Terry Fox Run

WILLIE DONOHOE

THE TERRY FOX RUN started in Ratoath and Ireland in September 1993. In Ratoath, the first run raised in excess of £1,000.00. Each year the event is held in Ratoath on the second Sunday in September. In the year 2000, Ratoath raised over £9,000.00. Over the nine years, we have raised over £40,000.00. Terry Fox was born on July 28, 1958 in Canada. In 1977, aged 18, doctors diagnosed a malignant tumour on Terry's right leg. A few days later, Terry's leg was amputated six inches above the knee and an artificial limb was fitted in its place.

Having seen the effects of cancer on other young people while attending hospital, Terry decided he would attempt to run across Canada to raise money for cancer research. After months of training, on April 12, 1980, Terry set off on his 'Marathon of Hope'. He ran an average of a marathon a day for 143 days consecutively. He had to battle with the elements, including searing heat and snow storms, as well as coping with great physical pain and problems with his artificial limb.

On September 1, having completed almost two-thirds of his journey across Canada (3,339 miles), and just weeks away from achieving his goal, Terry was forced to stop. The cancer had spread to his lungs. Despite intensive treatment, he died the following year on June 28, a month before his 23rd birthday.

Today, Terry's legendary physical feat lives on - the Terry Fox Runs are now the world's largest single-day fundraiser for cancer research. Terry Fox runs take place in 55 countries attracting almost 250,000 participants. Ireland currently ranks World No.2 with 81 runs and World No.6 with 9,500 participants. $21,500,000.00 was raised world wide in Terry Fox Runs in 2000, bringing the total raised since 1980 to $275,000,000.00. Over £1 Million has been raised in the Irish Terry Fox Runs since 1993 and a record £180,000.00 in 2000.

ASSOCIATIONS AND CLUBS

Royal Lopez Chess Club Ratoath

Established April 2005

DAVID ECCLES

IN EARLY 2005, it was evident that Ratoath's growing community must have some budding chess players living in the area. Experienced chess practitioners, Ernie McElroy and Michael Keating, set about enlisting interested Ratoath residents to set up a chess presence in the community. After a few phone calls, an advertising campaign and chess contact/database searches a group eventually met in the Ratoath Inn to discuss their options. On Wednesday 20th April 2005 in the function room of the Ratoath Inn Ernie McElroy, Michael Keating, David Eccles, Mark Gould and Ed Doyle amongst others founded a chess club for Ratoath. The name for the club was no ordinary club name. Members decided to use a combination of an infamous chess opening (Ruy Lopez) and their geographical location (County Meath-The Royal County) to launch Ratoath's Chess Club onto the chess scene as "**Royal Lopez Chess Club Ratoath**". The club originally met weekly in the **Ratoath NS school staff room** for social games of chess. It was not long before the club's membership and taste for competition grew.

In September 2005, the club decided to enter a competitive team into the Leinster Chess Leagues. The team, captained by David Eccles, was the outright winner of the 2005/2006 Bodley Cup League championship. The photo shows team members being presented with individual trophies and the perpetual cup by the Leinster League controller. In the inaugural year **Royal Lopez** had set the standard for the years to follow. Automatic promotion to the British Airways League 2006/2007 caused further excitement in the chess community when **Royal Lopez** were clear winners again.

As the chess club was now drawing members from as far away as Dunboyne and Kildare a larger venue was required. The opening of the refurbished Ratoath Community Center in September 2006 meant that the club could move to the **Lagore Room** in the Center for their regular 7.30pm Monday evening club night. The perpetual British Airways Cup was the first silverware to be displayed in the new trophy cabinet at the entrance to the center. The club has enjoyed the publicity gained from frequent editorial comment in the Meath Echo, Meath Post and air-time on radio station LMFM. A regularly maintained Website contains club facts and information about chess at http://royalchess.blogspot.com/.

Following the Senior team promotion to the O'Hanlon Cup league in 2007/2008 season the club continued their successful ways. Again they won the league and thus guaranteed a prominent location in the Community Center trophy cabinet for another year with the replacement Cup. However this time they won by the narrowest of margins. It is almost unbelievable, but Royal Lopez Senior Team claimed their 3rd Leinster League championship in a row. In the most dramatic fashion imaginable the team overtook the largest chess club in the country, Phibsboro, in the final round of matches by the smallest possible margin, a half point. In scenes of high drama, which required 3 hours of technical deliberation, adjudication and rulebook consultation – involving league controllers, tournament directors, even an international arbiter, the league declared and then redeclared for Ratoath, Phibsboro and then Ratoath again. But at the end, when the dust from the rulebooks had settled, it was the victorious Meath team who came through.

Junior members of the club mirrored their Senior mentor's successes by winning the Community Games 2007/2008 competition and they went on to represent Meath.

Achievements to date, September 2008:-
Senior: O' Hanlon League Champions, 2007/2008
Junior: Meath Community Games, 2007/2008
Senior: Killane Shield runners-up, 2007
Senior: BEA Champions, 2006/2007
Senior: Bodley Champions, 2005/2006

Photograph shows the 2008 Royal Lopez Chess Club, Ratoath Senior Team members (from left to right):- Ed Doyle, Michael Keating[Treasurer], David Eccles[Team Captain and Secretary], Ernie McElroy[Chairman] and Ed Malone. Absent from photo- Mark Gould, Pearse Dunne and John Farren.

HORSES FOR COURSES

Creakenstown Point-to-Point Races

GRETTA KELLY

RICHARD KELLY, having been a cowboy in Texas from 1906 and Rhodesia, now Zimbabwe, where he married Sheila Fletcher, returned to farm Creakenstown (located between Ratoath and Curragha) in 1925, on the death, following a hunting accident, of his youngest brother, Martin. Edward, his eldest brother was gassed in the Great War and was in poor health the rest of his life.

In 1932 the Ward Union Hunt Committee decided to move the Ward Union Hunt Point-to-Point from Mullinam, near Fairyhouse, and relocate in Creakenstown. The first few years the Point-to-Point was run in a large circle across Loughlinstown, Bodeen and Creakenstown. In 1943, the Bodeen lane was put in and the land divided. So the course was changed to a figure of eight; the start being in McCauley's now Colm Keogh's. This was a relief to many riders as the Loughlinstown ditches were enormous. The figure of eight course ran as follows: McCauley's - Creakenstown – Blackwater – Lower Creakenstown – Morgan's – turn in McCann's – back through Morgan's – McCauley's – Creakenstown – finishing in the Back Cruchan.

The late Richard Kelly

In the late 1950's more alterations were introduced with a Bush Fence replacing the second last ditch – a sign of things to come. The 1960's saw a move to an all Bush Fence course at Palmerstown. Sadly, the last Point-to-Point in Creakenstown, was held in 1962 but it was an historic day as it witnessed the first of the outside racing broadcasts made by RTÉ. The legendary broadcaster, Michael O'Hehir, then Head of Sport, wanted to try out the cameras at horse racing. Michael did the race commentary for many years at the Point-to-Point. That last Creakenstown meeting was shown on the RTÉ evening news with a recording of the first running of the Lobitos Trophy, sponsored by Shamrock Oil, later called Burma.

Preparations made for the Creakenstown Point-to-Point
The first Monday in March was a very important day in the lives of the local community as that was the day of the Creakenstown Point-to-Point. People came by bicycle, trap and any other means available. Children got the day off school. In the late fifties buses brought people from Dublin. For weeks ahead there was talk of which horses would win the Hunt Race and the Farmer's Race – both confined to local horses.

In the early thirties you had Paddy Leonard, Jim Ennis and Tom Dreaper, amongst others. Later, Denis Baggalley, Peggy Nolan, Willie Rooney from Northern Ireland, the Hoey brothers, three generations of the Craigie family from Merville Dairies, Harry Rooney, Pat Hogan from Limerick, Stan Cullen, Pat Taaffe, the Kelly brothers, Martin and Ted, Eddie Harty, Willie Robinson, Bunny Cox, Johnny Martin, Barney Lawless and Roy Craigie. They are only some of those who rode horses at the event.

Weeks before, Jemmy Monahan, grandfather of two leading National Hunt riders – Batty and Ross Geraghty, prepared the course, building up to frantic activity by hunt members the day before the races. The final touches included tents, fence flags and most important a horse and cart laden with sleepers going to each fence so that spectators could cross the ditches in safety. Paddy Morgan, grandfather of two more leading National Hunt riders, Tom and Kevin, did the very important job of course minder when Jemmy retired. There was no plough on this course, which was unusual because in the War Years there was compulsory tillage almost everywhere.

W.T. Cosgrave and sons following the hunt on foot

Newspaper picture showing the Farmer's Race and Ted Kelly with Brave Alice at the last fence

Farmer's Race with riders and spectators all wearing Top Hats

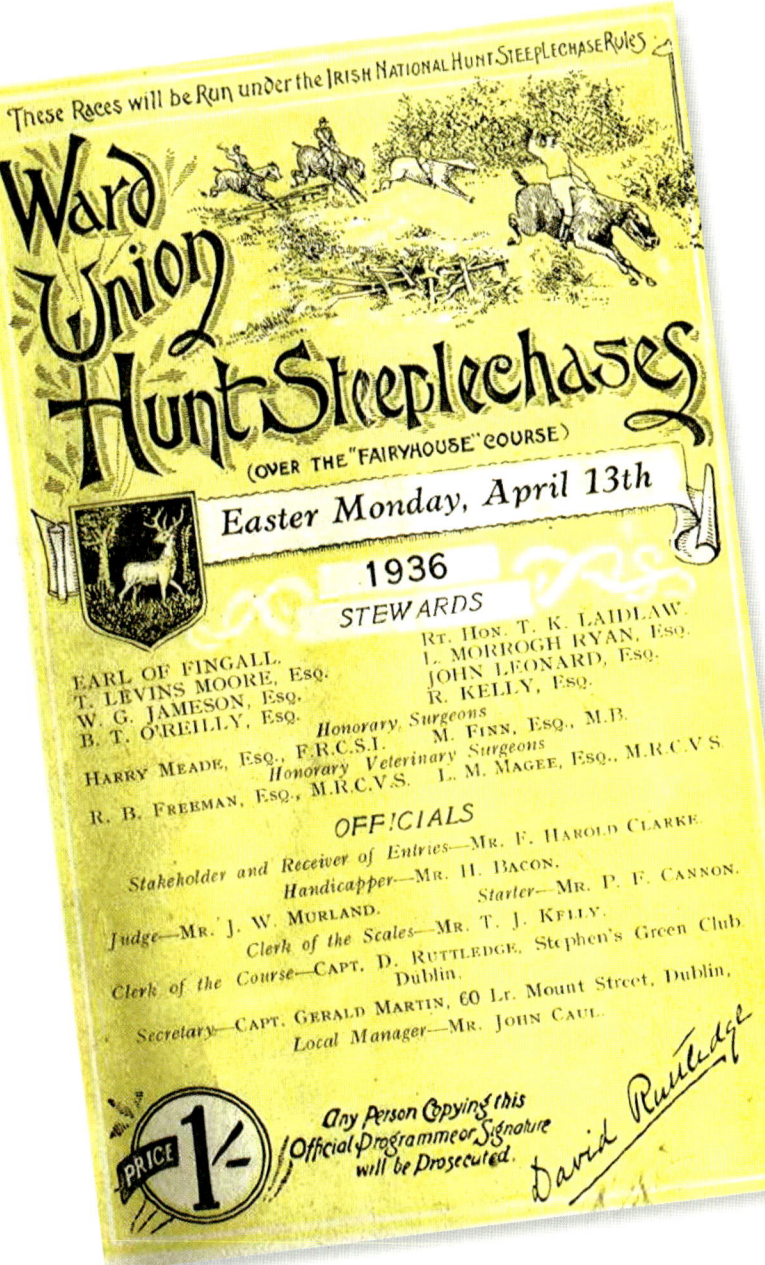

(Above): The Lobitos Trophy being presented by Mrs. Sidney Minch to E.J. Kelly, 1962

Reproduction of the Programme Cover for Ward Union Hunt Steeplechase at Fairyhouse on Easter Monday 1936

L-R: Roy Craigie, Eric Craigie, Standish Collen, Ted Kelly, George Malcolmson and Barney Lawless who were the six previous winners of the Ward Union Hunt Trophy. The picture was taken at a reception in Searson's Lounge, Dublin, prior to the 1969 Point-to-Point event which took place at Oldtown, Co. Dublin.

(Above): Ted Kelly and Tulley Chief winning the Ward Hunt Cup race in 1953 at Fairyhouse. This fine combination won again in 1954. The runner up was Pearls Peach ridden by Gordon Craigie in 1953. Pictured on the Steward's Stand was a delighted Dick Kelly.

(Above right): Ted Kelly being presented with the winner's Trophy in 1954

(Right): Party Piece II (Mr. J. R. Craigie) and Delaney (Mr. J. R. Bryce-Smith) on the open side, take an open ditch in the Mooretown Cup at Creakenstown Point-to-Point on Friday, March 9th 1962.

416

Brave Alice wins at Creakenstown in 1956

Brave Alice

Good fields, a large crowd and interesting finishes, all combined to make the point to point meeting of the Ward Union Hunt at Creakenstown in 1956 a highly successful affair, according to the late broadcaster, Michael O'Hehir.

The success of young *Brave Alice* in the Open Lightweight Race was not only impressive, but indicative of a bright future for Lord Bicester's daughter of *Fortina* and *Alice Rosethorn*. She was one of two winners for popular rider, Mr. E. J. ("Ted") Kelly, who completed his double when getting *Enfield King* home in front, in the Farmers' Race, which ended the day's sport.

Tom Dreaper bought *Brave Alice* at Ballsbridge from Mrs. Harper for the present Lord Bicester and to judge by the manner in which, this as yet inexperienced five year old mare jumped, challenged successfully and then fought back when momentarily troubled by *Bush King*, augurs well for the future.

Prospect was moving so well three jumps out that it seemed that he would be a force but from the second last fence he was faltering and unable to maintain his place as *Brave Alice* mastered *Bush King* and the always well positioned *Head Piece*.

HORSES FOR COURSES

The Ward Union Staghounds

JAMES BYRNE & ANN GAUGHAN

THE WARD UNION STAGHOUNDS are one of two such packs remaining in the country, the other pack being the County Down Staghounds. The Ward Union Staghounds hunt an area, which is bordered on the east by the Town of Balbriggan, on the west by the Dancing Tree at Moyglare, Kilcock, on the north by Duleek, and on the south by the Royal Canal. The Ward Union has long been associated with the Parish of Ratoath. Ratoath has always been a venue on the Hunt Card and the Ward Union has traditionally held its Point-to-Point meeting in the Parish. People from the parish have served as Joint Masters, and on the Committee. In 2001 there were three parishioners on the Committee and two more were Honorary Whips. The Ward Union Kennels are based at Greenpark, only three miles from the Village of Ratoath.

Looking back over the Years
The Ward Union Staghounds, as we know them today, came into existence in approximately 1854. We must, however, go back to 1828 when there were two foxhound packs in the area, The Dubber and the Hollywood. In fact a great-great-grandfather of Ted Kelly of Creakenstown, Ratoath, was a founder of the Dubber pack. In 1830, these two packs amalgamated and became known as The Ward Hunt, taking their name from a small river in Finglas. A Mr P. Alley was Master of this pack for 27 years and it was he who introduced Fallow Deer, and later Native Red Deer, (which we still hunt today) as the quarry. In 1840 Lord Howth imported a pack of Staghounds, from Leamington in England, and kept them until 1842, when they were bought by the Dublin Garrison, and became known as the Garrison Hounds. In or about 1854, The Wards and The Garrisons amalgamated and so The Ward Union Staghounds was found. In 1864 a committee took over the running of the Hunt and moved the Kennels to Ashbourne (The Hunter's Moon and adjoining shopping centre now stand on the site of the old Kennels). The Kennels remained in Ashbourne until 1978 when they were moved to the present location at Greenpark.

The 1864 Committee appointed Capt. Montgomery as Field Master and Charles Brindley as Huntsman, and so began the long tradition of the Brindley family involvement with the Hunt. Charles Brindley was followed as Huntsman by his son Jim, from 1879 until 1912. Jim's son Charles succeeded him having been Whip and Huntsman until 1922 when he was killed in a hunting accident. The monument erected at the nine-mile stone just outside Ashbourne is in memory of Charles Brindley. The Brindley family still live in the parish at Rathbeggan House, and members of the family continue to hunt with the Ward Union. A Mr William Strickland and then a Mr Charles Hall-Dare, followed Charles Brindley as Huntsman to the Ward Union. Tom Fitzsimons was appointed Huntsman in 1941. Tom had been Huntsman of the famous Galway Blazers, and with the East Galway's, before coming to the Ward Union. Tom remained Huntsman for over twenty-five years. Charlie

DOUBLE EVENT ON THIRD & FIFTH RACES

1.0 Percy Maynard Memorial Challenge Cup, value 100 sovs, With 130 sovs added.

Second receives 30 sovs, third 20 sovs, fourth 10 sovs. A farmers' race for horses not thoroughbred bred in the district, *bona-fide* property of farmers occupying land in Hunt district (defined by Stewards), in their possession on and since Jan. 27th. Exclusions— Winner of a race under any rules in any country. Four yrs, 10st 12lb; five, 12st: six & aged, 12st 7lb. Riders—"Qualified Riders" under Rule 95 (i.) or those elected under Rule 96 I.N.H.S. Rules. This Cup (presented by subscribers to Maynard Memorial Fund) to be run for each year and held by winner for one year, but must be returned to Secretary on or before February 13th. **ABOUT THREE MILES.**

No.	Owner	Horse	Age, etc.	Colours
1 { 1	E. Delany	ONE MORE	a 12 7	Black, gold cap
2	E. Delany	SLANTHE	6 12 7	Black, gold cap
3 { 3	J. A. Farrell	HOUDINI	a 12 7	Purple, purple & gold qtd cap
4	J. A. Farrell	MERRY CHERRY	5 12 0	Purple, purple & gold qtd cap
5 { 5	P. Maguire	CLASHFORD II.	a 12 7	White, blk sash & slvs, red cap
6	P. Maguire	TICKETS PLEASE	6 12 7	White, blk sash & slvs, red cap
7 { 7	R. Morrin	CHANCE II.	a 12 7	Pale blue, gold sash, blk & gold qtd cap
8	R. Morrin	JOHNSTOWN BEE	6 12 7	Pale blue, gold sash, blk & gold qtd cap
9	Jas. J. Ryan	MADAM DE LION	a 12 7	Chocolate, pink slvs & cap
10	L. Charls	OBERSTOWN	6 12 7	Green, gold stripes, sclt cap
11	J. M. Ennis	MORNA	6 12 7	Khaki, brown sash light blue slvs & cap
12	P. Kettle	NEW TIME II.	6 12 7	Cerise, green slvs & cap
13	L. King	EASTER BEAUTY	6 12 7	Scarlet, green sash, sclt cap
14	T. M'Donald	GRIOSACH	6 12 7	Yellow, green & blue hpd slvs, green cap
15	L. S. Ward	BRAVE EDNA	6 12 7	Maroon, turquoise blue cap
16	R. Ball	PADDY'S PRIDE	5 12 0	Amber, blk hoop on body & slvs, blk cap
17	R. Cargill	OBERSTOWN STAR	5 12 0	Pale blue, red & orange qtd cap
18	M. Duffy	DUKE	5 12 0	Blue, red cap
19	J. T. Ennis	CHICABOO	5 12 0	Green, primrose hpd slvs, blk cap
20	Jas. Geraghty	MISS MALONE	5 12 0	Maroon, black cap
21	T. R. M'Keever	HOLLYWOOD II.	5 12 0	Yellow & crimson slvs, sash & cap
22	T. M. Long	TEDDY SWORDS	5 12 0	Black & amber bars, blk cap
23	T. J. Mangan	GOLDEN SARRAIL	5 12 0	Yellow, yellow & purple qtd cap
24	D. Monahan	FLYING COURT	5 12 0	Green, yellow cap
25	Peter Murray	NOW THEN	5 12 0	Green, old gold cap
26	J. A. Morrin, jun.	GOLDEN LADY II.	5 12 0	Black, amber, gold cap
27	G. A. Reynolds	GREEN BACHELOR	5 12 0	Maize, purple btns, purple & green qtd cap
28	Jas. J. Rooney	MISTING	5 12 0	Mauve, blue slvs, blk cap
29	F. Delany	SHADOW II.	4 10 12	Black, green sash & cap
30	C. A. Rogers	CASTLE IRWELL	4 10 12	Blue, red sash, blue cap with red spots

McCann then took over the role of Huntsman for three years, having whipped in to T. Fitzsimons for the previous eight. Charlie a native of Ballyboughhill is now farming in Garristown and has hunted up until recently. In 1966, Eamonn Dunphy joined the Ward Union as a whip having been with the Kildare's for over seventeen years and he was appointed Huntsman in 1969. Eamonn lives at the Kennels in Greenpark, having retired due to an injury received in a fall, and keeps a close eye on the hounds and deer in the park. Pat Coyle, Eamonn's nephew, took over as Huntsman in 1982, and is well known in the hunting world. Pat, a native of Kildare, now lives in Curragha with his wife and family.

In 1891, Percy Maynard of The Manor, Ratoath (now Silverstream Nursing Home) was appointed Field Master, and with the exception of one season served for twenty-seven years, until his death following a fall when out hunting. T.L. Moore took over the mastership in 1919 until 1925. Mr Justice Wylie of Clonsilla took over in 1925 and remained Master until the outbreak of the World War II, when Andrew Moore took over. Andrew was a son of T.L. Moore and it was he who kept the Hunt going during the war years. The Moore family who lived in Old Fairhouse Stud (Tattersalls is now based there), are still involved with the Hunt through the Carberry family of Ballybin (trainers of Grand National winner *Bobbyjo*). Pamela Carberry is a niece of the above Andrew Moore, and her son leading National Hunt jockey Paul, seems to get as big a thrill out of hunting as he does riding winners on the racetrack. In 1949, George Malcolmson took over as Joint Master with Andrew Moore for one season, before becoming sole master for ten years. He was joined by Eric Craigie of Merville Dairies in 1959. George Malcolmson retired in 1962 to be replaced by Standish Collen. Since then Judge Frank Roe, Tom Mangan, Roy Craigie, Raymond Keogh, Fred Duffy, Denis Coakley, John Mangan, Pudser Toole, Curkeen, Ratoath, and James Toole, The Strand, Ratoath, have been Joint-Masters. In 2001, the joint-masters were Larry Rowan, Sean Byrne, John Duffy, Mick Bailey and Joe Bruton.

Ratoath and the Ward Union
Ratoath has traditionally been one of the better meets on the card for the Ward Union and the Auld Stand Pub formally known as Rory's, (and before that as Meagher's), was always a favourite meeting place for followers. In the last few years the village has expanded so much and has become so busy that the number of Meets held in the village has decreased. One of these Meets has been moved up the road to Fairyhouse at the invitation of Tattersalls. One of the three pre-season October Saturday morning hunts is held in Ratoath. The Ward Union Children's Meet which is held at Ratoath on the last Sunday in December is a very popular fixture where between 150 and 200 children arrive each year to participate. These meets are made possible due to the goodwill of the farmers and residents in the area.

The Ward Union Point-to Point has been one of the most constant connections the Hunt has to the Parish of Ratoath. Initially, it was held at Mullinam, Fairyhouse, which is just to the back of Fairyhouse racecourse. In 1932, the Point-to-Point was moved to Creakenstown, where it remained until 1962, after which it moved to the Garristown area. *(An article on the Creakenstown Point-to-Point races also appears in this publication)*. However, shortly thereafter it returned to Fairyhouse racecourse and initially was run in conjunction with the Fingal Harriers and later, solely, by the Ward Union. The actual races were run on the inside fields of the racecourse, where the all-weather schooling grounds are now. In fact it was due to the installation of this all-weather schooling track (also used by Sean Boylan to train the Meath Team during the winter), that the Hunt, in 1998, had to move the Point-to-Point across the road to Tattersalls Farm. The course built at Tattersalls has proven to be a very successful course for Point-to-Point.

Hunting and Point-to-Pointing are very important to the world of National Hunt racing and it is where many of the star horses of National Hunt racing commenced their careers, e.g. Imperial Call, Doran's Pride and Florida Pearl to name but a few. Many

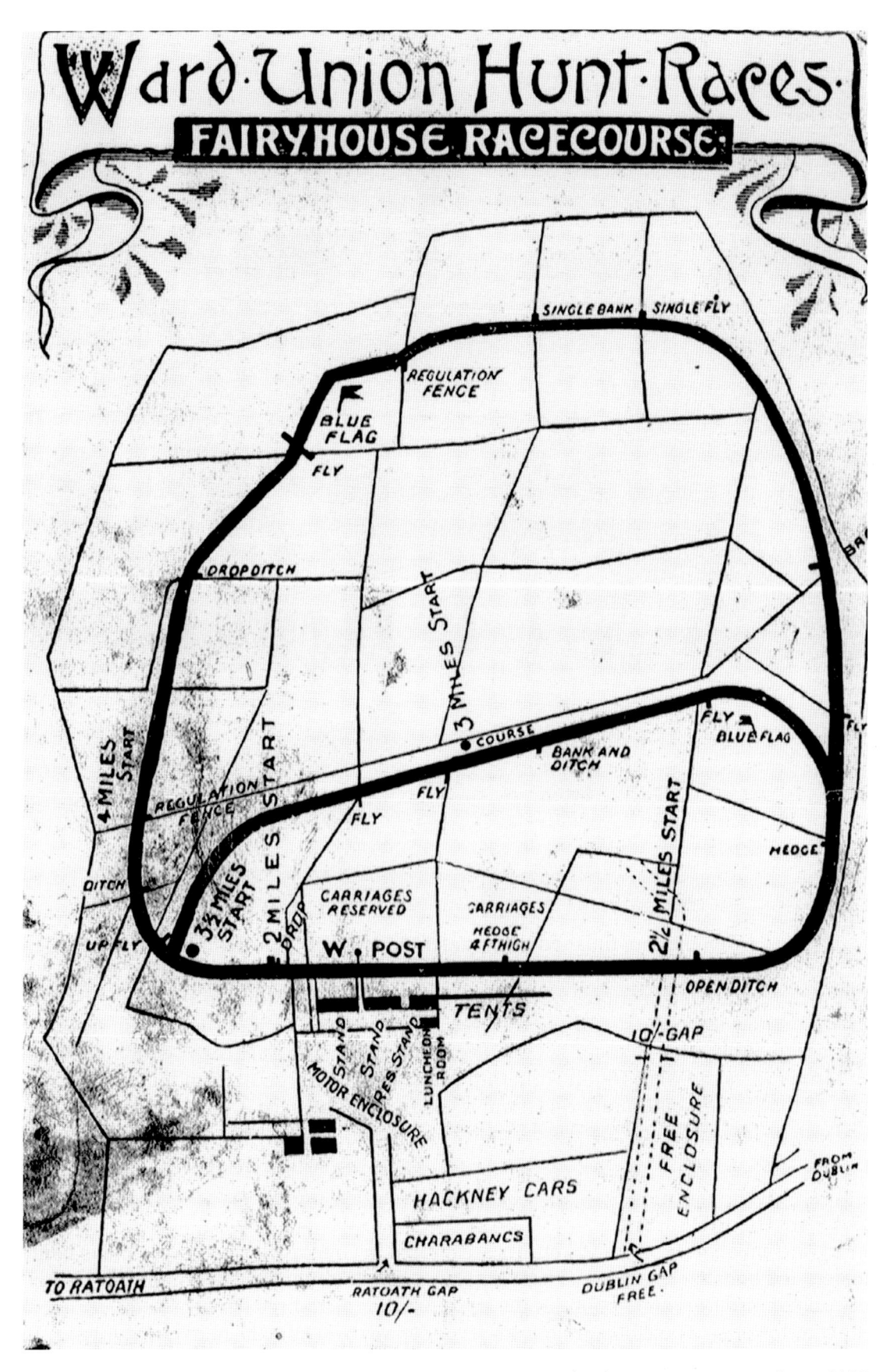

Ward Union Hunt Programme Cover, 1932

The Hunt gathering outside Rory's Pub, Ratoath, late 1990's

racehorses, when they are finished their career on the track, retire to the hunting field or to Point-to-Point/Hunterchasing. The Ward Union Hunt has a long association with Fairyhouse racecourse and members were closely involved in its foundation and have served on the committee up to the present time. Over the years, Roy Craigie, the former manager, was a Hon. Whip, Hon. Treasurer, Hon. Secretary and Chairman of the Ward Union Hunt. In former years the Ward Union Hunt Cup (the trophy is a large silver mounted stag) was part of the Easter Monday card on Grand National day. This race is held during the Point-to-Point at Tattersalls and the Ward Union Hunt trophy is very much sought after by participants.

The Ward Union Hunt Today
The Ward Union deer park and kennels are located in Greenpark since 1978, and is home to deer and hounds. The Ward Union Hunt has a long tradition of conservation and breeding of Irish Red Deer and has one of the last remaining pure-bred herds of Red Deer left in the country today; a breeding programme is under way to ensure the herd remains pure. In September, the hunting Deer and the breeding stock are separated. In November, sufficient hunting deer are separated from the herd to ensure that no deer is hunted more than

Huntsman Pat Coyle with Hon. Whip Con Kennedy and Kieran Ryan

twice in the season. A code of practise to protect the welfare of the deer has been specifically formulated by the committee and approved by the Dept. of Agriculture Food and Rural Development. All the hunting deer are tagged and records are kept of each deer hunted. When followers recapture a deer at the end of a hunt it is returned to the deer park that

Ward Union Hunt, RDS

evening. Any deer that is not recaptured is called an "outlyer" and remains in the countryside until it settles down and can be recaptured. Landowners usually report its location quite quickly. The deer is recaptured by the Huntsman using a sedative dart like that used in Zoos and Wild Life Parks for the sedation and treatment of wild animals.

The Ward Union Hunt also provides a subsidised collection service to farmers in the Hunt area for fallen animals and has one of the few licensed Knackeries in the area. The Ward Union shares the North Dublin and Meath countryside with other packs; to the east the Fingal Harriers and to a lesser extent the Louth foxhounds, and to the west the South Co. Dublin hunt. Most of the County Meath countryside is also shared with the Meath Foxhounds who actually own a fox-covert in Ratoath, at the back of Foxlodge Estate.

The Future
The mission statement embodied in the constitution of the Ward Union Hunt Club states *"The objects of the Club shall be to promote the sport of hunting on horseback and all incidental and ancillary equestrian activities and the promotion, research and development into the conservation, welfare and prosperity of Irish Red Deer and to ensure the continued unity, comradeship and social prosperity amongst Members, Subscribers and Landowners"*. The rapid urbanisation taking place in Ratoath and the surrounding area coupled with the new by-passes of Ashbourne and Ratoath have reduced the hunting country. The Hunt is continually adjusting to these changes. There are those, who predicted the end of hunting in every decade since the 1930's but I am confident that due to the popularity of the hunt with Irish people, and its secure place in the rural community, that its future is assured.

HORSES FOR COURSES

Fairyhouse – Home of the Irish Grand National

RATOATH HERITAGE GROUP

"Racing at Fairyhouse commenced in 1848. Twenty two years later, Mr. L. Dunne saw his horse, Sir Robert Peel, earn 167 sovereigns in winning the first Irish Grand National in 1870. The Irish Grand National quickly established itself as Ireland's premier steeplechase and each success had its own rich tale, none more amazing than the success in 1929 of a six-year-old mare, 'Alike', owned and ridden by 5'4" Frank Wise, who was missing three fingers and rode with a wooden leg!" **(Go Fairyhouse Racing)**

Founder of Fairyhouse Racecourse: Pictured here is Mr. Leonard Morrogh (1828-89) who was secretary of the Ward Union Hunt for 25 years and who played a crucial role in the establishment of the Fairyhouse Racecourse and the Irish Grand National.

FAIRYHOUSE as a racecourse first came into existence in the middle of the 19th century (1848) when the Ward Union Hunt Club transferred from nearby Ashbourne. 1870, was the first year of the Irish Grand National at Fairyhouse. In 1871 two new stands were opened at Fairyhouse and 1890 saw the opening of yet another new stand. Political events of the time meant that the meeting of 1919 did not take place. Again in 1941 the meeting was not held due to the outbreak of Foot and Mouth disease. The Power's Gold Label Stand was opened on 16 January 2000 by the then Minister for Agriculture, Food and Rural Development, Mr. Joe Walsh T.D. This fine stand improved yet again the facilities for those who love to go racing. In 2001, the Easter Festival was postponed until June due to an outbreak of Foot and Mouth disease.

Some Famous Horses
Arkle, Desert Orchid, Flyingbolt, Captain Christy, L'Escargot, Persian War, Monksfield, Prince Regent, Bobbyjo, Brown Lad, Tied Cottage and Rhyme 'N Reason are just some of the great horses that have graced this famous galloping track which is renowned for both flat and National Hunt racing.

Irish Grand National at Fairyhouse
Since it started in 1870. the Irish Grand National remains a limited extended handicap

Above: Arkle at Fairyhouse in the mid 1960's

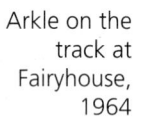

Arkle on the track at Fairyhouse, 1964

steeplechase for five-year-olds and upwards. In recent years it is a 3 miles 5 furlongs Handicap Chase over 24 fences. Recent race title prefixes were:

1970 – 1981	**Irish Distillers**
1982 – 1999	**Jameson**
2000 – 2007	**Powers Gold Label**
2008	**Powers Whiskey**

Irish Grand National Distances varied over the years as follows:

1870 – 1884	3 miles
1885 – 1891	3 miles 4 furlongs
1892 – 1909	3 miles
1910	2 miles 2 furlongs
1911 – 1918	3 miles
1920 – 1950	3 miles 4 furlongs
1951 – 1973	3 miles 2 furlongs
1974 – 1990	3 miles 4 furlongs
1991 – 2008	3 miles 5 furlongs

Irish Grand National: Winning Horses, Riders, Owners & Trainers 1870-2008

Year	Winning Horse	Winning Rider	Owner	Trainer
1870	Sir Robert Peel	John Boylan	Mr. L. Dunne	Private
1871	The Doe	John Boylan	Mr. T.Y.L. Kirkwood	Private
1872	Scots Grey	Garry Moore	Major Browne	J.H. Moore
1873	The Torrent	M. Toole	Mr. P.J. Reynolds	P.J. Reynolds
1874	Sailor	W. Ryan	Captain S. Gubbins	D. Broderick
1875	Scots Grey	Garry Moore	Major Browne	J.H. Moore
1876	Grand National	Mr. T. Beasley	Mr. Moses Taylor	H.E. Linde
1877	Thiggin True	Mr. T. Beasley	Mr. John Gubbins	H.E. Linde
1878	Juggler	Mr. John Beasley	Mr. John H. Moore	John H. Moore
1879	Jupiter Tonans	Mr. F.J. Lee-Barber	Mr. F.J. Lee-Barber	Capt. G. Joy
1880	Controller	Mr. H. Beasley	Mr. W. Brophy	H.E. Linde
1881	Antoinnette	S. Fleming	Mr. James Andrews	J. Gannon
1882	Chantilly	D. Canavan	J.H. Fanning	D. Canavan
1883	The Gift	T. Kelly	Mr. P.J. Reynolds	P.J. Reynolds
1884	The Gift	T. Kelly	Mr. P.J. Reynolds	Private
1885	Billet Doux	Mr. W. Murland	Count Zborowski	Private
1886	Castle Lucas	Mr. Atkinson	Mr. J.G. Blake	Private
1887	Eglantine	Mr. R. Brabazon	Mr. G.F. Gradwell	Private
1888	The Maroon	Mr. W. McAuliffe	Mr. J. Richards	W. McAuliffe
1889	Citadel	Mr. H. Beasley	Mr. H. Beasley	H. Beasley
1890	Greek Girl	Mr. H. Gore	Mr. H. Gore	H. Beasley
1891	Firewater	Capt J. Burn-Murdoch	Mr. Stephen Kelly	S. Kelly
1892	Springfield Maid	Mr. L. Hope	Mr. S.A. Leonard	N/a
1893	Thurles	L. Ryan	Major Bunbury	L. Ryan
1894	The Admiral	Mr. F.W. Mitchell	Mr. F.W. Mitchell	F.W. Mitchell
1895	Yellow Girl	Mr. J. Ennis	Mr. E. Rooney	Private
1896	Royston-Crow	Mr. G. M. Parsons	Mr. G.V. Briscoe	Walker

Year	Winning Horse	Winning Rider	Owner	Trainer
1897	Breemount's Pride	R. Hooper	Mr. J.O.C. Murphy	J.J. Maher
1898	Porridge	T. Collier	Mr. E. Delany	Private
1899	Princess Hilda	Mr. J. Clarke	Mr. L. Hope	L. Hope
1900	Mavis of Meath	J. Kelly	F.J. Kelly	L. Hope
1901	Tipperary Boy	Thomas Moran	Mr. T.B. Holmes	F.F. Cullen
1902	Patlander	J. Cheshire	Mr. M.J. Cleary	J. Cheshire
1903	Kirko	J. Scully	Mr. T.A. Hartigan	J. Scully
1904	Ascetic's Silver	T. Dowdall	Mr. P.J. Dunne	Sperrin
1905	Red Lad	C. Kelly	Mr. E.M. Lucas	J. Hunter
1906	Brown Bess	J. Bresname	Mr. V. Wall	N.J. Kelly
1907	Sweet Cecil	Mr. T. Price	Mr. M. Dawson	M. Dawson
1908	Lord Rivers	Mr. R. H. Walker	Mr. P. McLoughlin	P. McLoughlin
1909	Little Hack II	Mr. R. H. Walker	Mr. N. Markey	N. Markey
1910	Oniche	Mr. F. Malone	Mrs. F. McDonnell	T. Miller
1911	Repeater II	Mr. J.A. Trench	Mr. W.L. Goulding	Capt. Bacon
1912	Small Polly	Mr. R.H. Walker	Mr. R.H. Walker	G.L. Walker
1913	Little Hack II	S. Matthews	Mr. N. Markey	N. Markey
1914	Civil War	Capt. P.O'Brien Butler	Mr. L. King	L. King
1915	Punch	Mr. R.H. Walker	Mr. F. Barbour	R.H. Walker
1916	All Sorts	J. Lynn	Mr. J. Kiernan	R.G. Cleary
1917	Pay Only	Mr. W.F. Shankey	Mr. W.P. Hanly	W.P. Hanly
1918	Ballyboggan	C. Hawkins	Mr. E.W. Hope Johnstone	Fetherston
1919	———	———	———	———
1920	Halston	D. Colbert	Major H. Dixon	J. Ruttle
1921	Bohernore	D. Colbert	Mr. A. Willis	C. Brabazon
1922	Halston	J. Moloney	Major H. Dixon	J. Ruttle
1923	Be Careful	J. Moloney	Mrs. F. Blacker	Private
1924	Kilbarry	W. Horan	Lady Eva Forbes	M. Dawson
1925	Dog Fox	Joseph Doyle	Mr. J. Jackson	R. Fetherston
1926	Amberwave	Mr. J.E. O'Brien	Mr. E.A. Kirwan	W.P. Hanley
1927	Jerpoint	P. Powell	Mr. J.M. Barbour Jr.	A. Bickley (GB)
1928	Don Sancho	T.B. Cullinan	Mr. V.H. Smith	Withington (GB)
1929	Alike	Mr. F.W. Wise	Mr. F.W. Wise	Mr. F.W. Wise
1930	Fanmond	K. Lenehan	Mr. G.P. Gilpin	Mr. G.P. Gilpin
1931	Impudent Barney	Mr. F.E. McKeever	Mrs. B.M. Webster	C. A. Rogers
1932	Copper Court	T. Cullen	Mrs. B.M. Webster	R. Fetherston
1933	Red Park	D. Kirwan	Lady Helen McCalmont	J.J. Barry
1934	Poolgowran	R. Everett	Sir James Nelson	J. Ruttle
1935	Rathfriland	Timothy Regan	J.P. Markey	T.R. McKeever
1936	Alice Maythorn	M.C. Prendergast	P.J. Osbourne	J.W. Osborne
1937	Pontet	F.E. McKeever	G.V. Malcomson	C.A. Brabazon
1938	Clare County	T. Hyde	T.A. O'rman	M. Cunningham
1939	Shaun Peel	J. Wade	Nelson Dixon	C.F.P. Creed
1940	Jack Chaucer	J. Lenhan	H. L. Egan	C.A. Brabazon
1941	———	———	———	———
1942	Prince Regent	T. Hyde	J. V. Rank	T. W. Dreaper
1943	Golden Jack	D.L. Moore	Miss Dorothy Paget	C.A. Rogers
1944	Knight's Crest	M. Molony	Mrs. W. Malony	C.B. Harty
1945	Heirdom	J.P. Maguire	H. Quinn	J. Kirwan

Year	Winning Horse	Winning Rider	Owner	Trainer
1946	Golden View II	M. Molony	Mrs. L. Lillingtom	R. O'Connell
1947	Revelry	D.L. Moore	J. T. Doyle	R. O'Connell
1948	Hamstar	E.J. Kennedy	B. Hamilton	W. T. O'Grady
1949	Shagreen	E. Newman	J. V. Bank	T. W. Dreaper
1950	Dominick's Bar	M. Molony	Mrs. P. Kely	T. Hyde
1951	Icy Calm	P.J. Doyle	P. G. Grey	W.T. O'Grady
1952	Alberoni	L. Stephens	H.H.M. Stanley	M.V. O'Brien
1953	Overshadow	A. Power	Mrs. J. A. Woods	C. Magnier
1954	Royal Approach	P. Taaffe	Lord Bicester	T.W. Dreaper
1955	Umm	P. Taaffe	C. Rooney	G.H. Wells
1956	Air Prince	T. O'Brien	J. McClintock	J. McClintock
1957	Kilballyown	G.W. Robinson	Mrs. M. A. Lynch	P. Norris
1958	Gold Legend	J. Lehane	Mrs. P. J. Murphy	J. Brogan
1959	Zonda	P. Taaffe	Mrs. G. St-John Nolan	M. Geraghty
1960	Olympia	T Taaffe	Lord Donoughmore	T.W. Dreaper
1961	Fortria	P. Taaffe	George Ansley	T.W. Dreaper
1962	Kerforo	L. McLoughlin	F. J. Stafford	T.W. Dreaper
1963	Last Link	P. Woods	A. Craigie	T.W. Dreaper
1964	Arkle	P. Taaffe	Anne, Duchess of Westminster	T.W. Dreaper
1965	Splash	P. Woods	A. Craigie	T.W. Dreaper
1966	Flying Bolt	P. Taaffe	Mrs. T.G. Wilkinson	T.W. Dreaper
1967	Vulpine	M. Curran	T.W. Nicholson	P. Mullins
1968	Herring Gull	J. Crowley	Mrs. G.A. J. Wilson	P. Mullins
1969	Sweet Dreams	R. Coonan	P. Meehan	K. Bell
1970	Garoupe	C. Finnegan	Mrs. Frances Williams	F. Flood
1971	King's Sprite	A.L.T. Moore	R. McIlhagga	G. Wells
1972	Dim Wit	M. Curran	J. J. O'Neill	P. Mullins
1973	Tartan Ace	John Cullen	Mrs. Sean Graham	T. Costello
1974	Colebridge	E. Wright	Mrs. Peter E. Burrell	J. Dreaper
1975	Brown Lad	T. Carberry	Mrs. Peter E. Burrell	J. Dreaper
1976	Brown Lad	T. Carberry	Mrs. Peter E. Burrell	J. Dreaper
1977	Ballycan	M. Morris	V. Killkenny	A. Maxwell
1978	Brown Lad	G. Dowd	Mrs. Peter E. Burrell	J. Dreaper
1979	Tied Cottage	D. L. Moore, owner	D. L. Moore	D.L. Moore
1980	Daletta	J.P. Harty	Mrs. F. Watson	G. St J. Williams
1981	Luska	T.V. Finn	J. Brophy	P. Mullins
1982	King Spruce	G. Newman	R. Carrier	M. J. O'Brien
1983	Bit of a Skite	T. J. Ryan	J. P. McManus	E. J. O'Grady
1984	Bentom Boy	Mrs. A. Ferris	T. Dorrien	W.E. Rooney
1985	Rhyme 'N Reason	G. Bradley	Mrs. J. E. Reid	D.J.G. Murray-Smith(GB)
1986	Insure	M. Flynn	P. Hughes	P. Hughes
1987	Brittany Boy	T. J. Taaffe	J. C. Glynn	K.C. Hitchmough
1988	Perris Valley	B. Sheridan	M.W.J. Smurfit	D. K. Weld
1989	Maid of Money	A. Powell	Mrs. H. A. McCormack	J. R. H. Fowler
1990	Desert Orchid	R. Dunwoody	R. Burridge	D.R.C. Elseworth (GB)
1991	Omerta	Mr. A. Maguire	Mrs. E.C. McMorrow	M.C. Pipe (GB)

Year	Winning Horse	Winning Rider	Owner	Trainer
1992	Vanton	J. Titley	Noel McCabe	M. J. P. O'Brien
1993	Ebony Jane	C. F. Swan	James Lynch	F. Flood
1994	Son of War	F. Woods	Mrs. Vera O'Brien	Peter McCreery
1995	Flashing Steel	J. Osborne	C.J. Haughey	J.E. Mulhern
1996	Feathered Gale	C. O'Dwyer	M.D. O'Connor/E.P.King	A L T Moore
1997	Mudahim	J. F. Titley	In Touch Racing Club	Mrs Jenny Pitman
1998	Bobbyjo	P. Carberry	Robert Burke	T. Carberry
1999	Glebe Lad	T. P. Rudd	T.B. Conroy	M. J. P. O'Brien
2000	Commanche Court	R.. Walsh	D.F. Desmond	T. M. Walsh
2001	David's Lad	T. J. Murphy	Eddie Joe's Racing Syndicate	A. J. Martin
2002	The Bunny Boiler	R. Geraghty	Usual Suspects Syndicate	Noel Meade
2003	Timbera	J. Culloty	Mrs. J. M. Breen	D. T. Hughes
2004	Granite D'Estruval	B. P. Harding	W. J. Gott	F. Murphy (in GB)
2005	Numbersixvalverde	Ruby Walsh	O.B.P. Carroll	M. Brassil
2006	Point Barrow	Philip Carberry	Mrs. P. Clune Hughes/ Mrs. Michael O'Dwyer	P. Hughes
2007	Butler's Cabin	A.P. McCoy	J.P. McManus	Jonjo O'Neill (in GB)
2008	Hear the Echo	Paddy Flood	Michael O'Leary of Gigginstown House Stud	Michael 'Mouse' Morris

Planning for the Grand National Festival

For any event to be successful a lot of detailed planning is required to cater for all eventualities and so it is at Fairyhouse Racecourse. The **Four-day Easter Festival** at Fairyhouse is a major National event each year. Every effort is made to keep the track in excellent condition for the meeting. The spacious racecourse is managed so that fresh ground is provided on all four days of the Festival on the hurdles course. The chase fences are repositioned to the usual Easter chase course and fresh ground is provided on the Irish Grand National day.

What might the prize be for the winners on the day?

In 2002, the meeting opened on Sunday, 31 March. The feature race, the €170,000 Powers Irish Grand National, took place, as usual, the following day, Easter Monday, 1 April.

In 2006 the Irish Grand National Steeplechase was run over 3 miles and 5 furlongs (5,800 meters). The value of the race was €250,000. The race was a limited extended handicap steeplechase for five-year-olds and upwards. An Taoiseach Mr. Bertie Aherne, T.D. and Mr. Paul Duffy, CEO Irish Distillers, presented trophies to the winning owners (Mrs. P. Clune and Mrs. Michael O'Dwyer). The winning trainer, P. Hughes, was presented with the Tom Dreaper Perpetual Trophy and a cut glass memento.

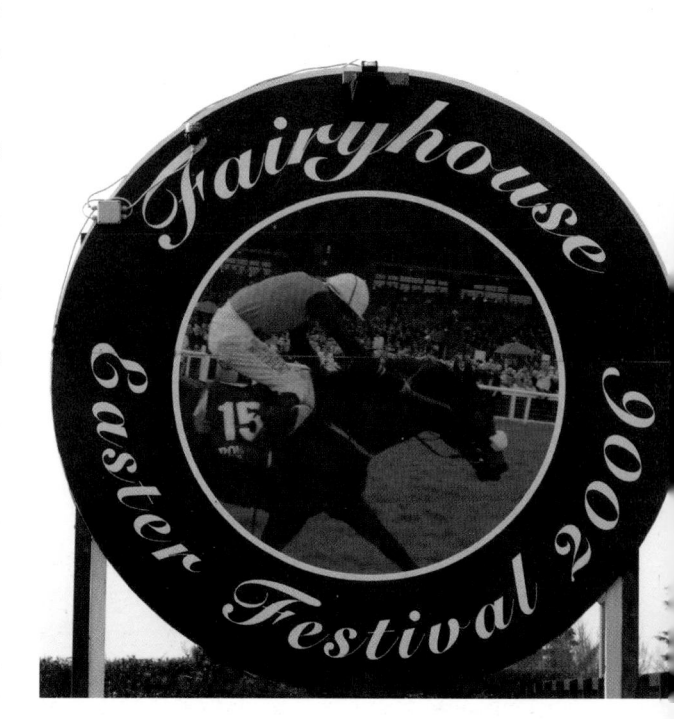

The winning rider, Philip Carberry, received the Eric McKeever Perpetual Memorial Trophy and a replica. The groom in charge of *Point Barrow*, the winning horse, received a cash prize.

Fairyhouse – Annual Prizes
At Fairyhouse in 1850 the Grand Military Stakes was held over a 3 mile Cross Country. Its value was £155 and the winner was *Shinrone*. In 1859 the Kilrue Cup was a 3 mile Chase valued at £150 and that year it was won by *Thomastown*.

The value of the Grand National Annual Prize changed over the years, increasing or decreasing according to the economics of the times. The changes are outlined below:

Year	Value	Year	Value	Year	Value
1870	£167	1920 - 1923	£640	1972	£9,162
1871	£250	1924	£690	1973	£9,305
1872	£255	1925 - 1926	£840	1974	£8,916
1873	£355	1927 - 1928	£870	1975	£8,643
1874	£507	1929 - 1931	£777	1976	£10,821
1875	£337	1932 - 1940	£740	1977	£15,954
1876	£272	**1941**	No race	1978	£15,544
1877	£320	1942 - 1943	£745	1979	£20,040
1878	£570	1944 - 1945	£740	**1980**	£20,938
1879	£320	1946	£745	1981	£24,185
1880	£290	1947	£1,115	1982	£29,928
1881	£280	1948	£1,467	1983	£28,462
1882	£307	1949	£1,485	1984	£28,578
1883	£287	**1950**	£1,455	1985	£27,522
1884 - 1897	£245	1951 - 1956	£1,485	1986	£34,320
1898	£242	1957	£2,043	1987	£62,700
1899	£245	1958	£2,017	1988 - **1994**	£55,200
		1959	£1,878	1995 - 1997	£62,700
1900 - 1901	£166	**1960**	£2,256	1998 - 2000	£78,350
1902	£165	1961	£2,301	2001	£81,500
1903 - 1904	£164	1962	£2,245	2002	€170,000
1905	£160	1963	£2,870	2003	€170,000
1906 - 1908	£164	1964	£2,630	2004	€180,000
1909 - 1910	£167	1965	£4,237	2005	€250,000
1911 - 1912	£245	1966	£4,470	2006	€250,000
1913	£167	1967	£4,537	2007	€250,000
1914	£245	1968	£4,758	2008	€250,000
1915	£167	1969	£5,047	2009	
1916 - 1918	£197	**1970**	£9,685	2010	
1919	No race	1971	£9,917	2011	

Go Racing at Fairyhouse!
Today, with the most modern stands in Ireland, completed in 1989, 1996 and 2000, and every up-to-date facility, Fairyhouse, members of the Association of Irish Racecourses, still retains the magic and romance of its history. It reflects the informality and friendliness, which makes Irish racing such an enjoyable day out. Just twelve miles to the north-west of Dublin beside the International Tattersall's Bloodstock Sales Centre, it is an easy location

Powers Gold Label Irish Grand National at *Fairyhouse* Easter Monday

(Right): Margaret Mannering and Patsy Mannering studying the form at the Easter Charity Race, 2001

to get to for racing. Of course if you live in Ratoath you just walk to the races especially for the bigger meetings as they did in 1848 and all the years since! No need to bring the car, someone will give you a lift home! Traditionally for the Ratoath people the Easter Racing Festival is an enjoyable event where one can study the form and enjoy a few hours each day catching up with family and friends.

Fairyhouse is within twenty minutes of Dublin Airport and within half an hour's drive from the ferry port so it is convenient for those who visit from overseas with or without horses. When upgrading the facilities at Fairyhouse Racecourse in 2000 one of the rooms was named the '*BobbyJo Room*'. Fairyhouse has acres of outdoor space and like most racecourses today, in order to earn additional revenue to help pay for the latest developments, it plays host to a variety of activities outside the racing calendar e.g. auctions, Sunday Markets, product launches, concerts (most notably Witness), conferences, seminars, team-building events, wedding receptions, parties, summer BBQ's, trade fairs, craft and antique fairs and location shoots.

"Witnness" Music Festival at Fairyhouse
During the August bank holiday weekend in 2000, Fairyhouse Racecourse hosted the first of the "Witness" Music festivals. Following local representations and local residents' expressions of concern, the two-day event was well managed and was held without any trouble to the delight of the enthusiastic locals, some of whom were fortunate enough to receive free passes to the entire event.

In 2001, building of the success of the first year, up to 35,000 people went to Fairyhouse racecourse for the two-day music festival. The event featured over 60 acts on five stages around the grounds. It was a fun weekend that was enjoyed by all.

To accommodate such a major music festival, Fairyhouse was converted into an entertainment arena and a campsite, complete with weather shelters, a fun park and bars. The organisers offered free handouts to the first 500 campers to arrive each day. Topping the bill on the first day were Faithless, Stereophonics, Charlatans, Muse, The Waterboys, The Frames, Tindersticks, Embrace, Evan Dando and Eagle Eye Cherry. The second day featured acts such as Ash, Texas, Fun Lovin' Criminals, Placebo, James, Feeder and Relish playing on the main stage. Super Furry Animals and David Kitt topped the bill on the

"Witnness Rising" stage, Stereo MCs were the main attraction at the "Witnness Dance" venue and Paul Weller, Teenage Fanclub and The Saw Doctors all played in the large "Witnness More" tent.

The festival was promoted by MCD and a spokesman described the festival as the "*biggest musical event in Ireland in 2001 in terms of acts. There were no other multi-stage, multiday outdoor events like it in Ireland.*" Day tickets for the festival cost £36.50. Weekend tickets cost £64 (£79 with camping). Dublin Bus operated a shuttle service between O'Connell Street, Dublin, and Fairyhouse for the event. Some 150 buses ran each day, departing from O'Connell Street every 20 minutes from 11:30 a.m. The return buses from Fairyhouse began to depart at 10.30 p.m.

The Witnness event was also held in mid July 2002, based on the successful formula of the two previous years.

Ever Adaptable to Local Needs
While waiting for a new building, Ratoath Community College found a temporary home at Fairyhouse Racecourse for its new students (2005-2007) with the agreement of the Department of Education and Science, Co. Meath Vocational Education Committee and the Management of Fairyhouse Racecourse and under the guidance of its new principal, Máire Ní Bhroithe. It was quite a challenge to make a racing environment suitable for educational purposes. Students travelled to this most unusual school from all directions. This was a wonderful temporary location for a school, out in the open countryside, with no distractions and lots of fresh air!

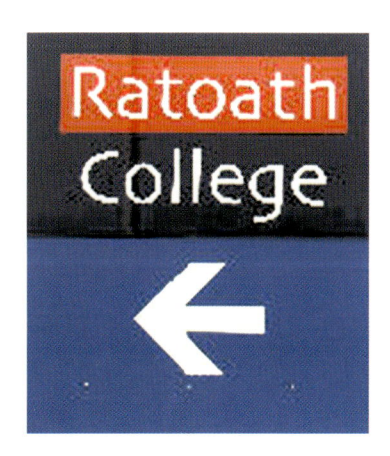

REFERENCES:
Jameson Irish Grand National. A history of Ireland's premier steeplechase. Authors: Guy St. John Williams and Francis P.M. Hyland. Published by The Organisation, Dublin 1995. ISBN: 0 9526902 0 9
The Sweeney Guide to the Irish Turf 1501-2001. pp 523-529. Authors: Tony & Annie Sweeney in association with Francis Hyland. Published by Edmund Burke, Blackrock, Co. Dublin. 2002. ISBN: O 946130 37 X

HORSES FOR COURSES

Jockeys
Native to Ratoath

JOE MANNERING

John Mannering
Born in the Paddock, Ratoath in 1944, John started to work for D.L. Moore, Fairyhouse at the age of thirteen and a half as a stable lad. He became a jockey when he was 16 and he went on to ride numerous winners for D.L. Moore. Later he worked in Limerick for P.P. Hogan where he rode a couple of winners. From there John went to England to ride in Tom Yeats' stables. After four months he had a terrible fall from a horse named *Manor House* and was unconscious for five days. That finished his horse riding career and he went to Canada to begin a new life.

Paddy Woods
Paddy Woods, Fairyhouse Road, initially worked for D.L. Moore with whom he stayed for approximately ten years. He then went to work for T. W. Dreaper where he rode many winners. The high points of his career involved riding two Irish Grand National winners, one in 1963 with *Last Link* and the other in 1965 with *Splash*; both horses were owned by A. Craigie. Paddy set up his own training yard at Greenogue with his wife Phyllis and has trained many winners over the years.

Liam (Jock) McLoughlin
Liam (Jock) McLoughlin, Crushen Road, worked with T. W. Dreaper stables, where he rode many winners. He was the first jockey to win a rate on the mighty **Arkle** at 20/1 in a race at Navan. Liam rode a winner at the Cheltenham Festival meeting and also rode in the English Grand National. Riding a horse called *Kerforo*, Liam won four principal races in one season (1962-1963), namely the D.L. Moore Chase at Thurles, the Thyestes Chase at Gowran Park, the Leopardstown Chase and the Irish Grand National at Fairyhouse.

Mick Ennis
Mick Ennis, Rathbeggan, Ratoath also worked for D. L. Moore as a stable lad for a number of years and as a jockey. He later worked for Ms. Jane Moore in County Kildare.

Martin O'Connor
Martin O'Connor from Ballybin Road, Ratoath, was a freelance rider. He worked for A. O'Connor, Luke Comer and other stables. Martin rode as an amateur rider.

Peter McLoughlin

Peter McLoughlin was associated with the Dreaper yard in Greenogue for 21 years. Some of the many races Peter won include the Leopardstown Chase (1966, 1967, 1968 on *Fort Leney*), the Troytown Chase, Navan (1966 on *Fort Leney*) and the Guinness Chase, Punchestown. Other horses that he rode include *Proud Tarquin* and *Lean Forward* on which he won fifteen races. Most of the winners were for the late Sir John Thompson in his famous white and orange colours. The first winner he rode over fences was a horse called *Foinavon*. A couple of years later (1967), *Foinavon* won the English Grand National at a price of 100/1. This was the year that the big pile-up happened at the fence after Beechers' Brook. Peter always enjoyed the thrill of the National Hunt Game!

Paul Carberry
Paul Carberry was born in Ballybin, Ratoath. Paul comes from a family that has always been involved with horses. He is a grandson of Jane and D.L. Moore former owners of Old Fairyhouse that is now the site of the Tattersalls Sales Complex. Paul is known as a great horseman whether it is flat racing, hurdles or chase. For instance, in 1993, he had a total of 54 Apprentice Wins and Titles. To date he has won two Grand Nationals. First he rode **Bobbyjo** to win the Irish Grand National on Easter Monday 1998. He won the English Grand National on 10th April 1999 on the same horse, *Bobbyjo*. The next day, Sunday, a huge welcome home party was held in the centre of Ratoath village near the then Rory's Pub (now rebuilt as the Auld Stand).

Sunday 11th April 1999: Delighted Ratoath fans welcome home Tommy Carberry (Trainer), Paul Carberry (Jockey) and Bobbyjo winner of the English Grand National at Aintree.

Philip Carberry
Philip Carberry is Paul Carberry's brother. Philip started his riding career as an amateur and he is now a successful professional jockey. Philip has ridden many winners for his father Tommy and other trainers.

Nina Carberry
Nina Carberry is a sister of Paul and Philip Carberry. In March 2005 at the Cheltenham Festival in England she followed in the footsteps of her father Tommy and brother Paul when she rode her first Cheltenham Festival winner on 20/1 outsider *Dabiroun* in the Fred Winter Juvenile Novices' Hurdle. Thus, she became the first woman in 18 years to win against the professional jockeys at the fiercely competitive festival.

HORSES FOR COURSES

My Time with D.L. Moore at Old Fairyhouse

PADDY WOODS

From the time I went to school, I wanted to work for D.L. Moore with horses, but my mother thought horses were dangerous. However, later on Dick O'Connell got me a job at Old Fairyhouse with D.L. Moore. He was a great trainer, worked his horses hard and had impressive winners including Free Brother. Mrs. Moore (Joanie) was a great help to him and she was most generous to the staff. On the day you had to drive to The Hunt, she would make a lovely tea before you left and the same was waiting for you on your return. The Moore's were very fond of hunting with the Ward Union Hunt. During Fairyhouse Races they entertained all their many friends and indeed gatecrashers. The Moore's had two children Arthur and Pamela.

D.L. worked his horses inside Fairyhouse Racecourse and on his own land. His schooling grounds were located on the lands now owned by Tattersalls. This was the only place *Arkle* fell over a small hurdle and in doing so broke Pat Taaffe's arm. D.L. Moore **designed great jumps** for his horses and it is considered that this training ground was a contributing factor to his racing successes in Ireland and England. Great jockeys worked for D.L. Moore; including Martin Moloney, T.P. Burns, G. Wells, his best friend R.J. Doyle, Tom Carberry and Mick Brown. **Jimmy Fitzgerald was another lad who worked for him but he**

House and schooling grounds at Fairyhouse formerly owned by D.L. Moore. The House and lands are now owned and managed by Tattersalls Ireland Ltd.

did not ride. Jimmy Fitzgerald went on to become a very successful trainer in England and he trained *Forgive and Forget* which won the Cheltenham Gold Cup with jockey Mark Dwyer.

Vets to the stables were Harry O'Leary, Maxie Cosgrove, and Jim Kavanagh. Some of the best horses associated with D.L. Moore included *Saddler's Well*, *Wild Delight*, *Royal Bridge*, *Miss Steel*, *In View*, and, in latter years, *L'Escargot*. Some of the men who worked for him in my time at Old Fairyhouse were Dick O'Connell, Joe Cannon, Dinnie Farrell, Tommy Kelly, Tony Everard, Bill Mannering, Andy Hessman, Burke Smyth and Tom Gannon. Christy Foley was the blacksmith. Girls who worked in the house were Molly Nulty, Agnes Nolan, Mrs. Walls, Nellie Rooney and Nellie Sheehy. They were all great to work with; two of his first workers were Dessie Donnelly and Harry Ellis.

Funny things that took place at Old Fairyhouse
D.L. Moore had an aeroplane. One day it broke down in the front field. He got spanners in the yard, fixed it and flew to Weston Aerodrome. He would let nothing best him. A horse developed a big wart on its leg, so Dick sent me to the kitchen for a knife to cut it off, but when Molly Nulty heard what he had used the knife for she never spoke to D.L. for a month. An old tramp used to call to Old Fairyhouse. Dick said to him, "*there is a field of spuds to be picked if you want work*", but the tramp asked him "*are they boiled?*" Not much work was going to be done by the tramp! Paul Flynn was getting a ride out one day and the lads met him on the road with the saddle on backwards. Dermot Darby went to Ratoath for cigarettes for Dick. He tied the horse's reins to the knob of Naughton's door. The horse pulled back, shut the door and the key could not be got out, so Dermot had to come home with the knob of the door on the end of the reins and no cigarettes! Life was not dull in Ratoath or at Old Fairyhouse! One evening D.L. sacked one of the lads for not doing the tack, so we thought it was not fair and walked out. Some of the lads returned but as Charlie Reilly got me a job in Dreaper's Stables I decided to move from Old Fairyhouse, but always remained friendly with D.L. Moore.

Two of the most memorable wins I had in Dreaper's yard were The Irish Grand National in 1963 on *Last Link* and again in 1965 on *Splash*. Today I live in Greenogue with my wife Phyllis and I work as a representative for Glanbia selling Gain Horse Feeds.

LAST LINK - Winning the Irish Grand National at Fairyhouse, April 1963 (Rider: P. Woods)

(Above): SPLASH – Winning the Irish Grand National at Fairyhouse, April 1965 (Rider: P. Woods)

1947: D.L. Moore riding 'Reverly', the winner of the Irish Grand National at Fairyhouse in 1947

Early Horse Transport on Aer Lingus Aircraft

1953: The first Irish horses that were transported from Ireland by Aer Lingus, on the Bristol 170 Wayfarer 31, were from the Old Fairyhouse Stud which was then owned by Dan L. Moore.
This picture was taken at Dublin Airport beside the Bristol 170 Wayfarer 31 aircraft that took the four horses to the UK three days ahead of a race meeting at Cheltenham.

Pictured leading the horses were L-R: Joe Cannon, Tommy Kelly, Dick O'Connell & Jimmy Fitzgerald. Note the Bristol 170 Wayfarer 31 aircraft in the background had a specially customised horse loading ramp fitted to its front loading cargo bay.

According to Eamon Power, in an interview with Beryl Donnelly in October 2008, Aer Lingus took delivery of a leased Bristol 170 Wayfarer 31 aircraft on 18th March 1952. This first cargo aircraft was used for crew training and service introduction. Later in June and July 1952 two aircraft were delivered ready for operational use, one was a Vickers Viscount 700 and the other was the Bristol 170 Wayfarer 31 which was a versatile aircraft that could be configured to carry multiple types of cargo. Aer Lingus soon expanded into new markets such as the carriage of small vehicles and race horses. With effect from 01 July 1952, these new aircraft were used on freighter and passenger services between Dublin and London, Manchester, Liverpool and Birmingham.

In 1953, the first Irish race horses, pictured below, from Dan L. Moore's stables, were transported on a freight flight from Dublin to Birmingham, departing Dublin at 15:00 and arriving at Elmdon Aerodrome, which is now Birmingham International Airport, at 16:25

1953: Pictured calming two of the horses on board the Aer Lingus Bristol 170 Wayfarer 31 at Dublin Airport were, L-R: Dinnie Farrell & Joe Cannon.
They were pictured standing in one of the two customised horse stalls that were fitted to the Bristol 170 Mark 31 aircraft.

p.m. From there the horses were transported by road to Cheltenham Racecourse, arriving there three days ahead of their scheduled races.

From January 1953, Aer Lingus operated a full fleet of four aircraft. However, at the end of the summer 1954 season, when Viscount aircrafts were integrated into all Aer Lingus services, it was decided to dispose of the Wayfarer aircrafts which had carried 119 horses on scheduled all-cargo services between Dublin and UK destinations.

HORSES FOR COURSES

Through The Years with Tommy Carberry

PAMELA CARBERRY

It was in 1956 that Tommy arrived from Garristown to work for Dan Moore at Old Fairyhouse, (now Tattersalls). At that time he stayed with his aunt Esther (Brindley) at Mullinam (between Kilbride and Fairyhouse), and he cycled from there to Fairyhouse. He had started off working with ponies but Dan Moore thought he would be better suited to a Flat trainer on the Curragh. Dan introduced him to his friend Jimmy Lenehan. So Tommy was on the move again!

It was arranged that Tommy was only on loan to Jimmy Lenehan and that Dan Moore wanted him back. While there, he had a great start to his career by winning the apprenticeship on his first year riding and he went on again to win another apprenticeship title in his second year. Then with Tommy's weight increasing Jimmy Lenehan sent him back to Dan Moore to further his career over jumps.

Sean T. O'Kelly greets a young Tommy Carberry at Phoenix Park Racecourse

Tommy's first winner over jumps was in 1962, when he won on *Tripacer* in a hurdle race, his first ride at Cheltenham. That success at Cheltenham was his first of 15 winners at the Festival over the years. His victories included four Gold Cups with L'*Escargot* twice, *Ten Up* & *Tied Cottage*. (*Tied Cottage* was disqualified because of prohibited feedstuff).

Tommy's best year was in 1975 when he won the Gold Cup on *Ten Up*, The Irish Grand National on *Brown Lad*, & The Aintree Grand National on L'*Escargot*.

Another highlight was winning the Jump Jockey Title in 1966. This was followed by another four years as champion later on in his career.

In 1970 he married Pamela Moore (Dan & Joan Moore's daughter) and they had six children:- Thomas (now with Robbie Osborne, Trainer). Paul who started off riding ponies at home with the Ward Pony Club and hunting whenever he could. Paul used to go everywhere on his ponies to visit his friends at the weekend. He didn't get a bike until later. When Paul was 16 he had his first ride in a Point-to-Point race in February 1990 at Glencairn, where he won on *Joseph Knibb* owned by Mrs J McGowan. Then in May of that year he went to Mr Jim Bolger to serve his apprenticeship. He stayed there for two years then went to Noel Meade. It was the following year that he got a ride at Cheltenham for Homer Scott and won the Bumper on *Rhythm Section* beating Noel Meade's horse *Heist*, which was the favourite for the race. He was champion apprentice and continued to ride successfully for Noel Meade when he got the offer to ride for Mr Robert Ogden in 1996 and for whom he rode in England for three years.

Nowadays when people talk about the Carberry's they normally have Bobbyjo on their mind. Bobbyjo was owned by Robert Burke who has had horses with Tommy since he started training. That wonderful horse has had a great affect on Tommy, Paul and the rest of the family. He first came to be a household name when he won the Jameson Grand National at Fairyhouse, his local track. After winning the Aintree Martell Grand National (the 10-1 winner was trained by Paul's father Tommy who rode the last Irish winner, L'*Escargot* in 1975). Father and son received many awards including the Texaco award for racing, an award from Jury's Hotel Group, Star Award, Biscuit/Independent award, Meath Weekender award, National Hunt distinction award and Goff's personality award.

Paul Carberry winning the Aintree Grand National on Bobbyjo, 1999, the first Irish winner of the race in 24 years

Nina & Philip Carberry celebrate their success at the end of the Irish Grand National at Fairyhouse, April 2006

Just to mention in case people think there are only two Carberrys, there are more of us! Mark is a carpenter and has been to America and Australia for a number of years. Then there is Philip who became a jockey after school, and in 2000 won the claiming jockeys National Hunt title and also represented Ireland as a member of the jockey team in Australia. He won a race on Grand National day in Aintree in 2000 on *Sharpeten* for Pat Hughes. Peter likes to play soccer and is also keen on the riding. Peter won Horse and Pony Racing Championship 2004. His passion is off-road biking.

Nina is an all round athlete, - winning gold medals for long jump and running in the Leinster competitions, she was also chosen for the All Ireland Basketball team. However, Nina was involved in pony racing, and the two sports clashed, and the pony racing was her first choice. In 2000 Nina won the Senior Horse and Pony Jockey title, the Ladies Champion Rider Title 2005 followed by Overall Champion Rider title in 2006. She also won at Cheltenham in 2005 and on *La Touche* in Punchestown in 2006. Philip won the Irish Grand National on *Point Barrow* at Fairyhouse in April 2006. In the same year he also won the French Prix La Haye Jousselin (referred to as the Grand Steeplechase) with *Princess D'Anjou*, trained by Francois-Marie Cottin and owned by Jean-Paul Sénéchal.

Philip Carberry winning on Point Barrow at Fairyhouse in 2006

Tommy, Paul and Bobbyjo
An Irish Fairytale

(i)
Come and listen to my story of how a race was won
It's all about two jockeys, a father and a son
The great Tommy Carberry - Aintree, L 'Escargot
Twenty-four years later, Paul on Bobbyjo.

Chorus:
Come on Bobbyjo, Go on Bobbyjo
The rest are under pressure, Oh they're looking very slow
History's in the making with just a fence to go
Ireland wins the national- Tommy, Paul and Bobbyjo.

When Paul was a baby sitting on Pamela's knee
His Dad was sitting on L 'Escargot, winning at Aintree
Red Rum was only second to a horse they called "The Snail"
This is the first half of an Irish Fairytale.
Chorus

(iii)
It started off at Fairyhouse - the national was the race
Bobbyjo jumped like a buck, Ruby took second place
At the stables down in Ratoath, Tommy said to Paul
"Next year we'll win at Aintree, Bobbyjo will beat them all."
Chorus

(iv)
Bobbyjo looked a picture, the going was just right
Tommy prayed it wouldn't rain - he was on his knees all night
The sun was shining brightly as they reached the starting gate
Said young Paul to Bobbyjo "We won't have long to wait."
Chorus

(v)
Double Thriller was the danger, very soon his bubble burst
The field was down to thirty-one when he fell at the first
It's over now to Tony O' Hehir as they cross the Melling Road
"Bobbyjo is only cruising! He's going to explode!"
Chorus

(vi)
Dunwoody is sitting pretty, so is Adrian Maguire
Blue Charm is on the bridle, ridden by Lorcan Wyer
Racing to the final fence, on the outside Paul says, "Go!"
Coming past the elbow, in front is Bobbyjo.
Chorus

(vii)
Bobbyjo is ten lengths clear, the Irish have a ball
Paul is hanging from the rafters - I hope he doesn't fall
In Ratoath they're celebrating - the bookie has no dough
All because of Tommy Carberry, Paul and Bobbyjo.
Chorus

(viii)
"And Bobbyjo wins the 1999 Aintree Grand National
Ridden by Paul Carberry and trained by his father - Tommy Carberry"
Go on Bobbyjo, Come on Bobbyjo
Easy Bobbyjo, Whoa Bobbyjo!

Ratoath Past and Present

(*Above*): Tommy Carberry on 'Bobbyjo' Receiving a warm "Welcome Home" from fans at the centre of Ratoath in 1999. After winning the Aintree Grand National

Tommy Carberry, George Wells, 'Bobbyjo' and Philip Carberry At the "Welcome Home" Celebrations at the centre of Ratoath in 1999

HORSES FOR COURSES

The Legend of Pat Rogers of Ratoath

RUTH ROGERS

At certain times during the year we think about all those who have been called to their eternal rest. Little did I know, when pondering at my family graveside in Ratoath cemetery on Christmas Eve 2006, looking across at the famous old cobbled yard which is now Donnelly's, that I would be privileged to meet Brendan Lynch and Daragh O Neill. Together we recalled so many memories of my family, especially my grandfather. It seemed like yesterday. We talked and recalled over 50 years of Rogers' horses that started their careers in Ratoath.

Looking towards the old Rectory where Archie Cooke and Tom McKeever had lived, I walked to Mick Flood's grave and reflected how he, and his wife Peggy, played such a big part in the success of so many horses owned and trained by my family. To this day many names spring to mind when I drive through Ratoath, above all Pat Rogers, my father George, uncles Charlie and Frank, Johnny Connor, D.L. Moore, Peter and Liam McLoughlin, Johnny Walls, a son of Paddy who worked for my uncle Frank at Glascairn, P.P. Hogan, blacksmith Christy Foley, Albert Power, George Wells, Molly Talty, Doran's of Glascairn, the Mannering family, Peter Riordan and above all Brendan Lynch.

In their own right each was a master of their craft. All were synonymous with great horses and awe-inspiring tradition. It is a huge honour to be asked to remember Pat Rogers in this book.

Pat Rogers of Ratoath 1866 - 1934
Pat had a brother John and a sister Annie; they were born at Piercetown, Dunboyne. It is believed that he came to live in the yard at Ratoath in the late 1800's with his bride Margaret Maher who had lived at Clounstown outside Dunhaughlin. Margaret's brother Joe and his wife Winnie lived at Vesington (midway between Batterstown and Black Bush) but their daughter Marjorie married into the Nugent family and resided at the old home. Their son Jimmy Maher kept up the family tradition as he worked for several years at the Irish National Stud.

Pat & Margaret moved to Park House later which became their family home. Early photographs suggest that they bought the house around 1890 and there they raised seven children: Gladys; Frank (died 1956); Violet; Hilda (died 1978); Charlie (died 1971); Willy (died 1919); Jimmy (died 1914) and my father George (died 1981). Pat died in 1934 after suffering from Parkinson's disease. His headstone can be found beside the gate of the old graveyard in Ratoath. Margaret died in 1958 and she is buried in the new section, and also Charlie's wife Josephine who died in approximately 1974.

Margaret had a pony and trap as transport. This was used for shopping, going to daily

Mass, and taking grandfather to the train station at Drumree when he travelled to buy horses down the country and also to collect the new arrivals.

One of my best childhood memories of Ratoath is when my grandmother visited Borranstown, Ashbourne, driving a brown pony called *Barney* that she bought from Edward Carey on the Fairyhouse Road. I was allowed to take the reins on the return journey and I borrowed Aunt Hilda's "High Nellie bicycle" to get home again. In those times this bike was the equivalent of the B.M.W. car of today; it even had a sheepskin saddle cover for extra comfort.

Pat Rogers did not believe in education, all his sons were put to work as soon as they were able to handle a horse. His policy that hard work kept everybody happy and out of trouble was accepted and fulfilled by his children. On reaching their teens they broke, schooled and hunted the horses from the yard at Ratoath. It was said that a Rogers hunted five days a week and hacked many miles to the meet and home again after a long day. Throughout his life Pat believed in perfection, presentation and above all, attention to detail. He had an understanding and passion for the horse itself that all his sons inherited. Willie died at the age of 23, his younger brother Jimmy aged 18 looked set to become a top jockey but sadly he was killed riding at Leopardstown on St. Stephens's Day in 1914. Both sons are laid to rest with Pat, and also his grandson the late Pat Moorhead.

Pat established the yard at Ratoath where he bought and sold horses dealing in "hunters, racehorses and troopers". Pat was always mounted on a typical Irish hunter; he rode mainly with the Ward Union Staghounds. He held a firm belief that all his young chasers should be educated over several days with the Meath Foxhounds. He had a passion for breeding and retaining good bloodlines; in his time he established several thoroughbred stud farms.

My grandfather believed with great enthusiasm and foresight, that to retain tradition we must also retain the native breed of the Irish hunter and never to mix foreign bloodlines into their genes. If it were felt that improvement to the typical Irish hunter was necessary he favoured the introduction of high quality thoroughbred blood crossed with pure Irish Draught as he was always conscious of temperament, especially if the offspring was required as a small hunter. The arrival of Arab polo ponies into Co. Meath did at times introduce quality within the smaller horses. In those days ponies and smaller horses were dual purpose; many were used in traps and were what we call today, cob horses.

Grandfather had a principle that he staunchly believed in, that of never refusing profit in a horse, he sold many in his day. He supplied many of the troopers to the British army, and high quality hunters to the blue-blooded wives of the gentlemen in the army who had a passion for hunting and more importantly a good horse. However, as most people know a good horse has to be made into a good mount; most clients wanted a hunter perfectly trained to a side-saddle. My father George was the one who had the job of training hunting horses to side-saddle in preparation for their new owners.

Pat Rogers was years ahead of his time; the people of Ratoath appreciated his vision and expertise. He was an outstanding judge of horseflesh. Over the years he purchased an acre or two of land when he sold an animal for profit. It is said that he bought pasture for as little as £10 an acre. Over the decades he accumulated a considerable parcel of land of approximately 2,000 acres around Ratoath, Big Lagore, Cheverstown, Tankardstown, the Paddocks and Balfestown. He provided huge employment in the area and left behind him, a legend that he passed on to his sons, all of whom were superb judges of horses. All the tack including saddles used in the Rogers yards were made in Kilrue by a Mr. Mulligan. Pat always maintained that there were only two saddlers in the world, Mulligan of Kilrue and Whippy of London.

Pat bought a farm at The Paddocks for his son Frank, who founded Glascarn Stud, the home of many famous stallions including *Knight of the Garter*, *Jamacia Inn* and *Mustang*. Up until his death Frank was a steward at Fairyhouse.

There was an additional yard at Tankardstown for the broodmares but Pat also bought most of the land on the road towards Kilbride including Balfestown, later the home and famous training yard of C.A. Rogers. A farm and house at Borranstown, Ashbourne, was purchased in 1913, when my father, George, married Eileen Woodbyrne who was born at St. Enda's in Rathfarnham. They commenced life together there, the house and farm was held in trust by Pat's wife Margaret who on her death, willed it to my brother, Pat's grandson the late Patrick Rogers. Part of **Borranstown** was later purchased in the nineteen-seventies by George and was my home where I was born, and where my father trained racehorses and greyhounds up to his death on Nov 2nd 1981. Unlike my ancestors I choose to become a professional photographer specialising in the early days in horse photography but not before assisting my father breaking and training horses and helping with my uncle's stud at Balfestown after his death and where I learned many trade secrets.

Today if Pat were alive he would be sad to see the changes that have become part of life in Ratoath but he would also be proud of the progress and the employment in the area. In his day he hated alcohol and still lived life to the full.

Pat's eldest daughter Gladys married Joseph Moorhead from Tullamore, their other daughter Violet remained in a convent at Woldingham in England where she died in her eighties. Margaret Rogers was deeply religious. As Hilda rode very well to hounds (side saddle) she came to the attention of Mr. Percy Maynard who was Master of the Ward Union Hounds and residing at the Manor. When Margaret discovered that Percy had romantic notions, Hilda, possibly against her will, was promptly sent off to a convent where she was to remain for 16 years. Hilda was one of the first nuns to come out of religious life and she later worked as Secretary to Charlie Rogers at Balfestown. She lived up to her death at Park House but died at the Manor Nursing Home in 1978. Hilda left Park House to her nephew the late Pat Moorhead a son of Gladys. His wife Sheila and some of their children still reside there.

The Yard in Ratoath
Pat Rogers kept his hunters at the yard in Ratoath; a steady flow of customers came to buy horses. His sons hunted every day and hacked to meets many miles away. Horses were well schooled and ready for clients. There was always great attention to detail and horses changed hands frequently. A regular visitor was Sir Harold Werhner and his wife Lady Zia who had a love for hunting. Pat's interest in hunting was not his only means of making a living; he was a successful owner and trainer of many racehorses.

Pat was deeply committed to racing, he owned and sold many steeplechasers and had many horses in training. The Rogers family had a remarkable connection with Leopardstown and in 1911 he won the feature chase with *Tobber*. He also had a burning ambition to win the Trim Cup at the Trim Races but keeping in mind the conditions, which stipulated that the same owner had to win it four times in succession. He managed to do so with *Oakstick, Pioneer, Chip of the Block* and *Sister Dear*. His famous navy blue colours with a green cap were seen at racecourses all over Ireland and I am pleased that I had the opportunity to register these same colours for life.

The National
There are so many links to the great race in my family. Pat bought *Scan Spadah* for £350 after he won his first race at Downpatrick in war time and sold him on to Frank Barbour who in turn passed him on to Sir Malcolm McAlpine who won The **National in 1921**.

Pat bought *Master Robert* for £50 from a Mr McKinly in Donegal who had bought him as a cast off from the Curragh because he was too slow. *Master Robert* was one of the only horses on record to have pulled a plough prior to winning at Aintree, but Pat Rogers saw his potential, and sold him on, he won The **National in 1924** trained by Aubrey Hastings.

Royal Mail was bred by Charlie who sold him as a three-year-old to Hubert Hartigan. He later sold him to Hugh Lloyd Thomas who won The **Centenary National** with this horse in 1937 (ridden by Evan Williams).

Charlie bought *Brown Jack* from Marcus Thompson in Cashel, Co.Tipperary, as a raw two-year-old by *Jackdaw*; he went on to win 26 races including the Champion Hurdle at Cheltenham and several major races on the flat at Ascot and Goodwood. On June 5th 1931 Charlie was a special guest at a dinner given by Sir Harold Wernher at the Savoy Hotel in London to celebrate the achievements of *Brown Jack*.

Flying Swallow
There is a Diamond broach and a painting in our family that was presented to grandfather by the owner of *Flying Swallow* around 1905; it stipulates that the brooch passes to the eldest male Rogers of each generation.

After Pat Rogers died, Charlie Rogers commenced training at Balfestown, Frank set up Glascairn Stud. My father George worked for Charlie at the yard in Ratoath. He travelled on a green bicycle 10 miles every day for many years and was given the job of breaking the young stock with the help of an amazing team of dedicated people all from around the area of Ratoath. They put hundreds of horses through their hands. It was often said that Charlie Rogers had an empire and I would never dispute this. Without the staff it would never have happened. The main stay at the yard was Mick Flood and my father, who worked "twenty-four-seven" in graceful bliss, taking on a variation of tasks associated with breaking and schooling young horses and with great help from Liam McLoughlin (Stash).

A full yard was around 40 horses and many people in Ratoath worked there. Johnny Connor, father of Nicky (Hen) and Scan, Johnny Walls, Peter McLoughlin, father of Liam & Peter, and Brendan Lynch who later went to Balfestown until C.A. died. P. P. Hogan rode many of the young horses at home and racing them prior to them travelling to Dorothy Paget's team of trainers in England; Frenchie Nicholson, Fulke Walwin or Harry Beasley and others.

Christy Foley was resident Blacksmith at the yard.

Tom McKeever from the Rectory was an outstanding horseman who also played a big part in the Rogers outfit. The family also had a keen interest in greyhounds and spent many a cold day coursing at Dunshaughlin and Big Lagore in the company of Harry Everard and Pat Thunder; men they all spoke of with huge respect.

Bridle Path
Later the yard was sold to the Fairyhouse Race Company and leased back to Charlie with a stipulation that every Easter the stables would be cleared to facilitate runners at the meeting. The horses were walked from the yard to Fairyhouse via the Bridle Path and it was a tradition that the runners from T.W. Dreaper's stables, and any others that came by train, would meet near Mr. Costello's shop and walk in tandem to the course.

Balfestown Stud
Charlie Rogers married Josephine Rooney a sister of the legendry Harry Rooney from Trevet, near Dunshaughlin. They had no children. So many great horses passed through his hands at Balfestown. Jockeys who worked there included Bobby Beasley, P. P. Hogan who rode all the bumper horses, Albert Power, and Dan Moore, father of Pamela Carberry. Charlie had a great friend in the late Charlie Weld and always had much admiration for his son Dermot Weld as a horseman and perfectionist. How right he was.

It was a loyal and dedicated staff headed by Brendan Lynch and John Smith who cared for the mares and stallions throughout his illness with additional help from a wonderful staff, and that I will always remember with deep gratitude.

Charlie managed and trained for Dorothy Paget a millionaire who liked good chasers. She always had around 200 horses in Ireland between Ratoath, Tankardstown, Flat House and the Curragh. Her total between the two countries was 450. Her most famous horse was *Golden Miller* who was originally bought from Lawrence Geraghty in Co Meath. After he won his fifth Gold Cup at Cheltenham, Dorothy gave Charlie a gold watch to commemorate the occasion. Two days before he died, he gave it to me at Balfestown along with the three-penny piece engraved and surrounded in gold in memory of two great horses he trained for her, *Distal* and *Roman Hackle*. This was one of his greatest possessions, and now is also mine!

Charlie loved Galway and he won many races there, I am proud to have won a race there with *Lady Nightingale* shortly before my father died in 1980. I also bred the Galway Hurdle winner, *I'm Confident*.

The Foundation Stud at Ballymacoll
The Rogers connection with Ballymacoll and Dorothy Paget came about when my father was taking tea in the Post Office in Ratoath with the Postmistress Mary Bruen wife of Jack Bruen. It has to be said that with no television and no communication other than the bush telegraph Mary sometimes had a hankering for listening into the odd conversation while people were on the phone. In those days all the calls had to be manually switched through by Mary so temptation came especially if the conversations were about horses.

On this particular day Mary put a call from the Army Headquarters through to Ballymacoll in Dunboyne where they were stationed. She overheard the conversation telling the Sergeant in Ballymacoll that the Army were being pulled out of Ballymacoll immediately. She passed on the news to my father George who jumped on his bicycle and headed to Balfestown to tell Charlie who was frantically looking for a yard for Dorothy Paget's mares. Here started an odyssey of great horses, great trainers and great people but above all great staff. Charlie Rogers bought Ballymacoll on behalf of Dorothy Paget for £28,000 and the rest is history. Once Miss Paget had a yard in Ireland she was happy.

Shortly after that phone call the Army were out and the Rogers horses were in. More foundation mares were bought and the young stock was put in place. Today many of the names still come up in pedigrees. Danny Daly took over the reins at Ballymacoll where he lived with his wife Sheila.

When Dorothy Paget died it was a sad day for Charlie and my father. Somehow it was the end of an amazing tradition that was handed down by Pat Rogers. Charlie continued on as manager to Sir Michael Sobell who bought Ballymacoll. In the late sixties, Mr Daniel Wildenstein, one of the most famous art collectors in the world and then living in Paris, purchased Killeen Castle Stud from Sir Victor Sassoon. He contacted Charlie to become his manager and advisor to transform Killeen into a state of the art stud farm. Charlie Rogers was facing the greatest challenge of his days with horses. I shared many of his dreams at Killeen as he refurbished and redesigned all the boxes and yards. Unfortunately he did not live long enough to fulfill his dreams of yet another foundation stud in Ireland.

What Pat Rogers Handed Down To My Father George
My grandfather had some golden rules about training young horses to jump, which he passed on to his sons, especially my father. He believed that you should never ever ask a young horse to jump a pole but always make him stretch over a wide obstacle such as two or three, bales of straw, the logic of this being that the steeplechaser has to stretch wide over a fence and if he learns the right way from day one he will never fall.

On the other hand if the steeplechaser is trained to go up over a pole to get height he will always do it, and will topple over when he takes off on his hocks at a chase fence.

It was said, and I have no reason to doubt it, that my father broke the 2nd, 3rd, 4th and 5th in one English National.

His favourite horses were *Legal Joy*, *Happy Home*, *Revelry*, *Distal* and *Roman Hackle*.

He was recognised as a supreme judge of a horse and some of the great chasers associated with him were *Royal Approach* which won the Irish Grand National at Fairyhouse as a six year old. Others included *Arctic Silver*, *Arctic Gold*, *Somerville*, (third in the National at Aintree) and *Charles Dickens* (third in the National at Aintree). Many more were symbols of his great knowledge. They were true ambassadors of his type of chaser, bone, substance and above all presence. He also bought and produced *Hartstown* to win at the RDS and at Cheltenham for his owner Joe McGowan. It was my father's policy, when buying a young chaser that he must have the presence to win at the RDS, the speed to win up the Curragh and the quality to win at Cheltenham. George also bought and produced the champion young horse at the RDS in 1970.

When working at the yard in Ratoath he met with a serious accident when schooling a horse named *Possible* in long reins. Consequently he was seriously ill for several years and after several operations he carried the burden of a colostomy for the last 30 years of his life. He never complained and he continued to love his horses and his greyhounds. George also had a good eye for a pony. He purchased 100 pit ponies just after World War II and some of the breed still exists around Co Meath.

Gay Kindersley contacted my father in 1959 with a request to buy him 10 horses to fulfill his ambition to win the Amateur Riders Championship in England, which he successfully achieved, but the brief also included that all of the youngsters would be broken and schooled in Ireland prior to joining his trainer Don Butchers. One of them was *Carrickbeg* who in 1963 as a seven-year-old jumped the last in front at Aintree but was caught in the last strides by *Ayala*. My friendship with Gay remains to this day.

George always said that Martin Moloney was the best jockey he ever saw in Ireland, with Dan Moore in close pursuit but he also thought that Vincent O'Brien was the only person to ever come near Pat Rogers in the perfectionist stakes. I believe if my father was alive today he would have the same views about Nina Carberry. Her ability to get horses running for her is everything my grandfather would have asked of a jockey.

A trip to Deauville
My last trip away with Charlie was to Deauville Sales. We met many people there and on leaving he asked me to accompany him to the beach. He told me he would never see it again because his health was deteriorating fast. He died at Balfstown on July 25th 1971 after fighting cancer bravely for almost two years. Following his coffin going down the avenue at Balfstown, the brood mares were watching and came to the stud fencing to stand in silence to pay their last respects. A great man and a great trainer had gone to his eternal rest forever.

Balfestown was left to my father but he had no option but to sell it to pay off huge death duties. Sixteen staff were let go and it was one of the saddest days of our lives in 1972, as the C.I.E. boxes rumbled down the famous avenue for the last time as the horses left Balfstown for a special sale in Goffs, bringing to a close another great chapter of a legend started by Pat Rogers.

Pat Rogers of Ratoath left behind him a tradition that only he himself could ever emulate. I deeply regret that I never had the ability to ride a horse like my grandfather, my father or my uncles. Perhaps I got too much of it from breaking big chasers in my early days, but I still look back and think of some great memories. Right or wrong, I choose to be a professional photographer and thankfully managed to succeed by winning eight National Press Awards and one International Press Award of which four were for Racing. My career gave me opportunities to cover every aspect of life but much was devoted to the equine sport. Above all as a news photographer, the opportunity to meet and photograph people from all over the world, from every walk of life, is something for which I am eternally thankful.

I have wonderful memories of Aintree and Cheltenham. You get 'a high' that money could never buy the moment you set foot on the turf heading towards the Melling Road or up the hill at Cheltenham.

Horses are in my veins and it will never leave me. My brothers, nieces and nephews choose careers, not involved with horses, but I am really proud of my grandniece Sorcha Rogers a daughter of my niece Mary, who is the only Rogers left to carry on the tradition set by Pat Rogers. Hopefully she will continue to enjoy all the pleasures, as she pursues the path of show-jumping and eventing. I suspect it could be said that although I failed not to carry on where my family left off, my greatest memories of my uncles and my father was their ability to judge a young horse.

I still think of them. Writing this article rekindles so much inside me. To this day I am unable to plait a horse with anything other than thread! In my heart I will try and carry on the example of perfection that was set in Ratoath by Pat Rogers. His passing and the death of his sons was the end of a great era and above all the extraordinary connection with the horses. Times have changed, but thankfully some will remain, like the legend of Pat Rogers of Ratoath.

HORSES FOR COURSES

Tom Dreaper and the Irish Grand-National

LIAM & PETER McLOUGHLIN

T OM DREAPER was second as an amateur rider in the 1938 Irish Grand National. The run of play on the whole was very much in his favour at Fairyhouse, the home of the Irish Grand National. Tom Dreaper trained his first winner of Ireland's most important chase on the 6th April 1942 when the mighty *Prince Regent* carried Tim Hyde and 12st. 7lbs. to victory in a race worth £745. *Prince*

Tom Dreaper's Staff in his yard at Greenogue in the mid 1960s.
Left to Right: Sean Barker, Willie McCabe, Paddy Woods, Paddy Browne, Nick Connor, Charlie Reilly, Paddy Murray (Head Man), Joe Finglas, Noel Carroll, Mark Roper, Benny Coldrick, Matt Kearns, Tom Flanagan, Val O'Brien, Eddie Wright and Paddy Mooney.

Regent, carrying the same weight was second in 1943 and 1944.[1] It was exciting times for Tom Draper and those who worked in his yard.

Another of Tom's winners came in 1949 with *Shagreen*. Perhaps the confirmation of Tom as an all time great trainer came in the 1954 running of the Irish Grand National when the six year old, *Royal Approach*, carrying 12 stone and starting even money favourite, won his sixth race of the season.

The 1960's record of Tom's achievements in the Irish Grand National is significant - he won the race seven times on the trot. His winners were: 1960, *Olympia*; 1961, *Fortria*; 1962, *Keforo*; 1963, *Last Link*; 1964, *Arkle*; 1965, *Splash*; 1966, *Flyingbolt*. The winning riders were T. Taaffe, P. Taaffe (3 times), L. McLoughlin and P. Woods (2 times).

His record of ten victories achieved between 1942 and 1966 with a string of never more than thirty-five horses is unlikely to be beaten. The handicapper by the late 1940's never did the Greenogue horses any favours and Tom's horses often carried top weight in Eire's greatest chase either to victory or a place. Tom Dreaper also helped strengthen the links between Irish race goers and the Cheltenham Festival. To this day Ratoath becomes a ghost town during Festival week in Cheltenham. Tom Dreaper turned out 26 Cheltenham winners.[2]

Fairyhouse Racecourse was the nearest course to Donaghmore and Greenogue. Tom had a very special relationship with it; he would have hunted over it with the Ward Staghounds long before he actually rode there as an amateur rider. He was very successful at Fairyhouse as an amateur rider. His record speaks for itself. Not only did he train the winner of the Irish Grand National ten times but he also trained winners of all the other big races regularly.

Tom Dreaper with his daughter Eva on the day she married Michael Kauntz in Dunboyne c. early 1970s.

---

[1] *Tom Dreaper & His Horses*. Bryony Fuller. Punchestown Books, Dublin. (1991).
[2] *Vincent O'Brien The Man & The Legend*, Raymond Smith. Sporting Books Publishers, Dublin (1997)

HORSES FOR COURSES

Tattersalls Ireland
A brief history of the Company and grounds at Ratoath

SOPHIE HAYLEY

Tattersalls – the beginning
In 1738 a fourteen year old English boy, Richard Tattersall bought a carriage horse behind his parents back and hid it in a barn. From that simple transaction started what was to become the world's first bloodstock auction house which Richard Tattersall officially founded in 1766. Hunters, hounds, carriage horses and thoroughbreds all passed under the gavel at the Tattersalls sales ground at Hyde Park Corner in London.

From London to Newmarket
In 1865 Tattersalls moved from Hyde Park corner to Knightsbridge Green; modern day visitors to London would scarcely be able to imagine that those two acres of prime real estate bustling with shops, restaurants and traffic in one of the capital's smartest area would have been devoted to the stabling and exchange of hundreds and thousands of horses even up to the Second World War. The expansion of the bloodstock sales and an ever increasing number of commercial breeders who wanted to sell their young stock – a relatively new concept among the established owner-breeders of the previous centuries – led to the need for more room for stabling and facilities. Racing's headquarters had long been established in Newmarket and the move from London to the existing site at Park Paddocks in Newmarket was a natural progression.

Ballsbridge Tattersalls
In 1975 the Ballsbridge International Sales Company was founded as a Bloodstock Auction house in Ballsbridge in Dublin with its sales being conducted at the famous Royal Dublin Society's showgrounds, which still to this day are the home of International Horse Shows. Many Irish breeders traditionally took their young horses to England to sell at Tattersalls in Newmarket, and many of the purchasers were Irish, so when in 1979 Tattersalls saw the opportunity to expand into Ireland, a 44% interest of Ballsbridge International was bought and the resulting Ballsbridge Tattersalls sales company came into being.

From Ballsbridge to Fairyhouse
By 1985 Tattersalls had increased their holding and the company was now known as Tattersalls Ireland Ltd, however many of the original directors of Ballsbridge International remained at the helm of the new company – Michael Hillman, David Pim, Denis Mahony (father of current chairman Edmond Mahony), Willie O'Rourke, Standish Collen, Matt

Macken. Again with an increase in business the need for more space became apparent and in 1986 the Old Fairyhouse Stud in Ratoath was acquired. The site of just over 200 acres of suitable land was on the other side of the road from Fairyhouse racecourse, home of the Irish Grand National. The sale ground with its stabling, barns, offices, auction ring, parking and many other facilities was developed from scratch, with much research having been done within Ireland and internationally and with the requirements of the Irish vendors and purchasers all being taken into account.

Old Fairyhouse Stud
Old Fairyhouse Stud had been bought by Tattersalls Ireland from Peter McDowell, a family of jewellers, famed for the Happy Ring House on O'Connell Street in Dublin, where many amorous young men have bought engagement rings in hopeful anticipation for their girlfriends. Previous owners of Old Fairyhouse Stud included the Purfields who farmed the land, the Hillmans (Michael Hillman is a director of Tattersalls Ireland); Dan Moore trained his well-known string of National Hunt horses here. The farm was also leased to the Irish National Stud for a period.

Great racehorses
Tattersalls has always been known with racehorses of the very highest calibre from the beginning. Founder Richard Tattersall owned the legendary racehorse *Highflyer*, who was foaled in 1774. Never beaten in twelve starts on the racecourse, *Highflyer* became an outstanding stallion at stud at Highflyer Hall, Richard Tattersalls home near Ely in Cambridgeshire, and was the sire of three Derby winners in the first ten years of the world's most famous race. Numerous legendary racehorses have been sold by Tattersalls – *St Simon*, *Flying Fox*, *High Top*, *Grundy*, and *Vaguely Noble*.

The Aintree Grand National
Tattersalls Ireland and Old Fairyhouse Stud have had a fascinating relationship with the Aintree Grand National. The McDowells owned *Caughoo*, trained by Herbert McDowell who was a shock 100-1 winner in 1947; while Dan Moore, who used Old Fairyhouse Stud as a training stable, was responsible for *L'Escargot* who beat the immortal *Red Rum* at Aintree in 1975. Between 2000 and 2006 five winners of the Aintree Grand National were bought at different sales at Tattersalls Ireland – *Numbersixvalverde*, *Hedgehunter*, *Amberleigh House*, *Monty's Pass* and *Bindaree*.

Tattersalls Ireland today
Tattersalls Ireland is the leading National Hunt sale company in the world. Sellers come from all over Ireland and buyers come from all over the world to Tattersalls Ireland to attend the auctions, which take place throughout the year. There are six different sales held at the Tattersalls Ireland complex – two for Flat horses and four for National Hunt (jumping) with nearly 6,000 horses ranging from mares and foals to older 3 and 4 year olds all going through the sales ring here. The biggest sale of all is the marathon November sale which takes place over a fortnight. Tattersalls Ireland em-

Part of the Extensive stable complex at Tattersalls

(*Above*): Typical Horse Auction at Tattersalls

(*Left*): Interior of one of the stable units at Tattersalls

ploys roughly 25 full time staff with many more joining the team leading up to and during the sales. The grounds are occupied by the main house which has been turned into the main office, facilities for buyers and sellers such as restaurants, bars and car parking, and of course the auction ring and parade rings where potential purchasers can view the horses; there is also more than 600 stables to house the horses while they are being inspected prior to the auction.

The thoroughbred and beyond
Although the thoroughbred auctions are at the heart of Tattersalls Ireland's business, there has been an ongoing policy to make the grounds at Fairyhouse into an equestrian complex of international standard, capitalising on the excellent location of the site and the recently refurbished facilities and services. Among the variety of other activities taking place are a point to point course, which is steeplechasing for amateurs and organised by the local hunts and a cross-country course designed by renowned Irish course designer Tommy Brennan for the annual international three-day event which attracts competitors from around Europe. The grounds and facilities are also used by local Pony Clubs and Girl Guides for their annual camps. The buildings also house the Somerville Rooms (named after Somerville Tattersall, one of the legendary directors of the original company), which given the beautiful surrounds and charm of the old house, provide a very popular setting for weddings, art and antique shows along with other functions, corporate and private.

Recent Events
Ratoath Heritage Group
Recent developments at Tattersalls (Ireland) include the construction of a Point-To-Point course, a Cross-Country Event course, an additional stable complex and redesign of the main entrance on the Fairyhouse Road. These improvements represent important steps in Tattersalls (Ireland) ongoing policy to uphold Fairyhouse as an equestrian complex of international standard, capitalising on the excellent location of the site and the recently refurbished ancillary facilities and services. The 2006 Tattersalls Ireland International Horse Trials featured dressage, cross-country and show jumping. From 29th May to 1st June 2008 Olympic riders from around the world took part in the Tattersalls Ireland International Horse Trials which included a World Cup Qualifier.

COMMUNITY

Ratoath Community Centre

The Early Years (1930's to the New Millennium)

NICK KILLIAN

A COMMUNITY CENTRE was established on a site where the original St. Oliver Plunkett Hall once stood. It started its life as a centre for stable lads, who worked in the adjoining property belonging to the Rogers family, and was taken over by the parish around the 1930's. It was used as a Dance Hall with a beautiful maple floor and many courtships started there! It survived until 1980.

The interior of St. Oliver Plunkett Community Hall showing the well polished wooden floor which was enjoyed by the dancers. This photo shows the addition of central heating (radiators).

The Exterior of the original St. Oliver Plunkett Hall

(*Above*): Drama Group rehearsing in the original Community Hall in Ratoath in the late 1930's with Mr. J.J. Kelly N.T. who was the musical director, at the centre of the picture.
Also included in the picture are: Margaret Duffy as Lucia; Jimmy Maher as Francesco; Patricia McLoughlin as Jacinta and May Costello as Our Lady. Others in the picture are: Phyllis and Christina Brennan, Mary Walsh, Lizzy Mannering, Lucy Browne, Katy Darby and Teresa McCann.

(*Below*): Left to right (from front to back): Christina Connor, Tommy Dolan, Dan Eiffe, May Hessmann, Paddy Walsh, Brendan Ralph, Mary Nulty, Tiny Everard, Colm Keogh, Peggy Flood, Agnes McCabe, Mick Flood, John Eiffe, Eddie Nulty and Christy Smith.

Following the Stardust disaster, which happened in 13/14 February 1981, the Meath County Fire Officer indicated in July 1981 that the Parochial Hall could no longer be used in its then condition. This, although in the offing, came as a stunning blow to the community. On 21 September 1981, Fr. Cogan (Parish Priest) called a meeting in the old Parochial Hall, outlined the Fire Officer's remarks, and asked the community to decide its needs for the future. A committee was formed charged with evaluating the development of a new hall on a new site, and/or replacing the existing hall on its present site.

Officers elected: Nick Killian, Ballybin, (Chairman); Des Brady, Lagore, (Vice-chairman); Annie Gogan, Village (Secretary); Mary Walsh, Glascarn (Assistant Secretary); Fr Mulvany C.C. (Treasurer); Nicky Keogh, Rackenstown (Assistant Treasurer); Joan Bolger, Commons (PRO).

Members of the Committee: Aidan Conway, Noel Eiffe, Joe Mannering, Lil Keogh, Sean Woods, Anne Reilly, Mary Flinter, Veronica Cullen, Joe Lynch, Jean Donnelly, Tom Wallace, Margaret Casey, Mick Mahon, Michael Gilchrist, Liam Burke, Willie Donohoe, Nuala Walls, Marie Reilly, Lena Naughton and Imelda Elliott.

Over the following two years the committee identified the needs of the community, where the Community Centre should be sited, and what fundraising would be required to finance a new centre. The dedicated committee set about the task of fundraising with steely determination and with a sense of fun. Lord Mayor competitions, a monster bingo at Warrenstown, a visit by Eric Bristow, the great Darts Player, (the Ratoath Inn was packed to overflowing with over 600 fans present on the night), a music night with the Wolfe Tones, a wrestling event in Ashbourne, turkey draws, poker classics and many more wonderful events all contributed towards the funding of the new Centre. Liam Burke and Joe Lynch were great **Lord Mayors!**

1982: Left to right: Michael Gilchrist, Pat Donnelly, Fr. Cogan, Nick Killian and Noel Eiffe at the formal signing of the Contract for the Construction of the former Community Centre.

Initially two sites were proposed, one at the school and the second involved the redevelopment of the old hall on the existing site. After much deliberation, it was agreed to redevelop the old hall site by purchasing additional land from Mollie Talty and Nan Moore. Arthur Lardner, who lived at Glebe House, was appointed architect and Pat Donnelly was the appointed builder.

The new Centre was built and the debt was completely cleared by 1986. Since opening on 16 March 1983, by Fr. Cogan Parish Priest, in the presence of the newly ordained Bishop of Meath, Dr Michael Smith, the Centre became a focal point for most of the community organisations and was in constant use by a variety of organisations until its redevelopment in the new millennium.

Over the years the Community Centre has been well served by the many individuals, from chair and committee members who have given selflessly, to persons keeping the Centre open, functioning and well maintained. In that time we have lost members who worked tirelessly for the Centre - Joe Lynch, Pud Mahon and Andy Eiffe.

Seated: Joe Connor, Sheila Farrell and Teresa Gorman
Standing: Ben Lynan, Paddy Dolan

The New Millennium
Once again, as we approached the millennium the committee included people with the same vision of 20 years ago, comprising both the oldest and newer members of our village. In 2001, the committee appointed local architect, Michael Lysaght, to plan a building that would serve the needs of this ever-growing community over the next 20 to 30 years. With the expansion of the Primary School to 1,000 students, and a new Post-Primary School for 700 students, the continued development of an inclusive and comprehensive social infrastructure is obvious and essential. As before, I have no doubt but that the new focal point for the population of this historic village on the edge of County Meath will underpin the continued success of this community.

Another make over for the Community Centre
With much work, fundraising and energy, yet again, the Community Centre went through its third cycle of redevelopment and expansion in order to cater for the needs of a growing modern community. In order to ensure that the building would meet the needs of the people of Ratoath the committee was charged with delivering a centre which would continue to promote a spirit of community and a sense of belonging. The heart symbol (instead of

O) included as part of the Ratoath name emphasises that this Community Centre represents the new "heart" or centre of Ratoath, a centre for all members of the community, and one which can be used by community organisations, clubs and associations.

Rat♥ath

The Community Centre encompasses a variety of facilities: a purpose built theatre called *The Venue Theatre*, *'As You Like It' Barrista Caffé*, several studios and meeting rooms. Finally, the most modern community facility, one of first of its kind in Ireland was officially opened by President of Ireland, Mary McAleese on 9 September 2006.

A New yet Old Vision
Our Community Centre which has all the benefits of modern building and technological advancements is in reality the culmination of a vision which began over 70 years ago as local community development emerged as a concept and was prioritised by people in Ratoath. They had no idea where that journey would take future generations or the costs involved! Our links with the past continue, we benefit in the present and hopefully build for the future. There are individuals who work tireless for the community in order that we can continue to enjoy the outcome of the vision of those previous generations. Ratoath Community Centre is a comfortable and adaptable venue and it is sitting on our doorsteps. As well as rooms to accommodate many activities, the Venue Theatre has already become home to plays, recitals, concerts, drama and radio/TV broadcasts.

Official Opening: President Mary McAleese cutting the ribbon held by Kiera Judge and Eoin O'Connor.

Community Centre Committee members with the President and her husband,
9th September 2006.
Front row: Noel Eiffe, Martin McAleese, President Mary McAleese, Jackie O'Brien, Ita Murray
Middle row: Garda Colm Curran, Nick Killian, Phil Bateson, Chris Maher, Joe Mannering, Sean Woods, Lil Keogh
Back row: Superintendent Charles Devine, Mary Walshe, Marian Simpson, Leo Cummins, Anne Brady, Ciaran Buckley, Tom O'Connor, Liam Burke.

LOCAL HISTORY   Chapter

The Staff of Ratoath Community Centre on Opening Day: Marie Rooney, Donna Byrne, Nicholas Killian, Aine Moore McCormack, Lorna Flood and Eilish Finch.

Trying out the scissors on Opening Day: Bill Byrne and Nicholas Killian

Noel Eiffe and Nick Killian with President Mary McAleese and Martin McAleese just before the official opening the new Ratoath Community Centre on 9th September 2006

COMMUNITY

Official Opening of Ratoath Community Centre 2006 by Uachtarain na hÉireann, Mary McAleese

ON A BEAUTIFUL warm and sunny autumn afternoon on Saturday 9th September 2006, amid a wide variety of locally produced street and indoor entertainment comprising of several varieties of music, song and dance, put on by the young and old people of Ratoath, the President was warmly welcomed back to Ratoath. She had previously lived for a time in Lagore which in the parish of Ratoath. She and her husband Martin were thanked by the newly appointed General Manager of Ratoath Community Centre, Nick Killian, for sharing the very special occasion with the people of Ratoath.

Just before she officially opened the Centre, the President made the following remarks:

> *The sun is shining down on the people of Ratoath and deservedly so. When I think of what this tiny village, just a short time ago, has lived with and experienced over the last 15 years.*
>
> *The huge explosion from a tiny little village where we all knew one another to this extraordinary metropolis now of going on for 10,000 people and growing.*
>
> *The big worry – the big, big worry always is 'Will you be able to hold on to community? Will you be able to create community; will you be able to embrace everybody, and draw them in, and create not just a bunch of houses; not just a bunch of people who happen to live together'?*
>
> *I have never opened a Community Centre like this. This is the most stunning Community Centre I can safely say I think I have ever seen.*
>
> *I now declare this wonderful Community Centre officially open. Use it and enjoy it.*

COMMUNITY

Ratoath Population Trends

PAUL HALTON

THE CENTRAL STATISTICS OFFICE, in an analysis of the 2002 Census data, stated that a quarter of the housing stock in Kildare and Meath was built in the six-year period 1996 to 2002. For example, in the towns of Ratoath and Sallins, Co. Kildare, 70 per cent of the dwellings were built during this period.

Socio-economic Scale

The 2002 Census data revealed that Malahide in north Dublin had the highest proportion of its population aged 15 and over classified to the socio-economic groups of Employers and Managers and Higher professionals. These groups combined represented a total of 41.3 per cent of the relevant population. Greystones (36.7%), Ratoath (36.6%), Oranmore (36.4%) and Enniskerry (35.7%) were next in line.

The CSO analysis of the 2006 Census of Population, Volume 2, reported that Dublin's commuter belt towns have the highest proportion of young people aged 0-14 years with Ratoath in County Meath having the highest in Ireland at 32 per cent.

Ability of Ratoath residents to speak the Irish language is summarised as follows:

Town	Tota	Irish Speakers	Non-Irish Speakers	Not Stated	Irish speakers as percentage of total
Ratoath	6,678	2,898	3,646	134	44.3%

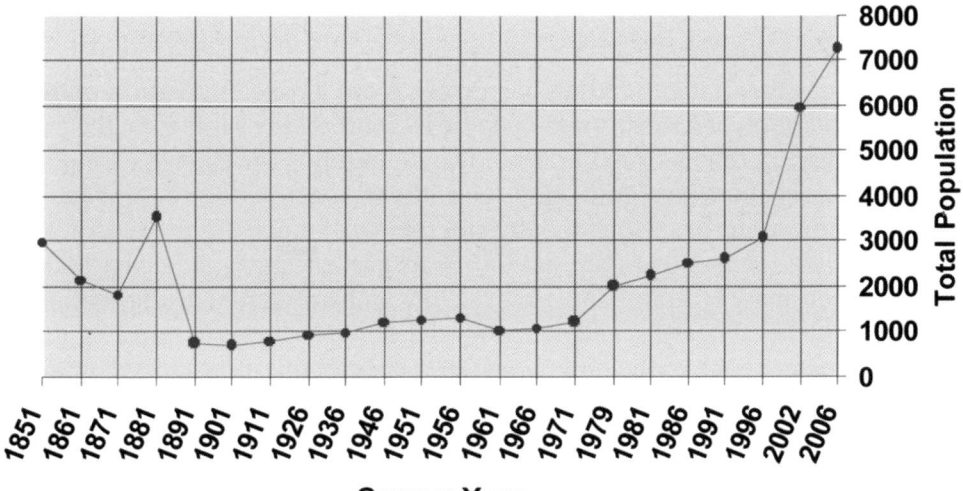

Population Trend Chart for Ratoath - compiled from data generously provided byThe Central Statistics Office

COMMUNITY

Ratoath 1993 to 2008 – A study of a rapidly changing community

RATOATH HERITAGE GROUP

Background

DURING THE *"Celtic Tiger Period"* Ireland as a whole experienced a major economic boost resulting from leading International High Tech firms accepting attractive incentives to set up their European headquarters in this country, particularly in the greater Dublin area. These "Foreign Direct Investment" companies provided well paid employment for tens of thousands of highly skilled employees and they generated demand for multiple spin off services to support their activities. Having reached a position of "full employment" (unemployment rate countrywide was sub 4%), Ireland welcomed over 400,000 migrant workers from all parts of the world, particularly Eastern European countries, who took up jobs mainly in the construction and hospitality services. Several of the software, electronic and bio-chemical firms required professional translators with advanced language skills to localise the English versions of the software products and user manuals into over 25 languages for onward sales to Europe, Middle-East and Asia.

Introduction

Over the past 15 years Ratoath parish has grown from a base population of around 800 people to a population of almost 10,000 people in 2008. At the same time the populations of the other adjacent towns of Ashbourne, Dunshaughlin, Dunboyne, Clonee and Blanchardstown have also grown significantly. Over the ten-year period 1997-2007, in particular, the local community has witnessed the emergence of much higher density, higher rise apartment blocks, a reduction in the size of private gardens and an increase in the amount of common open spaces (though limited in size) which are shared by the occupants of the adjoining complexes. Lifestyles and accommodation types have changed significantly resulting in a greater sense of the emergence of a cosmopolitan urbanised society on the edge of a rural landscape.

The rapid pace of change over a relatively short period has challenged planners, the local community, associations and organisations, local authorities and service providers alike. Ratoath became a major focus for developers who offered attractive prices to local land owners for land banks with development potential. Planning application signs popped up all over the area and local community groups and public representatives were hard pressed to keep pace with what the developers were planning and the likely consequences for the supporting infrastructure and fabric of the community itself.

In the 15-year period, almost 40 housing developments have been constructed in the Ratoath area, ranging in numbers from less than 10 units in the smaller schemes to almost 400 units in the larger development. At the same time the emergence, (even if at times somewhat slow!), of a wide range of new businesses and services has provided some of the services needed by the burgeoning population.

Sociological Studies of Ratoath
In 2002 Dr. Mary Corcoran, Dr. Jane Gray and Dr. Michel Peillon, National University of Ireland, Maynooth, carried out a survey that *"aimed to develop a profile of life in Ratoath"* and in addition to "identify *some of the problems and issues that concern local residents."* The findings of the survey and its analysis were published in February 2003.

Similar research surveys were also carried out by the group, from the sociology department of Maynooth University, in some parts of Lucan, Leixlip and in the new estates on the periphery of Mullingar. The group conducted a series of in-depth interviews, with selected respondents, around the theme of active engagement in the locality. The research involved the organisation of a series of focus-groups with school-children, mothers with young children, senior citizens, etc., in each location. Their in-depth analysis has provided a rich insight into local communities and the survey results have already been presented in a number of major publications, including:

- Mary P. Corcoran, Jane Gray and Michel Peillon, "Local sentiment and sense of place in a new suburban community", in M. Breen, E. Conway and B. McMillan (eds), Technology and transcendence. Dublin: The Columba Press, 2003. (Mainly focused on Ratoath)
- *NUI Maynooth Symposium on Civic and Social Life in the Suburbs* (April 8th 2005): Over one hundred academics, students, politicians, planners, local government personnel and people working in the voluntary and community sector gathered to debate the key issues relating to suburban development. Three papers related to the NUIM research project (they deal with the four locations) can be found at the following Internet address: http://sociology.nuim.ie/CivicSocialConference.shtml
- Michel Peillon, Mary Corcoran and Jane Gray, *Civic engagement and the governance of Irish suburbs*, Studies in Public Policy 21, Dublin: The Policy Institute, 2006. (focused on Ratoath)
- Mary P. Corocran, Jane Gray and Michel Peillon, "Ties that bind? The social fabric of daily life in new suburbs", in T. Fahey, H. Russell and C.T. Whelan (eds), Best of times? The social impact of the Celtic Tiger. Dublin: Institute of Public Administration, 2007 (comparison of the 4 locations)
- A book based on the study is currently being written and it will be published sometime in the future.

The Study
Mary P. Corcoran, Jane Gray and Michel Peillon (National Institute for Regional and Spatial Analysis Department of Sociology NUI, Maynooth) in their work "**New Urban Living: a study of social and civic life in Irish suburbs (2003)**" organised a summary of their findings into the following areas:

1. Population profile
2. Attachment to place
3. The pattern of everyday life
4. Household and family patterns
5. Local networks of social support
6. Access to and use of information technology
7. Local voluntary associations
8. Participation in local voluntary associations
9. Local problems
10. Local problems and collective action

A summary of their findings is given in the following report that the Maynooth researchers generously provided to us for inclusion in this publication.

COMMUNITY

New Urban Living: a study of social and civic life in Irish suburbs (2003)

MARY P. CORCORAN,
JANE GRAY and MICHEL PEILLON

National Institute for Regional and Spatial Analysis Department of Sociology NUI, Maynooth

Summary of findings of first stage of suburban study in Ratoath, Co. Meath

1 Population profile

RATOATH RECORDED the highest percentage population increase in the commuter belt of Leinster in the most recent inter-census period. Between 1996 and 2002, the population grew by 82 % to 5,585 (CSO 2002). Not surprisingly, only a small number of our respondents have lived in Ratoath all of their lives. Just under half of our respondents have lived in Ratoath for just five years or less. Although the population profile is dominated by newcomers, it is noteworthy that the vast majority of those surveyed expect to continue to live in Ratoath for the next five years. Looking to the future, this suggests that there will be a degree of stability within the community as families put down roots, develop social networks and begin to avail of facilities locally. The population is likely to continue to expand in the short-term, as planning permission has been granted for a further 700 housing units in the Jamestown area close to the village. Given the large number of families with small children in the locality, the needs of the population in terms of educational and recreational facilities will intensify over the coming years. Already, there is a considerable degree of dissatisfaction at the overcrowded and under-resourced national school in the village, and the absence of a local secondary school for children living in the area. Plans are currently afoot within the community to build a recreational centre, but crucially this will have a public-private funding structure, with locals being required to pay fees to utilise the facilities.

The majority of respondents (just under 58 per cent) moved to Ratoath from the Dublin metropolitan area. A further 15 per cent had migrated from Co. Dublin, Kildare or Wicklow, with just 13 per cent hailing from elsewhere in Meath. In some respects, Ratoath, formerly a sleepy rural village, is creating a new template for modern living. Locals are in the minority, while the population profile represents a cross section of migrants from the city, towns and rural outposts in adjacent counties. This indicates that new population flows are taking people out of built up urban areas and into peripheral urban localities, whereas historically the population flows were primarily from rural areas to the central cities. The growth of suburban areas in major cities of the United States has been shown to come from the depopulation from the centre as well as new growth from other regions. Not surprisingly, the children growing up in Ratoath had some difficulty in responding to questions regarding their primary identity. While most identify with the adopted county of Meath, they are frequently viewed as Dubliners by those whose families have a history in the County, and as "culchies" by their family and friends who still reside in the Dublin metropolitan area.

2 Attachment to place

The quality and nature of urban life depends in part on the way residents relate to their urban or suburban environment. This can be looked at from the point of view of residents' identification with their locality and usage of local facilities and resources. How do people perceive their neighbourhood, to what extent do they feel an attachment, and how is that sense of place attachment expressed? The ways suburban residents identify with the locality and make use of it determine in a fairly direct way the social relationships that develop there. How people feel about where they live has consequences for their capacity to form sustainable communities. Consumer tastes are an important element of the nature and evolution of urban areas.

There are very specific features with which people identify when thinking about and choosing Ratoath as a place to live. The most commonly cited features include the village character, country feel, friendliness and sense of community. Focus group data suggests that bigger houses at affordable prices was perceived as a big advantage that Ratoath had when compared to Dublin. Furthermore, many participants in the focus groups commented on the village character and country feel of the place. Ratoath's greenery- the hedges, fields and trees- act as important signifiers of the countryside and rurality for respondents, both young and old. Focus group participants were adamant that Ratoath did not form part of Dublin city, and the majority had little orientation toward the downtown. More than three quarters of respondents feel either strongly attached or attached to Ratoath.

The largest single group, 40 per cent of the sample, expressed a preference for socialising in Ratoath, with the next largest proportion, 24 per cent, preferring to socialise at home. This indicates that people have developed a strong local orientation, and are much more likely to remain in and around the locality than to seek sociability outside of it. At the same time, just under half of the respondents (46 per cent) expressed the view that Ratoath is a place that is changing, and as such is in danger of losing its character and tradition. While respondents generally appear to be fairly happy about where they live, a number of key problems were identified: 27 per cent of respondents expressed concern about traffic in the locality, 25 per cent expressed dissatisfaction about the lack of facilities locally, and just under one fifth said that they disliked too much development. Children in the locality who were invited to write short essays on the place where I live, repeated mentioned their fear of the deleterious effect on the environment of over-development, and the safety implications of traffic throughput in the village and on the surrounding roads.

3 The pattern of everyday life

The pattern of everyday life, in terms of accessing goods and services, also shows an orientation away from downtown Dublin. Respondents tend to operate within the matrix of Ratoath, Blanchardstown and the towns of Ashbourne, Navan and Dunshaughlin. Of those who attend church, the overwhelming majority do so locally. One quarter of respondents, however, do not attend church. This figure provides further evidence of the decline in regular church-going among the Irish population, which has been evident since the early

1990s. The majority of respondents use the shop, pub and restaurant facilities within Ratoath. Just over 40 per cent do their supermarket shopping in Blanchardstown, while more than two-thirds go to the cinema there. While more than two-thirds attend doctors' surgeries in Ratoath, the remainder travels to Ashbourne, Dublin and elsewhere for such services. This probably reflects the relatively high numbers that have moved into the area recently, and have yet to establish a relationship with a local GP. About half of respondents bank in Ashbourne, Dunshaughlin or Blanchardstown, and a further 24 per cent bank in Dublin.

Ratoath is an active community with 60 per cent of the respondents utilising sports facilities. Just over half of those who use sports facilities, do so locally while the remainder travel primarily to Dublin, Ashbourne, Blanchardstown and Dunshaughlin to avail of such facilities. In the focus groups with children, it emerged that the GAA plays a crucial role in providing a recreational outlet for boys and girls from Ratoath. This role is rendered particularly significant in the absence of sports and recreational facilities locally.

Of the seventy children who participated in focus groups, not one expressed an interest in visiting any downtown city facility when describing their perfect day out. Rather, they wanted to visit adventure centres, shopping malls, skateboard and motor tracks located well beyond the perimeter of the city and generally accessible only by motor car. A picture emerges of a community that is constantly on the move, but crucially people are commuting between different country towns and suburban localities, rather than from the periphery into the core, in order to fulfill every day social, personal and recreational needs.

4. Household and Family Patterns

A number of classical sociological studies showed how 'traditional' family and kinship networks formed a central thread in the web of sociability in urban communities. The great majority of our respondents (85 per cent) in Ratoath are married, and describe the composition of their households as 'two parents with dependent children' (75 per cent). Part of the explanation for this may lie in the age structure of the population: almost 60 per cent of our respondents are aged between 26 and 39 years. Sixty-eight percent had one or more young children living in their households. On the Monday preceding the interview, when they were not at school, most of those children were at home in the care of a parent or other relative. After 1 p.m., sixty-five percent of children under-six years of age were cared for at home, while more than ninety percent of six to twelve year olds were at home after 3 p.m. However, nearly one third of children under six years attended a nursery, crèche or preschool between 9 a.m. and 1 p.m., while over ten percent were cared for in a similar location between 1 p.m. and 5 p.m.

Patterns of childcare in Ratoath are linked to the household income strategies of the children's parents. Just 19 per cent of our respondents were members of dual-income households, where both partners work full-time. Twenty-seven percent either work part-time or their partners work part-time, while 32 per cent of our respondents are either full-time homemakers or their partners are full-time homemakers. The labour force participation rate of Ratoath women (at 58 per cent) appears to be somewhat higher than the national average of 48% (Central Statistics Office, Statistical Abstract of Ireland, 2002). This is probably also a reflection of the relatively young age of the people in our sample. However, 57 per cent of employed women in our survey are working part-time, compared to 31 per cent nationally. The proportion of women engaged in full-time home duties (35 per cent) is about the same as the national average.

5 Local Networks of Social Support

The new suburbs emerging in and around Dublin, and other urban centres, provide challenging new constraints and opportunities for meeting family goals. These include the physical use of space, the availability of employment, services, and leisure facilities, and the demographic profile of suburban housing estates. Clearly, families will have to find ways of adapting to these challenges, which may lead to the emergence of new family forms and kinship networks. On average, our respondents reported between 5 and 6 (mean=5.76) people that were important to them, and on whom they could call for help and support. Nearly fifty-six percent of all the people mentioned by our respondents live in Ratoath, while more than eighty percent live within an hour's journey (including those living in Ratoath). Thus, most people rely to a large extent on people living nearby. Over two-thirds of the people they rely on are non-relatives, while sixty percent of them are female. Our respondents keep in touch with nearly 4 members (mean=3.85) of their network by visiting at least once a week, and with about 2 members (mean=2.23) by telephone at least once a week. On average, they can call on about 3 people (mean=3.34) in their network to help out when they are sick, nearly 4 people (mean=3.61) if they need to borrow something, nearly 3 people (mean=2.72) if they are worried about something, and more than 4 people (mean=4.50) for socialising. Parents of young children can call on an average of about 2 people (mean=2.28) to help out with childcare.

6 Access to and use of Information Technology

As a community, Ratoath is very much tuned into information and communications technology. More than half of households have three or more televisions. Although a relatively new technology, slightly more than half of households own a DVD machine. Only a handful of respondents do not possess a mobile phone, with the majority of households boasting two or more. Indeed, the vast majority of the sixth class children, who attend the local primary school, reported that they personally own mobile phones. They primary reasons they cited for ownership was safety and being able to contact their parents in an emergency.

More than 80 per cent of households are equipped with a Personal Computer, and a further 30 per cent also own a laptop computer. Three-quarters of all households are connected to the Internet. Both statistics are significantly above the national average: in 2000, about one third (32.4 per cent) of all households in Ireland had a home computer and about 63 per cent of those households were connected to the Internet (Quarterly National Household Survey, 2000).

In Ratoath, we found that personal computers are primarily used to access information, for email and for word-processing. About 40 per cent of respondents also use their computer to play computer games. Just over a quarter of respondents (29.6 per cent) bank on-line, while almost the same proportion (27.7 per cent) shop on line. The relatively low level of take up of ecommerce services suggests that even in 'wired communities' people prefer to conduct their business in more traditional ways. Despite all the hype about new technologies and the interactive possibilities they offer, most respondents (53.7 per cent) cite the television as their preferred medium. The personal computer comes in second (preferred by 12.9 per cent of respondents) followed closely by the mobile phone (12.4 per cent). The most frequently cited reasons for keeping an item was it's entertainment value and usefulness as an information and communication tool.

According to Wellman (1999) the most significant social relationships are said to occur increasingly outside residential neighbourhoods. Local communities are being replaced by "personal communities." The networks of support and social ties that count are widely dispersed spatially: they focus on family, kin, friends, and, some would add, on emerging "virtual communities". In this regard, it is noteworthy that for those who use email, about two-thirds of the respondents, the main purposes to which it is put is to stay in touch with family and friends. Indeed, three-quarters of respondents see technology generally as allowing them to be more flexible about keeping in touch with people, and accessing places and communities other than Ratoath. While slightly more than two-thirds of people feel happy about the new communications technology in their lives, about a third say they sometimes feel overwhelmed and wish they could get back to a more simple way of living. Two-thirds of those surveyed also believe that there is excessive hype about new information technologies that make them seem more important than they really are.

7 Local voluntary associations

Support, trust, membership and commitment determine the level of collective competence which a group or a community enjoys. The extent to which a locality or neighbourhood acquires a collective, social existence depends in part on the cooperation of local residents and their ability to address a range of issues or perform a set of services. This is achieved mainly through the activity of voluntary associations in the locality. A question prompted respondents' awareness of such local voluntary organisations. It made it possible to identify the voluntary organisations which operate at the local level, and also tested their profile in the locality. Most respondents were aware of voluntary organisations active in Ratoath and only 14 percent of them did not give at least one relevant name.

Over all, **thirty-seven local voluntary organisations** were indicated and recorded during the interviews. It must be noted that churches were rarely mentioned and not referred to as "voluntary organisations". For instance, the Catholic Church is not perceived as a voluntary organisation, although technically it falls within that category and is certainly "active" in Ratoath. On the other hand, church-related organisations were included in the list (St Vincent de Paul, choir group). These 37 organisations were classified into the following broad categories:

Charitable	3
Political	1
Recreational, leisure	11
Quality of life in locality	7
Religious	2
Parents	1
Sport	12

Sport clubs, followed by recreational and then resident associations make up the bulk of them. This classification should be seen as ad hoc and does not follow any particular rationale. Nevertheless, it underlines the predominance of service organisations, as opposed to organisations which articulate and promote particular interests or goals. This is further reinforced by the information relating to the overall number of references to individual organisations:

Charitable	18
Political	14
Recreational, leisure	174
Quality of life in locality	91
Religious	7
Parents	16
Sport	293
Other	18

Local sport clubs enjoy a very high profile, and this statement applies more particularly to the G.A.A. and the Harps (the soccer club), but it also extends to more recent types of sport activity such as martial arts.

We were also interested in finding out how respondents became aware of the existence of these local organisations. Thirty respondents stated that they obtained this knowledge through formal channels: such as leaflets (12), newsletters (12) and canvassing (12). Informal channels were slightly more prominent, when respondents got this knowledge from friends (10), neighbours (18) and family (18). But many (54) obtained this information through different channels. It appears, on balance, that informal channels play a more significant role in the awareness of the existence of local organisations.

8 Participation in local voluntary associations

The awareness of the existence of voluntary organisations operating at the local level represents only one indicator of the importance of such associations in the life of the locality. More crucial perhaps is the associational density, which is measured by the level of membership in such organisations. Sixty seven (34 percent) of the respondents in this representative sample indicated that they belonged to a local organisation. One may note that most of them have joined only one such association, with 10 percent participating in more than one. This piece of information is interpreted only with great difficulty, as we possess very few points of reference. The figure of a third of enlisted residents would rise sharply if membership of all voluntary organisations (not only local) had been included.

The level of membership varies considerably from one country to another, and Ireland is ranked among the low membership countries in such league tables. A notional two-third membership gives a rough measure of organisational density, but it takes on board membership of all voluntary organisations, not simply local ones. Furthermore, the organisations which are classified as voluntary vary a great deal (e.g. churches, unions, etc.). A few studies of American neighbourhoods have sought information about membership in local organisations and pointed to a level of around 30 percent membership. Ratoath would then be in line with these findings. But we have no way, at the moment, of rating the figure as high or low (compared for instance to established suburbs, urban neighbourhoods or even rural localities). The total membership of 101 is distributed in the following manner:

Charitable	2
Political	1
Recreational, leisure	17
Quality of life in locality	36
Religious	2
Parents	5
Sport	35
Other	3

The profile of membership does not quite correspond to the profile of awareness. For instance, sport and recreation, although still very significant, now lag behind membership in organisations dealing with the quality of life in the locality. This category includes, almost exclusively, residents associations. In fact, it is quite surprising that only 36 of the respondents mentioned their membership in the relevant resident associations. In some cases, the resident association is involved in the management of the estate and every household belongs to it and contributes to the cost of maintenance. This "membership" is either taken for granted or not considered as a membership as such. It remains that only three types of voluntary organisations really matter in Ratoath, as far as membership is concerned: resident associations, sport and leisure/recreation.

How did these respondents become members of such local organisations? The formal (canvassed 12) and informal (friend, neighbours, family: 12) channels play an equal role. Thirteen respondents stated that they joined by themselves approaching the organisations (self-approach). This type of initiative points to an act of individual agency.

Membership of local voluntary organisations does not represent, for many of the respondents, a merely formal matter. Forty of them (that is around two-thirds) are actively involved in the associations of which they are members. For the whole sample, this means that roughly 20 percent are actively engaged in such voluntary organisations. They typically spend a few hours every month in performing various tasks:

- Attending meetings   24 (out of 59)
- Fundraising   18 (out of 58)
- Committee members   8 (out of 62)
- Distributing newsletters   3 (out of 59)
- Secretarial work   11 (out of 59)
- Organising events   13 (out of 44)
- Participating in events   9 (out of 59)

Membership in voluntary organisations in Ratoath is to a large extent associated with volunteerism. This means that while only a third of the local residents participate in voluntary associations, they are quite active when they do so.

9 Local problems

Four main problems were frequently mentioned by local residents. Half of them referred to traffic and infrastructure problems.

- The heavy **traffic** which passes through Ratoath (commuters but also numerous lorries which use Ratoath as a shortcut) is compounded by the fact that one accedes to Ratoath through what has remained country roads. Numerous accidents are reported, and the death of a young girl occurred while the survey was being conducted.
- The lack of **infrastructure** was also stressed by many; the number of housing estates has multiplied in the last few years, and continues to do so. But the basic infrastructure has not been put in place in order to sustain this growth.
- A similar comment can be made in relation to the provision of basic **amenities**. Close to a third of respondents reported the general lack of amenities and another quarter of them pointed to the lack of amenities for children (play areas, etc) as a major issue. Development has taken place without much forward planning. Services which sufficed for a small village can no longer cope with a population which has grown rapidly. For instance, no bank had yet opened a branch in Ratoath and, at the time of the survey, only one ATM was operating in a petrol service station. A purpose-built small supermarket was being constructed.
- Another quarter of the respondents mentioned the lack of a particular **amenity**: that of a school. The ground of the primary school has been covered with numerous prefabricated structures and could not adequately cope with the situation. Ratoath has no secondary school.

Other problems were indicated by respondents, but far less frequently: some (14 percent) complained that Ratoath was being overdeveloped and others (12 percent) denounced the inadequacy of public transport. It must be noted that very few respondents (3 percent) made a reference to vandalism, which is not considered to be a problem.

These problems were widely talked about in the community, with only 15 percent of the residents indicating that they have not talked about these problems with anybody. A large majority of respondents stated that they talked about such problems with their neighbours (71 percent) and friends (60 percent). They raised the issues with canvassers in 40 per cent of cases. Such problems had also been discussed with shopkeepers for 24 percent of the respondents. It is then clear that local residents have clearly defined the main problems in the locality and that they talked about such problems widely.

10 Local problems and collective action

Although much talked about, to what extent do these problems prompt local residents to address them and do something about them? Many residents express awareness that some action took place in the past to address the problems they mention. Less than 5 per cent of them indicated that they were not aware of any action. Most of them indicated that local politicians had been approached (62 percent). Petitions were also sent to the relevant authorities, mainly the local county council (41 percent). Actual delegations were dispatched (13 percent), but demonstrations seem to have been an extremely rare occurrence in Ratoath: only 5 respondents mentioned such an action.

Although nearly half of the respondents (47 percent) declared that they had done nothing in relation to such problems, more than half of the local residents stated that they engaged in some kind of action. This action consisted mainly in approaching local politicians (22 per cent) and in signing petitions. A higher level of activism was triggered for some people, when they joined an organisation to deal with these problems (7 per cent) or sought to mobilise other people (7 per cent). All this points to a fairly high level of concern, and involvement in dealing with these problems, but also to a generally low level of activism.

The action of respondents, when it took place, was not perceived as very effective. Of those who stated that they did something about local problems, two-thirds of them (68 per cent) did not think that their action had improved the situation. This points to a low level of feeling of empowerment and political competency.

Sense of Place

In another article entitled "Finding your place: forging identity and a sense of belonging in new suburban communities" Mary P Corcoran, NUI Maynooth, states that:

> "In Ratoath where we recorded a very high level of attachment to place (79%) respondents identified very specific features which had attracted them to Ratoath as a place to live. The most commonly cited features that attracted people to Ratoath include the village character, country feel, friendliness and sense of community. Ratoath's greenery- the hedges, fields and trees- act as important signifiers of the countryside and rurality for respondents, both young and old. Older children remarked that despite all the development, and the fact that a lot of people don't know each other, Ratoath has not lost "its country look." A participant in the Mother and Toddler group remarked that she liked the "ruralness of the place" especially the green fields and the fact that it was "not all concrete". Both comments suggest that it is the aesthetic of rurality to which people are attached, rather than to the countryside itself. For the reality is that the countryside around Ratoath is under threat from development and that the very reasons that attracted people in the first place, are fast disappearing. The general consensus among women in that group (most of whom had moved out to Ratoath from Dublin) was that Ratoath was part of the country. The "countryside" formed the crucial environmental backdrop".

In their joint paper entitled "Civic Engagement and The Governance of Irish Suburbs" published by The Policy Institute in Studies in Public Poilcy:21, Michel Peillon, Mary Corcoran and Jane Gray explain that:

> "While suburbs are often presented as soulless and uniform places, the findings of the Ratoath study present a picture of a community in which many residents are attached to the place where

they live, belong to local networks of family, friends and neighbours, participate in local voluntary associations and want to be involved in local public affairs. Residents are particularly keen to be involved in tackling what they perceive as key issues impacting on the quality of life of their community for example the unregulated nature of development, a lack of basic amenities, access to school facilities and high traffic volumes on inadequate road infrastructure," "Despite many Ratoath residents attempting to do something to address these problems, they were aware of the ineffectiveness of their action. Residents of new suburbs such as Ratoath face an uphill struggle in this as they have encountered an institutional void – that is, a lack of institutions of local government at that level. Hence residents rely heavily on local political networks and politicians to ensure access to the formal structures of local government. Rarely consulted and unable to participate in the decision-making process, they can only uphold their views and interests negatively, through various forms of resistance to external pressures and interests".

In "Finding your place: forging identity and a sense of belonging in new suburban communities" Mary P Corcoran, NUI Maynooth, notes that older residents reported that

"the proximity of Fairyhouse to the village has historically been an important symbol for the area. The racecourse is an important source of identity and pride for the community generally. Historically, on Grand National Day (Easter Sunday) it was known as "the day of the year". People would whitewash their houses in acknowledgement of and participation in the event. They concede that the increased frequency of race meetings throughout the racing year at Fairyhouse has lessened their significance as major days of celebration and pride for the local community today, (Active Age, Ratoath), but nevertheless, the "Fairyhouse factor" continues to have currency locally".

Mary Corcoran observes that "In describing the place where they live, local children in Ratoath utilise a rural/urban continuum, positively evaluating the former and negatively evaluating the latter. In short the respondents do not want Ratoath to be "Dublin." Not surprisingly, the children growing up in Ratoath had some difficulty in responding to questions regarding their primary identity. While most identify with the adopted county of Meath, they are frequently viewed as Dubliners by those whose families have a history in the County, and as "culchies" by their family and friends who still reside in the Dublin metropolitan area. One informant explained that as an out-migrant from Dublin he had to balance the identity positions of both his father and his son. When his father comes to visit in Ratoath, the informant's son- a naturalized Meath supporter- must don a Dublin jersey over his Meath jersey so that the Grandfather will not be upset!"

Final Observations from a Local Perspective
The results of the NUIM survey in 2003 were fascinating to all who participated the previous summer. Only a small number of participants lived in Ratoath all their lives. The majority of people, new to the area, moved from the Dublin area and 90% expected to remain living in Ratoath for the next five years at least. Corcoran, Gray and Peillon stated that "The Ratoath population is also distinctive in terms of its socio-economic profile. More than half of those gainfully employed belong to the Class 2 (managerial and technical) of the Census Population."

When one reads the summary of findings from Mary P. Corcoran, Jane Gray and Michel Peillon and the other works which they have written it is clear that what has happened in Ratoath is replicated in other locations in Ireland as small villages experience an explosion of population and an urgent need for the relevant infrastructure to build new integrated communities empowered to participate in, and contribute to, the welfare of everyone in these communities. The people of Ratoath are attached to Ratoath and many came to live here in recent times because they were attracted to the rural characteristics but yet the closeness to the city environment continued to provide easy access to that which was familiar. In doing so it has emerged that individuals and families grapple with the reality of sharing identities of being from other places (within and outside Ireland, from urban and rural areas) with different cultural perspectives. It was a lifestyle choice with children at different stages of development. New networks had to be established to replace those which they left behind.

When asked about sources of help and support, Ratoath demolished another stereotype. Most people surveyed by the Maynooth sociologists mentioned five or six people on whom they could call and, rather surprisingly, more than half of these live locally. There was also surprisingly little orientation towards the city, with most choosing to operate within the triangle of Ratoath (local community/recreation), Blanchardstown (shopping, cinema), and Ashbourne and Navan and Dunshaughlin (swimming, library, doctor). Of the 70 children who attended focus groups, not one expressed an interest in visiting any city centre facility when describing their perfect day out, preferring adventure centres, malls, skateboard and motor tracks, all located on the urban periphery.

The new residents of Ratoath also have plenty to occupy them in the home. Well over 50 per cent have three or more televisions, more than 80 per cent have a computer, a further 30 per cent own a laptop and a higher than average 75 per cent are connected to the Internet. As in all burgeoning communities, the battle to create adequate infrastructure is continuing. In Ratoath, the campaign is carried on at a muted but sophisticated pitch.

A new study has suggested the stereotypical image of unhappy commuters feeling isolated in the burgeoning dormitory towns around Dublin is untrue. Nearly 60 per cent of the 2,000 families who have moved into Ratoath, Co Meath, in recent years are relatively affluent and working in information technology or at Dublin Airport, according to the research carried out by the sociologists at NUI Maynooth.

Ratoath, once a small village near Fairyhouse racecourse, has become the fastest growing centre in Dublin's commuter belt, the new "*suburban frontier.*" Its population soared by more than 82 per cent between 1996 and 2002, to reach 5,585 and it has continued to grow to reach 7,249 in April 2006 and approximately 9,600 in 2008. While we all know that it is a changing place, people still consider that it has a village atmosphere, friendliness and a sense of community according to Corcoran, Gray and Peillon. However, there is a fear which has been voiced that Ratoath could be in danger of losing its rural character and traditions.

The study, carried out by Dr Mary Corcoran, Dr Jane Gray and Dr Michel Peillon, found that most of those now living there moved to Ratoath from Dublin, in many cases purchasing detached homes for less than the price of a terraced house in the city. Although 85 per cent of households are married couples with young children, they confound the stereotype of double-income, commuting parents who leave their children in crèches. Instead, what emerges is a picture of comfortable, conventional family life.

Fewer than 20 per cent of households have both partners in full-time work and just 10 per cent of children are in full-time crèche care. Even though labour force participation for women, at 58 per cent, is higher than the national average.

The NUI Maynooth study of Ratoath in 2002 is now six years old (in 2008) and in that time there have been additional significant changes around the Ratoath area, most notably further increases in population, a very young population, increases in commuter traffic each morning and evening, but still people are happy to get back to Ratoath at the end of the day. The new N2 motorway, opened in May 2006, and associated roundabout at the nine-mile-stone junction have improved travel time to the city and beyond. The impending new M3 motorway, under construction in 2008, will greatly improve access to Fairyhouse and Ratoath

Shopping facilities, business enterprises, community and sporting amenities, identified as lacking in the 2002 survey, have since improved beyond expectations in and around the village to provide what most families need. A thirty to forty minute journey will take residents of the area to the coast, Dublin city, the mountains, ferry terminals or to Dublin airport. Everything is quite convenient to the village of Ratoath. A new purpose built theatre – *The Venue*, in the Ratoath Community Centre, provides a variety of dramas, music (popular, pop, classical, traditional and others), cinema, clubs and societies. Park the car and just walk around the corner or up the road along the much improved footpaths that are regularly cleaned and maintained. Walk down the Dunshaughlin Road to Sean Eiffe Park, the 27 acre home to the local GAA Club or down to the Ratoath Harps grounds on the Skryne Road, or down to the new Rugby Grounds on the Curragha Road, or to the new running track next to the Ratoath Community Secondary School in Jamestown, and you will see how a community can work together to ensure that modern sporting facilities become a reality for all of the community to enjoy. All these new amenities are easily accessible around Ratoath in 2008.

COMMUNITY

Ratoath Independent Living Initiative [RILI] 2008

Arkle House, Steeplechase, with its 12 specially fitted units, was created for the benefit of people with physical disabilities.

County Manager Tom Dowling, right is pictured with Sean Reilly, Managing Director of Developers McGarrell Reilly, who donated the land to Ratoath Independent Living Initiative, with founder of the project Nick Killian. Also in the picture at back row are John Scott, Project Manager, Brian Reilly, Eamonn Walsh, Michael McGarrell and Dr. Fergal Quinn, Chair of the RILI (Ratoath Independent Living Initiative) Committee.

During his time as CEO of the Irish Association of Spina Bifida and Hydrocephalus, Nick Killian founded the project and the local RILI Committee under the chairmanship of Dr. Fergal Quinn was formed. The first occupants moved into Arkle House in summer 2008.

COMMUNITY

Pride of Place in Ratoath

RATOATH HERITAGE GROUP

PRIDE OF PLACE was initiated in 2003 by Tom Dowling, County Manager of Meath County Council. The competition is hosted by *Co-Operation Ireland* under its Local Authority Programme in partnership with an all-island Local Authority Steering Committee. Its success is evident through the enthusiasm and hard work which community groups are investing in their projects each year. Ratoath community groups have enthusiastically participated in this initiative from the beginning.

Meath County Council encourages local communities throughout the county to participate. The Chairman of the Meath Pride of Place Committee is Tom Dowling. Improvements in towns and villages are recognised annually as local community groups come together to identify the local needs, shape and improve their area in order to make a positive impact on their environment and within their community. The Local Authority nominates the towns and villages.

Despite the rapidly changing landscape of Ratoath a variety of community orientated projects and activities involving all age groups have been undertaken which benefit the environment and community in which we live.

Pride of Place Awards for Ratoath 2005-2007

Ratoath Housing Estates Awards 2005:
1st *Place*: Meadowbank Hill
2nd *Place*: Clonkeen Estate
3rd *Place*: Jamestown Park

Best Overall Housing Estate Awards in County Meath 2005:
3rd *Place*: Meadowbank Hill, Ratoath

Harvest Walk Winners 2006: Best Clean up Effort:
Ratoath Heritage Group

The Harvest Walk category of the competition encourages rurally based community groups in their efforts to improve and enhance a specific aspect of the local landscape. Ratoath Heritage Group was rewarded for the work done in enhancing the natural beauty of a mile long stretch of The Lough Lane off the Dunshaughlin Road. The work involved many hours of voluntary labour all through the summer months of that year.

Best Overall Housing Estate Awards in County Meath 2006:
3rd *Place*: Meadowbank Hill, Ratoath

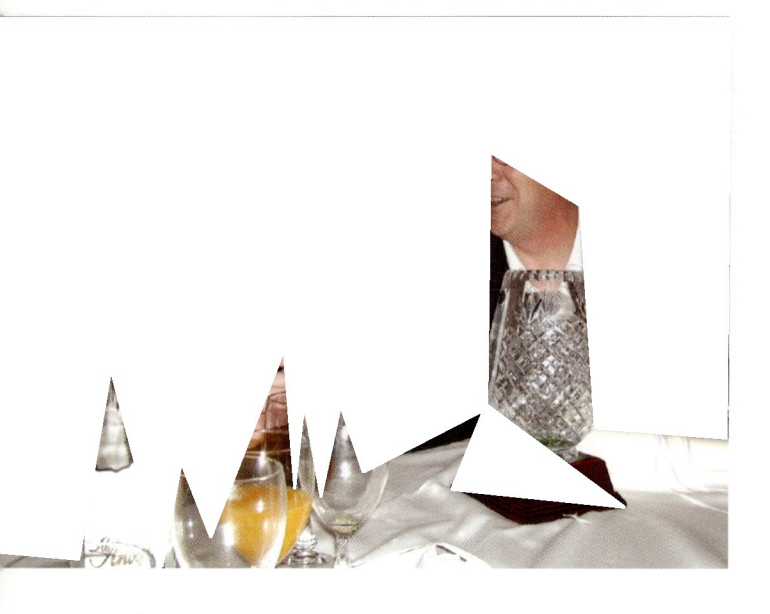

Ann Gaughan, Tony Darby and Noel Kelly, previous Chairperson of Meadowbank Hill Residents Association, at the Pride of Place Awards Ceremony in Warrenstown College, 2006

Residents from Meadowbank Hill, Yvonne Murray and Deborah McQueen receiving a 2007 Pride of Place Award (Best Kept Overall Housing Estate Award) from Mary Wallace T.D. Also in the photograph are Nick Killian and Tom Dowling, Meath County Manager.

Ratoath Housing Estates 2006 Awards:
1st Place: Meadowbank Hill
2nd Place: Clonkeen Estate

Towns with Populations over 2,000 people in 2007:
3rd Place: Ratoath

Best Overall Housing Estate Awards in County Meath 2007:   Pride of Place Awards
3rd Place: Meadowbank Hill, Ratoath

The Waterways Award 2007
2nd Place: Ratoath Forest River Walk

Prizes Awarded at the Judges Discretion 2007:
Meath County Council's Cathaoirleach's Prize: Community Centre, Ratoath

Pride of Place for Schools 2007
3rd Place Overall Winner: Ratoath Senior National School

Best Use of Art in the School Ground
2nd Prize: Ratoath Junior National School

COMMUNITY												Pride of Place in Ratoath

Noel Martin is pictured receiving the Pride of Place Cup for Best Kept Garden from the Cathaoirleach of Meath County Council, Councillor Nick Killian, in November 2007 for his wonderful gardens on Well Road. Noel was also awarded the Pride of Place Cup in 2004 and he was awarded a plaque for second place in the competition in 2005.

COMMUNITY

Community in Action in the New Millennium

Local School Dramas
Ratoath National School

St. Paul's National School

Community Development
Ratoath Community Sports Campus

Playground at Happy Days Community Childcare located in the Community Centre.

This area will be home to Ratoath Athletic Club, Ratoath Tennis Club and 9th Meath Scouts Troop.

COMMUNITY — Community in Action in the New Millennium

Official Opening of the Playground at Steeplechase, Saturday 6th June 2008

COMMUNITY

Know Your Neighbour Event Ratoath, Saturday 14th July 2007

THE *"Know Your Neighbour"* event, inspired by Macra na Feirme, nationally was a wonderful opportunity to meet new neighbours and keep in touch with friends one may not have seen for a while. In times past it was easier to know everyone as most people lived, worked and socialised near home. The majority of people walked or cycled everywhere as most families did not own cars. It was more likely that one remained close to home among families who had known each other for generations either in the local parish or adjoining parishes unless one went to work in other counties, into the City of Dublin or emigrated to England, USA or Australia.

This event also provided opportunities for Ratoath people to meet those who are responsible for running key services which protect and assist the community in times of crisis e.g. Gardaí and the Fire Service. Mary Wallace T.D. was on hand to support the event.

Mary Wallace, then Minister of State at the Dept of Agriculture, Fisheries and Food, with Siobhan Connell, Annette Farrell and Fergus O Riordan of the Mill Tree Park Residents Association, enjoying the fun at the "Know Your Neighbour" event in Ratoath on Saturday 14th July 2007

PHOTOGRAPHIC GALLERY — A Ramble Down Memory Lane

A Ramble Down Memory Lane

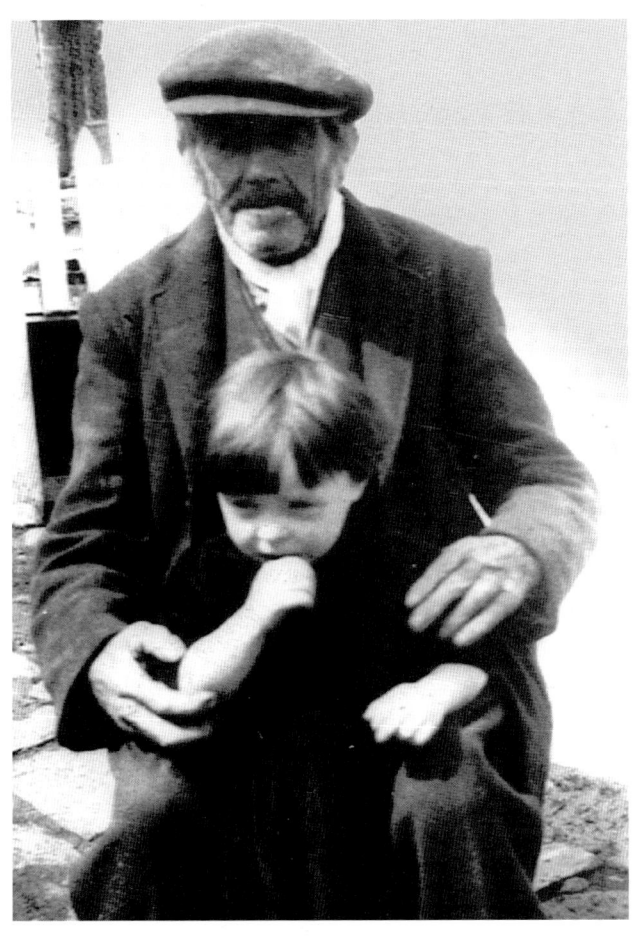

1926: Peggy Flood with her Grandfather, Mick Elliot of Summerhill, Co. Meath.

Summer 1957 in Ratoath
Mrs. Margaret Collins (Frances Maher's grandmother) and Mrs. Catherine Donohoe from Fairyhouse Road, Ratoath

William Barry Mooney in uniform in 1922.
Photo Courtesy of Larry Mooney.

Getting Out and About

James Ralph (Granduncle of Jimmy Ralph) and Nan Moore. Picture taken c. 1930's.

Lizzy and Molly Mannering in mid 1930's

PHOTOGRAPHIC GALLERY — Getting Out and About

Ratoath group pictured outside the home of JJ Kelly, Principal Ratoath NS, in early 1950s
Back Row: L-R: Paddy Moore, Mary Ingoldsby, May Keogh, Bridget Kiernan, Ruby Keating and Gerry Keogh
Middle Row: L-R: Alice Dolan and Nan Moore (nee Robinson)
Front Row: L-R: Molly Mannering, Maud Foley, May Dolan, Sheila McLoughlin, Molly Walls (nee Flood), Kathy Brennan and Lizzie Mannering

Picture shows L-R: Tommy McLoughlin, Maud Foley, Tommy Foley and Molly Mannering in the early 1950's

491

Holidays in Ireland

Rita Martin, Pauline Kennedy, Joanie Barker, Mona Collins and Tiny Nulty. Picture was taken in the mid 1950's in Glendalough.

Tommy McLoughlin and Paddy Woods Date of picture 1950's.

L-R: Jimmy Ralph, Paddy Woods, John Mannering, Brendan Ralph and Liam Mannering. Picture taken in Tramore, Co. Waterford in early 1950's.

PHOTOGRAPHIC GALLERY   Holidays in Ireland/ Close to Home

Close to Home

Above: Luke & Margaret Ralph at home by the fireside in the 1950's

May Costello outside her family business then trading as B. Monahan Wine & Spirit Merchant

This house, formerly owned by Paddy and Rita Martin, was demolished to make way for the entrance to Streamstown development off Pullwee Street (Dunshaughlin Road).

Childhood Memories Revisited – The Dunshaughlin Road

The Swing Bar that was in Clover Hill Woods for over 40 years between two mature trees that were removed to make way for a roundabout in 2005. Pictured in the springtime of 2002 were members of the Heritage Committee, Tony Darby, Ann Gaughan & Beryl Donnelly, revisiting their childhood playground!

Tree-lined Dunshaughlin Road

Primroses in Clover Hill, Spring 2002

(*Below*) House in Lagore where Molly and Stephen Blake lived (*Photo Courtesy Padraig Halton*)

Ratoath Lads on Holiday in the Canary Islands during the summer of 2000

Back L-R: Sean Killian, Barry Nally, Damian Ryan, Stephen Coby, Garry Maher, Paddy Cummins, David Maher.
Front L-R: Conor Killian, Sean Ryan, Barry Crowley, name unknown, Maurice Brown, Colin Phelan, Terry Maher, Fiacra O Neill.

Street Life

Former Ratoath Harps players after Sunday morning Mass in Ratoath in 1970's
L-R: David Foley, Martin Dolan, Dominic O'Neill, Mick McGrail, Paddy Donoghue and Mark Flood

(*Above*): Pictured on the family farm at Kilrue, Co. Meath, in 1981 were L-R: Brian White, Eamon White, Suzanne (baby daughter of Brian and Anne White) and Mary White

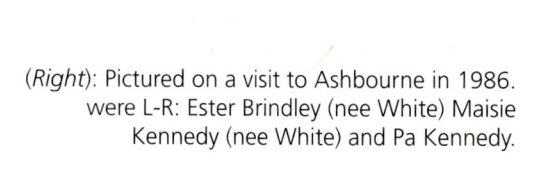

(*Right*): Pictured on a visit to Ashbourne in 1986. were L-R: Ester Brindley (nee White) Maisie Kennedy (nee White) and Pa Kennedy.

LOCAL HISTORY   Street Life/Celebrations

Ratoath Club/Cub Celebrations

Former members of Ratoath Badminton Club at a Dinner Dance in Ashbourne House Hotel c. 1980s
L-R Tom Watters Martin Mannering and Mark Watters.

Ratoath Cubs participating in the Cub Fun Day outing in Portumna Co. Galway in 1985.

The Lough Lane Flora – A Walk on the Wild Side

Mary Moore's Sweet Shop

Moore's Sweet Shop in mid 1970's which was situated adjacent to the small entrance gate to Ratoath Cemetery. It later became the site of the two De Lacy Court houses that were built in the mid 1990's.
Photo Courtesy Owen Hackett

Ecclesiastical and Social Functions

1933: Eucharistic Procession around the Congressional Cross at the centre of Ratoath with home of Jack Sherlock, Irish Street, in the background

Front L-R: Molly O'Neill, Fr. Pat Browne and Cardinal Basil Hume in Ratoath Church grounds. Pictured in the background L-R: Noel Ryan, Tom Wheeler and Frank Begley.
This picture was taken circa June 1986, just after Cardinal Hume had fulfilled a promise to visit The Most Holy Trinity Church in Ratoath to concelebrate Mass with Fr. Pat Browne, who was then Cardinal Hume's Private Secretary.

PHOTOGRAPHIC GALLERY   Ecclesiastical and Social Functions

Late 1970s: Pictured at a PTAA Function in Ratoath were:
L-R Standing: Sonny Martin, Noel Ryan, Peadar Nugent, Pat Donnelly
L-R Seated: Frances Maher, Michael O'Hehir (Sports Commentator) and Florrie Martin

Ratoath Motte. Picture taken on 6th December 2008

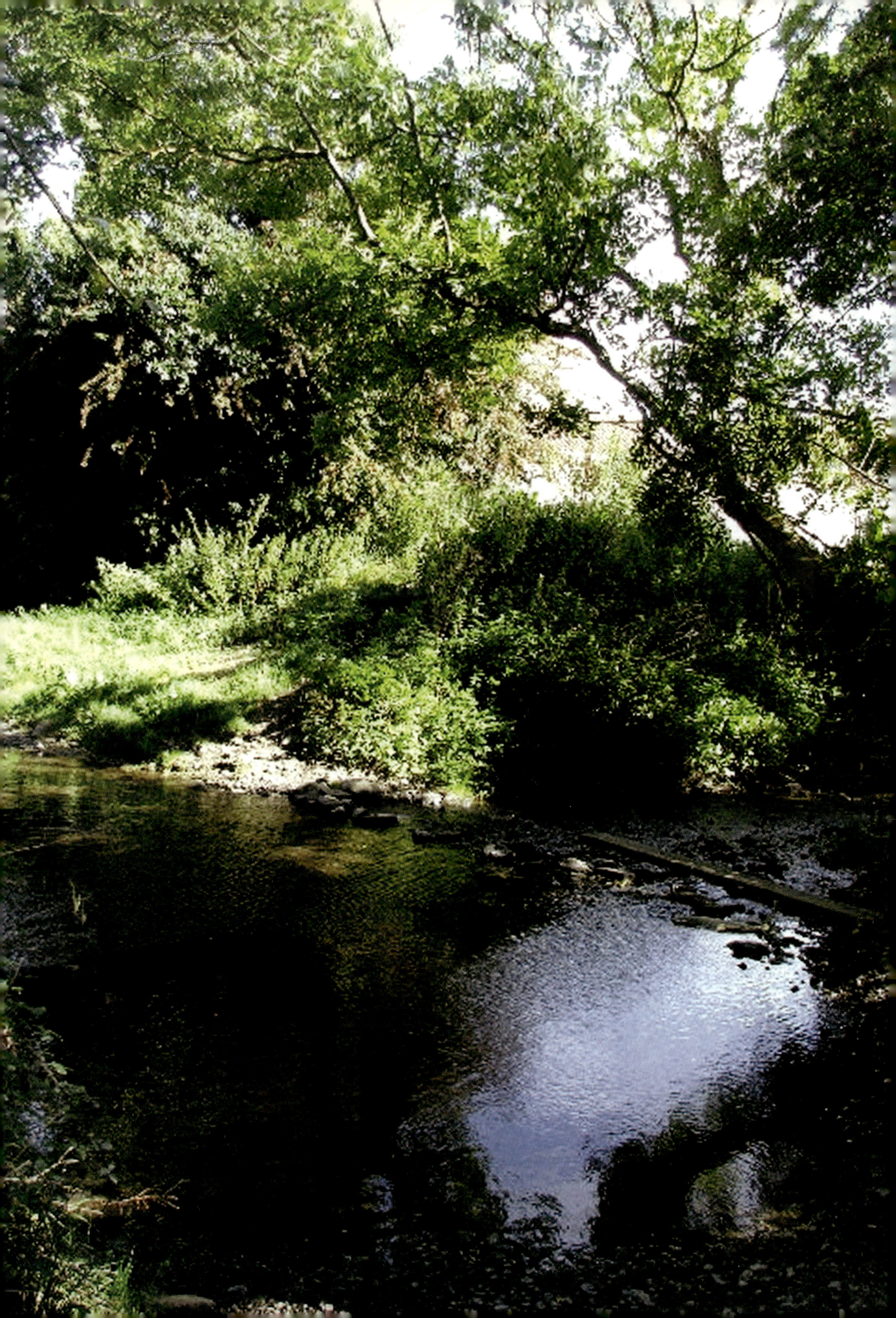

Conclusion

RATOATH HERITAGE GROUP

As we come to the end of the journey of this new book on and of Ratoath we begin to realise that Ratoath is a very different place to that which was portrayed in the first historical accounts by Frances Maher and Tony Darby. Indeed the journey the people of Ratoath have taken over the centuries to arrive at this particular moment in time has been a momentous one. The historical, social, educational and cultural challenges have been extraordinary, particularly in the last fifty years. The essays, articles, family memories and stories throughout the book serve to illustrate the transformation which has taken place in Ratoath. The book will add to the knowledge, appreciation and enjoyment of those who take an interest in the local heritage of this corner of Co. Meath.

All of us need to understand what it is to belong but also to understand what is involved in helping others to belong to new communities. And as we have entered the early years of the twenty-first century the rate of the changes and challenges are much faster than in the past. In Ratoath there is a vibrant young population, who are the future of this community, they are our future and it is our responsibility to ensure that they can cope with the journey ahead of them in this rapidly changing and diverse world by understanding where they have come from within this and other communities. Ratoath has been forcefully propelled into modern times without real reflection on the past and without true preparation for the future. We hope that this book will help them on their journey.

Our links to the world are far more diverse than those of Norman and Viking times and far wider. Each year, family, friends and visitors from every continent come to Ratoath, from every culture, historical and political area. We have immediate links with at least twenty five other nations which enrich this community and the life that unfolds here for all of us. It is our responsibility to ensure that this community continues to contribute to the development of its own locality and to the enrichment of the wider community at national and global levels through its links.

Those involved in protecting heritage and all that it entails can take heart from the fact that there are supportive official structures in place which enable new initiatives to be undertaken by local groups. The strength of the local community and its care for heritage lies in the work that has already been achieved and the willingness of individuals to become involved. Motivation, enthusiasm, perseverance and hard work in conjunction with official agencies help to build a solid basis for community-based heritage projects. New members are warmly welcomed by Ratoath Heritage Group.

Bibliography
AND OTHER REFERENCES

BOOKS:

"A Topographical Dictionary of Ireland". Author Samuel Lewis. In two volumes. Published by S. Lewis & Co. 87, Aldersgate Street, London. 1837.

"Fair Day - The story of Irish Fair Days and Markets". Author: Patrick Logan. Published by Apletree Press Ltd, Belfast. 1986. **ISBN**: 0-86281-146-5

"The Ward Union Staghounds". Author: Ralph Greaves. Published and Produced for the Ward Union Staghounds by Reid-Hamilton (Ireland) Ltd. 3 College Green, Dublin. 1950.

"An Irish Sporting Life". Author: Eric Craigie. Published by Liliput Press, Arbour Hill, Dublin 7. Paperback. ISBN: 1 874675 40 6

"Politics and War in Meath 1913-23". Author: Oliver Coogan. Published by Folens and Co. Ltd., Dublin. 1983.

"RATOATH" Author: Very Rev. John Cogan, P.P. Published by Drogheda Independent Co. Ltd. c. mid 1960's.

"Ordnance Survey Letters Meath". Edited with and Introduction by Michael Herity MRIA, Published by Four Mater Press, Dublin 2001. Hardback. ISBN: 1-903538-03-3

"Ordnance Survey Letters Meath" Edited by John O'Donovan. 1836.

"Short History of the Parishes of the Diocese of Meath, 1867-1937" Author: Rev. John Brady. No. 2. in continuation of THE DIOCESE OF MEATH ancient and modern by Rev. Anthony Cogan. Published by Meath Chronicle Printing Works, 1937.

"The Medieval Towns of Co. Meath." Royal Society of Antiquaries of Ireland, June 1921.

"The Barony of Ratoath" Authors Adam Maher & Laurence Kearney with Stephen Lane, Colin White and Derek Orr. Former pupils of Ratoath National School.

"A brief History of the Parish of Ratoath". Author: Gina Conway former pupil of Ratoath National School. Local History Project completed in 1990. Unpublished.

"The History of Ireland" Author Stephen Gwynn. Publishers Macmillan & Co, London, 1923, pp 3-10, 12, 43-44. ISBN:

"Early Irish History and Mythology", Author: Thomas F. O'Rahilly; Dublin Institute for Advanced Studies. Published in 1946.

"A History of the Abbeys, Priories and Other Religious Houses in Ireland" Author: Mervyn Archdall, A.M. 1873.

"Medieval Religious Houses in Ireland". Authors: A. Gwynn and R. N. Hadcock. Circa 1873.

"The Story of the Irish Race". Author: Seumas MacManus. Publisher: The Devin-Adair Company, Old Greenwich, Connecticut; Revised edition, 1966. ISBN: 0-517-06408-1

"Timetables of Irish History. An Illustrated Chronological Chart of the History of Ireland from 6000 BC to Present Times". Authors: Patrick C. Power and Seán Duffy. Published by Worth Press Limited, London. 2001.

"Jameson Irish Grand National. A history of Ireland's premier steeplechase". Authors: Guy St. John Williams and Francis P.M. Hyland. Published by The Organisation, Dublin 1995. ISBN: 0-9526-9020-9

"The Sweeney Guide to the Irish Turf 1501-2001." pp 523-529. Authors: Tony & Annie Sweeney in association with Francis Hyland. Published by Edmund Burke, Blackrock, Co. Dublin. 2002. ISBN: O 946130 37 X

"Secret Sights – Unknown Celtic Ireland". Author: Rob Vance. Publisher: Gill & Macmillian Ltd. 2003. pp100. ISBN: 0-7171-3664-7

BIBLIOGRAPHY

"*The Buildings of Ireland, North Leinster*". Authors: Christine Casey and Alister Rowan. Published by Penguine Press. 1993.

"*Tom Dreaper & His Horses*". Author: Bryony Fuller. First Published by Punchestown Books, Ormond Court, 11 Ormond Quay, Dublin 1, 1991. ISBN: 187391900X

"*The History of Ireland*" Author: Stephen Gwynn. Publishers Macmillan & Co, London. 1923. pp 3-10, 12, 43-44.

"Archaeological Inventory of County Meath." General Editor: P. David Sweetman, OPW. Published by The Stationary Office. 1987. ISBN: 0-7076-0031-6

"*Philips' Handy Atlas of the Counties of Ireland*" Constructed by: John Bartholomew, F.R.G.S. Published by: Geroge Philip & Son, 32 Fleet Street, London. 1885.

"*The Heritage of Ireland, Natural, Man-Made and Cultural Heritage*". *Edited by Neil Buttimer, Colin Rynne, Helen Guerin*. Published by: The Collins Press, West Link Park, Doughcloyne, Wilton, Cork, Ireland. 2000. ISBN: 1-898256-15-2 (paperback)

"**Urban Archaeological Survey of County Meath**". Author: BRADLEY, J. Dublin: Archaeological Survey of Ireland. (1984).

"*The Diocese of Meath: Ancient and Modern*". Volume I, II and III. Author: Cogan, Anthony. **Publisher:** Four Courts Press Ltd. (Nov 1992). **ISBN:** 1851821082

"*Lagore Crannog: An Irish Royal Residence of the 7th to 10th Centuries A.D*". Author: Hencken, Hugh. 1950. PRIA Vol.53 C, 1-247.

"*Archaeological Assessment Report, Ratoath, Co. Meath*". Arch-Tech Ltd. McCabe, S. & Johnston, S. 2002. Unpublished report submitted to Archaeological Section, Department of Environment Heritage and Local Government (DEHLG) and to the National Museum of Ireland.

"*Annals of the Kingdom of Ireland from the Earliest Times to the year 1616*". By The Four Masters. Editor: O'Donovan, J. 1990 (1856). 3rd Edition. Publisher: De Burca Rare Books, Dublin.

"*Archaeological Monitoring Report Licence No.03E1300, Ratoath, Co. Meath*". Wallace, Angela. 2003. Unpublished report submitted to Archaeological Section, Department of Environment Heritage and Local Government (DEHLG) and to the National Museum of Ireland.

"**Dublin Historical Records, 1952-53**". Rev. Maurice Dufficy

"*Ratoath Pitch & Putt Silver Jubilee*". 25th Anniversary Booklet 1972-1997. Pitch & Putt Union of Ireland (P.P.U.I). 1997.

"*Victorian Doctor: Being the Life of Sir William Wilde*". Author: Wilson TG. New York, LB Fisher, 1946

"**The Medieval Towns of Co. Meath**". Royal Society of Antiquaries of Ireland, June 1921.

"*The Barony of Ratoath*". Unpublished work by Adam Maher & Laurence Kearney, both former pupils of Ratoath School, also Stephen Lane, Colin White, Derek Orr.

"**A Brief History on the Parish of Ratoath**". Unpublished work by Gina Conway. 1990.

"**Survey of the Church of the Blessed Trinity and of the Old Graveyard, Ratoath**". Completed by Michael J. Kenny, Dunboyne, Co. Meath. 1982.

"**Survey of the Church of the Old Graveyard, Ratoath**". Completed by Derek Darby, Ratoath, Co. Meath. 1990.

"*The Story of Dunsany Castle*". Authors: Carty, Mary-Rose and Lynch, Malachy. Publisher: Publisher: Carty/Lynch, Dunsany. Published on 26 July 2000. ISBN (978)-0-95173821-4.

"*Meath of the Pastures*". Jim Gammons. A collection of verse by his late father Philip Gammons. Book launched at a commemoration of Francis Ledwidge, World War 1 poet, in Slane, Co. Meath on Sunday 30th July 2006.

"*Strong Farmer – The Memoirs of Joe Ward*". Ciaran Buckley and Chris Ward. Published by Liberty Press. 2007. ISBN: 978-1-905483-24-2

JOURNALS
Proceedings of the Royal Irish Academy (PRIA), Dublin.
"Lagore Crannóg: an Irish royal residence of the 7th to 10th centuries A.D". By Hencken, Hugh: With sections by Liam Price, M.R.I.A. and Laura E. Start, M.A., (1950). *PRIA Volume 53 (1950-1951), Section C, pp. 1-247.*
Also published in:
"Lagore Crannog. An Irish Royal Residence of the Seventh to Tenth Centuries A.D." by Hugh Hencken. Review author[s]: William H. Forsyth. *American Journal of Archaeology*, Vol. 57, No. 2 (Apr., 1953), pp. 156-157
And published in:
American Anthropologist, New Series, Vol. 55, No. 5, Part 1 (Dec., 1953), pp. 732-733
"Lagore Crannog: An Irish Royal Residence of the 7th to 10th Centuries A.D." by Hugh Hencken. *PRIA Volume 78 (1978), Section C*
"Iron 'Slave Collars' from Lagore Crannog, County Meath." B. G. Scott. 1978. pp 213-230. Proceeding of the Royal Irish Academy, Dublin. (Blue wrappers with title on front cover).

Journal of the Royal Society of Antiquaries of Ireland (JRSAI)
"A bronze double-edged knife-dagger with openwork handle and ring terminal from Lagore, Co. Meath, and its affinities." Eogan, George. JRSAI Vol.96 (1966). Part 2. pp. 147-156
John Waddell, JRSAI Vol. 104 (1974)

Report of the Council of the Leeds Philosophical and Literary Society, 1866-7, p.10

Antiquaries Journal Volume 9 (1929). Lily Frances Chitty

'*Religion and metal working at Mine Howe, Orkney*'. Card, N, Downes, J, Gibson, J & Sharman, P. Current Archaeology, Vol. 17, No. 199, 322–7. 2005.

'*Excavations at Poundbury 1966–80 Vol. II: the cemeteries.*' Farwell, D E & Molleson, T I. Dorset Natural History and Archaeology Society Monograph Series No. 11. Dorset Natural History and Archaeology Society, Dorset. 1993.

'*A Neolithic house at Newtown*'. Gowen, M & Halpin, E. Archaeology Ireland, Vol. 6, No. 2, 156. 1992.

'*Site 1, Coolfore*'. Ó Drisceoil, C. In I Bennett (ed.), Excavations 2000: summary accounts of archaeological excavations in Ireland, 214–15. Wordwell, Bray. 2002.

'*Valley bottom and hilltop: 6,000 years of settlement along the route of the N4 Sligo Inner Relief Road*'. MacDonagh, M. In J O'Sullivan & M Stanley (eds), Recent Archaeological Discoveries on National Road Schemes 2004, 9–23. Archaeology and the National Roads Authority Monograph Series No. 2. National Roads Authority, Dublin. 2005.

'*Iron Age toe-rings from Rath, County Meath, on the N2 Finglas–Ashbourne Road Scheme*'. Schweitzer, H. In J O'Sullivan & M Stanley (eds), Recent Archaeological Discoveries on National Road Schemes 2004, 93–8. Archaeology and the National Roads Authority Monograph Series No. 2. National Roads Authority, Dublin. 2005.

'*Maiden Castle, Dorset*'. Wheeler, R E M. Reports of the Research Committee of the Society of Antiquaries of London, No. 12. 1943.

"**The New Faces of Europe**". Secondary Education. Michel Foucher. Strasbourg: Council of Europe. 1995. ISBN: 92-871-92-871-2621-6

BIBLIOGRAPHY

NATIONAL PERIODICALS

Dublin Historical Records. Article by Rev. Maurice Dufficy. 1952-53

"**Ríocht na Midhe.**" Article with Ratoath Diary extracts. Rev. Peter Mulvany, P.P. Ardcath and former C.C. Ratoath. 1975

"**Ríocht na Midhe.**" Various extracts from records of Meath Archaeological & Historical Society. Article by: C.C. Ellison M.A Vol. IV, #5, 1971.

"**Ríocht na Midhe.**" Peter Mulvany. 1975, 1988, 1989.

"**Ríocht na Midhe.**" Records of Meath Archaeological and Historical Society Vol. XII 2001.

"*One Hundred Years of Life and Times in North Leinster*". Edited by **The Meath Chronicle**. pp37; © Meath Chronicle Publications, 1997.

"**The Parish of Kilbeg**". Jack Fitzsimons, 1974. The Leinster Leader. Royal Society of Antiquaries of Ireland, 63 Merrion Square, Dublin 2.

LOCAL PERIODICALS

Village Voice
Ratoath Echo
Meath Echo
Meath Chronicle
Weekender
Fingal Independent
Drogheda Independent
Ratoath Parish Newsletters
Dunboyne News, Vol. 2, No 27, 1973. An article submitted by Chris Ward.

REFERENCE RESOURCES VISITED:

Navan Library
Dunshaughlin Library
National Library
Department of Irish Folklore, University College Dublin (UCD), Belfield, Dublin 4
National Archives of Ireland, Administration Bonds, Diocese of Meath, T2427
Dunshaughlin Parish Records. NLI Pos. 4177
Registry of Deeds, Henrietta St., Dublin. Cahill/Barry Deed, 1869, Book 38, No.215 Wilkinstown, Rathbeggan, Co. Meath.
Registry of Deeds, Henrietta St., Dublin. Barry to Barry Deed, 1873, Book ? No. 72
School Registers from 1861. Kilcoole, Co. Wicklow. Compiled by G.H. O'Reilly. Irish Genealogical Sources. No. 16, 1999

Rathbeggan – Unpublished work – By Rev. Hamlet McClenaghan

REFERENCE WEB SITES

Song about Bobbyjo:	http://www.mp3ireland.com/patgood/
Fairyhouse Racecourse:	http://www.fairyhouseracecourse.ie/
Witnness Music Festival:	www.witnness.com
Ratoath Parish Web Site:	http://www.ratoathparish.ie/
Ratoath Parish Bulletin:	http://www.ratoathparish.ie/parish-bulletin
	Web page accessed on Sunday 28 September 2008.
Ratoath Community Centre:	http://www.ratoathcc.ie/
Ratoath National Schools:	http://homepage.eircom.net/~ratoathNS

Central Statistics Office: http://www.cso.ie/census/documents/2006PreliminaryReport.pdf
Irish Townland Maps https://secure.pasthomes.com/mydownloads.php
Web page accessed on Sunday 19 October 2008.

Griffiths Valuation of Ireland - Ratoath, County Meath. 1855:
http://www.failteromhat.com/griffiths/meath/ratoath.htm
http://www.failteromhat.com/griffiths/meath/rathbeggan.htm

County Meath Ireland Genealogy Project:
http://www.rootsweb.com/~irlmea2/Church/parish_of_ratoath.htm

Missionary nun honoured in home town:
http://www.ratoathparish.ie/index.php?option=com_cifeed&task=newsarticle&artid=4083
Web site accessed on 21 December 2007

Diocese of Meath: http://www.dioceseofmeath.ie/parishes/index.html
Web site accessed on 18 September 2008

Meath County Council: http://www.meath.ie/
Web site accessed on 27 September 2008

Ratoath Chamber of Commerce: www.ratoathisalive.ie Web site accessed on 08 October 2008

Ratoath Tennis Club: http://www.ratoathtennisclub.com/
Web site accessed on 11 October 2008